SOCIOLOGICAL THEORY

FROM THE CLASSICAL TO THE CONTEMPORARY

Fourth Edition

John J. Leveille

West Chester University

Blue Faucet Press. Philadelphia, Pennsylvania

Copyright 2020, 2021, 2024, 2025 John J. Leveille

All Rights Reserved
No part of this book may be reproduced, or stored in a retrieval system, or transmitted in any form or by any means, electronic, mechanical, photocopying, recording, or otherwise, without expressed written permission of the publisher.
ISBN: 978-1-7355120-9-9 (ebook)
ISBN: 978-1-7355120-8-2 (paperback)

Contents

Chapter One: Introduction to Sociological Theory
Chapter Two: Marx
Chapter Three: Durkheim
Chapter Four: Weber
Chapter Five: Simmel
Chapter Six: Tocqueville – Democracy and Sociological Theory
Chapter Seven: Structural Functionalism and Conflict Theory
Chapter Eight: Later Marxists – Gramsci, Lukacs, Althusser – and the Frankfurt School
Chapter Nine: Micro-Sociological Theories – Symbolic Interactionism, Goffman, and Phenomenology
Chapter Ten: Exchange Theories, Network Theories, and Rational Choice Theory
Chapter Eleven: Integrative Theories – Bourdieu, Giddens, and Habermas
Chapter Twelve: Postmodern Theories
Chapter Thirteen: Critical Identity Theories – Race, Gender and Queer Theories
Chapter Fourteen: Theories of the Changing Present World – from Wallerstein to Castells

Chapter One: The Project of Sociological Theory

Sociology is the systematic study of the patterns and patternings of social behavior, particularly of the patternings of social relationships of individuals and groups. Sociological theory is the branch of sociology that seeks to explain how and why these patterns and patternings emerge, how and why they are sustained, and how and why they fall apart or are changed. On its surface, these definitions seem obvious and reasonable. The field as defined here seems to have an indisputable reality. Yet it is striking to me and perhaps to many sociologists how contemporary American society is invested, knowingly or not, in denying the reality and relevance of sociology. It is as if many people wish to believe that sociology does not exist, or at the least that it is insignificant in its analyses; as a friend of mine once said, that "sociology is the intense study of the obvious." This is particularly noteworthy given the myriad of significant social issues that are afflicting the United States today. We see this denial of sociology in every corner of society. We see it, for example, in a statement made a while ago by Supreme Court Justice John Roberts when sociological evidence was presented to him in a case related to inequalities and race. Roberts refused to consider the merits of this sociological research in that case, calling it "gobblegook." We see this denial in all sorts of places today.

We see it in terms of current understandings of such things as crime and mental illness. Here the focus in popular culture, in politics, in policies, etc., when discussing or analyzing such things, is not in understanding the patternings of social life – of the organization of the social -- which may produce such things. It is not oriented toward an understanding the patternings of social life which may prevent such things from occurring. Instead, the focus incessantly is on the individual – and only the individual -- rather than on the social; on the psychological or biological (e.g., "his genetic makeup" made him do it; "neurochemical imbalances caused it"), rather than the systematic sociological forces. Can we really pretend to understand the incredibly high murder rate in America without looking at the social, whether it is in terms of gun legislation or in terms of things such as economic inequality or race? Can we really ignore the realities that the perpetrators and victims of gun violence tend to come from some groups rather than others? Can we ignore that certain areas of the country have more gun violence than others? Similarly, can we really understand the massive growth in the numbers of Americans identified and treated as mentally ill without recognizing the social forces – those related both to the mentally ill patients and the mental health professions diagnosing them -- that work to produce this reality? For example, the rates of people diagnosed and treated (often with medication) for anxiety and depressive disorders have risen markedly in the closing decades of the twentieth century into the present. This is not even to mention the sharp rise in things such as autism. Why? What is it about the social organization of American society that may produce such realities, such increases, and such treatments? Should we not be focusing on the systematic workings of society, using sociology, rather than, or in conjunction with, psychology (or biology), to understand and respond? In any event, it is clear that this individualistic type of explanation has been woefully ineffective in society's efforts to understand and respond to such things.

This individualization of understandings has long and deep roots in American society. Individualism, after all, is a long-standing, stereotypical cultural trait of Americans. Sociologically, not only do such things as crime and mental illness cry out for understandings other than individualized ones, but the very tendency or need to draw upon or fall back upon the individual and to ignore or deny the social also cries out for a sociological explanation. Why is it that Americans seemingly have a need to deny the social and to focus exclusively on the individual? What systematic social forces exist in history and into the present that have produced and sustained such things? These are just a few relevant sociological questions.

The denial of sociology in America – of its reality and its need -- goes well beyond the penchant to individualize reality. We can see it in other aspects of social reality today. For example, the push for STEM education also reflects the denial or negation of the relevance or importance of sociology, sadly at a time when arguably it is sociology (and the liberal arts in general) rather than STEM that is more needed if contemporary America wishes to understand and to address its current fundamental crises – related to politics, culture, morality, meaning, etc. STEM stands for science, technology, engineering, and math. The push for an increased focus on STEM in education is rooted in the belief that America may be falling behind other societies in these areas and as a result might decline compared to others in terms of technological advances, or wealth, or influence, or power, if policies and practices in the educational arena are not changed. At a time when AI (artificial intelligence) might turn the entire society into one big paperclip factory -- as AI could perhaps be programmed to do -- to use an example often given by those AI experts who have become alarmed at its ethical implications, might it not be better for people to focus more on understanding the organization of the social world, of understanding sociology, of understanding the social patterns and patternings that have produced AI and that might help or hinder an appropriate social response to it?

It is striking that at a time when American society is in a state of crisis, not only in terms of the myriad of conventional social ills, such as crime, mental illness, health, etc., but more significantly in terms of the cultural and political divide most emblematically seen in the power of Donald Trump and his radical, right wing cult followers and supporters in the new Republican Party, that the reality and importance of sociology is so denied. Moreover, in what has been called the American "culture wars" sociology is often, albeit implicitly, the target of wrath. The radical right wing assault on "liberal" or "woke" [sic] education and sensibilities belie this animus toward sociological understandings. For example, the assault on "critical race theory," (see Chapter Thirteen) however much this term is misused by its detractors, is often based upon the rabid rejection of the existence of any form of systematic racism. (Critical race theory has its origins in critical legal theory and is, often if not typically, misunderstood by its critics. Is it really far-fetched to call, as these theorists do, the attempts by white legislators in Alabama in the early nineteen hundreds during the Jim Crow era racist when they sought to impose such things as literary tests or poll taxes or residency requirements to deny black Americans the vote? Afterall, the white legislators would say their actions are not based on race and are not racist. Clearly, their actions were based on race. Clearly, their actions were racist. So too we find state legislators in Alabama and other places today doing similar things (now that the Supreme Court has thoroughly thrown out the major provisions of the Civil Rights Act of 1964 – a seminal piece of civil rights legislation). Today, the racism often is cloaked, in this instance, in terms of gerrymandering – designing electoral districts to favor white people and to diminish the voting power of black people. And again the white legislators argue their actions are not based on race and are not racist!)

Perhaps the thing that infuriates the arch-conservatives today most about "woke" efforts and about critical race theory are the claims by many advocates of this theory that "we are all racists." "Conservative" critics reject out of hand such claims, and by extension reject the reality of the systematic patternings of race and race relations. Critics rail against any suggestion that they, as individuals, may be racist without knowing it. In short, this is a rejection of sociology and sociological theorizing, not because it denies individual culpability, but because it denies the reality of social patternings which are unfair or which produce unequal outcomes. But it is not simply the conservatives who implicitly or explicitly eschew sociology because of the issues surrounding race and racism. One finds a curiously similar rejection of sociology by the very people, i.e. "liberals," who embrace the claims of the realities of such things as systematic racism and critical race theory. That is, one finds the need to turn the sociological into the psychological, the social into the individual. I am here speaking of the penchant of such supporters, for example, when they cry out that "we are all racists" (whether individuals know it or not), to claim that racism can and does appear in individual behaviors as the result of the individual's *un*conscious. One does not have to believe oneself to be a racist and one does not have to self-consciously act in ways that are racist to be racist, one need only do things that directly or indirectly maintain the subordinate position of minority groups, or so this logic goes. In short, "liberals" in this mold draw upon the same individualization tendencies noted earlier in relation to American culture. The problem, the argument goes, lies within the individual rather than with social organization. Sociological theorizing, I wish to suggest, may help to illuminate these issues in a more full and more fruitful way.

Sociology and sociological theory are perhaps more relevant and arguably more needed in America today than at any time in the last many decades. Not only because they might help illuminate and perhaps even effectively address some of the issues noted above, but because they may help to understand the overarching state of crisis in which America currently finds itself. The crisis is reflected in the reality of the power and influence of Donald Trump and his supporters. Trump and his cult-like followers who have remade the Republican Party into their own image are more than a threat to the continued maintenance and stability of American society as a democracy. (One needs no further evidence of this claim than the January 6, 2021 insurrection by Trump supporters who refused to accept the reality that Trump lost his first re-election bid to be president.)

We can mention several sociological issues of relevance here: the denigration of trust; the demise of virtue in public life; the use of fear; the gross violation of political, social and institutional norms of democracy. Many scholars have said that Trump and his supporters actively denigrate the value of trust and significantly contribute to the destruction of virtue in public life. Thirty years or so ago, the American public tended to trust professionals – professors, journalists, scientist, and, yes to an extent, politicians, at least far, far more than they do today. (One may object to this statement. One might wish to claim that Americans have always been mistrustful of professionals, notably of politicians. But the depth and breadth of the mistrust in decades past pales in comparison to its pervasiveness today.) The public would generally trust in the past that the professionals would say things that are true or would say things that the professionals believed to be true. If a scientist in the past said something was a danger, people in general would tend to believe this to be the case. (One might be tempted to present the example of the Scopes monkey trial of 1925 to argue that my claim here is wrong. One might wish to say that this trial shows that the mistrust of scientists or experts is not of recent origin, that it has a long history in America. Yet it does no such thing. Not only was the Scopes monkey trial simply one instance, but the very nature of the case shows that the trust in science at the time was actually growing. The famous case, pitting prominent lawyers against one another, was about a Tennessee teacher who was disciplined for teaching Darwin's theory of evolution to his students, at a time and place where the religious beliefs of creationism held supreme. It was a violation of school policy to teach evolution. Scopes was found guilty, but the verdict was overruled on a technicality. Importantly, the case was in Tennessee, not in New York City or some other such place. The teaching of evolution was widespread throughout much of the industrialized and urbanized parts of the country at the time, and the trial did not reflect any widespread antipathy toward Darwin's theory in much of the country. As such, the case does not reflect a widespread and long-standing mistrust of science in America. At best, it perhaps reflects a mistrust found in poor, rural areas or in the South. The teaching of evolution spread without much controversy in much of America in the early nineteen hundreds.) Today, it is not the case that the public overwhelming accepts the pronouncements of professionals -- scientists or others. Large sections of the American public – many are those who support Trump – reject the assumptions that professionals say things that are true or say things that are believed by the professionals themselves to be true. Instead, there is now the assumption that everyone – including professionals – routinely lie or manipulate. Everyone – including professionals – are thought to use proclamations of truth to serve one or another biased end, for example to advance one's interest or to gain power.

    We see this rejection of a conventional trust in truth and of the rejection of the professionals responsible for proclaiming truths over and over again in contemporary America. The denial of the truth that Donald Trump soundly lost the 2020 presidential election by seven million votes (and by a large number of votes in the electoral college) is an example of this. His supporters deny that journalists and politicians are or can be truthful when they say such things. The denial of the reality of global warming and climate change and their dire implications – realities that are overwhelmingly accepted as truths by the scientific community – by supporters of Trump is another example. It is claimed by these deniers that scientists have an agenda and are not being honest and truthful when they make such claims. Trust is gone; truth is gone. The rabid denial of the safety and effectiveness of the Covid vaccines, and now other vaccines as well, by so many millions of Americans – most though not by any means all of whom are Trump supporters – is yet another example of the rejection of trust in scientific proclamations of truth. We saw the rabid rejection by Trump and many of his supporters that the thirty-seven count indictment of Trump for his attempts after he left office to obstruct the government from regaining control over numerous classified documents which he illegally possessed was issued in a fair and impartial manner. Again, Trump and his supporters denied that the prosecutor and his office acted in a professional, unbiased manner. We were told by Trump and sadly by people at the heart of the United States government – from Republican candidates for President to the former Speaker of the House Kevin McCarthy -- not to trust the Justice Department, the FBI, etc.

The rejection of the trust in truth can be seen very clearly in many of the actions taken by Trump in the first few months of his second term (at the time of this writing). He has purged the federal government of thousands and thousands of non-partisan experts and replaced them with loyalists who are willing to do his bidding. (This was all done under the delusions of the existence of a "deep state", a belief that the government is filled with workers who have a "liberal agenda." The purges also seem directly influenced by the policy program of Project 2025, produced by the conservative think tank the Heritage Foundation.) Whether it is in the FBI or in the Department of Health and Human Services, he has filled these divisions not with the most competent people but with people who will do his political bidding. He has thoroughly politicized most major branches of the federal government, all under the guise of de-politicizing the federal government. (One cannot help but to think of postmodern theory here, where truth no longer matters. See Chapter 12.) No longer is the government bureaucracy to produce objective, scientific truths, for example, in the fields of vaccines or health care or environmental matters. Instead, the bureaucracy is and will presumably now continue to do things that are decidedly opposed to objectivity and conventional science. When conspiracy theorists are running the federal government divisions of justice; when anti-scientists are running the divisions of public health; etc., when the government launches an all out assault on Harvard University – which the government is doing as of this writing – simply because Harvard refused to bow down to the inappropriate demands of the Trump administration, then trust in truth is eroded. All that is left is power. Truth is not objective; truth is power.

In short, trust has and is being eviscerated; trust in professionals proclaiming truths is being rejected. As I note in Chapter Six on Alexis de Tocqueville's study of American democracy, this does not bode well for the future of American democracy or for the stability of American society. (On the other hand, it is worth noting that some sociologists believe that the lack of trust is actually a good thing. Mistrust fosters and contributes to the maintenance of social order rather than threatening it. This is the position taken by the exchange theorist Karen Cook and her colleagues (2005, 2009)(see Chapter Ten).) A democracy cannot be maintained if the populace does not trust professionals – scientists, journalists, professors, etc. -- to speak truths to the best of their abilities, even if these truths are unpalatable. (This does not mean that the populace should accept uncritically everything told to them by professionals. Indeed, a measure of skepticism is indeed a healthy and needed thing for a democracy. But a rigid, blank and automatic rejection of professionals is of a different order.)

Trust is tied to another important idea: virtue. Some sociologists such as Robert Bellah, and his colleagues, whose ideas are discussed in Chapter Six, follow in the footsteps of Tocqueville (see below), and argue that virtue, and specifically civic virtue, is also needed for democracies to survive. As Bellah et al. note, James Madison and Alexis de Tocqueville and many, many others all "believed that the survival of a free people depends on the revival of a public virtue that is able to find political expression" (1996:271).

Numerous "conservative politicians" in recent years, towing the Trump line, such as Ron DeSantis, the governor of Florida, who when running for the office of the President, sadly abandoned the commitment to civic virtue and to trust and truth. (DeSantis ran against Trump in the 2023-24 Republican primary. As such, one might question the claim that he was or is marching in line with Trump. Yet his orientations and actions, despite formally being opposed, indeed have been and continue to be clearly embracing the new Republican perspective and positions – the new ways of being a Republican, the new anti-democratic way -- advanced by Trump.) This is evident in their blind support for Trump several years ago after he was indicted during his first term for attempting to block the government from regaining the classified documents Trump had taken. These politicians lambasted the U.S. Department of Justice and have decried President Biden, who assumed the presidency after Trump's first term, for "weaponizing" the judicial process. Along the way, DeSantis proclaimed that the founding father James Madison would be turning in his grave if he were alive to witness the putative abuses being conducted here by the leaders of the Democratic Party against Trump. To be clear: the Justice Department was not weaponized by the Democrats. For our purposes it is relevant to note that DeSantis and others have and are significantly weakening American democracy through their actions. They are corroding the public's trust and faith in truth. They – or at least DeSantis -- are also wrongly invoking the founding fathers in their support for Trump. They are demonstrating the very lack of civic virtue noted by Bellah al. and discussed at length by James Madison and others in the *Federalist Papers* (2003 [[1787]).

This discussion warrants a brief digression into the ideas of the founding fathers and what they actually said. Specifically, we can turn to James Madison's writings in the *Federalist Papers*. The *Federalist Papers* were a collection of articles published in the 1780s in newspapers by James Madison, Alexander Hamilton and John Jay after the new U.S. Constitution was written but before it was passed and enacted into law. The intent was to convince the public to support the newly proposed Constitution. The new Constitution was meant to replace the then existing Articles of Confederation, as almost all believed that these Articles were too weak and would not be sufficient to maintain a stable, unified, national, political system. At the time, in the the 1780s, were two major political camps in the United States, one of these was the federalists who embraced the new Constitution and who embraced a strong, central government. The other, championed by Jefferson and others, were called republicans. They favored a weaker central government. They favored more power to the states. (It is rather curious that in the last several decades a group of arch-conservative political activists with significant power have come together in an organization called the Federalist Society. The basis of the existence of this Society ostensibly is the embrace of the ideas put forth in the *Federalist Papers* – presumably its appeal for this Society lies in the authors' championing such things as property rights (including slavery!) as well as liberty (rather than equality). Ironically, the original authors of the *Federalist Papers* were making the case for a strong central government, whereas arch-conservatives today are against such things.)

In the *Federalist Papers*, Madison systematically assesses the new draft of the Constitution and explained to the public why it should be adopted – why it would work as the foundation of the country and why the public should support its passage. When DeSantis said that Madison would be appalled at the recent indictment of Trump, he is suggesting that Madison was well aware of the possibilities of corruption and abuse in any form of government, most notably in a democratic form of government. DeSantis is right to note that Madison was aware of such things and that the Constitution was built in a way, most notably with endless "checks and balances" and with a diffusion of power, to ward against corruption or abuse. But for our purposes it is important to note that DeSantis ignores the more important and more relevant parts of the *Federalist Papers* as they pertain to the current situation in America. This has to do with Madison's views about the personal character of the elected representatives.

Madison claims that direct democracies cannot work, only a representative democracy can work. A society in which the people make all of the decisions will not work. A main reason he says that this would not work is because of the passions of the public. He argues that the public often times acts on emotion or impulse rather than through the use of cool, detached reason, and these irrational and unenlightened passions would not allow for a stable government to exist. Instead, Madison champions a "republic," i.e. a representative democracy. Elected representatives would be chosen to make decisions for the public and this would be a check on these irrational passions of the public (see *Federalist Papers*, No.10, 43, 48, 49, 51, 52, 55, 57, 62, 63).

Madison repeatedly states that the new democratic republican form of government would work, would only work, because in the last analysis the personal character of the elected (and appointed) representatives – the senators and the representatives – would be noble. These men serving as representatives would have the intelligence as well as the virtuous character to act in ways to champion the public good rather than to endlessly act in ways to advance their own self-interests, or their own party's interest. (The founding fathers were particularly concerned about the growth of political parties and "factionalism" and how they might destabilize the society.) When push comes to shove, Madison says, it is the "enlightened" character and the knowledge of the elected representatives – their knowledge, virtue, honesty, integrity – that would protect democracy from the passions of the mob. (The fear of the passions of the masses originally led the founding fathers to place in the Constitution a provision to have the Senate members appointed by state legislators rather than being elected by the populace as it is now, as it was believed that the legislators would use reason rather than passion in selecting what they viewed as the most competent, virtuous Senators. The irrationality and passions of the public would therefore be tempered. Both the elected representatives and the Senate members are deemed to have certain "abilities and virtues" and are seen as "enlightened and respectable citizens." As John Jay writes about the Senate in *Federalist Paper* No. 64: "As the select assemblies for choosing the President, as well as the State legislatures who appoint the senators, will in general be composed of the most enlightened and respectable citizens, there is reason to presume that their only attention and their votes will be directed to those men only who have become the most distinguished by their abilities and virtue...." 2003:389).)

We can see Madison's concerns about direct democracy and the passions of the mob and his belief that the character of the elected representatives would be such to protect democracy from them time and again in the *Federalist Papers*. In writing about the organization and election of the Senate, he writes in No. 63 that:

> such an institution [i.e., the Senate] may be sometimes necessary as a defense to the people against their own temporary errors and delusions. As the cool and deliberate sense of the community ought, in all governments, and actually will in all free governments, ultimately prevail over the views of its rulers; so there are particular moments in public affairs when the people, stimulated by some irregular passion, or some illicit advantage, or misled by the artful misrepresentations of interested men, may call for measures which they themselves will afterwards be the most ready to lament and condemn. In these critical moments, how salutary will be the interference of some temperate and respectable body of citizens ... [by which he means the Senate]. (2003:382)

Elsewhere in the *Federalist Papers* Madison repeatedly falls back on the noble character of the elected representatives to explain how the proposed government would work if and when the various checks and balances somehow failed to fully contain threats to it. Public "passions" which potentially threaten the stability of the government should be controlled by the representatives: "The *passions* ... not the *reason*, of the public would sit in judgement. But it is the reason, alone, of the public that ought to control and regulate the government. The passions ought to be controlled and regulated by the government" (2003:315 [emphasis in the original]).

This digression into a discussion of democratic political theory may at first glance seem not very central to a discussion of sociology or sociological theory. But I argue that it is. The stability and instability of social orders may be caused by dynamics in many different areas of society, whether these are cultural, social, economic, or political. Today in America, political issues are, and must be, central to a sociological understanding and analysis of the society at large.

When arch-conservatives such as DeSantis and others invoke Madison in ways that corrode the trust of the public, that corrode the trust in truth held by the public, they ironically are showing how wrong Madison was in believing that the character of the elected representatives would temper the passions of the mob and would serve as a protection of democracy (or a democratic republic). Instead, we see impassioned elected representatives such as DeSantis encouraging and fostering, not suppressing, the passions of the mob. We see them nurturing a greater and greater mistrust in professionals. We see them championing a negation in the belief in truth. Madison would indeed by rolling in his grave if he witnessed what was happening in America today, so too would Tocqueville (see below), but not for the reasons given by DeSantis. All of this bodes ill for the future stability of democratic American society, and all of this should be central to sociological analysis and sociological theorizing today.

Trust and virtue are not the only sociological forces that have been significantly damaged with Trump's second term. The very foundations of democratic government, as has been practiced in America for centuries has been and now is being significantly undermined in two specific ways: through the use of fear and through the eradication of institutional norms of governance. A few words can be said about each of these.

The Trump second term is decidedly different from his first term as president in two ways. First, in this second term, unlike the first, the Republican Party controls all branches of government – the judiciary, the legislative, and the executive. The unwillingness of member of the Republican Party in any of these branches to meaningful oppose Trump has given the latter almost endless power. Second, and presumably in part of product of the first issue, Trump has acted far, far more like an autocrat, disdainful of most aspects of democracy in his second term, whereas in his first term he seemed somewhat more reserved, comparatively speaking. Fear and the rejection of fundamental democratic, institutional norms characterize this second term.

I think of Max Weber's typology of dominance and authority (see Chapter Four) when considering Trump's reliance on fear to get things done.

For Weber, a person might comply with a request out of coercion or fear, or because the person believes the request to be legitimate. Legitimacy is what Weber sees as the basis of authority. He identifies three types of authority: traditional, charismatic, and rational legal. Democratic societies are largely anchored in rational legal authority and traditional authority. They are not grounded in charisma or on coercion. Yet charisma and coercion are foundational to Trump's leadership.

Commentators often note that Trump followers resemble a cult in their rabid devotion to their leader. In a religious cult, members abandon their rational and moral autonomy and willingly comply with the commands and dictates of the leader. Cults tend to have charismatic leaders. While it may be difficult for non-believers to understand the charismatic appeal of Trump, it seems rather clear that the loyalty of his followers is anchored in what they see as his charisma.

Charisma is fused with coercion in his leadership. Trump employs coercion regularly in his second term and eschews traditional and most importantly rational legal authority. In short, he is using forms of dominance which are anti-democratic. (Charismatic authority in itself is not anti-democratic. Many democratic leaders arguably have had charisma. But if charism is used or paired with such things as coercion, it gives coercive power much more potency.) His use of fear is clearly seen in many, many of his actions. For example, in the first few months of his second term he has threatened prominent universities in the country with significant financial penalty if they did not accede to his wishes regarding such things as direct (Trump-led) government involvement in regulating and policing academic policies to ensure that "diverse perspectives," i.e. conservative academic orientations, are being presented at the university – and to silence "liberal" voices, among many other intrusive demands which clearly threaten the autonomy of the universities. Some universities, such as Columbia University, have complied with these inappropriate demands. But one university in particular has resisted: Harvard University has refused to comply with the inappropriate political interference by the Trump administration. As a consequence, Trump and his administration has withheld funding, has threated to revoke the tax exempt status of the university, has blocked international students from attending, and has done numerous others things, to force Harvard to bow to his will. All of these actions are clearly meant to intimidate the university and to force them, out of fear, to comply with Trump's demands. This is decidedly not adhering to any mainstream understanding of democratic values. This is merely one example of Trump's use of fear. One could cite many, many others, as it is a fundamental tactic in his political actions.

Lastly, we can mention Trump's incessant violation of institutional norms of governance here as another major threat to democracy that cries out for sociological understanding. It is generally recognized today – at least by most mainstream scholars -- that a modern, meaningful democracy must have a governmental, institutional scaffolding that is relatively impervious to the whims or wishes of individuals in power. Thus, medical doctors and researchers employed by the government must be allowed to make scientific claims, based upon scientific research, without fear of political retribution if their findings go against the wishes of the person in power. Similarly, the Department of Justice must be directed by people committed to the rule of law and not by loyalty to a president. Environmental scientists must be allowed to make objective scientific claims about global warming. The head of the Federal Reserve must be allowed to make decisions regarding interest rates without political interference. At least, this is the conventional theory of how modern democracy in America should work.

Trump and his supporters, championing such fanciful ideas as the "deep state" have turned reason on its head and have complained that government scientists and other government workers are not being objective and unbiased, but instead have and are advancing their own moral and political agendas. As a result, Trump has set about to cleanse the deep state. He has fundamentally politicized most departments of government in the name of de-politicizing them. (Post-modern theory would undoubtedly site such oddities as evidence of the post-modern condition. See Chapter Twelve.) In short, he has consistently violated these and countless other institutional norms, much to the detriment of democracy.

All of this cries out for sociological understanding. By becoming informed of the various theories presented in this text, it is hoped that the reader will better be able to understand and to respond to what is happening in and to America today and perhaps be better able to defend democracy.

Overview of the Book

This textbook describes twenty or so sociological theories, all of which could be used in their own ways to make sense out of the issues discussed above. All could be used to better understand the sociological causes and consequences: of the destruction of trust and truth so foundational to a democracy; of the elevation of individualistic sensibilities and the negation of the social; of the perilous state of American society today; of the use of fear; of the eradication of institutional norms of democracy. For example, the sociological theorizing of Emile Durkheim (see Chapter Three) could illuminate current realities. One of Durkheim's concerns was with the central role of morality in maintaining social order. For Durkheim, writing over one hundred years ago, morality consisted of the shared evaluations and judgements, shared understandings, of right and wrong, good and bad, proper and improper. Shared morality, for Durkheim, was the social glue that holds many societies together. If a society does not have such sharedness, its stability will be threatened. He also focuses on the relationship of a people's set of moral expectations and the actual social realities in which they live. If there is a gap between expectations and realities, then tensions will likely arise. If a people, or a large segment of a people, expects one thing to happen, and instead another thing happens, then there will be confusion and social strife. The relevance of Durkheim's ideas to American society today is clear. Alternatively, we might draw upon the ideas of Karl Marx (see Chapter Two), to present just one other example, to make sense out of the confusions in America today. For Marx, the economic structure of a society is the key determinant of the major things happening in any society. Capitalism is the economic structure in America today. Marx believed that capitalism produces an almost endless series of conflicts which will eventually cause the entire system to collapse. For him, the central conflict was between the rich people, who he sees as the ruling class -- even in a democracy the rich, he says, are running the society – and the working class. While this class conflict may not be evident in America today, is there really any question that the rich class wields enormous power? Is there much question that the economic system of capitalism is a major determinant of what happens throughout society – whether in the economic or the political arenas? These are just two short suggestions about how sociological theory might be applied in understanding American society. I will leave it to the reader to see how one might apply the various other theories described in the chapters ahead to better understand and address the crises in America today. Here is a brief description of the coming chapters.

In the first part of this book, the classical theories of Marx, Weber and Durkheim are reviewed. Georg Simmel's theory, which was once rather influential, is also described here. This is followed by a chapter on Alexis de Tocqueville's analysis of American democracy. A few words need to be said here about this chapter.

Chapter Six provides a description of the theoretical ideas related to democratic culture in America (and how this culture affects individual personality) by the Frenchman Alexis de Tocqueville and by the American sociologist Robert Bellah and his colleagues. Of all the thinkers covered in this book, Tocqueville and Bellah et al. arguably are the ones that most explicitly address the concerns noted above about the crises of contemporary American democracy. These scholars see it as their tasks to understand American democratic culture and how it works. They seek to understand the individual forms of being, the personality or character types, produced by American democratic culture, and they wish to understand how these forms of being work to maintain or to threaten the future stability of American society.

Tocqueville (1805-1859) was not a sociologist, at least not formally, though his analyses are thoroughly sociological in nature. He was instead an astute observer and commentator of social and political life. In the early 1830s, he was awarded a grant to study prisons in America. He traveled to America soon after, but he did not focus on prisons. Instead, he investigated the social life of Americans and how this related to democracy. Throughout his travels in the United States, he met and talked to countless Americans. His central concern was a desire to understand American democracy. Specifically, he sought to understand how it was that democracy in America seemed to work, while in France the attempts to create a modern, stable democracy led to chaos and oppression during and after the French Revolution. In stark contrast to the United States, France experienced decades of turmoil in their attempts to establish a democratic society. First there was the chaos and bloodshed of the French Revolution of 1789. In the midst of the Revolution came Robespierre's Reign of Terror when opponents of the Revolution were sent in a seemingly endless stream to the guillotines (which eventually took Robespierre himself as one if its victims!). Everything was turned up-side-down during and after the revolution, for decades. Eventually, Napoleon came to power and led France and the entire continent into war. This was followed by an attempt in France to restore the monarchy, which was violently defeated during the Revolution, and this was followed by another attempt at democracy. It took decades and decades for France to establish a stable democracy – long after Tocqueville died. In short, Tocqueville sought to understand why it was that democracy managed to work in the United States but it could not do so in France. What was it about the United States? Importantly, he not only sought to understand how democracy managed to thrive in America, he also wished to understand its strengths and weaknesses, and wished to understand the threats intrinsic to this form of society.

Tocqueville published his report as a book titled *Democracy in America* (2003 [1835]), a book that became very influential in American intellectual circles in the eighteen hundreds and continues to be so today. His book is really about the political culture of the American public, about individuals and social relations in a democracy, as well as the social life that fuels this culture. He offers numerous insights into the workings of democracy in America and into possible threats to it. At the heart of his analysis is the idea that the central element of democratic societies, and specifically of American society, was the concept of "equality of conditions." As we discuss in Chapter Six, this notion of equality is not quite the same as other notions such as equality of opportunity or equality of outcomes. Instead, it refers to a large extent to the philosophical idea that citizens in American democracy all see themselves as fundamentally as having the same value, worth and dignity as everyone else. A poor person is *essentially* the same as a rich person.

Tocqueville sees this value as a centrally important force shaping Americans' personality and shaping American society, for good and ill. Along with this equality of conditions, he says, comes a society that is thoroughly mobile in the economic and social spheres. People are constantly moving up and down the economic ladder. The equality of conditions, and the love of this equality that he sees, causes Americans to be endlessly restless, constantly in motion. It also curiously causes them to be actively involved in social concerns of the community, through for example voluntary associations. But the positives of American democracy also are accompanied by negatives. For example, Tocqueville says American democracy produces few intellectuals – scientists, poets, artists, etc. It levels everyone down. The love for equality, he says, also potentially could lead to tyranny, as Americans love equality more than liberty and would surrender the latter if they need to do so to maintain he former. But this fear of the surrender of liberty, he argues, is significantly tempered by many cultural forces at work in America, as is described in Chapter Six. These are simply a few of the many features of democracy he analyzes.

Chapter Six also presents an overview of Robert Bellah et al.'s influential book *Habits of the Heart* (1996), a book deeply influenced by Tocqueville's ideas. Bellah and his colleagues interviewed numerous Americans in the nineteen eighties. They sought to understand how Americans understood themselves in relation to society. Theirs was a study of culture and personality, of individualism and commitment. They argued that in the history of the United States there have been four basic individual cultural types or traditions, and these are embodied in four character types. Americans traditionally fall into one or another of these four, though these are merely abstract types, and most people would likely embody elements of more than one or another of these four. The four dominant character types related to individualism and commitment are: utilitarian individualism, expressive individualism, the civic republican tradition, and the biblical tradition. The main argument of their book is that in the closing decades of the twentieth century two of the character types have become dominant, and the other two have receded, and this is posing a threat to American (democratic) society. The two that have become dominant are expressive individualism and utilitarian individualism. The two that have receded are the civic republican tradition and the biblical tradition. As the latter two traditions explicitly orient individuals toward a concern for realizing the "public good" and the former two do not, Bellah et al. express concerns about the present and future state of American society. In short, if everyone is focused only on themselves, who will focus on the collective good?

Bellah et al. express great concerns about the then state of American democratic culture, concerns which eerily resonate today. Thirty years ago, they wrote an "Introduction to the Updated Edition: The House Divided" to

Habits of the Heart, which was originally published in 1985. The authors expressed alarm at what they saw as a growing crisis in America: "Most Americans agree that things are seriously amiss in our society – that we are not, as the poll questions often put it, "headed in the right direction" – but they differ over why this is so and what should be done about it" (1996:xxii). America had become deeply divided and the prospects of overcoming the divide seem questionable. Again, this was written thirty years ago. The crack in American society has now become a chasm. The reader will have to assess whether the deep divisions in America today can be attributed to the forces described by Bellah et al. or whether they are caused by some other sociological forces.

The next section of the book includes chapters that examine the developments in sociological theory that emerged in the middle years of the twentieth century. These include the structural functionalist models of Talcott Parsons, conflict theories, and the symbolic interactionist tradition. Some of these approaches continue to be widely embraced today. Some have grown in influence. Others have declined. This is followed by several chapters that focus upon a number of recent trends in theorizing including: the integrative theories of Bourdieu, Giddens and Habermas; postmodern theories; critical race and gender theories as well as queer theories; and theories which we shall call theories of the changing present, including theories of globalization, the environment, and post-industrial and post-Marxist theories.

A few words can be said here about these last chapters. Integrative theories are described in Chapter Eleven. These theories produced by people such as Bourdieu, Giddens, and Habermas seek to overcome the main conceptual divides and thorny issues in theory construction. For example, should theorist think of individuals as free agents capable of making choices or should they think of individuals as if they are something like puppets on a string who are programmed and determined by their social environment to act in one way or another? Of course, in America the gut reaction to such a choice is to automatically assume that individuals are free agents (as we discussed earlier). And there is no question that people make choices. Yet as we see below, the issue becomes far more complicated when one peels back the layers. For example, if you are a student, ask yourself why you and your fellow students tend to sit in the same seat in class every day? Why is it that you do not sit in a different seat each class? Couldn't one predict where students are going to sit after the first week of class? You might say the students make the choice to sit in the same seat, but the reality is they are acting like puppets or programmed machines. In Chapter Twelve we look at the theories of postmodernism. Postmodern theories challenge most of the basic assumptions of traditional theorizing. This form of theorizing is, as we shall see, very controversial and largely is rejected by mainstream sociology. Nevertheless, postmodern theorists provide many provocative and challenging ideas which theorists today should not ignore (and these theorists have influenced some of the current cultural issues and controversies, particularly around the issues of sexuality and gender and identities). Critical race and gender theories are also covered in Chapter Thirteen, as are queer theories. These theories do not simply provide theoretical accounting of race and gender but claim that the task of theory is to challenge existing systems of inequality by showing how they operate. Queer theories not only take a critical look at systems of inequality, but they argue that the conceptual binary of the gender divisions of male and female maintain inequalities and as such should be challenged. In Chapter Fourteen, several examples of recent development in sociological theories anchored in understanding recent and pressing issues of the world today are described. We look at several globalization and environmental social theories, and we describe several theories which could perhaps best be described as post-industrial or post-Marxist theories. These latter theories, created by Beck, Touraine, and Castells, argue that the essential dynamics of the world today are fundamentally different than those of industrial capitalism. Beck, for example, argues that risk rather than class conflict is the essential dynamic of the world today. Touraine argues it is the control over what he calls "historicity." Castells claims the essence of the world today is to be found in the concept of networks. He sets about analyzing networks and how they work in the world today. An essential conflict in the world today according to Castells concerns the tensions over what he calls spaces of flows and spaces of places. Spaces of flows are defined in terms of things or ideas that flow through them, whether it is money, digital things, goods, etc. The networks controlling the spaces of flows have power today.

Modern History and Sociological Theory

Sociological theory should be understood within a historical context. One needs to appreciate the historical context that gave birth to the various forms of theories that have emerged, and one should recognize that theorists develop their ideas because they are trying to understand the context within which they live. History provides a framework of understanding. We can identify three historic eras of significance for the development of modern, sociological theory: The Enlightenment, the industrial era, and the post-industrial period.

The Enlightenment

The Enlightenment, also known as the Age of Reason, was a hugely important period in European and world history. It occurred roughly between 1600 and 1800. It is characterized by new ways of thinking. Philosophers, scholars, and scientists of the time throughout western Europe wrote articles and books harshly critical of the then existing ways of thinking about the world and about how the world was organized. Some of the more famous of the many, many persons identified with the Enlightenment include the following philosophers and social thinkers: Immanuel Kant (1724-1804) in Germany, John Locke (1632-1704) in England; Adam Smith (1723-1790) and David Hume (1711-1776) in Scotland (the northern part of the Great Britain); Rene Descartes (1596-1650), Montesquieu (1689-1755), Condorcet (1743-1794), and Jean-Jacques Rousseau (1712-1778) in France. (Rousseau was born in Switzerland but lived and died in France). In addition, it was during this period that the birth of modern forms of science also emerged. Many early and important scientists appeared, and through their research established some of the most basic principles of science that are accepted today. Scientists such as Joseph Priestly (1733-1804) in England and Antoine Lavoisier (1743-1794) in France, for example, conducted research in their chemistry laboratories that established the modern understanding of the basic chemical elements (e.g. oxygen, helium, etc.). Among other things, they set the foundation for the creation of the periodic table of elements that we use today to classify all of the basic chemicals known to exist. How different the world had to have been before a knowledge of these things emerged. How might one have explained fire or rust without knowing about oxygen?

It is the philosophers of the period however that are more central to our concerns. These Enlightenment philosophers reacted against the conventional ways of understanding the social world. Prior to the seventeenth century, the principles of traditional and religion governed much thinking. Farmers selected the crops they planted not because science told them the crops would be the best to plant, but because the parents of the farmers planted those same crops. Tradition dictated decisions. In the political arena, Europe was dominated by aristocratic nobility. This was the era of kings and queens, and the vast array of nobles. How does one become a king? One inherits it. It is because of tradition. But it was not simply the practical concerns of the farmer or the organization of the political system that was governed by tradition or religion, science too was ruled by these things. As we see in Chapter Two, Galileo (1564-1642), the great Italian scientist of the late Renaissance, created a lot of trouble by conducting and publishing research about the solar system that contradicted the dominant theories of the day. His scientific research challenged the claims of the Roman Catholic

Church, and this religious body reacted harshly to this challenge. The scholars of the Enlightenment looked at all of these types of things and more and questioned whether the use of tradition and religion should be the guiding principles of knowledge. They looked about the social world, the political world, the natural world, and questioned whether religion and tradition are the best principles upon which to understand their world. They concluded that these basic principles should be rejected and should be replaced by a new set of principles. These principles are rooted in the three major themes embraced by the Enlightenment thinkers: Reason, the primacy of the individual, and optimism.

Reason

In general, most of the major figures of the Enlightenment were passionate supporters of reason, and particularly for the free use of reason. They repeatedly championed its use and repeatedly called for it to be elevated above all else. As Kant wrote: "For enlightenment ... all that is needed is *freedom*. And the freedom to make *public use* of one's reason in all matters" (2003 [1784]:46). For Kant and for many of the Enlightenment thinkers, reason should replace tradition and religion as the guiding principle of knowledge and the guiding principle of practice. If we are allowed to freely use reason, logic, to understand our worlds, rather than tradition or religion, we would have a better world. We would be better able to understand and therefore control the natural world through science, because science is based upon reason. We would have better political systems. After all, if one reflects upon the history of the aristocracy in Europe one sees that some kings and queens were good or benevolent, but others were cruel, evil, mentally ill, or incompetent. Relying upon tradition or religion as the basis for political organization is not the best way to go about organizing the political system. Instead, we should use reason, the Enlightenment figures proclaimed. What would be a more rational, more reasonable form of political system than aristocracy? Modern democracy. What is more logical than a system in which everyone is equal and the majority rules?

The Enlightenment gave birth also to modern social science. Perhaps, the thinkers argued, we could use reason to develop theories of behavior and social organization such that we could create a more just and more rational world? Modern economic theory, sociological theory, psychology, and other modern social sciences emerged at this time and in this spirit. Adam Smith, for example, wrote the *Wealth of Nations* (1776). The book has become something like the bible of capitalism. It provides a reasoned, scientific explanation for why capitalism would be the best economic system to have. It would provide the most wealth. It would be the most just. And it is rooted firmly in the idea of reason. It assumes that individual economic actors are rational in their activities. Individuals rationally act in self-interested ways, and when an economic system is organized to allow this to happen then good things result.

At the heart of all of this was the belief that reason could or should be the road that people follow to create order in their worlds such that they can control this world. Reason and science would allow us to better understand the natural and the social worlds such that we could control the forces of these worlds to produce a good and just order. The world should not be controlled and ordered by tradition or religion but by systematic use of reason.

The Individual Self

The individual became a major focus during the Enlightenment. Philosophers set about trying to understand the individual self by systematically applying reason to it. This led to the great epistemological debates of the era. Epistemology is the branch of philosophy concerned with knowledge, specifically it is concerns with how we know. How do we know the difference between an apple and a rock? How do we know that we can eat one and not the other? Locke, Descartes, Kant and others all put forth theories about these matters. We need not concern ourselves here with the particulars of their theories. What is of concern here is that they elevated concerns about the individual and how the individual works to a central place in philosophy. On a related note, these same philosophers build their political theories, including theories of democracy, on assumptions about the value of the individual, and about the essentially same value of each individual. That is, they built their political theories on assumptions of essential equality. They asked: What would be the most rational political and social system that we could imagine if we begin with the assumption that all individuals have the same value, that all individuals are essential equal? Of course, this led to the emergence of modern democratic theories.

The focus on the individual also contributed to the birth of modern social science. Among other things, it contributed to the birth of modern psychology, and modern theories of the self. Many have argued that John Locke's *An Essay Concerning Human Understanding* (1975 [1689]) is the first major philosophical work that paved the way for modern psychology. It also paved the way for the emergence of the modern human sciences and of modern sociology, as we see below.

Optimism

The third major theme of the Enlightenment was optimism. The Enlightenment scholars were incredibly hopeful about the future. They believed that if people embraced the principles of reason and embraced the primacy of the individual, they could develop understandings and practices that could understand and organize their worlds in a way that was more just and was more beneficial to the people. The world of the future for these men was a world of greater liberty, more prosperity and more justice, if the principles they espoused were embraced. The French Enlightenment figure Marquis de Condorcet captures these sentiments in his essay on the *Progress of the Human Mind*, written in the midst of the chaos of the French Revolution:

> We have watched man's reason being slowly formed by the natural progress of civilization; we have watched superstition seize upon it and corrupt it, and tyranny degrade and deaden the minds of men under the burden of misery and fear. One nation alone escapes the two-fold influence of tyranny and superstition [presumably he is speaking of France here]. From that happy land where freedom had only recently kindled the torch of genius, the mind of man, released from leading-strings of its infancy, advances with firm steps toward the truth. But this triumph soon encourages tyranny to return, followed by its faithful companion superstition, and the whole of mankind is plunged once more into darkness, which seems as if it must last forever. Yet, little by little, day breaks again; eyes long condemned to darkness catch a glimpse of the light and close again, then slowly become accustomed to it, and at last gaze on it without flinching; once again genius dares to walk aboard on the earth, from which fanaticism and barbarism had exiled it. (2003 [1793]:63)

The light of reason, he tells us, cannot be stopped. It can only be temporarily halted. Religion, tradition, tyranny, superstition, all will give way to reason. Condorcet rails against religion in this essay and against any forces that prevent reason from being embraced. He identifies his "battle cry": "reason, tolerance, humanity."

Counter-Enlightenment and Critics

It bears mentioning that not all of the major thinkers of this period embraced all of these themes. Not all championed reason, and not all believed that democratic revolutions would lead to better worlds. Not all believed in the unfettered themes and values of the Enlightenment. For example, Jean Jacques Rousseau, the influential philosopher who was noted for among other things the concept of the social contract, was harshly critical of "civilization" and of the growth of knowledge and reason. He began his philosophy by imaging human beings in a state of nature, in a world before civilization. He saw man in this state as good and as free. He believed civilization along with the growth of knowledge and reason could well lead to oppressions. Knowledge and reason, rather than liberating, could shackle people. These things could enslave people and prevent them from living their true nature. Rousseau believed that man in nature was good. As he says in the opening lines of Chapter One of *The Social Contract*: "Man was born free, but is everywhere in bondage" (1954 [1762]:2). Rousseau perhaps shows his concerns more fully a few years earlier: "While the government and the laws see to the safety and well-being of assembled men, the sciences, letters and the arts, less despotic and perhaps more powerful, spread garlands of flowers over the iron chains with which they are burdened, stifle in them the sense of the original liberty for which they seem to have been born, make them love their slavery, and turn them into what is called civilized people" (2003 [1750]:33).

Despite his concerns, Rousseau has been historically closely associated with the many Enlightenment figures who helped usher in the modern world. Other figures from the seventeen hundreds however were clearly opposed to the Enlightenment. They were part of what is called the Counter-Enlightenment. For example, the English-Irish philosopher Edmund Burke was critical of many facets of the Enlightenment. He was particularly critical of the French Revolution and its excesses. He found value in the embrace of tradition. He championed a number of conservative ideas, including an embrace of tradition. These things ran counter to Enlightenment thought. Similarly, in France people such as Joseph de Maistre (1753-1821) and Louis de Bonald (1754-1840) opposed the essential tenets of the Enlightenment. They bemoaned the elevation of reason and the decline of God. They saw the French Revolution (see below) not as a glorious, positive event, but instead as a seriously wrongheaded thing. Traditional institutions, these intellectuals claimed, should be embraced and should not destroyed as they were in the French Revolution. In short, the Counter-Enlightenment was essentially a conservative reaction to the wellspring of change brought with the Enlightenment.

Consequences of the Enlightenment

The Enlightenment led to the great revolutions of the late seventeen hundreds: The American Revolution in 1776 and the French Revolution in 1789. Both were directly inspired by Enlightenment ideas. This is reflected in the founding documents of these countries: The Declaration of Independence, the United States Constitution, and the French Declaration of the Rights of Man. While the American Revolution came first, it was the French Revolution that had the more significant impact in many ways. After all, France was a world power in the late seventeen hundreds. Before the Revolution it had an aristocracy, a system that was in place for over five hundred years. The King inherited his thrown and was the ultimate ruler. The French revolutionaries, schooled in Enlightenment thinking, sought to replace this system with a democratic and capitalist one. It was a dramatic change to society. The Revolution was not a tidy affair. In contrast to the American Revolution, the French Revolution was bloody and chaotic, and the country was in turmoil for twenty years. Unlike in America, the French Revolution sought a total remaking of society. First there was the Revolution, then came the Reign of Terror in which the more radical wing of the Revolution came to power and killed anyone who opposed the new regime. In the early revolutionary years, soon after 1789, the revolutionaries sought to make radical changes not simply to the government, but to all facets of society. Among other things, the revolutionaries changed the days and numbers of the days of the week. They changed the years of the calendar (1792 became Year One). They abolished all of the privileges of the nobility and confiscated all of the extensive Church properties. (The Church owned a large percentage of all of the land before the Revolution.) They did all of this and more in the spirit of embracing the principles of reason and more generally the principles of the Enlightenment. After all, the names of the days, weeks, months and years were based upon a Christian calendar. They were based upon ideas rooted in religion and tradition. And the revolutionaries in France saw the Catholic Church as much as the nobility as their enemy. Eventually Napoleon came to power in the early eighteen hundreds and proceeded to wage war throughout Europe. It was only after his defeat and only after a brief attempt was made to restore the monarchy that France developed some stable form of democracy.

With the French and American Revolutions paving the way, democracy and capitalism rooted deeply in Enlightenment thought came to conquer much of the developed world.

Industrialization and Urbanization

The Enlightenment ushered in the modern era. At the heart of this modern era lies democracy and capitalism. These political and economic systems in turn are closely associated with other forces that were unleashed by the Enlightenment. These include industrialization, urbanization, and the consolidation of the nation state system. One cannot truly understand sociological theory – either the classical theories of the late eighteen and early nineteen hundreds or any of the more recent theories – without understanding and appreciating these historical developments. We begin here with industrialization.

Prior to the late seventeen hundreds there were no factories as we know them; there was no mass production to speak of. The economies before this time were largely agricultural. Most people in the United States in 1776 were farmers, living in rural areas. Clothing, furniture, pots and pans, and all of the other material things were produced in small shops (perhaps one might wish to call these early factories) or at home. The first modern factories then emerged in the late seventeen hundreds in New England and in northern Europe. Early textile mills, where cotton and wool were processed into clothe, began to appear, as did other things such as the growth of iron works and the spread of grist mills to grind the wheat and corn into powder. Though clothing, iron, and milled wheat had been produced for centuries prior to this period, it was in this period that the systems of production increased in efficiency, size, and scope. They were successful economic enterprises and they grew, and they led others to begin other types of factories which produced an ever-increasing array of goods. This process continued through the eighteen hundreds and exploded by the end of that century.

One cannot underestimate the extent of social change that accompanied the growth and spread of factories in America, England, and in the rest of northern Europe in the eighteen and early nineteen hundreds. Huge American cities appeared almost overnight. Chicago, for example, grew from a tiny settlement to a city of millions in the space of fifty years in the late eighteen hundreds. The other major cities in the Eastern and Midwestern parts of America also exploded in size. Probably less than fifteen percent of Americans lived in urban areas in 1776. Most lived in rural areas, and there were only a few cities such Boston, New York, and Philadelphia that even had populations in excess of one hundred thousand people – the size of a small town today. This was basically reversed in the short space of one hundred years. By the nineteen hundreds well over seventy-five percent of Americans lived in or near cities. It went from being a rural society to an urban society and remained so throughout the century.

In the midst of this, America experienced massive population changes. There was an immigration boom. From 1890 to 1920 an enormous number of people immigrated to America from Europe. These immigrants were largely Roman Catholics and Jews, largely from southern and eastern Europe -- from Italy, Poland, Russia, Ireland, and many, many other countries. They came to America, a country that was until then overwhelming dominated by Protestants who traced their ancestry to Great Britain (i.e., England, Scotland, Wales, and Northern Ireland). Immigrants also came from Germany and Scandinavia during this wave, though many from these countries came earlier. These groups were not the only ones on the move. African Americans in the South who were liberated from slavery at the end of the Civil War (1865) only to find themselves quickly subjected to the oppressive brutal system of Jim Crow which lasted through the 1950s, also moved in great numbers North to the cities. Many experienced a set of push and pull factors that led them north. Many African Americans in the late nineteenth and early twentieth centuries saw the prospects of moving to the North as a means of escaping the brutality of the south, but they also saw the industrializing North as a possible site of comparably good work. The booming factories needed laborers.

The changes that came with industrialization were profound. Technological, social, economic, cultural, and global changes all were significant. Automobiles did not of course exist in the nineteenth century; they did exist by the opening years of the twentieth. Electricity was just beginning to be understood in the early years of the nineteenth century, but by the twentieth century, it was commonly found in major cities. Technological inventions and innovations abounded. The way one listened to music was fundamentally alerted with these changes, and movies did not yet exist in the nineteenth century. Social changes also were dramatic. Working farms and families of the early nineteenth century were dramatically different from the families and factories of the second half of that century. This inevitably altered social relations. The economic situation also changed. Life for the poor and working classes of the late nineteenth and early twentieth centuries was brutal, but there was a sense amongst at least many of them that their lives were getting better or that they could get better if they worked and worked and worked in the factories and their brutal conditions. Changes also came to the national and global political order. The nation state system, the international system of national governments that we now have, was consolidated in the nineteenth century (though it was not until the end of World War Two that it was finally settled). Prior to the late seventeen hundreds many countries did not exist as modern nation states. The notion of citizens engaged in some sort of "social contract" with others and the state did yet exist. In countries ruled by kings and queens and aristocracies, the nature of the state was fundamentally different. With this came an ever-increasing awareness of global interconnectedness, through trade, political contacts, wars, etc. But the most significant change of all that occurred in this period was change itself. Before the modern era, social life from one generation to another, from one year to another, did not change much or dramatically. In Europe, the peasant farmers rode horses and plowed their fields in 300 A.D. They likely had some king or some other nobility ruling over them. This was little different in the seventeen hundreds. They continued to ride horses and continued to have royalty ruling over them. Life was characterized not by change, but by stability. It was largely static, and change was slow to non-existent from generation to generation. All that changed in the eighteen hundreds. Change itself characterizes the industrial era. Things are expected not to remain the same, but to change. And of course, the rate of change increased throughout the twentieth century and into the present.

In the first half of the twentieth century, America and Western Europe experienced a number of major historical events that accompanied the above changes. Most notably, the rapid expansion of capitalism and wealth that occurred in the 1920s was followed by the Great Depression, which began with the stock market crash of 1929 and continued throughout the 1930s. The economy fell apart. Unemployment went through the roof, with up to twenty-five percent of the population out of work. Waged declined. Capitalism was not working. Franklin Delano Roosevelt was elected President in 1932 and instituted the New Deal, which basically consisted of large federal programs to aid the economy and to provide jobs, health, welfare and security to American citizens. Roosevelt's programs laid the foundation for social security, Medicare, and a whole host of other federal programs. At the same time, an ominous threat was emerging in Europe. This was the threat of fascism. European societies in the early nineteen hundreds were being torn apart by polarized political fights, between the radical left and the radical right. The radical right, in the form of the fascist movements of Hitler's Nazis in Germany, as well as Mussolini's fascists in Italy and others throughout Europe who shared such thinking, won out in the conflict and took over much of Europe. Hitler began by aggressively taking back a part of France (the Alsace), then he invaded Bohemia (a part of Czechoslovakia), Austria and eventually Poland, not to mention many other countries and areas of Europe. His conquests led to World War Two and the Holocaust. America joined the war effort to defeat Hitler (and Japan), and eventually succeeded in doing so in. In 1945, American was the sole dominant military and economic power in the world, all other major countries were destroyed by the war.

The industrial era reached its peak in the post-World War Two era. American society was getting increasingly wealthy in the 1940s, 1950s and into the 1960s. Each generation seemed to be getting wealthier than the earlier one. A middle class was growing (though it never was or is anywhere as large as popular imagery suggests). The changes which were noted earlier expanded. American was also becoming more and more a consumer society. Things continued to be produced on an ever more massive scale. Automobiles and Coke-a-Cola, washing machines and television sets, were being produced like never before. Fast food, shopping malls, and suburbs began to appear on the social landscape. This led to the 1960s, a period of social protest and social strife. A number of great social movements appeared. The Civil Rights Movement, for example, started in the 1950s but grew in size and acceptance in the 1960s. The student protest movements, the anti-Viet Nam war movement, environmentalism, the women's rights movement, and many more emerged in this era.

The Post-Industrial Era

America and the western world entered a new historical era starting somewhere in the 1970s, and these societies continue in this new era through the present. We live now in a post-industrial era. (Some scholars and commentators use the term postmodern to describe this present era. However, that term is fraught with problems. We discuss the postmodern in Chapter Twelve).) The world today is very different from the world of the 1950s. This new post-industrial era is characterized by several key developments. The first of these is the changing basis of the economy. The economy of the industrial era was based upon increasingly large-scale manufacturing. The number as well as the size of factories grew through that period. Moreover, the number and percent of jobs in the economy that were in the industrial sector, rather than in the agricultural sector or the service sector, was large. The industrial sector was the largest part of the economy and had the largest work force of any other sector in the 1940s and 1950s, at its height. In other words, more Americans were working in factories than in any other setting in this period. All of this has changed, and dramatically so. The vast majority of factories in America have been shut down. America, particularly the northeast and Midwest, is littered with abandoned factories that once teamed with workers busily making anything from automobiles to washing machines to custom jewelry.

What has replaced the factories? We now live in a service and information-based economy. That is the core of the post-industrial economy. It is not things as much as services and information that are produced now in America. Things of course are still being produced. Automobiles and washing machines are still being made, but more so now in Mexico, in India and in China than in Philadelphia or Detroit. Services include anything from a McDonald's worker providing service to the customer at the counter to a tax accountant providing services to someone filing their taxes. Information includes anything from college professor's giving lectures and publishing articles and books to pharmaceutical researchers and software engineers developing new programs. It is the service and information sector that is the largest today. More jobs are found here than anywhere else. This sector has replaced the industrial one as the largest. There are many differences between these types of economies. Most notably, while the industrial sector produced a growing working class that was relatively prosperous (thanks in no small part to unionization) – a class that is often identified as the "vast middle class" – the post-industrial society of today is characterized not by the growing middle but by the shrinking middle. The post-industrial economy is more bifurcated, more split between the wealthier groups and the poorer groups. This is made plain when we recognize that service and information jobs come in two distinct types. Some are high end, high paying jobs that require high education and provide good benefits, and some are low end, low paying jobs that do not require high education and do not provide benefits. The former are jobs such as software engineering jobs at Apple or Google. The latter are jobs at McDonalds's and Walmart.

Post-industrial society is also characterized by consumption and technology. Consumption has replaced production both in terms of its importance to the economic system and as a main focus of social life. Our economy and much of our lives are driven by, and organized around, consumption. And it is not simply consumption. It is consumption within a capitalist society. This means that a major element of society is the management of the consumption process. A significant part of this involves the manipulation of signs and symbols. From advertising and promotion to market research designed to allow producers of things and ideas with the knowledge need to effectively control the sales and consumption process, the organization of control over signs and symbols has become a theme of the post-industrial era. Consumption and the organization and manipulation of signs are closely tied to another theme of post-industrialism. This is the theme of technology, and specifically digital and high-technology. The internet era has had an enormous effect on society.

Nature and the environment and globalization are additional features of concern if not of prominence in the post-industrial society. As the result of technological developments and social changes brought about with or because of democratic capitalism, a new relationship to nature and the environment is arising, though there are currently major contests over what this relationship is and should be. These contests reflect the changes in the role of nature and the environment in our lives. Technology, whether through new drugs or bio-technological devises, has infused itself thoroughly within medicine and medical practices. Technology, of course, was a major characteristic of the industrial era. We see this is all areas of life. For example, birth control, a technological development, arose during that period and clearly had a significant social impact. But now the marvels of technology and biotechnology abound. These have contributed to a reassessment of what nature is, what people are and what the relationship is between the two. Gay liberation emerged in the post-industrial era. This is a form of questioning traditional conceptualizations of nature. The environment too has assumed a very different place than it once had. No longer might we think as Benjamin Franklin once did that it would be better to mine coal than to cut down a forest for fuel to heat houses because cutting down the forest would be so unsightly. We know and appreciate – at least many do – the finite nature of the environment. We can only warm the planet so much before dire things happen. All of this is related closely to the globalization. Consumption, nature, technology, are intertwined with the increasingly interconnected and interdependent character of the global society.

Some Early Theorists, Theories, and Traditions

New developments in sociological theorizing emerged in the nineteenth and early twentieth centuries. Some of these, such as the ideas of Marx, Weber and Durkheim, continue to have a major impact upon sociology today. These are described in detail in coming chapters. But a number of other theories and traditions are worth mentioning here, if for no other reason than many of these serve as the backdrop for more recent theorizing. In this section, the early theories of Comte and Spencer are described. Also, the importance of the German intellectual traditions of this period for subsequent theorizing is noted. This section ends with a brief but important note concerning several important theorists writing in the eighteen hundreds and early nineteen hundreds who were until rather recent decades largely ignored by mainstream sociology. The works of Harriet Martineau and W.E.B. Du Bois are described. Of central significance, Martineau was a woman, and W.E.B. Du Bois was African American. (Their ideas are discussed more in Chapter Thirteen.)

Auguste Comte (1798-1857) was a French philosopher and social theorist who is widely seen as the first, modern sociologist. He was an assistant to another prominent social theorist, Henri Saint-Simon (1760-1825). Saint-Simon was a well-known political philosopher. Saint-Simon was not interested in developing a science of sociology. Instead, he was interested in developing a theory of society, and specifically a theory of a good society. He particularly focused upon what he called "the laboring classes" and upon what role the government should play in society. The laboring classes consisted of anyone who worked. This would include farmers, shop owners, factory workers, and intellectuals. The laboring classes were seen as noble. He contrasts the laboring classes with the idle classes, a class that does not work. The aristocracy would be considered part of this class. Saint Simon saw this class as part of the problem in society. He did not like this class. He also saw a limited role for the government in society. The government should exist to address the ills associated with the idle class, and it should exist to ensure that a liberal market economy was working.

Comte developed his own approach which he called "social physics." He sought to create a new academic discipline that was scientific and that was devoted to understanding the workings of the social world. In effect, he sought to develop a scientific sociology. Of note, he believed there was one and only one form of scientific knowledge, and all scientific disciplines, whether chemistry or sociology, should use the same approach in their studies. This approach was the scientific one. Only one true scientific approach exists, and sociology should embrace it. Toward this end, Comte embraced a **positive philosophy**. Positivism is a type of philosophy that assumes one and only one correct scientific approach exists and that is the approach used by the likes of chemistry, physics, biology, etc. It assumes that the scientist should systematically apply logic to understanding empirical, observable things, and that he or she should look to explain causal relationships based upon these observations. Moreover, Comte saw the task of the scientist, at least the most fundamental task, was to discover the natural laws governing the world. There are natural laws of physics -- laws of gravity, laws of the speed of light, etc. The same with chemistry and biology. Comte believed the task was to discover the natural laws governing all things, including social things. The task of sociology, or social physics, was to discover the natural laws of society and the social world. (The claim that the social world is governed by some sort of natural laws is widely if not universally rejected by scholars today. Indeed, even the philosophers who developed far more sophisticated approaches to positivism in the late nineteen and early twentieth centuries (see Chapter Eight) quickly abandoned any claim that any such laws exist. We must remember however when he was writing. He clearly was a son of the Enlightenment.)

Comte also developed an evolutionary model of the history of intellectual development. He argued that in the course of the history of intellectual development, whether in a society at large or in an individual academic discipline, thinking goes through three stages. The first is what he calls the theological stage. At this stage, people tend to claim that the fundamental cause of some reality, whether it is an earthquake or a rainbow, is some sort of religious being. This could be a god or gods, or spirits. God causes things to happen. The second stage is what he calls the metaphysical stage. This is similar in some respects to the theological stage. In the metaphysical stage people explain things in terms of magical or mysterious forces hidden within the realities of one or another thing. Specifically, nature is used as the essential explanation of things at this metaphysical stage. The forces of nature are mysterious and unchanging, much like god, and are fundamentally unknowable. In the course of intellectual development, the metaphysical stage gives way to the third and final stage, the positive (or scientific) state. He describes this stage: "[In] the positive state, the human mind, recognizing the impossibility of obtaining absolute truth, gives up the search after the origin and hidden causes of the universe and a knowledge of the final causes of phenomena. It endeavors now only to discover, by a well-combined use of reasoning and observation, the actual laws of phenomena – that is to say, their invariable relations of succession and likeness" (1988:2). In keeping with the sentiments of the Enlightenment, Comte was optimistic that a science of society could be developed, and he believed it would be extremely important for the future political and social development of the world.

Another important, early thinker in the sociological tradition is Herbert Spencer (1820-1903). Spencer was a British political philosopher and social theorist. He became quite popular in England in the second half of the nineteenth century, and his ideas became very influential in many countries, from the United States, to France, to England. He was most famously influenced by Charles Darwin (1809-1882), the father of modern evolutionary theory (though Spencer also influenced Darwin in turn). Darwin's theory, which is almost universally accepted by scientists today, says that evolution occurs as the result of genetics and adaptation. If a lizard has the gene for green skin and the green skin allows the lizard to effectively hide so that the birds who wish to eat it cannot see it, then the lizard will more likely survive and pass on the gene for green skin to its offspring. This is the main idea. The genes that are the most adapted to the environment are the ones that will be carried on in future generations, and the genes that are the least adapted to the environment will not be passed on. The slowest or weakest deer in a herd – the one with the worst genes -- that is running away from a wolf that is chasing them will be caught and eaten by the wolf and as a result the weak deer's genes will not be passed on. Thus, the herd itself is strengthened. The gene pool of the herd is strengthened because it is no longer burdened with the prospects that the weaker genes will be passed on to the next generation. (The dead deer cannot reproduce.) In short, Darwin (and Spencer) embraced the claim of the "survival of the fittest." Spencer was also influenced by the British demographer, or population theorist, Thomas Malthus (1766-1834). (Curiously he was also influenced by Jean-Baptiste Lamarck (1744-1829), the French scientist who developed a theory of evolution which was contradictory to that of Darwin. Lamarck embraced the theory of the inheritance of acquired characteristics. If something happened to you physically to alter your biological makeup, the theory says that your children would inherit this. For example, if you exercise a lot and build your muscles, the Lamarckian might say that your children will have bigger muscles than they otherwise would. Today this is almost universally rejected. Darwinian evolutionary theory says that acquired traits are not inherited.)

Spencer applied the Darwinian ideas, particularly the evolutionary ideas of Charles Darwin, to an understanding of society and social evolution. He is often associated with the concept of **Social Darwinism**, which is the application of Darwin's theory to social evolution. Social evolution, he argues, operates under the same laws as natural evolution. Just as in nature, where the fast and strong and healthy deer survives and produces offspring and the slow and weakly and sick deer are eaten or otherwise die, so the same principle applies to human societies. There are smart and rich people, and dumb and poor people. Inequality exists, and this is the result of nature, Spencer argues. Moreover, just as in biological evolution where there is a development from simple to complex organisms and systems – evolution from single celled organism to more and more complicated organisms such as mammals – so to in social history there is an evolution from the simple to the complex. There are simple societies and complex societies. Modern,

---

Herbert Spencer

It would be a mistake to think that Spencer was nothing more than a Social Darwinist or to think that he was simply someone who created, in hindsight, a revolting racist theory. The situation is more complicated than this. It is true that he did not favor governmental intervention to aid the poorer classes, but he did so not only because of his political philosophy. He favored small government and he championed the ideas that humans have rights that should be protected, because these, he believed, were the right moral positions to take. We have rights to liberty and prosperity. A limited government should ensure these rights. In many ways, he was influenced by and embraced the "liberal" ideas of utilitarianism and libertarian political philosophy of his time.

It would also be a mistake to think that he looked with nothing but disdain on the poor and the working classes. On the contrary, he complained about the "unjust condemnation of the working classes" (1888:251). He writes: "It is a pity that those who speak disparagingly of the masses have not the wisdom enough, or the candor enough, to make due allowances for the unfavorable circumstances in which the masses are placed" (1888:250). It would also be a mistake not to recognize the fullness of his sociological theory, however now dated. He relied upon the biological metaphor and upon the theory of evolution to explain what he saw as the natural course of social evolution. Indeed, he not only saw society as if it was like a biological entity, for Spencer it was a biological entity: "society is an organism" (1967 [1876]:3).

industrial societies are complex, i.e. more advanced on the evolutionary ladder, and simple societies are basic and not very far along the evolutionary ladder. Spencer looked favorably upon social evolution and claimed to have outlined the laws that governed its development. He looked favorably upon the modern western world, as the most evolved. In addition to comparing one society to another, Spencer compared one or another aspect or group within a society to another within the same society. For example, there is inequality in society, and just as inequality exists, and is a necessary and beneficial thing in the natural world, so too inequality has the same place in the social world.

In hindsight, the ideas of Social Darwinism are now rightfully associated with several horrendous historical episodes. These ideas are now seen as contributing, if not leading, to a number of terrible periods of history. For example, the fascist movement of Hitler's Nazis embraced Social Darwinism and used to perpetrate the Holocaust, and to slaughter millions and millions of Jews and millions of other innocent people. But it was not simply Hitler. Social Darwinism contributed to racist theories of human races that were common in the eighteen hundreds and first half of the nineteen hundreds. Just as there are different species of ants, or dogs, or birds, so too there are, it was claimed, different races of people. "Caucasians" were fundamentally different than "Negroid" (i.e. people descended from Sub-Sahara Africa). Some races were smarter, more advanced than others, and this explains why some races were more wealthy and more powerful. Not surprisingly, this theory was championed by Europeans and European Americans, which were the dominant powers in the world. Americans in the early nineteen hundreds used this form of thinking to develop policies regarding immigration from Europe by Southern and Eastern Europeans. For example, at the time many thought that Italians were biologically distinct from people who came from England. They were a different race. In the late eighteen and early nineteen hundreds, there was a massive immigration into the United States from Eastern and Southern Europe, and the dominant group in America at that time was the White Anglo Saxon Protestants (those who descended from Great Britain). One of the reasons the immigration door was shut in the early twentieth century was the arguments raised by those inspired by Social Darwinism that claimed that allowing Italians and others inferior groups into the country would weaken the gene pool.

Social Darwinism also leads to a political position that asserted the government should not provide health or welfare services or even education to the poorer classes, or at least to those "idlers, criminals, etc." from those classes, as this would violate the natural order of things and would harm the evolutionary process, which Spencer deemed good and natural. Spencer writes:

> Fostering the good-for-nothing at the expense of the good, is an extreme cruelty. It is a deliberate stirring-up of miseries for future generations. There is no greater curse to posterity than that of bequeathing to them an increasing population of imbeciles and idlers and criminals ... The whole effort of nature is to get rid of such, to clear the world of them, and make room for the better ... If they are not sufficiently complete to live, they die, and it is best they should die. (quoted in Abrams, 1968:74)

Spencer's social theory is rooted in the application of the theory of evolution to social history and social organization. The principles of evolution are the same as the principles of social evolution and of human history. Much like the earliest forms of life billions of years ago were simple organisms that gradually evolved into modern, complex life forms, including human beings, so too early human societies were simple in organization and these gradually evolved into the modern complex societies found in the modern western world. The principles underlying both processes are essentially the same. Spencer identifies several main aspects to this evolutionary process. As things evolve, they become more differentiated and specialized. Specialized and distinct parts that have their own distinct functions emerge. A one-celled animal does not have eyes, lungs, kidneys, etc. A human body has many specialized parts. Different parts emerge that have their own specialized functions, and all the parts work harmoniously to keep the entire organism alive and healthy. Spencer claimed the same thing occurs in social evolution. He writes, "It is also a character of social bodies, as of living bodies, that while they increase in size they increase in structure. Like a low animal, the embryo of a high one has few distinguishable parts, but while it is acquiring greater mass, its parts multiply and differentiate. It is thus with society" (1967 [1876]:3). The earlier societies were, he claimed, less differentiated and had less specialization. In traditional agricultural societies most people did the same form of work. Most were farmers. But today, the range of specialized occupations is vast. Spencer argued that social evolution involved increasing structural differentiation. More evolved societies have more and more specialized social institutions. Think for a second about government. What was the form of government in a traditional Native American tribe who lived in what is now Kansas one thousand years ago? Did they have a White House? No. Did they have anything like a distinct institution called government? No. They perhaps had a chief and other forms of leaders. But the decision making was not distinct and separate from the rest of the workings of the society. Think of education. There were no schools to speak of ten thousand years. Any education that occurred likely occurred in the home. Schools were not differentiated from the home. Today of course they very much are separate.

In short, Spencer saw these processes of social evolution as being ruled by natural laws very much like the natural laws governing biological evolution. In the same way, he saw a natural tendency for systems – social and biological – to gravitate toward states of balance or harmony. The human body has a normal body temperature of 98.6, but when sick or disturbed it may rise or fall. The natural tendency for social systems is to maintain this balanced state. Yet at the same time, the process of evolution calls out for change.

Thus far we have encountered a British scholar, Spencer, and one French scholar, Comte. Many, many other British and French scholars of the Enlightenment era and of the nineteenth century also contributed greatly to the emergence of modern sociological theory. Many Germans of the era did the same. One cannot understand sociological theory today or the history of sociological theory as we know it today without appreciating the enormous contributions made to its development by German intellectuals of the seventeen, eighteen, and early nineteen hundreds. A few words can be said about this German heritage here. One of the greatest modern, western philosophers was the German Immanuel Kant (1724-1804). Kant was not a social theorist. He was a philosopher. Yet his thinking has had a great influence on sociological theorizing, from its impact upon German nineteenth century sociological theory to its impact on much theory today. This is not to say that all theory today embraces Kantian ideas, but it is to say that it is hard for sociological theorists today to ignore and to not address some of the many philosophical issues raised by Kant. His thinking influenced sociological developments concerning rationality and morality, and most importantly he influenced the epistemological and methodological perspectives taken by more recent scholars. For example, in the late eighteen hundreds German sociologists, influenced by Kant, engaged in debates about how social science should be conducted. Should it copy the methods of the natural sciences, or should it embrace a different type of method, one based more in interpretation? Should sociology be more like a science, such as biology, or should it be more like one of the humanities, such as the field of literature?

Kant, in the true Enlightenment spirit, embraced the concepts of reason, autonomy and freedom. Reason was the tool through which all fundamental understandings was to be accomplished, whether these are moral or scientific or artistic. Kant also has an enormous impact upon the branch of philosophy called epistemology. Epistemology is the branch of philosophy that concerns itself with the question of how we know things. How is it possible that we know that we can eat an apple, but cannot eat a rock? In the Enlightenment there were major debates on such questions. Some said every fundamental category of understanding is learned. We are able to know things because of our experiences. We learn the difference between an apple and a rock, a square and a triangle, heavy and light, red and blue. Others said that we know things naturally. The world outside of ourselves somehow reveals itself to us. We simply know. But this is not a great answer. How is it that we know? Kant claimed the argument needs to start with the acceptance of the assumption that there is an objective world outside of us, and that we interpret this world. This separation of the world and our interpretations is central. But this does not in itself explain how we know things. Kant argued that humans have built into them, built into their minds, forms or categories of thought that allow us to understand the world, however imperfectly. It is, for example, only by having a category of time that we can tell whether it is six o'clock or eight o'clock. Perhaps an easier example is that of the category of classification. We are able to classify things. We can classify an apple as edible and a rock as inedible. We can classify some things as birds and others as trees. We can do so because we have the natural ability to classify. So too do we have other conceptual forms, such as the form of time, that allow us to understand the world. As we will see in later chapters, theories of epistemology are centrally important in many forms of sociological theorizing and have become even more so in recent years. For example, how and why do people act as they do? Do people act based purely upon their constructed understandings of the world, whether this understanding reflects the true reality outside of us, or do people instead act on the basis of what the true reality outside of us is?

Kant was followed by many important German philosophers and social theorists in the nineteenth century which have had a major impact upon theory through the present. One of the more influential of these was G.W.F. Hegel (1770-1831). The ideas of the philosopher Hegel were very popular amongst German intellectuals in the early years of that century. Hegel (see Chapter Two) greatly influenced Karl Marx. Hegel's philosophy was less oriented toward the individual and was more oriented toward developing a theory of history and human evolution. He saw this evolution as a process of progressive development that comes about through conflicting and competing ideas. The battle of ideas produces changes in history, and these changes lead to progress, as reflected in western history. Kant, Hegel, and Marx ultimately set the table for later important developments in German sociological theory, most notably those found in the ideas of Max Weber (1864-1920) and Georg Simmel (1858-1918) (see Chapters Four and Five).

German scholars in the second half of the nineteenth century within the fields of social philosophy and social theory were incredibly productive and creative. They engaged in many of the foundational questions regarding theory and method that scholars today continue to debate. One such debate concerned the philosophical issues of nominalism versus realism. This issue can be traced back to the ancient Greek philosophers, but in modern times social theorists have had to address it specifically in terms of understandings of the social world. Realism is the philosophical perspective that a thing can be identified as a particular thing in its relation to being a member of a general class of things, and this general class is real. An apple is both an individual apple and an apple because it shares traits with apples in general. Reality then deals with the relationships between the particular and the general. For realism, the general exists. Nominalism rejects this claim and instead insists that only the particulars exist in reality. The general exists not because it is real, but because it has been labeled or constructed as real. Applied to sociology, this question becomes very important. For example, does society exist? Is it nothing more than a collection of individuals or some constructed idea (nominalism), or does society have a distinct reality (realism)? The answers to such questions directly shape the types of sociological theories that are created.

German scholars also engaged in debates about methodology, and about the relationship between theory and methods. Theory tends to explain why something happens. Methods, in contrast, is about how the scientist should go about discovering the facts of the world and their causes. Methods then is concerned with the types of research approaches the sociologist should use. Should the researcher conduct an experiment, like a physicist, or should they conduct a participant observation study in which the researcher tries to get a sense of the group he or she is studying by spending a lot of time, months or more, with the group. What is the proper method? And how does method relate to theory? These are some of the questions that engaged the German scholars, and that continue to engage sociological theorists today (in American and elsewhere). The nineteenth century Germans asked themselves whether sociology should aspire to be like the hard sciences, such as chemistry and biology and physics, or whether it should strive to be more like disciplines such as history. (This debate is called the "methodenstreit" (see Chapter Four).) Those who claimed sociology should embrace the same scientific approach of physics, etc., asserted that there is one and only one right way to do science, and the methods used in the hard sciences are that right way. As such, sociology should copy these other disciplines, particularly in the methodology it uses. On the other hand, history is very different. History is the study of particular events in the past. Like the sciences it relies upon objective facts to make claims, but unlike the sciences it does not seek to discover natural laws of history. History in ways serves as a stand-in for a larger issue. That issue is whether or if sociology should be an interpretive discipline or a scientific one. Historians, after all, interpret, the past. But how? Many German social philosophers and sociologists at the time came to believe it was important to develop a theoretical understanding of the proper ways of interpreting social reality, including history. Toward this end, many believed it was vital for the sociologist to try to understand the meanings of the social actions for the actors, and to do this they believed it was necessary to try to imagine how the social actors developed meaningful understandings of their worlds. As we can see, this form of sociology is distinct and in conflict with the scientific approaches of physics, chemistry, etc.

Ignored or Overlooked Theories in History

In recent decades, sociological theorists have come to recognize that some important and insightful theorists in history have for far too long been ignored or at least not accorded their proper place amongst scholars. Of note, these theorists were women and minorities. In recent decades it is common, accurate, and appropriate, to recognize the contributions of theorists such as Harriet Martineau and W.E.B. DuBois to sociological theory, and it is equally acknowledged today that the slighting of their work must be attributed in no small measure to the fact they were not white men. The ideas of each of these theorists is described at greater length in Chapter Thirteen. Here a brief introduction is in order.

Harriet Martineau (1802-1876) was a British intellectual. She was a descendent of French Huguenots (Protestants), who fled France to avoid religious persecution. She was raised in the Unitarian Christian faith. This is of note because Unitarianism is a very liberal, unorthodox Protestant denomination. Her religious sensibilities continued throughout her life, though her religious convictions declined as she grew older. Martineau wrote a number of important works in sociology including the books *How To Observe Morals and Manners* (1989 [1838]) and *Society in America* (1962). In addition, she translated into English August Comte's *Positive Philosophy*, a translation that was widely praised (so much so that the work was re-translated into French and that re-translation was widely seen as being an improvement over the original). She spent much of her life as a journalist and social commentator, often criticizing the injustices of the age. For example, she championed the anti-slavery abolitionist cause.

Martineau never presents a systematic sociological theory of society in any of her works. However, her theoretical ideas come through in many of these. Moreover, her theoretical ideas are often fused with her methodological ideas. Indeed, the book *Morals and Manners* arguably is one of the very first books on research methods in sociology to appear. In that book, she puts forth an argument concerning how sociologists, or "travelers," should observe and understand social realities. The sociologist should be objective. He or she should embrace a scientific orientation to what is being studied. The observer should seek to understand the morals of a people. By morals she is referring to the notions of right and wrong, good and bad, a people have. Morality she believed was at the heart of society and should be at the heart of the sociological enterprise. But one cannot study morality directly (Hill in Martineau 1989). The sociologists should examine social "things" to understand the morality of a people. They should study facts. Things and facts are concrete entities, such as statistical documents, the inscriptions on tombstones, suicide data, economic and political data, criminal justice reports, etc. Relatedly, the sociologist should not rely upon interview data, as this is partial, incomplete, and does not lend itself readily to generalizations. This understanding of sociology was quite advanced for its time, and sociologists really did not begin to make use of such formulations until many decades after her death. Martineau saw morality as the central force in society and she saw it as the cornerstone of an analysis of society. The social scientist then should analyze the world he or she is investigating by comparing the realities of the world to the moral standards held by the social scientist. Martineau did not quite phrase this view in this manner, but that was the direct implication of her approach. The moral position she held, quite unreflectively, was the position emanating from a fusion of Enlightenment ideals and a liberal Protestantism. She subscribed to the notion, seen in British utilitarian philosophy, that the ultimate determinant of goodness is happiness. The greater the happiness, the greater the good. She layered on top of this the full embrace of the values of equality and liberty, of democracy, and uses these as measuring rods to assess the realities she observed.

Toward that end, she provided a nuanced understanding, and fervent moral condemnations, of the workings of slavery in America. Her book *Society in America* (1962), written in the 1830s, is a sociological analysis of America. It was based upon her travels to the United States. In it she commented at length about the moral character of Americans and the benefits and drawbacks of this to the newly created democracy. The book describes various features of American society but gives special attention to slavery. She embraces the anti-slavery abolitionist cause and provides significant insights into the workings of the slave system and specifically upon what it does social psychologically to the slaves and the slave owners. She writes, for example, about how the white southern slave owner unconsciously is forced to address the contradiction of his love of liberty and his support and participating in slavery, a system directly at odds with liberty: "One of the absolutely inevitable results of slavery is a disregard of human rights; an inability even to comprehend them. Probably the southern gentry, who declare that the presence of slavery enhances the love of freedom; that freedom can be duly estimated only where a particular class can appropriate all social privileges; that, to use the words of one of they, "They know too much of slavery to be slaves themselves," are sincere enough in such declarations; and if so, it follows that they do not know what freedom is." She continues, "Another of my reasons for supposing that the gentry of the south do not know what freedom is, is that many seem unconscious of the state of coercion in which they themselves are living" (1962:233). Martineau then shows how this way of thinking infiltrates the relations of the slave owner men and the women. It perverts the men's understanding of and relations to women. The distortions or the moral character done to the slave owner as the result of the system of slavery impacts and perverts all social relations and "degrades" other groups in addition to slaves, most notably women. Relatedly, Martineau is rightly called a feminist (Yates 1985) as a result of her critical assessment of the ways in which women were treated in an unequal and degraded fashion at the time. Her feminist theorizing is described in Chapter Thirteen.

Another essential element of Martineau's theoretical orientation is her overarching embrace of what would today be clearly seen as a conservative view of history. Much like Comte, she saw history as a march of progress, with the western world being the most advanced form of society. She repeatedly presents ideas noting that the western world is more advanced in an evolutionary sense than the rest of the world, and that it is in effect morally superior to the rest. The western bias is clear throughout her writings. In discussing the superiority of modern responses to law and criminal justice, for example, she writes, "Recklessness of human life is one of the surest symptoms of barbarism, whether life is taken by law or by assassination. As men grow more civilized, and learn to rate the spiritual higher and higher about the physical life, human life grows sacred" (1989:134). Also, the "degree of civilization" of a people is associated with the dominant type of "idea" held by that people. She presents a theory of history in the following: "The prominent idea of savages is the necessity of providing for the supply of the commonest bodily wants. The first steps in civilization, therefore, are somewhat refined methods of treating the body. When, by combination of labour and other exercises of ingenuity, the wants of the body are supplied with regularity and comparative ease, the love of pleasure, the love of idleness, succeeds. Then comes the desire of wealth; and next, the regard to opinion. Further than this no nation has yet attained" (1982:246).

Another scholar whose work was largely ignored, certainly throughout his life by mainstream sociology and for many decades after, was W.E.B. Du Bois (1868-1963). Du Bois, an African American, was raised in Massachusetts. He earned a Ph.D. from Harvard University and spent his life as an academic and political activist. He was a co-founder of the National Association for the Advancement of Colored People (NAACP), the important civil rights organization. He was a very productive scholar, having published hundreds of articles and books throughout his life. Much of this work focused on race and race relations, and specifically upon the inequalities between African Americans and whites. There were two central legs to Du Bois' theorizing. On the one hand, he came to embrace Marxism, though he never systematically employed the theory in his research. On the other hand, he fully recognized that one cannot sociologically understand America without recognize the centrality of the concept of race in American society. The opening lines of Chapter Two of what is probably his most popular book, *The Souls of Black Folks*, makes this point: "The problem of the twentieth century is the problem of the color-line" (1969 [1903]:54). He spent much of his career working on multi-dimensional, empirical investigations into the conditions of African Americans in the early and mid-nineteen hundreds. His creative, multi-method studies, using quantitative and qualitative data, documented in detail the great inequalities that existed between African Americans and whites. His ideas are further discussed in Chapter Thirteen.

Some Current Themes in Theorizing

When reading the following chapters, you should keep in mind several thorny issues or themes that have hounded sociological theory in the past and continue to do so through the present. These issues are sets of conceptual contradictions that appear to be unavoidable in sociological theorizing. While some today may claim, as many in the earlier periods did as well, that these issues have been resolved or overcome, or that they are not in fact significant issues or problems, many if not most scholars today recognize these as centrally important, if not troubling, themes that need to be addressed in one way or another in any current theory. These themes are: 1) agency vs structure; 2) the micro-macro divide; 3) facts vs values; and 4) objective versus interpretivistic approaches.

The first issue concerns the divide between agency and structure. Agency is the term sociologists use to describe individuals as choice makers. Individuals are not puppets or machines. They can and do assign meaning to their worlds. They interpret their worlds, and act based upon the meanings and interpretations of their worlds. Structure refers to an organized set of forces that are imposed upon individuals and that cause individuals to act in one way or another. All sorts of structures exist. Language can be thought of as a structure, so too can institutional arrangements. There is a structure to the family or to a university. In these settings there are organized sets of roles, rules, etc. in which people operate. There is also a structure to morality, as we see in coming chapters, and morality is viewed by some if not many sociologists are a key factor in social behavior and social order. Much as if one is performing in a play, the structure of the play, the script, the setting, etc. determines how the performer acts. The issue here concerns the ultimate nature of social action. Are people puppets or are they choice makers?

There are agency sociological theories and there are structural sociological theories. Some sociologists claim that theories should begin with the assumption that people have agency. Others claim that theories should begin with the assumption that sociology is not some form of psychology or philosophy that seeks to understand individual choice making, rather sociology should seek to explain social behavior and social order by understanding and explaining the structural forces that are imposed upon individuals. The question becomes: which perspective is the right one? How should we explain social behavior and order? Should we say that people are choice makers or that they are puppets, slaves to the structures around them? Each perspective has its own problems. Agency theories tend in the direction of psychology and/or in the direction of philosophy, though it is important to note that agency should not be equated with psychology. After all, many forms of psychological thinking, such as behavior psychology, are anything but agency theories. That is, behavioral psychology is rooted in the idea that behavior can be explained in terms of things such as reinforcements and punishments, and in effect this approach ultimately rejects the idea of agency. People are not choice makers, according to behavioral psychology. Instead, the choices people make are dictated by the experiences of reinforcement and punishments the person has experienced. (See for example the works of noted psychologist B.F. Skinner.) If we leave behavioral psychology aside, and focus instead on forms of psychology that imply choice making, we might as: If psychology is all there is, then does sociology exist? What would it mean to say that sociology exists if people have agency? Likewise, when sociologists focus on choice making, meaning making, interpretations and the like, how are they really to determine what causes people's actions? Isn't any such claim little more than speculation or guesswork? Can we really know the true cause of people's behaviors? Structural perspectives also have their fundamental problems. For example, common sense says that people in fact are not puppets, and that people do indeed make choices. Similarly, what is structure? And does it make any sense to talk of structures that are in any way independent of living individuals? Do structures have an existence independent of individuals? If so, what does that mean? If it does not make any sense to say that structures are independent of individuals, then doesn't that mean we have to return to the individual and agency?

A second set of issues for theory is the micro-macro divide. This concerns the focus of attention of the sociologist. Is the sociologist seeking to explain real, lived interactions, or is he or she seeking to explain larger social phenomena, such as historical currents and the like? Is the focus of attention on explaining the organization of society itself or on the organization of small-scale social settings and interactions? Is the sociologist seeking to understand the immediate interactions of people in the present, or is he or she seeking to understand not the immediate present but the larger organization of society? Micro perspectives focus their attention on understanding and explaining lived social behaviors in the immediate context. Thus, a micro sociologist studying divorce would not focus his or her attention on data on divorce rates and upon how and why these rates may have changed. Instead, he or she would focus on living families and how and why these families break up. In effect, macro sociologists look to explain large-scale social realities, like the emergence of modernity and modern society, or the spread of capitalism, while micro sociologists focus their attention on immediate and small, lived interactions.

At first glance one might think that the two sets of concepts just discussed – micro-macro and agency-structure are parallel. One might think that the micro and agency perspectives are somehow naturally paired, and that macro and structural perspectives are likewise associated. But the issue is more complicated than this. The agency structure divide refers to the causes of social behavior and order while the micro macro divide refers to the object or focus of attention of the sociologist. As we see in Chapter Eleven, many scholars believe it is possible to create a theory that combined the micro with agency. Symbolic interactionist theories tend to do this (see Chapter Nine). One might alternatively create a theory that combines the micro with structure. Erving Goffman (see Chapter Nine) does this, particularly in his work on frame analysis. Georg Simmel also does this (see Chapter Five). In the same way, it is possible to create a theory that combines the macro with agency. Arguably, Max Weber's approach does this (see Chapter Four). And it is also possible to develop a theory that combines the macro with structure. Perhaps the clearest example in this text of a theorist who does this is Durkheim (see Chapter Three).

Our third set of themes or issues concerns facts vs values. In sociology there is a long and ongoing debate about the relationship of facts and values in sociology. The debate, in the present context of sociological theory, revolves around objectivity and bias. Can or should the sociologist be objective and unbiased when he or she is creating a theory, or can or should the sociologist be biased? Should the sociologist allow his or her own personal or religious or political views distort or influence the way that he or she sees, understands and explains the world, or should the sociologists be objective, impartial and value-free in his work? The traditional view of the sociologist as scientist is that he or she should be unbiased and objective. Who would want a scientific researcher doing an experiment on a new drug to treat cancer to somehow distort the facts of his or her work or the facts of his or her research findings to fit with a set of moral values? The heart of science today is objectivity. It is perhaps not hard to see how a chemist or a physicist may easily put aside their values in much of their work. It may be easy to see how they can and should be objective. Their task is to let the facts speak for themselves. But what about social scientists? Sociologists? Sociologists do not study rocks and things. They study people. As such, isn't it the case that the sociologists will have feelings, will have values, moral values and otherwise, related to the things he or she studies? If I grew up poor or in a divorced household, might I not have strong and passionate feelings about such things? Perhaps I will value equality more so than someone who grew up in a wealthy home? Perhaps I will think that society should be one in which the wealth is not concentrated in the hands of a small group of people but instead spread more equally amongst the people, including the poor? One can see here that the values held by the sociologists are not as easy to put to the side as the values held by the chemist, the physicist, etc.

What role then should values play in sociology and in sociology theory? As we see in Chapter Two, Karl Marx once famously said "Philosophers think about the world, the point is to change it." Marx is saying here that the point of theory is not simply to describe the world, the point is to use theory to change the world. But the traditional, non-Marxist view is that scientists are supposed to describe and explain the world. They are supposed to be objective. They are not supposed to try to change the world directly through manipulating their understandings of it. Knowledge and practices should be kept separate. Politicians, moral leaders, revolutionaries, on the other hand, are not scientists. They embrace and are led by their values. From the traditional perspective, the position of these people is fundamentally different than the position of the social scientist, and the wall between the two should be high and firm. As we see throughout this book, sociological theorists have taken vastly different views about the relationship of facts and values. Some such as Durkheim (see Chapter Three) believe that the sociologist can and should be no different than the chemist or physicist. The sociologist can and should keep facts and values separate from each other in his or her work, and that this is not a significant problem for the social scientist. Other theorists we encounter (particularly those writing in more recent years) believe the issue is far more complicated than Durkheim would have us believe. Some such as the critical race and gender theorists (Chapter Thirteen) and the postmodern theorist (Chapter Twelve) as well as some theorists of the environment (Chapter Fourteen) see the whole point of theory today is not only to understand the social world but also to change it.

Another way of thinking about the fact vs value debate concerns the role of justice in theorizing. What role does or should the sociologist's belief in issues such as justice play in his or her theory, and in his or her understanding of the social world? Should the sociologist seek to put to the side his or her beliefs about what is just and unjust and simply try to look at the world as objectively as possible? Should the sociologist not consider what he or she thinks is or is not a just society? Or, like Marx, should the sociologist embrace his or her view of justice and allow this to guide his or her understandings?

Another set of themes related to the fact-value debate concerns the perspective the sociologist should take in understanding the world, and specifically which academic discipline should sociology model itself upon in creating a perspective? That is, should sociology seek to be more like chemistry, biology, and physics, or should it be more like literature or art criticism? The issue here concerns objectivity versus interpretivistic approaches. Fundamentally, the issue comes down to different forms of knowledge found in the different academic disciplines. The chemist produces knowledge about the chemical world when he or she does experiments. When the experiment is done, the chemist proclaims to have discovered new knowledge about the world. But doesn't the art professor also have knowledge about art? Doesn't an art professor know the art of Picasso or of some other great artist? But the art professor doesn't subject the art to a scientific experiment, does she? The knowledge is of a different sort than the art of the chemist. The question for sociology is: Which form of knowledge should the sociologist seek? Different sociological theories suggest different answers to these questions, as we see in the various chapters of this book.

Summary

This chapter opened with expressions of concern if not alarm at the current state of American society. It was argued that part of the problem lies in the current political culture, and that to address this issue one would need to embrace a sociological understanding, i.e. to understand and explain the patterns and patternings of social behavior. The exclusive focus on individualistic explanations for social realities that is common in American society was identified as part of the reason that Americans tend not to see things sociologically. Another part involves the erosion of trust and virtue in contemporary politics in America. Donald Trump and his followers were identified as contributing to this. Specifically, current trends are threating the continued existence of democracy in America. It was argued that sociological theory – broadly including theories of democracy such as Tocqueville's and Bellah -- might help us to understand how this contemporary reality appeared, and what might be best done to address it.

To understand sociological theory we should recognize that it was and is a product of its times. As such, a historical understanding is needed. In this chapter we traced the historical origins of modern social theory. Modern sociological theory has its origins in The Enlightenment (The Age of Reason), a period of intellectual history in Europe from the sixteen hundreds through the seventeen hundreds. The Enlightenment is characterized by three themes: Reason, the individual, and optimism. The Enlightenment gave birth to modernity in the eighteen and nineteen hundreds. Modernity is characterized by dramatic changes, including industrialization, urbanization and rationalization. These changes greatly influenced the development of the classical sociological theories of Marx, Weber, and Durkheim, as well as many of the important sociological theories that arose in the early and mid-nineteen hundreds. By the late nineteen hundreds new social conditions emerged, and social change became an even greater force in society. This was the beginning of the post-industrial era, the era in which we now live. This period is one in which the economy became based more on service and information jobs, and less on manufacturing. American and western societies since the nineteen sixties are markedly different from the societies of the industrial era. The post-industrial society is characterized by consumption, by high technology, and by globalization. All of these have impacted recent developments in sociological theory.

The description of history was followed by an introduction to a number of early sociological theorists. The ideas of Comte and Spencer were briefly presented, and the importance of nineteenth century German philosophy and social theory was noted. Comte is associated with positivist philosophy, and Spencer is associated Social Darwinism and with the quest to develop a model of society and social evolution. The overlooked theories of Harriet Martineau and W.E.B. Du Bois were also described. The last part of this chapter describes several of central problematic themes that sociologists have faced and continue to face as they try to create theories. These themes include: 1) agency vs structure; 2) the micro-macro divide; 3) facts vs values; and 4) objective versus interpretivistic approaches.

Discussion Questions

1. Is it true as it is claimed in the opening pages of this chapter that contemporary America is confronted with a number of crises? And is it true as suggested that American individualism works against the acceptance of sociological theorizing today? If so, is it true that sociology and sociological theory in particular are needed now more than ever to aid in understanding and responding to these crises? How might sociological theory explain what is happening in America today?

2. Some recent theories, such as postmodern theories, suggest or claim that the root of the problems of the world today are to be found the Enlightenment, and these theories claim that the solution lies in abandoning the Enlightenment Project. They claim we should reject the fundamental principles of the Enlightenment and build a new set of principles. What do

you think? Should we strive to salvage the Enlightenment Project or should we abandon it? Why?

3. Are the theories that were developed in the industrial era of the eighteen and early nineteen hundreds relevant today, or has the world changed so much that the basic claims of these theories no long applicable? Explain.

4. The agency-structure question concerns two issues: 1) are people puppets on a string or do they make choices in their behaviors, and 2) does society exist independent of the living individual? How do you answer these two questions, and do your answers affect the type of theory you think is best suited to explain social reality?

Chapter Two: Karl Marx

I was raised in a working class household in Providence, Rhode Island, an old industrial city, near Boston. My father, who had less than a sixth grade education, worked in factories his whole life. When I was growing up, Providence was the custom jewelry capital of the world, or so this is how the city promoted itself. Factories were everywhere in the city, cranking out cheap, mass produced jewelry – rings, earrings, necklaces, watches, and more. In high school and in college I needed to work both to survive and to pay for college, so I worked in the jewelry factories for several years. I hated those jobs. One of the jobs that I had was in a foundry, a jewelry factory in which raw metal – large slabs of steel, gold, brass, etc. -- was brought in, heated up to some ungodly temperature, melted down, and then poured into the cast molds of the jewelry, much like one might pour cookie dough or chocolate into a mold to make cookies or chocolate bunnies, or some such thing. After the metal cooled and hardened the molds would be cracked opened and removed, and the raw jewelry would need to be finished. I worked with the brass finger rings, the kind used for high school rings and the like. The liquid metal was poured down into the molds in which the rings were standing vertically in the mold with the face of the ring at the bottom. After the metal cooled, the molding was cracked open and the raw rings were removed. But a little nub remained where the metal was poured into the mold, on the back side of each ring. That is, a nub remained on the part of the ring that would face what would be the palm of your hand. Each nub was about an eighth of an inch long or so. My job was to cut off the little nub from each brass ring so that the ring could then be polished and finished. I was given a seat, and a very large box of brass rings with their little nubs was placed on the floor to my left. There must have been thousands of rings in each box. I was also given a pair of pliers or snippers to cut the nubs off. My job was to pick up one of the rings from the box and cut the nub off. Then I was to place the ring into an empty box (soon to be filled) to my right. I then was to pick up another ring from the box on the left, cut the nub, and place it in the box to the right again, and I was to do the same thing, again and again and again. When the box was empty, when I finished with all of the rings in the box, they would bring me another one, and then another one. That was my job. My entire job. I could cut through thousands and thousands of these rings in a day.

    I did not like that job. It was anything but fulfilling for me. With every fiber in my body, I hated it. It was mind-numbing, and I had absolutely no control over any part of it. But I had to work, and it was a job. Yet when I looked around the factory, I saw many older people doing one or another job that was comparable to the ring job. They had worked in that factory for years, quietly complying with the drudgery of this labor. They seemed content or at least complacent with their work. I also saw many others of my own age, teenagers and people in their young twenties working there. Many of these, it seemed, would be unable to go to college and as such faced a life of factory work. Many of these would go out at lunch and get drunk.

In hindsight, I think of Karl Marx and my work in the factories. Karl Marx was not writing about jewelry factories in New England in the mid to late nineteen hundreds. He was instead writing about industrializing European societies in the mid to late eighteen hundreds. Yet I can only imagine that the factories of his time were that much harsher, far more brutal, and that much more trying than the factories within which I worked. But my experiences raise a couple of important points to consider when you are reading about Marx's theory. One of these concerns Marx's claim, described below, that industrial work in capitalism was and is dehumanizing. Yet the fact is that so many of the workers in my factories seemed content or at least complacent with their work and work situation. (I did not.) How is it that I could be so upset personally with this work and others could so easily and quietly accept it? The second point is perhaps even more significant: The factories have all closed down. None are left, at least in Providence. But this seems at odds with Marx's ideas. Marx saw industrial capitalism as causing the working class to organize and then to lead a revolution that would topple capitalism. But how can this occur without any more factories? I was working at a time when the jewelry factories were beginning to close or to move to Mexico, or China, or elsewhere. Today, Providence is filled with so many empty factories, as is the case with so many cities, particularly in the American Northeast and Midwest. We now no longer live in an industrial economy. One hundred years ago, factories were the major source of work for people. Today, they are not. Today, we live in a post-industrial society. We live in a society in which the jobs are increasingly service or information jobs, jobs at Apple Computers, or health care, or Home Depot or McDonald's.

When I first read Karl Marx, in college, my experiences of working in the jewelry factories jumped off the pages. I could see what he was saying when he complained that the workers were alienated and oppressed. I was alienated and felt oppressed. But what of those who did not seem so? What of those who worked quietly for years and years in these places? What sense does Marx's theory have today, now that the factories have all closed down? Is his theory relevant today? After all, a worker in health care or at Home Depot does not do the same repetitive task, such as cutting off the nub of thousands of brass rings that I did.

In the following pages, you will be presented with an overview of Marx's theory. Ask yourself if the theory is relevant today? You might also ask yourself, in light of what was just said, why most sociologists today consider Marx important (more so than American sociologists did in the industrial era of the mid-nineteen hundreds!)? What might sociologists today think is worthwhile in his theory, in a world so different from the one he was writing about? Why, after all, are you being taught Marx in the course you are taking right now? Clearly, sociologists believe he must have something of value to say. The question is, what is it?

Themes in Marx's Theory

Why in the world would anyone today believe Marx has anything of value to say? It is not only that the post-industrial world we live in is so starkly different from the industrial world in which Marx lived. It is also a question of what Marxist theory has produced in political and social realities. After all, one need only look at the disasters that were spawned in the last one hundred years by those professing to be following his ideas. Who in their right mind would want to live in North Korea today? It is an oppressive, poor, totalitarian regime, run by a dictator who is the leader for no other reason than his father was the leader. North Korea proudly proclaims itself to be communist. It proudly proclaims to be the embodiment of Marx's ideas. The Russian Revolution in Eastern Europe in the early nineteen hundreds also was made in the name of Marx, as was the totalitarian, oppressive system called the Soviet Union and its satellite countries in Eastern Europe that was born out of it, only to wither away in the late nineteen hundreds. Examples of failed communist systems abound in the twentieth century. Even China today which claims to be communist in fact has a capitalist economy. Doesn't this prove the wrongheadedness of Marx's theory? Yet curiously, at the time when communism was collapsing in many societies at the end of the century, Marx's theory was gaining strength in American sociology.

Prior to the 1960s, Marxism was not taught as a major theoretical tradition within American sociology. It was dismissed or ignored. Since then Marx has regularly been embraced by sociologists as one of the three major classical sociological theorists, along with Durkheim and Weber. While there are likely many reasons, including many sociological reasons, that could be cited to account for this we can here identify several theoretical reasons. Marx's theory is a conflict theory (though sociologists often use the term to describe some non-Marxist approaches, see Chapter Eight), and conflict theory is one of several main, competing approaches to sociological inquiry today. (Other approaches include symbolic interactionism and structural functionalism.) Many scholars since the 1960s believe one must understand the basic conflicts in society if one is to understand American society itself. Marxism is anchored in the assumption that conflict lies at the heart of capitalist society. For Marx, the conflict between economic classes is central to understanding society. Many scholars also see Marx's macro orientation as the proper one to understand and explain social realities. He provides tools for understanding how the large-scale organization and forces in society, specifically the economic structure, influence, if not determine, other seemingly independent aspects of society, from family structure to the entertainment industry. The claim that the economic structure of a society is central to an understanding of a society appears to have resonance with many sociologists today.

Another aspect of Marx's theory that likely contributes to its popularity in sociology today lies in the methodological perspective taken by him. In his

> ## Karl Marx
>
> Karl Marx (1818-1883) was a German, Jewish intellectual and revolutionary. He was raised in a middle class household, one of nine children. His father was a lawyer and vineyard owner who converted to Lutheranism in reaction to the anti-Semitism of the times, though the family was not religious at all. The conversion was for political expediency and not religious conviction. Karl Marx earned a doctorate from the University of Berlin where he became exposed to the ideas of Hegel. After graduating he became a journalist and a revolutionary, spending much time writing and researching in the libraries. He married Jenny von Westphalen in 1843, seven years after they were first engaged. He met Friedrich Engels in 1844, and they became lifelong friends for the rest of their lives. Marx and Engels co-wrote a number of works. As Marx's political writings called for revolution, he was increasingly censored by the government fearful of his ideas. He was forced to move from one European country to another as the result of his writings and his radical politics. He spent time in France, Belgium, Germany, and finally in England. He moved to London in 1849 and remained there for the rest of his life, spending considerable time writing and doing research in the national library. He died at the age of sixty-four and was buried at Highgate Cemetery in London. Only ten mourners or so were at the funeral, a stark contrast to the millions of supporters he garnered in the decades after his death.

Eleventh Thesis on Feuerbach, he wrote, "Philosophers have only interpreted the world in various ways; the point, however, is to change it." The point here concerns the relationship of facts to values. That is, what should sociology be? Should it model itself upon the natural sciences, such as physics, biology and chemistry? These fields separate facts from values. That is, the chemist puts his own personal beliefs, values, moral sentiments aside when he or she does chemistry. He or she is supposed to look at the world objectively in an unbiased, objective way. Facts are here separated from values. Sociologists who claim that this discipline should model itself upon the likes of chemistry and physics and should strive to be the same sort of science as these also say that they should separate fact from value. The sociologists should not let their beliefs about justice, morality, etc. influence and distort their understandings of the world. In short, they should not try to change or alter the world. Instead, they should try to objectively try to understand how the world works and should leave it to politicians or others to try to change the world. Marx believed the theorists should try to change the world. However, he also claimed that the mode of understanding which led to the separation of fact and value had to be overcome with a different mode of understanding. A new form of science was needed, one based on dialectics and materialism (see below), one that he claimed overcome problems associated with the conventional scientific approach being applied to an understanding of humanity, societies, and history.

This leads Marx to embrace the cause of justice. Theory should not simply be about describing the world, but it should be about helping to change it. It should be about fostering social action that advances the cause of justice. (Though of course this leads to the philosophical problem concerning what is justice.)

Hegel's Influence

Marx was greatly influenced by G.W.F. Hegel (1770-1831), a very influential German philosopher. Hegel was interested in developing a philosophy of history. Three of his ideas in particular were influential on Marx. Marx embraces some of these and dramatically revised others. One of Hegel's ideas was that of idealism. Hegel was an idealist. He believed the human world consisted of two interrelated parts, the realm of ideas and the realm of material conditions. Together they constituted human reality. The realm of ideas includes beliefs, ideas, attitudes, and other such things. It is comprised of human reality that cannot be experienced through the senses (e.g. touch, smell, etc.). The realm of material conditions includes all that can be experienced through the senses. The easiest way of thinking of this is that a major part of the material world is the physical reality in which we live. Our bodies, the chairs upon which we sit, our houses, etc. are all part of the material world. The ideational and the material interact and intersect. For Hegel, the question becomes which of these two aspects is the driving force in social change and more generally in history? Remember, he wanted to develop a philosophy of history. What propels history forward, ideas or material conditions? One way of thinking of this is to ask why political revolutions happen. Do political revolutions happen because people develop new ideas about how society is organized and how it should be organized, or do revolutions happen because people are hungry, or unemployed, or homeless? If you argue that the driving force in history is ideas, then you are an idealist. An idealist would say revolutions happen as the result of new ideas emerging and then people act in ways to put these ideas into practice (in the material world). If you say that the driving force in history is material conditions, then you are a materialist. A materialist would say revolutions happen because people are hunger, or unemployed, or are experiencing some other unwanted material condition. These material conditions lead people to develop new revolutionary ideas.

The second of Hegel's ideas that had an impact upon Marx was Hegel's embrace of dialectics. Dialectics is a philosophy of change that assumes the world is made up of contradictions. Each reality is made up of contradictions. Dialectics assumes that each present, each moment, is comprised of opposing forces. These opposing forces, or contradictions or conflicts demand resolution. They force a change to happen, a resolution to the conflict. But within this new reality emerges new sets of contradictions, which in turn demand resolution. One force presses against another, and something has to give. A new reality is born, with new conflicts. History, Hegel says, can be explained using dialectics. An example of dialectics might be an explanation for the earth's orbit around the sun. The earth moves around the sun; that is, it changes its location, as the result of opposing forces. One force – the sun's gravity – is pulling the earth toward the sun. But the earth does not crash into it. It remains in orbit. Another opposing force, centripetal force, seeks to push the earth away from the sun, much like when one twirls a ball at the end of a string and lets it go. This is a force of nature. As a result of the opposing forces, the earth moves from point to point around the sun.

Hegel also focuses much of his attention on history and its relationship to his present. For Hegel history constituted a story of the march of progress. Germany in the early eighteen hundreds was greater than it was two hundred years earlier, and it was greater two hundred years ago than it was five hundred years earlier. The history of the west is one in which there has been a relentless progress – in the arts, in science, in knowledge, in politics, etc. History for Hegel was nothing but a story of progress, and European society in the early eighteen hundreds was the culmination of this history. He looked around and saw a great civilization. He saw the progressive rise of "reason" through history and was particularly enamored with The Enlightenment. In sum, history was seen as the development of ideas brought about through dialectics. All was well with the modern world, for Hegel. For him, history was a dialectical process of ideas, in which the ideas of Reason in the modern era rose to prominence. The values of the Enlightenment and the associated developments in science, art, politics, etc. all attest to the flowering of Reason brought about through the dialectics of history.

Marx critically assessed and responded to these three key ideas of Hegel – idealism, dialectics and history. He embraced Hegel's notion of dialectics but revised the other two. (As with so much of Marx's theorizing, there are debates about whether he actually did embrace dialectics or not. Some scholars (Elster 1985; Cohen 1978) make the case that in fact his theorizing was not dialectical.) Marx agreed with Hegel that history was important, and he agreed it was important to try to discover the mechanisms of history, to try to unlock the riddle of history. He also disagreed with Hegel's view of the modern world and of the trajectory of history. Marx looked about and saw the emergence of industrial capitalism. He saw the factories, the brutal factories where children of all ages worked all hours, where children and men and women lost life and limb, where they worked for pennies while the owners became more and more prosperous. The danger, the pollution, the horrid conditions of early industrial capitalism caused Marx to see a different world than that seen by Hegel. True, Marx recognized capitalism was incredible productive, but its fruits did not go to the people. Instead, the fruits of capitalism were reserved for one small group, the rich. Moreover, the economic system itself was being driven not by the will of the people, but by the needs of capital itself. He wanted to understand the logic of history that produced this reality, such that he could understand where society should and will go in the future.

To understand history, Marx turned to the other ideas of Hegel. He claimed Hegel got it upside-down when he said that the realm of ideas was the driving force in history. For Marx, the material conditions were the bedrock of social life. Marx was a materialist. Revolutions, he might say, do not happen because people first develop new ideas, i.e. the realm of the ideal. Instead, they happen because people are hunger, or unemployed, or homeless, i.e. because of material conditions. Marx then sought to understand the key material conditions that shape and determine social life. He looked about and saw that a universal material condition shared by all societies throughout the history of the world was the need to produce – to produce food, to produce clothing, to produce shelter, to produce babies, etc. He also recognized that production is fundamentally a social rather than an individual enterprise. A society needs to organize its system of production if it is to survive.

We are of course talking about economics. Marx saw economics as the central material fact and concluded that the ways in which a society organizes its economy was the fundamental determinant of all else in that society. He recognized that throughout history there have been many different types of economic systems, from slavery, to feudalism, from "primitive communism" – such as the hunting and gathering societies of pre-Columbus Native Americans – to modern day capitalism.

We can now put Marx's ideas of dialectics, materialism and history together. He wished to understand the logic of history that led to the modern world, and he wished to understand where this logic should and would take the world into the future. The key was to be found in contradictions (dialectics) rooted in material conditions, and the key material condition was the economic structure of a society. The contradictions found in the economy then are the main thing to identify. But what are the essential contradictions in economies that propel history forward? What, for example, caused feudalism, the economic system found in Europe before the modern age, to give rise to capitalism, the system we now have? Marx dug deeper and sought to discover the essential element of economic systems throughout history that produced contradictions that toppled the systems and gave birth to new one.

Economic Contradictions

We have already seen that the economic organization of a society was the overarching material condition in any society. Marx of course took this much further. He looked at history and saw that the ways that societies organized their economies in one period of history were very different from those of another period. What was produced and how it was produced differed from one historical period to another. The type of economy that a society has is called the **mode of production**. Capitalism is a mode of production, but so too is feudalism – the economic system of the Middle Ages in Europe. Slavery is a mode of production, as is the hunting and gathering economies of some of the Native American tribes before the Europeans arrived. (Marx would call these types of societies primitive communism.) These modes of production differed in many ways. For example, while feudalism was largely a rural, agricultural type of economy, one that is based upon ownership of land, capitalism is largely an urban and industrial type of economy, which is based not upon ownership of land, but on ownership of this thing called capital, which is discussed below. The modes of production are very different from one another. Yet each mode of production does share things with each other. For example, each mode of production has a particular **means of production.** The means of production are the things within each mode or production that are needed to produce whatever it is that is being produced. In a feudal agricultural economy food is produced. One needs land, tools, perhaps animals, and one needs to organize the workers such that they can produce. These are all parts of the means of production. Marx notes that each means of production contains the **instruments (or forces) of production** and the **social relations of production**. The instruments of production are the things that are needed to produce whatever is being produced. In capitalism, it would include such things as factories, tools, materials, etc. But to produce things, people have to be socially organized. These are the social relations of production. In a factory, the owner of the factory has to organize the workers and managers and their relationships to each other and to him.

Marx also chronicles the history of Western Europe (and he would say the world), and he notes that one mode of production has given way to another, and then that mode has given way to another, and seemingly on and on. Capitalism, for example, has replaced feudalism. He then seeks to identify the key thing that is propelling history forward. Why did capitalism replace feudalism? Why has history been filled with a series of modes of production, one being replaced by another throughout history? Why have there been these conflicts and revolutions? What is the essential driving force in this history? The answer is private property. Specifically, Marx sees private property as a social and historical creation, and not something that is simply universal or not something that has always been around in history. It is worth emphasizing here that he is focusing specifically on the private ownership over the means of production, and not so much the private ownership over your iphone or car or house. If one thinks of the nature of property in many non-capitalist societies, for example, if one things of the Native Americans living in what is now Kansas one thousand years ago, they did not have private property as we know it. Did they have a written deed to their land? When the hunters went out and killed a buffalo, did they bring it back to the village and sell the meat to the members of the village? The buffalo and the meat were communal property, not private property. This is what Marx is thinking about here. In short, it is a social and human creation it is not a natural creation, and as such much as it could be created by people it – the concept and the reality of private property itself -- could also be ended by people.

Private Property and the Division of Labor

The creation of private property is the key that unlocks the riddle of history. As soon as private property emerges, specifically the private ownership over the means of production, in history, many other fundamental things happen. One of the things that happens is the emergence of the **division of labor**. The division of labor refers to the parceling out of specialized tasks to produce something. In an automobile factory, one person does not build the entire car from scratch. Instead, one person puts one part onto the car, and then the same part on to the next car, and the same part onto the next car, etc. Another worker puts another part into the car, and then another. One can think of Henry Ford's assembly line, where workers are lined upon next to a conveyor belt and each worker has his own special task as the car being built moves down the line. If one reflects upon early modes of production, such as hunting and gathering, one can see that in contrast to modern, industrial capitalism there was not much of a division of labor present. Most of the men were hunters, etc. There of course was some division, for example, between men and women, and between the chief and others, but by and large the amount of the division was small and, Marx would say, it had a radically different nature because it was not related to private property.

In modern, industrial, and post-industrial societies, the division of labor is enormous, and it is not simply in factories, but elsewhere. One can see the division of labor in universities, where some faculty teach sociology, while others teach chemistry. Moreover, some sociologists teach or specialize in sociological theory, while others teach the sociology of the family. Likewise, in medicine today there are numerous specialists, from oncologists, to pediatricians, to psychiatrists. Three hundred years ago these divisions did not exist. There were medical doctors, not gynecologists and neurologists, etc.

In the seventeen and eighteen hundreds and into the nineteen hundreds, philosophers and social scientists saw the increasing division of labor that was occurring as a centrally important feature of the modern world and one that was having and would have significant social consequences. Marx saw the emergence of the division of labor in history as occurring simultaneously as the emergence of private property. They are the same. As Marx notes, the "division of labor and private property are ... identical expressions" (The German Ideology, 1978 [1856]:160). With private property comes the division between people who own the means of production and those who do not. Those who do not own the means of production -- whether it be the land in feudalism or the capital and the factories bought with the capital in capitalism -- have to work for those who do own the means of production if they wish to survive. In capitalism, the worker has to sell his labor to the owner of the factory to survive. Moreover, as we see below, the opposing groups, e.g. workers and owners have conflicting interests. In the most basic terms, the worker wishes to get paid more, and the owner wishes to pay him less. We will return to this a bit later, for now let us look at a few of the other consequences of the emergence of private property and the division of labor. As we see below, the emergence and spread of these things is directly related to many other aspects of Marx's theory, including his ideas related to alienation, the state, and ideology.

Labor and Alienation

As we have seen, Marx is a materialist and he believed that the social organization of production was a central element of society. Economic production specifically was key. He examines production more closely and more philosophically. When we speak of production, we are speaking of labor. People labor, they work, to produce things. Marx then goes on to examine philosophically the nature of labor. The nature of human beings is that human beings must labor to survive. They must engage productively with the world to get their needs met. It is a universal aspect of mankind that people labor. As such, Marx examines this more closely. What are people doing when they labor? Humans *externalize* themselves through their labor. They express themselves through their work. Perhaps the easiest way of thinking about this is to imagine an artist. An artist paints a painting and holds it up once it is completed and says, "This is me." The painting is an expression of who the artist is. The artist externalizes himself in his painting. Much the same perhaps when a Native American a thousand years ago crafted his own pipe or bow and arrow. He too could perhaps hold it up and with pride note that his labor is an expression of himself. But now imagine a worker at McDonald's. Can you imagine a worker at McDonald's who just finished making, or putting together, a BigMac, hold up the burger and say, "This is me!". The worker is not expressing himself through his labor. What would happen to the worker if he decided to be creative, if he decided to express himself, and he cut off the edges of the round burger and made the patty square? He could then perhaps hold the burger up and say it is an expression of himself. But if he did so he undoubtedly would get fired. In the same way, I had no control over the jewelry that I made in the factories. I did not hold the brass rings up with a note of fulfillment or accomplishment.

This is alienation. **Alienation** is the inability of the worker to express himself as a genuine and full human being through his labor. It is a perversion of the externalization process. The cause of alienation is private property, and the division of labor is most fully realized in modern capitalism. Private property creates a situation in which the owner controls the labor of the worker, and the worker loses that control. Marx identifies four specific aspects of alienation (which he also calls estrangement). The first form of alienation is that the worker is alienated from what he is producing. A worker in an automobile factory cannot drive the car home. He cannot use or sell it. He has no control over what is produced. The second form of alienation is that the worker is alienated from how the thing he makes is produced. The worker has no say into how to make the burger at McDonald's, or how to make the brass ring in the factory. He is told how to do the work. He has no control over the process. The third form of alienation is that the worker is alienated from other people. He is forced to treat other workers, and other people generally, as things to be used to accomplish the task assigned. Imagine working on an assembly line in a factory. You must think of others as part of the machinery. They are not human but are things. They are means to an end and not ends in themselves. The last form is that workers are alienated from what Marx calls their *species being*. This refers to one's own humanity. Just as the worker must turn other workers into things, into means to be used to achieve an end, so to the worker must turn himself into a thing, a machine-like entity, which is drained of its humanity. The worker's humanity, his sense of what it is to be human, fully human, is emptied.

Separation of Mental and Physical Labor

The emergence of private property has other consequences of note. One of these is the separation of mental and physical labor. This is also associated with the emergence of the division of labor. Together this produces consciousness and ideology, as is noted below. Marx writes:

> The division of labor only becomes truly such from the moment when a division of material and mental labour appears. From this moment onward consciousness *can* really flatter itself that it is something other than consciousness of existing practice, that it *really* represents something without representing something real; from now on consciousness is in a position to emancipate itself from the world and to proceed to the formation of "pure" theory. (The German Ideology, 1978:159)

He is here describing the origins of ideologies. The separation of mental labor from physical labor refers to the situation in which one person thinks about how work is to be organized and conducted and another is the person who actually does the work planned by the first. This separation produces the seeds of conflicts that have been seen throughout history.

Marx is also describing here the origins of ideologies, and as we see below his ideas regarding consciousness and ideology are today sometimes if not often seen as some of his more relevant ideas for sociology.

The State

Private property and the division of labor are also directly connected to the creation and maintenance of the state, or national governments, according to Marx. Private property, as we have seen, produces two groups, one that owns and controls the means of production, i.e. the rich people, and the other that does not own and does not control the means of production, i.e. the working class. The working class in order to survive must work for the rich people, but their interests are opposed. The worker wants a higher income, better working conditions, more control or say in the working situation, the owner wants the opposite. Two points should be noted here. The first is that like private property the state does not exist in nature. It is a human creation, and like private property as a human creation it does not always have to exist, at least in the way that we today think of the state or national government. If it only exists because private property exists, then logically it will disappear if and when private property is abolished. This is discussed further below. The second point is that with the power to control the economy, comes the power to control the state, according to Marx. The state always exists as a tool of the ruling class. It exists to serve the interests of the ruling class (the rich) and not the people in general.

You might wonder how this relates to modern democracy. At first glance doesn't it seem that the modern democratic state, such as found in the United States or Western European countries today, show that Marx's claims are wrong? After all, democracies are societies in which the popular will determines state actions. In democracies, the ruling class does not control the state. Instead, it is the people who rule. So how could Marx say the state exists to serve the interest of the rich in democratic capitalist countries? He argues that modern democracies in capitalist societies do not give the power to the people. Instead, it merely looks that way. In matters of importance, the rich people, even in democracies, are in fact controlling the state. Modern democracies are democracies in name only, and not in genuine practice. Marx would say it is not really possible to have genuine democracies in capitalist economies because the nature of capitalist economies (or any economic system based upon private property) inevitably produces a situation in which one group, the rich, controls the state. Moreover, he would say that modern democracies serve to maintain capitalism, and a system of inequality, by convincing people that democracies are legitimate systems by which the majority rule. They are an ideological force used to maintain the economic system. Ideologies are discussed below.

Classes and Class Conflict

The opening lines of the first part of Marx's *Communist Manifesto* are as follows:

> The history of all hitherto existing society is the history of class struggles. Freeman and slave, patrician and plebeian, lord and serf, guild-master and journeyman, in a word, oppressor and oppressed stood in constant opposition to one another, carried on an uninterrupted, now hidden, now open fight, a fight that each time ended, either in a revolutionary re-constitution of society at large, or in the common ruin of the contending classes. (1978:473-74)

Social classes are at the heart of Marx's theory. He looks at history from a dialectical and a materialist perspective, and he looks at the contradictions that have repeatedly arisen throughout history due to the existence of private property and the division of labor and concluded that all of the major developments in history can be traced to conflicts between social classes. To begin, we must recognize how and why Marx sees social classes as so important, and to do this we must first begin by noting how he defines social classes. He recognized that in any society that are many different classes, but he also believed that in each society thus far in history there have been two distinct and opposing classes that have been central to historical development. In other words, within each mode of production (remember the mode of production is the type of economy a society has) there are two distinct classes. One of these owns the means of production, the other must work for the owners of the means of production in order to survive. In order to survive this class must sell their labor to the owners. Thus, in capitalism, the workers have to sell themselves to the factory owners for eight, ten, twelve hours a day. In exchange for this, they get a paycheck. Again, Marx is not saying that only two classes exist in any society, but he is saying that these two classes are the ones that are and will be historically significant, as long as private property continues to exist. Because private property exists, the two classes have opposing and antagonistic interest, as was suggested earlier. The worker wishes for better pay and better treatment, the owner wishes to pay the worker the least amount as possible and treats the worker as little different from an animal or a machine. The worker, from the perspective of the owner, is nothing more than a means toward the ends of making a profit.

In capitalism, the two central classes are the proletariat and the bourgeoisie. The proletariat are the industrial working class. These are the factory workers. The bourgeoisie are the owners of industry. They own the factories. The proletariat are far, far larger in number than the bourgeoisie. The conflict of interest between these two groups will lead, Marx believed, to a revolution that overthrows capitalism. This will occur in part because of the contradictions associated with the two classes. That is, he claims the bourgeoisie will be their own "gravediggers." By this he means that the bourgeoisie as much as the proletariat are subject to the demands of capitalism. To survive they have to follow the rules of capitalism. The rule of capitalism for the bourgeoisie includes the constant need to produce a profit and to outdo their competitors. When successful, the bourgeoisie get wealthier and their factories get larger. More and more and more workers are brought under the same roof to work in the factories. Thousands of people working together under the same oppressive conditions would eventually recognize their strength in numbers and would form unions and eventually create a revolution.

Part of the historical puzzle for Marx was what would happen to the proletariat in the factories. Specifically, would capitalism produce lower wages and poorer conditions for the workers, or would it produce the opposite? Marx has a famous line in which he claims that the workers will become immiserated as capitalism proceeds. But what does the phrase "the immiseration of the working class" actually mean? Did he mean that the workers would become poorer and would suffer worse working conditions as capitalism advanced? Did he mean that the workers would become poorer relative to the wealth and power of the bourgeoisie? Or relative to the worker's productivity? Or did he mean the working conditions would render then less and less human? Marxists have argued ever since about the meaning of this phrase. But it seems rather clear that Marx thought that indeed the workers would become poorer and would suffer worse working conditions as capitalism advanced (Wage Labour and Capital, 1978 [1856]:206). The economic logic of capitalism which treats the workers' labor as the same as any other thing that could be bought and sold led Marx to believe that the reduction of the cost of labor, as a thing, was something the bourgeoisie would have to do in capitalism, as they were limited in the other ways of reducing expenses. (If you buy a machine to make something, you cannot reduce the cost of the machine after you have bought it.)

Whether Marx believed the proletariat would become poorer or not does not essentially challenge the core of his theorizing regarding class conflict. It would only at best require some modification. Marx describes what he saw as the steps toward revolution produced by capitalism. The workers in the factory at first are put together en masse and are placed in a common situation. But at first, they do not realize their commonalities and the powers that can come with coming together as a group. Marx writes about the consciousness of the working class here. He notes that the workers are first a **class-in-itself** in the factory. That is, the proletariat are all placed in the same objective situation. But they are not yet fully conscious of its meanings. Eventually, the objective (material) conditions will lead to the proletariat forming a **class-for-itself.** They will realize their shared circumstance and will realize their power as a group. They will come together to confront the owners, first to form unions and then to radicalize the unions. A class-for-itself then is a class that is self-consciously aware of itself, of its situation, of its power, and Marx might say, of its historical situation.

View of History

We can now tie some of the above ideas together by looking at how Marx saw history. Marx believed he uncovered the key to solving the riddle of history. He believed he discovered a "science" of history through his fusion of dialectics and materialism. There is only one science and "natural science … will become the basis of human science" (Economic and Philosophic

Manuscript, 1978 [1856]:90). And we might add, history too with the embrace of dialectics and materialism will be scientific. For Marx, there is a logic to history. There is a logic to the path that history has taken up until now, and this logic will continue through the future. The logic is a series of modes of productions, which have thus far contained the "seeds of their own destruction," that is, they have thus far had at their heart fundamental contradictions that demanded resolution. These contradictions are rooted in the existence of private property and in the creating of economic systems that necessarily produce classes with opposing interests.

None of this, however, is to suggest that Marx saw people as having no freedom to choose one path or another. Marx wished to unlock the riddle of history. He wished to understand "scientifically" the rules governing history. However, we should note that Marx did not see history as some sort of automatic process by which the logic of history lead in a certain direction regardless of what people do. Marx recognizes that people are not puppets of history. They are not machines enslaved to some sort of laws of historical development. In a well-known passage, he addresses this point: "Men make their own history, but they do not make it just as the please; they do not make it under circumstances chosen by themselves, but under circumstances directly found, given and transmitted from the past" (The Eighteenth Brumaire, 1978:595). Here he is saying that people make choices, but the choices that people make are defined by and limited by the circumstances in which they live.

Marx provides a summary account of his view of history in *The Communist Manifesto*. There he describes the contradictions that led to the end of feudalism, and he describes the contradictions that will spell the end of capitalism. Briefly, feudalism, which was the type of economy found in Europe for over one thousand years, from the decline of the Roman Empire in 300 A.D. through the fifteen and sixteen hundreds. This was the economic system found in the Middle Ages. It was an agricultural economy. Ownership of land was the key form of ownership then. It was the basis of the dominant mode of production, which largely consisted of agricultural products. The political system was an aristocracy. This was the era of kings and queens, and peasant farmers. The royalty owned the land, and the landless peasants to survive had to live and work on the feudal lords, i.e. the aristocracy's land. The peasants and the aristocracy of course had conflicting interests. But this was not the central conflict, according to Marx. In the Middle Ages, cities in Europe expanded as trade expanded and as surpluses were produced on the farms. This led to the emergence of a new class, a new trading class called the burghers, which were the forerunners to the modern bourgeoisie. The burghers were the wholesalers and financiers, the importers and exporters, the large-scale merchants. There also were of course the craftsmen and guild workers. There were ironsmiths, and blacksmiths, pottery makers and cabinetmakers, but for Marx, the burghers were the most important. As they grew in power and number through the Middle Ages, their interest began to increasingly come into conflict with the ruling aristocracy. While the burgers sought more economic independence and freedom from the control of the aristocracy, the aristocracy sought to create more and new laws and regulations controlling the burghers' activities and money. This conflict eventually led to the great revolutions of the late seventeen hundreds, specifically, the French Revolution and the American Revolution.

Modern democratic capitalism was born as a result. And with the new mode of production comes a new set of conflicts. The aristocracy, which was the powerful class, rooted in ownership of land and rooted in an agricultural economy, gave way to the newly emerging bourgeoisie class, which has its historical roots in the burgher class. The bourgeoisie set about ushering in industrial capitalism. Factories grew in size and number throughout Europe and the United States, and with this the industrial working class, the proletariat also grew. Marx saw the major conflicts between the proletariat and the bourgeoisie emerging in Europe in the eighteen hundreds. He believed the working class would eventually organize into unions, and the members of the unions would increasingly come to realize their own power and they would increasingly come to realize the source of their problems. The source, Marx says, is not the individual factory or the individual factory owner and it is not even the entire industry within which the workers worked. It was not the mining industry or the steel industry or the timber industry. The workers would eventually realize the problem was with capitalism itself.

At some point, the proletariat would lead a revolution to topple capitalism. Once they succeeded with their revolution, they would take control of the state. In Marx's infamous words, there would be a **dictatorship of the proletariat** (Critique of the Gotha Program, 1978:539). This would be the period of socialism. The state still exists but it would be in the hands of the proletariat. (The term "dictatorship" of course shocks many people to this day. It implies that the leaders would not be responsible to the people in any way and that the leaders – the proletariat – would do as they want to the people. Indeed, this is what Marx suggests, but one must be careful not to exaggerate this. Marx believed the proletariat at the time of the revolution would embody the essential sentiments of the people and as such would reflect the genuine will of the people. He believed the proletariat in power would not then act in their own interests against the interests of the people. In hindsight, it is clear that those who gained power in "communist revolutions" in the last one hundred years or so did in fact become a group or class that did not act in the interest of the people but instead acted in the service of their own ends, i.e. to remain in power.)

> ## Marx and Anarchy
>
> Marx had some interesting debates with the anarchists of the time over the issue of the dictatorship of the proletariat. Anarchy is a political philosophy that says the source of all problems in the modern era is the existence of the state, i.e. the government, and not the existence of capitalism per se. As such, the goal for anarchy is to abolish *all* government. Anarchy as a political perspective had a good number of supporters in the eighteen hundreds. One of the more prominent anarchists at the time was the Russian Mikhail Bakunin. Marx argued with him. In one essay, Marx quoted Bakunin and mocked him. Bakunin writes that in anarchy, "The entire nation will be governors and there will be no governed ones … Then there will be no government, no state, but if there is a state there will be governors and slaves…. This dilemma has a simple solution in the Marxists' theory. By popular administration they [that is, Bakunin] understand administration of the people by means of a small number of representatives elected by the people" (Debates with Bakunin, 1978:545). Bakunin is saying that Marx's theory will lead to an oppressive government, if for no other reason than governments by their nature are oppressive and if you give a group power, they will hold on to it and do self-serving things to keep themselves in power. Marx rejects his argument. He writes: "This is democratic nonsense … Elections are a political form …. The character of elections depends not on these designations but on the economic foundations, on the economic ties of the voters amongst one another, and from the moment these functions cease being political (1) no governmental functions any longer exist; (2) the distribution of general functions takes on a business character and involves no domination; (3) elections completely lose their present political character" (1978:545). Government, Marx says, will no longer look like government, once private property is abolished. It will no longer be political in nature, but administrative in nature. Bakunin rejects such thinking.

One of the first tasks of the proletariat once they take power is that they will abolish private property, specifically private ownership over the means of production. Thus, if the revolution were to occur in America today, the proletarian rulers would take over General Motors, Microsoft, Wall Street, etc. and turn these into publicly, i.e. government, owned entities. Recall our discussion about the state and private property above to see what is to happen next. Once private property is abolished, what becomes of the state? Once private property is abolished, according to Marx's logic, there is no need for the state to continue to exist. After all, the state exists only because private property exists. The state exists to serve the interest of the ruling class (the bourgeoisie, in capitalism). But once the proletariat take over the state, there will no longer be classes because private property has been eliminated. There will no longer be class conflict. And the basis for the state also will disappear. At this point, Marx says the **"state will wither away"** and then true communism emerges.

What exactly does this communist society look like? Marx wrote extensively about history and about capitalism, but he only wrote a few pages about this new society called communism. As such, while one can imagine some elements of what he thought a communist world would look like, it remains highly speculative. I imagine that his vision might consist of a fusion of the better elements of those societies he called "primitive communism," such as Native American societies of the Plains Indians, with the technological developments of the modern world. Native Americans with iphones, perhaps?

Human Needs and Nature

It is rather common for students who first hear of Marx's theory of history and his notions about a future communist society, one without private property and without a state, at least as we know it, to say "It would never work. People are naturally greedy, or naturally lazy." Or, "Why would someone work hard for something, if they could get that something for no work at all?" There are actually two sets of questions here. One of these concerns human needs; the other concerns human nature. Let's start with needs. What are human needs? Do we need a new iphone? Do we need food and shelter? Do we need to be happy? Or to be fulfilled? Or to be allowed to be fully human? How are needs determined? While our animal needs, our biological needs, are little different from those of other animals, all other needs are fundamentally different, and fundamentally social according to Marx. Moreover, our understanding of what our needs are themselves fundamentally socially produced. Without diving too much into his philosophical positions regarding needs here, it is sufficient to point out that Marx believes capitalism, and other systems based upon private property, distort our understandings of what needs really are. In communism, he says, we will then be allowed to see our true needs, and we will be able to fulfill these. Marx once famously said that in a communist society it would be a situation in which the following principle will be applied: "From each according to his abilities, to each according to his needs" (Critique of the Gotha Program, 1978:531). Thus, a person might become a doctor not because he or she thinks he will make a lot of money, and not because he or she thinks others will think highly of him or her for being a doctor, but because that someone realizes what they are capable of and realizes they wish to help people as medical doctors and they have the ability to do so.

The issue of human nature is equally complicated. What is human nature? Today, it is not uncommon for people to have debates about human nature. Are people naturally selfish, naturally aggressive, naturally generous, etc.? These debates tend to be based upon the assumption that there is some definitive set of animalistic instincts hardwired into our being that propel us forward. A number of problems arise with thinking of human nature in these terms. One of these is that phrasing the problem in this way never allows for a scientific answer to the question. The question falls within the metaphysical realm, the realm beyond science. It falls within the field of opinion. After all, can anyone really say that people are naturally selfish or not, and what does this mean in a scientific sense? As such, these types of claims should be understood as ideological (see below) rather than scientific. They serve not to enlighten, but to reaffirm existing beliefs and existing social arrangements.

This is not to deny that people are naturally selfish, or naturally greedy, or what have you. People by nature are all of these things and more. People are built with an enormous number of potential forms of behavior. The question is: which of these are encouraged, supported and produced by society?

For Marx, human nature should be thought of in terms of human possibilities and potential. What are the potentials of humans? We get a glimmer of his thinking on this matter when we reflect back upon the earlier discussion of labor and alienation. Specifically, humans seek to realize their humanity through their activity in the world. They externalize themselves through their labor and through this process realize or not their full humanity. For Marx, there are two key elements to the understanding of human nature. First, one must recognize that people are first and foremost social creatures. As such, social relationships lie at the heart of our being and at the heart of our nature. We are created and defined through our interactions. His concept of *species being*, noted earlier in our discussion of alienation, refers directly to this point. Second, the structure of these social relationships changes through history, particularly as we move from one mode of production to another, and because of these changes in structure, human nature also changes. Wall Street Bankers sometimes say, "greed is good." This implies that greed is natural and good, and it should be rewarded. But would greed be good in a tribe of Native American Plains Indian living one thousand years ago?

Culture and Consciousness

Scholars sometimes distinguish the "young Marx" from the "old Marx." That is, scholars sometimes say that Marx tended to think about things differently when he was younger, say in his thirties and forties, than when he was older. When he was younger, he tended to be more philosophical in orientation. He focuses more on the individual, on culture, and on consciousness. In this period, he sought to understand the impact capitalism was having on the individual and his or her humanity. When he was older, he tended to focus more on economic theory. He became more of a radical economist. This is most clearly seen in his last major work, *Das Capital* (*Capital*), a detailed economic analysis in which he attempted to demonstrate the contradictions rooted in the economic workings of capitalism.

Today, more sociologists in America draw upon the ideas of the young Marx than the old. To understand the importance of culture and consciousness for Marxist theory one should reflect upon how and why revolutions do or do not happen. Specifically, if Marx is right in saying that capitalism is an oppressive and exploitive system (see below), and if he is right in saying that the proletariat is the group that most centrally experiences this oppression and exploitation, then how is it that the proletariat have not yet had a revolution in the most advanced capitalist countries? (The major communist revolutions in the twentieth century all occurred in less advanced capitalist countries, or even pre-capitalist, agricultural and feudal societies, such as Russia, China, Cuba, etc.) How might a Marxist explain how an oppressive and exploitive system of capitalism, with all of its contradictions, is able to maintain itself? One might wish to claim that the working class and the poor have not and do not work toward revolution because they know that if they did, they would get killed by those in power or by the military and police supporting them. But is fear really the reason that they do not revolt? It is possible if not likely that some percentage of poor and working class people in America today would wish to have such a revolution, but it is far more likely that most people in these classes do not believe that the capitalist system is oppressive or exploitive and they do not believe that a revolution should occur. Most people likely believe capitalism is a good system, or at least better than any other imagined. Marx's theory of culture and consciousness has been and is used to account for such things. This theory explains how and why people think and believe what they do, and specifically it explains how and why people who are said to be victims of capitalism tolerate if not support its continued operation.

At the heart of his understanding of culture and consciousness is his **base-superstructure model**. This is his explanation for how and why people in any society think and believe as they do. Ask yourself how and why some ideas are accepted as true and others as false. Ask yourself how and why some work of art is seen as beautiful and as deserving a place in a great museum of art and other art is deemed otherwise. His base-superstructure model seeks to explain such things. He summarizes the model in the following passage:

> In the social production of their life, men enter into definite relations that are indispensable and independent of their will, relations of production which correspond to a definite stage of development of their material productive forces. The sum total of these relations of production constitutes the economic structure of society, the real foundation, on which rises a legal and political superstructure and to which correspond definite forms of social consciousness. The mode of production of material life conditions the social, political and intellectual life process in general. It is not the consciousness of men that determine their being, but, on the contrary, their social being that determines their consciousness. (Preface to the Critique of Political Economy, 1978:4)

The **base** is the economic structure of a society. The economic arrangements (in systems that have private property) produce a system of inequality in which one group has a great amount of money and power. The **superstructure** for Marx technically consists of the laws, politics, and culture of a society, and along with the culture it consists of the consciousness of the people. That is, the way that people think is influenced by the economic structure of a society. In a nutshell, the base determines the superstructure, and the superstructure, when operating in a normal fashion, reinforces the base. But what does this mean? This model seeks to answer the question: Where do ideas and beliefs come from? Where does art and culture come from? Where do laws come from? Where do political arrangements come from? And why?

It means that the common and accepted understandings of the world held by people in general, specifically poor and working people, are ultimately shaped or determined by the understandings, beliefs, values, ideas, etc. held by the powerful groups in society, i.e. the rich. Marx writes:

> The ideas of the ruling class are in every epoch the ruling ideas: i.e., the class which is the ruling *material* force of society, is at the same time its ruling *intellectual* force. The class which has the means of material production at its disposal, has control at the same time over the means of mental production, so that thereby, generally speaking, the ideas of those who lack the means of mental production are subject to it. (The German Ideology, 1978:172)

In short, those in power, i.e. the ruling class, ultimately get to say which ideas, beliefs, etc. are acceptable and correct. They get to say what is true, good, and beautiful. The ruling class determines whose tastes are right, and whose are wrong. The ruling class because they have the power dictate to all that their understandings of the world are the right and only legitimate understandings of the world. Marx is not suggesting in any way that this is some sort of conspiracy on the part of the bourgeoisie. They are not sitting in a back room somewhere conjuring up belief systems to give to the proletariat and the public at large to dupe them into believing that the system of inequality is good, necessary and just. Rather he is saying the structures of the world produce this reality that the rich will naturally act in ways that support their understandings of the world. We can see many examples of Marx's model in history.

One can find countless examples from history that illustrate these ideas. For example, we can turn to the case of Galileo (1564-1642) to show this, though Marx did not as far as I know use this case to illustrate his point. Galileo was the great Italian scientist, philosopher, inventor, and astronomer. At that time, the accepted scientific theory of the solar system was the geocentric view. The geocentric view claims that the earth was the center of the solar system and that the sun, the planets, and all of the other bodies in space revolved around the earth. Elaborate maps and theories were developed to explain the movement of the sun, the planets, and these other bodies. The explanations had to be increasingly complex, and from our perspective today rather odd, because they were based on the faulty belief that the earth rather than the sun was at the center of the solar system. Galileo challenged this view. He embraced the heliocentric view put forth by the Danish astronomer Copernicus (1473-1543). The heliocentric view says the earth and all the planets revolve around the sun. This of course is what we believe today. Galileo went further, and he built one of the first telescopes to look at the planets. What he saw, convinced him that the heliocentric view was correct. He noticed, for example, that the shadows on the moons of Venus could only be explained if one used the heliocentric theory rather than the geocentric theory. He published his results, and they were immediately attacked. They were specifically attacked by the Roman Catholic Church which at the time wielded enormous power. It was Church teaching that the geocentric view was correct. After all, if God saw humans as the apple of his eye, then how and why would he place earth as the third rock from the sun rather than at the center of the universe? Theologically, it did not seem to make sense. Galileo was arrested and convicted of heresy. He was sentenced to prison but was ordered under indefinite house arrest instead.

But it is not simply that the ruling ideas in any society are the ideas of the ruling class. Marx goes further and argues that these ideas tend to be accepted as true by the poorer and working classes, and by accepting them, these classes believe the world as it is is as it should be. The poorer and working classes who accept these ideas believe the existing system of inequality is good and just and should not be changed. They believe the rich and powerful should be the rich and powerful. In other words, the superstructure reinforces the base; ideas help maintain the economic system.

Perhaps one of the clearest examples of this process is Marx's views on religion. He writes: "Religion is the sigh of the oppressed creature, the sentiment of a heartless world, and the soul of soulless conditions. It is the *opium* of the people" (Critique of Hegel's Philosophy of Right, 1978:54). Religion as a set of ideas, as part of the superstructure, reinforces the base. Religion works to maintain the system of inequality and ultimately serves the interest of the rich. How does it do so? Much like the geocentric view of the solar system was once believed to be true but is and was false in reality, Marx would say that religion is also false. Religion serves to maintain the system of inequality by acting like a drug, opium. Opium is the plant that is the source of heroin. When one is high on opium or heroin, one is happy and content, blissful. One does not have a care in the world. One is certainly not thinking critically about the social order. One is not thinking about how to address any social injustices through revolutions.

One can look at some of the main themes in Christianity to get an understanding of what Marx is getting at here. Christianity routinely extolls the virtues of the poor and chastises the rich. As the Gospels tell us: "It is easier for a camel to go through the eye of a needle than for someone who is rich to enter the kingdom of God" (Matthew 19:25). (Some contemporary conservative Christians might take issue with this interpretation, noting that "the eye of a needle" refers in ancient times to a doorway and not our contemporary understanding. Nevertheless, the point still stands.) One could site numerous other passages from the Bible that makes similar points. We are encouraged to be humble, and not to engage in politics. We are encouraged in the Bible to endure the sufferings of this world because if we do so properly, a wondrous world of eternal happiness awaits us in Heaven.

Other examples not from Marx could be offered to illustrate his model. Take the idea of individualism. Individualism is a classic element of the American belief system. It is the belief that individuals succeed or fail in life, that is, they become wealthy or poor, due to their own natural abilities and their own motivations and determinations. Thus, someone who is rich is believed to be so because he or she is naturally smarter than others and is also driven or motivated to work hard and to succeed. Similarly, someone who is poor is believed to be so because they are naturally not as smart and are not as motivated. But we can see how the workings of Marx's model can become more complicated here. That is, a rich person would likely embrace the idea of individualism because it allows him or her to believe he should be rich. But a poor person would also likely embrace the idea of individualism, but for the opposite reason. The poor person would likely say he is poor because he is not smart enough or is not motivated enough. Both explanations focus upon the individual and do not focus on society or social arrangements. Neither explanation allows for any criticisms of the social or economic structure, so the social order can go on without any challenge. As such, these beliefs serve to maintain the system of inequality.

Ideology and False Consciousness

What I have been describing is closely related to Marx's notion of **ideology**. Ideology is a confusing term. It is used to mean many different and conflicting things in popular usage. It is also used in different and conflicting ways when people use it in the sense that they thought Marx intended. The situation becomes that much more confusing when we realize that his usage itself is complicated, and arguably contradictory. In general, Marx views ideology as a shared belief system that is used to maintain existing systems of inequality. All of the examples given above – Galileo, religion, individualism – are ideologies in this sense. But Marx sees ideologies as arising in two distinct ways. The first way that he describes ideology concerns the shared belief systems of the bourgeoisie and the spreading of these beliefs to the population at large. This, of course, refers to the discussion earlier of the ruling ideas and the ruling class.

The second way is that ideologies emerge naturally or organically out of the workings of the economic system, and specifically in capitalism this system naturally produces a distorted understanding of reality. Capitalism produces a way of thinking, he says, that is upside-down. He uses the metaphor of a camera obscura to make his point. He writes:

> Consciousness can never be anything else than conscious existence, and the existence of men is their actual life-process. If in all ideology men and their circumstances appear upside-down as in a camera obscura, this phenomena arises just as much from their historical life-process as the inversions of objects on the retina does from their physical life-process …. We set out from real, active men, and on the basis of their real life-process we demonstrate the development of ideological reflexes and echoes of this life-process. The phantoms formed in the human brain are also, necessarily, sublimates of their material life-process, which is empirically verifiable and bound to material premises. Morality, religion, metaphysics, all the rest of ideology and their corresponding forms of consciousness thus no longer retain the semblance of independence . . . Life is not determined by consciousness, but consciousness by life. (The German Ideology, 1978:154-55)

Here ideology consists of ideas that percolate up from the material arrangements, i.e. from the economic structures of inequality. These ideologies invert a true understanding. A camera obscura turns everything upside-down. This is a common theme in Marx's overall theory. He regularly notes how things have been turned upside-down. For example, he complains that Hegel's idealism, discussed earlier, does this. Similarly, capitalism turns things upside-down, and through this process prevents people from easily seeing how this economic system really works.

False consciousness is closely related to the concept of ideology. Marx says that one of the reasons that the working class does not revolt is that they accept unquestioningly the ideologies they are exposed to. That is, they believe their situation is somehow good, just or necessary, and believe they should not seek to change it. This is false consciousness. When a worker believes that capitalism is a good system that should be defended, he is said to be suffering from false consciousness.

Analysis of Capitalism

Labor and Value

The starting point for Marx's analysis of capitalism lies in his understanding of labor and value and the relationship between these two things. Earlier we described the importance of the concept of labor to his overall theory. Labor, it will be recalled, was a natural and central element of human existence. We externalize our being; we express ourselves and our humanity through the laboring process. We tell the world who we are, and we tell ourselves who we are through this laboring process. But Marx saw this process corrupted in history with the emergence of private property. And this corruption takes its full form in capitalism, where the worker becomes nothing more than an animal or an appendage to a machine, or even a machine-like thing him or herself. The concept of alienation noted earlier addresses this point. But Marx also understood labor in relationship to his economic theory of capitalism, and to the contradictions he saw in capitalism.

To understand his view of labor in this context, we must understand a bit about how he looked at value. Value is a concept central to economic theory. But what is value, and what is the value of labor? Value is the worth of something. But how is something assigned worth? And how does one assign worth to labor? These are some of the questions Marx sought to answer, and he answered them by engaging in disagreements with the conventional, capitalist economists of his time. Marx, like other economists of the time, distinguished between different types of value. There is use value, exchange value, and surplus value. The use value is the usefulness of something. If I own a lawn mower but live in a rented apartment complex, what use is that mower? It certainly is not useful to me, particularly when compared to its usefulness if and when I owned a home with a lawn. Exchange value is different. Exchange value is the worth of something based upon how much I could buy or sell it. If I lived in a rented apartment, perhaps I could sell the mower to someone else. I could exchange it for money, or perhaps even barter it for something else that I would want. This is its exchange value. It bears noting that the exchange value and use value of a thing are not the same. Adam Smith, the author of *The Wealth of Nations*, which is widely considered to be the first major, modern description of the theory of capitalism, notes the difference: "The things which have the greatest value in use have frequently little or no value in exchange; and on the contrary, those which have the greatest value in exchange have frequently little or no value in use. Nothing is more useful than water; but it will purchase scarce any thing; scarce any thing can be had in exchange for it. A diamond, on the contrary, has scarce any value in use; but a very great quantity of other goods may frequently be had in exchange for it" (1776:33).

Marx picked up on these concepts, as well as the concept of surplus value. Surplus value is the value of an object that goes beyond the value of the labor put into making it. This can happen through the process of creating value through labor. When a worker builds something out of parts, the new something has more value than the parts by themselves. It can also happen through the introduction of more efficient machines. When a worker makes ten things in an hour using a machine, and then that machine is replaced with one that allows the worker to make one hundred things in the same hour, then the surplus value has increased. In some ways, surplus value is similar to the profit of an object, though technically the two ideas are distinct.

Why are the concepts of use value, exchange value and surplus value important to Marx's theory? In capitalism the value of the labor of a worker becomes equivalent to a thing that can be bought and sold. That is, labor, which you will recall is a central means through which people can and should be able to realize their own humanity, becomes an object no different from any other object, such as a table or chair. The essential difference between the value of labor and the value of a thing gets eliminated in capitalism, Marx says, and this is problematic for philosophical and economic reasons.

Marx is concerned that capitalism turns the qualitative thing of the worker's labor into a quantitative thing no different from any other thing. An equivalence is established between the worker's labor and things, and this equivalence is rooted in the exchange of money. Money can buy an hour's worth of labor or a bushel of apple. They are equivalent. But he says labor is essentially different. Labor is part of the experience of being human. Turning labor into a quantitative thing negates this difference. People and their experiences are rendered thing-like.

But here the thing-like nature of this process concerns the workings of the economic system. As capitalism treats the value of a worker's labor as no different than the value of any other thing, i.e. all can be turned into money and used to exchange one for another, the bourgeoisie in their decision making see the worker's value as simply another line on the accounting sheet. It is equally subject to be cut or eliminated if need be. Moreover, Marx argues that capitalism produces pressures to reduce, either in absolute or relative terms, the cost of labor because the costs of labor are variable rather than fixed. The cost of equipment is fixed. Once the owner buys the machine the price he paid or is paying (if bought with credit) is fixed. He cannot reduce this cost. Labor, on the other hand, can be reduced. Marx explains that this logic and associated forms of logic required by capitalism cause various sorts of economic crises that ultimately will lead to revolution.

Absorption

For Marx, the essential conflict in capitalism lies between labor and capital. This conflict is intensified in part because of absorption. Specifically, Marx sees the expansion of the division of labor combined with the increase in the use of machinery, with capital as its foundation, as endlessly forcing the value of social labor to be transferred from the worker himself to the machine and to capital itself. That is, for the factory owner to survive in industrial capitalism he has to continually introduce new and more efficient machines in the production process. Each worker is then able to produce more than before in the same amount of time, using the same amount of labor. But the work becomes increasingly simplified. "Modern industry always brings with it the substitution of a more simple, subordinate occupation for the more complex and higher one" (Wage Labour and Capital, 1978 [1856]:215). In effect, the machines are absorbing the value of the social labor. As the machines become more sophisticated and more powerful; the worker becomes less so, less human. The machines are absorbing more and more of the workers' humanity. But this was not the central feature of the dynamic of absorption in capitalism. For Marx, capital itself absorbs the value of social labor. "The accumulation of knowledge and of skill, of the general productive forces of the social brain, is ... absorbed into capital, as opposed to labour, and hence appears as the attribute of capital" (The Grundrisse, 1978 [1856]:280). The human value of social labor thus becomes hidden when it is transferred to capital, making it that much harder to see, to understand, and to combat.

Commodities and Commodification

A **commodity** is something that can be bought and sold. An iphone is a commodity. A cow is a commodity. Your car is or can be a commodity. Your labor can be a commodity. Water can be and typically is a commodity. One of the things about capitalism is its need to expand. Capitalism must expand. If it does not, it dies. One way in which it expands is by creating new markets. This can be done by turning things that were once not commodities into things that now are commodities. This is **commodification.** It is the process of turning things into objects that can be bought and sold in the marketplace. Capitalism has an insatiable appetite for commodification. Think about water. Did Native Americans one thousand years ago living in teepees in what is now Kansas, buy their water? Where did they get their water? They got the water for free at local rivers, streams, and lakes. Today, we buy water. I am not simply talking about bottled water, but regular tap water. People have to pay the water company for water. It is a commodity. Another example: How about childbirth? Did people ten thousand years ago pay a doctor to have a baby? Perhaps they had midwives, but the delivery of a child was not commodified as it is today. Today, you pay the doctor and the hospital money in exchange for delivering your baby. Relationships of all sorts have been commodified today. Childcare, for example, is paying someone to take care of your children.

Marx saw commodification as a feature of capitalism, and just as labor is commodified, as we noted above, all facets of human existence become subject to commodification. And with this comes dehumanization. People become objects to one another, to themselves. Objects are things that are used and are not ends in themselves. But as Marx notes people are in essence ends in themselves or should be allowed to be so.

Things Turned Upside-Down

A theme in much of Marx's writings is that capitalism is a very unusual economic system. Not only is it fundamentally a dynamic system that has to constantly change – in contrast to most economic system in history which generally do the opposite. Other systems generally foster stability and a lack of change. But capitalism also turns things upside-down. It turns many things upside-down. We saw an example of this with the camera obscura, where consciousness in capitalism gets turned around. We can see this in terms of the worker and his labor. The worker becomes a thing, a machine-like thing, an object, but at the same time capitalism places more and more power, knowledge, control into things other than human beings. The things in our

world take on the characteristics of people. Your computer tells you what to do. We are enslaved to the dictates of machines. Capital tells you what to do.

Many other examples of this process of turning things upside-down can be noted. Marx's concept of commodity fetish can be thought of in this sense. The term fetish is typically associated with psychology. In psychology it is a non-sexual object that becomes the object of sexual attention and gratification for someone. Someone, for example, might develop a foot fetish, in which he or she gets sexually aroused by feet. Marx suggests that capitalism produces a similar orientation with commodities. (Keep in mind he was writing one hundred and fifty years ago. Think about what he would say if he walked around an American shopping mall today!) A **commodity fetish** is the excessive attraction that people have to objects of consumption. The act of buying and consuming becomes so gratifying that all else becomes secondary or non-important. Specifically, a commodity fetish helps blind people from thinking critically about the organization of the world, about capitalism, about the ten-year old children in Viet Nam who make the Nikes that you are thinking of buying. The value of the commodity then becomes exclusively the sensual pleasure one gets through its purchase and consumption. The true value of the labor that went into its production is ignored or denied. Our human priorities get turned-upside-down in capitalism.

Marx also wrote about the philosophical and economic problems of thing getting turned upside-down that are associated with the relationship of commodities to money. He contrasts pre-capitalism with capitalism. In pre-capitalist societies, such as ancient Rome and the Roman forum – the central marketplace in the city -- two thousand years ago, a farmer would bring his grapes to the marketplace and sell them. The grapes are a commodity. The farmer sells his grapes and gets money in exchange and then he turns around and buys something else, perhaps seeds, or shoes, or whatever. Marx represents this in the form of C1-M-C2, where C1 is the grapes, M is the money, and C2 is the new thing that was bought with the money. This was the central process of exchange in pre-capitalist economies. But things get turned upside-down in capitalism. Now we have M1-C-M2. Perhaps the easiest way to understand this is to imagine how someone buys and sells "pork bellies" on Wall Street. Pork bellies are the symbolic name for pigs (technically "pig futures") that are bought and sold. If you wished to buy one hundred pigs say in three months, you could place an order on Wall Street for these pork bellies. So the Wall Street broker buys the one hundred pork bellies. What does he do with them? Does he eat them? No. He buys them so that he can sell them for a profit. In other words, he has some money (M1) and buys the pork bellies (C), and then turns around and sells the pork bellies for a profit (or loss)(M2). One of the issues here concerns the difference in the nature of these exchanges. In the pre-capitalist mode of exchange (C1-M-C2), whose interest and needs are dictating the transaction? The needs of the people involved in the production and exchange, e.g. the farmer, are what is driving this process. In capitalism, however, it is capital, the needs of capital, which are driving the process, not the needs of people. The exchange process is driven by and for this abstract thing called capital, and it is not driven by and for human beings.

The Many Versions of Marx and Marxism

An enormous amount of Marxist scholarship has been produced over the years. But not all Marxists agree upon what Marx was actually saying, and not all agree upon what Marxist theory actually is. Throughout history there have been many different, and sometimes contradictory, versions of Marx and Marxism put forth. A few of these can be briefly mentioned here. To begin, we should note that scholars and commentators often distinguish between the young Marx and the old Marx (see Chapters Seven and Eight). That is, some argue that the theory that Marx developed when he was younger was substantially different from the theory he championed when he was older. Specifically, the young Marx, it is said, was more philosophically and culturally focused. He was more oriented toward understanding how capitalism was negatively affecting the individual, social relations, and humanity. The older Marx was said to focus less upon such things and more upon the actual workings of the capitalist economic system, and specifically upon the contradictions inherent in it that will lead to its collapse. (It perhaps should be noted here that many scholars argue that the differences between the perspectives of Marx when he was younger compared to when he was older is minimal at best. These scholars say it is a false understanding to make such a division and that Marx's theory was the same in his younger years and when he got older. The only thing that changed was his focus.)

Another pair of opposing views of Marxism is the structuralist versus the instrumentalist readings of Marx (see Chapter Eight). Structural Marxism (most classically seen in the writings of the French scholar Louis Althusser (2005)) assert that Marx's focus was on the conceptual organization of society defined by capitalism and not on individual psychology. The structures of the world, anchored in economics, exist and operate autonomously from individual agents, and it is the structures and their contradictions that must be studied. This approach basically claims that fundamental actions of people in society – including such things as revolutionary change -- are determined not by individuals making decisions but by the structures of the capitalist system itself which are governed by set of rules, as identified by Marx. The workings of capitalism in effect are on auto-pilot, outside of the control of individuals. Or perhaps a better way of saying this is that individuals are merely puppets of the dictates of capitalism. The task then is to identify the contradictions inherent in the structures of capitalism that will produce its downfall. In contrast, instrumentalist Marxists say that a Marxist understanding needs to recognize that individual actions cause things to happen. For example, the bourgeoisie act in rational, self-interested ways, and it is this individual decision making that needs to be at the center of the analysis. As the bourgeoisie are in control of the state, they have the state do things that are in their interests. Instrumentalists would reject the structuralists claim that Marx viewed society as if it was on auto-pilot, outside of the control of individuals.

This is related to another set of conflicting Marxist interpretations. These revolve around whether Marxist embrace a view that claims that individuals are fundamentally rational, self-interested actors or not. That is, some claim or imply that Marx believed that it was a universal aspect of the human condition that individuals act in rational, self-interested ways. People do so now, and they did so a billion years ago. The proletariat unionize and then revolt, so this line of thinking goes, because they see that it is in their interest to do so, much as people living in earlier modes of production acted in their interests to either maintain or challenge the existing social arrangements. The claim is that it is a timeless quality of human beings that they are rational and self-interested. Other Marxists would reject this claim. Marx, they would say, says that the forms of human beings – the forms of being human -- are necessarily shaped by the particular economic structures within which they live, and as the structures change in history so too do the forms of being. As such, the claim that humans are by nature rational and self-interested mistakenly is based upon the idea that the forms of being seen in capitalism, i.e. individuals are thought to be and required to be rational and self-interested, are mistakenly believed to be timeless traits when in fact they are produced in and by particular historical circumstance, i.e. capitalism (see Chapter Eight).

Numerous other opposing sets of understanding can be identified. For example, one set of opposing views of Marx is that between humanistic and structural Marxists. We have just described structural Marxist briefly above. Humanistic Marxists (see Chapter Eight) are those who tend to embrace the writing of the young Marx and tend to be focused upon how capitalism affects individuals and social relations, specifically, in how it was turning human beings into things, denying them of their humanity. Humanistic Marxists often focus on the workings of culture and such things as ideology. Still another set of opposing views of Marxism is that between those who believe Marx embraced dialectics and those who believe he did not. Specifically, the different perspectives revolve around whether Marx actually embraced Hegelian dialectics or whether he rejected this and embraced a traditional, non-dialectical scientific perspective (i.e., one more in-line with the philosophy of positivism or scientism)(see Elster 1985; Cohen 1978).

Summary

Marx was responding to the growth of industrial capitalism in the eighteen hundreds in Europe. He sought to understand the logic of history that produced the modern world. He did so with the intent of trying to understand what the future would be like. He was greatly influenced by the German philosopher Hegel. Hegel developed a philosophy of history rooted in idealism and dialectics that saw history as one of progress in which the modern world was more advanced and better than earlier worlds. Marx embraced some of Hegel's ideas and turned others upside-down. He embraced Hegel's notion of dialectics, and this became a central concept in the theory. The world consists of contradictions that cry out for resolution. Each reality is composed of opposing forces and this conflict produces change. It produces a new reality, which then contains a new set of contradictions, and again this leads to change. As such, identifying the essential conflicts in a society should be the starting point for any analysis. Marx rejected Hegel's idealism and instead embraced materialism, which states that materials conditions were the fundamental cause of social realities and social change. The key material condition was the organization of the economy, specifically the social organization of production. The economy in any society was the key to understanding the entire society, and it was the key to understanding history. The task was to identify the central conflicts or dialectics embedded in the economy.

Marx identifies private property as the key factor that explains the logic of history. Private property does not exist in nature, rather it is a social and historical creation. As soon as private property was created, society automatically became divided into two opposing camps. On the one side is the group or class that owns the means of production, that is, the class of rich people. On the other hand, there is the group that does not own the means of production but only own their ability to work. This second group must work for the first in order to survive. But this creates a conflict between the interests and needs of the two groups. This conflict has been the source of all major historic change. In capitalism, the working class is called the proletariat and the rich people, the owners of the means of production, are the bourgeoisie. Marx believed the industrial working class was exploited and alienated as the result of capitalism, and they would eventually organize into unions, and they would become radicalized. This would eventually lead to a revolution to topple not only the bourgeoisie but capitalism itself. Once in power, the proletariat will abolish private property, then all the elements of oppression and exploitation that characterize capitalism will vanish. Class conflict will disappear, as there will no longer be classes. The state (as we know it) will also disappear as there is no longer a reason for its existence in a society without classes.

An influential part of his theory is his view of culture and consciousness. Marx developed a base superstructure model to explain how and why people think as they do, believe as they do, appreciate art and culture as they do. The base is the economic structure of a society, and the superstructure consists of the law, politics, and culture (including consciousness) of society. In any society, the base determines the superstructure and the superstructure, when operating in a normal fashion, reinforces the base. This maintains the existing system of inequality. Culture and consciousness, and law and politics, are produced in ways that convince people that the existing system of capitalism and of inequality is just and necessary. This provides an important way in which, he says, such an exploitive and oppressive system is able to survive and flourish. The ideas that people hold have been manipulated by the organization of the economic structure. Marx says that the working class will eventually come to see how this works, and he believed this class would eventually develop a class consciousness. They would come to recognize how the accepted understandings of the world – the ideas spread through capitalism and supported by the rich – are factually wrong and opposed to the interests of the working class. The working class will then develop alternative ways of thinking that challenge the conventional ways.

Marx also devoted considerable attention to an economic analysis of capitalism. He saw the economic logic of capitalism as harmful to individuals and he saw it as riddled with economic contradictions that would eventually cause the system to experience economic crises which would lead to revolution. To understand how capitalism is harmful to individuals, one must recognize Marx's philosophical approach to the concept of labor. Humans by nature must labor. In any society through the world, humans have to work. Society could not exist if this was not the case. Marx saw labor as a process through which individuals engaged with the world and expressed themselves. (They externalize themselves.) It is through labor that people should naturally be able to realize their humanity, to be fully human. However, this process has become perverted in history as the result of the emergence of private property. With this emergence in history the individual no longer has the ability to control his or her own labor. He must work for someone else. Someone else, i.e. the owners of the means of production, now tell the worker what to produce, how to produce, etc. As a result, his ability to express his humanity through his work is denied. This is also associated with the concept of value. At the heart of his analysis of capitalism lies the notion of value, and the belief that the essential fact of capitalism was that it turned the qualitative value of human labor, and human experience, into a quantitative thing no different from any other thing. In capitalism, labor is also turned into a commodity. This is a dehumanizing process. It negates our humanity. This is the core of alienation. Labor value is one of many different types of values. Exchange value and use value are two other forms of value.

Discussion Questions:

1. Is Marx's theory still applicable today? We live in a post-industrial society. The size of the industrial working class today in America is very small, as there are very few factories left in America. Does this mean his theory is outdated? How might a Marxist respond to this issue? Would a person working at a McDonald's be considered a proletariat? Why or why not? What class would a software engineer at Apple be considered?

2. Marx was writing at a time when there were not many stock holding companies. Most companies at the time were owned by individuals or families. His theory is based upon this. However, today most big companies are stock holding companies. That is, they are owned by thousands of shareholders. They are not generally owned by one person or one family. Anyone can buy a piece of a corporation by buying a share of a company. If I own a share of stock of Microsoft Corporation, am I a member of the bourgeoisie? What does this change say about Marx's theory? Is it still relevant today?

3. Many conflicts in America and in the world appear to be based on religion or race and not on economic conflicts. How might a Marxist explain these conflicts that do not appear to be economic ones? For example, how might he explain radical Islamist terrorists?

4. Is Marx's base superstructure model right? Are the ruling ideas of any society the ideas of the ruling class? Is religion the opium of the people? How would Marx explain the fact that religion has and is often used to foster change, rather than to support the existing system? The American Civil Rights Movement was led by religious leaders. Radical Islam is driven by religious beliefs? Moreover, Marx claims that people have false beliefs about the world because they have been duped. If someone is happy working at McDonald's or in a factory, who is to say whether they are suffering from false consciousness?

5. Marx believed the two main classes in capitalism, the bourgeoisie and the proletariat, would be in conflict with one another. He also believed the proletariat class would grow larger and larger with industrialization. He did

not see the middle classes as very important to history. Yet through the first half of the nineteen hundreds the middle classes in American became large and powerful (though nowhere near as large as popular images suggest). At one point, Marx claimed the middle classes, of medical doctors for example, would fall into the proletariat as capitalism advanced. Is it a fatal flaw in his theory that he did not recognize that the middle class is or was such a large and influential part of society?

Chapter Three: Durkheim

When I think of Emile Durkheim, I think of Disneyland and all the things associated with it, such as Disney World, EuroDisney, Mickey and Goofy. Disneyland is a wonderfully ordered and happy place. It is, I am told, the happiest place on earth. The world of Disney is a world of unity and order in which values and moral sentiments are reinforced, specifically the moral sentiments associated with being an American, a good American. In the world of Disney, whether at the theme parks or in the movies or through the dolls and puppets and the endless Disney merchandise, everything is pure and good, and ordered. Everything is the way it should be. Moreover, we are taught by the characters and by the stories how to be good and pure. We are told that we too can be real persons if we just listen to Jiminy Cricket, the mouthpiece of conscience, as he instructs Pinocchio on how to behave. And through our visits our image of ourselves as good Americans, as members of a good community, is steadily reinforced. In the world of Disney, one does not see inequality, racism, poverty, war, pollution. One does not see massive prisons, nuclear weapons and police, at least not as they are.

If we can get past the realization that the world of Disney is not real (though Disney seeks to get us to suspend judgment on such matters), and if we look behind the curtain at the world of Disney, we would see a far more complicated and messy reality: a reality that includes the animation workers at Disney Corporation going on strike in the 1940s; a reality of Disney today producing R-rated movies; a reality of Disneyland and Disney World holding "Gay Days" where gay families are celebrated, a world in which Walt Disney created and produced the film Song of the South in 1946, which is generally considered highly racist. If we appreciate or understand the differences between the appearances and realities, then we could perhaps see some similarities between Disney and Emile Durkheim and his theory of society. Both worlds – that of Disney and that of Durkheim – start with an image that the social world is a united place. It is a moral place, and a morally ordered one. There is unity and goodness in this order. Both also start with the assumption that this is how it should be. But hidden within each is a more complicated reality.

One might then ask, if we conjure up these images, if indeed Durkheim's views somehow are echoed in the landscape of Disneyland, then how and why do sociologists today continue to see Durkheim as a significant figure in sociology, as one who has something of relevance to say? Isn't his theory then no less fanciful than Disney? Isn't he just another dead white guy, writing about a dead reality of over one hundred years ago, or writing about a dead reality imagined by others sixty years ago, or perhaps writing about an unreal, mythical image held by some today? Why would a theorist who seemingly has an image of a society reminiscent of a fantasy land still be accorded significance today? The answer is that while some of his ideas could reasonably be seen as conservative and fanciful (though at the time of his writing he was generally seen as being liberal), and while some of his ideas might seem out of place or outdated in the contemporary world, many if not most of his theoretical positions arguably can help us a good deal in understanding our world today. Most sociologists today do not see many of his ideas as outdated, but instead they see them as having great value in helping us to make sense out of our current world.

For example, as I am writing this in the summer of 2020, America is experiencing numerous crises. The covid-19 pandemic and the odd American responses to it; the protests and riots (some would say these are acts of rebellion rather than riots) related to the Black Lives Matter movement and the demands to an end to racism in general and police brutality directed at black people in particular; and of course the bizarre and highly divisive presidency of Donald Trump, an unstable, authoritarian leader, all paint a picture of America today as highly disordered and contentious. Disneyland it is not. For Durkheim, society should be seen as a unified moral entity. Morality consists of judgments and evaluations about how the world is and how the world ought to be. When these two sets of judgments are aligned, when people understand the world as it is, is the same as it ought to be, then social order is produced. But when there is a gap between the two, then social tensions arise. When expectations and realities do not align, then order breaks down. We see this today.

Take another example, his theorizing might help inform an understanding of the terrorist attacks on September 11, 2001 and the subsequent and ongoing and barbaric Islamist terrorist attacks around the world since then. Durkheim might begin an explanation of such things by focusing on the question of social order and how and why it was or is disrupted. Terror attacks might be signs of a disruption in the moral order. They might be symptoms of a diseased social body. In this case, arguably it is the global social body rather than the national order that is at question. He might focus on the role that morality plays in maintaining social order. But which social order? And whose morality? The social order of a family? Of a city? Of New Jersey? Of America? Of the world? Of the terrorists? The social order arguably now is on an international scale, at least as it pertains to global terrorism. It is one of globalization. The world has become highly inter-related. The terrorist attacks suggest strongly that there is something wrong or dysfunctional with the present global order. Durkheim would likely say as much if he was alive today.

There is something wrong perhaps with the morality of this order. At the heart of Durkheim's theorizing is the belief that morality is (or should be) a fundamental force in the creation and maintenance of social order in the modern world (even more so in pre-modern worlds). But whose morality? It is clear that the terrorists are attacking not simply the western world, but western values, western morality, western ways of being. Even more so, they are attacking the value of the Enlightenment which have played such a vital role in the western world, as well as the entire world, over the last three hundred years. These include the secular values of liberty and equality and the values of the individual and of the community. The expectations and desires, the values and morality, of Americans today are largely at odds with those of radical Islamists who behead people for being non-Islamic. Ultimately, the terrorists are attacking modernity, a modern world build upon the moral values of the Enlightenment. Durkheim's theory can indeed be used today to help account for the rise and the spread of terrorism. His theory continues to have much import for the world today.

Take one last example: Crime is a big topic of conversation, rightfully so, in our society. Whether it is street crime or the all too common mass shootings, crime saturates our world. When commentators appear on the news talking about crime, particularly mass shootings, they almost always focus on the individual criminal, or upon what the police can or should do about crime, or upon debates about gun control. When an individual goes into a movie theater and guns down many people, commentators look to understand the individual psychology of the shooter. Was he mentally ill or not? What was his motivations? Do they ever talk about how the organization of American society might produce crime? Do they ever talk about the social conditions – conditions external to the individual that may nurture crime, or the social conditions that might work to reduce crime? Do they ever talk about sociology? For Durkheim crime could be thought of as a sociological thing rather than a psychological thing. Crime, or at least excessive crime, reflects an imbalance in the society, an imbalance in the moral order. It is a symptom of an illness in the body social. As we see in the following pages, he might see high crime rates as indications of a problem with the social order, much like a fever is an indication that the human body is sick. He might talk about confusing or conflicting morality in society and how such things might relate to crime. Again, a morally ordered world is one in which most people in a society expect something to happen and then see their expectations realized in reality. Something should happen, and it does. This is a moral world. When everyone or when most people do not share a perspective about how the world is and how the world should be, i.e. about morality, then one might find crime rising. Moral confusion fosters crime and mass shootings. When expectations and reality are not inline, then confusions arise about how to act. These are a few of the things that make Durkheim relevant today, and they are just a few of the things that make a comparison between Disney and Durkheim's theory worth pondering.

Main Themes

Several main themes can be identified in Durkheim's theorizing. One of these concerns science and methods. Durkheim saw one of his main tasks to be the development of a science of sociology. Toward that end, he turned to the hard sciences – biology, chemistry, physics, etc. – for inspiration. The science of sociology should use the same methods as these other sciences. More will be said on this below. A second main theme, one that was touched upon above, is morality. One cannot understand Durkheim's theorizing unless one appreciates the centrality of the concept of morality to his work. He saw sociology as a **science of morality**: "We do not wish to deduce morality from science, but to constitute the science of morality" (1984:xxv). We should understand however that he uses the concept of morality in a way that is significantly different from the way that this word is used today in popular discourse, in public discussions. Today, morality is often viewed narrowly; often it is associated with religion. Morality now concerns the right and the wrongs of some behavior. Is it moral to have an abortion? To allow or to condone gay marriage? For Durkheim, morality has a different meaning. In some respects, one can hear echoes in Durkheim's usage of the ways that morality was written about in the late seventeen hundreds and early eighteen hundreds, a hundred years before his time. Morality then had a more expansive definition than it does now. Then morality was defined as proper evaluations and judgments, and it was fundamentally social in character. A moral action was one in which a person's behavior based upon evaluations and judgments was in accord with group standards. Durkheim shared this understanding of morality. He writes: "Morality is the sum total of the inclinations and habits which social life, depending upon the manner in which it is organized, is developed in the conscience of individuals" (1982:169). For him, morality was social, and it involved the evaluation and judgments of people.

A second main theme is the **collective conscience**. To understand this concept, it is helpful to recognize that the word "conscience" has two different meanings in French. Conscience refers to the capacity for moral evaluations. Thus, one is said to have a conscience if one can distinguish right from wrong. The second translation is consciousness. Here conscience means awareness. Arguably, when Durkheim uses the concept collective conscience, he is suggesting that we should understand it in both ways, both as a moral concept and as awareness. So what is the collective conscience? Some sociologists define it as a "group mind." This is somewhat awkward, but it does capture some sense of the concept. Durkheim defines the

Emile Durkheim

Emile Durkheim was born in 1858 in Epinal, a small town in Eastern France (in the Lorraine/Vosges region). He was born into a long line of Jewish rabbis. As a child he was enrolled in rabbinical (religious) schools, but he soon decided against a religious career, and as an adult he was not religious at all. He was a very good student and earned his doctorate from the prestigious Ecole Normale Superieure in Paris in 1882. At the time there were no sociology departments at the universities, so he could not get a degree in sociology. Instead, his degrees were in philosophy and education. One can perhaps understand why he pursued these areas. He had an interest in science, morality, social order and psychology. After earning his degree, he taught from 1882 to 1887 at various secondary schools in France and then earned an appointment as a professor in philosophy at the University of Bordeaux in the southwest of France. It was there that he taught the first course in sociology at any university in France. He published a number of his major works (including *The Division of Labor*, *The Rules of Sociological Method* and *Suicide*) in the period from 1893 through 1897. His academic reputation grew, and he eventually was hired as a professor at the famous, ancient Sorbonne University in Paris in 1902, where he remained for the rest of his life. At the Sorbonne he taught courses in education, in moral education, and in sociology. He published his last major book, *The Elementary Forms of Religious Life*, in 1912. Durkheim died in 1917, a few months after his son Andre died fighting for France in World War One (1914-1918).

collective conscience as follows:

> The totality of beliefs and sentiments common to the average members of a society forms a determinate system with a life of its own. It can be termed the collective or common [conscience]. Undoubtedly the substratum of this consciousness does not consist of a single organ. By definition it is diffused over society as a whole, but nonetheless possesses specific characteristics that make it a distinctive reality. In fact, it is independent of the particular conditions in which individuals define themselves. Individuals pass on, but it abides. It is the same in the north and south, in large towns and in small, and in different professions. Likewise it does not change with every generation but, on the contrary, links successive generations to one another. Thus it is something totally different from the consciousness of individuals, although it is only realized in individuals. (1984:38-39)

For him, it is as if this thing, this collective conscience, hovers above us, enshrouds us like an umbrella, and has a life of its own, independent of the individuals in the society. The collective conscience has a reality independent of individuals and has or can have a power over individuals. It is comprised of "beliefs and sentiments." In some, if not many, societies, as I discuss below, religion is often times the embodiment of the collective conscience. Whether religious or not, one can imagine that a social group or society must share certain understandings, certain perspectives, if it is to survive. For Durkheim, these shared understandings are key to understanding how or if a society is able to survive.

The idea of the collective conscience is closely associated with another one in his theory. This is the idea of **sui generis**. The concept of sui generis refers to a distinctive reality that emerges when parts or elements are combined to form a whole. This new whole then operates under its own set of rules, rules that are different from the rules that govern the operation of the individual parts. In some ways, the saying "the whole is greater than the sum of its parts" can be used to illustrate this concept. A human being consists of many different body parts. The liver, the kidney, the heart, etc. all operate under different rules. Different rules govern the individual operations of the individual organs and parts. But when all of these are combined, a living human organism arises, complete with consciousness, and this living human is governed by rules that are distinct from the rules that govern the individual parts making up this whole. Likewise, an automobile is more than simply the sum of its parts. When put together, the automobile is governed by its own set of rules that are distinctive from the rules governing the individual parts that comprise the auto. In much the same way, Durkheim sees the collective conscience as well as society as having a sui generis reality. Sociology, for Durkheim, is the scientific study of this sui generis reality. Sociology should be focused upon understanding the rules that govern this totality, rules that are different than the psychological rules governing the individuals that make up that society.

A third theme that ripples through much of Durkheim's theorizing concerns the relationship of the individual to society. He does not explicitly focus much on this theme, but it is found throughout his writings. The issue concerns the nature of the relationship of society to the self. To understand his thinking, one could imagine three types of societies, characterized by different relationships of the individual to society. One could imagine these in terms of big and little circles where the larger circle stands for the society and the smaller circle stands for the individual within the society (see Figure 3.1). In Society A, the little circle is completely located within the larger circle. This means that all individuals act, think, behave alike. The individuals all have the same beliefs, the same language, the same race or ethnicity; they all dress alike and talk alike. The Amish, North Korea and cults are examples of Society A. In Society B the small circle lies completely outside of the larger circle. Society B is one in which individuals do not share anything with

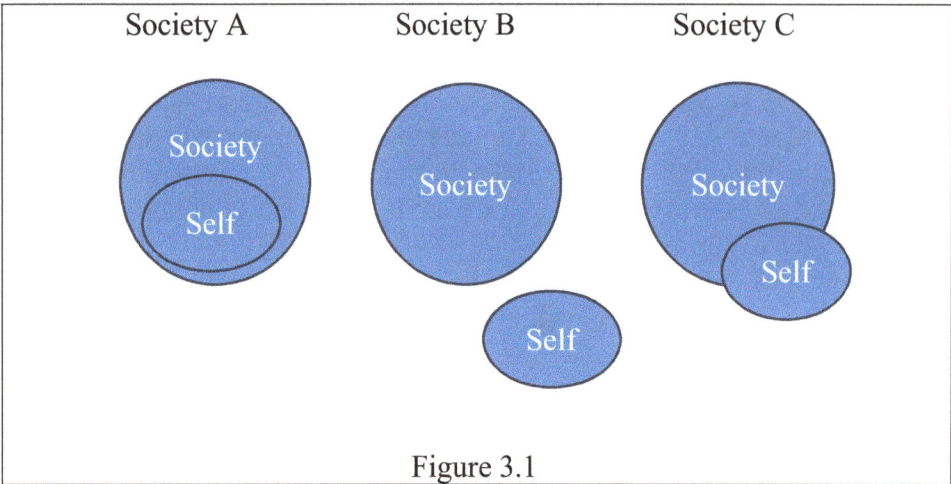

Figure 3.1

other individuals in the society. They do not share morality, values, language, etc. It is hard to imagine a society of this order, or perhaps it is hard to imagine how such a society could even exist. Society C is when the small circle lies on the edge of the larger circle. Part of the small circle (the self) lies within the larger circle (society) and part of the small circle lies outside of the larger circle. Society C is one in which individuals share some characteristics with others in society, but at the same time maintain their individual distinctiveness. Thus, they might share language, values, morality, tastes, etc. but they hold distinct and different views of the world, different religions, different ethnicities, etc. Arguably, modern, urban societies, such as the United States, are examples of this.

Durkheim, as is noted below, saw Society C as the optimal society for the modern world. He saw the other two as abnormal or unhealthy. Durkheim liked to use biological metaphors in his description of society – terms such as healthy and unhealthy. Here we can get a sense of Durkheim's assumptions of balance or order. Societies A and B are not balanced, but Society C is. We return to this point below.

A fourth theme found in his theorizing is **functionalism**. Functionalism assumes that society is a unified whole that is comprised of specialized parts, and that these parts exist to keep the whole going. Functionalism is the position that assumes that if something exists and endures over a period of time it must have a reason to exist and endure. Otherwise, it would not. It would fade away. The heart exists because of its function to pump blood such that the body can survive and can maintain health. In the same way, the lungs exist because of their function to process oxygen. The biological analogy is apt here. (One can also see echoes of Darwinian thinking here: those traits that are functional will endure; those that are dysfunctional will wither away.) Society is like the human body. Much like the human body consists of numerous specialized parts which when working normally function to maintain the health of the body, society also has parts that exist to function to maintain the health of the social whole, i.e. of society. For example, the family exists. All societies have families of one sort or another. As such, the family must serve a function. A functionalist might say the family has many functions, which contribute to maintaining the social order of society. It socializes children into conforming to the norms and values of society. It protects children emotionally and physically, etc. Likewise, a functionalist might look at education and claim that educational institutions, whether K-12 or higher education, function to keep a large, complex society, such as ours, stable and whole.

At the heart of functionalist reasoning is the assumption that societies have a natural tendency to maintain some healthy balance or equilibrium. Much like the human body has a natural tendency to maintain a balance, society does as well. The human body naturally maintains a healthy body temperature of 98.6 degrees and a normal healthy heart rate, but when one runs around the block the heart rate goes up. When one has a fever, the body temperature rises, but under normal conditions the body returns to its natural state of equilibrium or balance. Much as the fever produces symptoms of an ill body, so too society in Durkheim's way of thinking can become sick. Excessively high crime rates or excessively high suicide rates, for example, might indicate such sickness of the social body.

Using Durkheim's reasoning, if some social formation exists and endures over a stretch of time it must exist for a reason, and that reason is that it contributes to the maintenance of the stability of the existing social order. That is its function. Some social formations can almost intuitively be understood in this way. Education, family, and religion, for example, can be seen as existing to maintain the stability of the whole. However, the functionality of other formations seems less intuitive. What about crime, for example? Every society has crime of some sort or another. As such, a functionalist would need to claim that crime paradoxically serves some function. Durkheim actually wrote explicitly about crime in this way. He noted that in a society of saints, even the smallest of infractions would be considered criminal and would be treated as such. He noted that "crime is normal." But it is not only normal, "crime is necessary" (1982:101). So what functions might crime serve? There are several. One function is that crime sometimes illustrates, clarifies, and reinforces the society's understanding of right and wrong. Without someone being arrested, convicted, imprisoned, a society might not easily understand what is morally acceptable and what is not morally acceptable. Crime also reinforces solidarity. It brings people morally together as a community. I think of the immediate days after September 11, 2001. In those days Americans felt as if they were one. There was a unity, a shared sense of grief and anger. The terrorist crimes bound Americans together (though this communing was disrupted by President Bush's decision to invade Iraq). One can see this often when one or another heinous crime comes to light. Members of a society feel a sense of solidarity in the face of such things. Crime also can serve, can function, to help a society to evolve. Crime can help a society change and adapt to changing circumstances. Many examples could be provided in which people engage in illegal acts only to ultimately have the laws changed to render what was once illegal now legal. From women smoking cigarettes a hundred years ago, to gay rights and gay marriage, to the legalization of marijuana, criminals often function to push changes in moral and legal codes of behavior.

Method

Durkheim wanted very much to create a science of sociology that was modeled upon the hard sciences, e.g. physics, chemistry, etc. He believed there was one and only one proper approach toward the production of scientific knowledge. (This approach is sometimes called "scientism.") The ways that chemist produce their knowledge about the chemical world is the same as the ways that biologists produce their knowledge about the biological world. And the way that chemists and biologists produce knowledge is the same way that sociologists should follow. Sociologists should not be engaged in an interpretive project, such as that found in the humanities, in literature, in art. An art professor knows a work of art. He or she can explain what a Picasso means. But this professor does not use a scientific approach to develop scientific knowledge. For Durkheim the form of knowledge that sociologists should embrace is the form of knowledge found in the sciences.

He could loosely be said to embrace a "positivistic" form of reasoning. **Positivism** means many things to many people, but here we can think of it as the logic (or more specifically the philosophical logic) behind conventional science. How is it that we can have confidence in the proclamations of a medical researcher when the researcher claims to have discovered a new drug that effectively treats one or another disease? We assume the medical scientist followed certain logical methods. These methods are rooted in positivism. Here we can say that positivism is a form of reasoning that says that a claim of fact (or a hypothesis about the factual world) can only be made if this claim is subject (at least) potentially to empirical (e.g. observable and measurable) verification or falsification. Positivists claim that scientific claims must be based upon objective observations of facts in the world that relate to one another. One fact may cause something to happen, and it is observable. Water freezes at thirty-two degrees. One can empirically verify this through an experiment. Durkheim fully embraced this form of understanding. In short, he wanted to be a scientist, and he wanted to demonstrate that sociology could be and is a scientific field of inquiry.

Durkheim wished to create a science of society and a central part of this consists of explanations of human behavior. Yet other sciences out there are tasked with explaining human behavior. Specifically, psychology is a field that is designed to do just that. Yet if psychology is a field that explains social behavior, then what need is there for a sociology? If psychology can explain why people do what they do, then why should one develop a sociology? One might argue from a scientific perspective, i.e. the perspective that Durkheim very much wishes to embrace, that sociology does not exist. After all, doesn't every explanation of social behavior ultimately come down to psychology? From explaining revolutions to explaining why people marry, are not all explanations of social behavior fundamentally psychological? To explain behavior, don't we ultimately have to examine scientifically the internal workings of the psychology of individuals to understand their behaviors? If so, then does sociology even exist? Is it really a legitimate enterprise? These questions were very much at the forefront of Durkheim's mind when he was creating his sociology.

In sum, he was driven in part to convince people that sociology was a legitimate and distinct scientific discipline, distinct from psychology. He did this in part by embracing the concept of the collective conscience, noted earlier. He also did it by championing a science of morality. For Durkheim morality, as we saw above, was key to understanding society. Society is fundamentally a moral enterprise. The task then is to develop a science of morality. But how? To address this issue, he turned to the important concept of **social facts**. Social facts, for him, are the proper object of study of sociology, and the study of social facts are a major thing that distinguishes sociology from the other social sciences, most notably psychology. So what are social facts? Durkheim famously tells us that "social facts are things," by which he means they are things that can be scientifically identified and measured much like the height of a tree in a forest can be measured or the speed of light can be measured or the pull of gravity could be measured. They are objective and observable.

Durkheim says social facts have two essential characteristics: They are external to individuals, and they are coercive upon the individual. That is, social facts are things that are outside of the individual that cause the individual to do or not to do something. If I hold a gun to someone's head and demand they give me the money in their pocket, the gun is external to the individual and it is coercive upon that individual. It is a social fact. If my mother who lives five hundred miles away calls me up and asks me to come visit her for the weekend and I comply with her request, is that a social fact? Yes. It is external to me and coercive upon me. These two examples illustrate two types of social facts identified by Durkheim. There are material social facts, such as guns, or physical things, and non-material social facts. Non-material social facts are things like language, morality, the collective conscience, norms, etc. If anyone has any doubt that language is external to and coercive upon an individual, I suggest that the next time one is driving down the road and see a stop sign that they do not stop. Clearly, the written word "stop" is a social fact. Language is routinely used to coerce people into doing things. But so too are the more subtle forms of social facts such as norms and morality. Why is it that students generally do not disrupt their classes? Why do they follow (generally) the directions of the professor in class? There are likely many reasons for this, but one of these is certainly that the norms, the sets of expectations associated with being a student in a classroom contribute to regulating the behaviors of the individual students.

An important issue arises here about social facts. You will recall that Durkheim wished to create a science of sociology (a science of morality), and as such he wished to explain causal relationships between social facts. Yet the issue becomes a bit more complicated when one recognizes that one cannot often observe non-material social facts directly. Where is the norm governing or regulating students' behavior in a classroom? Where is morality? The collective consciousness? These concepts seem beyond the realm of the observable, and yet these are what he wishes to study. How can this be? The easiest way of understanding his answer is to draw upon the analogy of the physical sciences. Many concepts in the physical sciences cannot be seen. Can a physicist see gravity? No, but they can see the effects of gravity. Gravity can be identified and measured by proxy. If one drops a ball in an experiment, one can measure how fast the ball drops, etc. to assess the principle of gravity. Durkheim is thinking along the same lines when writing about social facts. One might not be able to see one or another of these directly, but one can see their effects. Students sitting quietly in a classroom might be an effect of the social fact of a norm. In a similar way, Durkheim might argue that a high crime rate (or an excessively low crime rate) might be an indicator of lack of social order or social solidarity.

The Division of Labor

The concept of **the division of labor** refers to the breaking down of work tasks into its particular components. It is related to the concept of specialization. The division of labor is the changing organization of work such that workers no longer constructed an entire object from start to finish, but instead devoted all their work to constructing only one part of the entire object over and over again, while another worker devoted all his or her work to constructing another part. For example, in an automobile factory with no division of labor, one worker would build an entire car from scratch. He or she would make the chassis; he or she would place the doors on the car, the steering wheel on the car, etc. Similarly, a pre-Columbian Native American might make his own bow and arrow from start to finish. This is a low division of labor. But industrial, capitalist factories increasingly relied upon an increasing division of labor. The autoworker does not build the entire auto. Instead, he or she focuses on one task. Perhaps the worker specialized in putting the bumpers on the cars. He would put the bumper on one car, then another, and then another. Another person might put the windows on a car, then another car, etc.

The division of labor extends far beyond the factory. One finds an extensive division of labor in schools and in medicine, for example. Universities have academic departments, and within the departments faculty specialize in certain areas of their academic discipline. In sociology, a faculty might specialize in the study of the family, or in the study of deviance and social control, or in social theory. In medicine too specializations abound. Three hundred years ago, if you were to go to a medical doctor, you would not generally go to a specialist. There were none. Now the medical field is filled with specialists, whether they are gynecologists, oncologists, psychiatrists, etc.

Scholars in western Europe from the seventeen hundreds through the early nineteen hundreds recognized the growing division of labor as one of the central characteristics of the modern industrial world. From Adam Smith to Karl Marx, from August Comte to the German sociologist Ferdinand Toennies, social thinkers tried to understand this phenomenon and they tried to understand what sort of future the growing division of labor in society would produce. Many of these earlier thinkers were concerned about the consequences of the growing division of labor. Marx and Toennies, for example, saw this growth as harmful to social solidarity, albeit for different reasons. All in all, a number of critics were concerned that the increasing division of labor would cause society to become fragmented. If you are specializing in your task, and I am specializing in my task, what do we have in common? What do we share? Moreover, critics were also concerned about what this growth was or will do to the individual. Marx's concept of alienation (see Chapter Two) speaks to this point, though he ultimately attributes the cause of alienation to the existence of private property rather than to the division of labor itself. (Marx said private property and the division of labor arose in tandem.)

Durkheim wrote his book *The Division of Labor* in Society in 1893 in response to such critics. It was his doctoral dissertation. It was an analysis and critique of existing arguments concerning the growing division of labor in the industrial modern world. He ultimately concluded that the fears associated with the growing division of labor were wrongheaded. Moreover, he said the critics had it backwards. The division of labor was not a problem that would lead to social breakdown in the modern world. Instead, the division of labor, Durkheim said, could under normal circumstances actually serve to cement social bonds in the modern world. It was a force, or at least could be if it operated normally, for social stability and social solidarity.

He builds his argument by imagining and identifying two distinct forms of society, one with a low division of labor and another with a high division of labor. One might imagine a Native American tribe living a thousand years ago in Kansas, or for that matter any of countless societies throughout the world in throughout history living in small, non-industrial, "primitive" groups. Such groups are characterized by a low division of labor. While there of course was some division of labor, the men did certain things while the women did others, there were some specialized tasks, there was a chief, etc., on the whole most adult men did the same things, and most women did the same things. The man in one teepee likely was a buffalo hunter. He likely made his own bow and arrows and hunted buffalo. The man in another teepee likely was a buffalo hunter. He likely made his own bow and arrows and hunter buffalo. The woman in one teepee likely cleaned the buffalo skins and cooked. The woman in another teepee likely cleaned the buffalo skins and cooked. There was little specialization, little division of labor. This situation stands in stark contrast to the world of the United States in the industrial or in the post-industrial era. One person is a professor, another an auto mechanic. One person is an accountant, another is a fry cook at McDonald's. Moreover, there are specializations in specializations.

Many of the scholars that Durkheim was responding to in his book believed that the Native American types of societies fostered greater solidarity and stability than the modern societies. These "simple" societies fostered solidarity in part because of the similarities of the people and their tasks, and in part because of their shared beliefs, such as shared religious beliefs. When you are doing the same things that I am doing, doesn't this foster a sense of attachment, understanding, togetherness? I can relate to your work as a buffalo hunter because I too am a buffalo hunter. But now? In industrial or post-industrial capitalism, can these bonds be sustained? We no longer have this shared-ness of tasks. Moreover, many if not most social thinkers in the eighteen hundreds and early nineteen hundreds believed that religion declines with modernity. This is the idea of secularization (see below). As people are introduced to more and more different beliefs and as science has replaced religion as a basis of explanations of more and more phenomena, religion was said to be in decline. Scholars therefore concluded that the growing division of labor was a threat to social order and social stability.

Durkheim argued otherwise. He claimed that the modern industrial societies with a high division of labor actually had greater not less solidarity and were more inclined to be resistant in the face of threats to social order and stability. He makes the argument by identifying the types of solidarity that keeps the two types of societies together. Societies, such as the Native Americans living in teepees, which have low division of labor are held together by **mechanical solidarity**, and modern industrial societies with high division of labor are held together by what he calls **organic solidarity**. He describes the essential features of these two forms of solidarity and then shows how and why societies with organic solidarity are in fact more cohesive, more stable than those held together by mechanical solidarity.

Societies characterized by mechanical solidarity are those in which people are very similar to one another. They are held together by "solidarity of similarities." They are also characterized by a strong collective conscience. That is, the people have strong shared, moral belief systems, perhaps typically expressed through some form of religion. One might imagine other characteristics of these types of society, though Durkheim does not explicit note these: Societies characterized by mechanical solidarity are small, rural, and homogeneous. Moreover, because of the low division of labor members were somewhat self-sufficient, independent of others. The Native American who makes his own tools does not have to rely upon others for these tools. In contrast, societies with organic solidarity are built not on similarities but on difference. With difference, comes a greater dependence. A professor likely will have to depend upon a farmer to provide him with eggs and milk, as he likely does not have chickens and cows in his back yard. In addition, the collective conscience weakens. Religion becomes less, perhaps far less, powerful in modern, industrial societies. He writes:

> If there is one truth that history has incontrovertibly settled, it is that religion extends over an ever diminishing area of social life. Originally, it extended to everything; everything social was religious – the two words were synonymous. Then gradually political, economic and scientific functions broke free from the religious function, becoming separate entities and taking on more and more markedly temporal character. God, if we may express it in such a way, from being at first present in every human relationship has progressively withdrawn. He leaves the world to men and their quarrels. ... In short, not only is the sphere of religion not increasing as that of the temporal world, nor in the same proportion, but it is continually diminishing. ... This means that the average intensity of the common [collective] conscience is itself weakening. (1984:119-120)

Durkheim believed that it was the similarities and the strong collective conscience that was fundamental to maintaining social solidarity in societies with mechanical solidarity. But these decline in the modern world. So what then was the glue, the solidarity, in the modern world? What keeps these societies together in the face of the decline of the collective conscience and the increase in differences? The answer, he says, is the growing division of labor itself, which fosters increased mutual dependence. The auto mechanic needs the farmer; the farmer needs the software engineer; the software engineer needs the auto mechanic.

Earlier it was noted that one of Durkheim's intents was to create a science of sociology, a science of morality. As part of this effort, he embraced a commitment to not simply developing abstract theories, but instead to offer empirical evidence of his theoretical claims. He does just that in *The Division of Labor*. Durkheim turns to forms of law as indicators of the two types of solidarity described above. There are forms that are **repressive laws** and there are **restitutory laws**. Repressive law is akin to criminal law. If someone today is charged with committing murder, the person will be brought before a criminal court because the person has violated a criminal law. Restitutory law is civil law. It is the law of contracts. This is the law that is typically on display on television court shows, such as Judge Judy. When someone rents a house from someone else and believes the landlord has not lived up to the conditions of the lease, then the person may take them to civil, not criminal, court to seek justice.

The nature of the two forms of law is quite different. Whereas violations of criminal law are against the society itself, violations of civil law are private and against individual parties rather than society itself. Durkheim argues that the predominant form of law found in societies characterized by mechanical solidarity is criminal law, and the type of law more often found in societies characterized by organic solidarity is civil (restitutory) law. Criminal law is predominant in societies with mechanical solidarity because of the strong collective conscience. The strong collective conscience consists of strong moral sentiments about the collective. He notes that "an act is criminal when it offends the strong, well-defined states of the collective [conscience]" (1984:39). On the other hand, in modern, industrial societies with weakened a collective conscience, the paramount legal concern is not with affronts to the moral sentiments of the community, but instead with private, contractual relations. As such, Durkheim says one should expect to find more criminal law in societies characterized with mechanical solidarity, and one should expect more civil law in societies characterized by organic solidarity.

In sum, Durkheim saw the growing division of labor in modern society not as a problem but as a solution to concerns about modernity. Organic solidarity that comes with the increasing division of labor fosters interdependence and strong ties. But it does so, according to Durkheim, not at the expense of the individual. Marx, you will recall, saw the division of labor built upon private property as causing fundamental harm to individuals. Individuals become alienated, Marx says. Durkheim disagrees. Near the end of his book, he takes explicit aim at Marx's criticisms and notes that the division of labor "has often been accused of diminishing the individual by reducing him to the role of a machine" (1984:306). But then argues that this does not happen under normal states of affair, "but only in exceptional and abnormal circumstances" (1984:307). He then refutes Marx: "The division of labor supposes that the worker, far from remaining bent over his task, does not lose sight of those co-operating with him, but acts upon them and is acted upon by them. He is not therefore a machine who repeats movements the sense of which he does not perceive, but he knows that they are tending in a certain direction, towards a goal that he can conceive of more or less distinctly. He feels that he is of some use" (1984:308).

While Durkheim saw the increasing division of labor as a good thing in the modern world, he nevertheless identifies a number of potential concerns or problems that could arise and threaten social order. Much like the human body can become sick, the social body can also become sick. Four such problems can be identified. Three of these he calls types of **"abnormal forms" of the division of labor**. The first abnormal form he calls the **anomic division of labor**. The word anomic (the noun is anomie) is a central concept in Durkheim's theory, and one we see again in his work on suicide. Anomie refers to a state of normlessness. It is a social situation in which moral regulation has broken down. It is a state of moral confusion. It is a description of a social situation, and not of a psychological state. It is a situation in which expectations of a group do not match up with realities. When people expect one thing to happen and another happens, or when one person expects something and another expects something else, these are anomic situations. Such a state is abnormal and imbalanced. Though Durkheim does not say so in his book, one could imagine the types of chaos and confusions that might arise in an anomic situation. A riot is perhaps the most glaringly apparent example, but so too arguably are various other forms of social problems, such as crime, mental illness, homelessness, etc.

The second abnormal form is the **forced division of labor**. Here Durkheim is referring to a situation in which people are placed in the division of labor, or more broadly considered in a place within a system of inequality in which they are by "nature" not properly suited. If the best and the brightest minds of society are prevented from gaining access to the highest levels of education and are prevented from filling those positions which require the best and brightest minds, such as medical doctors and scientists, then the system is not running as it should. Likewise, if someone is placed in a position not because of their talent or natural abilities but instead because of their personal connections, then the division of labor is not working properly.

When people are placed in positions in which they are ill-suited, e.g. when they are placed in jobs above or beneath their abilities and talents, then they may become unhappy. As Durkheim notes, "if the institution of class or caste sometimes gives rise to miserable squabbling instead of producing solidarity, it is because the distribution of social functions on which it rest does not correspond, or rather no longer corresponds, to the distribution of natural abilities" (1984:311). He envisions a stable modern society as a meritocracy, a society in which inequality is determined by merit, by natural abilities, by motivations, and not by other things.

The **lack of coordination** is Durkheim's third abnormal form. This refers to situations of inefficiency. If an organization creates a position and then does not assign adequate work to the person filling the position such that the person is continually and productively engaged, then this produces instability. Of particular importance here are the consequences this has for others. He argues that the lack of work in one position negatively affects the interactions with others and makes the entire system less efficient.

In addition to the three abnormal or "pathological" forms of the division of labor, Durkheim cites another important concern. The high division of labor produces a situation in which the "individual becomes the object of a sort of religion" (1984:122). When describing organic solidarity, he notes:

> There is indeed one area in which the [collective conscience] has grown stronger, becoming more clearly delineated, viz., in its view of the individual. As all the other beliefs and practices assume less and less religious a character, the individual becomes the object of a sort of religion. We carry on the worship of the dignity of the human person, which, like all strong acts of worship, has already acquired its superstitions. If you like, therefore, it is a common faith. Yet first of all, it is only because of the collapse of other faiths and consequently it cannot engender the same results as that multiplicity of extinct beliefs. There is no compensation. Moreover, if the faith is common because it is shared among the community, it is individual in its object. If it impels every will toward the same end, that end is not a social one. Thus it holds a wholly exceptional position within the collective [conscience]. It is indeed from society that it draws all this strength, but it is not to society that it binds us: it is to ourselves. Thus it does not constitute a truly social link. (1984:122)

At the end of the book, he picks up the same theme and expresses concerns about the **"cult of the individual"** (1984:338). But here he focuses more so on the moral elements of this elevation of the individual to a form of religious worship. When the moral focus in society is upon the individual rather than the society, how is the society going to be able to be maintained?

Might social order be threatened when the moral order becomes focused on exalting the idea of the individual?

Suicide

Durkheim's book *Suicide*, published in 1897, captured many of the themes found in his other works. In this book he presented a sociological accounting of suicide by focusing on social rather than psychological conditions as forces to account for suicide. He was interested in understanding suicide rates rather than individual suicides. His argument was based on the assumptions that suicide rates rise when social conditions become imbalanced in one way or another. It was also based on the assumptions of the sui generis reality of society and of the collective conscience. Society exists and operates independently of the individuals that make up the society, and society operates under rules that are distinct and different from the rules that govern individual behaviors. This work was an earlier example of the extensive use of statistics in sociological research. (Albeit the level of sophistication of the statistics was quite limited by today's standards which employ highly advanced statistical methods.)

Durkheim was motivated in writing this book to demonstrate and to convince the reader that sociology was a legitimate and distinct social science, distinct particularly from psychology. How could he most convincingly argue that sociology was legitimate and distinct from psychology? He reasoned that if he selected a topic of study conventionally understood to fall squarely within the domain of psychology and then if he could demonstrate that he could account for this topic sociologically, then he believed the skeptical reader would have to accept that sociology is indeed a legitimate and distinct social science. This is precisely what he did when selected to study suicide. After all, what could be more psychological than suicide? Wouldn't a social scientific explanation of suicide necessarily be psychology, rather than sociological? Durkheim argued that suicide could be explained psychologically, and it could be explained sociologically. It was the latter he followed in the book. The key difference here has to do with the object of study of the two disciplines. For psychology, the object of study is the individual actor, his individual behavior, and/or his internal psychological processes. For sociology, he argues, the object of study, you will recall, is social facts, i.e. things external to and coercive upon the individual. His book on suicide sought to demonstrate how social forces, e.g. the collective conscience, morality, society itself, are determinant factors in human behaviors.

Durkheim wished to understand and explain changing and varied rates of suicide in France and in other parts of Europe. He collected a wealth of data on suicide from various countries in Europe for second half of the eighteen hundreds, focusing on France in particular. Many of these countries, France in particular, kept extensive records of suicide (as well as other social data). These records provided statistics about the relationship of suicide rates to many social factors. The records showed the rate of suicides by religion, by marital status, by city versus rural areas, by countries, as well as a host of other factors.

He analyzed the data and explained the variations and then concluded that suicide rates vary because of two sociological factors. Suicide rates vary based upon the relative **social integration** of the setting, and they vary based upon the degree of **moral regulation** of the setting. Social integration refers to the amount and the strength of social connections or attachments individuals have to others. A person with many friends is more integrated than a person with no friends. Moral regulation refers to the relationship between expectations and reality. A highly regulated situation is one in which what one expects to happen actually does in fact happen. A poorly regulated environment is one in which people expect one thing to happen and it does not happen. In keeping with his functionalist assumptions, and with his assumptions of the normal healthy society as one that is in balance, harmony or equilibrium, Durkheim argued that suicide rates rose when there was too much or two little social integration, and when there was too much or two little moral regulation. Conversely, suicide rates were lower when there was just the right amount of integration or regulation.

Durkheim's Types of Suicide

	Too Little	Too Much
Social Integration	Egoistic Suicide	Altruistic Suicide
Moral Regulation	Anomic Suicide	Fatalistic Suicide

Figure 3.2

He calls the form of suicide that occurs under situations of low social integration **egoistic suicide**. He used data collected on suicide rates amongst different religious groups as well as data on issues related to marriage and family to make his argument. Protestants, he notes, commit suicide at rates higher than Roman Catholics. (He also discusses Jewish rates of suicide, which he says are even lower than Catholic rates.) Moreover, it is not simply that countries that are overwhelming Protestant, such as Denmark, have higher rates than countries, such as France, which are overwhelmingly Catholic. Even within countries, Protestants commit more suicide than Catholics. He provides evidence from Germany which indicates, for example, that the rates of suicide in highly Catholic, southern German state of Bavaria is much less than the highly Protestant northern German states. Protestants commit more suicide, he argues, because they are less socially integrated than Roman Catholics. But what does that mean? It does not mean that Protestants have less friends or less social bonds than Catholic. It does mean that there is something about the Protestant form of religion that causes a lack of social integration. But what is it?

Durkheim identifies a number of differences that account for the higher rate of Protestant suicide. He says the "nature of the two religious systems" are different. The Protestant faith encourages if not requires its followers to critically and independently assess their own religion. Unlike Catholicism in which Church officials dictate the truths of the religion to the followers, and then the followers are supposed to passively accept these truths, in Protestantism the followers have to actively develop their own individual understandings. As he notes, "The only essential difference between Catholicism and Protestantism is that the second permits free inquiry to a far greater degree than the first" (1979:157). It is this "spirit of free inquiry" that causes Protestants to commit more suicide than Catholics. The openness of the Protestant faith and the lack of centrally shared beliefs amongst Protestants weakens social bonds.

Similarly, the institution of the Roman Catholic Church as well as the rituals involved in Catholicism also foster integration of the followers. In contrast, for Protestants the institution of the Church is seen not in itself as a sacred force but instead as a man-made creation. The importance for Protestants is their relation to God, not their relation to their Church. In short, the individualizing nature of Protestantism produces less social integration than the communal nature of Catholicism, and this accounts for egoistic suicide.

Durkheim uses data about marriage and family to further make his points about egoistic suicide and the lack of social integration. He presents and analyzes this data and argues that those who are unmarried are more likely to commit suicide than those that are married, and those that are married without children are more likely to commit suicide than those that are married with children. The amount and nature of the social bonds explains these differences. Unmarried people are less integrated. This condition produces egoistic suicide. (It is worth noting here the rampant sexism Durkheim displays in his analysis, though perhaps he may, or may not, be forgiven considering that he was writing at another time. He says that while marriage helps to ward off suicide in both men and women, it is far more effective in preventing suicide amongst men than amongst women. He explains this in part by claiming that women by "nature" are different than men, and this difference explains the suicide rates. But he is not simply saying women are different. He is saying that women are inferior. He could not be clearer about this. For example, when discussing how social bonds ward of suicide among different groups, he notes that suicide is rare among children, among the elderly, and among animals. Egoistic suicide is also rare in "primitive" society. He explains this by noting these groups feel "a lesser need for self-completion through something not themselves, they are also less exposed to feel the lack of what is necessary for living" (1979:215). He continues:

> This is also why woman can endure life in isolation more easily than man." When a widow is seen to endure her condition much better than a widower and desires marriage less passionately, one is led to consider this ease in dispensing with the family a mark of superiority; it is said that woman's affective faculties, being very intense, are easily employed outside the domestic circle, while her devotion is indispensable to man to help him endure life. Actually, if this is her privilege it is because her sensibility is rudimentary rather than highly developed. As she lives outside of community existence more than man, she is less penetrated by it; society is less necessary to her because she is less impregnated with sociability. (1979:215) (Such sexism in itself however should not cause the reader to reject the entirety of his theorizing.)

Altruistic suicide is the second form Durkheim identifies. Altruism means selfless. It means sacrificing your needs for the needs of others. Altruistic suicide is the opposite of egoistic. Altruistic suicide occurs under social conditions in which there is too much social integration. When individuals lose their individuality in the collective, altruistic suicide may result. Islamist suicide bombers, cult suicides, Japanese pilots who committed hara-kiri by crashing their planes into American ships during World War Two all could be considered examples of altruistic suicide. Altruistic suicide is often born out of sense of "duty."

Durkheim distinguishes egoistic from altruistic forms of suicide and notes there are several forms of altruistic suicide. One of these is described as follows:

> We thus confront a type of suicide (altruistic) differing by incisive qualities from the preceding one (egoistic). Whereas [egoistic suicide] is due to excessive individualization, [altruistic suicide] is caused by too rudimentary individuation. One occurs because society allows the individual to escape it, being insufficiently aggregated in some parts or even the whole; the other, because society holds him in too strict tutelage. Having given the name *egoism* to the state of the ego living its own life

and obeying itself alone, that of *altruism* adequately expresses the opposite state, where the ego is not its own property, where it is blended with something not itself, where the goal of conduct is exterior to itself, that is, in one of the groups in which it participates. (1979:221)

This is what Durkheim calls "obligatory altruistic suicide," and it is the form found in "primitive" societies. But he also notes that altruistic suicide in a different form can and does appear in modern societies. He presents evidence of high suicide rates in the military services to support his case. In either case, whether in primitive or modern societies, too much social integration is ultimately the source of this form of suicide.

The third form of suicide is **anomic suicide**. Anomic suicide occurs in social conditions in which there is insufficient moral regulation. In social situations where expectations and reality do not line up people may become confused, disoriented. This may produce anomic suicide. "No living being can be happy or even exist unless his needs are sufficiently proportioned to his means" (1979:246). When the stock market crashed in 1929, suicides went up. They went up because investors expected that they would continue to make more and more money as they had through the 1920s. But the new reality was otherwise. Durkheim begins his analysis of anomic suicide by noting that "it is a well-known fact that economic crises have an aggravating effect on the suicidal tendency" (1979:241).

Anomic suicide is largely a modern phenomenon. It is produced by a weakening of social controls that regulate the relationship between expectations and reality, between means and ends. When what is expected to occur does not occur, confusion and perhaps suicide results. The decline of religion, he says, in the modern era is one example of an aspect of the modern world that fosters this form of suicide. Religion serves to regulate the relationships.

The last form of suicide is fatalistic. Durkheim devoted most of his book on suicide to an explanation of the first three forms and he only briefly mentions **fatalistic suicide**. This form of suicide is produced in social conditions that are too highly regulated. Excessive moral regulation leads to lives of emptiness and fatalistic suicide. There was an episode of the old television show The Twilight Zone that illustrates some of this. The story begins with this criminal, low life character getting killed. The next scene finds the man sitting at a bar in a restaurant. He is confused. He thought he had died. He then thought to himself that he would like a drink. The waiter then walks over to him and gives him a drink. The man tries to reach into his pocket to pay the waiter. The waiter says it is free. Then over and over again the man wishes for one thing or another, and his wishes are granted. He gets whatever he desires. He begins to think he somehow has made it to heaven, rather than to hell where he thought he would be. After all, heaven is supposed to be the place of peace and happiness, and here he is getting whatever it is he desires. He is happy and content. This goes on for a while until the man starts to become a bit bored. When each and every desire is met, the wonder, the joy of existence is drained. He eventually realizes he is in fact not in heaven, but in hell, stuck in an eternal state in which expectations and reality are identical. He may not commit suicide in the show (after all he is already dead), but the point is clear. In a similar way, the middle aged, middle class businessman who seemingly has everything – a wife, children, a house in the suburbs – but who now also realizes that there is nothing more to be gotten, no more raises or promotions, no more changes in life, may kill himself. If so, this would be an instance of fatalistic suicide.

The Sociology of Religion

Many scholars have said that Durkheim's book on religion, *The Elementary Forms of Religious Life*, written in 1912, is his most profound and important work. This book demonstrates an intellectual sophistication and nuance that many say go well beyond his earlier work. Durkheim sought in this book to develop a universal sociology of religion, one applicable to explaining religions in any and all societies. He did this by selecting to study "primitive" religions in the belief that these societies are simpler than modern industrial societies and the essential workings of these societies could more clearly be seen. The workings of these societies could be more clearly seen because the societies were not filled with the complexities of modern life.

Durkheim did not do any anthropological field work for this book. Instead, he based it upon several anthropological studies, specifically of religions and cultures amongst native peoples of the Arunta tribe in Australia. He critically analyzes the existing anthropological literature and developed a universal sociological theory and a sociological accounting of religion. The importance of his work, in his mind, was not the depiction of religion in primitive society, but instead it was the universal sociological workings of religion in all societies, and in particular modern, industrial society. Durkheim was driven in this work to address the questions about why religion exists and what functions does it serves? After all, if religion exists in all societies, it must be for some reason. It must serve a function.

As he wished to be a scientist, in the mold of all other types of scientists, whether in chemistry, biology or physics, he first identified and defined the object of his study. The object of his study was religion. As such, he presents, what has now become a classic, **sociological definition of religion**. He writes: "A religion is a unified set of beliefs and practices relative to sacred things, that is to say, things set apart and forbidden – beliefs and practices which unite into one single moral community called a Church, all those who adhere to them" (1965:62). The four key components to this definition are: 1) beliefs; 2) practices; 3) the sacred; and 4) moral community called a Church. We can begin by looking first at the third and fourth component and then can return to the first two. The concept of the **sacred** is central to Durkheim's understanding of religion, and it is a concept that in one way or another that has been widely used by anthropologists and by some sociologists ever since. All religions conceptually "divide the world into two domains, the one containing all that is sacred, the other all that is profane" (1965:52). The realm of the sacred is the time, place, beliefs, event that is not simply extraordinary, but transcendent. The sacred is the site in which one removes oneself from the ordinary day-to-day experience and becomes intimately connected with the holy. All religions have things that are sacred. Christianity has the sacred days of Easter and Christmas. Islam views the city of Mecca as a sacred place. Christian rituals, from baptism to marriage, are sacred. The sacred is special and is clearly demarked from the **profane**. The profane is the ordinary, the commonplace, the mundane. It is the realm of experience of the day-to-day life.

Some later scholars have built upon this sacred-profane distinction and claimed that much of social life can be understood using it. Perhaps humans are structured to partition their entire worlds, not simply their religious worlds per se, into these two domains. Why is it, for example, that many housewives are so insistent that their homes be so clean, so pure? As the old adage goes, cleanliness is next to godliness. The home is viewed by some as sacred, as pure, as good. In contrast, the outside is viewed as dirty, as impure, and profane. Likewise, one can look at food systems. Why is it that some cultures are repulsed at the thought of eating certain foods, while others are not? Why is it that Americans are generally aghast at the thought of eating a dog, but in some countries eating dog is not so odd? Why is it that in Southern Mexico they eat fried grasshoppers and beetles, but in America it would seem quite strange to do so? Social scientists following in Durkheim's footsteps might say humans have a need to conceptually parcel out their worlds into these two domains, the realm of the sacred and the profane. For example, the anthropologist Mary Douglas has followed in Durkheim's footsteps. She wrote the book *Purity and Danger* in which she expanded upon the sacred-profane distinction and showed how this divide overlaps with other divides, such as purity-dirtiness and good-bad. That which is pure and good is sacred; that which is dirty and bad is profane.

It is worth noting here that Durkheim's definition of religion included the concept of the sacred, but it does not include the concept of god. As such, a religion does not need to have a god or gods. This may seem strange at first, but when one recognizes that there are many religions today that arguably do not have gods, then one might more easily see his point. Several of the major religions in China and in East Asia, for example, arguably do not have gods. One of the main religions in China is Confucianism, and this religion follows the moral teachings of the philosopher Confucius. Another religion in China is Taoism, which is more of a philosophy of opposing forces, i.e. the yin and yang, than it is a religion in the conventional western sense. Buddhism too, a religion practiced in many areas of Asia is a religion, and it arguably is godless, though some if not many might argue that the goal of the Buddhist is to reach the god-like state that Buddha himself achieved. Nevertheless, all of these are social in nature, and all involve beliefs and practices relative to sacred things. Thus, if one uses Durkheim's definition, then all of these are religions.

The fourth element of his definition is that religions necessarily have moral communities (called a Church). The fundamental point he is making here is that religions are fundamentally social rather than individual enterprises. Religion is inextricably tied to the social, and the social is inextricably tied to religion. It cannot be, according to Durkheim, an individual thing. He says that "magic" (perhaps like voodoo) used in some societies is not a religious thing because it is individually practiced. There are no social rituals, and no community associated with it. The first and second elements are that religion involves a set of beliefs and practices relative to sacred things. Religion consists of a particular set of ideas, such as ideas about morality, the social, and sacred. Practices involve things like rites and rituals, public enactments and expressions of the group's religion.

In his analysis of the Arunta's religious practices, he focused upon the concept of totems and clans. A clan is a group "united by a bond of kinship, but one which is of a very special nature" (1965:122). It is like a very extended family, but much, much more. A clan demands far more if its members. Clan members have duties, obligations to uphold as members of the group. Each clan has a totem. A totem is a unifying, symbolic and sacred emblem of the group. Plants and animals are typically used as the totem of a clan. Thus, for example, one might find a bear clan. Each member of this clan identifies as a member of this bear clan and recognizes each other as members.

Several main themes can be identified in Durkheim's understanding of religion. One of these is the claim that society emerges from religion rather than religion emerging from society. For him religion and society are inextricably linked. Both are essentially moral and social phenomena. Religion allows for society to exist, and society requires religion. Society then is fundamentally a religious concept. As he notes, "If religion has given birth to all that is essential in society, it is because the idea of society is the soul of religion" (1965:466). It should be noted here that he bases these claims on his overarching understanding of what religion and morality are. If one looks at these claims without recognizing the basis for them, one might well simply dismiss them.

A second main theme is that when people engage in religious practices and when people embrace religious beliefs, they are in fact not worshiping some god or some removed sacred thing. Instead, people are worshiping their society, their group. They are worshiping their shared we-ness. When a member of a bear clan worships the bear, they are in fact, Durkheim says, not worshipping the bear but instead are worshiping the social group and their membership in this group. It is this group and the membership in the group that is the sacred thing. We can see here why Durkheim believes that public rites and rituals are so essential to religion. Through these rituals and rites people come together and reaffirm their religion, and most importantly they reaffirm the membership in the group. Participants enter a "state of effervescence," a collective effervescence, through these practices, a state of heightened, shared emotional experience that reinforces social bonds to the community in deep and profound ways. In sum, religion serves a fundamental function in society. It serves to foster social solidarity.

Perhaps the most interesting if not the most provocative aspect of his sociological analysis of religion concerns **the categories of understanding**. Here Durkheim is engaging in a debate about epistemology, i.e. the philosophy of knowledge. To understand his claims, we need to first understand what this issue is. Philosophers from the Enlightenment through the present have presented competing arguments to explain how it is that humans are able to know things, to know anything. How is it that we know the difference between an apple and a rock? How is it that we know that one can eat an apple, but that one cannot eat a rock? In the western philosophical tradition of the Enlightenment, two opposing explanations arose. One of these claimed that our ability to know things is learned through our individual experiences. At birth we do not have such abilities. It is only through experience that we develop an understanding of the basic categories of things. It is only through individual experience with the objective world that we can parcel out the world into categories, of things, time, places, etc. A very different and competing theory says that this is not how we know things. This second theory says we know things because our brain is wired, is biologically constructed, to allow us to know such things. We are hard wired, for example, to know the concepts or categories of time. We intuitively know the concept of past, present, and future. We do not learn such things through experience.

Durkheim engages with this argument and proposed a radically different solution. He proposes a sociological explanation for epistemology. The very basic building blocks of consciousness – the categories of understanding – are not rooted in our biology or in our psychology but instead are developed through social engagement, through society. Moreover, these basic categories are produced through religion. He writes:

> For a long time it has been known that the first systems of representations with which men have pictured themselves were of religious origin. There is no religion that is not cosmological at the same time that it is a speculation upon divine things. If philosophy and the sciences were born of religion, it is because religion began by taking the place of the sciences and philosophy. But it has less frequently been notices that religion has not confined itself to enriching the human intellect, formed beforehand, with a certain number of ideas; it has contributed to forming the intellect itself. Men owe to it not only a good part of the substance of their knowledge, but also the form in which this knowledge has been elaborated.
>
> At the root of all our judgments there are a certain number of essential ideas which dominate all our intellectual life; they are what philosophers since Aristotle have called the categories of the understanding: ideas of time, space, class [classification], number, cause, substance, personality, etc. They correspond to the most universal properties of things. They are like the solid frame which encloses all thought: this does not seem to be able to liberate itself from them without destroying itself, for it seems that we cannot think of objects that are not in time and space, which have no number, etc. Other ideas are contingent and unsteady; we can conceive of their being unknown to man, a society or an epoch; but these others appear to be nearly inseparable from the normal workings of the intellect. They are like the framework of the intelligence. Now when primitive religious beliefs are systematically analyzed, the principal categories are naturally found. They are born in religion and of religion: they are a product of religious thought. (1965:22)

He is claiming that the basic forms of thought, not the content, are socially produced. Moreover, they are produced by and through religion. The very ways that people think about the world are determined by society. Society structures our consciousness, and it does so in a way that leads us to see the world in one way rather than another. This is a significant claim, and one that has many, many sociological implications. It means that people in different places, in different societies, and people in different times can understand their worlds, at the most basic level, in fundamentally different ways, and that these differences are caused by different social arrangements. For example, not too long ago a researcher compared the ways in which school children in Japan and in the United States classified things. Classification is one of the categories of understanding. The researchers showed students in Japan three pictures – a picture of a banana, a monkey, and a panda. Then the students were asked, which of the two pictures are related. Which go together? The researchers did the same with students in the United States. In Japan, the students said the monkey and banana go together because monkeys eat bananas. In the United States, the students said the monkey and the panda go together because they are both animals. Why would students in different countries classify things differently? Durkheim's theorizing might help to account for such things.

A last major element of his theory of religion concerns his view regarding the future of religion. Earlier, it was noted that Durkheim believed with many of his contemporaries that modernity brought with it secularization, the decline of religion. Yet at the same time, he also believed that every society must have a collective conscience, and every society must have some shared moral sensibilities. Otherwise, it would not be a society, but instead some other form of group, such as a business, a factory, or some such thing. Durkheim addresses these issues near the end of *The Elementary Forms* when he writes:

> There is something eternal in religion which is destined to survive all the particular symbols in which religious thought has successively enveloped itself. There can be no society which does not feel the need of upholding and reaffirming at regular intervals the collective sentiments and the collective ideas which makes its unity and its personality. Now this moral remaking cannot be achieved except by the means of reunions, assemblies and meetings where the individuals, being closely united to one another, reaffirm in common their common sentiments; hence comes ceremonies which co not yet differ from regular religious ceremonies, either in their object, the results which they produce, or the processes employed to attain these results. What essential difference is there between an assembly of Christians celebrating the principal dates of the life of Christ, or of Jews remembering the exodus from Egypt or the promulgation of the Decalogue, and a reunion of citizens commemorating the promulgation of a new moral or legal system or some great event in the national life? (1965:475)

Here he is quite clear. Religion is always going to be around. (It serves a function.) But the form that religion takes can and will change. Beliefs and practices which are conventionally understood as religion, such as going to church, participating in religious rituals, etc., are not different from some beliefs and practices typically identified as non-religious. Specifically, here he says when citizens gather to celebrate the founding of a country, and a new legal system, or some other great national event, they are engaged in religious practices. What does he mean by this? In France, he likely is referring to Bastille Day, the French version of America's July 4th. In America of course holidays such as July 4th, as well as Thanksgiving, and others, are perhaps what he would have in mind. We can take his ideas even further and look at various elements of patriotism in America. Are there not sacred symbols associated with patriotism? The Pledge of Allegiance, the flag, etc.? Don't Americans celebrate their patriotism in various social ways, at designated times and places? Don't Americans reaffirm their sacred we-ness through such things? Is patriotism a religion?

Summary

Durkheim sought to develop a science of society called sociology. As a science, sociology should use the same positivist approach used in all of the other sciences, such as physics, chemistry, etc. He believed there was only one form of scientific knowledge, and that was the form found in these disciplines. Any science must have a clearly defined object of study. Sociology wishes to explain social behavior, but so too do all of the other social sciences, including psychology. Durkheim argues that the main thing that distinguishes sociology from psychology and the other social sciences is the object of study. The object of study for sociology was social facts, things external to and coercive upon the individual. There are material and non-material social facts. Durkheim was mostly interested in non-material social facts, including, morality, language, norms, the collective conscience. Morality was particularly important for him. He believed sociology should be a science of morality. Society was essential a moral thing. Moreover, he argued that society itself should be an object of study for sociology. Society existed as a real and unified whole, and it had a sui generis reality. It existed independently of the individuals who comprised the society, and it operated under sets of laws that were distinct and different from the sets of laws governing individual psychological behaviors. The task then was to understand how and why societies held together and how and why they fell apart. Toward that end, he relied heavily upon biological metaphors, and he embraced the concept of functionalism.

Durkheim was a functionalist. Functionalism is the theoretical claim that social things that exist over a long period of time must have a reason for existing. Otherwise, they would cease to exist. The reason for their existence is that they serve a function. They somehow contribute to maintaining social order. The task of the sociologist is to identify the functions of social things.

All of these elements are found in his major works. One of these is his book *The Division of Labor*. There he examines the social consequences of the growing division of labor in the modern world and says that the conventional arguments that express concern for ongoing social stability as the result of the increasing division of labor are wrong. Instead, he argues that social stability and social order are enhanced by the increasing division of labor. To make his argument he distinguishes between pre-modern societies which are characterized by mechanical solidarity and modern societies which have organic solidarity. Societies characterized by mechanical solidarity are held together by a strong collective conscience. But the collective conscience is weakened in the modern era, in societies characterized by organic solidarity. The increased division of labor now becomes the main force of social solidarity. This brings about interdependence. However, there are four potential problems with the increase of the division of labor in the modern world. He identifies three of these as abnormal forms of the division of labor: forced division of labor, anomic division of labor, and the poorly coordinated division of labor. The fourth problem is excessive individualism. His book *Suicide* was an empirical study of suicide rates which was meant to demonstrate the legitimacy of sociology. Suicide, a seemingly individual action, could be explained sociologically. Suicide rates go up when there is too much or too little moral regulation, and when there is too much or too little social integration. Later he turned to a study of the sociology of religion. Religion is a fundamentally a social phenomenon, not an individual phenomenon. Society is born out of religion. Religion will always be around. All religions distinguish the realm of the sacred from the profane. Religion is the source of the categories of understanding, the building blocks of our consciousness, which allow us to understand the world.

Discussion Questions

1. Durkheim sought to convince people that the discipline of sociology was distinct from that of psychology. But both psychology and sociology seek to explain why people do what they do. So how are they different? Durkheim claims that sociologists have a different object of study than that of psychology. Psychologists study individuals and individual motivations. They seek to get inside the heads of people to understand why they do what they do. In contrast, Durkheim seeks to explain social behavior without getting inside people's heads. The object of study for sociology is social facts. Durkheim says he can explain social behavior without needing to understand individual psychology. He says he can explain social behavior by looking at the forces outside of the individual. The question is: Is he right? Can we ignore psychology if we wish to explain social behavior? But if we say we must include psychology in any explanation of behavior, then can we do it scientifically? How can one scientifically study someone's motivations? Don't we act based upon the meanings we give to the world? Is it possible to scientifically study this meaning making?

2. Durkheim says, or suggests, that the worker in a factory (or today in a McDonald's) is not alienated. Instead, when society is healthy, and when there is a healthy and well-functioning division of labor, the worker will "feel he is of some use." Marx, on the other hand, says the worker in capitalism is alienated, and is not allowed to be fully human in the workplace. The question is: Who is right, Durkheim or Marx? Are the workers at McDonald's alienated, or do they get satisfaction and fulfillment through their work?

3. Robert Bellah (1927-2013) was a prominent American sociologist who wrote a great deal on the sociology of religion and on American culture. He was greatly influenced by Durkheim. Bellah seemingly agreed with Durkheim's claim that there is "something eternal in all religions" and that most members of a society must share some common moral perspective if the society is to survive. (It should be recalled here how Durkheim defines religion broadly.) Bellah also recognized that the modern era did not cause religion to disappear or to dramatically decline, at least in America, as many European social theorists (including Marx and Durkheim) believed it would. Instead, Bellah saw religion in America today as alive. But he saw something else. He saw a particular form of religion in American, which he called "civil religion." This idea builds upon Durkheim's ideas about the future of religion. What difference is there between getting together on the Fourth of July and celebrating Christmas? Civil religion, Bellah says, is a form of "religion" that many if not most people in America practice, whatever their individual faiths. Civil religion combines elements from the Judeo-Christian tradition, e.g. god, the Ten Commandments, etc., with basic elements from the Enlightenment, from democratic sentiments, e.g. tolerance, equality, individualism, etc. In short, as Americans, whether we are Protestants, Jews, Catholics, Muslims, or whatever, share certain moral perspectives, we share a civil religion. The question is: Is Bellah (and Durkheim) right? Is patriotism a form of religion? Does civil religion exist?

4. This question is about the logic of functionalism. Durkheim's functionalism was and is criticized for claiming to be an objective and unbiased form of theorizing when in fact – or so says the critics -- it is a theory that is at its heart biased. It is a conservative theory. It begins with the assumption that the existing social order is normal and healthy, and as such any threats or challenges to this existing social order are deemed unhealthy or dysfunctional. Are we to belief that (the relatively few) Germans who engaged in defiant opposition to the German Nazi's in the 1930s were "abnormal," as is suggested by functionalist reasoning? Who is to say what is a normal and healthy society? The question is this: What is a healthy society? What are the indications of a healthy or a sick society? Does functionalism require that a theorist make a claim that one or another society

is healthy or sick? Is this a good way to understand sociology? Why or why not?

Chapter Four: Weber

To understand the sociological theorizing of Max Weber (1864-1920), it might be helpful to start at McDonald's restaurant. McDonald's started in the 1950s and has grown to well over thirty thousand restaurants. Twenty years or so ago, the American sociologist George Ritzer wrote a book titled *The McDonaldization of Society*. The book has become very popular and has gone through many editions. Ritzer argues that the organizational form and characteristics of McDonald's restaurants can increasingly be found in more and more organizations in America today. There are McSchools, McUniversities, McDentists, etc. Ritzer says there are four elements of McDonaldization: 1) Efficiency; 2) Calculability; 3) Predictability; and, 4) Control by non-human technologies. McDonald's is organized to be as efficient as it possibly can. Efficiency "means choosing the optimum means to a given end." Thus, the process of buying a hamburger is supposed to be as fast as possible. Drive-throughs were created with this intent. Everything at McDonald's is calculated. Without a doubt, the McDonald's Corporation knows exactly how much each hamburger weighs; how many fries in each bag; how long the average customer sits in the restaurant; how long it takes to make a hamburger. McDonald's is also focused on predictability. When one enters a McDonald's, one knows exactly what to expect, whether one is in New York or Kansas or Berlin. Lastly, both workers and customers at McDonald's are controlled by non-human technologies, whether it is the fry cook machine or the computers at the counter.

This form of organization allows for incredible productivity. It has many positive elements to it. Ritzer, however, notes that there are also some negative aspects to McDonaldization as well. It produces an "irrationality of rationality." McDonald's is organized along rational lines, but it can and does produce things that are irrational. For example, Ritzer argues it can produce inefficiencies and high costs. One thinks here of the common complaints about bureaucracies, such as state Department of Motor Vehicle offices or waiting in the TSA security lines at the airport. These large, formal organizations are designed to be efficient, but in fact are anything but. McDonaldization also produces homogenization. Everything becomes the same -- bland and common. A burger is the same, as noted, in Berlin and in Los Angeles. All in all, McDonald's fosters, Ritzer argues, dehumanization. Dehumanization is the process whereby human beings are treated as things, as non-human, as objects rather than as people. When the person behind the counter cheerily says, "Welcome to McDonald's, can I take your order?" is this person acting in a genuine manner? No. They are reading a script. The qualities of humanity are drained from individuals and from social relationships in McDonaldized entities.

Ritzer's ideas about McDonaldization, both the description of its elements and its harmful consequences, come from the theory of Max Weber. McDonaldization is simply another word for what Weber calls rationalization. Rationalization, rationality, and other associated ideas are major themes in Weber's theorizing. (When sociologists use the term rationalization it should be noted that this term means something very different, as we see below, from the meaning it has in psychology or even in some circles amongst the general public. In psychology and in the general public, rationalization refers to a psychological defense mechanism (first proposed by the psychoanalyst Sigmund Freud – see Chapter Eight).)

Weber lived at the same time as Durkheim, in the late eighteen and early nineteen hundreds, though his theory could not be more different in so many ways, as we will see. One significant difference concerns the national and cultural context within which Weber wrote. Durkheim drew inspiration largely from French intellectuals and from French intellectual history. Weber drew inspiration mostly from German intellectuals and from German intellectual history. He was, for example, influenced by Kant, Nietzsche, and Marx, among many others. Some scholars today say that to truly appreciate Weber's work one should see much of it as an extended dialog or debate with the ideas of Marx. Weber did not have a real dialog with Marx. Marx died when Weber was in his twenties and they never met. However, one can see in Weber's writings the echoes of Marx. It is not that Weber was a Marxist. He strongly rejected most of Marx's main claims. But he did believe it was important to respond to Marx's arguments, to engage with them, to modify or reject them.

Max Weber

Max Weber was born in Erfurt, Germany on April 21, 1864. He was the eldest son of Max, Senior, and Helene Weber and grew up in a middle class household in the Berlin area. His father was a mid-level bureaucrat and politician. His mother was a well-educated, deeply religious woman, a Protestant influenced by (liberal) Unitarian traditions. It is often noted that the contrasting orientations of his father and mother are seen as significant influences on Weber's life and on his theorizing. Bureaucracy and religion are common themes in his writings. Weber was a good student. He entered the University of Heidelberg when he was eighteen but left after three semesters to fulfill his mandatory military service. He completed his doctorate at the University of Berlin. His intellectual focus there and for the rest of his career was upon economics, history, politics, and sociology,

> and his doctoral dissertation was on trade associations in the Middle Ages. He taught at several universities over the course of his life, though mostly at Heidelberg, and he developed a reputation in Germany as a sought after intellectual. He spent his career as an academic, though he was also involved in political matters (notably concerning Germany's surrender in World War One). Weber could be described as a workaholic.
>
> His academic work however was hampered by a long lasting nervous or mental illness. The illness prevented him from doing academic work for months or years at a time. The nature of his illness is somewhat unclear. Some have described it as a "mental breakdown," or perhaps nervous exhaustion. Others say it was a form of major depression (cf Marianne Weber 2017).
>
> Weber travelled extensively, mostly throughout Europe. One of the more notable trips was to the United States in 1904, when he was invited to give a talk at the world's fair in St. Louis. On that visit, he travelled across the eastern parts of the United States, visiting New York, Chicago, Philadelphia, and New Orleans, among other places. America had a great impact upon him. He saw positive as well as negative things. Commenting on Chicago, he said the city itself was like watching sausage being made. Upon his return to Germany, he completed his influential book *The Protestant Ethic and the Spirit of Capitalism*.
>
> He married Marianne Schnitger in 1893. She was an intellectual in her own right and wrote a well-known biography of her husband. The couple never had any children of their own but adopted several young relatives near the end of Max's life. Max Weber knew, and was friends with, many of the important intellectuals of his day, and his household was the site of many gatherings of intellectuals where they discussed and debated matters of mutual concern. Some of his notable friends included Ernst Troeltsch, Georg Simmel, Georg Lukacs, Werner Sombart, Ferdinand Toennies, among many others. Weber died of pneumonia in 1920.

Three sets of ideas ripple through much of Weber's theory. The first is the importance of meaning and interpretation in sociology. He believed that the task of the sociologist was to understand meaningful social behavior, and to do so requires that the sociologist engage in an interpretive process. The second set of ideas concerns rationality and values. Weber believed it was crucial to understand the concept of rationality and to understand the role that rationality plays in sociological research. It was necessary to recognize the increasingly dominant role rationality plays in the organization of the modern world. From science to technology to government, rationality increasingly is a force of organization in the modern world, for good or ill. But our world is not simply one of rationality. Values too are central. Values are an important concept not only for Weber but for much of sociology today. Values are things that are deemed important. What is of value to you? Do you value a college education? Do you value your relationship with your family members? Do you value your smart phone? Do you value religion? Do you value honesty? Do people act in the world based upon value judgments, however biased or distorted they may be, or do people act like machines, using nothing more than rational calculations? What is the relationship between values and rationality? Moreover, how are values and rationality related to doing social science? Can or should the social scientist leave his or her values and biases to the side when he or she does research? All of these questions lurk within Weber's theorizing. A third set of ideas is the importance of history. Sociology should be historical. Weber was particularly interested in understanding how and why the modern world, specifically the modern western world, came about, and where it was headed.

Meaning, Methods and Modernity

Meaning

Closely related to the above, Weber's theorizing revolves around three interrelated themes: Meaning, methods, and modernity. First, **meaning**. He wished to create a sociological science, but he did not wish to do so in the way that Durkheim did. For Durkheim, the social scientist should understand the world in the same way as a natural scientist, such as a biologist or chemist, does. The implication of Durkheim's approach then is that social behavior should be understood as billiard balls on a pool table or rocks rolling down a hill, simply mechanically responding to their environment. Weber's theorizing begins with a flat rejection of such an approach. An understanding of social behavior requires that one recognize the essential differences between a billiard ball and a human being. Human beings may act automatically at times, but they also typically assign meaning to their worlds and act based upon the meaning they give to their worlds. Humans interpret their worlds and then assign meaning to it, and then they act. When a student walks into a classroom on the first day of class, he or she on one level or another assesses the classroom and says, "This is what it means." He or she then acts accordingly. If a student walks into a classroom on the first day of class and all of the chairs are facing backwards, away from the front of the class, what would the student think? He or she is compelled to try to understand the meaning of the situation and then to act based upon that meaning. Perhaps the student would turn a chair around and sit in it. Perhaps he or she would simply sit it the backward chair and assume the professor arranged the chairs that way for a reason. Whatever the case, the student will search for a meaning and then act based upon it.

Weber argues that the task of the sociologist is to understand meaningful social behavior. Meaningful behavior is behavior that makes sense to the person doing the behavior, and as such it is at least possible that an observing social scientist could understand the meanings of that same behavior. But is all behavior meaningful? Some behavior is crazy, and by definition this behavior is not meaningful. These types of behavior are not capable of being understood scientifically, according to Weber.

He begins by trying to understand the basic components of meaningful behavior. He does so by imagining different types of behavior. Why does someone work at McDonald's? Perhaps they do so because they need a job to pay their bills. But is this sort of rational behavior the only type of meaningful behavior? If someone shoots someone in a lover's quarrel, is that rational? Is it meaningful? It is not rational, but it is meaningful. The shooter likely was enraged, driven by raw emotion. One could understand how emotions sometimes drive behaviors. Weber then tries to imagine different basic types of behavior, or social action. He identifies four types. The four basic types of social action are: 1) Traditional action; 2) Affective action; 3) Instrumental (or means-ends) rational action; and 4) Value rational action. **Traditional action** is action that is habitual. People often engage in habitual behaviors, from drinking a cup of coffee in the morning to sitting in the same seat in class. Why is it that students after the first week of class tend to sit in the same seat for the rest of the semester? Do students make a rational calculation and choose to sit in the seat for that reason? Perhaps some do. Perhaps a student sits in the front row to hear better or to see the blackboard better. But it is likely that most students sit in the seat they have selected out of habit. It is traditional action. **Affective action** is emotional behavior. The shooter killing someone in a lover's quarrel is an example of affective action. Weber was far less interested in these first two types of action – traditional and affective – than he was in the next two. The next two are forms of rational action. To understand them, one needs to understand what he means by rational action. The essential components of a **rational action** are means and ends. It consists of identifying an end, or a goal, and then logically deciding upon a course of action to reach that end. The lining up of means and ends in a rational way is the definition of a rational action. If one wishes to graduate from college, this is an end (goal). How is one to rationally accomplish this goal? What means should one embrace to achieve this goal? Taking and passing the right classes is one of the means of doing so. It is the rational thing to do. It would not be rational for someone to have a goal of graduating from college and then for that person not to take the exams in classes needed to accomplish this goal (i.e. the means). **Instrumental rational action** (also called means-ends rational action) lines up means and ends in a rational way without any consideration of values. The absence of value considerations is central here. The behavior of producers and consumers in the marketplace is an example of instrumentally rational action. It is logical. It is the rationality of a machine. **Value rational action**, by contrast, is the lining up of means and ends in a logical or rational fashion while considering values. One's values determine the ends, the means, or the relationship between them. Think about your interactions with members of your family -- your brothers and sisters, your parents. Do you treat your brother or sister as a customer, as you would if you were using instrumental rational action? Do you interact with them as you would with the person behind the counter at McDonald's? Likewise, your interactions with your parents are not based purely on the same logic as the logic one finds in the marketplace. One would not treat these interactions as instrumental. Instead, the value of brothers, of sisters, of sons and daughters, of mother and father, of family influence your rational actions in the family. It is not that people act irrationally within families (at least most of the time!). It is that the form of rationality is different. It is value rationality. You act toward your brother and sister, or mother or father, based upon the value you have for them as part of the family. These values in themselves define the actions.

Methods

The task of the sociologist, at least in part, is then to explain **meaningful social behavior** by identifying the type of social action that is occurring. But this raises a thorny issue. How is the sociologist to know which form of social action, of the four just described, an actor is doing? The answer takes us to the heart of Weber's significant contributions to the methods of social science. If someone wished to know why students sit in the seats they are sitting in, how would they go about getting the answer? How can one explain the social action of the students in their decisions to sit in the respective seats? Simply observing the students will not do. Simply observing their behaviors will not tell us why they chose the seat they chose. Observation of behavior is one necessary part of an explanation, but it cannot be the entire explanation. The person would have to come to understand the meanings of these behavior by imagining how the students understood their immediate situation. The person would have to try to understand the meanings the students gave to their immediate situation.

Another example might be as follows: Imagine you are walking down a country road and you see a man chopping wood in his yard. Why is the man chopping wood? He might be chopping the wood for exercise. He might be doing it to sell the wood. He might be doing it to heat his house. He might be doing it to let off steam after getting into an argument with his wife. How is the observer, i.e. the researcher, to know which of these reasons is the "true" or right reason? Whether it is the example of the students or the example of the woodsman, the explanation is the same: The researcher has to place himself or herself in the shoes of the persons being observed and he or she has to imagine what it is like to be that person. This is what Weber calls verstehen. **Verstehen** is empathic, interpretive understanding, and is central to his sociology. Only by trying to imagine what it is like to be that other person can one get a sense of the types of social action the person is doing. One can imagine, for example, that a student sits in the front row of class because he may be able to see and hear better and thus be in a better position to get a good grade (instrumental rational action). Or one might imagine that the woodsman just got into an argument with his wife and he is chopping wood to let of steam (affective action).

How then does the observer, i.e. the researcher, know why the person is doing what he or she is doing? One might imagine what it is like to be the person observed, but this is mere speculation. Though this is a necessary part of the process, it is hardly a scientific enterprise in itself. Science calls for objective, empirical data. Scientists look for facts and look to explain causal relations between facts. Weber, as is described below, very much believed sociology is a science and should strive to be a science, though the type of science it is and should be is distinctive different from the form of science that people such as Durkheim envisioned. Weber sought to develop an interpretive science of sociology. The task then is to interpret empirical evidence. One should not make claims, as a social scientist, based merely on imaginations. So how then is one to know, from a scientific perspective, why the student is sitting in the seat he or she is sitting in, or why the woodsman is chopping the wood? What sort of observable evidence is needed to answer the question? Perhaps one obvious form of evidence might be that the observer could simply ask the student or the woodsman why they are doing what they are doing. They might tell you what they believe to be the reasons. You might write the answers down. These reports are empirical data. They are observable factual data, data that any other observer could agree occurred as the first observer said.

If the woodsman tells the observer he is chopping the wood because he wanted the exercise, how are we to know that is really the reason he is doing so? Couldn't he be lying? Or couldn't he be telling the observer something that is not true, even if he is not intentionally lying? The woodsman might say he is doing it for the exercise but in fact is too embarrassed to say that he is really doing it because he just got into an argument with his wife and is doing it to let off steam. What then is the observer, the researcher, to think? The answer is that the observer, if he wishes to be a social scientist, can only go by what he has observed, e.g. what the woodsman or student tells him, recognizing that it might not be true or complete. The only thing the observer can do is to recognize this limitation and to collect more data to confirm or refute his explanation. Social scientific knowledge for someone following Weber's theorizing is therefore open ended and subject to change as more factual data becomes available.

There is another problem: Might not people do things for reasons they do not know? Do people always know exactly why they do what they do? If a person claims to be chopping wood for exercise, and they tell someone else that and they believe it to be true, can one say with certainty that this is in fact the reason they are chopping the wood? The answer again is the researcher cannot know with complete certainty one way or the other. The only thing the investigator can go on is the factual evidence before him or her. The researcher, for example, may find evidence from the woodsman's wife or from other sources that conflict with the woodsman's own explanation of his behavior. Ultimately, the researcher must interpret the facts and make a judgment. This is how the researcher should proceed.

This takes us to the question of values and objectivity. Values were discussed above in terms of the values that influence a social actor's behavior. Here we need to focus on the values of the sociologist doing the observing. This relates very much to what sociologists refer to the issue or the debate of "facts and values." What role does or should the values of the sociologist play in his or her understanding of the world? If I am firmly opposed to abortion, and I am a sociologist studying abortion, can or should I allow my view, my moral position, my values, to influence and distort my scientific understanding of the situation? Or should I let the facts speak for themselves, and leave my values to the side? Durkheim, as we saw, embraced this latter position. He believed it was possible without problem for the sociologist to look at the world objectively and for the sociologist to leave his or her biases and values to the side. Weber believes it is more complicated than this. As we are fundamentally moral beings, as we fundamentally interpret the world through our particular value perspectives, we may knowingly or more likely unknowingly distort the facts observed. The best the researcher can do is to be vigilant and on guard for any distortions he or she might make. The sociologist should strive to be as objective as possible. It is a goal not a fact. Weber calls this **value freedom** or value neutrality. The researcher should strive to be value neutral in his or her work, in the interpretations he or she makes about the social world.

There is one place where Weber says it is possible and it is inevitable that values can and do enter into the research process, and he says it is fine for this to occur. This is in the selection of the research topic by the social scientist. Why do some sociologists study divorce and other study mental illness? Why so some study race or gender and others study education? It may be for many different reasons. The selection of topics of study on one level or another is inevitably based upon one's value preferences. This is called **value relevance**. Once the researcher selects the topic of study, then he or she should strive to maintain value neutrality.

The descriptions given above regarding methodology might give the reader the impression that Weber was focused mostly, if not exclusively, upon understanding meaningful individual action. But this hardly sounds like sociology. It sounds perhaps more like some form of psychology. At the least, it sounds very much like he is advocating some form of micro-sociology rather than a macro-sociology. It is important to understand that his interest in understanding meaningful individual action is merely a step toward understanding the large-scale workings of society. His central concerns were in understanding macro-sociological issues. To understand Weber's methods more and to understand how he moves from a concern in explaining individual action to explaining large-scale social phenomena, we should understand the intellectual context within which he was writing. In the late eighteen hundreds, there was a significant academic debate occurring in the social sciences in Germany regarding what the social sciences should strive to be. That is, the debate concerned whether the social sciences should embrace the methods of the natural sciences, such as biology and physics, or whether they should strive to embrace some of the interpretive disciplines in the humanities such as history.

This debate is called the methodenstreit and largely revolved around the issue of whether sociology and the social sciences should strive to produce **idiographic** knowledge or **nomothetic** knowledge. Idiographic knowledge is the knowledge that is unique and particular. It is a form of knowledge that seeks to understand completely the unique elements of a particular reality. It strives to capture the elements of this particular reality that make it distinctive, unlike any other particular reality. Nomothetic knowledge, on the other hand, seeks generalizations. This form of knowledge looks for patterns or laws that are reflected in particular realities. It does not seek to understand how each reality is unique, but instead seeks to understand how one particular reality shares qualities with other particular realities. It seeks to develop an understanding of the general rule or laws that govern the particular reality.

The natural sciences, such as biology and chemistry, are nomothetic in character. When a chemist does an experiment, he or she seeks to discover laws about the workings of the chemicals. History and the humanities are largely idiographic. Historians by and large do not seek to discover the laws of history. Instead, they seek to develop a full, rich understanding of the unique historical events, and they seek to explain these events through this understanding.

In Germany the methodenstreit debate tended to revolve around the disciplines of economics and history. Some argued that the field of economics is and should be a nomothetic science, one that seeks to establish laws governing economic behavior and economic systems, and some argued that the field of history should be idiographic. That is, some argued that there is and should be a recognition of two distinct forms of knowledge about human behavior. Others argued that all systematic studies of human behavior, from history to economics, from psychology to sociology, should be nomothetic while still others argued that all studies of human behavior should be idiographic.

Weber was very much focused on developing a historical sociology. So where did he stand on this issue? He argued for a third approach. Sociology was different from economics and history, and it should not strive to be either idiographic or nomothetic. It should take the best elements of each approach and combine them, while leaving the worst elements of each to the side. Both approaches sought to provide causal explanations of observable phenomena. Weber too believed sociology should strive to do this. But the forms of causation in chemistry are fundamentally different than the forms of causation in sociology. The chemicals in a test tube automatically do things. They automatically or mechanically react. They do not think or interpret or assign meanings to their world, and then act based upon these understandings. Human beings however engage in motivated behaviors. Their actions are caused by human interpretations. As such, values must be central to an understanding of social action. Humans make value judgments about things and act based upon these value judgments. The task of sociology is to scientifically understand motivated social actions and the values associated with these through the observation of empirical realities.

A major different between the idiographic and nomothetic forms of knowledge is seen in relation to the concept of laws – not the laws passed by Congress or some such political body, but the laws of nature. Nomothetic forms of knowledge are based on the desire to discover laws from the observations of particular realities. A physicist, for example, through experiments has established laws related to gravity, or to the fact that water freezes at thirty-two degrees. Weber rejected any suggestion that sociology should strive to discover laws – like natural laws -- of social behavior. They simply do not exist. It would be fool-hearted and misguided for the sociologist to seek to discover these laws because humans are meaning-making creatures and are motivated by an endless variety of things, and specifically by and endless variety of value constellations.

Thus far, it may seem that Weber continues to favor the idiographic rather than the nomothetic side of the argument. However, this is not quite true. He sees a clear distinction, for example, between history, an idiographic discipline, and sociology. Weber did see sociology as a discipline that can and should strive to make generalizations, though these generalizations were certainty not law-like in character. But how could he do so, given the above? How could a sociology proceed and be anything but a form of history or a form of some other interpretive enterprise?

Weber solves these problems by developing his concept of ideal types. An **ideal type** is an abstract concept or model of some aspect of social reality. They are conceptual tools that the sociologist uses to understand social reality. The sociologist should develop in his or her own mind an image of the core features of the reality he or she wishes to understand before he or she actually does an empirical study. For example, if a sociologist wished to understand why it is that college students tend to sit in the same seat again and again after the first few days of the semester, he or she might seek to develop a set of ideal types of this behavior prior to actually studying it. As we saw above, a student may sit in the same seat out of habit, or he or she may sit in the same seat because he or she wishes to see the blackboard better. Indeed, the types of social action noted above are in fact ideal types. Similarly, if the sociologist wished to study and to understand the sociology of the family, he or she would create in his or her mind types of families. He or she would imagine the various forms of families that might reasonably exist and then would outline the main features of these types. One might imagine a nuclear family, with a biological mother, biological father, and children, each with their own roles and expectations attached to these roles. Or one might imagine a single parent family, with a different composition and different roles and expectations of the members.

When Weber uses the term "ideal," he is not claiming that the ideal type or types he has constructed are somehow or other the best form of social organization. He is not making a value judgment about the goodness of some social formation. Thus, as we see below, he constructs an ideal type of bureaucracy, but he in no way means to say that the ideal type of bureaucracy that he created should be used somehow as a model that people should follow to create or implement bureaucracies. Weber did not believe that bureaucracies in themselves were unequivocally good. Perhaps a better way of thinking about his concept of ideal types is through the concept of "pure types." Again, they are methodological tools that the sociologist can use to understand social realities. But how then does he or she do so?

Weber says that once the sociologist has created the particular ideal type, then he or she can then look at a social reality and compare that social reality to the ideal type. Typically, there will be a difference; often there will be a major difference, between the concept of the ideal types and the reality being observed. How many bureaucracies, for example, in real life actually reflect the essential elements of an ideal type of bureaucracy? Do students sitting in a classroom reflect clearly and unequivocally one or another of the four ideal types of social action noted above (i.e., traditional, affective, instrumental rational, and value rational action)? Might it not be the case that more often than not students have more than one reason for sitting where they do? In short, there tends to be a gap between the ideal type and the reality being observed. This goes to the heart of Weber's sociology: The task then is to explain how and why there is such a difference. For example, one of the characteristics of the ideal type of bureaucracy is impersonality. Decisions about personnel, about hiring, firing, disciplining, etc., in a bureaucracy should be made based upon objective criteria and not upon personal friendships, loyalties, etc. But is that really how bureaucracies work? It does not take much to imagine that in the real world decisions are often made in bureaucracies that violate this ideal type condition. Is it hard to come up with an example or two of how someone in some organization was promoted, or was not disciplined, due to personal connections rather than due to objective assessments of the facts? (On a related note, one of the things Weber noted about American democracy from his visit was the machine politics of the cities, such as Chicago. The formal rules of democracy that are supposed to dictate how decision making occurs in American cities were at odds with the actual practices by city leaders, who doled out favors and manipulated the government to serve their own ends. The ideal type of city government, one based perhaps upon an abstract understanding of democracy was at odds with the real workings of city government.) The sociological question then is how and why does this occur? Why do particular social realities depart from the ideal types? This is the quest of sociology.

Modernity

A driving force in much of Weber's sociology was a desire to understand **modernity**. The modern world of capitalism, of industrialization, of great cities, of science and technologies, of ever-increasing change was a concern for all of the classical theorists, whether Marx, Weber, or Durkheim. Weber wished to understand how this modern world came about, and he wished to understand its consequences. Would modernity lead to a better or to a worse world in the future? What are the essential forces in the modern world propelling it forward? One specific issue of concern for Weber in this regard was how and why did the modern world first develop in Europe and America and how and why did it not develop in India or China or in some other part of the world. How was it that the western world became so wealthy, so powerful, so scientifically and technologically advanced, so dynamic in the last few hundred years and other parts of the world did not? He concluded that it had much to do with culture and specifically with religion. Below I describe his famous argument put forth in the book *The Protestant Ethic and the Spirit of Capitalism*, in which he attributes the emergence of modern, rational capitalism in the western world to Protestantism.

But there is another more important theme in his understanding of modernity. This is his concerns about **rationalization**. Scholars over the last few decades have come to realize that his focus on rationalization is central to his entire theoretical project. However, Weber's understanding of the concepts of rational, rationality, and rationalization are confusing and are understood by different scholars today in different ways. Earlier the concept of rational action was briefly discussed, as was the concept of McDonaldization, which is akin to the concept of rationalization. Weber believed that rationalization lies at the heart of modernity. But what is it? Rationalization is the historical process by which the world is increasingly being organized along formally rational lines. Another way of thinking about this is that rationalization is the historical process by which formal rationality is taking over from substantive rationality. **Formal rationality** is the lining up of means and ends in a social context without considering values. **Substantive rationality** is the lining up of means and ends in a social context while considering values.

One might note that these definitions of formal and substantive rationality sound similar to the two types of social action – instrumental rational action and value rational action. After all, instrumental rational action is the lining up of means and ends in a rational or logical way without considering values, and value rational action is lining up means and ends in a rational or logical way while considering values. The difference is the focus. For Weber, the concept of rationalization, both formal and substantive, refers not to abstracted individual behaviors but instead to the social context or the social environment and its relationship to the individual. The social context is organized and bears down upon the individual. It is this context and this relationship that are at the heart of formal and substantive rationality. Thus, one could identify a social context as more or less formally rational in organization. The army or a McDonald's restaurant are examples of entities that are formally rational. Perhaps the easiest example of formal rationality is the capitalist economy. In all of these settings participants are expected, demanded in some cases, to act in a rational way without considering their values. The values of a private in the army, whether he or she thinks the war he or she is fighting is just or not, whether he or she thinks a command given by a superior is right or not, should not affect his or her actions. Indeed, the social actor in such settings is not to consider values at all. They are to be machine like in their ways of being. Similarly, one could identify social contexts that are more substantively rational in organization. Families and the Amish community in Pennsylvania are two examples of settings that are substantively rational. In such settings people are to act rationally, but only within the context of their own values. The values of the setting dictate the means, the ends, and the relationship between the two. Arguably, the Amish do act rationally when they refuse to use recent technologies, such as their decision not to have electricity in their homes, or their decision to ride horses and buggies rather than automobiles, but their rational actions are shaped and determined by their values, in this case by their religious convictions.

For Weber, rationalization began in earnest in the western world in the sixteen hundreds and has continued ever since. Moreover, it has increased in scope and intensity as capitalism, technology, bureaucratization, and other elements of modernity have grown and spread in the last few hundred years. Rationalization was occurring in various areas of social life. For example, he wrote about the rationalization of the economy. Capitalism was organized along formally rational lines and it replaced economic systems rooted in substantive rationality, whether those found in traditional hunting and gathering societies or those found in the feudalism of the Middle Ages in Europe. He wrote about the rationalization of law. Law in the modern western world is based upon formal rationality. It is based on the idea that if a legal system is created and maintained on the basis of just rules, regulations and procedures, and if people – lawyers, judges, etc. -- working within the system conform to the rules and regulations in their actions, then the outcome of justice will be served. This is the case whether the individual case provides a "just" verdict or not. If someone commits a crime but is found innocent, has justice been served? If all the rules and procedures were properly followed, then indeed justice has been served. He contrasts this, for example, with the system of "Qadi" justice found in traditional villages in the Arab world. That system is rooted not in formal rules and regulations, but instead is based largely upon the individual discretion of the judge. The judge is not constrained by rules and regulations. His task is to arrive at a true and just verdict, no matter what must be done to determine it. It is a form of substantive justice. Weber also shows that rationalization has occurred in political systems, in cities, and in art forms such as music, art and architecture. He notes how rationalized western classical music, and art, and architecture became in the modern era. Here he is thinking of how technical the art has become. Great art is determined by technical mastery, rather than by other things, such as concerns of beauty or other substantive concerns. The criterion is the effective use of rational technique. For example, the invention of the use of perspective in western art was a rational technique by which three dimensional spaces are displayed on two dimensional canvases. If one has ever seen a painting in which people meant by the artist to be seen as far away in the distance are depicted as smaller in the painting than people closer to the viewer, one has seen an example of perspective in use. This traditionally was hailed in western history as a technical and aesthetic advancement in art.

Formally rational institutions increasingly dominant the social landscape, from private businesses to governmental agencies, from the military to the judiciary, from the economy to schools. One can find formal rationality relentlessly growing. While Weber was writing a hundred years ago, we can see in the last twenty or thirty years an embrace of formal rationality in many areas of social life. The testing movement in schools as well as the charter movement attest to the embrace of formal rationality. The very idea of marketization of social issues is rooted in an embrace of formal rationality as the proper basis of social organization. Marketization is the belief that the capitalist marketplace, i.e. competition and allowing supply and demand to dictate the amount, quality and types of products and services available, is the optimal way of allocating value in society. Thus, to improve schools we need more competition. Thus, we need charter schools, etc. All of this is based upon an implicit belief that formal rationality is a good thing. Rationalization here is viewed favorably.

Weber however had a far different and far more nuanced understanding of rationalization. He recognized both the positive and negative consequences of it. Formal rationalization does indeed produce good things. It allows for the growth of science and scientific discoveries. (After all the scientific laboratory is organized along formal and not substantive rationality.) It allows for the growth of corporate businesses. (Bureaucracies are formally rational in organization.) And it allows for the mass production of things like iphones, Facebook, and airplanes. Moreover, it is hard to argue logically against the principles of rationalization. Who would want a scientific laboratory organized along substantively rational lines, one organized, for example, on religious principles? But Weber was concerned about the growth and spread of formal rationality. The modern world is a **disenchanted world**. In pre-modern worlds, societies were enchanted. An enchanted world is filled with wonder and awe. One might think of natural phenomena such as a rainbow or an earthquake and ask how people living in hunting and gathering societies, people living in pre-technological societies, might explain such things? They might say that such things are caused by spirits or Gods or some other supernatural forces. They would most certainly not explain an earthquake by notions of plate tectonics or other scientific concepts. When we see a rainbow today, most of us realize that the existence of the rainbow can be explained by light refracting through the air. One might not know exactly how it happens, but one knows today that some scientist or other could provide a scientific explanation if asked. All of the magic, wonder, and awe of the world has been drained from it due to formal rationality taking over. This is a disenchanted world.

Weber also writes about the **iron cage of rationality** which has been imposed upon us by the conquest of formal rationality. We cannot see this metaphorical cage, but it is real. It traps us. It traps us into thinking about the world in a particular way, in a way that excludes values. It leads us to think and act mechanically in an unreflective way. As a consequence, we become little more than producing and consuming, soulless machines.

The disenchanted world and the iron cage of rationality foster an emptiness in the modern individual self. It is dehumanizing. What is the point of living if there is no longer any mystery? These things produce a loss of meaning, an emptiness in the self which cries out to be filled. I think of the bumper sticker that was popular, at least in California, a few decades ago. One would sometimes find these on the massive SUVs that were popular. The bumper sticker read, "He who has the most toys wins," suggesting that the SUV is just another needless toy. It is a satiric commentary on American consumerism. The idea is that we endlessly buy the newest and latest gadgets, iphones, autos, etc. But why? We are compelled to do so. Using Weber's ideas, one might say we are trying to fill the void in our lives that is produced by disenchantment and rationalization. But, of course, this way of fulfilling the void is not an effective means, at least in the long term. It is short-lived and ultimately futile.

There are numerous implications with this argument about rationalization and the loss of meaning. One of these concerns the future of democracy. If a population becomes psychologically lost, that is, if it becomes emptied of meaning and purpose, might the people not seek some charismatic leader who will give them a sense of purpose, who will restore their sense of meaning? We discuss charisma below. Here we can note that such a process actually did arise in Germany within a few years after Weber's death: the fascist Hitler and the Nazis came to power on the back of his charismatic leadership and his fanatic German nationalism. He said he would make Germany great again!

There are other implications as well with this argument about rationalization, most of which remain implied or suggested in Weber's work. He, like many other intellectuals of the early nineteen hundreds, was concerned about the loss of meaning that accompanies rationalization, disenchantment, and the iron cage or rationality, but that is not all. A number of commentators invoking Weber worry about **the irrationality of rationality** that comes with a blind embrace of formal rationality. When a population swears allegiance to formal rationality, then we might create an incredibly destructive situation. Some people note that the German Nazi regime under Hitler was very rational, at least in some respects. It is sometimes said, as a simultaneous, back-handed compliment and insult to the Germans, that in Germany the "trains run on time." By this it is meant that the railroads in Germany run very efficiently. They run on time and in a smooth manner. The trains depart and arrive on schedule. This is good. However, the trains also metaphorically if not in reality ran on time during World War Two to Auschwitz and the many other extermination camps. Six million Jews and millions upon millions of others were slaughtered in these camps in a highly methodical fashion. The German death machine was very efficient. Was it rational? Yes, and yes and no, and this is the point. We do not have to look back sixty years to see such irrationalities of rationality. Whether it is the existence of nuclear bombs and the strategy employed by the United States in the post-World War Two era in which the deterrence was the threat of annihilation of the Soviet Union (and the United States) or whether it is the fact that modern rational capitalism is destroying the environment, evidence abounds about the irrationality of rationality.

The Protestant Ethic and the Spirit of Capitalism

Weber wrote the book *The Protestant Ethic and the Spirit of Capitalism* as part of a larger project. This larger project was an attempt to understand why modern, rational capitalism emerged in the West and not in other parts of the world in the sixteen and seventeen hundreds. Why did the western world come to be so rich, so dominant in the modern era? In addition to the book he wrote a number of essays on religion in India and religion in China in which he attempted to show why modern capitalism did not emerge in these places. For example, he says that China did not develop capitalism for many reasons. One of these was the social organization of the community in China. It was organized by strict kinship bonds, and this fostered economic relations that were not conducive to capitalism. The organization of the Chinese government also was an impediment. The basis of the governmental rule was in tradition and was largely patrimonial. Formalism in governmental actions was not very prominent, and this too did not foster a context in which capitalism could thrive. He also argued that the structure of the Chinese language itself was an impediment. The Chinese used a character based language system in which a word is a character or a number of characters superimposed. It was radically different from the western languages which relied upon alphabets. This worked against rational and systematic thinking, which was necessary for the growth of capitalism. He also cited the Chinese religions as factors that worked against capitalism. Confucianism embraced tradition. It championed tradition at the expense of social change. It fosters a scholarly orientation that emphasizes literary education and not technical education, and this focused the attention of the intellectuals not on problems of the world, not on economic matters, but instead on things like the skillful use or art of language or in things like memorization. All of this works against the intellectual orientation that fosters capitalism.

In *The Protestant Ethic* Weber sought to answer the following question: Why did modern, rational capitalism emerged where and when it did? To answer this question, one needs to first understand a few things. The first thing concerns modern, rational capitalism. He says that capitalistic activities, e.g. the buying and selling of things for a profit in a marketplace, has been around for thousands of years. In the Roman forum, for example, grape farmers from the countryside brought their grapes to the market in Rome market to sell. Weber notes that this form of capitalist activity, traditional capitalism, is starkly different from the modern, rational form that appeared in the last few hundred years. In traditional capitalism, people are motivated by emotion, by hedonism and by the pursuit of pleasures. In the capitalism of the modern world, people are motivated by almost the opposite. Economic actors – think here of people on Wall Street or in a corporate boardroom and not of people shopping in the malls -- now are supposed to be cold and calculating. They are supposed to be emotion-less and disciplined. Not rash and impulsive. The modern man is characterized by restraint, not by impulsiveness. The economic actor in the modern world who embodies the spirit of modern, rational capitalism is the man on Wall Street in a suit. For Weber the question was how and why did this type of capitalist man emerge?

He says that modern, rational capitalism emerged in the sixteen and seventeen hundreds in two places: in a part of New England, specifically the Massachusetts Bay Colony, and in parts of England. What were these societies like such that they served as the seedbed of modern capitalism? What was unique about them? What made them different from other places? Weber noted that several features of western societies paved the way for the emergence of capitalism. The separation of business from the household was one of these that he argued was present. So too was the existence of "formally" free labor. Modern capitalism requires a population that is "formally" free to take or to leave a job. Thirdly, he says the rational bookkeeping employed in the West also helped provide a foundation for capitalism. But above all else the main factor concerned religion. It was the Protestant ethic that fostered the growth of the spirit of capitalism. This ethic was the key to understanding the growth and spread of capitalism.

To understand his argument, one must be clear about what Protestantism is. The two major types of Christianity in western Europe and in America are Roman Catholicism and Protestantism. (A third form of Christianity exists in Eastern Europe. This is Orthodox Christianity. This form does not concern us here.) Prior to the fifteen hundreds Protestant religions did not exist. If you were a Christian before that time, you were a Roman Catholic. Roman Catholicism traces its roots back to Jesus Christ. Beginning in the late fourteen hundreds and continuing for the next two hundred years the Protestant Reformation occurred. This was the period in which Protestant faiths emerged. The Protestants broke away from, they protested against, the Roman Catholic Church and formed their own, new Christian Churches. Thus, today, if someone is a Christian but is not a Roman Catholic, they are likely a Protestant. Methodists, Baptists, Episcopalians, Presbyterians, Quakers, etc. are all Protestant churches. There are now hundreds of Protestant denominations.

In the late fourteen hundreds and into the fifteen hundreds, Catholic priests and others began to complain loudly against the corrupt practices of the Roman Catholic Church. Priests such as Martin Luther (1483-1546) – the founder of what was to become the Protestant denomination of Lutheranism -- stood up and loudly complained about such things. Luther, for example, complained about the practice of indulgences created in the Roman Catholic Church in the Middle Ages. Indulgences were documents written by the Church to forgive members who have sinned. If someone sinned, they could buy an indulgence from the Church and all will be forgiven with God. This seems patently unfair. If one is rich, one could commit a sin and then buy an indulgence, and all is forgiven. But if one is poor, one cannot. This is but one of the many, many complaints leveled against the Catholic Church. This eventually led Luther and many others, such as John Calvin, to renounce the Church and to create their own Christian churches, i.e. Protestant churches. In addition, non-religious persons were also rebelling against the Catholic Church. Henry the Eighth, the King of England, broke away from the Catholic Church and created the Church of England, i.e. the Episcopal Church, but he did not do so for theological reasons. He did so because he wished to have a male heir to his thrown and his wife could not provide him with one. As a result, he wanted a divorce, which was against Roman Catholic policies. He rejected Catholicism so that he could remarry with the hope of having a son.

Weber noted that modern capitalism began in Protestant countries – in England and in the United States – and did not begin in Catholic countries. He concluded that the explanation for the rise of capitalism must have something to do with religion. So he asked, what was the difference between Protestantism and Catholicism? Moreover, he wanted to understand how the different faiths caused people to think and to act differently. He then noted that capitalism arose in Protestant countries, but it arose in specific places within these Protestant countries. It arose where one group of Protestants tended to live. This group was the Puritans or the Calvinists, i.e. the followers of Swiss reformer John Calvin. Weber then asks, what was it about Calvinism that caused its followers to work in ways that produced modern capitalism? To answer this question, one must appreciate how important and significant the Reformation was to the faiths and to the faithful. Prior to the Reformation, if one had a question about what Jesus or God believed or wanted, one would turn to the Catholic Church, to the priests, the bishops, the pope, for answers. The centralization of the authority of the Church in the Church hierarchy was central to the faith. Indeed, it was not until the Reformation that the bible was translated into local languages. It was traditionally written in Latin, a language only the priests could read. In the Reformation, the bible was translated into German and into other European languages, thus giving the people direct access to the holy book and thus allowing them to develop their own understandings. The point is that once Christians broke away from Catholicism, they were then faced with the issue of what their faith means and with the question of how they should behave. How should one interpret the faith? How should one interpret the Bible? Should on treat the stories in the Bible literally or metaphorically? Was the earth created in seven days? Or were the stories metaphors or allegories? These and many other issues had to be addressed by the new Protestants.

Weber wished to understand (verstehen) the Protestants and specifically the Calvinists, how they viewed their new religion and how this prompted them to act in ways that were supportive of the rise of capitalism. As a result, he examined closely the Calvinist faith. Calvin as well as the other reformers set about to re-interpret the Bible and the fundamental meanings of Christianity. One of the elements of that Calvinist belief was predestination. Predestination is the idea that if God is all knowing and all powerful, then he must know if someone is going to be going to heaven or hell even before the person is born. Otherwise, one would be saying that God is not all knowing and all powerful. Another element was the embrace of asceticism. Asceticism is an orientation to the world that shuns or rejects pleasure. An ascetic would not drink alcohol, dance, party, or eat ice cream. Calvinists were ascetics. Calvin interpreted Christianity to mean that God wished for people to be ascetic in their lives. They are to live sober and simple lives.

But Weber notes that there are two forms of asceticism: this worldly asceticism and other worldly asceticism. Other worldly asceticism is an orientation which calls upon the believers to remove themselves as much as possible from the day-to-day mundane world. This calls upon the followers to retreat from the world. A group of monks living in isolation on a mountain top in an ascetic fashion is an example of this. Their spirituality is realized by removing themselves as much as possible from this world. In contrast, this worldly asceticism calls upon the followers to be ascetic while they engage and participate in the day-to-day world. They are not to flee from the world; they are to participate in the world, all the while in an ascetic fashion. The focus of this worldly ascetics is upon being religious through participating in the activities of this world, albeit in an ascetic fashion. The Calvinists were this worldly ascetics. They did not seek to retreat from this world, but instead sought to engage in the world.

The Calvinists also embraced the idea of the calling. Each of us is placed upon this earth to do God's work. As God was all knowing and all powerful, he must certainly know what the Calvinist should do with their lives. The calling is the vocation, work, job, career, that the Calvinists believed God wanted them to do. God might wish for someone to be a carpenter, and another to be a doctor, and yet another to be a farmer. This is their calling. One of the tasks of the Calvinist is to find their calling. But how do they know if God wishes for them to be a carpenter or a doctor? After all, God never tells them. They are left to figure this out on their own. Weber argues that the Calvinists figured it out by determining whether they were good or not good at their selected occupations. If someone became a carpenter, and he was not good at it, then he might conclude it was not his calling. If someone became a farmer, and he was good at it, he might conclude it was his calling.

This is closely tied to another concept – signs of election. The Calvinists, according to Weber, embraced and lived their faiths deeply. They believed in heaven and hell and the horrors of eternal damnation. This faith produced great anxieties. After all, the Calvinists believed God knows what was to happen to them, and they did not, and they most certainly did not wish to spend eternity in hell. Rather, they wished to go to heaven. How then is one to get to heaven? The point is that one cannot do anything to get to heaven, as God already knows where the person will end up. The anxiety that all of this produces in the believer leads him to try to convince himself and to convince others that he is one of the elect, that he is one that has been chosen by God to go to heaven. And how does one know if one has been elected? One looks for signs, signs of election. Finding your calling, working very hard in a sober and serious way, being successful in your work, living an ascetic life all will convince you that you are one of the elect, and that you will be going to heaven.

In short, this Protestant ethic leads the faithful to work very hard and very well in their career. The Calvinist furniture maker will make good furniture and he will make a good deal of money because of his economic orientation. But he cannot spend the money on pleasures. What does the Calvinist then do with all of these profits? He reinvests the money in his business. He grows his business. He hired more people. The business expands, and all of this is driven by the religious ethic. Moreover, his orientation makes him a more efficient, better worker and businessman than his competitors or others who do not share this ethic. These others then are forced then either to go out of business or are forced to adopt the orientations of the Calvinists. This does not mean that the others need to convert to Calvinism, but it does mean that they need to emulate the work ethic and practices of the Calvinists if they are to remain economically competitive.

Weber argues that this ethic set the working of modern capitalism in motion. Increasingly, people had to adopt the practices and orientations of the Calvinists if they were to survive economically. There was what Weber calls an **elective affinity** between the Protestant ethic and the spirit of capitalism. By this mean means that the orientation of the Calvinists, e.g. their beliefs and practices, fit neatly like a glove on a hand with the orientation that was demanded of modern capitalism. This overlap of orientations is the elective affinity.

Of note, one of the great ironies of his argument is that religious sentiments fueled the growth of modern capitalism, but modern capitalism then fuels the decline of the religious sentiments. Weber say rationalization, as discussed earlier, produces secularization or a decline in religion.

Disenchantment and the iron cage of rationality lead people away from the enchanted beliefs in religion. And modern rational capitalism fits neatly with rationalization, disenchantment, and the iron cage.

Some of Weber's Ideal Types

Power, Dominance and Authority

We can now turn our attention to several of Weber's more well-known ideal type formations. The first we will address is his ideas about power, dominance and authority. **Power** (macht) "is the probability that one actor within a social relationship will be in a position to carry out his own will despite resistance" (1978:53). **Dominance** (herrschaft) "is the probability that a command with a given specific content will be obeyed by a given group of persons" (1978:53). Weber was most interested in dominance: "Dominance in the most general sense is one of the most important elements of social action" (1978:941). He sought to understand how and why people follow commands, and particularly why people in many situations willingly do so. People follow commands for various reasons. Sometimes people are forced or coerced to do so. If someone puts a gun to another's head and demands money from them, the second person will likely give the first person the money. He or she is being forced. This is a form of illegitimate power or coercion. The person being robbed does not see the robber's actions as legitimate. Weber was far more interesting in understanding legitimate dominance, which he calls authority, rather than illegitimate power. Legitimate dominance or **authority** is when a person complies with a request because the person believes the person making the request has the right to do so. It is a legitimate request.

There are three forms of authority: traditional, charismatic and rational-legal authority. **Traditional authority** is rooted in tradition. It is rooted in the acceptance as legitimate of the way things have always been done. When a person follows the command of another because that's simply the way things have always been done, then this is traditional authority. The authority of a king or queen in the Middle Ages in Europe might be traditional when he or she asks the peasant to do something, though this would depend upon whether the peasant recognizes the request as legitimate. (It very well might not be viewed as legitimate but instead as a form of illegitimate dominance, e.g. force or coercion.) Similarly, if a mother asks her adult son to do something, the son may comply with the mother's request because he believes that sons should do what their mother asks. Or a student may comply with the directions of a professor because the student has come to believe he or she should follow the directions of a person in the role of teacher. **Charismatic authority** rests upon the personality of the person making the request. The person has charisma, which is that indefinable, personal quality that causes others to like, to admire, to follow them. The leader embodies certain traits that cause others to follow their commands. History is filled with charismatic leaders. From Martin Luther King to Hitler (though the latter relied of course on force or illegitimate dominance as well), from Jesus Christ to cult leaders, the commands of the charismatic leaders are followed because of the unique personal quality of the leader.

The third form of authority is **rational-legal authority**. This is not rooted in tradition and is not rooted in the person of the leader. Instead, it is rooted in an impersonal sets of rules. When one does what another asks because the second person is following the rules of the given situation when they make their request, then this is rational-legal authority. Rational-legal authority is when a person complies with a request because the person believes the request to be in accord with a set of rules, regulations, laws, or ideas, which are supposed to be followed. When a policeman pulls someone over for speeding and then asks the driver for his license and registration, the driver will likely provide this information to the policeman. If the driver does so because he believes the policeman is following the law when he pulled the person over for speeding, then this is legitimate authority. Of course, the driver may comply because of the power of the policeman, or because of traditional authority. One can only know by looking at the real live situation at hand. (This is an illustration of how ideal types works.) An important feature of rational-legal authority is that it is often associated with bureaucracies, a concept described below, and more generally with the workings of the modern world. People often comply with requests in bureaucracies, or in formal organizations more broadly, because they believe that those making the request have the right to make them because of some set of rules or regulations which are deemed to be legitimate.

Of the three forms of authority, charismatic is least able to be sustained for very long, at least for very long in the broad scope of time. As charismatic authority is rooted in the person, when the person dies, what happens to the authority? The charismatic authority dies with the person. But sometimes the charismatic leader will create rules and regulations that are independent up the individual leader. This then leads to a change from charismatic authority to another form of authority, to traditional or rational-legal. Weber calls this **the routinization of charisma**. For example, Jesus Christ arguably had charismatic authority, but when he died Christianity did not die. It did not die in part because the form of authority shifted. When Jesus was alive, he instituted what later was interpreted as rules that were followed after his death, that instituted some of the rules of the Catholic Church. The leadership structure of the Catholic Church, i.e. with the pope at the head, is said to trace its origins to Jesus' designation that Peter would be the first pope. In the Gospel Matthew Jesus is reported to say: "Peter, upon this rock, I will build my Church." Rules of succession, as well as other organizational rules, were created and instituted and continued on long after the charismatic leader dies.

It should be remembered here when thinking of these ideal types of authority that the concepts themselves do not reflect realities. Instead, they are tools that are used to understand realities. As such, it is not the case that in any particular situation one will find one or another form of authority or domination. In any particular situation it is possible if not likely that one will find more than one form of authority or dominance present. For example, several presidents of the United States might be said to have charisma, perhaps John F. Kennedy, but this does not exclude the possibility that people might follow the directions of these persons for reasons of rational-legal authority or for traditional authority.

Class, Status, Party

Class, **status** and **party** are Weber's ideal types of stratification. Stratification refers to the layerings of society. In short, it refers to types of inequalities. Different groups have different access to power, resources, and rewards. Weber developed this typology of class, status and party in response to Marx's understanding of stratification. For Marx, all forms of stratification ultimately come down to economic inequality, and specifically inequality between economic classes. Weber saw this as too limiting, and as a distortion of the real workings of the world. He saw the world as more complex than Marx understood it. Weber identified three areas of social life in which stratification occurs. In the economic arena class is the central element, but Weber defines class very differently from that of Marx. For Marx, the principal classes are defined in terms of the relationship to the means of production, i.e. a person is part of the class that owns the means of production (in capitalism this is the bourgeoisie) or is part of the class that does not own the means of production (in capitalism that is the proletariat), but only own their ability to sell their labor. People in this class are forced to work for the owners. Weber recognized class as an important concept, but he defined it more broadly than Marx. Weber defines classes in terms of economic positions and in terms of "life chances." Life chances are "represented exclusively by economic interests in the possession of goods and opportunities for income" (Weber, 1958:181). As such, it does not matter if two people have fundamentally different types of jobs, as long as they have comparable incomes and are afforded comparable access to goods and opportunities, then they are in the same class.

Status groups are located within the social arena, and not within the economic arena. Status is anchored in the social esteem or honor accorded a group or membership in a group. Some groups are thought of more highly than others. Some groups have more prestige than others. He says that a key feature of status groups is their "styles of life." As Weber notes, "with some over-simplification, one might thus say that "classes" are stratified according to their relations to the production and acquisition of goods; whereas "status groups" are stratified according to the principles of their consumption of goods as represented by special "styles of life" (1958:193). Today, the term lifestyle is widely used, and this is not that different from Weber's concept of styles of life. Different groups have different styles of life. Membership in a street gang entails a certain style of life. Membership in an exclusive club for rich people also has a distinctive style of life.

The third form of stratification is party. Weber here is referring to inequality in the political arena, and specifically he is referring to the relative amounts of political power a group has. Parties "live in a house of 'power'" (1958:194). Formal political parties fall within his understanding of party, but so too do many other forms of groups. Lobbying groups, for example, are parties in this sense. Thus, some groups, i.e. parties, have political power and others do not.

This is, arguably, a more sophisticated understanding of stratification than the one Marx proposed. Weber's categories allow us to understand perhaps more clearly some of the complex realities of inequality more clearly than Marx does. For example, one could use Weber's typology to understand what otherwise might be some confusing realities. That is, it is possible, if not quite common, for someone to rank high in one of the three types – class, status, party – and low in another. A leader of an organized crime family, for example, would rank high in the class stratification, but would rank low in the status system. He or she would likely be wealthy, but the leader would likely not have high prestige in the eyes of the general public (though within certain limited circles, the local community might think favorably and highly about the criminals). Similarly, it is possible to be high in status and lower in class position. One thinks here of some religious figures, such as Mother Theresa, and the like.

Bureaucracy

Bureaucracies are everywhere in the modern world. Bureaucracies are formal organizations. From universities to the military, from the government to big business, this organizational form has come to be a major force in the modern world. Weber knew this and tried to understand this organizational form. He developed an ideal type of bureaucracies. Some of the main features of this ideal type include: 1. Specialization, technical knowledge and training; 2. Hierarchy of offices; 3. Impersonality; and 4. Written rules and regulations. One of the characteristics of an ideal type bureaucracy is specialization, technical knowledge and training. In a bureaucracy there are different specialized jobs and these jobs require particular skills. These skills are acquired through training, particularly through educational institutions. In Microsoft Corporation, for example, there are software engineers, salespersons, accountants, etc. They all have their special, technical knowledge and have all been trained accordingly. A second characteristic is the hierarchy of offices. Bureaucracies are characterized by a chain of command, where there is a boss, and that person has a boss, etc. Impersonality is a third feature. This refers to how decisions are made in these settings. Decisions regarding personnel matters, e.g. should a person be hired, fired, or promoted, and more general decisions in the organization, are to be made objectively and are not to be made based upon personal loyalties. A person is not hired because he or she is a friend of the owner of the corporation. Lastly, bureaucracies are characterized by written rules and regulations. Written documents and files are a common feature of this form of organization.

As was noted earlier, it should be remembered that this is Weber's ideal type of a bureaucracy. As an ideal type it is not a form of organization that Weber says the modern world should strive to put into practice. Bureaucracies, as noted, may have positive features, but they also have negative features. The main point however is to remember that his depiction of the ideal type of a bureaucracy is meant to be a tool that the sociologist could use to understand social realities. One could take this ideal type and compare it to realities, and if one did so one would likely find that the reality is different from the ideal type. The question for the researcher then is how and why is a difference? An example that illustrates this is the United States government's response to Hurricane Katrina. In 2005, a massive hurricane named Katrina swept over New Orleans. The force of the hurricane destroyed the levees that kept the sea waters from flooding the city, which is below sea level. The city was flooded. For days, Americans watched on television thousands of people, mostly African Americans stranded and desperate in New Orleans crying out for help. Help was not coming. The management of the crisis by President George W. Bush and by the government was widely criticized. The administrator in charge of the U.S. government agency Federal Emergency Management Agency (FEMA) was Michael Brown. Brown was a political appointee. He was a lawyer with little to no emergency management experience or training. This is clearly an instance in which several of the ideal type characteristics of bureaucracy were violated. Impersonality was violated, as was specialization, technical knowledge, and training. As such, the question that Weber might ask is what caused this gap to arise between the ideal type and the reality?

It is important to recognize the relationship between bureaucracies and many of the other themes in Weber's work discussed above. The theme of rationality in particular relates here. Bureaucracies really are the embodiment of rational organization. Specifically, they are the embodiment of formally rational organizations. But it is not simply rationality that is relevant here. His understandings of dominance and authority also relate. For example, which form of dominance or authority might fit most neatly, or might be most compatible, with bureaucratic forms of organization? Admittedly, and of the forms of dominance and authority may be compatible with bureaucracies, but rational-legal authority appears most in line with the dictates of bureaucracy. When one considers the concerns about modernity and specifically about rationalization expressed by Weber implicitly and explicitly, e.g. disenchantment, the iron cage, the loss of meaning, etc., one might also consider how these things may be amplified when bureaucracy is fused with these other things.

Summary

The concepts of meaning, methods, and modernity are at the heart of Weber's sociology. Meaning was central to his theorizing. Humans are essentially meaning making creatures, and as such this should be the focus of any understanding of social life and social organization. When someone enters a classroom for the first time, they assign meaning to the situation and act upon it. On one level or another, people assign meanings constantly to their worlds and they act upon this meaning. If one enters a classroom and finds all the chairs facing the wrong way, the person will give the situation a different meaning than if the chairs were facing the right way. But it is not simply the meaning that social actors give to the world that is of importance to Weber, it is also the realization that the sociologist him or herself also assigns meaning to the world he or she is observing. This inevitably led Weber to develop a methodology which was rooted in the idea that sociology is an interpretive science. As such, in order to adequately explain social reality, the social scientist must use empathic understanding, or verstehen. The social scientist must try to place him or herself in the shoes of the people he is studying to try to understand their worlds. His method also involves the use of ideal types. An ideal type is an abstract model of a social phenomenon. By "ideal" he does not mean "best" in any sort of morally evaluative way. Instead, he means the purest. An ideal type seeks to capture the essential features of some social reality. By comparing what actually occurs to the constructed ideal type, the scholar can then begin to ask how or why there are differences between these. This is one of the foundations of his method. Weber created numerous ideal types. He created an ideal type of social action, in which he identifies four types of action: traditional, affective, value rational action, and instrumentally (or means-ends) rational action. Bureaucracy is another of his ideal types. Still another is his conceptualization of power, dominance and authority, as well as the three forms of authority: traditional, charismatic, legal-rational authority. He created ideal types concerning stratification. Here he identifies class, status, and party as the main ideal types.

Weber was interested in understanding how the modern world came about, and where it might be headed. At the heart of modernity lies rationalization. Rationalization is the historical process by which formal rationality is becoming dominant. He identifies two main types of rationality: formal and substantive. They differ in terms of the place of values in the decision-making process. Formal rationality excludes value considerations. The modern world, dominated by formal rationality, has produced many wonderful things, such as scientific advancements. But it also has produced a crisis of meaning. Rationality produces disenchantment and a loss of meaning, and we are increasingly living within "an iron cage." Weber wrote extensively about the role of religion in history, and specifically in the development of modern, rational capitalism. His book *The Protestant Ethic and the Spirit of Capitalism* argues that modern, rational capitalism began in Protestant areas of England and New England in the sixteen hundreds. He argues that the Puritan (i.e. Calvinist) ethic was instrumental to the early spread of modern rational capitalism. The Puritans embraced a set of ideas and practices which were supportive of the growth of modern rational capitalism. Weber conducted research on other civilizations of the world, such as those of India and China, and he sought to explain how and why modern, rational capitalism did not develop in these other places. This is a project that mirrors his work on *the Protestant Ethic*. While he identifies many factors to account for this, one of these factors is the religious ethic of these other civilizations. This ethic contributed in part to the prevention of the growth of capitalism.

The themes of rationality and values and the relationship between the two ripple through much of his work. For Weber these themes are more complicated than one might think. Many forms of rationality exist. One form is found in rational action. Rational action is one of several forms of social action. The task is to identify the various forms and then to compare social realities to these forms. Moreover, the relationship of rationality to values is also central to his analyses. People are meaning making creatures, and as such use values routinely in their assignment of meanings. But people are also rational. Sometimes they act in instrumentally rational ways. Sometimes they act in value rational ways. The task again is to understand the social context and how this influences the forms of actions the social actor takes. The theme of rationality and values also arise in his understanding of the role of the sociological researcher. The researcher, as a value assigning creature, must recognize this. But if he is to be a social scientist, the researcher must strive to recognize and to manage or control his value commitments when doing research. The researcher should strive to be value free.

It was noted that many scholars say that a good way to understand Weber's theorizing is to think of him as having been engaged in one long (metaphorical) dialog or debate with Marx. Both were focused upon understanding the modern world, how it came about, and where it was headed. Both were interested in understanding conflicts in society. However, Weber disagreed with Marx on these issues and on many, many others. For example, he rejected Marx's materialism, and he believed Marx's future communist society would lead to political oppressions as the result of the centralization of power in the hands of one party, the proletariat. Similarly, while he wished to understand the modern world and the emergence and spread of modern rational capitalism – themes similarly found in Marx's theorizing, he rejected Marx's claims to have developed a science of history that can track and predict the course of history. Weber complains that such an approach wrongfully force-fits social realities into the scholar's pre-set theory or ideology. Like Marx, he was concerned about the impact that modern rational capitalism was having upon the individual, but unlike Marx the source of Weber's concerns was rationalization and not capitalism, at least not capitalism in itself. After all, it is possible to have a rationalized political or social system that is not capitalist, the Soviet Union, for example. Had he lived in the middle decades of the century, Weber would undoubtedly have bemoaned the rational bureaucracies at the heart of the Soviet society – which became so infamously recognized by so many as oppressive nightmares. Likewise, he saw Marx's views on class as too simplistic. Stratification, as we saw, has many dimensions. It is not simply based upon an economics, as Marx claims. He complained as well about Marx's understandings of culture. Marx's base-superstructure theory of ideology and culture was wrong-headed. Again, Weber complains that it imposed a theoretical framework on reality and forces reality to conform to the framework. As a result, it distorts reality to justify the theory. For Weber, it is not that the base never determines the superstructure. He recognizes that at times it can. But it is also not the case that the base always determines the superstructure. This point is made in the closing paragraph of *The Protestant Ethic*, where he implicitly responds to Marx: "[I]t is, of course, not my aim to substitute for a one-sided materialistic an equally one-sided spiritualistic [i.e. cultural] causal interpretation of culture and of history. Each is equally possible, but each, if it does not serve as the preparation, but as the conclusion of an investigation, accomplishes equally little in the interest of historical truth" (1976:183).

He also saw conflict and class very differently from Marx. Conflict relates to power, and for Weber to understand such things one should recognize the different forms of dominance and authority. In contrast to Marx, he says these may or may not be anchored in economic conflicts. Likewise, his understanding of class is different. Marx, Weber might say, viewed class too simplistically. Not only that, but Marx saw class as the only determinate and important form of stratification. Weber defined class differently and saw three distinctive forms of stratification. The world is more complicated, he seems to say, than Marx thought, and one should not demand that social realities conform to a pre-set theory. Instead, one should be driven by an understanding of the facts and only then develop a theoretical understanding of these facts.

Discussion Questions

1. Is Weber an idealist, in the Marxist sense of the word (See Chapter Two)? Specifically, in his work *The Protestant Ethic and the Spirit of Capitalism*, Weber seems to suggest that changing ideas, i.e. the emergence of Protestantism, caused changes to occur in the "material" conditions of society, i.e. it caused the spread of modern, rational capitalism. This suggests he is an idealist. Yet, as we saw above, he claims that he is neither an idealist nor a materialist, and he argues that the scholar should not proclaim themselves to be one or another prior to engaging in their research. Instead, he suggests that the research topic should determine whether one seeks an idealist or a materialist explanation. Do you think his approach is sound or not? Why?

2. Weber, quoting Tolstoi, once wrote, "Science is meaningless because it gives no answer to our question, the only question important for us: "What shall we do and how shall we live?" " Elsewhere, he writes, "Who – aside from certain big children who are indeed found in the natural sciences – still believes that the findings of astronomy, biology, physics, or chemistry could teach us anything about the *meaning* of the world?" (1958a:142-143). What does Weber mean by these things? Why can't these things provide meaning for us? What does it mean to say science is meaningless? If science cannot provide meaning, then how are we to find meaning in the modern world? Is there any possible way for this to happen?

3. Weber presents a rather pessimistic view of the modern world. It is a world dominated by formal rationality. It is a world in which disenchantment, the iron cage of rationality, and the loss of meaning have taken over. This sounds rather bleak. Is Weber right to say that formal rationality has taken over, and

that it has led to disenchantment, the iron cage, and the loss of meaning? Why or why not?

4. Weber wishes to create scientific sociology. But his understanding of a scientific sociology is significantly different from Durkheim's views of a scientific sociology. Weber seeks to create an interpretive science of sociology. Compare and contrast his understanding of a scientific sociology with that of Durkheim. How are they alike and how are they different? Which of the two approaches is better? Why?

Chapter Five: Simmel

When I think of Georg Simmel (1858-1918), I think of an athlete being in the "zone." Being in the zone is a term used to describe a particular form or type of being an athlete sometimes experiences. It is an experience in which everything the athlete does at that moment is experienced as being right and successful. When in the zone the athlete is at one with his activities. Sometimes people report that time slows down when they are in the zone. In the zone one knows what will happen. If playing basketball, someone in the zone knows when he or she is shooting that the ball will go through the hoop even before he or she shoots it. When playing baseball, one knows he or she will solidly hit the ball no matter what. It is a mode of experience in which the athlete loses himself completely in the action. At these moments he or she is not thinking, not thinking of anything. Instead, he or she is simply being and simply excelling at being. When I was young, I was quite athletic and can count on one hand the number of times I experienced being in the zone. One time was during a baseball game. It was a playoff game when I was a teenager. I usually played first base or outfield (as I am left handed, I had few options!). But in this game, I was called upon to pitch. I had not pitched for a couple of years, but the team ran out of pitchers and I was the only one left. I was not a very good pitcher, but on that day I excelled. It was not so much that I had a good assortment of pitches. Rather it was that I knew exactly where each pitch was going to go before I even pitched it. I knew the batters would miss. I was in the zone. We easily won the game. I pitched a two hitter. The point here is about modes of experiences, or forms of life.

Simmel never wrote about zones and being German he never wrote about baseball. But this example illustrates one aspect of his theorizing. He looks to understand forms of behavior. Much like one might be in a zone in a baseball game or in a basketball game, so too the forms of behavior that Simmel seeks to understand go beyond the particular setting and can be applied elsewhere. Perhaps they can even go beyond the same type of setting and can be applied to many different types of settings? The examples above are about sports, but perhaps one might be in the zone in other domains of life. For example, it is possible to conceive that one might be in the zone while working on Wall Street? There are different forms of life and Simmel spent much time trying to understand these.

Simmel is one of the most unique social theorists covered in this textbook. He certainly was one of the most unique theorists writing in the late eighteen and early nineteen hundreds. He was more of a social philosopher than a scientific sociologist. He also was and is important. While today, Marx, Weber and Durkheim are generally considered the three classical sociological theorists, Simmel is generally left off this list. It would be wrong however to ignore his importance. While he perhaps does not have the influence of these others today, he had and continues to have an impact upon sociology.

When he was alive, he was well known by other sociological theorists, and he influenced many of them. Some knew him personally; others knew his work. Simmel personally knew many of the influential German theorists of the age, including Weber. Durkheim also knew of Simmel's work, and he included many of the latter's essays in his influential journal L'Annee Sociologique. Georg Lukacs, the Hungarian Marxist, often explicitly acknowledged the influence Simmel's writings had upon his own sophisticated theorizing. Simmel also had a significant impact upon the founders of American sociology. The earliest major figures in American sociology, including Albion Small, Robert Park, and Ernest Burgess at the University of Chicago, which was the first major American school of sociology, were explicitly influenced by Simmel. They included his writings in their own journal, the American Journal of Sociology (which is today one of the two most prominent journals in the field). In addition, Simmel also had an impact upon the thinking of George Herbert Mead (see Chapter Nine), the American philosopher whose ideas were the foundation of the sociological theory called symbolic interactionism. It has been claimed, for example, that Mead may have attended Simmel's lectures while he was studying in Berlin.

Georg Simmel

Georg Simmel (1858-1918) was born and raised in Berlin, Germany. He was Jewish. He was the youngest of seven children. His father, the founder of a chocolate factory, died when he was a boy, and Georg was raised by his adopted parent. His father left him a sizable inheritance, which allowed him to engage in academic work throughout his life. Simmel studied philosophy and earned his doctorate from the University of Berlin in 1881. His dissertation was titled "The Nature of Matter according to Kant's Physical Monadology." He married Gertrude Kinel in 1890, and they had one son. Simmel spent his career as a lecturer and professor, though through most of his career he did not have a regular faculty appointment, partly due to the wide-spread anti-Semitism in Germany. Much of his career was spent as a privatdozent, as an outsider in the academic world, where he lectured often without pay, or with pay by the students in attendance. He gave lectures to students in classes, but also gave lectures attended by the general public. He was an interesting and popular lecturer. He gave talks on a wide range of subjects including the history of philosophy, modern philosophy, Kant, other philosophers, Darwin, ethics, the philosophy of art, the philosophy of religion, social psychology,

psychology, and sociology (Wolff, 1950). It was only in the last years of his life that he was given a full-time faculty position. Simmel published a number of books and many articles over the course of his life. He often would publish articles in non-scientific journals and newspapers meant to be read by the educated general public. He was a friend and colleague of a number of important German sociologists, including Max Weber, and his work was known and cited by many of the founding members of American sociology. Along with Weber and Ferdinand Tonnies, Simmel cofounded the German Society for Sociology. He died in 1918 in Strasbourg, shortly before the end of World War One, of liver cancer.

His influence upon American sociology over the past one hundred years or so has ebbed and flowed. That is, while he had an appreciable influence in the early years of the twentieth century, particularly through the Chicago School, his impact declined in the middle years of that century as Talcott Parsons and his structural functionalist theory (see Chapter Seven) came to almost completely dominant American sociology. Parsons and his students and colleagues built a macro theory that all but ignored the likes of Simmel. (Parsons dismisses Simmel's theory in *The Structure of Social Action* (1949:772-773).) It was not really until the 1960s that Simmel's influence began to rise once again. In the last forty years there has been a slowly growing appreciation of his work. And while he is not routinely cited in the sociology literature today, one finds that more and more scholars directly or indirectly are drawing upon his works (Levine, 1971a). Perhaps most prominently, his influences can be seen clearly in the various theoretical formulations of Erving Goffman (Chapter Nine).

Overview of the Theoretical Framework

Perhaps a major reason for Simmel's relatively lack of impact is the form that his theorizing took. Unlike Durkheim and Marx who developed unified theories of society in which the diverse aspects of society could be cohesively tied together under one overarching theoretical framework, Simmel's theorizing does not lend itself easily to this. Marx, for example, developed a materialist theory of history. In that theory, all of the various pieces of society could fit. One could use the theory to understand and to locate anything from religion to movies to economic structure and activities, from politics and inequality. The mode or production determines all else, and it produces conflicts that give way to new modes of production. Durkheim too with his focus on moral cohesion and functionalism can conceptually place all the parts of society into one unified theory. Simmel does not give us anything remotely like a unified picture of society in itself, and indeed he explicitly rejects such an approach. For Simmel society should be thought of as a form, not as a thing, and social formations within society should also be understood as forms. The task for Simmel is to understand these forms. How and why did one or another emerge? How are they used? What are the contradictions found in the various forms? The reader might now be wondering how the discussion of forms is in any way different than the discussion of societies or any other social thing used by other theorists. Aren't they the same? This is the point. They are not the same in Simmel's view. Forms are described below.

Another reason for Simmel's lack of impact lies in the way he approached sociological theory. He was first a social philosopher, and only secondarily should one consider him a sociologist. That is, even in his own lifetime critics complained that his theorizing did not readily lend itself to empirical, scientific research. It was not easy, to say the least, to turn his abstract concepts, ideas and explanations into testable hypotheses or in any way to objectively assess the merits of the concepts. Moreover, on a superficial level, and perhaps even on a more foundational level, it is hard to see a unity to his method. Much like the problem noted above concerning a lack of a coherent unity to his view of the social or of society, so too does he not provide a clear and unambiguous way in which to do sociological theory. This again stands in contrast to most other theorists who present a clear and unambiguous method.

Despite the apparent lack of order and cohesion in Simmel's theorizing, it is possible with a bit of effort to identify some of the overarching ideas and concepts which can be strung together in an organized way to give the theory some sense of conceptual clarity, if not order (see Levine, 1971a). His entire theorizing revolves around the concept of **forms**.

Simmel here is influenced in part by the eighteenth century German philosopher Immanuel Kant. Kant spent some of his time developing a philosophy to explain how we know things or how we are able to know things. Like Kant, Simmel begins with a distinction between the world external to the individual and the world as understood by the individual. We develop an understanding of the world outside of us. We do so through the construction of forms in our minds. Forms are like generalized concepts. When I see a dog, how do I know it is a dog? I know it is one because the dog that I see conforms to my image of what a dog is. It conforms to the form of a dog that I have in my mind. This understanding has a shape or a form to it, and this form may or may not be similar to the world outside. In the normal operations of the world, our forms of understanding approximate the world outside of us, i.e. the real world. This is probably truer when we consider the physical world outside of us. Most of us would understand the difference between an apple and a rock. But the issue becomes more complicated when we think of the forms of the social world. What is the form of friendship? Of society? Of inequality? It is the social forms that particularly interested Simmel.

When we think of mostly anything we assign realities to forms. There are forms of culture, of society, of personality types, of history. Any social reality consists of these forms that are produced by individual consciousness and are shared or not by others. But Simmel was not interested in simply defining the various forms of social life, whether it is the form of exchange, or of the stranger, or of prostitution or of domination, or of the forms of life in the city (all of which he does analyze, along with many, many more). Indeed, he was not really concerned with developing precise definitions of these or of any other social forms. Instead, he was interested in how these forms relate to social life, and importantly social life occurs in time and as a result the forms become fluid, changing and changeable. It is the dynamic relations between the forms and the lived social realities that most interested Simmel.

Conceptual Scheme

It is possible to identify a number of central concepts in Simmel's theorizing which can be cohesively strung together. Some of the main concepts are described here. The first main idea concerns the relationship of form to lived social experience. The easiest way of thinking about lived social experience is to equate this with the content of the forms. Simmel often uses examples from geometry to illustrate this idea. For example, we have a concept of the form of a square, or triangle, or some other shape in our head. We know what a square is. We can think about it abstractly. We can also identify some real object in the world as being square. A table might be square shaped. The face of dice is a square. The dice and the table are the contents, and the square is the form. Simmel, of course, was less interested in non-human forms and contents. He was instead interested in understanding social forms and contents, and as we see below here it gets more complicated.

Before we move on, we need to say a few more words about content. The word **content**, in relation to form, is an important one to use to describe Simmel's theorizing. However, it gets confusing because he uses the word content in a narrower way than the way I am using it here to describe his theory of forms. Simmel, for example, wrote about the "content of social life." There he describes content as the "material" of social life. Content is comprised of "drive, interest, purpose, inclination, psychic state, movement" (1971a:40). But content has a broader understanding in his theorizing. I am using it in this broader way. Donald Levine, a Simmel scholar, captures this broader understanding best when he writes that "contents are those aspects of existence which are determined in themselves, but as such contain neither structure nor the possibility of being apprehended by us in their immediacy" (1971a:xv). In effect, content is the real of un-reflected, lived experience. They are the experiences through which forms intersect. For example, as we see below, Simmel develops the form of the stranger. The content of the stranger would be an imagined lived embodiment of this form or type. A stranger might be an individual in a particular time and place who fits to one degree or another the broad characterizations of the form of stranger. It is the dynamic interplay between form and content that is at the heart of much of Simmel's theorizing. Typically, in real life gaps or tensions exist between the form and the content, and these gaps or tensions cry out for resolution.

A second concept central to Simmel's theory is that of **sociation**. The proper object of study for sociology is what he calls sociation. Sociation is the structure of lived social interactions. Whether it is the structure of the interaction of two or three people or of an entire society, he uses the concept of sociation to describe it. This leads Simmel to embrace a broader and a narrower understanding of society than is sometimes thought. Sometimes we think of society as existing out there, this big thing existing independent of individuals. But Simmel sees society and sociation as the structured interactions of people. He goes so far as to say that sociation is simply another word for society. We see this below in his discussion of whether society or social structures exist independently of living individuals. He writes:

> The large systems and the super-individual organizations that customarily come to mind when we think of society are nothing but immediate interactions that occur among men constantly, every minute, but that have become crystallized as permanent fields, as autonomous phenomena. As they crystallize, they attain their own existence and their own laws, and may even confront or oppose spontaneous interaction itself. At the same time, society, as its life is constantly being realized, always signifies that individuals are connected by mutual influence and determination. It is, hence, something functional, something individuals do and suffer. To be true to this fundamental character of it, one should properly speak, not of society, but of sociation. Society merely is the name for a number of individuals, connected by interaction. (1950:10)

But how then does sociation relate to forms? For Simmel, much of social life is structured through the forms of life. Sociologists should seek to identify and understand these forms and to see how they operate in daily live. Of note, the nature of these forms transcends the particular situations in which they appear, and they transcend the particular fields of social life in which they may appear. Thus, Simmel was not interested particularly in the forms of life one may find in an office or a bureaucracy. Instead, he was interested in understandings the structure of a common form of life that might be found in a bureaucracy as well in another setting, perhaps a religious organization, or a baseball team. For example, he notes that the sociologists might be well served by understanding the common forms of life shared by religious communities and members of a labor union. Members of both types of groups he suggests demonstrate a "readiness to sacrifice in terms of their devotion to an ideal" (1950:14-15). Both also may "ascribe the conduct of life, inspired as it is by the hope in a perfect state beyond the lives of the existing individuals." The structured similarities of the forms of life found in different social settings is one of the things Simmel says that the sociologists should study.

Another theme found in Simmel's theorizing, which is closely related to sociation, is that of **relations**. Simmel tends to conceptualize social life in terms of relations. But when we talk about relations in his theory, we are talking about far more than social relations, though this is part of it. Simmel sees the relationship of concepts to one another, the relationship of forms to one another, and the relationship of experience to concepts and forms, as all of central importance. Reality must be understood in terms of the relationship of one thing to another. Closely related to the concept of relations is that of distance and reciprocity. Levine describes each of these. **Reciprocity** means that "no thing or event has a fixed, intrinsic meaning; its meaning only emerges through interaction with other things or events" (1971a:xxxiii). One cannot understand anything without understanding the dynamic interactions something has with other things. The meaning exists only in the dynamics of the relationship and not in the abstracted thing in itself. This applies not only to ideas, but to people. Thus, an individual must be understood, at least from a sociological perspective, through his or her social relationships with other. Distance is the idea that "the properties of forms and meanings of things are a function of the relative distance between individuals and other individuals or things" (1971a:xxxiv). When seeking to understand the social world, one must recognize that the distance of one thing from one another, or the distance of individuals from things, etc. directly impacts how these things will be understood and how they will be engaged. As Levine writes, "All social forms are defined to some extent in terms of the dimensions of interpersonal distance. Some forms, like conflict, bring distant people into close contact. Others, like secrecy, increase the distance between people" (1971a:xxxv).

Dialectics is another concept central to Simmel's theorizing. For Simmel, seemingly every reality and every form of sociation consists of dialectics or contradictions. These contradictions fuel social action. We have encountered the concept of dialectics in an earlier chapter on Marx as well as in our discussion of Hegel. Simmel, however, does not use dialectics in exactly the same way. While he does see the world as riddled with contradictions, he does not see the contradictions rooted within the framework of materialism or idealism. Materialism or idealism are not the sources of the contradictions. The sources of the contradictions are found in the relations of forms to other things: forms to sociation; forms to content; forms to being. In short, the contradictions arise from the nature of the forms as they are encountered in the practice of social life. Forms are rigid and inflexible; reality is fluid and in flux.

An example of his use of contradictions is found in his essay "The Conflict in Modern Culture":

> Life must either produce forms or proceed through forms. But forms belong to a completely different order of being. They demand some content above and beyond life; they contradict the essence of life itself, with its weaving dynamics, its temporal fates, the unceasing differentiation of each of its parts. Life is inseparably charged with contradiction. It can enter reality only in the form of its antithesis, that is, only in the form of *form*. This contradiction becomes more urgent and appears more irreconcilable the more life makes itself felt. The forms themselves, however, deny this contradiction: in their rigidly individual shapes, in the demands of the imprescriptible rights, they boldly present themselves as the true meaning and value of our existence. ... (1971b:392)

Simmel is writing here about the desires of some mystical religions and some forms of modern art to get past the mediations of forms and to an immediate experience of reality. He says this is not possible: "Life wishes here to obtain something which it cannot reach. It desires to transcend all forms and to appear in its naked immediacy. Yet the process of thinking, wishing, and formatting can only substitute one form for another. They can never replace the forms as such by life which as such transcends the forms" (1971b:392-393). Here he is describing an overarching contradiction based upon the human condition in which humans must use forms to understand and socially engage in and through the world. Our immediate engagement with the world is inevitably confronted with the mediation of forms, forms which are fixed and imposed upon us. As individuals we are more than simply robots mechanically responding to the forms, yet this volitional or free side of human beings inevitably is forced to engage with these forms.

The concept of dialectics goes much farther in Simmel's theory however. We see it in much of his work, from his analysis of money or fashion to his descriptions of types of people, such as the stranger. Some of these are described below.

The last set of concepts central to Simmel's theorizing that will be mentioned here are subjective experience and objective culture. To understand Simmel's way of thinking, one must begin with the individual experiencing the world. When the individual uses thought, he or she creates a distance and creates forms. These thoughts, organized as forms of thought, stand in relation to, at a distance from, experience. Individuals create understandings and do things in the world that convey this understanding. A painter imagines a painting and paints it. In ways, this process is quite similar to the process of externalization described by Marx (see Chapter Two) and many others. We externalize our understandings of the world. We produce forms of understanding and then act in the world based upon these understandings. These products that are directly and immediately connected to the individual experience are called **subjective culture**. However, subjective culture cannot be understood alone. It must be understood in relation to the world within which an individual experiences life. Specifically, subjective culture can only be understood in its relationship to **objective culture**. Objective culture, again using Marx's terminology, is the objectified world. Objective culture engages with the individual from the outside. Objective culture consists of the forms that people have produced and that the individual inevitably has to engage with in his or her production of subjective culture. The original writers of the Bible, for example, embodied their subjective understandings and used their conceptual forms to create, to write, the Bible. They wrote what they personally thought. They put their thoughts into objective form, in the book called the Bible. But once the Bible was written, and reproduced, and once people from near and far found it to be meaningful, it assumed a reality of objective culture. In short, subjective culture cannot be understood separately from objective culture. These are defined in relation to one another.

Yet while "There can be no subjective culture without objective culture" (1971c:234), a central theme in much of Simmel's theory is that objective culture "comes to constitute an autonomous realm" (1971c:234) particular in the modern world. Objective culture becomes a force detached from the individual that is imposed upon the individual. (In other words, objective culture is reified. The concept of reification is discussed in Chapter Eight.) It assumes a life of its own. But it nevertheless can only be understood in relation to subjective culture. As we see below, this is a central claim in Simmel's analysis of money and the modern world.

Another feature of Simmel's theorizing concerns its relativism. Simmel presents a philosophical argument in favor of an epistemological position of relativism. Epistemology is the branch of philosophy concerning how we know things. How do we know what is true or false, for example, about the world? How do we know we can eat an apple, but not a rock? How do we know that if we throw a rock in the air, it will come down? Simmel notes that there is a difference between concepts and reality. Concepts represent reality. (They do so by being constituted through forms.) We can never know reality directly. We can only know it through the concepts we use. The conceptual forms are the intermediaries between us and the world. In other words, the objective world can never be known directly. It can only be known through conceptual forms. But these forms are diverse and changeable. They are relative and may or may not accurately represent reality. There is no certain anchor through which we can see with certainty that this is the reality of the world. All realities are mediated by conceptual forms. "Truth means the relationship between representations .... Relativity is not a qualification of an otherwise independent notion of truth but is the essential feature of truth" (1990:114-16). Simmel notes that this philosophical perspective could lead to skepticism, but it does not have to. It could lead to a view that no claim is better or more accurate or truthful than any other and therefore that no one idea should be believed rather than any other. All are equally legitimate. But he argues that relativism does not necessarily have to lead here.

He makes his argument by embracing dialectics and by embracing the claim of heuristics. Human understanding is fundamentally dialectical in nature. On the one hand, we make sense out of the world by focusing on particular elements in it and understanding them in their particularities. On the other hand, we make sense out of the world by locating the particulars within an overarching general framework of the world. We synthesize the particulars into a general. The first of these is a view of pluralism or multiplicity. The second is a view of unity. He notes that "the development of philosophy, and of individual thinking, moves from multiplicity to unity and from unity to multiplicity. The history of thought shows that it is vain to consider any of these viewpoints definitive. The structure of our reason in relation to objects demands equal validity for both principles ... Our innermost vital consciousness oscillates between this separateness and the solidarity among the elements of our existence" (1990:111). As a result, he rejects any arguments that favor one side or the other of these and goes on to argue that the solution to relativism then is to see this problem, and other associated ones, as problems of heuristics. "The essential point is not that these two trends constitute life, but that they are interdependent in a heuristic form" (1990:111). By "heuristic" he means that these ideas should be seen as tools of understanding rather than claims about the factual workings of the world. They are concepts that can help us understand our world, and nothing more.

He makes a similar argument when defending his position against charges that it is an idealist one. Idealism is the view that knowledge of the world is dependent first and foremost on the way the mind works rather than upon the way the world external to the individual actually is. (The use of the word idealism here should not be confused with the way it is used in Marxism (see Chapter Two). The word refers to something quite distinct here.) Idealism is traditionally said to be riddled with the problems of relativism.

But when one considers dialectics and heuristics this is no longer a problem. He begins by distinguishing the different viewpoints:

> The mind creates the world – the only world that we can discuss and that is real for us – according to its receptivity and its ability to construct forms. But on the other hand, this world is also the original source of the mind ... Considered historically, the mind with all its forms and contents is a product of the world – of the same world which is in turn a product of the mind because it is a world of representations. If these two generic possibilities are rigidly conceptualized they result in a disturbing contradiction. This does not come about, however, if they are regarded as heuristic principles which stand in relationship of alternation and interaction. ... The principal contradiction is dissolved by an interpretation of both as heuristic principles; this transforms their opposition into an interaction and their mutual negation into an endless process of interaction. (1990:113)

In short, he argues that criticisms that his theory is relativistic are misplaced. When one reconceptualizes the basic matter at hand, one sees that the only viable approach to take in understanding human knowledge, and social behaviors, is to begin with the dynamic interactions between forms and modes of being.

Fashion

In one way or another the dialectic between objective culture and subjective being is found in much of Simmel's writings. It is found, for example, in his essay "Fashion" (1971d). Here Simmel argues that fashion operates within the poles of uniformity and distinction, or unity and the particular. That is, fashion, in clothing, in consumer goods, etc., is the reflection simultaneously of an individual's attempt to be at one and the same time part of the group while being distinct from it at the same time. As he notes:

> Fashion is the imitation of a given example and satisfies the demand for social adaptation; it leads the individual upon the road which all travel, it furnishes a general condition, which resolves the conduct of every individual into a mere example. At the same time it satisfies no less degree a need of differentiation, the tendency toward dissimilarity, the desire for change and contrast, on the one hand by a constant change of contents, which gives to the fashion of today an individual stamp as opposed to that of yesterday and of tomorrow..." (1971d:296)

Individuals simultaneously externalize their individual sense of who they are through the use of the objective cultural elements of fashion. Different groups approach fashion in different ways. People in traditional, non-modern societies do not have the need that modern people do to express their individuality (see below). Conformity is instead cherished, and this works against the embrace of fashion. In the modern, industrial world, the embrace of fashion is not uniform across social classes and fashion operates in different ways in different classes. For example, the poorer classes are less inclined to be fashion conscious than the rich classes. The upper classes use fashion to distinguish themselves from the lower classes. Simmel notes the particular importance of fashion for the modern "middle class." The "increased social and political freedom" of modern society in general and specifically as these apply to the "middle class" have created condition whereby this class is inclined to embrace fashion to express itself. The middle class is a class that embodies the changing times and changing circumstance, and "classes and individuals who demand constant change, because the rapidity of their development gives them the advantage over others, find in fashion something that keeps pace with their own soul-movements. Social advance above all is favorable to the rapid change of fashion …" (1971d:318).

Fashion, Simmel notes, is fleeting. It is not permanent. Things constantly go in and out of fashion. It also has an interesting relationship to time. "Fashion always occupies the dividing-line between the past and the future, and consequently conveys a stronger feeling of the present …" (1971d:303). This is a reason that explains why fashion was not such a major focus of concern for people in traditional and non-modern societies, and why it is indeed such a focus in modern, industrial societies:

> We can discover one of the reasons why in these latter days fashion exerts such a powerful influence on our consciousness in the circumstance that the great, permanent, unquestionable convictions [in the modern era] are continually losing strength, as a consequence of which the transitory and vacillating elements of life acquire more room to display their activities. The break with the past, which, for more than a century, civilized mankind has been laboring unceasingly to bring about, make the consciousness turn more and more to the present. (1971d:303)

Fashion fits this bill nicely. He goes on to note the great power of fashion in the modern world: "It may almost be considered a sign of the increased power of fashion, that it has overstepped the bounds of its original domain, which comprised only personal externals, and has acquired an increasing influence over taste, over theoretical convictions, and even over the moral foundations of life" (1971d:303-304).

Overcoming Antinomies

We have encountered and described a number of antinomies, or contradictions, found in much social theory in Chapter One of this book (e.g. micro-macro, agency-structure, etc.). In one way or another, theorists are forced to address somehow these issues. They may simply ignore them, or they may create theoretical ways of managing or overcoming them. But these antinomies are part of theorizing. Simmel routinely claims to have overcome many of the central antinomies in sociological theorizing. We have already seen above how he addresses the micro-macro issue, that is, the issue of the individual and society. Society, he says, "merely is the name for a number of individuals, connected by interaction" (1950:10). Yet the issue is not so simple. It becomes more complicated when we consider how Simmel addresses the conceptual antinomy of realism versus nominalism. This is a classic philosophical issue. Realism is the claim that an aggregate of particular things becomes a new total thing that has a distinct reality separate and above the particular things. The particulars together do not form a new entity, which is a new united thing distinct from those parts. Nominalism is the claim that an aggregate of particular things does not become a new total thing. Reality instead is comprised of these individual things. In the context of sociology, the issue is whether society is a real and distinct entity, or whether it is nothing more than the sum total of individuals. Do only individuals exist, or does society exist? Above we have seen Simmel's views on this matter. From this it appears that Simmel is embracing a nominalist perspective. However, that is not quite right. As Levine and others argue, Simmel claims to have developed an approach that overcomes this divide. Levine writes that,

> Simmel rejects both views, arguing on the one hand that the idea of a societal substance, of an independent collective entity, does not correspond to anything that can be observed. The place where all societal events occur is within the minds of individuals. On the other hand, there is a way of looking at those psychic events that is not psychological, but that is able to perceive the synthetic realities of processes and relations through which individuals act upon and with one another. (1971a:xxxiii-iv)

Simmel uses the example of the Gothic style of architecture to make his point. Just as the Gothic style of architecture is real and is distinct from the individual buildings that have this style, so to society is real. "When we inquire into the Gothic style, its laws, its development, we do not describe any particular cathedral or place. Yet the *material* that makes up the unit we are investigating – "Gothic style" – we gain only from a study of the details of cathedrals and palaces" (1950:5). In much the same way, the sociologist can speak of society as a distinct entity, distinct from the individuals that constitute it.

Take another example: His views of Marx's materialist perspective. You will recall that Marx is a materialist. He based his materialism on a reaction to Hegel's idealism. Both Hegel and Marx saw the world as being comprised of these two realms: the realm of material conditions and the realm of ideas. They of course disagreed on which is foundational to social life. Simmel engages with Marx on this point. At first glance it may appear that Simmel's approach might be best characterized as an idealist perspective. But one must recall that he grounds his understandings, of forms and of all else, in experience. As such, what does he think of Marx's materialism? Simmel addresses this point in his intriguing book *The Philosophy of Money*. He argues that Marx's formulation of materialism is wrongheaded because it conceptually collapses "having" into "being" and as a result cannot see that this relationship and this dialectic – between having and being -- is central: "Marx's question of whether the consciousness of men determines their being or their being determines their consciousness is here answered in one sphere of existence since men's being in Marx's sense includes having" (1990:307). Simmel here is noting that just because someone owns something does not mean he will automatically relate to that thing in only one way. The relationship a factory owner has to his factory is different from the relationship someone who owns a share of stock in the Apple Computer company has with the stock. Simmel is saying that one must appreciate the particular forms of relations an individual has to ownership, or for that matter to any relation in the economy. Marx wrongfully collapses these elements into one – ownership.

History and the Modern World

Two central themes in Simmel's sociology are history and the impact or consequences of the modern world. He believed history was a central part of the sociology project. "The first problem area of sociology ... consisted of the whole of historical life insofar as it is formed societally" (1950:22). The social scientist should understand history using the same concepts Simmel developed to understand all parts of the social world. That is, the task of the sociologist studying history is to identify forms in history. The task was not to understand the particulars of a historical event or period, but instead to relate this historical event or period to forms such that one might see common patterns of behaviors in the social actions of groups operating at different times and places. As he notes, "social groups [in history] which are the most diverse imaginable in purpose and general significance, may nevertheless show identical forms of behavior toward one another on the part of their individual members." He goes on to list some of the forms that are relevant to the study of history, forms which he identifies and employs in other contexts: "We find superiority and subordination, competition, division of labor, formation of parties, representation, inner solidarity coupled with exclusiveness toward the outside, and innumerable similar features in the state, in a religious community, in a band of conspirators, in an economic association, in an art school, in the family. However diverse the interests are that give rise to these sociations, the *forms* in which the interests are realized may yet be identical" (1950:20).

Simmel's approach to the sociological understanding of history is based in part upon the idea that any form of knowledge, about history or about anything, is limited. Any knowledge selects certain features of reality and focuses upon these to the exclusion of others. History is a movement of forms that emerge, synthesize, and decline, only to be replaced or altered by other forms. When writing about the history of culture, he notes that "history, as an empirical science, concerns itself with changes in the forms of culture" (1971b:376). This gives the impression that Simmel is embracing some sort of perspectivism. That is, it suggests history can be understood in many ways, depending upon the perspective the scholar takes and depending upon what specific feature of the historical landscape the scholar focuses upon. While it is true he does embrace such thinking (see above), he also claims, on the other hand, that it is possible to identify some universal tendencies and forces in history. He says, for example, that the history of culture could be seen as an endless struggle between "life" and "form." By life he is referring to the essential mode of being that exists independent of, or primary to, the forms which we create to understand our realities. He explains the relation between life and form:

> Life ... can manifest itself only in particular forms; yet, owing to its essential restlessness, life constantly struggles against its own products [i.e. forms], which have become fixed and do not move along with it. This process manifests itself as the displacement of an old form by a new one. This constant change in the content of culture, even of whole cultural styles, is the sign of the infinite fruitfulness of life. At the same time, it marks the deep contradiction between life's eternal flux and the objective validity and authenticity of the forms through which it proceeds. It moves constantly between death and resurrection – between resurrection and death.... Life as such is formless, yet incessantly

generates forms for itself. As soon as each form appears, however, it demands a validity which transcends the movement and is emancipated from the pulse of life. (1971b:376-377)

Simmel builds upon these ideas and develops a theory of history which is comprised of a set of distinct stages or period. In each historical period, at least in the cultural realm, there is a central idea or theme that propels action forward. In the ancient Greek world, the central is "idea of being, of the uniform, the substantive, the divine." In the Middle Ages, being was replaced by God as the central concept of the age. God was "at once the source and goal of all reality." From the Renaissance through late seventeen hundreds, the central concept was nature. Nature "appeared as the only being and truth." Beginning in the late seventeen hundreds a new central theme arose. The "ego" or "spiritual personality" emerged as the new central concept: "Some thinkers represented the totality of being as a creation of the ego; others saw personal identity as a task, the essential task for man. Thus, the ego, human individuality, appeared either as an absolute moral demand or as the metaphysical purpose of the world." In the eighteen hundreds, there was no one central theme "unless, perhaps, we give this title to the idea of *society*, which for many nineteenth century thinkers epitomized the reality of life." This then gave way at the end of the century to a new theme: "The concept of life was raised to a central place, in which perceptions of reality were united with metaphysical, psychological, moral, and aesthetic values" (1971b:378-379).

A more important idea in Simmel's theorizing was that of modernity. Simmel, like many others of his age, and particularly like many other intellectuals from the German speaking world, such as Weber, was greatly concerned about what modernity was doing to individuals. Like Weber and Marx, Simmel believed modern, urban, industrial society was not simply changing the individual and his or her relationships, but it was harming the individual and his or her relationships. Simmel identifies a number of forces that impact the individual in the modern world and shows the dialectical effects these have had. The division of labor is one such force. He notes that the "unlimited competition and individual specialization through the division of labor have affected individual culture in a way that shows them not to be its most suited promoters" (1950:84). The division of labor creates problems for many reasons. One of these is that while it enhances individualism by allowing individuals to do things that are distinct from others it also negates individualism by necessarily creating hierarchies and power. The division of labor creates objectivated powers that command the individual. Thus, the individual is negated (1950:82). Another force in the modern world that dialectically and negatively impacts the individual is the changing relationship of the individual to forms, more specifically of life to objective culture. Modern culture is fundamentally objective culture. We discussed objective culture earlier. It is the objectified understandings of the world. The central point here is that objective culture imposes itself upon the individual, as if from the outside. Objective culture, particularly in the modern world, has become reified. Reification was discussed in Chapter Two. It is the process by which ideas and things created by humans exist independently of humans and assume a life of their own in relation to humans. They become like elements of nature. In the modern world objective culture has grown stronger, and the individual in turn has grown weaker. That is, the individual in the modern world is increasingly at the mercy of objective culture. And yet at the same time, the modern world liberates the individual from the shackles of earlier times. The modern individual thus has more choices.

This argument directly bears on his overarching theme regarding modern life. This concerns the relationship of life to forms in the modern era. The essential force of life has become a central element in the modern western world. Simmel describes the philosophies of Nietzsche and Schopenhauer to make his point here. He also describes modern art movements. The modern world has produced a seemingly endless desire for the individual to experience life in its fullness. Yet at the same time, the modern world has produced objectivated culture. It has produced more and more, and stronger and stronger forms, through which individual necessarily have to engage. It is this conflict – between the boundless self-seeking to experience life and the constraints imposed upon it by objective culture – that is central to the modern era.

The modern world produces another set of conditions that negatively impacts the individual. This is the matter of necessarily reducing complex and full human interactions to simplified interactions through which individuals engage in only one dimension. For example, as we see below, Simmel describes money and the economic exchanges of money in the modern world as a way in which individuals interact based upon one single, quantified dimension. The complexities of social interaction based upon human interactions have increasingly been replaced by the narrowing down of the relationship into channels that can be quantified, such as money. This has a sterilizing effect upon individuals and their relations.

Many of the themes related to the effects of modernity just noted are seen in his essay "The Metropolis and Modern Life" (1971e), originally published in 1903. For Simmel, urban life, i.e. the life in a metropolis, is as central to the modern world as is the division of labor. He identifies a number of specific features and consequences of urban life and examines the impact this form of life has for the individual. In cities, the individual's psychological foundation changes. The individual must resort to an "intellectualistic" or rational orientation toward life as the result of the overwhelming stimuli, emotional and otherwise, encountered. The individual resorts to cool, rational, calculating ways of being in order to cope with the overwhelming amount and diversity of stimuli. This fosters a detached, non-emotional and uncaring mode of being. The rational, calculating personality is further nurtured by the money economy. In addition, urban life produces a "blasé" attitude. It produces an attitude of indifference. The individual distances himself from personal engagement with his or her world. Money becomes the great leveler: "To the extent that money, with its colorlessness and indifferent quality, can become a common denominator of all values it has become the frightful leveler – it hollows out the core of things, their peculiarities, their specific values and their uniqueness and incomparability in a way which is beyond repair" (1971e:330). In effect, urban life has a dialectical impact upon the individual. On the one hand it frees the individual through the division of labor and through the nature of urban life, but on the other hand it causes individuals to become less and less individuated and causes them to be all alike in their cold, rational engagements with each other.

Social Types

Simmel describes and analyzes a number of social types in his writings, including the stranger, the poor, the miser and the spendthrift, as well as the adventurer. We see many of the themes described above in each of these essays. Here we briefly describe a couple of these social types.

The Poor

In the essay "The Poor" (1971f), Simmel applies his conceptual formulations to an understanding of the social type identified as poor. At the heart of the analysis lies the relationships through which the poor are defined. He specifically focuses upon the relationship of the poor to the rest of modern society, and upon the nature of welfare given to the poor. This relationship is one defined by rights and obligations. In the modern world, the poor are deemed to have a right to financial support. In contrast, the rest of society is not oriented toward the poor by rights, but by obligations. The rest of society has an obligation to aid the poor. Simmel analyzes the various implications of this imbalance. For example, he contrasts the form this relationship took in the pre-modern era with the form it takes in the modern era. In the pre-modern era, the relation between the poor and the non-poor was local and personal. The alms to the poor were given by the local community and not by a distant state. The relationship of rights and duties then was also personal, and the obligation was a moral one. But in the modern era, the impersonal state provides for the needs of the poor. The relationship changes. It is no longer one based on morality, and the notion of obligation takes a different form.

As with all of his work, he identifies a number of essential contradictions in the nature of the poor, and he shows how the type, or form, of the poor, can be compared with other types such as the stranger (see below) or with being poor in various social contexts. For example, the poor are at one and the same time part of society and are external to society. "[T]he poor are located in a way outside the group; but this is no more than a peculiar mode of interaction which binds them into a unity with the whole in its widest sense" (1971f:158). He also shows how the form of the relationship between the poor and the non-poor is replicated in various social settings, such as the family, where there are richer members and poorer members, and religious congregations, and societies at large. The answer to the question, "Where does the poor belong?" will be different in the different social settings.

The Stranger

We see similar themes of dialectics and relationships and forms in his essay "The Stranger" (1971g). The stranger is not a traveler. Instead, it is an outsider person living amongst a group of people. The stranger is embedded in a set of dialectical relations with others. The stranger is at once close to others and is remote or distant from them. He writes: "The union of closeness and remoteness involved in every human relationship is patterned in a way that may be succinctly formulated as follows: the distance within this relationship indicates that one who is close by is remote, but his strangeness indicates that one who is remote is near" (1971g:143). Simmel identities a number of characteristics of this role. One of these is that the stranger is not "Bound by roots to particular constituents and partisan dispositions of the group" and as such is able to maintain a "distinctly "objective" attitude." This objectivity places the stranger in the position of being the one that members of the community feel comfortable in sharing their secrets. The stranger is a safe person in this regard. The objectivity of the stranger also gives him or her more "freedom": "the objective man is not bound by ties which could prejudice his perceptions, his understandings, and his assessment of data" (1971g:146). As such, the stranger is able to "examine conditions with less prejudice" and is sought after in this regard. Another characteristic of the stranger and his or her relationship to the community lies in the commonality and distance he simultaneously has with others. "The stranger is close to us in so far as we feel between him and ourselves similarities of nationality or social position, of occupation or of general human nature. He is far from us insofar as these similarities extend beyond him and us, and connect us only because they connect a great many people" (1971g:147). In sum, the social location of the social type of the stranger is one riddled with contradictions that determine the nature of the stranger and his relationship with others.

The Philosophy of Money

Simmel's book *The Philosophy of Money* (1990) is not very much about economics, despite what the title suggests. It is not even very much about money in itself, though of course money is superficially the focus. Instead, this book can in some ways be understood as a summary of some of the main aspects of Simmel's overarching sociological theory. Many of the themes noted earlier are present in this book. The significance of the division of labor, the changes brought about with modernity, the dialectics of social realities, the centrality of exchange in understanding social life, the objectification of the modern world and its impact upon individuals and upon social relations, these are just a few of the recurrent themes found in this work. Similarly, one can see many themes Simmel shares with other German social theorists of the eighteen and early nineteen hundreds. His concerns about the negative effects of money on individuals and social relationships most certainly echoes that of Marx. Weber concerns about rationalization are also paralleled here. But *The Philosophy of Money* is different in a number of respects from his other works, and it is making an argument that is distinctive from Marx and Weber and others. At its heart, it is a book about value and how value is organized in the modern world. And the analytic depth by which Simmel examines the ways in which money impacts the individual and social relations distinguishes his work from that of Weber and Marx.

We can think of *The Philosophy of Money* as being organized along three topical themes. One aspect of the book is devoted to a philosophical understanding of the abstract qualities of money and specifically how money and value relate to each other. Value rather than money is really the central concern of this book. A second aspect of this work concerns the ways in which money affects social relationships. Money, Simmel tells us, "is entirely a sociological phenomenon, a form of human interaction…" (1990:172). The third aspect concerns the ways in which money affects the individual. We can look at each of these in turn.

The heart of *The Philosophy of Money* is about value, and the relationship of money to value in the modern world. Money is "the objectification of subjective values" (1990:65). The individual human subject values this or that and does things in the world that reflects this valuing. He or she might buy or sell something. He or she might put a price on something. This is objectification. It is putting out in the world the ideas and values held by an individual. By putting a price on something, the individual is moving the realm of value from the individual, subjective level to the social level. As the value is out there in the social world, it is now in relations with others. Individuals now are in relations with others, and most significantly individuals are in relation to money. Money is not simply the medium through which individuals interact with others to decide upon value (as embodied in money). Money takes on a different role as a consequence. It becomes a value in itself.

Simmel identifies a number of themes and concepts related to this objectification. One of these is the concept of distance. Distance plays a crucial role in his analysis of money. It does so in various ways. One way it does so is that money creates distance between the individual and the objects that are represented through the value of money. This is part of a larger pattern in the modern world that has increasingly become objectified. A greater and greater distance is created between the objective culture and the individual. Simmel also makes a curious comment about the relationship of distance to value: Things lose their relative value if they are too easy to obtain, i.e. are too near, and they lose their value if they are too hard to obtain, i.e. are too far. Things that are between these two extremes are given the highest value (1990:72).

Money also is greatly responsible, along with the growth of the division of labor, for the flattening or leveling of the modern world. Money turns things that have different qualitative characteristics into things that have the same quantitative characteristics. Oranges and dust brooms now become somehow equivalent through the use of money, when in fact they are fundamentally distinct. All the distinctiveness of objects is rendered unimportant with the use of money because all the distinctiveness is erased through the quantitative valuation of money. This argument is quite similar to that raised by Marx, though Simmel locates the source of the dynamic not in capitalism (or more broadly within a dialectical materialist perspective) but instead in money, in modernity, and in the division of labor.

Another couple of general elements of money and its relation to value in the modern world is rationalization and reification. We have discussed these themes in one way or another above, but in *The Philosophy of Money*, they become central to the argument. Money as the overwhelmingly dominant form of value in the modern world produces an objective culture that assumes a life of its own, separate and apart from the individual. This objectified culture imposes itself upon the individual as an overwhelming and alien force. It is outside the control or production of the individual. Closely associated with this notion is the idea of rationalization. The modern world is characterized, in no small measure as the result of money, by rationalization. Money forces individuals to think in quantitative terms rather than in qualitative terms. Simmel notes "the calculating character of modern times" (1990:443). It forces individuals to have an "intellectual" rather than an "emotional" orientation to the world. Buying or selling something in the marketplace demands or at least calls upon the participants to rationally calculate the price of the goods. Emotions are deemed not merely irrelevant but harmful in this process.

Money significantly impacts social relations. For Simmel, exchange is an essential concept in sociology, and the main vehicle of the exchange of value is money. As such, money is central to an understanding of social relations in the modern world. He describes the relation of money and exchange to social relations: "The interactions between the primary elements that produce the social unit are replaced [in money exchange relations] by the fact that each of these elements establishes an independent relation to a higher or intermediate organ. Money belongs to this category of reified social functions. The function of exchange, as a direct interaction between individuals, becomes crystallized in the form of money as an independent structure" (1990:175). Simmel goes on to note that exchange, and by implication money, is the essence of society:

> The exchange of the products of labour, or any other possessions, is obviously one of the purest and most primitive forms of human socialization; not in the sense that "society" already existed and then brought about acts of exchange but, on the contrary, that exchange is one of the functions that all the individual relations of its members ... can develop within its framework or be represented by it: it is only the synthesis or the general term for the totality of these specific interactions. .... It is ... almost a tautology [that is, a circular argument] to say that exchange brings about socialization: for exchange is a form of socialization. It is one of those relations through which a number of individuals become a social group, and "society" is identical with the sum total of these relations. (1990:175)

In the modern world, money has a particular effect upon social relations. Money, particularly as it is paired with the division of labor and urbanization, produces increasingly impersonal forms of relations. When money, particularly in its modern form, is used people interact with others in cool and detached ways. We interact more with the role of the person with whom we are interacting than with the individual person. Money removed the personal, the emotional, from the interaction and replaces it with a detached, mechanical form of relation in which individuals interact with one another as if interacting with objects or things. The particular individual with whom one interacts in an economic exchange becomes inconsequential to the form of the relationship, which is one of quantitative exchange.

This increase in impersonal interactions is closely related to another effect of money on social relations. Simmel argues that individuals become increasing "indifferent" to others. That is, individuals no longer see and act toward others as full human beings who have value distinct from other values. Instead, individuals are treated as simply other things in the world that one uses in the process of exchange of money. The uniqueness of other humans becomes drained. As economic exchanges are necessarily oriented toward one dimension, i.e. the value of the thing being exchanged, the total personality of the individuals is negated. The total personality "is almost completely destroyed under the conditions of the money economy" (1990:296).

The modern money economy also greatly impacts the individual. An individual's freedom is affected in contradictory ways. On the one hand, the individual is allowed more autonomy in a money economy. For example, Simmel describes a hypothetical example from the Middle Ages: "The lord of a manor who can demand a quantity of beer or poultry or honey from a serf thereby determines the activity of the latter in a certain direction. But the moment he imposes merely a money levy the peasant is free, is so far as he can decide whether to keep the bees or cattle or anything else" (1990:286). With the introduction of the medium of money, the nature of social relations changes and some elements of this enhance human freedom. But equally as important, the individual's freedom is harmed in the money economy. The objective culture which necessarily assumes ever increasing power in a money economy in turn bears down upon the ever increasingly isolated individual. The individual becomes relatively more powerless, less free, as the objective culture assumes greater and greater power over him. The individual becomes "atomized" in the face of objective culture.

According to Simmel, the modern world with its money economy is characterized by intellectual rather than emotional engagements. The modern world has a "rationalistic character" to it (1990:443). "One may characterize the intellectual functions that are used [in the modern world] in coping with the world and in regulating both individual and social relations as *calculating* functions. Their cognitive ideal is to conceive of the world as an arithmetical problem…" (1990:444). This modern way stands in contrast to the "more impulsive, emotionally determined character of earlier epochs" (1990:444).

All of the above leads the individual in the modern world to assume a "**blasé attitude**." Specifically, the "leveling" effects of money turns everything into one form of equivalence, money. Things that were once qualitatively different are now quantifiably comparable. This process makes all things the same at a basic level. Everything is equivalent in that everything can be exchanged the same way that everything else can be exchanged. The blasé person of the modern world "has completely lost the feelings for value differences. He experiences all things as being of an equally dull and grey hue, as not worth getting excited about, particularly where the will is concerned. The decisive movement here … is not the devaluation of things as such, but indifference to their specific qualities from which the whole liveliness of feeling and volition originates" (1990:256). In short, the money economy affects the entire personality, and it fosters a blasé attitude in the entire individual.

Summary

Simmel was a German Jewish social philosopher writing in the late eighteen and early nineteen hundreds who developed a speculative, micro-approach toward the understanding of social behavior and social order. His thinking was influential on American and German sociology in the early nineteen hundreds, but this influence declined in America in the middle parts of the last century. It has increased once again in recent decades, at least according to some. He sought to understand the forms of social behavior and social interaction and the essential dynamic nature involved in the ways these forms were realized in lived social realities. The dialectical realities created by all forms propels social action forward. Much of his theorizing sought to identify the many contradictions found in various forms of social life. Toward that end, he identified and analyzed various forms of social types, including a study of the concept of the poor, of the stranger, of life in the city, etc.

His theory is anchored in several concepts, including: content and forms; sociation; relations; reciprocity; dialectics, and subjective and objective culture. The concepts of form and content are central to his approach. We understand our worlds through the forms we assign to it. Forms are like generalized concepts in our minds. Forms give shape to the real world; they allow us to understand the real world. Content is comprised of "drive, interest, purpose, inclination, psychic state, movement" (1971a:40). Content is the point of experience within which forms are realized. Sociation is the structure of lived social interactions. It is associated with the idea of society. Sociation is the structure through which form and content are realized in lived social interactions. Relations and reciprocity are also significant concepts in Simmel's theorizing. Relations involve not only social relations, but relations between forms and between forms and contents. Reciprocity means that any thing or event can only be understood in relation to other things and events. It cannot be understood independently. As a result, the meaning of a thing or event is never fixed or static. Simmel embraced the concept of dialectics. Every reality and every form of sociation consists of dialectics or contradictions. Contradictions fuel social action. Subjective culture and objective culture are two further concepts important to this theory. Subjective culture is the immediate and direct experience and expression of culture. Objective culture consists of the forms that people have produced, and that the individual inevitably has to engage with in his or her production of subjective culture. Objective culture consists of the objectified world, external to the individual. Subjective culture cannot exist without objective culture. However, one of the themes in Simmel's theorizing is that objective culture in the modern world has come to "constitute an autonomous realm." Objective culture is or has become detached from the individual. Simmel embraces the epistemological position of relativism.

He also was acutely interested in understanding life in the modern world. Content, forms, sociation, etc. could all be used toward that end. He was interested in understanding modernity and the impact the modern world was having upon the individual. He specifically was concerned with the growth of power in objectivated culture, as well as the structural forces external to the individual and the impact these have on the individual. The modern world is alienating. The modern world is characterized in part by urban civilization and by money, and Simmel saw both of these as alienating. The growth of objective culture and the tension of objective culture with subjective culture is another characteristic of modern life, which has consequences for individuals and for social relations. His concerns about modernity led to his studies of life in cities. They also led to the production of his most influential book, *The Philosophy of Money*.

Discussion Questions

1. Many of Simmel's ideas are rather abstract and speculative. This might make his theoretical approach difficult to assess using social scientific research. For example, how would one develop and then test one or another hypothesis related to his concepts? The issue becomes even more complicated when one considers the dialectical and relational nature of his theorizing. Is his theory capable of being scientifically tested? If so, how? If not, is this a major flaw in the approach?

2. Much of Simmel's theorizing seems to revolve around the notions of perspectivism. We saw this in his approach to history. This suggests there are many different and competing ways of understanding one reality. Is this correct? If so, what does this suggest for the traditional view of sociology being a social science based upon empirical evidence?

3. According to Simmel, does "society" exist? What is society? Does it exist as a reality independent of the individuals who comprise this society? Does his answer to these questions pose any conceptual problems or contradictions for his theory? If so, what might these be?

Chapter Six: Tocqueville, Democracy, and Sociological Theory

What should sociology and sociological theory be today? Should they be aloof from contemporary world events, or should they engage directly with trying to understand and relate their approach to the social realities of today? It is arguably the case that at some points in history it may be morally defensible to adhere to the former position. But at other points, I believe it is a moral imperative to orient sociology and sociological theory to the matters of the day. One of the central issues confronting American society today, and for that matter many other democratic societies, is the rise of authoritarianism (some would say fascism) which stands in stark opposition to, and is a threat to, democracy. As many scholars have argued, the rise of Donald Trump to the leadership of America, for a second time, embodies this threat. Sociology and sociological theory have a moral obligation to assess and to address this threat with the intellectual tools available to them. It is in this light that I present a chapter on the sociological works of Alexis de Tocqueville (1805-1859). If one wishes to intellectually defend democracy against authoritarianism, a good place to start would be with an understanding of Tocqueville's analysis of democracy.

Most, if not almost all, American sociologists today would undoubtedly claim that Tocqueville's approach is not sociological and should not be considered as such. Most would likely claim his work lies with the field of political science. I wish to argue otherwise and at times such as this his work cries out for attention. And I am not alone in believing that Tocqueville's studies should be regarded as works of sociology as much if not more so than as political science. Perhaps the sociologist most well known for claiming Tocqueville as a sociologist is the influential mid-twentieth century French sociologist Raymond Aron. Aron is most well known for his scathing indictment of French sociology in the post-World War Two era. In *The Opium of the Intellectuals* (2001), he sharply criticizes French sociology for being overwhelmingly Marxist. To be anyone in French sociology one had to be a Marxist. The ideological blinders put on by such a situation impedes sociology, Aron says. (Lest one think that Aron was a conservative, he was in reality a liberal, in the classic rather than the popular sense of the term.)

Aron wrote several books in which he also argued that Tocqueville, as well as Comte and Montesquieu and others, should be located with the sociology canon of great thinkers (1998). He argues that the methodology of

Tocqueville as well as the objects of study put him squarely within the terrain of sociology. For example, Aron argues that Tocqueville regularly employed ideal types – specifically the ideal type of democracy – in his writings (see Weber), even though he did not identify them as such. Tocqueville also focused on groups and group behaviors, a decidedly sociological approach. We see this specifically in his analysis of the *The Old Regime and the French Revolution* (1955) where Tocqueville identifies four classes in pre-Revolutionary France – the nobility, the bourgeoisie, the working classes, and the peasants. He systematically assesses how these classes were organized or not and how they interacted with each other. This is a decidedly sociological analysis. These are just two of the many themes and topics that Aron identifies within Tocqueville's works that he believes makes the latter a sociologist.

Some American sociologists also recognize Tocqueville for his sociology. Perhaps most notably are Robert Bellah, Richard Madson and their colleagues. I discuss below their classic sociological work *Habits of the Heart* (1996) – the title itself is a phrase from Tocqueville's *Democracy in America*. Here it is worth noting that the authors see Tocqueville as providing a theory of democratic culture, and they show how Tocqueville's understandings can be useful in understanding American society.

Before exploring Tocqueville's ideas, a few words should be said about his biography. Alexis de Tocqueville (1805-1859) was born and raised in a lower aristocratic French family soon after the French Revolution. To understand Tocqueville and his views on democracy it is important to recognize this biographical fact, and it is equally important to recognize the historic times in which he lived. The 1789 French Revolution was a dramatic event that overthrew centuries of aristocratic government. Moreover, it overthrew the entire established social order, anchored in such things as tradition, religion, aristocratic privilege, etc. Until then, French society was ruled by the nobility and the Catholic Church. In contrast to the America experience where there was no established aristocratic order prior to the American Revolution, the French Revolution was a dramatic upheaval of not just the political, but the social and cultural, order. France experienced decades of chaos and turmoil after the Revolution before any sense of a stable democracy was established there. The Revolution was bloody and chaotic and last several years. This was followed by Napoleon Bonaparte taking over and marching across Europe with his military (twice). This was then followed by attempts at establishing a workable democracy. At one point, the French reinstituted a monarchy, seeking to establish a republican monarchy, hoping for stability. This collapsed in 1848 and in the early 1850s, Louis Napoleon, the great nephew of Napolean Bonaparte was elected to the Presidency. He promptly called himself emperor and cancelled future elections. He ruled until 1870 and the Franco-Prussian war. In short, the first half of the nineteenth century in France, showed that they had great difficulties establishing a stable democracy.

Tocqueville was born and raised in this tumultuous environment. He was an aristocrat by birth, living in a time of nascent democracy. (His father was an aristocrat who never lost faith in aristocracy.) Nevertheless, Tocqueville embraced democracy. He saw it, or at least the values of "equality of conditions," as described below, as an almost inevitable engine of modern history. He championed the ideals of the Enlightenment, of democracy, equality, liberty, and embraced the necessity of the French Revolution (though he was harshly critical of its excesses). But he wondered how or if democracy could work. It obviously was having trouble getting established in France. On the other hand, the country in which the other great democratic revolution of the late 1700s occurred – the United States – seemingly managed to create and maintain a thriving democracy. Tocqueville wondered how and why this happened. How was it that America was able to create and maintain a flourishing, working democracy while France could not? What was it about America that allowed this to happen?

He decided to go to America to find answers to his questions. He managed to get a grant from the French government to travel to the United States ostensibly to study prison reforms. In 1831, Tocqueville along with his friend and colleague Gustave de Beaumont set sail for America. They arrived in Newport, Rhode Island and for the nine months Tocqueville traveled all around what was then the United States, basically as far west as the Mississippi River. He went all around the then existing country, from New England to Wisconsin, from New York to New Orleans, and places in between. In his travels, he talked to countless people and attended various events; he observed and interacted with all sorts of Americans, all with the intent of understanding American society, specifically American political culture; all with the intent of understanding and analyzing American democracy: How was it that democracy seemed to work in America, as opposed to France, and will it continue? What are the strengths and weaknesses of American democracy? What are the threats to democracy and is America organized in a way to ward off these threats? These are just a few of the guiding questions that oriented his investigations.

It is important to emphasize here that his entire analysis of democracy in America is based upon what he saw in the northern, free states rather than in the southern, slave states. He believed the heart of democracy in America lay in New England, New York, and the free states of the northeast – rooted ultimately in the Puritan sensibilities of the settlers of Massachusetts in the 1600s, and his observations and assessments of democracy were almost all based upon what was happening in these states. He believed the settlers of the "west", what we now would call the mid-west, largely came from the northeast and took with them this culture of democracy. They planted the seeds of democracy there – in Ohio, Wisconsin, etc. He clearly did not believe that the south with its slavery embodied the sensibilities and actions of democracy, and clearly did not believe slave society was the wave of the future. I discuss his views of American slavery below. Moreover, ever the optimist (except perhaps when thinking of the future of race relations in America!), he believed the democracy found in the north was the irrepressible wave of the future. It was this he was thinking about when he says "democracy in America."

He returned to France and wrote up his observations and analysis in his two volume work *Democracy in America*. By the early 1900s the book became widely read and discussed in American academic circles and continues to be to this day. It continues to be viewed as a classic by most scholars.

It is in this book that Tocqueville's sociological theorizing is most clearly evident. (Though as I suggested earlier, one might argue that his book comparing French society before and after the French revolution, *The Old Regime and the French Revolution* (1955), published after *Democracy in America* and a few years before his death, was even more sociological.) Here we will focus on *Democracy in America*. In that book Tocqueville describes and analyzes how democracy works, and how it does not work, in America. He is particularly interested in understanding how democracy shapes the culture and social psychology of Americans, and how the culture and psychology of Americans shapes American democracy. But he is also interested in understanding how democracy, not simply democracy in America, works. He moves back and forth throughout the text in stating he is making claims about the specific workings of democracy in America and the general workings of democracy.

Democracy in America made Tocqueville a celebrity in France. He then became involved in politics, being elected and appointed to several offices. Near the end of his life, he wrote a second major work *The Old Regime and the French Revolution*. When Louis Napolean came to power by election and then announced a new empire -- and a fundamental rejection of democracy, Tocqueville retired from politics. He died prematurely of an illness in 1859.

Some Dominant Themes

The overarching theme in his writing is his critical analysis of the seemingly unstoppable historical movement towards democracy – in France and everywhere else. Tocqueville embraces this movement, but it is important to note that he also critically assesses democracy. He found it had numerous wonderful qualities, but it also was flawed in many ways. On the other hand, while he recognized the flaws in the old, aristocratic order, he also saw this old order as having virtues that the new democracies did not have. For example, in *Democracy in America*, he complained that democracy did not and would not produce great scholars and intellectuals whereas aristocracies produced these in abundance. (We can leave to the side the fact that American democracy in the 1800s and 1900s did increasingly produce great scholars, scientists, and intellectuals.)

The dominant theme throughout his work, and specifically in *Democracy in America*, was democracy: How it worked and how did not work; its strengths and weaknesses; and the threats posed to it. He saw the values of democracy – specifically equality and liberty – to be at the heart of democracy, and it was these forces that animated much of society, that propelled society forward. We can begin with equality. He specifically argues that it is the "equality of conditions" found in America that defines its democracy and its political culture, and its social conditions in general. To understand his concept of equality of conditions, we should first describe several other, contrasting meanings of equality. One meaning of equality is the equality of outcome. This is a social situation in which everyone, or at least most people, have roughly the same income, wealth or life circumstances. If there was a society in which everyone earned $40,000 a year in salary no matter what they did for work, whether a medical doctor or a garbage man, then this would be a state of equality in this sense. Equality of opportunity is a second meaning. Equality of opportunity is a social situation in which everyone has the same chance to success or to do what they wished as everyone else. For example, in such a situation, everyone would have the same opportunity to go to school and to succeed at school, and then everyone would have the possibility of getting a better job and becoming wealthier. What happens to one –whether one becomes rich or poor -- is dependent upon one's natural abilities and one's motivations. As such, in a state of equality of opportunity, there can and likely will be some people who are rich and others that are poor. This is akin to the metaphor of a foot race where everyone is starting at the same time and place at the starting line, but everyone finishes in different positions. Some win; others lose. In contrast, the equality of outcome is akin to the finishing line of such a race. Equality of opportunity traditionally has been the form of equality most championed in America, both today and in history. A third form of equality is equity. This is a more philosophical concept and revolves around the issues of fairness, justice, morality. A society is equal in this sense when all or most members are treated fairly. This concept is more complicated than the others and arguably is riddled with thorny issues, such as, what does it mean to say a situation is fair? This does not in itself negate the legitimacy or the utility of this concept. But it does demand that anyone employing it have a more sophisticated understanding of its meaning and ramification.

A fourth meaning of equality is the one used by Tocqueville – equality of condition, or as he sometimes writes "equality of social conditions." This is the equality that is at the heart of American democracy. The precise meaning he gives to equality of conditions is rather slippery, but it appears to have several components. One of these concerns a philosophical or psychological notion of equality in which all individuals believe themselves to be essentially of equal value or worth to everyone else and everyone else believes themselves to be of equal value or worth to the individual. We are all inherently the same. (He is not saying that we all have the same natural abilities. He of course recognizes differences. But on the philosophical as well as on the social level, we all have equal, inherent value.) This contrasts with aristocracies in which there are essential differences – etched by birth and privilege -- in value and worth between people, and more precisely between categories of people, e.g. between nobility and serfs. Thus, in a democracy such as the United States, Tocqueville says that a poor person would interact with a rich person as if the former was of the same social status as the latter. But this is only one dimension of his meaning of equality of social conditions. He also means, or at least strongly suggests, by this a social situation in which there is generally not much wealth inequality. It is a situation in which most people have about the same amount of wealth. Here he is not saying that there are no rich people in America. He does recognize that there are indeed rich people in America, but he argues that the nature and existence of the wealthy class is very different and is less of a true and impactful reality than it is in aristocracies. (See the discussion below on social classes). At one point he writes: "There are just as many wealthy people in the United States as elsewhere …" (2003:64), though a few paragraphs later he suggests something else: "In America there are few rich people" (ibid.:65).

At its heart, Tocqueville is claiming that equality of conditions is anchored in the existence of social mobility or the possibilities of mobility, upward and downward. America is a meritocracy. America, he believes, has an open mobility system in which people are constantly moving up and down the economic ladder; People born poor become rich, and people born rich become poor. "In America, most wealthy people start from poverty…" (2003:65). Because of the incessant mobility, America does not have established, self-interested, self-conscious social classes as they do in aristocracies. "There is no class … in America which passes to its descendants …. its wealth" (ibid.:65) Elsewhere he writes in contrasting democracy to aristocracies: "Things are very different when all privilege is dead, all classes intermingle, and all men move constantly up and down the social scale" (ibid.:538). He also suggests that because of this mobility, the possibilities of classes becoming identified as such is greatly diminished: "Classes still exist but it is not easy to distinguish clearly their members at first glance" (ibid.:655).

Despite the recognition of the existence of wealthy people and of economic inequality in America, one encounters repeated suggestions scattered throughout *Democracy in America* that the equality he is discussing refers at least to some large degree to the actual amount of economic equality present in America and not merely to the psychological or philosophical orientation of the people. He constantly notes the similar social status of most Americans. For example, when writing about the "influence of democracy on wages," he notes that: "As the rules of social hierarchy are less strictly observed, while the great sink and the humble rise, as poverty along with wealth ceases to be inherited, every day sees the lessening of the gaps between workman and masters both *in actual fact* and in men's mind" [italics added](2003:675). He continues, "I think that … it can be said that the slow and gradual rise in wages is one of the general laws of democratic societies. As conditions become more equal, wages rise; as wages increase, conditions become more equal" (ibid.:676).

In sum, Tocqueville's notion of equality of conditions seems to fuse elements of the equality of opportunity with some social psychological and philosophical elements, i.e. where individuals feel a sense that everyone is essentially equal – having the same value or worth -- to everyone else. But we should not escape his beliefs that equality of conditions also is suggestive of a society that does not have significant amounts of actual economic inequality.

But equality alone does not make democracy, and this is one of his central points. It is only when equality (of conditions) is paired with liberty (specifically political liberty) that one can have democracy. But these are independent forces and he says they must be understood as such. One of the many threats he identifies to democracy is the possibility that a democratic people might surrender their liberty to maintain their equality. He notes that while Americans cherish both of these democratic values, they are more attached and committed to equality than to liberty, and they would rather live in a state of equality that has no liberty than a state that has liberty and no equality. In a section of the book titled "Why Democratic nations display a more passionate and lasting love for equality than for freedom," he writes: "I think that democratic nations have a natural taste for freedom; left to themselves, they seek it out, become attached to it, and view any departure from it with distress. But they have a burning, insatiable, constant, and invincible passion for equality; they want equality in freedom, and if they cannot have it, they want it in slavery. They will endure poverty, subjection, barbarism but they will not endure aristocracy" (2003:587).

One of the reasons he gives for this is that freedom "if carried to the excess, damages peace, property and the lives of individuals" (2003:587). Freedom can produce readily apparent and immediate problems. On the other hand, the potential problems (or "evils" as he calls them) of equality are subtle and gradual and not readily seen. Conversely, the advantages of liberty "become visible only in the long term" but the "advantages of equality are felt immediately, and you can observe where they come from daily" (ibid.:587). In short, if not careful, democratic societies might lead to a situation of equality without freedom, either in the form of slavery or some form of aristocracy.

It is within this context, that Tocqueville analyzes American democracy. What was it about America that allowed democracy to work so well, in contrast to France? And what were some real and potential limitations and problems and threats to democracy in America? To begin, he notes that the particular constellation of geography, laws, customs, and mores provided the seedbed for its success. Geographically, America did not have many dangerous countries or empires at its borders, in contrast to France. This provided a context for political and social stability. But it was the laws, customs, and mores that were far more central to his explanation. He identified a number of character traits and habits of the Americans that contributed to their successful realization of democracy.

One of these was the materialist focus and the endless acquisitive nature. By materialism, Tocqueville does not mean what Marx means. Marx uses the term to describe an epistemological position, seeing the world as comprised of the realm of ideas and the realm of material conditions, with the latter being central to the course of history (see Chapter Two.) Instead, for Tocqueville it refers to a practical orientation that Americans had toward life. Americans were not focused on abstract and general ideas, but instead were focused on practical, hands-on issues of daily life. They wished to improve their concrete, material situation – getting wealthier, getting a bigger house, etc. This is combined with a restlessness in the population. Everyone was constantly on the move. There is an endless unsettledness amongst the people. "[A]n aimless restlessness permeates democratic societies" (2003:246). Americans are constantly in motion. They are unsettled, constantly changing, constantly looking to change. This dynamic feature is central, and it is largely driven by self-interest. Americans he says are driven, constantly driven to better themselves, and by extension their communities. (Note the contrast to aristocracies which are based upon the opposing principle of stagnation.)

In America, materialism is fused with what Tocqueville calls "self-interest well understood." To understand this we need to distinguish, as Tocqueville does, the concepts of selfishness, individualism, and self-interest well understood. Individualism is different from selfishness, or egoism. He writes:

> Individualism is a recently coined expression prompted by a new idea, for our forefathers knew only of egoism. Egoism is an ardent and

> excessive love of oneself which leads man to relate everything back to himself and to prefer himself above everything. Individualism is a calm and considered feeling which persuades each citizen to cut himself off from his fellows and to withdraw into the circle of his family and friends in such a way that he thus creates a small group of his own and willingly abandons society to its own devices ... Individualism is democratic in origin and threatens to grow as conditions become more equal. (ibid.:587-588)

Tocqueville believed that Americans embraced and lived the concept of individualism. But individualism unchecked, he says, would lead to the destruction of democracy.

In America, this modern form of individualism is controlled or contained. He champions this form of individualism and sees it as prevalent in American democracy. But, again, he sees individualism as being both potentially beneficial and harmful to the maintenance of democracy. It could threaten democracy and social stability if everyone retreats into their own private realm, e.g. family and friends. If this happens, no one will be concerned about the society at large – who will be concerned about "us"? -- and democratic society will perish. But he does not see this happening in America. On the contrary, individualism fosters a curious commitment to others and to the social good (ultimately because of the existence of liberty. See below). "As soon as communal affairs are treated as belonging to all, every man realizes that he is not as separate from his fellows as he first imagined and that it is often vital to help them in order to gain their support. When the public is in charge, every single man feels the value of public goodwill and seeks to court it by attracting the regard and affection of those amongst whom he is to live" (2003:592). Later, he writes, "I must say that I have seen Americans making great and sincere sacrifices for the common good and a hundred times I have noticed that, when needs be, they almost always gave each other faithful support" (ibid.:595). Paradoxically, he argues, individualism fosters actions oriented to the realization of the public good.

It is the value of liberty that is central to this orientation:

> The free institutions belonging to the inhabitants of the United States and the political rights they employ so much, provide a thousand reminders to each citizen that he lives in a society. They constantly impress this idea upon his mind, that it is the duty as well as self-interest to be useful to one's fellow and, as he sees no particular reason to hate others, being neither slave nor their master, his heart easily inclines toward kindness. Attention is paid, in the first instance,

to the common interest out of necessity and later out of choice. (2003:595)

In America, individualism is contained or controlled by the embrace of "self interest well understood." He believed Americans were largely driven by self-interest, but it was a particular form of self-interest. It is not a self-interest of selfishness or egoism. Rather it is one that simultaneously seeks to better oneself and one's family while bettering society.

Self-interest well understood is a qualified form of self-interest. It is one that leads the individual to focus on the community as well as upon the individual. The goal is to simultaneously advance the interests of the self and the society. He notes that in modern American democracy "the belief is born that man helps himself by serving others and that doing good serves his own interest" (ibid.:610). He elaborates: "Americans … are delighted to explain almost all the acts of their life in the light of self-interest properly [well] understood. They are quite willing to show how enlightened self-love continually leads them to help one another and inclines them to devote freely a part of their time and wealth to the welfare of the state" (ibid.:611).

He notes that the doctrine of self-interest well understood does not lead Americans to make great sacrifices but instead infuses their daily lives with a form of being that contributes to the maintenance of democracy. "The doctrine of self-interest properly [well] understood does not inspire great sacrifices but does prompt daily small ones; by itself it could not make a man virtuous but it does shape a host of law-abiding, sober, moderate, careful, and self-controlled citizens. If it does not lead the will directly to virtue it moves it closer through the imperceptible influence of habit" (ibid.:612).

The embrace of self-interest well understood is one force that maintains democracy in America. But Tocqueville identifies many others. One of these is religion. Tocqueville was a Roman Catholic and a believer, though the depths of his beliefs and religious practices can be questioned. His faith surely influenced, if not distorted, his understandings of the role of religion in American democracy. He saw religion as a powerful and necessary and positive force both in the production and maintenance of democracy, in direct and indirect ways. (Of note, he does not readily distinguish the effects of Protestantism compared to Catholicism on democracy. He sees these together as Christian churches having comparable effects on democracy in America, and possibly elsewhere. This is a rather curious position and one that implicitly stands at odds with many sociological formulations. Weber, for example, sees Protestantism having a profoundly different impact upon people than Catholicism (see Chapter Four).) To begin, he rejects the secularization hypothesis that was a widely held product of the Enlightenment (and was dramatically seen in the French Revolution). Religion was not declining and was not going to decline in modernity. (It perhaps is worth noting that in France, the revolutionaries widely despised religion and specifically the role played by the Catholic Church in supporting the old order.) There is, he argues, a universal human need for religion. It fulfills basic human psychological (and social) needs. Moreover, he argues that religion is not only compatible with equality but is deeply supportive of it. In a section titled "Religion considered as a political institution which powerfully supports the maintenance of a democratic republic among Americas," he argues that Christianity is "one of the most supportive of the equality of social conditions" (2003:337) and religion "should ... be regarded as the first of their basic political institutions" (ibid.:342). Religion provides the foundation for the mores and customs held by Americans that maintain democracy. But it is not only the shaping of the social and political orientations of Americans by religion that maintain democracy, it is also the formal organization of the political system. Specifically, he says the separation of church and state is foundational to the maintenance of democracy. Tocqueville notes his surprise at how widespread the support of this basic doctrine was in America. He says that he interviewed "the faithful of all communions," and talked to many "priests" of various faiths to find out what Americans thought about the separation of church and state. They all "attributed the peaceful influence exercised by religion over their country principally to the separation of Church and state. ... I did not meet a single man, priest or layman, who did not agree about that" (ibid.:345).

The freedom of the press is another thing that serves to maintain democracy in America. As with most of the social formations and social realities identified by Tocqueville that are associated with democracy, there are aspects of the free press which simultaneously are positive and negative, helpful and potentially harmful, and again as with his analysis of most of the other social formations, the positives of the free press certainly outweigh the negative, particularly in terms of supporting democracy.

Perhaps the most discussed feature of American democracy presented by Tocqueville in recent and contemporary sociology is the concept of civic or voluntary associations. He says the presence of countless voluntary associations is an important factor in contributing to the stability and success of American democracy and American society at large. As he notes, equality of conditions and individualism tend to lead citizens inward and away from concerns about the public good. He writes, "[A]mong democratic nations all citizens are independent and weak; they can achieve almost nothing by themselves and none or them could force his fellows to help him. Therefore they all sink into a state of impotence, if they do not learn to help each other voluntarily" (2003:597). Voluntary associations in the broadest sense consist of non-governmental organizations that citizens join for a common purpose. Voluntary associations in democracies are vital elements of civil society. One may thing of three central sites of public, social activity: the political sphere, the economic sphere, and the civil society. When people vote, when representatives raise taxes, etc., they are engaged in the political sphere. When people work or go to the mall and consume, they are engaged in the economic sphere. When people engage with others in other organized ways with the intent of a common goal, often to advance an image of the public good, then they are engaged in civil society, and specifically within voluntary associations. Broadly speaking, voluntary associations include a wide array of groups such as: protest movements – engaging in political action outside of the legal political institutions, environmental groups, parent teachers' groups, little league, the Boy Scouts, the Knights of Columbus, the Shriners, religious groups, etc. He was struck by how many and how often Americans joined together in voluntary associations:

> Americans of all ages, conditions, and all dispositions constantly unite together. Not only do they have commercial and industrial associations to which all belong by also a thousand other kinds, religious, moral, serious, futile, very general and very specialized, large and small. Americans group together to hold fetes, found seminaries, build inns, construct churches, distribute books, dispatch missionaries to the antipodes. They establish hospitals, prisons, schools by the same method. (2003:596)

Tocqueville (2003:283) identifies the temperance movement – the anti-alcohol movement – as an example of a voluntary association. The temperance movement, particularly later in the nineteenth and early twentieth centuries sought to make alcohol illegal. This evolved into an explicit social movement aimed directly at affecting political change. But voluntary associations do not necessarily need to be focused on political change. Instead, they may be focused on anything concerning the public good.

He was amazed at the extent of the creation and participation of voluntary associations, and he contrasts this with France, and particularly with aristocratic France, which had an absence of such associations and activities. Associations bind a people together in a democracy and work against the centralization of power and thus the destruction of democracy. Associations also instill in individuals a sense of ownership over the collective and a sense of democratic empowerment. Associations nurture a sense that the citizen is and should be engaged in realizing the public good. They are essential to a democracy. He suggests that a democracy without a vibrant sector of voluntary associations would be one that may fall prey to anti-democratic forces, such as tyranny.

Another feature of American democracy is the leveling of the population. That is, the equality of conditions spawns a way of being in which one does not find many exceptional scholars, scientists, poets, etc. (Again, in contrast to aristocracies which produce individual excellence.) Democracies produce mediocre talents, he argues. Yet at the same time, they are industrious and hard-working, echoing the earlier claim of restlessness. As such, "men are industrious but they do not foster the science of industry" (2003:353).

Democratic citizens also tend to be highly conformist, and they tend to be "weak" rather than independent (2003:542). They are not deep and independent thinkers and are not deeply committed to one or another idea. In democracies, "men are insignificant and very much alike" (ibid.:61). "[T]hey are almost always plagued by doubt ... In their ever-shifting circumstances, the fickleness of their fortunes persuades them never to hold firm to any of their opinions" (ibid.:558).

The reader might come to believe from the above that Tocqueville has a very negative view of democracy and specifically of American democracy, particularly on what it does to the individual character. But it would be a mistake to believe this. Tocqueville in fact admires democracy. He is here, as he does throughout *Democracy in America*, identifying some of the many social psychological consequences of this system. As he does throughout, he tends to employ an analysis that is almost dialectical, repeatedly identifying the strengths and simultaneous weaknesses of each of the elements of democracy. For example, while he sees Americans are weak and individualist and having a predominant focus on themselves as individuals, he also sees them as hard working, productive, and committed to social participation.

Another theme found in *Democracy in America* is the importance of work and the economy in American life. He locates, perhaps implicitly, the economic organization of American society at the center of his analysis. Yet he does not discuss the organization of capitalism per se. Nevertheless, it is ever-present. The economic structure of capitalism is not a consequential cause of the political culture of democracy, but it is a central part of the society. It is in effect a product of democratic culture rather than a cause of it. The democratic values of equality and liberty produce a people that are economically motivated by self-interest (well understood) to succeed. The assumption of Americans driven by self-interest is a central feature of the analysis. The economy in democracies, he says, will inevitably grow. The society will become wealthier.

Two themes stand out in his discussions of the economy: the value of work and the place of the rich and of social classes in America. We discuss the latter below. Here a few words can be said about the value of work. Tocqueville repeatedly notes that Americans value work. They see work very favorably. They see work as an essential positive thing, as honorable, and not as burdensome or as evil. Work is "held in high esteem" (2003:639). This is captured in his discussion of "servants" and employers: "American servants do not believe that they are degraded for working since everyone around them is working. They do not feel humiliated by the idea of receiving a wage ...

All honest occupations are honorable" (ibid.:640). The cause of this orientation is a bit ambiguous in Tocqueville's writings. On the one hand, he attributes this ethos to the existence of equality, liberty, and democracy, but on the other he alludes at times to the religious and specifically (New England) Puritan source of this orientation.

The value of work is reflected in his discussions of the differences in orientation to work between the free northern states and the slave-holding southern states. He says it is in the north, anchored in the original Puritan settlers of New England, where this honorable view of work is held, and this is the view that is spreading west as the country expands. On the other hand, he says the existence of slavery had destroyed the honorable view of work – both for white and black southerners. In slavery work is seen as an oppressive thing, forced upon someone against their will. Work is seen as something one is forced to do and as something that benefits those that do not work, the slaveowner. It is something to be avoided. This has caused the southerners – both black and white -- to take a negative view towards work and he says it explain at least in part why it is that the north has become so much wealthier and industrious than the south.

Two Significant Threats

Of the many problems with and threats to democracies identified by Tocqueville two stand out: the tyranny of the majority and soft despotism. The term the tyranny of the majority is a widely quoted concern but is often used in a way that fails to capture Tocqueville's full meaning. Often people discuss the concept in terms of the readily apparent problem for a democracy when there is a situation in which one group that is a majority of people in the society, even fifty-one percent, always or almost always vote in favor of their own interests and disregards or oppose the interests of the minority. As such, the rest of the society, even forty-nine percent, are subjected constantly to the will of the majority without any recourse. The minority becomes powerless. This is not democratic. While Tocqueville describes this as one of the features of the problem of the tyranny of the majority, there is, he says, another of importance. This is his moral concern. For him, the moral sensibilities of people living in a democracy with equality of conditions are weakened. People become pliable and uncertain, and they do not commit deeply to one or another position, he says. Morality becomes flabby and fluid. And he says that in the democratic process whereby the majority wins, the minority might come to see this victory not simply in terms of an instrumental victory in which the majority gets what it wants, but also a moral victory in which the moral position of the majority is actually seen as the correct and proper moral position to take, and by extension the moral position of the minority is wrong. This is anchored in part on the idea that "the moral ascendancy of the majority is partly founded upon the idea that more enlightenment and wisdom are found in a group of men than in one man alone and that the number of legislators counts for more than who is elected" (2003:288). It is also founded on something mentioned above: The equality of conditions nurtures a weakness of the individual: "[T]he majority is endowed with a force both physical and moral which affects people's will as much as their actions and which at the same time stands in the way of any act and the desire to do it. I know of no other country where there is generally less independence of thought and real freedom of debate than in America" (ibid.:297). As a result of such things, the minority will bow to the wishes of the majority, believing that the latter are morally correct in their decisions.

A second potential problem is soft despotism. Soft despotism is closely associated with another set of themes Tocqueville focuses upon, perhaps more so in *The Old Regime and the French Revolution*. These are the themes of centralization and bureaucratization. (Such themes became central issues of concern for sociologists writing over fifty years after Tocqueville died and continue to remain so through the present.) He was concerned about the growth of a centralized and bureaucratized government in modern democratic societies. But he was less concerned that the growing democratic state might resort and rely upon obvious, oppressive forces to maintain social order. Instead, such modern democratic states would produce a "soft despotism," a form of oppressive government that appears to be otherwise. He writes, "If despotism were to be established in present-day democracies, it would probably assume a different character [that earlier forms of despotism]; it would be more widespread and kinder; it would debase men without tormenting them" (ibid.:804).

Soft despotism could emerge when centralization and bureaucratization fuse with equality of conditions in a state without liberty. Everyone is equally enslaved and happy: "When I consider the trivial nature of men's passions, the mildness of their manners, the extent of their education, the purity of their religion, the gentleness of their morality, their industrious and tidy habits, the restraint they almost all display in their vices as in their virtues, I have no fear that their leaders will be considered as tyrants but rather as guardians" (ibid.: 805).

He provides an image of a world of soft despotism:

> I see an innumerable crowd of men, all alike and equal, turned upon themselves in a restless search for those petty, vulgar pleasures with which they fill their souls. Each of them, living apart, is almost unaware of the destiny of all the rest. His children and personal friends are for him the whole of the human race; as for the remainder of his fellow citizens, he stands alongside them but does not see them;

> he touches them without feeling them; he exists only in himself and for himself; if he still retains his family circle, at any rate he may be said to have lost his country.
>
> Above these men stands an immense and protective power which alone is responsible for looking after their enjoyments and watching over their destiny. It is absolute, meticulous, ordered, provident, and kindly disposed. It would be like a fatherly authority, if, fatherlike, its aim were to prepare men for manhood, but it seeks only to keep them in perpetual childhood, it prefers its citizens to enjoy themselves provided they have only enjoyment in mind. (ibid.:805)

The concept of soft despotism foreshadows a theme that has been common in sociology for over the last one hundred years: The potentially harmful effects of the administered society.

On Religion

Tocqueville believed religion, and specifically Christian religions, to be foundational to democracy. One cannot help but wonder if this is an artifact of his aristocratic upbringing. He was not very religious in his personal life, but in his analysis and theorizing of democracy – particularly American democracy – he saw religion as playing a vital role. As he notes: "It is religion which has given birth to Anglo-American societies: one must never lose sight of that; in the United States, religion is thus intimately linked to all national habits and all the emotions which one's native country arouses; that gives it a particular strength" (2003:496). I wish to make two points about his views on religion here. The first is how he fore-shadowed Weber's classic *The Protestant Ethic and the Spirit of Capitalism*. The second is a summary of the role religion plays in democracy.

Tocqueville believed that American democracy worked – at least in the early 1800s – for numerous reasons, some of which have been discussed herein. One of these reasons was the economic industriousness of Americas. They worked. They worked constantly. They worked hard. Why? Where did this ethic of hard work derive? While he says freedom and democracy are foundational to the work ethic of Americans, he strongly suggests that it was also the ethos towards work and towards life brought to America, particularly to New England in the 1600s, by the Puritans that laid the seedbed for the industriousness of American society that Tocqueville witnessed. Religion dictates that they be disciplined and hard working, that they be serious and austere in their lives. All of which fostered great economic prosperity.

Tocqueville also believed that religion played an important role in the social and political organization of America. Religion, he says, is a universal need and it is the seedbed for democracy. As he notes: "In my opinion, I doubt whether man can ever support at the same time complete religious independence and entire political freedom and am drawn to the thought that if a man is without faith, he must serve someone and if he is free, he must believe (2003:512). But many different forms of religion exist and these different forms relate to democracy in different ways. Monotheistic religions he believed, however chauvinistically, were more supportive of democracy than other forms. And Christianity in particular was particularly conducive to democracy. He believed that the general moral tenets of this faith simultaneously bound people together morally and allowed and encouraged freedom. The rules of Christianity were general, not specific. They did not regulate particular daily behaviors, but instead provided an overarching moral roadmap, or so Tocqueville believed.

He contrasts Islam with Christianity in this regard and concludes – in however much a biased manor – that Christianity rather than Islam is supportive of freedom and democracy. He writes: "Mohammed drew down from heaven into the writings of the Koran not only religious teachings but political thoughts, civil and criminal laws and scientific theories. The Gospel, in contrast, refers only to general links of man to God and man to man. Beyond that, it teaches nothing and imposes no beliefs in anything" (2003:513).

In short, Tocqueville believed that religion was centrally important to the success of American democracy and of democracies in general. He discussed the role of religion throughout *Democracy in America* and clearly is quite sympathetic to it. He also discusses religion in *The Old Regime and the French Revolution* and there too he says things that to the ear of many, non-believing current sociologists would seem at best as anachronistic and at worse simply wrong. For example, he claims the French revolutionaries did not see religion – and specifically Catholicism – as an object of their wrath, as a symbol of the old order. Instead, he claims the revolutionaries, at least in the early years of the movement, were not hostile to religion but were hostile to how religion was used by the aristocracy to oppress the people. While religion is undoubtedly important to understand if one wishes to provide a sociological explanation of the social world – see Weber or Durkheim! – Tocqueville's analysis, at least to this author, appears to be one of the weaker aspects of an otherwise highly astute analysis of democracy.

On Mores

Arguably, one of the most sociological dimensions of Tocqueville's analysis of democracy is his focus on what may be called the forms of being of democratic citizens. Not unlike Weber's analysis in *The Protestant Ethic and the Spirit of Capitalism*, Tocqueville is seeking to understand the character of the democratic citizen, specifically in America. What shapes this character? How does this character type, this form of being, influence the actions of Americans in terms of politics, economics, morality, social order, etc.? All of these are questions animating his analysis. Law, customs, manners, and mores are often discussed in Tocqueville's *Democracy in America* with the intent of answering such questions. Customs, manners and mores combines provide the foundations for the form of being.

Tocqueville distinguishes between manners and mores. He writes, "Manners generally issue from the very same substance of mores; and in addition, they sometimes result from an arbitrary convention among certain men. They are at the same time natural and acquired" (2000:578, Mansfield and Winthrop translation). Tocqueville describes *customs* and mores as follows: "By customs I mean the term used by classical writers when they use the word *mores*; for I apply it not only to customs in the strict sense of what might be called habits of the heart but also to the different concepts men adopt, the various opinions which prevail among them and to the whole collection of ideas which shape mental habits. Thus, I include in the use of this word the entire moral and intellectual state of a nation" (2003: 334-335). Mores are the moral cornerstone of forms of being, and an analysis of democracy, freedom, and equality necessitates their study. This is arguably Tocqueville's sociological position.

For Tocqueville, mores are at the heart of American democracy. Mores are anchored in democracy. They emanate from democracy, and most notably from the embrace of equality of conditions. Mores shape the formal institutions such as law, but more importantly they create the form of daily living in which American democracy can thrive. In writing about the role of religion, he notes, "It is in the East [Northeast] that the Anglo-Americans have been longest accustomed to democratic government and that they have shaped the habits ad conceived the ideas which most favor its maintenance. Democracy has gradually permeated their customs, opinions, and social habits ... What are all these usages, opinions, habits, beliefs, if they are not what I have named "customs" [mores]? (2003:360). He continues, "Thus, of all Americans, it is especially the customs [mores] of Americans ... which make them capable of supporting a democratic government; and it is customs [mores] again that cause the various Anglo-American democracies to be more or less orderly and prosperous" (2003:361).

Views on Social Class and Inequality

Tocqueville's works were decidedly not analyses of economic structures or of social class or of economic inequalities. They instead focused on politics, culture, the social, and the institutional and bureaucratic features of modern democratic societies. And yet throughout his writings we find discussions of economics and of social class. A major part of the success of American democracy is due to its economic success and due to the industrious habits of its citizens. The economic focus of the population was central to the workings of nineteenth century America.

He wrote often about economics and social class. But unlike Marx, he did not see the economy nor class as the key forces propelling history forward. They instead seemed to simply exist for Tocqueville or at best seemed to be products of the cultural forces of democracy at work.

So what did he think of capitalism and of class, specifically in America? Though he did not identify and systematically assess the economic system, he gives clear views on what he thought of capitalism and how it worked in early to mid-eighteen hundreds America. He saw the American economy as incredibly dynamic and changing. People were constantly creating new businesses. For Tocqueville, the American economy was populated largely by small rather than large businesses. There was a dynamic energy related to economics as everyone seemed to wish to be productive. He saw the economy expanding, and he saw all of this as the result of the cultural ethos of democracy, of the embrace of freedom and equality.

As for social classes in America, he did not believe they existed in any significant sense. Or perhaps more accurately, they existed but they were not very meaningful: "Classes still exist [in America] but it is not easy to distinguish clearly their members at first glance" (2003:655). Similarly, he writes: "Men who live in such a society [as America] could not possible draw their beliefs from the opinions of the class they belong to, for there are not, so to speak, class divisions any more" (ibid.:494). In a society of equality of conditions there is endless mobility (see above). The poor and the rich constantly moved up and down. As people could and did move up and down the economic classes, moving from one class to another, there was less chance of the classes solidifying, and less chances of people identifying as a group with one or another class. Of course, we should recall that America at that time was a largely rural and agricultural society, with industrialization just starting to take root.

He also believed that the degree of economic inequality was less, if not far less, than that found in Europe, though this needs to be qualified as he says contradictory things on this matter throughout *Democracy in America*.

He says on numerous occasions that the amount of economic inequality in democratic America is not very great. "As classes intermingle and very large as well as very small fortunes become rarer, as the days go by there is less distance between the status [social conditions] of the landowner and that of the tenant farmer" (2003:672). Any yet, sounding almost Marxist, writing at a time of an emerging industrialization, the growth of factory workers and the growth of a small class of rich industrialists, he does recognize the reality that the emerging industrial world is producing two opposing classes: the workers and the wealthy industrialists. For the worker, factory work causes the worker to lose his humanity, or as Marx would say it produces alienation. In passages that could have been written by Marx himself, Tocqueville complains about what factory work is doing to the worker. He writes:

> When a craftsman is constantly and solely engaged upon the making of one single object, he ultimately performs this work with unusual dexterity; but at the same time, he loses the general capacity to apply his concentration on the way he is working. Day by day, he gains in skill but is less industrious; one may say that as he, the workingman, improves, so does he, the man, lose his self-respect." (2003:645)

He continues:

> What can be expected of a man who has spent twenty years of his life making pinheads? ... When a workman has spent a considerable part of his existence in such a manner ... he no longer belongs to himself but to the profession he has chosen .... As the principle of the division of labor is applied more completely, the worker becomes weaker, more limited and more dependent. The craft makes progress, the craftsman ships backwards. ... [S]cience constantly lowers the standing of workers, it raises that of the bosses ... The one increasingly looks like the administrator of a vast empire, the other a brute. (2003:646)

Tocqueville issues a warning about the future if these two classes – workers and the rich – coalesce within themselves: "[I]f ever aristocracy and the permanent inequality of social conditions were to infiltrate the world once again, it is predictable that this is the door by which it should enter" (2003:648). But ever the optimist with a boundless faith in democracy, he believes the rich will not consolidate and act as a unified class. As noted earlier, he says, social mobility weakens the possibility of entrenched classes arising. Moreover, he claims that the relationship between the rich and the workers in industrial capitalism is different from the relationship between the aristocracy and the serfs and this difference helps to prevent class consolidation in industrial capitalism. That is, in aristocracies the nobility had a paternalistic relationship with their serfs. They were morally tied to them. But in industrial capitalism, there is absolutely no moral connection between the rich and the workers. The rich do not care at all about the workers. The rich "aim not to rule them but to use them" 2003:648).

At first glance, this is a rather curious argument, and it may appear that it contradicts Tocqueville's actual intent. That is, it appears that it would foster greater not lesser class antagonisms when the industrial rich have no connection, no relationship, with their workers. But Tocqueville says the opposite: The breaking of the relationship will contribute to a weakening of social class formation. This is so presumably because the self-identification of the aristocracy is in relation to the serfs. But in industrial capitalism where there is no comparable relationship, the foundations of class identification amongst the rich is weakened. In short, he seems to suggest that classes are anchored in self-identification with classes and classes are defined in terms of relationship – particularly with other classes. When the relationship breaks down – as it does in industrial capitalism – so too does the foundation for the existence of class.

Views on Slavery, Black Americans, and Women

It is perhaps rather common today for students, and to a less extent faculty, reading historical social thinkers to focus on how these thinkers thought about such things as race and gender, specifically about black Americans, women, and the relationship of these groups to white males. (Sadly, often readers today who take this perspective are too quick to reject the entirety of a scholar's work from hundreds of years ago due to perceived faulty perspectives regarding things such as race or gender. The political and moral purity of the author generally should not be the criteria used to assessed the value of historical or contemporary works.) As such, we should perhaps say a few words about Tocqueville's views on such things. To begin, *Democracy in America* is largely about the experiences of white men as they practice democracy. That said, he does discuss black Americans, slavery and women, as well as Native Americans. He explicitly does so in several sections. One of these is titled, "A few remarks on the present-day state and the probable future of the three races which live in the territory of the United States." "The position of the black race in the United States; Dangers to the whites from its presence." Still another is titled, "How the Americans view the equality of men and women."

Regarding American women, he writes, "I have shown how democracy destroyed or altered the various inequalities which originate with society. But is that all? Will it not succeed ultimately in affecting that great inequality between men and women which has appeared, up to the present time, to be based on the timeless dictates of nature herself?" (2003:696). He answers this question by noting that American men believe "that since nature has established such a great variation in the physical and moral make-up of men and women, ... she clearly intended to give different employment to their different faculties" (ibid.:697). American men believe there are "distinct spheres of action" for the two sexes, and that "both are required to walk at an equal pace but along paths that are never the same" (ibid.:697). He continues: "Americans, then, who have allowed the social inferiority of women to remain, have done their utmost to raise her intellectually and morally to man's level. In this way, they seem to have admirably understood the true concept of democratic progress" (ibid.:700). He concludes this section with a few personal observations: "[I]f I am asked how we should account for the unusual prosperity and growing strength of this [American] nation, I would reply that they must be attributed to the superiority of women" (ibid.:700). In short, he seems to recognize the contradiction between his views on women, democracy, and nature, but refrains from engaging in the philosophical discuss that such contradictions cry out for. A similar view emerges in his discussion of black Americans.

In terms of black Americans and specifically slavery, Tocqueville takes an unequivocal stand: Slavery is an abhorrent and reprehensible system. He notes that he "witnessed evils I would find it impossible to relate" (2003:380). It is a system, he says -- thirty years before the Civil War -- that cannot and will not survive. The tide of history – anchored in the spread of Enlightenment thought upon which democracy rides – dictates that slavery will come to an end. He says that the "most fearsome of all the ills threatening the future of the United States stems from the presence of the blacks on their soil" (ibid.:399).(I must leave aside any discussion of the obvious racist language and tone of this line, i.e. in the use of the word "their": why are blacks considered to be occupying or living on white land?) He speculates about the possible outcomes of black-white relations in America, and provides no optimistic forecast. "[E]ither Negroes and whites must blend together completely or they must part" (ibid.:417). He notes that the former option will not happen. As for the latter: "I do not think that the white and black races will ever mange to live in any country on an equal footing" (ibid.:418). At one point, he suggests a "civil war" might be the result of slavery, but it would not be between the north and the south. It would be between southern black slaves and southern whites. In short, he provides no clear image of the future of race relations. He provides no happy picture of the future of race relations or their impact upon the maintenance of democracy in America.

Diverse and Competing Receptions of Tocqueville

Upon reading Tocqueville, one might take issue with whether his accountings of democracy and specifically of American democracy were accurate. One might say he was wrong in his description and analysis of American society in the 1830s. Or one may say that his analysis, even if it was correct for America in the 1830s, is not correct or relevant to American democracy today. Certainly, some if not many of the things he said about American democracy in the 1830s were distorted if not wrong. And many of his ideas about American democracy if applied to America today would strain credulity – for example, his claims about the relative incoherence and impotence of the rich class in America can be seen as at best quaint in their oddity and at worst a crass misunderstanding of American society. Another example: history clearly shows that his claims that American democracy fosters mediocrity rather than excellence in the sciences and more generally in the fields of advance knowledge was simply wrong. Nevertheless, he provides numerous insights into the workings of democracy and into the social implications of having a society anchored in the equality of conditions; one would be wrongheaded simply to dismiss the entirety of his argument due to such errors.

Relatedly, when one considers how Tocqueville has been received by "conservatives" and by "liberals" over the years we see competing interpretations both as to the merits of his work and as to what he was actually saying. (Note that I place the words conservative and liberal in quotations because the meanings of these words today -- in the Trump era -- are starkly different than the meanings of these words forty or fifty years ago. This applies to both conservative and liberals, but far more so to the former than the latter.) Conservatives and liberals alike have at various times championed and criticized Tocqueville. Conservatives often focus on his embrace not only of liberty and the equality of conditions – typically defined by conservatives as meaning the equality of opportunity – but on his beliefs in the importance of such things as religion and private property rights to the maintenance of democracy. Liberals, on the other hand, often focus on the themes of equality, and on individualism and commitment, as well as upon the importance of such things as voluntary associations and the like. This is seen clearly in

Robert Bellah et al.'s classic work *Habits of the Heart* (1996), discussed below.

On the other hand, conservatives may criticize *Democracy in America* for the author's views and for the implication of his views on such things as equality and individualism. After all, individualism suggests a tolerance – of such things as difference -- that seems anathema to many conservatives, particularly today. Similarly, they may reject Tocqueville's warnings of the potential threat posed to democracy by the wealthy class, as discussed earlier. Liberals too might reject or at least criticize Tocqueville. They might claim that he takes a conservative view on many matters, from religion to property rights, and that he ignores or pays insufficient attention to the centrally important role played by such things as race and gender in all of society. Also, while he warns about the prospect of the wealthy becoming a threat to democracy, he argues they are not a powerful and cohesive group and as such are not, at least at the time of his writing, such a concern. Liberals would certainly protest his views on such matters. Liberals might also complain, perhaps wrongly, that he is merely another dead white guy writing about history, about the white man's history, from the white man's perspective, and only gives attention to people other than white men when these others stand in relation to the white man.

However one wishes to read and to criticize Tocqueville, I believe he has many important things to say that may be of use in these troubled times of a failing, contemporary American democracy. It is up to the reader, of course, to identify what if anything he writes that is of value. One many only say in times when democracy is under threat, it behooves Americans to think more, and to think more deeply and more critically, about American democracy then and now, at least if one wishes to maintain it.

Tocqueville and *Habits of the Heart*

Tocqueville has had a relatively small but consequential and enduring influence upon American sociology through the decades. Here I describe one of the better known and more influential works that is directly influenced by *Democracy in America*. I am referring to *Habits of the Heart* by Robert Bellah and four of his colleagues (1996, originally published in 1985). For this work, Bellah et al. interviewed numerous Americans with the intent of discovering how Americans understood and practiced the ideas of "individualism and commitment." They sought to discover how Americans understood themselves and their relationship to American society at large. They wanted to comprehend the culture, really the personality and culture, of American democracy. They also sought to know how Americans understood and sought to realize the public good in their practices.

The book is based upon a research project conducted by Bellah and his colleagues. The authors interviewed numerous "white, middle class Americans" throughout the country. (We can leave aside the obvious limitations or concerns with making claims about American culture based upon interviews with this selective sample.) They sought to understand, in the tradition of Tocqueville, how Americans connected the personal to the public, in thought and in social action. They wished to know American character types and the relationship of these to culture and to cultural practices, i.e. to the mores of the people, and more broadly to social stability in American democracy. They sought to know how people understood themselves morally and politically and how they saw their relationship to society, specifically to political society. The focus was on understanding "individualism and commitment". That is, the authors wished to understand how individuals thought of themselves as individuals in relationship to their concept of the public good, i.e. what is deemed best for us and the authors wanted to understand how Americans "use private and public life to make sense of their lives" (1996:20). Their analysis led them to believe that there were and are four dominant cultural traditions in America, or four different general way in which Americans throughout history and into the present understood and practice the above sensibilities. Of note, it is not that Americans embrace one or the other of these traditions to the exclusion of the other three. Individuals may embody aspects of more than one or another of the four traditions. It is that one or another of these is often if not typically dominant in individual lives.

The first of the four cultural traditions is utilitarian individualism. They define this in their glossary: "Utilitarian individualism is a form of individualism that takes as given certain basic human appetites and fears – for Hobbes, the desire for power over others and the fear of sudden violent death at the hands of another – and sees human life as an effort by individuals to maximize their self-interest relative to these given ends. Utilitarian individualism views society as arising from a contract that individuals enter into only in order to advance their self-interest" (1996:336). Benjamin Franklin is used as an example of this character type. Today, we may think of many businessmen as embodying this form of being. The individual here views society in effect as one large social marketplace where individuals exchange things for their personal benefit, and by doing so all or most benefit. Society benefits when people act in rational, self-interested ways. This tradition ultimately is anchored in the concept of enlightened self-interest, whereby the selfish pursuit of individual self-interest is believed to be morally good and morally justified because the public good will benefit, i.e. most people will benefit, as a result.

The second cultural tradition is expressive individualism. Expressive individualism stands in contrast to utilitarian individualism. Whereas utilitarian individualism is anchored in rational, self-control, and in measured acts designed to maximize one's interests, expressive individualism is based upon the expression of feeling. Expressive individualism "holds that each person has a unique core of feelings and intuition that should unfold or be expressed if individuality is to be realized" (1996:334). The authors use Walt Whitman, the notable nineteenth century poet, to capture a historical example of this character type. They note that this form of individualism is historically associated with nineteenth century romanticism, though it is pervasive in recent and contemporary America. Individuals today who go to or believe in the values of such things as psychotherapy reflect this type as well. The hippies from the 1960s and many members of the LGBTQ+ community today arguably embody this tradition. The focus for expressive individuals is to try to be genuine, real in their being. It is focused on being authentically who you really are and allowing others to do the same.

The biblical tradition is our third dominant American character type. This tradition is "carried primarily by Jewish and Christian communities" (1996:333). In this form of being, individuals seek to live their faith in both their personal and public lives. They are oriented toward seeking to realize their understanding of themselves through their faith in their daily practices. The focus is also on realizing a concept of the public good through practices that are based upon religious sensibilities. Bellah et al. (echoing Tocqueville), accord Puritanism a particularly influential role in the history of this tradition. America has deep religious roots, going back to the Puritans of New England. Contemporary sociologists of religion have repeatedly noted that religion continues to be much more influential in American society than in other industrial or post-industrial society. Whether it is in terms of surveys asking whether people believe in god or whether they attend church services, Americans are much more religious than other countries. (It bears noting however that data from recent decades has shown a marked decline in religiosity in America. Secularization which has been a noted feature of most industrial societies would appear to be happing historically rather late in America.) (Notably absent from these assertions is the reality that the religiosity of America is not evenly spread throughout the country. Some parts of the country – the South, the Bible Belt – are far, far more religious than other parts – for example, the urban, industrial or post-industrial northeast or far west. The religiosity of the latter while still a bit higher than other post-industrial countries is not significantly so. As such, scholars should be careful about making such bold pronouncements that Americans are more religious than others.) Throughout American history we can see the importance religion has played in countless public issues, from the temperance movement to the civil rights movement, as well as in countless laws, customs, and practices of Americans. Religion has clearly played a huge role in American life throughout history.

The fourth and last main character type is based on what Bellah et al. call the republican (or civic republican) tradition. (The term of course should not be confused in any way with the Republican Party. There is absolutely no connection between the two.) Here is how Bellah et al. describes this tradition: The republican tradition "originated in the cities of classical Greece and Rome. [It] was expressed in the civic humanism of late medieval and early modern Europe, and contributed to the formation of modern Western democracies. It presupposes that the citizens of a republic are motivated by civic virtue as well as self-interest. It views public participation as a form of moral education and sees its purpose as the attainment of *justice* and the *public good* ..." (1996:335; Emphasis in the original). The central emphasis in the republican tradition is the secular, moral duty of individuals to be oriented toward self-governance and toward the advancement of the public good. (Echoes of Tocqueville's notions of self-interest well understood and voluntary associations are clear.) Bellah et al. gives Thomas Jefferson as the exemplar of this tradition.

Bellah and his colleagues did not merely wish to describe these four main cultural traditions. They wished to understand how these have evolved in history and specifically into the present. Indeed, the central theme of *Habits of the Heart* is a stark warning or alarm at how the relative salience and significant of each of the four traditions have changed in the late nineteen hundreds. While one could find each of the four as living and dynamic realities throughout American history into the present, in recent decades two of the four have become dominant and the other two have receded, and this, they argue, is perilous. The authors express concern if not alarm that the traditions of utilitarian individualism and expressive individualism have taken over and that the traditions of civic republicanism and the biblical tradition have declined and have become far less influential. Further, a sharper divide or fragmentation has occurred between all of these traditions.

The four cultural traditions have manifested themselves within American political economic ideologies in the late nineteen hundreds, as they have done so throughout the history of the United States. In recent decades – at least prior to the rise of Donald Trump and his followers, the authors argue that these traditions have consolidated around two opposing orientations – neocapitalism and welfare capitalism – which could roughly be associated with traditional "conservative" and "liberal" sensibilities. Ronald Reagan is used as an exemplar of someone embracing neocapitalism and John Kennedy is the one used to reflect welfare capitalism. The authors make the prediction in the original edition of *Habits of the Heart* that these competing images of the public good will not be able to endure, and these may be replaced by a new set of competing ideologies of what is and should be the public good. The new pair is the administered society versus a society of economic democracy. They write: "The Administered Society is above all a vision of social harmony among different and unequal groups cooperating for the goals of improving individual security and widely shared economic growth. To accomplish these ends, it would link private groups, especially business and labor, with governmental agencies to steer economic development through this period of technological and international change ... One key to this vision is the idea of "partnership" among various sectors of the economy and society, brought together through governmental boards, commissions and agencies" (1996:268). Economic democracy is the alternative. This is simply a form of democratic socialism. The authors describe the writings of Michael Harrington, a prominent American democratic socialist in the middle of the nineteen hundreds, as an exemplar of this orientation. "Harrington proposes an active government role to bring about a "democratization of the investment function." Such a policy would lead eventually to "introducing democracy from the shop floor to the board room" " (ibid.:269). Economic democracy calls for decentralization of economic power and for the democratization of the economic decision making process.

In short, the authors argue in the original edition of *Habits of the Heart*, that these competing ideologies will result in either an "administered society" or an "economic democracy" (1996:267). But as they note in their Introduction to the Updated Edition: The House Divided, written ten years later, their earlier predictions did not occur. Instead, neocapitalism has taken over (ibid.:xxv). They express concerns if not alarms at this. Neocapitalism (anchored solidly within the utilitarian and expressive individualism traditions – largely to the exclusion of the civic republican and biblical traditions) was producing "severe strains ... for the nation." They continue: "We are convinced ... that the extreme position of the United States compared to other countries on matters such as income inequality and the attack on public provisions [that come from neocapitalist ideologies] is due in important part to the culture of individualism [of both types], with its inability to understand the capacities and responsibilities of government" (ibid.:xxviii).

It is quite telling that in the Introduction to the Updated Edition they also express alarm at the state of America almost thirty years ago: "Most Americans agree that things are seriously amiss in our society – that we are not, as the poll questions often put it, "headed in the right direction" (1996:xxii). Again, this was written almost three decades ago, well before the very deep political, moral, social and cultural chasms we see and experience in America today. American society today is far more "seriously amiss" today than it was even then. The crisis today is far more precarious. In the late nineteen hundreds, we did not have almost half the country believing in delusions and lies – about Trump winning an election, about the Covid vaccine, about the Jan. 6th insurrection as being insignificant, etc. Thirty years ago, we did not have millions of Americans rejecting any trust at all that professionals – whether they are professors, scientists, journalist, or politicians – can or even do speak the truth, or even more importantly that these people even self-consciously seek to speak the truth. Thirty years ago, presidents did not routinely draw upon fear to get others to comply with their wishes. Today, fear – a decidedly anti-democratic mechanism – is one of the foundational tools of the current presidential administration. In the America of a few decades ago, we had people largely believing in the truth, believing in the reality that truths exist, and believing that professionals for the most part can and do speak the truth or at the least sincerely try to do so. Now truth is deemed by many simply to be a mere proxy or tool of power. Power not truth is what matters. Democracy cannot be sustained in this environment. The crisis that Bellah and his colleagues argued was present decades ago is far more serious today than it was then and is cast because of circumstances in a decidedly different light.

Whether this crisis is of the same form or whether it can be attributed to the same causes identified in *Habits of the Heart*, e.g. the conquest of individualism – both utilitarian and expressive, and the decline of the republican and biblical traditions -- one could debate. Similarly, one could debate the causes of the rise and conquest of individualism, or of particular forms of individualism. Bellah et al. are committed to a cultural and historical explanation of this. Many other sociologists – going back one hundred years – have presented alternative explanations. Often these are based on changes in the political economy. Scholars in the Marxist tradition perhaps are the most obvious example (see for example the Frankfurt School theorists (Chapter Eight).) Such scholars see the pernicious form of individualism that has taken over, according to Bellah and his colleagues, as the direct product of the structure of capitalism. Capitalism in a myriad of ways fosters, produces and requires a particular way of being and way of thinking that nurtures and requires individualism, and this has consequences. I will leave it to the reader to decide whether Bellah, Marx, or others are correct in their assessments about contemporary American culture and the negative consequences of particular forms of individualism.

We can end by noting the importance seen by Bellah et al. of civic virtue – a particular moral way of individuals being oriented and connected to the goal of realizing the public good (see Chapter One). The authors note that democracy was and is dependent upon the rulers and the ruled embracing and enacting civic virtue. James Madison and the other founding fathers clearly recognized this. Bellah et. al. note:

> that our form of government was dependent upon the existence of virtue among the people. It was such virtue that [was] expected to resolve the tension between private interest and the public good. Without civic virtue [the founding fathers thought] the republic would

decline into factional chaos and probably end in authoritarian rule. Half a century later, this idea was reiterated in Tocqueville's argument about the importance of the mores – the "habits of the heart" – of Americans. … The tensions between private interests and the public good is never completely resolved in any society. But in a free republic, it is the task of the citizen, whether ruler or ruled, to cultivate civic virtue in order to mitigate the tension and render it manageable. As the twentieth century has progressed, that understanding, so important through most of our history, has begun to slip from our grasp. (1996:270)

And today, what are we to think of civic virtue in America?

Discussion Questions

1. Should Tocqueville be considered a sociological theorist? Is he a sociologist at heart or is he a political scientist? Is he more or less of a political scientist than Marx? What makes a theory a sociological theory? Does sociological theory need to locate the workings of the political order, e.g. democracy, at the center of any analysis of the social or cultural order?

2. What did Tocqueville get right and what did he get wrong in his analysis about how democracy works and specifically about how American democracy works in the early 1800s and in contemporary America?

3. As noted, some might dismiss Tocqueville's theorizing because he ignores or downplays issues of race, class and gender. Is his theorizing fatally flawed because of this, or is his analysis still legitimate despite this? How can his theorizing about the equality of conditions and mores help to explain issues of race and gender and inequalities today?

4. Is Tocqueville a liberal or a conservative? What do these terms mean? What do these terms mean in relation to social theorists and to Tocqueville's ideas of democracy and equality?

5. In light of the current crisis in American society, and specifically related to the crisis of political, cultural, and social divisions, what if anything can we take from Tocqueville to help us to understand these divides?

Chapter Seven: Structural Functionalism and Conflict Theories

When I think of the structural functionalist theory, I think of days gone by; The America of the 1940s and 1950s comes to mind. World War Two ended in 1945. Before the war, America experienced the Great Depression, a time when the economy fell apart. The Depression began with the stock market crash of 1929 and the economy did not really begin to recover until the war, which began in 1939. For fifteen years or so, from 1929 to 1945, America experienced profound troubles, first economic, then military and political. But the war ended and the troops returned home. America was the only major industrial country left standing after the war. It was the only one not destroyed. The economy expanded and America became wealthier, more prosperous. The "middle classes" were growing in size and in wealth and there was movement up the economic ladder. More and more people were attending college, fueled in part by the GI Bill. The world was well again, and the future was bright. Science and technology were providing new and more convenient, helpful, and useful things to people. Technological innovations could be found throughout society. This is not to deny there were major concerns pressing on Americans at that time. Most notably, the cold war emerged between the United States, and its Western allies, and the Soviet Union. Both sides produced more and more nuclear weapons, and Americans were well aware that any nuclear war would be horrendous. This was the era in which school children in America were taught to "duck and cover" in drills at school to prepare them for a nuclear attack (as if hiding under a desk could save one from nuclear weapons). Yet despite such concerns, America was in a time of happiness and optimism.

Or so that is the image one might have had in watching the news of the time or in watching the television shows. This image however was not the image of reality. It was the image of the dominant and aspiring groups of the time. It was the image that white, male Protestants of English ancestry (i.e. White Anglo-Saxon Protestants – the WASPs) embraced. It was also the image embraced by the hoard of second and third generation white Europeans, largely Catholic and Jewish immigrants, who saw their prospects better than those of their parents and grandparents who arrived in the late eighteen and early nineteen hundreds. There was hope they could rise from the poorer classes. The American Dream was alive and well in the images in their minds. But wait. What about the others? What about African Americans and other minority groups? What about women? The poor? The deep discontent that these groups felt or may have felt was absent from this image. The inequalities and oppressions were hidden from view, or if and when they surfaced as issues of interest, they were not seen in ways that would challenge the accepted views of the good and hopeful state of America.

Structural functionalism emerged and then went on to become the dominant sociological theory at this time and in this context, not at the time when the voices of minorities and women were heard but at a time when white America warmly embraced the image of America as a country of greatness and purity, as a country marching forward toward a "more perfect union." The overwhelmingly dominant figure associated with the creation and spread of structural functionalism was Talcott Parsons (1902-1979), who spent most of his career at Harvard University. Parsons set out to create a grand theory of society. A grand theory is one that explains everything in society, big and small. It is one that explains the relationships of all of the elements in society to one another. A grand theory could explain why wars happen, and why individuals get married, and why one of these things affects the other. Grand theories are all encompassing. The theory he created, called structural functionalism, is a classic grand theory. In building his theory he was greatly influenced by a number of earlier European theorists, including Durkheim, Weber, and the Italian economist Vilfredo Pareto, among many others. Parsons was instrumental in introducing or facilitating the expansion of the ideas of Durkheim and most significantly Weber to American sociology. For example, he was the first to translate Weber's classic work *The Protestant Ethic* into English. In some ways, one can view Parsons' theorizing as an attempt to combine what he considered the better parts of Durkheim and Weber's theory into one grand theory.

Structural functionalism emerged and came to dominance in the mid-nineteen hundreds in America. But this was not the only influential theory to arise during this period. Indeed, numerous others did so. For example, the micro-theories discussed in Chapter Nine arose during this period as well. So too did conflict theory. Conflict theory stands in direct opposition to Parsons' structural functionalism. While structural functionalism begins with an assumption of a natural tendency for society to maintain or to strive for social order, one based upon consensus, conflict theories begin with the opposing assumption that conflict, rather than consensus, lies at the heart of society. But unlike Marxists (see Chapters Two and Eight) who also accord conflict a central place in their theories, conflict theorists reject the claims that all conflict has its roots in the organization of the material conditions, specifically of the economy. For conflict theorists, conflict is anchored in competing and conflicting group interests, whether these are economic and class based or whether they are based on other things, such as status groups, race, etc. Below we describe the conflict theories of Ralf Dahrendorf and Randall Collins.

Talcott Parsons

Parsons spent much of his career developing a model of society, much like one might create a model airplane, or perhaps like an architect might create a model or a blueprint of a building to be built (though he knew well that the metaphor of a model should be understood as just that – a metaphor – and should not be taken for reality itself). The model is much like a model or blueprint of the workings of the world, much like a biologist, chemist or astrophysicist might build a model of the natural environment, the chemical environment, or the objects in space, to understand their worlds. It is an abstract totality representing the true way the world is said to work. His model building set out to identify the parts of some whole and sought to identify how the parts relate to each other and to the whole. Parsons' grand theory sought to create a model of the entire social world, a theory that could explain the workings of all societies at all times, from small Native American societies in the pre-Columbus era, to the workings of industrial America in the 1950s. Alternatively, one might think of his theorizing as puzzle building. Much like a jigsaw puzzle has many distinct parts that fit together to make a unified whole, so too society has many parts that fit together to do the same. The task then is to identify the pieces of the puzzle and to understand how they all fit together. How does the family, as a piece of the puzzle of society, fit in with other parts of society, such as education and schools, the economy and work, culture and the arts, etc.? Using this approach, the task then is to identify the basic elements of the family and see how, why or if, it works to make the whole society function properly or normally.

Several themes ripple through Parsons' theorizing. One of these is culture. He believed the cultural component of society, including that domain of norms, values, beliefs, morality, etc., was central to an understanding of human societies. Also, in keeping with his commitment to model building, he was very much interested in understanding the relationship of parts to the whole. But the parts too could also be considered wholes that in turn are comprised of parts. Society can be thought of as a whole, as a united entity, but within society there are parts like the family, and the family could also be considered a whole. The family too is a whole and is comprised of parts. The family is made up of roles – the father role, the mother role, son, daughter, etc. And each person is a whole, a whole psychological and biological entity. What holds these things – the family, society, other entities -- together? These are the sorts of questions Parsons sought to answer.

Talcott Parsons

Talcott Parsons (1902-1979) was the dominant figure in American sociology in the post-World War Two decades. He was born in Colorado Springs, Colorado. His father was a Congregationalist minister and college professor and administrator, first at Colorado College and later at Marietta College in Ohio where he became president. His family tree on both his mother's and father's sides traces its lineage back to the early British settlers in New England in the sixteen hundreds. Talcott graduated from Amherst College in 1924, studying economics, biology and philosophy, and had initially thought of becoming a medical doctor. He began his graduate work in sociology and economics at the London School of Economics but transferred to the University of Heidelberg in Germany where he received his Ph.D. in 1927. He returned to the United States, and after a year working as a professor at Amherst, he became a professor at Harvard University where he remained for the rest of his working life. He retired in 1973 and died in 1979 of a stroke.

Over the course of his career, Parsons worked with and developed friendships with many, many important social scientists and theorists of the time, including Alfred Schutz, Kenneth Burke, Karl Mannheim, among many others. While in Germany, he met Marianne Weber, Max's wife, and attended and participated in scholarly discussions with notable academics at her home. (Max Weber died several years before Talcott arrived, but the former's influence was still very present.) At Harvard Parsons was instrumental in the development of the interdisciplinary Department of Social Relations, which brought together sociologists, cultural anthropologists, and social psychologists in one academic department. Many of Parsons' students, including Robert Merton, went on to become influential figures in American sociology; Many went on to lead the major sociology programs in universities throughout the country. Parsons was President of the American Sociological Association in 1949 and was given numerous awards throughout his career.

While the above description may suggest that Parsons viewed society in some sort of mechanical way, and it may also suggest that he viewed individuals as simply mechanical puppets. But this was not his intent. He was focused upon creating a theory that did not treat people as if they were mechanical robots or puppets or billiard balls that automatically reacted without making choices in response to the world around them. He sought to create a theory that did not negate agency. People make choices; people have agency. Part of the task in theory building was to build this assumption into the entire model.

The following description of Parsons' theory is organized into three parts. His famous AGIL model is described in the first part. In the second part, his analysis of agency is presented. Here his "voluntaristic theory of action" is described. In the third section his views about social change, evolution and functionalism are covered.

The AGIL Model

Parsons begins his theory by focusing on systems. A system is an organized whole comprised of parts that relate to this whole. These parts work toward keeping the whole going. The world is filled with systems – society, families, universities, the law, friendship, religion, economics, the human body, human psychology, and so many more. The natural ecology is a system. All systems share a number of features. Systems are unified wholes with parts that are integrated and that work together to maintain the whole. Systems are self-regulating. Systems have a tendency toward maintaining a harmonious balance or equilibrium. The structure of any one part of the system impacts the structure on the other parts. Systems have a relationship with their environments; they maintain boundaries. Systems are driven by adaptation and integration.

One can think of the forest as an ecological system. It is filled with trees, and other plant life, as well as birds and other animals. In a normal state of affairs, the forest will maintain itself in a stable and healthy manner. This does not mean that in a natural state there will not be changes to this system, but in a normal state of affairs, the forest will be able to maintain the natural diversity of plant and animal life in proportions that allow for the forest to continue to exist in a healthy manner. The forest could be harmed or altered by any number of factors. Global warming, for example, might lead to the growth of some plants that might not otherwise be present in the forest, and these new plants might successfully compete with already existing plant life such that the already existing plants die off. And this die off might affect the number and types of animals that lived in the forest. If one species of animal lived off the plant that died off, then that species might decline or disappear. Similarly, the introduction of invasive plants and animals into an ecology could significantly alter the ecology. In the northern Mississippi River, the Asian carp has been accidently introduced. This carp has eaten all of the other native fish and has significantly altered the ecology. In short, the whole exists and is maintained, but it also changes.

At the heart of this form of understanding – whether applied to natural environments or to human societies – is an assumption that things exist and are sustained because they serve a function. Something exists because it helps somehow to maintain the normal and healthy whole. Wolves exist in an ecosystem because they limit the number of deer by killing and eating some. If the wolves did not exist, the deer population would grow, and the entire balance of the ecological system would be changed or destroyed. (See Chapter Three on Durkheim for a fuller description of functionalism.)

Parsons says that all living systems need to be able to provide for four basic necessities if they are to survive. Whether it is a family, the natural ecology of the ocean, a human cell, or a society, or any other system, each system requires four things if it is to survive. That is, there are four "functional requisites" for all systems. The four things are abbreviated as **AGIL**. The A stands for **adaptation**. The system needs to have some way to adapt to its external environment. Specifically, it needs resources from the external environment to survive. The human body needs air and food and other things from outside of the body if it is to survive. The university as a system needs many things from outside of it too survive. It needs money, students, perhaps the approval of at least some segments of the population, etc. The G stands for **goal attainment**. A system must be oriented towards some goal. It must be directed in one way or another toward some end, toward accomplishing something or other. For biological agents, the goal tends to be survival or life itself. For the economic system the goal is something else. What might the goal of the economy in a capitalist society be? The goal, arguably, in an economic system is to provide for the needs and desires of the populace. In capitalism it is perhaps to provide increasing prosperity over time. In capitalism, the goal is also profit. The I stands for **integration**. Integration concerns the mechanisms in the system that regulate the relationships of the different parts of the system to each other, including the mechanisms that relate the functional requisites of the four parts of the AGIL to each other. A system must be integrated or coordinated if it is to survive. Money, for example, is an integrating mechanism for the economic system. How are the different parts in a system coordinated? That is the question addressed by the integrative element of a system. The L stands for **latent pattern maintenance**. In any system, there has to be some way to get all of the parts to do what needs is needed for the system to continue. Moreover, for systems to survive this requirement must be done in a way that the parts do not constantly have to be concerned with it. The word latent means quiet or hidden. The patterns of the system are maintained in part because the parts do things to keep the system going often without being aware they are doing so. In human societies, Parsons focuses upon motivation as a key feature of latent pattern maintenance. For a human system (that is, for a "healthy" society) to survive, the individuals in it need to have the proper motivations to act in ways to keep it going. The proper motivations come through proper socialization. Individuals are taught through social interactions how they should be motivated in the world. As such, socialization is a central element of latent pattern maintenance.

Parsons applies the AGIL model to human society and asks what are the functional requisites needed for any society to survive? What things are needed for any and all societies to survive? How do societies, as systems, satisfy the needs of AGIL? He identifies the structural systems in society that are in place to meet the needs of each of these four requisites. These are the **four major systems** in society. The first major system is the **behavioral organism**, i.e. the biological individual. The behavioral organism meets the needs of adaptation. This is the first system. The most basic needs related to adaptation are organic or biological in nature. One can find this need in human societies and in nature. A polar bear would have a hard time living in Florida (outside of a zoo) because its environment is not supportive. The lack of cold, the lack of snow, the lack of traditional food source, and more, would surely be harmful to the continued existence of the bear. (For that matter, a polar bear would have a hard time surviving in the north pole if all the snow and ice melts as the result of global warming, as is happening now.) In the same way, it has been argued that some ancient human societies collapsed because they could no longer provide for the basic biological necessities of life. A society that exists in a dry area that has occasional rain and has a river running nearby, might collapse if the rain stops coming and the river dries up. Similarly, a society that cannot feed its people or that cannot provide for basic necessities will not survive. The **personality system** is the second major system. Parsons says the functional requisite of goal attainment is met in human societies through the personality system. Specifically, individuals need to have a psychology, a way of seeing and acting in the world, which is supportive of the society. Could an industrial or post-industrial democratic capitalist society such as ours, for example, survive unless the individuals in the society were oriented in particular ways? In America, children are taught to be individualistically oriented and success oriented. Americans are taught the values of individual initiative and the desires to work hard to achieve success. Could American society survive if people embrace an alternative set of values, such as one that focuses more on community and compassion, or ones that focus more upon contentment, than it does on individualism and competition? The personality system is basically a form of psychological orientation that is needed for a society to survive.

The **social system** is the third system. Parsons devoted more time to understanding this system than he did to the others. His book *The Social System* (1951) describes how this system works. The social system is basically the structural side of society. It consists of religion, education, family, law, politics, and the economy. The social system is largely responsible for the integrative needs of society. This system contains the institutional framework that integrates the various elements of society. For example, it is not hard to see how laws in a society serve the function of integrating the various parts of society together. Without laws, how would disputes be resolved? The fourth and last major system is the **cultural system**. This exists to provide for the needs of latent pattern maintenance. It is through this system that the norms and values of a society operate, and norms and values for Parsons are centrally important in maintaining a society. For a society to survive, people have to embrace and to share one or another sets of values and beliefs, and they must accept the norms of the society. They must incorporate these norms and values into their behaviors. These things motivate the individuals to act in ways that maintain the society, and at the heart of the cultural system is socialization. Individuals have to be socializing into accepting the norms, values, beliefs, etc. of the society. If not, the society will have trouble maintaining stability.

We can now ask about the functional requisites within each of these four systems – organic, personality, social and cultural. If all systems need to have built into them ways to meet the four basic needs (AGIL), and if these four major systems are not only part of a larger system of society, but are also individual systems in themselves, then within each of these one should be able to identify the four basic needs. In other words, for the personality system to function effectively, it would need to have parts that fulfill the adaptive function, the goal attainment function, etc. The same holds for each of the four major systems. It was noted above that Parsons wrote about the needs of the social system. In the social system the economy is said to fulfill the functional requisites of adaptation. The political arena is said to fulfill the functional requisites of goal attainment. The law is the major institutional domain that fulfills the integrative requirement. And religion, education, and family are the institutions said to be tasked with fulfilling the requirements of the cultural system.

There are then systems within systems, and systems within systems within systems, much like the Russian wooden dolls in which one doll is placed within another larger one and then another one, etc. For societies to function the system requirements need to be met for each system and for the relations between one system and another (see Figure 7.1).

Parsons' AGIL Model

Adaptation	**Goal Attainment**
Latent Pattern Maintenance	**Integration**

Figure 7.1

The Cybernetic Hierarchy of Control

The systems in a society are integrated with each other through what Parsons calls the **cybernetic hierarchy of control.** (It is also called the general system of action). Cybernetics is the study of automatic systems whereby an action in one part of the system automatically ripples through and affects the entire system and causes actions to occur in the other parts. Much like a light switch turns a light on and off, a cybernetic system is one in which when one part is activated; it then activates other parts; and these other parts in turn activate still other parts. Parsons arranges the four systems in order. At the top is the cultural system. This is followed in order by the social system, the personality system and the organic system. As such, changes in the cultural system will then impact the social system, and changes to the social system will in turn affect the personality system, and this in turn affects the organic system. The same is true for the other way around. Changes in the organic system will impact the personality system, which will then affect the social system, and then in turn the cultural system (see Figure 7.2). For example, what might happen in a society if the norms and values break down? What might happen if people no longer shared a particular way of believing and acting? What might happen if people were not motivated in a way that would allow the society to continue in an orderly way? In America, what would happen if people stopped believing that the American dream was true? What if Americans came to believe the American dream was not true? The American dream is the idea that through hard work and fair play one could become wealthier than one's parents. It is the belief that one could succeed through individual initiative, and one could have a better life than one's parents. This is based on the assumption that there is a level playing field such that poor people have the same opportunities, or at least have reasonable opportunities, to become wealthy through individual initiative and hard work as do rich people in maintaining their wealth. If these norms, values, and beliefs break down, then this might affect the social system. For example, it might impact the family or the law or the political stability. If people come to have values and norms that are at odds with the official pronouncements of politicians, then the people might challenge the institutional arrangements in society. They might challenge the legitimacy of the political system or legal system. These in turn might affect the personalities of people in society. They will no longer be motivated to work hard to get ahead. And this in turn might affect the organic system. When one is unemployed, one might be hard pressed to provide for the basic necessities of life.

But it works the other way as well. The example of a Native American tribe that ran out of water, a basic organic necessity, would perhaps not survive, and would at least be forced to make substantial changes. Surely, the biological stresses would force a change in the personality systems of the individual members of the group, and this in turn would affect the social system and the cultural system.

Parsons identifies two primary mechanisms that direct or steer the relations between systems in the cybernetic hierarchy. The first is **information and control**. This moves from the cultural system down through the social, personality, and organic system. Complex systems, such as modern industrial (or post-industrial) societies, rely heavily upon information and control. In these systems the cultural beliefs, norms, and values are centrally important, and the control function of these are crucial for the maintenance of order. Beliefs, for example, about liberty and equality that emerged in the Enlightenment and spread through modernity are widely held today, and these certainly affect the organization of the social system. Among other things, they shape the types of economic, legal and political systems that appear in democratic capitalist societies. These in turn shape the personality and organic systems. But it is not simply political beliefs that trickle down into the other systems. Beliefs about science and history, and beliefs in other domains of social reality also do the same. On the other hand, there is another mechanism that works its way in the other direction – from the organic, through the personality, social and cultural systems. He calls this second primary mechanism the **energy for action**. At its most basic, the human body needs energy to survive. It needs food. The food provides the body with energy to affect the personality system. The personality system then provides the energy, the force, which propels the social system, etc. When the information and controls or the energy mechanisms are disrupted or when they are unable to function properly, this will have ripple effects throughout the system, and the social order of the entire society will be disrupted.

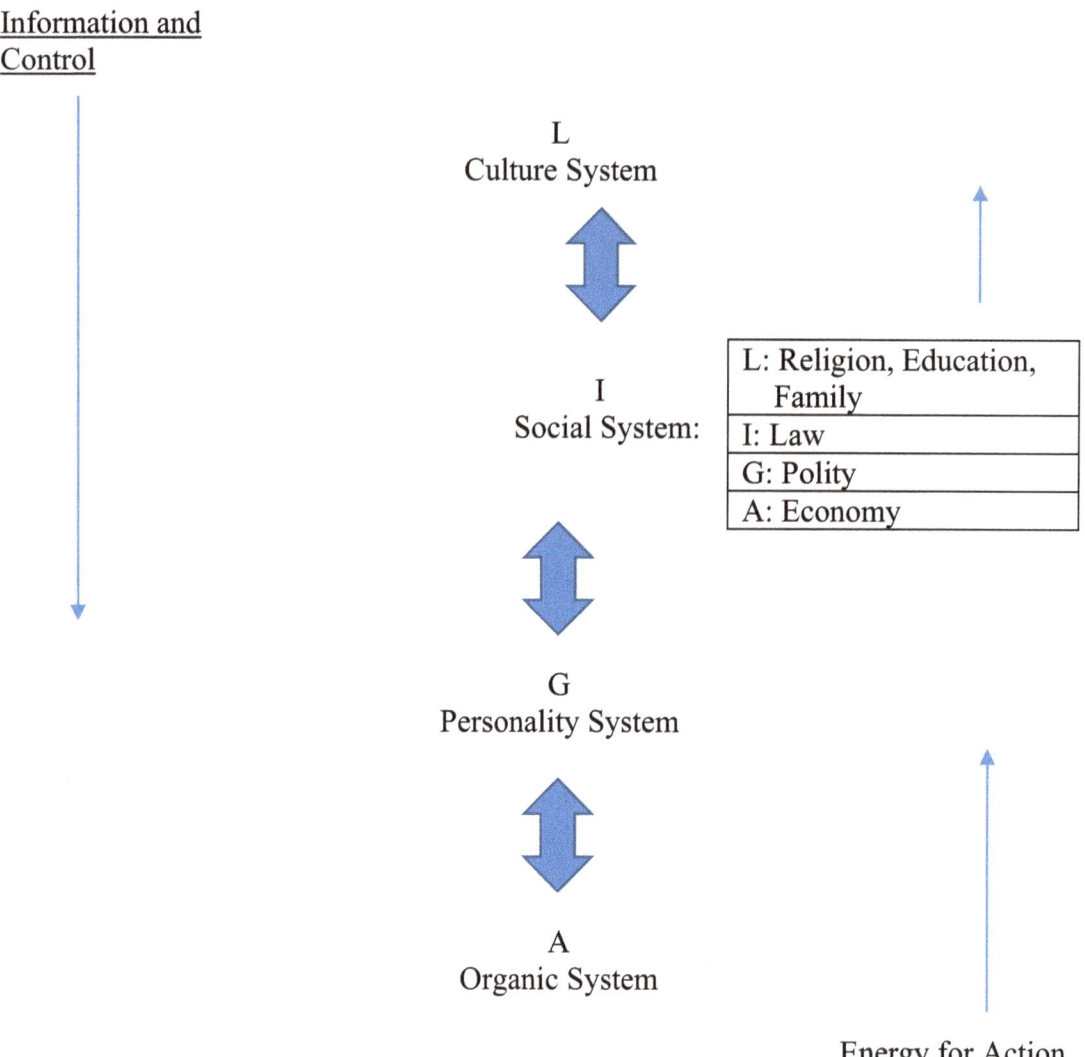

Figure 7.2

Parsons argues that information and control as well as energy move through the system of cybernetic hierarchy of control by way of generalized **media of exchange**. That is, specific things carry information and control as well as energy up and down the systems. Language, for example, is a generalized mechanism of information and control in modern, complex societies. It is and can be used, for example, in the cultural system to state the proper beliefs, values, and norms of a society. And it can then be used through the institutions of the social system to establish and legitimate systems such as law and politics. Parsons also identifies money, power, and influence as other vehicles through which energy moves up through the system and information and control moves down. (He also associated these various things with one or another of the four components of the AGIL system. Money is associated with adaptation; Power is associated with goal attainment; Influence is associated with integration; and language is associated with latent pattern maintenance. These mechanisms he says contribute to social stability, particularly when the norms and values of one system such as the economic system are in conflict with another system such as the family system within the overall society.)

Status Roles, Norms and Pattern Variables

Parsons recognizes that a complete picture of society must include an understanding of the basic elements of the various systems, and specifically the social system. The social system is largely comprised of institutions (politics, law, religion, family, education, economy). To understand society, we must then look more closely as the basic elements of these institutions. The basic elements include status roles and norms. By status role Parsons means the combination of the concept of status and that of role. Status refers to the position in a society. Role refers to the organized set of expectations associated with a status. Father is a status, as is soccer player or criminal. Status traditionally is associated with prestige or honor. The father role is defined in terms of the expectations attached to this position. In the traditional American, patriarchal family, the father was expected to be the breadwinner. Status role combines together the position and the expectations. Norms are shared understandings of expected behaviors. They are maintained by either positive or negative sanctions. The status role of the medical doctor has sets of norms associated with it. The doctor is supposed to act in certain ways and is not supposed to act in other ways. When the doctor conforms to the expectations of the role, he will receive positive sanctions, perhaps in terms of money or prestige. When the doctor violates the expectations, he will likely receive negative sanctions, such as being subject to a lawsuit, or being fired, or being shunned by his or her colleagues, etc. Status roles and norms, when organized in a formal and sustained way produce institutions.

Parsons also wished to understand how reoccurring social behaviors such as those found in formal institutions (e.g. you generally know how your doctor will behave before you meet with him or her) are patterned or organized. Specifically, he sought to identify the essential variables associated with the concept of status role. One status role is different from another. Roles differ in terms of the specific types of value orientations and expectations attached to them. The father's role is different from the mother's role. The doctor's role is different from the patient's role. These status roles are all different, but at the same time because they are all status roles they must share some things. That is, they differ along a number of variables that can be identified. These "pattern variables" are described below. Before describing this concept further, it would perhaps help here to describe how he came up with this notion. Here he is influenced by Durkheim's distinction between societies that are characterized by mechanical solidarity and those that are characterized by organic solidarity. (He is also influenced by a similar distinction made by the German sociologist Ferdinand Toennies, between gemeinschaft (community) and gesellshaft (society).) You may recall that the types of social bonds and interactions in societies having mechanical solidarity, such as pre-modern African villages, are quite different from those found in New York City, or some other setting today, which are characterized by organic solidarity. In societies with mechanical solidarity, individuals have personal relationships with one another. In contrast, modern societies characterized by organic solidarity are large and impersonal. People interact in quite different ways in these two types of societies. In societies with mechanical solidarity one would perhaps find status roles defined by personal connections. In societies with organic solidarity, one would perhaps find status roles defined by impersonal connections. The status role of a friend or relative is different from the status role of a bureaucrat because of the value orientations found in each role. The types of status roles developed in the societies differs. Parsons uses these distinctions to develop a set of "pattern variables" or concepts that define status roles and that describe the ways in which people can and do develop sustained relationships with each other.

He identifies five sets of **pattern variables**, all of which define the basic elements of status roles (see Figure 7.3). The first is affective versus affective neutrality. This refers to whether a role in a social relationship, particularly as it is institutionalized in a status role, is supposed to be emotional or not. Does the role allow for or encourage emotion? Is the person in the role expected to focus on emotions or not? For example, a professional such as a medical doctor is generally supposed to be affectively neutral. The doctor is not expected to show his or her emotions and is not supposed to allow these emotions to influence his or her actions. The doctor is not expected to embrace any emotions at all. Quite the contrary. The doctor should avoid being emotional in his or her decision making and in his or her behavior. In contrast, the role of mother (in Parsons' understanding) does have within it the expectation of affectivity. It is conforming to the role of wife, for the mother to be emotional. For example, it is acceptable if not expected that she will be emotionally supportive of others. The second set of pattern variables is collectivity versus self. Does the role focus mostly on the needs of the collective or on the needs of the individual? In the roles of the capitalist marketplace, the expectation is that the seller (and buyer) will be focused not on the collective and what is best for it, but on the individual and what is best for him or her. In contrast, some situations or roles call for the individual to act out of concern for the collective. The role of parent in a family, for example, is structured along the collective rather than the individual lines. Mothers and fathers are supposed to act in the interest of the family collective and not in their own selfish interests, or at least they are expected to place the needs of the family ahead of their individual needs.

Pattern Variables

Expressive Orientations:	Instrumental Orientations:
Ascription	Achievement
Diffuseness	Specificity
Affectivity	Neutrality
Particularism	Universalism
Collectivity	Self

Figure 7.3

Particularism versus universalism is the next set. The main issue for this set of pattern variables is whether a person will engage in social action based upon some universal and objective criteria (universalism), or whether a person will engage in actions based upon the particular, subjective assessments regarding the unique qualities of other person and of the relationship between then (particularism). When someone goes to a convenience store as a customer and buys something, the expectation is that the person behind the counter, in the role of worker, will treat the customer as he or she treats all customers. The worker will not treat the individual as a unique person. He holds a universalistic orientation. In the same way, the role of a scientist is patterned in a universal way. In contrast, the role of friend is oriented toward particularism. Friends interact with friends in particularistic ways. They act based upon their friendship and knowledge of the uniqueness of the other person. The fourth set is diffuseness versus specificity. This set of variables concerns the range of obligations that is expected in an interaction. The role of mother in relation to her child is diffuse. The child relies upon the mother for a wide array of things. In contrast, the policeman's orientation is specific. When the policeman pulls you over for speeding, you are not expecting that he will care about whether you are having a bad day or not. He is supposed to care only about whether you were speeding and whether you have or are breaking any other laws. A role oriented toward one specific thing or one specific attribute of another is specific.

The fifth set of pattern variables is ascription versus achievement. Ascription refers to characteristics that are assigned to others based upon some characteristic, often produced at birth or by nature, which are deemed by members of a group as significant. Sex, race, age, etc. are ascribed characteristics, but so too might be a king in political system in which the king becomes king because he is the son of a king. In contrast, the role of medical doctor today is an achieved role. The assumption is the person earned the title of doctor. In pre-modern societies, the assumption is that there were far more ascribed roles. In modern societies, achieved roles are the more common type.

The Voluntaristic Theory of Action

What about the individual? How should a theorist understand an individual's intentional action? Parsons begins by imagining the characteristics of any single, intentional social behavior. What are the building blocks or essential components of any such act? This is what he seeks to understand. If one wishes to understand and explain behavior (from a social scientific perspective), one must create abstract models of things. Toward that end, he develops a model. His model of the most basic elements of intentional social behavior is called the **unit act**. The unit act has several basic elements. A unit act consists of an initial state and an end state. That is, the actor is goal directed in his behavior. The act has a starting point and an end point or a goal, toward which he or she is directed. But the actor does not automatically achieve his or her goal. The actor also has choices as to how he or she seeks to achieve these goals. As such, the agent's actions are limited by the conditions of action found in the initial state. If I want to fly to Florida for vacation, but I am in prison in Montana serving a life term, the conditions do not allow me to easily reach my goal. In addition to the conditions of action, the normative orientation found in the situation of the unit act will influence the behaviors directed toward the goal. This is not to say that people automatically conform to normative expectations. Parsons says that individuals have agency; they make choices. This model is called the **voluntaristic theory of action**, which is described in his book *The Structure of Social Action* (1949). (One perhaps can see the influence of Weber in Parsons' model. Specifically, Parsons draws upon Weber's analysis of ideal types of social action.)

Patterns of Social Behavior

Parsons does not stop with a description of the unit act. He also analyzes various possible types of social action (see Figure 7.4). He begins here by identifying what he calls modes of orientation. These consist of three types of motivations and three types of values, and the interrelationship of motives and values. We are motivated by one or another of three types of needs. We have a need for objective knowledge. Here we are motivated by a need for truthful understandings of the world. We are also motived by the need for emotional attachment. We seek human connections with others. Thirdly, we are motived by a need for evaluation. We have a need to make judgments or assessments about the world. In addition to these three types of needs, there are three types of value that orient us. The first is the value of objective knowledge. We have a need for objective knowledge, but we also can value it. A second type of value is on aesthetic feelings. We can value taste and art and beauty. Thirdly, we can place a value on evaluative standards. We may make value judgments.

Types of Action

Modes of Orientation	Types of Action

Motives:
  -Cognitive (Toward Objective Knowledge)
  -Cathectic (Toward Emotional Expression)
  -Evaluative (Toward Evaluation)
	Strategic (or Instrumental) Action
	
	Expressive Action
	
	Moral Action

Values:
  -Cognitive (Objective Knowledge)(Truth)
  -Appreciative (Aesthetics)(Beauty)
  -Moral (Evaluative Standards)(Goodness)	

Figure 7.4

The three types of values and motivations intersect with one another to produce three types of cultural patterns, which in turn produce three types of action. The need for objective knowledge combines with the value of objective knowledge to produce belief systems of cognitive significance, and these create conditions for strategic action to occur. Action motivated by a need for emotional attachment combines with the value of aesthetic feelings to produce systems of expressive symbolism and expressive types of actions. Finally, the need for evaluation combines with the value of evaluative standards to produce systems of value orientations, which lead to moral types of actions.

Change, Evolution and Functionalism

Parsons was widely criticized in the 1960s and in later decades for not adequately addressing or incorporating theories of social change into his overall theoretical framework. His theory seems in some ways to be based upon the absence or lack of change. Societies and their parts have a tendency, he says, to maintain, establish, or re-establish states of equilibrium or balance or harmony. All of the parts are supposed naturally to work, to function, together to make the whole ordered and healthy. However, it is a bit too simplistic to say that he ignored theorizing about change. He wrote about change on several occasions. He wrote about the conditions of revolutionary change (see for example 1966). He also wrote a good deal about evolutionary change, and his theorizing was both influenced by and was a reaction against the evolutionary theorizing of Herbert Spencer. Nevertheless, more sophisticated critics complain that while he did theorize about change, he did so in a way that seemed to view it as an automatic or mechanical process, much like the changes in biological evolution. Social history then is seen as a natural process not unlike evolution. Humans it would appear have little say in determining history.

Parsons applies some of the principles of evolutionary biology to an understanding of changes in human societies in history. For example, life began in nature with simple, one-celled organisms many, many millions of years ago, and it evolved into more and more complicated biological entities. Humans are biologically far more complex than simple one-celled organisms. In the same way, early human societies could be seen as comparatively simple in organization, whereas modern societies can be viewed as complex.

The evolution of human societies is based upon several basic principles. The first of these is **differentiation**. That is, as evolution proceeds things become more complicated and more specialized, and within and between organisms (or systems) there is increasing differentiation. A one-celled animal does not have a liver or a kidney, but humans and other mammals do.

More and more as we walk up and through the evolutionary tree, we see increasing differentiation. Organisms increasingly have more and different specialized parts, and these parts and their interrelationships also become increasingly complex. In human societies, for example, we now have educational institutions. These did not exist when humans first roamed around this earth millions of years ago. There were no schools back then. Learning occurred, but it did so within the family or the social group. Similarly, governments as we know them today did not exist millions of years ago. Yet the tasks assigned to educational institutions and to government today still had to be fulfilled in one way or another many millions of years ago. The tasks were built into and not differentiated from other sectors of society. The village chief, for example, might be both the political leader and religious leader and he might be the military leader as well. All of these are largely differentiated today.

A second characteristic of social evolution is adaptation, or what Parsons calls **adaptive upgrading**. As evolution proceeds, if organisms are to survive, they have to develop increasingly sophisticated means of adapting to increasingly differentiated environments. In social evolution, those institutional formations or social actions that are not adapted to the environment will disappear, much as the tails of human primate ancestors who lived in trees ceased to exist as apes began to walk on the group rather than swing through the trees. The apes with the most adaptive genes were the ones able to reproduce, and those with the least adaptive genes vanished from evolutionary history. Another example perhaps could be human's use of clothing. The fact that humans wear clothes and other animals do not gives humans much more flexibility in where and how they live. Humans live in the artic and in the desert. A polar bear cannot live in the desert, or in Florida.

Parsons notes that several other factors arise within the process of evolution that must be understood if one is to understand social evolution. One of these is the increased need for **mechanisms of integration**. As organisms and systems become more and more complicated, there is an increasing need for them to develop effective means of integration, both within the organisms and within and between systems. Otherwise, the entire society would not function. It would fall apart. Mechanisms of integration become more important as increasing differentiation and adaptive upgrading proceeds. Also, Parsons noted the importance of culture, and specifically of values, in this evolutionary process. Social evolution creates an increasing need for value systems to be more general in scope. As differentiation causes partitioning and specialization, this in itself could threaten the unity of a society. The unity in complex societies must be anchored in shared generalized value systems. (One can hear echoes of Durkheim here.)

Structural-Functionalist Theory of Stratification

One of the more controversial elements of structural functionalist theory concerns inequality. Specifically, structural functionalists claim that because inequality exists in all societies it must be functional for the maintenance of society. The controversial elements of this argument are discussed below when some of the main criticisms that have been leveled against this theory are reviewed. Here, I describe one of the most well know structural functionalist statement on inequality. This statement was made in an article that was published in 1945 by Kingsley Davis and Wilbert Moore. (Davis and Moore were both students of Parsons at Harvard.) The article, titled "Some Principles of Stratification" (1945), presents an argument for the need for having a system of inequality, i.e. its functional necessity, in society, and for the benefits of it. Inequality in short is said to be necessary and beneficial to society. Unequal rewards (e.g. money, prestige, etc.) are needed to place the right people in the right jobs. Davis and Moore make a number of points in their argument. The first is that certain positions are functionally more important than others to the maintenance of society, and that these positions require special skills. A medical doctor is more important to modern society than is a cashier at McDonald's. Second, not everyone has the talents needed to fill these positions. Only some people in any society have the abilities needed to work effectively in these positions. Not everyone has the ability to become a brain surgeon, but most people have the ability or talent to be a clerk at Walmart. Third, the education and training needed to get into one of the selective positions requires much sacrifice, both in terms of money and time. It takes many years, for example, of advanced education to be a medical doctor, a professor, or a scientist, and this entails great sacrifice. Fourth, motivations or inducements in the form of valued things (e.g. high salaries, prestige, etc.) are needed to entice those with talents or abilities to undergo these sacrifices and to get this training. Fifth, the resulting inequality therefore is both inevitable and positively functional for any society (taken from Tumin, 1953:387-388). In sum, as Davis and Moore note:

> If the rights and perquisites of different positions in a society must be unequal, then the society must be stratified, because that is precisely what stratification means. Social inequality is thus an unconsciously evolved device by which societies insure that the most important positions are conscientiously filled by the most qualified persons. Hence every society, no matter how simple or complex, must differentiate

persons in terms of both prestige and esteem, and must therefore possess a certain amount of institutionalized inequality. (1945:243)

Davis and Moore's argument came under significant attack in the 1950s and 1960s and in more recent decades (see for example, Tumin, 1953; Huaco, 1966). Many if not most of the criticisms were based upon the functionalist assumptions used by Davis and Moore. One criticism concerns the claim that the functionally more important positions in society will be rewarded more than the less important positions. But is this true? Is it really true that a professional athlete is functionally more important to the smooth workings of American society today than a childcare worker who takes care of two-year olds each day? Relatedly, how is one to know which positions are functionally more important than others? The functionalist argument claims one will know because these positions will be given the greatest rewards. But this is a circular argument and thus a flawed argument (see criticisms of functionalism below). Critics also note the obvious political bias embedded in the Davis and Moore argument. The authors claim their argument is unbiased and objective, but it lends intellectual cover or support to existing systems of inequality and supports and legitimates the positions of the wealthier classes. Critics also challenge the assumption that there is in America an open mobility system whereby people who are poor and who have talent, ability and motivation have equal chance of getting access to the education and training needed to get into the higher positions in society. Rich people can and do send their children to private schools and can afford their children educational opportunities that are blocked to poorer children. (This situation is even more strikingly apparent today than it was forty years ago.) Another criticism concerns the assumption that the positions that require the most education and training and that require the most sacrifice in time and money to acquire this education and training will be rewarded the most. If this was true, then college professors, particular college professors teaching in the humanities (literature, history, philosophy, etc.), would be making more money than stockbrokers on Wall Street. But this is certainly not the case. Very often people with less education and training make more, if not much more, than those with a great deal of education and training. Lastly, the issue of motivation is troubling to many critics. Davis and Moore assume that people have self-interested motives of money or prestige that lead them to sacrifice time and money to get the training or education necessary to get high end positions. But do people act in this way? Motivations are complicated, and certainly people do things for many reasons that may be in addition, or as alternatives, to the self-interested motives of money or prestige. People may select occupations based upon their desire to help others, for example, or they may be driven to live fulfilling lives. Moreover, what motivations *should* someone have? Davis and Moore suggest that the self- interested motives are the motives that people do have and that these are the motives they should have. But is it true? Is the best doctor going to be the one that enters the field because he or she wants to make money and wishes to get the respect of others, or is the best doctor one who becomes a doctor because he or she wishes to help people and to save lives? Or, is the best doctor perhaps one who wishes to contribute first and foremost to the advancement of the science of medicine?

Robert Merton and Structural Functionalism

Robert Merton (1910-2003) was a student of Parsons who went on to become a prominent sociologist in his own right. He spent most of his career teaching sociology at Columbia University. He believed sociology should be an empirical science and believed it was vital for sociologists to engage in research and not to simply develop abstract ideas. His focus of interest throughout his career was quite broad. He studied such diverse topics as the sociology of science, the sociology of deviance, and the socialization of medical students, to name but a few of his interests. While Merton (1968) embraced many of the overarching ideas of structural functionalism and while he identified as a structural functionalist, he differed from Parsons on several main points. Parsons sought to understand the entire workings of a society from a functionalist perspective and as such wished to explain all facets of society as having functions that serve to maintain the stability of the entire society. Merton, on the other hand, believed functionalism should be narrower in scope. Not everything in society should be understood as existing to help maintain the entire social order. Moreover, Merton claims that every social formation should not be assumed to be functional for society. Many things exist that are not functional and indeed are harmful to the stability of society. In addition, some things exist in society that are neither helpful nor harmful to the maintenance of society.

Merton (1967) built his own version of structural functionalism. One of the central themes in this theory is the focus on the middle range. **Middle-range theory** was developed in part as a reaction against the grand theory of Parsons. But it was also a reaction against those who believed sociology as a science should reject any and all forms of theorizing and instead focus exclusively upon testing specific and particular hypothesis about specific and particular events in social life. Middle range theory seeks to develop explanations for more narrowly defined social phenomena than "society," and it seeks to create generalizations from empirical studies of these phenomena. For example, the task of sociology is not to provide a theory to explain the emergence of democratic capitalism or modernity, but instead to explain reoccurring patterns, for example, within one or another institutional context, such as a bureaucracy. In sum, middle range theories should be abstract, but not too abstract, and they should be rooted in understandings of facts, of empirical realities, but not so much that one is simply explaining the immediate facts and ignoring theory building.

As noted above, Merton disagreed with Parsons and others who claimed that social formations that last over a period of time exist because they serve a function, and that function is to help maintain social order, balance, or harmony in society. Merton notes that some things in society can be understood as being functional. Families, for example, arguably serve a function in societies. However, other things he says are **dysfunctional**. That is, some social things are not good for society. Some of these harm or threaten the stability and balance in society, or some prevent society from being as functionally balanced as it could be. Discrimination against races, ethnicities, or genders, arguably has prevented society from operating most effectively by restricting the potential pool of people available for various jobs. High crime rates, as we saw in the chapter on Durkheim, could be seen as dysfunctional to society. Similarly, religion might be viewed as functional in some respects in that it fosters social solidarity, but it could become dysfunctional if it threatens the social order. Islamic radicals today understand and embrace their religion in a way that seems highly dysfunctional to many societies, and to the world system. In addition to functional and dysfunctional outcomes, Merton recognizes that some social things may exist without having a function or dysfunctional element. These are **nonfunctions**. These are things that have consequences that neither help nor hurt the social order. They simply exist.

Another set of concepts Merton develops that are directly related to functionalism are manifest and latent functions. A **manifest function** is one that is the conscious and recognized function of a social formation. It is the stated purpose of a social thing. If one asked a teacher, why do schools exist? The teacher might say they exist to educate students. This is the manifest function. But in many things, hidden or latent elements exist that also contribute to the maintenance of the social order. These are **latent functions**. Schools, for example, help to socialize students into the proper norms and values of society. Similarly, some argue that schools contribute to the maintenance of a system of inequality, and thus to social order, by bringing together students from similar social classes. As students may date and then marry from within their own school and from within their own class, schools then serve to maintain the system. These are latent functions.

Merton also notes the importance of recognizing that there are very often **unintended effects** of social actions. Not all actions have intended effects. Many produce situations that are not planned and not foreseen. They create unintended effects. Some of these arguably are functional. Latent functions are examples of unintended effects. He gives the example of an American Indian rain dance. Why would a tribe of American Indians engage in rain dances if they do not produce rain? Wouldn't the people simply stop doing the dances once they realized they did not work? Yet they continue to do the dances. There must be a reason for this. The reason is that the dance fosters social solidarity. It is a latent function of the dance, and it is an unintended consequence. But not all things that have unintended effects are latent functions. Something might produce unintended effects that are dysfunctional or nonfunctional as well. One need not look any further than the workings of bureaucracies to see that they often have unintended effects that are dysfunctional.

So how are we to know whether something is functional, dysfunctional, or nonfunctional? How are we to know whether something produces latent as well as manifest functions? How are we to know whether something produced unintended effects? The answer to all of these questions for Merton lies in empirical research. The point is to conduct research on the real world to see whether or not one or another of these things is present. This goes back to his embrace of middle range theorizing. The sociologist should seek to discover through research whether one or another claim is verified or not.

Merton is also known for his theory of deviance and social problems. He initially presented this theory in an article, "Social Structure and Anomie" (1938). The theory came to be called the **strain (or anomie) theory of deviance** (Figure 7.5). It is based upon his interpretation of Durkheim's concept of anomie. Anomie is the social condition in which expectations and reality are not lined up properly. Specifically, it is a social situation in which peoples' expectations are not met in reality. This produces confusions and alternative behaviors meant to address these confusions. He frames the argument by focusing upon two sets of concepts: cultural goals (or ends) and institutional means to reach these goals. For a society to exist and for it to remain stable, its members must generally share certain values and certain goals. If a society does not have such unifying cultural elements, it will be unable to function normally. According to Merton, financial success was the generally agreed upon goal in America (in the middle of the nineteen hundreds). It was the normative goal. Seeking to have more money is a major unifying goal and value in American society. On the other hand, not everyone in society is placed in a position such that they can reach this goal, at least not through conventional and legal channels. Whether one can achieve the goal of financial success is dependent upon the structural position one finds oneself in society. Some people have the institutional means to succeed, others do not. Institutional means to achieve the cultural goals of success might include such things as having the access or money or resources needed to attend schools and colleges.

But not everyone embraces the cultural goals of financial success, and not everyone has the institutional means available to them. As such, Merton creates a table of the relationship between cultural goals and institutional means, and identifies five types of groups of people based upon: their structural situation in society; whether they accept the cultural goals of financial success; and whether they have institutional means available to them to achieve these goals and/or whether they use these means. Using this model, he identifies five types of people. The only group that Merton identifies as not being deviant are the conformists. The conformists embrace the cultural goals in society, i.e. financial success, and have access to and make use of the institutional means of gaining financial

Merton's Strain (or Anomie) Theory of Deviance

Types of Adaptation	Means	Ends (Goals)
Conformist	+	+
Innovator	--	+
Ritualist	+	--
Retreatist	--	--
Rebel	--/+	--/+

Figure 7.5

success. An example of a conformist might be someone who was raised in a middle class household who goes on to earn a college degree and then works as a mid-level manager. He seeks to advance in his career. He works nine to five, perhaps longer, and perhaps is married with two children. He is successful and does not engage in any illegal actions. The innovators are those who also embrace the goal of financial success, but do not have the conventional, institutional means of achieving this. They are blocked. For example, someone who grew up in a poor environment with no access to decent schools and certainly with no money to attend college, may resort to illegal activities to make money. The head of an illegal drug cartel or a mafia head might be examples of an innovator. Even a low level drug dealer would be considered an innovator. The ritualist has abandoned the cultural goals of financial success, even though he or she has available to him the institutional means of getting ahead. Thus, a person who is from the middle classes may go to college, then get a middle level job, but by the time the person is in his thirties or forties he or she realizes that he or she will not be getting any more promotions. He has gone as high up the financial ladder that he can. The ritualist accepts this and stops trying to get further ahead financially. He becomes resigned to his station in life. This is a controversial category of deviance in that the ritualist is not doing anything illegal. He or she goes to work, comes home, goes to work again. But he has abandoned the American value of seeking to financially advance. The retreatist rejects the cultural goals of financial success and does not use or does not have access to the institutional means of getting this success. Merton has in mind here the alcoholic or the mentally ill. The last category is the rebel. This is arguably more controversial than the ritualist. The rebel rejects the cultural goals and replace these with alternative sets of cultural goals, and they do the same with the institutional means. They reject the conventional institutional means and replace these with alternatives. Revolutionaries and those who join communes (and perhaps cults) are examples of this orientation.

Some Criticisms of Structural Functionalism

Structural functionalism came under sustained attack beginning in the 1960s and 1970s and has been unable to adequately or effectively respond to these ever since. As a result, this form of theorizing is not embraced by very many scholars today. Nevertheless, many prominent theorists today recognize that Parsons and the structural functionalists offered many significant insights into the workings of society, and many of these contemporary theorists have drawn upon some of their ideas. (One such scholar is Jurgen Habermas, who we discuss in Chapter Eleven.)

Many of the criticisms of structural functionalism are directed at those parts of the theory that are taken from Durkheim's theorizing. Specifically, many of the problems of structural functionalism revolve around the many thorny problems associated with the idea of functionalism itself. One of these problems concerns conflict. Structural functionalism is often called a consensus theory. It is built on the assumption that societies have a natural tendency to seek to maintain harmony and balance. The parts (e.g. family, the economy, etc.) of the society are seen to work smoothly with each other to produce a balanced, healthy and harmonious whole. Something exists because it fosters harmony, rather than because it challenges it, according to structural functionalists. The opposite of consensus is conflict, and structural functionalists see conflict in society as the exception. Conflict is not seen as a common, normal characteristic of society. However, many sociologists complained that one cannot accurately understand society if one assumes that things exist to produce consensus. These critics are often associated with what has come to be called conflict theories. Some of these are described in the next chapter.

The problem of consensus is associated with several other problems, problems related to power, change and history. Conflict theorists and others complained that structural functionalists do not adequately address the issue of power. Power is not a central concern for Parsons or others, and when he writes about it, he does so in ways that suggest it operates not to produce conflict, but to produce solidarity. He describes power, for example within the economic arena or the political arena, in terms of how it functions. It functions to contribute to the maintenance of the harmonious society. It contributes to the maintenance of the status quo. He does not see power as a force that is independent of this functional role. As such, he cannot see power as a tool used to oppress or to wrongfully dominate another. (One can hear Marx's criticisms here.) Parsons' understanding and explanation of social change has also widely been criticized (though when he was alive, he recognized these criticisms and tried to address them). How should we understand social change? How and why does it happen? If the parts of society exist to maintain the current system, then how and why does change occur? For Parsons, change happens to further integration and harmony (to further adaptation and differentiation). If change happens for other reasons, then it is dysfunctional. But critics ask, is this really the right way of thinking about such things? If change occurs that is oriented to, or leads to, a radical challenge of the status quo, is it dysfunctional. Are political revolutions automatically dysfunctional?

Structural functionalists have also roundly been criticized for ignoring history. Parsons' model is fundamentally ahistorical. That is, it neither presents a theory of history, nor does it recognize the importance of appreciating the historical situation of a particular society in order to understand it. Structural functionalism presents a model that is removed from and is outside of real history. But critics complain that any such model will fundamentally distort an understanding of real social life. History matters, critics say. We must determine how history affects the present. Any understanding of society must be historical. To ignore history is to distort our knowledge. Structural functionalism only really addresses the issue of history when it incorporates the evolutionary model. But is this an accurate or appropriate model to understand history? Much like biological evolution, structural functionalists seem to say, there are forces at work behind the scenes which propel history forward. But should we understand history as an automatic process? Over the last one hundred years, scholars from all quarters have abandoned such theories of history. (This related to the problems of teleology. See below.) If nothing else, the structural functionalist embrace of evolutionary models of history turns people into passive, mechanical pawns simply conforming to the demands of evolution. But history is not on autopilot, critics might say, and we need to understand how and why it works.

This criticism is closely related to another: Critics sometimes complain that Parsons fails to adequately incorporate the notion of agency into his theories. Much as people appear to be pawns in evolutionary history, so too do people in general operate in mechanistic ways in the structural functionalist theory, at least according to critics. Parsons refuted this criticism and indeed was very focused upon building a "voluntaristic theory of agency" into his theory, as described above. Nevertheless, critics complain that when his explanations are examined closely, one is left unsatisfied that he adequately accounts for things such as agency and social psychology.

In addition to the above, critics have leveled many philosophical complaints against the theory. One of these is that the theory claims to be an objective, scientific and unbiased theory of society, but in fact it is a biased and politically conservative theory. The theory supports and legitimates the existing democratic capitalist society, or any existing society, and it supports the inequalities found there, but it does so under the guise that it is an objective, scientific theory. In other words, the theory says that it separates out facts from values, as all science proclaims to do, but in fact it does not do so. The conservative values rooted in functionalism lay implicitly beneath the theory, while the theory itself gives the impression it is unbiased and scientific. (Curiously, like Durkheim, Parsons believed himself to be liberal, and believed his theorizing itself to be, if anything, liberal rather than conservative. Parsons was actually, and bizarrely, called a "communist" by the McCarthy-era anti-communist House of Un-American Activities Committee.) For example, are we to believe that (the relatively few) Germans who engaged in defiant opposition to the German Nazis in the 1930s were "abnormal," as is suggested by functionalist reasoning? And should we assume that Nazi Germany was a functional and healthy society? Of course not. Who is to say what is a normal and healthy society? This problem here, critics say, is rooted in the use of models, and specifically biological models to understand society. The issue of objectivity and of facts and values raises a whole host of thorny problems for theorizing, problems which to this day have not been resolved. However, critics maintain that at the very least a theorist must recognize such problems and should not ignore them in their theory building, as structural functionalists are said to have done.

Perhaps the most classic philosophical problems weighing down structural functionalism are those associated with **teleology**. Teleology is the idea that there is some (hidden) goal or end state of society that is driving action forward. Teleology is the perspective that assumes actions are directed automatically towards a particular end. The actions are caused by the end state; action is automatically pulled by and toward the end state. The end state directs the actions toward it. (An example of this is the concept of instrumental rationality (see Weber). This form of rationality is basically cold logic. In logically driven action the ends determine or pull the action forward.) We saw this above with the concept of social change and evolution. In the evolutionary model of structural functionalism, societies become more complex. Elements become more integrated and specialized, and there is an embrace of adaptability. This all leads to a harmonious end state, in which all of the parts work seamlessly together into a unified, wonderful whole. Structural functionalism has as one if its basic elements the claim that change and history are directed toward this harmonious state. The problem with teleology is that there is no basis for making such assumptions about the social world. Why would one or another social formation exist to help society march toward some end state? Teleology assumes there is some hidden or magical force propelling history forward, whereas critics rightfully note there is not such force. We as a society, and as a human race, could just as well be heading to a world of social hell as we are headed to a world of social heaven. The point is that we cannot say that either is what in fact is propelling social action.

Another criticism is the problem of **tautology**. Tautology is nothing more than circular reasoning. That is, it is a faulty way of arguing in which the conclusion of an argument is based on parts of the premise, often upon implicit parts of the premise. A tautology is an argument in which the conclusion says the same thing as the premise. Another way of thinking about tautologies is that it is saying the same thing twice while using different words. (One cute example of a tautology is: A tautology is a thing which is tautological.) An example of a tautological argument might be: The Red Sox are favored to win because they are the better team. So how is structural functionalism tautological? The theory claims that one can know why some social formation exist and why it does what it does based upon its function in contributing to the maintenance of social order or social stability. For example, a structural functionalist might argue that the nuclear family (e.g. married man and woman and two children living in the same house) is functional for the maintenance of social order. But how do you know this? You know this, the structural functionalist might say, because one of the things that indicates social order is the existence of a nuclear family. In short, tautologies appear to be making logical points, when in fact they are not saying anything at all.

A last criticism of note, which is closely related to, and which overlaps with the above, concerns the ways in which structural functionalists rely upon models and model building to understand society. This problem goes back to Durkheim's functionalism. Durkheim relied heavily upon biological metaphors, biological models, to understand human societies. But human societies are not biological entities and do not necessarily operate in the same way. Functionalism was criticized for treating the biological metaphor as if it was a fact and not a metaphor. Society may be like the human body, but there is no logical reason to think that social formations exist, like the heart exists, to maintain the existing social order. Critics rightly note that society is not the human body. The heart is biologically programed to function as it does. There is no comparable program in society that dictates how the various parts operate. Moreover, it is not logically possible to say whether some social formation is functional or dysfunctional. The human body might have a healthy and normal body temperature or heart rate, but should we think society operates in this same way? For example, Durkheim says crime is normal, but how much crime is normal and how much crime is abnormal?

Conflict Theories

Women are oppressed in Saudi Arabia today. They wear the head to toe burqas and their social and political activities are incredibly restricted. It is against custom or law for women there to drive a car and to participate in much of the public life of the country. One could provide a lengthy list of things they are prohibited from doing simply because they are women. Why then do the Saudi women accept this? It would seem to be in their interest to be able to drive and to do the other things now banned. On the other hand, in America one often finds people protesting. In the last few years, for example, in many American cities young African Americans and whites and others have engaged in numerous protests against the police shootings and killings of young black men. How are we to account for these two very different circumstances? In the first, women are not acting to further their interests; in the second, African Americans and their supporters are. In both situations, you have groups in conflict over issues of authority. In both groups the theme of interests is central. What are interests, and when do people do things to advance them? These are just a few of the themes found in some of the conflict theories we cover in this chapter.

Conflict theories stand in opposition to structural functionalism. The latter might assume that a sociological understanding of women in Saudi Arabia or of people protesting police violence against black Americans should be understood in terms of maintaining social order or social cohesion. Women complying with dictates that keep them subservient to men in Saudi

Arabia may contribute to social order. Conversely, protests against the police might be a symptom of threats to social order. Conflict theories reject such claims and instead see conflict whether overt or hidden as a central part of social life. Conflict theories are a diverse group of theories that all share the belief that in order to sociologically understand society one must recognize the central importance of conflict in social life.

Conflict theory arose in the 1950s and 1960s, and newer versions have appeared since then. Scholars including Dahrendorf, Coser, and Collins are conflict theorists in this tradition. They – at least the earlier ones -- were writing largely in response to structural functionalist theories and in reaction to and against Marxism. They saw pitfalls in each approach. Structural functionalism became very popular in America sociology in the middle decades of the twentieth century. It is often identified as a consensus theory. Built into this form of theory is the assumption that groups and individuals are in agreement or seek to be in agreement, and there is a natural drive for harmony and balance in society. Some conflict theorists such as Dahrendorf saw structural functionalism not so much as fundamentally wrong but as limited in its ability to adequately explain much of social reality. Blanket assumptions about widespread consensus are misguided, conflict theorists claim. Dahrendorf saw conflict theory as an alternative theory that could address these limitations. Other conflict theorists such as Coser (1956) believed conflict theory should fuse the ideas of structural functionalism and conflict theory into one unified theory. Coser identified a number of "functions of social conflict." Conflict theorists were also often reacting to the perceived limitations or flaws in Marxism. They tended to look around the social world and see that Marx's claims were largely not supported. For example, conflict theorists tend to believe that class conflict was not the only, or necessarily the major, source of conflict in society. Other forms of group conflict can and do appear.

Dahrendorf's Conflict Theory

Ralf Dahrendorf (1929-2009) was born in Germany. His father was a politician who was arrested first by the Nazis and later by the Soviets, who took control over Eastern Germany during and after World War Two. Both Ralf and his father were imprisoned by the Nazis. His father eventually managed to escape from Eastern Germany to England with his son. Ralf returned to West Germany after the war and earned his Ph.D. in philosophy from the University of Hamburg. He taught at various universities in West Germany through the 1960s. He also served as a politician in the West German parliament and later served as a commissioner in the European Commission in Brussels. He later became the director of the London School of Economics, where he stayed from 1974 through 1984. In the late 1980s he became a British citizen and served as a member of the House of Lords (the upper chamber of the British parliament).

Dahrendorf first and foremost wished to create a scientific sociological theory. A scientific theory was one that was capable of being empirically tested. A scientific theory necessarily had to be shaped in a way such that the claims of the theory could be judged to be true or false by conducting research studies about the real world. As such, theoretical concepts had to be clear and concise. They had to conform to social realities, and they had to be capable of being tested. If a theory did not conform to such standards, then it was not a scientific theory. For example, the concept of social class was (and is) quite unclear. How should we define class? How many classes are there, and who is in what class? If one cannot clearly define class, then one cannot build a scientific theory with claims about class. This has been a thorny issue throughout the history of sociology and continues to be so. It is much easier to study, for example, how a drug affects the human heart. One can easily define the drug and the human heart. This scientific impulse shaped Dahrendorf's overall approach.

Dahrendorf developed his conflict theory in reaction to and against two major sociological currents in the 1940s and 1950s: structural functionalism and (at least in Europe, though not in America) Marxism. He accepted and agreed with some elements of the two theories, and he incorporated some of their features into his own. But he rejected outright other parts of the two theories. One of the things he accepted from structural functionalism was the overarching desire found in that theory to create a model of society, specifically a scientific model of how society works. Another thing he accepted was the legitimacy of the theory of structural functionalism itself, at least within limits. He believed that structural functionalism was an effective theory that could explain some social phenomena, but not all. It was simply too limited, and it needed to recognize its limits. As we see below, Dahrendorf argues that his conflict theory also can explain many social phenomena, particularly those which cannot be explained by structural functionalism, but of note he says that this does not mean that conflict theory should replace structural functionalism. Rather they both should be accepted. It should be recognized that each provides legitimate bases of explanation for different social phenomena (1959:159). On the other hand, he criticizes structural functionalism on a number of counts, and indeed his theory in many ways can be viewed as the mirror opposite of structural functionalism. Dahrendorf identifies four assumptions of structural functionalism and then shows how his conflict theory takes the opposite position (1959:161-162). Whereas structural functionalism assumes that "Every society is a relatively persistent, stable structure of elements," conflict theory says that every society is in flux, and in a process of change. Whereas structural functionalism is based on the claim that societies are composed of "well-integrated structures of elements," conflict theory says that "social conflict is ubiquitous." Societies are filled with conflict. Whereas structural functionalism assumes that "every element in society has a function," conflict theory notes the opposite: "Every element in a society renders a contribution to its disintegration and change." Lastly, whereas structural functionalism assumes that societies are based on "a consensus of values" among the people in the society, conflict society is based "on the coercion of some of its members by others." The glue that holds society together is not shared agreement about values, but instead is based upon coercion or force.

Despite these glaring differences, Dahrendorf's theory is far more sympathetic and supportive of structural functionalism than it is of Marx's theory. Indeed, he is sharply critical if not dismissive of much of Marx's theory. On the other hand, he did recognize some things of value in Marx's theory. Specifically, he accepted Marx's claim that the key to understanding societies and specifically social change was to recognize that conflicting groups have opposing interests. But he rejected most of Marx's other claims. Dahrendorf complained that economic classes and the conflicts between them were not always the key source of social change, as Marx had claimed. Group conflicts can be found in many other places in society, within and between many various groups and types of groups. It is not restricted to economic conflicts between social classes. Moreover, Dahrendorf claimed that Marx's theory is not applicable to the ways that capitalism in the twentieth century works. It may have been applicable to the capitalism of the nineteenth century world in which Marx lived, but capitalism has changed fundamentally since then. We now live in a **post-capitalist society**. This post-capitalist society is very different from the earlier one in several major respects. First, when Marx was writing the owners and managers of private corporations were one in the same. The owner of a factory in the eighteen hundreds by and large managed the day-to-day operations of the factory. This was a world largely of privately owned companies. In contrast, capitalism now, and for the last one hundred years, is dominated by publicly owned companies. That is, companies today are more often than not owned by stock shareholders. A stock is a piece of ownership of a company. A company that is a public shareholder company is owned by the stockholders and not by the managers of the company. One can buy a share of stock of Apple or Home Depot and thus own a small piece of the company. Or if you are richer, you can by thousands of shares of stock of a company and thus own a larger piece. The point is that many, many people, i.e. the shareholders or owners of the stock, now own companies. As a result, the ownership and management of the corporations is now divided. They are not in the hands of the same people. If I own some shares of Apple, this does not mean I run or manage the company. This complicates Marx's claims about the bourgeoisie and how they operate. They are no longer this central, all powerful force. Power is divided between the stockholders and the mangers of the corporation who run it on a day-to-day basis.

A second difference according to Dahrendorf between the capitalism of today and the one in existence in Marx's life is the rise and growth of the middle classes. Managers and bureaucrats that work in corporations today do not fit neatly into Marx's class dichotomy of bourgeoisie and proletariat. These mid-level employees of large corporations are, or should be thought of as, a different class than the two opposing ones Marx identifies. This new middle has interests that may support the bourgeoisie at one time on one issue, or they may support the proletariat at another time or on another issue. The point is that they are a large and important force, and one that was largely ignored by Marx. A third problem concerns mobility. Marx saw class conflict as central, and Marx believed the two opposing classes will become more clearly organized. The classes will come into direct opposition to one another. However, the increased mobility present in twentieth century capitalism greatly weakens the prospects of class solidarity which according to Marx would be needed for the proletariat to rise up and create a revolution. If people who are born into the working classes can and do move up into the middle or upper classes, and if people move down -- Dahrendorf claims the research says this happens, then one will have many people in the classes who do not have loyalty to them. It is only through the proletariat remaining proletariat, and it is only through the sons and daughters of the proletariat remaining proletariat, or believing they will remain so, that group cohesion or solidarity could occur. Mobility greatly weakens the prospect of significant class conflict. In short, Dahrendorf says that Marx was wrong to claim his theory of history could explain all changes in all societies.

Dahrendorf frames his theory in relation to the classic Enlightenment debates about the sources of social order: How is social order created? In the history of sociology, going back to the Enlightenment, scholars have created two opposing answers to the question of social order. The theme of social order goes back to the writings of Thomas Hobbes. Hobbes believed that without social constraints placed upon people, by such things as norms, laws, etc., that society would fall apart because everyone would act in their own selfish interests. Life would be "brutish and short." The question then is how can society and social order survive? This is what has come to be called the Hobbsian problem of social order. Sociologists since then have made two opposing arguments to address this problem. Some embrace an "equilibrium approach." This is the approach taken by structural functionalists like Parsons. Social order is created as the result of shared norms, values, and beliefs. These things constrain people's behavior and allow for social order to occur. On the other hand, other scholars embrace a "constraint approach." These scholars claim that social order is imposed by some authority. The norms, values, and beliefs held by people are imposed upon them by one or another source of authority. Dahrendorf largely follows the constraint approach in his theorizing. The source of social order comes from some legitimate authority imposing the norms, values, and beliefs upon a people.

His theory can be summarized as follows: Society is comprised of groups that are in conflict with other groups. These conflicts are rooted in differences in amounts of legitimate power or authority the groups have, and the conflicts are driven by the interests of the groups. This is a universal condition. "Any society, and, indeed, any social organization, requires some differentiation into positions of domination and positions of subjugation" (1959:219). Groups have an interest in maintaining or in gaining legitimate power in relation to other groups. The defining element of these groups is the relationship between them and the degree to which one or the other had legitimate power in the relationship. He uses the rather awkward term **imperatively coordinated associations** to describe these groups (1959:167). By "imperatively coordinated" he means authority. Moreover, group conflicts are defined in dichotomous terms. There are always two distinct groups that could be identified as being in conflict – not four or five, but two. Perhaps the easiest example of all of this can be found in labor conflicts in the earlier industrial capitalist era. In these conflicts the industrial working class was in conflict with the owners of the factories. Two groups were in conflict. They had differing amounts of legitimate authority, and they had competing interests. For example, the working class wished perhaps for better wages or better working conditions or better benefits (health, retirement, etc.), and the owners wished for the opposite so that they could make more money.

Conflict groups can be found in all sectors of society. There are conflict groups within the political arena, within the industrial arena, within the religious arena, and more. Sometimes membership in one conflict group overlaps with membership in another. For example, someone in America in the 1920s might be a Catholic and might be part of the working class, working in a factory. Sometimes these memberships might not overlap and indeed could be at odds. Their commitment to their religion might put them at odds with their commitment to their union. The church might support the owners, for example. Society is comprised of a network of overlapping conflict groups.

As noted, the fundamental conflict lies in competing interests. For Dahrendorf a central interest revolves around the status quo, or the way things current are. Does a group have an interest in maintaining the way things currently are, or does the group have an interest in seeking to change this situation? The powerful groups more likely than not have an interest in keeping things as they are. The less powerful groups have an interest in trying to change things. He writes: "Our model of conflict group formation involves the proposition that the two aggregates of authority positions to be distinguished in ever association, one – that of domination – is characterized by an interest in the maintenance of a social structure that for them conveys authority, whereas the other – that of subjection – involves an interest in changing a social condition that deprives its incumbents of authority. These two interests are in conflict" (1959:176).

A key element of Dahrendorf's theory is its structural bent. He seeks to develop a sociological rather than a psychological theory of conflict groups and is not interested in understanding individual motivation or agency. He is not interested in understanding why an individual might actively proclaim allegiance to a group and participate with this group in conflict with another. Instead, he wishes to develop what he sees as a sociological theory -- that is, a theory that could be used to account for or explain conflicts between various groups at various times. He is seeking to develop a scientific model of conflict groups, and a key part of this is to examine not the psychological factors but the sociological ones. Toward that end, the concept of role is central. A role is a set of expectations. Roles are important in part because authority, or legitimate power, is "always associated with social positions or roles" (1959:166). It is within the concept of role that one can find the seeds of conflict:

> One of the central theses of this study consists in the assumption that [the] differential distribution of authority invariably becomes the determining factor of systematic social conflict of a type that is germane to class conflict in the traditional (Marxian) sense of this term [but which goes far beyond class conflicts]. The structural origins of group conflicts must be sought in the arrangement of social roles endowed with expectations of domination or subjugation. Wherever there are such roles, group conflicts of the type of in question are to be expected. (1959:165)

Group conflict can lead to change or attempts at change, and this is or can be driven by the less powerful group having an interest to push for the change. And yet not all less powerful groups do in fact push for change. Often times, people in groups having little to no power do not fight for change. Dahrendorf proposes an explanation for how and why groups do or do not set about trying to make these changes. Toward that end, he makes the distinction between latent and manifest interests. The concepts of latent and manifest are taken from the structural functionalist Robert Merton, but he significantly modifies them by grafting some elements of Marx's distinction between false and true consciousness. **Manifest interests** are those the members of the group are consciously aware of. If I am an African American living in Alabama in the 1940s, I am aware that it is in my interest to be allowed to attend the University of Alabama if I am academically qualified to do so.

During this period, during the Jim Crow era, African Americans were banned from attending the University of Alabama. It was segregated by law and custom. **Latent interests** are real interests that are not known to the group members. Latent interests are not conscious. People are not aware of them. This might seem odd to the reader. How can someone have an interest that they are not aware of? Yet sociologists have long provided countless examples of such things. The chapter began with a brief note about Saudi women wearing the burqas and sometimes believing they should be submissive to males. This is just one example.

If group members have latent interests but not manifest interest, it is hard to see how they might do things to further their interest. Dahrendorf sees one of the tasks of his theory to explain how groups move from having latent to manifest interests. Here he identifies two types of groups: quasi-groups and interest groups. These two are closely associated with the concepts of latent and manifest interests. **Quasi-groups** are characterized as having latent interests. They are a group that is composed of individuals who are not aware of their collective interests. A key element of quasi-groups is that while they are composed of individuals in similar structural positions, they are not organized as a self-conscious entity. In contrast, **interest groups** are characterized as having manifest interests. They are composed of individuals in similar structural positions that are self-consciously aware of their interests and are social organized. "They are the real agents of group conflict. They have a structure, a form of organization, a program or goal, and a personnel of members" (1959:180). Dahrendorf draws directly upon Marx's distinction between a class in itself and a class for itself to make his argument. He quotes Marx and the latter's explanation for why the peasants of nineteenth century France who had latent interests did not rebel:

> The small independent peasants constitute an enormous mass, the members of which live in the same situation but do not enter into manifold relations with one another. Their mode of production isolates them from each other instead of bringing them into mutual intercourse. This isolation is by the bad state of French means of communication and by the poverty of the peasants ... Every single peasant family is almost self-sufficient ... and thus gains its material of life more in exchange with nature than in intercourse with society. (Marx quoted in Dahrendorf, 1959:183)

The point for Marx and for Dahrendorf is that structural conditions of life can prohibit or can be supportive of a group changing from being a quasi-group to an interest group. So what sort of conditions will determine whether a quasi-group becomes an interest group? He identifies three types of conditions: technical, political and social. **Technical conditions of**

organization include things like "charters" and ideology, and personnel and norms. A charter is a system of values (1959:185). This system can be organized and codified into some written format, or it could be an ideology, a shared value system. Technical conditions also include personnel. By personnel, he is referring to leadership groups within the larger group. For a group to move from being a quasi-group to an interest group it needs to have leadership. In short, ideology and leadership are the key technical conditions needed here. **Political conditions of organization** include the political opportunities available in a society for a group to organize. Protest groups in totalitarian societies, such as the Soviet Union, do not exist because the political system does not allow for any. For quasi-groups to be able to turn into interest groups there also has to be present **social conditions of organization**. These are much like the structural condition referred to above in the quote from Marx. Social conditions include such things as means of communication amongst members. The concrete physical location of people is another social condition. As Marx claims, factory workers can organize because they are herded together daily for work in large factories. Dahrendorf also argues that a major, if not the major, social condition is the "structural pattern" that is present. That is, the structural conditions in society must distribute people – in time, space, in society -- in a systematic way that allows for their organization.

If a group develops manifest interests and it organizes, what determines whether it will act upon those perceived interests and what determines whether it will succeed? How and why does social change occur and what factors influence and determine how the conflict will appear? There are two main factors or variables in conflicts: intensity and violence (1959:210-212). Intensity refers to the "energy expenditure and degree of involvement of conflicting parties" (1959:211). Energy expenditure concerns the costs associated with an activity. Some activities cost more than others. They cost more in terms of money, time, risks, life, etc. Whether a group with little legitimate power will be inclined to challenge another group with power is influenced in part by the perceived costs of the activities. If the cost is low, then the probability is higher that the group will act. The degree of involvement is the amount of attention devoted to the conflict. Some conflicts involve relatively little involvement. Playing a casual game of chess, Dahrendorf notes, does not demand that the participants put their whole heart and soul into it. It is just a game. However, a labor union member who decides to go on strike with his fellow union members necessarily has to be more involved. Involvement concerns the personal commitment given to the particular conflict. Violence is also a variable, and it is independent of intensity. There can be situations of high intensity and great violence, but there can also be situations of high intensity and a lack of violence. For example, Mahatma Gandhi in his revolutionary actions in India against

British colonization was intense but non-violent. Violence is quite variable. Some conflicts may be non-violent, some may be slightly violent, and others very violent. Violence refers to "the types of weapons that are chosen by the conflict groups to express their hostilities" (1959:212).

A number of factors determine whether a conflict will be intense or violent. One of these is "pluralism versus superimposition" (1959:215). By this Dahrendorf is referring to the degree of concentration of authority in one or another side of the group conflict. If authority is diffuse, if it is not concentrated, then the probability of increased intensity or violence is not high. For example, it was earlier noted that the capitalism of the twentieth century is different from that of the earlier century in part because of the growth of publicly owned stock companies. Publicly owned stock companies create a distinction between owners and managers. Thus, the authority is diffused and not consolidated in one class, e.g. the bourgeoisie. This diffusion reduces the intensity of group conflict, in this case class conflict, because it works against the rich class having total, consolidated control. A second factor that will influence whether a conflict will become more intense or violent concerns mobility. In situations where there is greater mobility between groups or classes, there is less likelihood of increased intensity of group conflict. "There is an inverse relation between the degree of openness of classes and the intensity of class conflict. The more upward and downward mobility there is in a society, the less comprehensive and fundamental are class conflicts likely to be" (1959:222). The reason for this is that when members of a group come and go, it will be less likely for them to feel strong attachments and allegiances to the group. On the other hand, he suggests the effects of mobility upon the possibilities of violence is slight. The regulation of class conflict is a third factor. Several things that are needed for a class or a group conflict to be effectively managed, regulated, or contained. The first of these is the shared recognition of the legitimacy of the opposing group's position. This comes down to a recognition of shared values. When groups share values, the likelihood of violence is diminished. The second factor is the organization of interest groups. The more organized the two groups in conflict are, the less likely they will be to engage in violence. Third, the more that the two parties agree to "certain formal rules of the game," the less likely will violence occur.

The three factors just listed are prerequisites for effective regulation of conflicts. That is, they are seen as effective ways in which to reduce the possibilities of violence. The various forms of regulation can emerge once these prerequisites have been put into place. Dahrendorf identifies three of the more common forms of regulation: conciliation, mediation, and arbitration. Conciliation refers to some type of parliamentary process by which the two parties could engage in democratic debate on the issues at hand. Mediation, the second form, consists of a third-party mediator, who does not have the power to impose binding rulings on the two parties. In this situation, both parties will present their cases and then the mediator makes a ruling. Lastly, arbitration, like mediation, calls for a third party to be present, but in arbitration, the arbitrator's rulings are binding. The implementation of any of these contributes to the decreased probability that violence will result from the group conflicts.

Collins' Conflict Theory

Randall Collins (1941-) is an American sociologist who presents a very different sort of conflict theory than that of Dahrendorf. While both seek to develop abstract and scientific models of social formation, Dahrendorf ignores micro-sociology while Collins actively incorporates micro-sociology into his theorizing. Arguably, he is more influenced by those sociological traditions that believe one should begin an understanding of social reality by focusing primarily upon lived, small-scale social interactions. He seeks to merge elements of the micro and the macro into one encompassing theory of society. Collins also create a multi-causal, complex model of society. He built many nuanced ideas into his model, and the model of society is itself complex.

In his major work in this area, titled *Conflict Sociology* (1975), Collins begins with the assumption that conflict lies at the heart of society: "For conflict theory, the basic insight is that human beings are sociable but conflict-prone animals. Why is there conflict? Above all else, there is conflict because violent coercion is always a potential resource, and it is a zero-sum sort" (1975:59). That is, conflict exists. People battle over resources, and for one to win in this battle another must lose (i.e. the zero-sum game). His theory focuses on conflict as it appears in, and influences, two major dimensions of society: stratification and organization.

In *Conflict Sociology* he presents hundreds of propositions or hypothesized rules about social action and social order. To get a sense of these propositions, I have listed just a few of these below from his discussion of organizational control. In the section on organizational control, he notes that the "most fundamental determinant of how men influence each other [in organizations] is the type of sanction they apply. The main types are coercive threats, material rewards, and loyalty to ideals" (1975:298). Here is his list of propositions related to coercion within organizations:

10.1 Coercion leads to strong efforts to avoid being coerced.
10.11 If resources for fighting back are available, the greater the coercion that is applied, the more counter-aggression is called forth.

> 10.12 If resources for fighting back are not available but opportunities to escape are, the greater the coercion that is applied, the greater the tendency to leave the situation.
> 10.13 If resources for fighting back and opportunities to escape are not available, *or* if there are other strong incentives for staying in the situation (material rewards or potential power), the greater the coercion that is applied, the greater the tendency to comply with exactly those demands that are necessary to avoid being coerced.
> 10.14 If resources for fighting back and opportunities to escape are not available, and there are no strong positive incentives for staying, the greater the coercion applied, the greater the tendency to dull compliance and passive resistance. (1975:298-299)

Here are a few more of his propositions related to the "different determinants of occupational class culture":

> 1.0 Experiences of giving and taking orders are the main determinants of individual outlooks and behaviors.
> 1.1 The more one gives orders, the more he is proud, self-assured, formal, and identifies with the organizational ideals in whose name he justifies the orders.
> 1.2 The more one takes orders, the more he is subservient, fatalistic, alienated from organizational ideals, externally conforming, distrustful of others, concerned with extrinsic rewards, and amoral.
> 1.3 The more one interacts with others in egalitarian exchanges, the more he acts informal, friendly, and tends to accept others' ideals.
> 1.4 The more one *both* gives and takes orders, the more he combines both formality, self-assurance, and organizational identification with subservience and external conformity; he is little concerned with the long-range or abstract purposes of the organization (in whose name he is given orders), but strongly identifies with his own short-term order-giving rationale; he attempts to transform order-taking situations into orders that he passes on to others. (1975:73-74)

His theorizing is highly influenced by Durkheim, Weber, Goffman, and the micro-traditions of phenomenology, ethnomethodology, and symbolic interactionism. As a conflict theorist he also is influenced by Marx, though this influence is decidedly smaller than those of these other scholars and traditions just noted.

Collins anchors his theory in the concept of status groups, which he takes from Weber. A status group is a collection of people sharing a similar position in society. One can find status groups throughout society. There are political status groups and economic status groups. Families are status groups. People who embrace one or another fad or fashion could be considered a status group. Membership in a neighborhood or some other community, based upon geography, sex, sexual orientation, race, etc. are all status groups. Conflict theory focuses upon the conflicts between status groups. Perhaps the most obvious is between economic classes, as Marx noted. But Collins rejects the exclusive emphasis in Marxist theory upon economic class and instead seeks to develop a model of how status groups of all sorts conflict with one another.

At the heart of the conflict lies interests and resources. The conflict perspective "grounds explanations in real people pursuing real interests" (1975:21). Whether a person realizes his or her interests is dependent upon the resources available to him or her and the resources available to others: "everyone pursues his own best line of advantage according to resources available to him and to his competitors" (1975:89). This sets up conflict. One person or group may have an interest in one or another thing but may not have the resources needed to successfully get this thing. I may have an interest becoming friends with the President of the United States, as this would likely open doors for me in various ways, such as getting a good job, but I do not have the personal connections, the money, the personal status, etc., e.g. the resources, needed to get past the front door of the White House. "Material resources" in particular are crucial if a group is going to effectively pursue its interests. Material resources include such things "communication and transportation, as well as weapons (in the case of military conflicts), supplies to sustain persons while they are engaged in action, and the money to be used to convert all these" (1993:292). Material resources also include things like "devices for staging one's public impression, tools, and goods." However, he says there are many other forms of resources. The ability to coerce someone is a resource. Access to people with whom to negotiate is a resource, so too is sexual attractiveness and physical arrangements.

Another set of concepts central to Collins' conflict theory are emotions and rituals. Emotions and rituals stand in contrast to rationality. People are not rational machines, or at least they are not simply rational machines. Sociologists should not look at people and assume they act in cool, rational ways, at least much if not most of the time. In the same way, sociologists cannot assume that people act based upon thought alone. People are fundamentally emotional beings. Thoughts are deeply tied to emotions and to lived interactions. To understand social behavior, we must understand how all of these are tied together. Emotions are an essential cornerstone of social life. Emotions often are binding agents of social interactions. But situations vary greatly in the intensity and qualities of emotions involved. One might have passionate emotions about one's lover, but one likely does not have many feelings about the checkout person at the local Target store. Emotions are an important source of social order -- specifically, emotional connectedness. This is where rituals come in. He draws heavily upon

Durkheim and Goffman's understandings of rituals here. Rituals are central in creating, maintaining and reaffirming social order. Rituals are found everywhere, from saying "hello" or holding the door open for someone to the inauguration of a president. At the heart of rituals are emotions. Through rituals individuals emotional bond with others. As Durkheim claims, solidarity is fostered through this binding process. A collective effervescence, an intense emotional arousal occurs in rituals that bind the members of the collective together.

The degree to which a group acts to further their interests is based upon their ability to mobilize, and this is based upon the resources they have. Mobilization is dependent upon solidarity, and solidarity requires rituals. Moreover, rituals foster the growth of moral emotions:

> The key ingredient which produces a group identity are the conditions that brings persons together to perform collective rituals. These include both the interaction rituals of everyday life, which mold some persons together as friends and status equals while excluding others from personal intimacy, as well as larger official and public rituals, which bring together a church, an organization, or a social movement. According to the familiar Durkheimian model, rituals produce not only a sense of social membership, with boundaries between those who belong and those who do not, but also moral feelings, dividing those who believe they are right from those whom they believe are wrong. Individuals are energized by group rituals, filled with what I refer to as emotional energy. (1993:291)

Rituals serve to stabilize social relations, and they contribute to social solidarity of a group.

He then identifies a number of sociological factors that structure the higher status groups differently from the lower status groups, and he notes that these factors can be seen as helping to maintain systems of inequality. Four of these will be described here: culture, social density, surveillance, and communications. The culture of a group consists of, among other things, beliefs, ideologies, world views, and ritual. The upper class, for example, has a distinct culture from the working class. Moreover, within and between classes rituals exist which help to maintain the inequality between them. For example, there are rituals of deference and demeanor (1975:161). But the higher status groups also disproportionately control the ideologies of the general public as well, and these ideologies help to maintain the system of inequality (as Marx said). Collins uses Durkheim's concept of social density to further understand conflicts between status groups. The upper status groups are denser and more cohesive than the lower status groups. The members of the upper classes interact and socialize with one another. This greater density provides the upper groups with greater abilities to maintain their position as the upper groups. On the other hand, the lower status groups, such as the working class, are fragmented and do not socialize with each other very much. The lower status groups are also subjected to much more surveillance than the upper groups, and this too contributes to the maintenance of the system of inequality. Lastly, the nature and amounts of communication is a difference between the higher and lower status groups. Specifically, the higher status group members necessarily communicate with far more people than members of the lower status groups do. An owner of a factory must communicate with a wide array of people – people who are also from the higher classes – on a regular basis. Whether the owner talks to other factory owners, or store owners, or politicians or civic leaders, he or she necessarily has to engage with many, many diverse people. In contrast, the working class and other lower status groups do not. In short, the upper class has a "cosmopolitanism of communication" that helps them maintain their status positions.

Collins summarizes his theory in an article written in 1993. He writes that "multiple dimensions of social resources each generate potential conflicts between haves and have-nots. Potential interests become effective to the degree that they are mobilized, relative to the mobilization of opposing interests; such mobilization depends upon both (1) conditions of ritual solidarity with a conflict group and (2) material resources for organizing" (1993:289). There are "four main points of conflict theory." The first is that "each social resource produces a potential conflict, between those who have it and those who do not" (1993:290). Different types of resources must be considered here. One of these consists of economic resources, as Marx says, but there are also power resources, e.g. who "controls networks," and status or cultural resources, e.g. "control over social rituals producing group solidarity and group symbolism." Second, "potential conflicting interests become effective to the extent that they are mobilized, relative to the mobilization of opposing interests" (1993:290). There are "several ingredients which mobilize interests." These are: emotional, moral and symbolic mobilization, and material resources for mobilizing. The third main point is that "conflict engender subsequent conflicts" and that "conflict turns the wheels of history, because the endpoint of one conflict is a new lineup of resources, which in turn becomes the basis for the formation of new interests and new conflicts" (1993:292). The fourth and last point is that "conflicts diminish as resources for mobilization are used up" (1993:292). Conflicts decrease by the opposite processes involved in the mobilization of conflict. For example, when the "material costs of conflict are too high to continue," conflict will decrease. Also, a de-escalation of conflicts occurs when "conflict groups lose the conditions for identity rituals" (1993:296). That is, identities are nurtured through the emotional bonding that occurs in rituals. Without such mechanisms for bonding, a group will be less likely to engage in conflict because it has less of a sense of solidarity.

Summary

Talcott Parsons was the dominant figure in American sociology in the post-World War Two era. He developed the theory of structural functionalism, which became the dominant theory in American sociology through that time. It is a form of grand theory. The theory combines elements from Durkheim, Weber, and Spencer, as well as ideas from the economist Wilfredo Pareto into a unified model of society and all of its parts. The theory presents a model of society and its parts, and it explains how and why the whole and the parts operate and how they interact. Three major elements of the theory are: the AGIL model; the voluntaristic theory of action; and the themes of change, evolution, and functionalism.

Parsons builds his theory on the concept of systems. Society is a system and all of the parts of society are systems. The world is filled with systems. Society, families, personality, individual biological humans, etc., are all examples of systems. The AGIL model is a form of a systems model. All systems if they are to survive need four things. These are represented by AGIL. All systems have to have some ways to adapt (A) to their environment. Specifically, they need to be able to access and use relevant resources. All systems also must be goal oriented (G). The system must be directed in one way or another toward one or another thing. Systems have to have instituted ways in which the various parts of the system relate and are integrated (I) with each other. Lastly, each system has to have ways to maintain (L) and reproduce the system otherwise it would not survive. There are four major systems in society: the organic, personality, social and cultural systems. All of the systems in a society are interrelated through a cybernetic hierarchy, in which a change in one system has an effect on the other the systems. Parsons identities two main steering mechanisms – 1) information and control, and 2) energy – that drive the changes up or down the cybernetic hierarchy.

The voluntaristic theory of action lies at the heart of Parsons' theory. This aspect of his theory sets out to explain human behavior under the assumption that people have agency. Parsons seeks to identify the basic and universal elements of the most basic social behavior. The basic building block is called a unit of action, and it has several parts. A unit act consists of an initial state and an end state. The act is influenced by the conditions present and by the norms. Parsons identifies various types of social action. These differ from one another in terms of their modes of orientation. Action can be oriented toward the satisfaction of one or more of three types of needs: objective knowledge, emotional attachment; the need for evaluation. Action can also be orientated toward the realization of one or more of three types of values: the value of objective knowledge, aesthetic feelings, and evaluative standards. The three types of values and motivations intersect to produce three cultural patterns, which produce three types of action. The need for objective knowledge combines with the value of objective knowledge produces belief systems of cognitive significance, and these create conditions for strategic action to occur. Action motivated by a need for emotional attachment combines with the value of aesthetic feelings to produce systems of expressive symbolism and expressive types of actions. The need for evaluation combines with the value of evaluative standards to produce systems of value orientations, which lead to moral types of actions. He also identifies and describes five variables that pattern the value orientations associated with different roles. These are the basic elements of status roles: affective versus affective neutrality; collectivity versus self; particularism versus universalism; diffuseness versus specificity; ascription versus achievement.

Parsons provides us with a theory of social change and social evolution based upon functionalist reasoning. Systems change; they evolve; they may die. Building upon ideas not unrelated to Spencer and Durkheim, he identifies several evolutionary principles propelling the forces of system change. Two sets of factors are central to the social evolutionary process: differentiation and adaptive upgrading. As systems grow and expand, they become more complex. As they become more complicated, they develop specialized parts. The increasing differentiation of systems within systems based upon the increased specialization is an element of the evolutionary view of structural functionalism. A second principle is adaptive upgrading. As with biological evolution, systems of the human world adapt, and with this adaptation comes increasing specialization and differentiation. All of this leads to the process of increasing complexities in systems, such as social systems and societies.

The functionalist theory of stratification created by Davis and Moore was presented to illustrate how functionalism could be used to understand inequality. Inequality is seen as a necessary and beneficial quality of modern, complex societies. Davis and Moore identify the various needs that such societies have and show how unequal rewards must be allocated for the societal needs to be fulfilled.

Robert Merton was a student of Parsons who went on to become an influential sociologist in his own right. He largely embraced Parsons' structural functionalism, though modified it in some respects. Merton championed the idea of middle range theorizing. He also sought to specify more precisely the elements and nature of social behaviors and whether they could be considered functional. He describes a number of concepts toward that end: dysfunctions, nonfunctions, latent and manifest functions, and unintended effects. Merton is well known for developing a structural functionalist theory of deviance called strain (or anomie) theory, in which deviance is defined in terms of the structural relationships between the normatively accepted goals of a given society and the structural means in place to achieve these goals. When goals and means are not lined up favorably, one or another form of deviance will arise.

Structural functionalism has been widely criticized over the last fifty years. It is said to have problems associated with the concepts of tautology and teleology, and it is said to have an implicit conservative political bias, despite its claims that it does not.

In stark contrast or opposition to structural functionalism, conflict theories try to identify the essential conflicts at the heart of society. Scholars such as Dahrendorf and Collins champion this approach. Dahrendorf seeks to provide a sociological rather than a psychological theory. Conflict for him is a universal feature of social life. Groups compete over power and interests. These groups are called imperatively coordinated associations. These groups are found in all sectors of society, not only the economic sector. They have manifest and latent interests. There are different types of groups depending upon the form of interest. There are quasi-groups and interest groups. Groups may or may not act upon their interests. This is dependent upon a set of conditions: technical, political and social. Intensity and violence are the main factors that determine how a conflict between groups will appear in reality. Collins' conflict theory was more influenced by the micro traditions in sociology, and those traditions emphasizing agency, than was Dahrendorf's. He starts with the assumption that people are motivated by interests and resources. Status groups compete for these things. Conflict results. Conflict can be found in two main dimensions of society: stratification and organization. Collins argues that people are not simply rational machines, and that emotions, symbols, and particularly rituals are important in social conflict. Mobilization of status groups depends upon solidarity, and solidarity requires rituals. The sociological factors of culture, social density, surveillance, and communication structure competing status groups.

Discussion Questions

1. Parsons' theory is widely rejected today (though some influential theorists today, such as Habermas – see Chapter Eleven -- see some value in some of its parts). Should theorists today reject Parsons' entire theory, or are there parts of it that could and should be used today in theorizing? If so, which parts of his theorizing do you think are worthwhile? Why?

2. Parsons sought to develop an abstract model of society. This model is a metaphor, seemingly based upon the same sort of model building one sees in the natural sciences, e.g. a model of biological evolution. Should sociologists seek to build models? Is there a danger in creating a metaphorical model of reality and then treating the model as reality rather than as a metaphor? What is this danger?

3. If functionalism is conceptually flawed, as so many critics have said (see Chapter Three), and if we then remove functionalism from Parsons' theory, then what are we left with? Is Parsons' theory left with nothing more than being a collection of analytic concepts? This hardly seems like a coherent theory. Without functionalism, can Parsons' theory survive? Explain.

4. Parsons presents a theory of change and social evolution. It is based on the assumption that societies become more complex as they evolve, much like animals become more complex as they move through the evolutionary ladder. He identifies two principles driving this process: differentiation and adaptive upgrading. Do societies evolve as he suggests, and is he right in his claim that these are the driving forces of evolution in society? Why or why not?

5. Structural functionalism and conflict theories make opposing assumptions about society. One says consensus is the natural tendency of societies; the other says that conflict is the natural tendency. Which one is right? Alternatively, does one have to assume one or another of these positions? If one does not assume one or another of these, then what should be the foundation for a sociological theory?

Chapter Eight: Later Marxist Theories (Gramsci, Lukacs, Althusser) and the Frankfurt School

A rich intellectual heritage has developed within the Marxist tradition. (Whether the theoretical positions are accurate or not is another matter.) Two dominant forms of Marxism arose in the twentieth century: Humanistic (or cultural) Marxists and structural Marxists. Both of these share an acceptance of many of the key ideas found in Marx's writings, but these two camps tend to understand the meaning of Marx in very different ways. The two camps also emphasized very different parts of Marx's theory. Scholars like Georg Lukacs and Antonio Gramsci who developed Marxism in the cultural or humanistic direction tended to focus on things like consciousness, beliefs, the symbolic realm, and culture as the key concepts to use in understanding society. Humanistic Marxists tend to see social life as dynamic and not pre-determined. Marxists like Louis Althusser, on the other hand, took the theory in a structural direction and focused on the intersection of social structures in capitalism and how these worked.

In addition to these two groups – i.e., the cultural and structural Marxists – who claimed to adhere to Marx's ideas, there was another important Marxist group that emerged in the twentieth century. This was the Frankfurt School and their development of critical theory. The Frankfurt School arguably has wielded much more influence upon critical American sociologists in the last several decades than other Marxists scholars proclaiming to be following the ideas of Marx in a more orthodox fashion. The Frankfurt School were not committed to an orthodox Marxism. Instead, as we see below, they fused philosophical and sociological and psychological ideas together, taking the ideas of such people as Marx, Weber, Freud, Heidegger and many others, and developing their own unique form of theorizing.

We look at each of these two schools of Marxist influenced theorizing. First, we examine humanistic and structural Marxism, then we turn our attention to the Frankfurt School's critical theory.

Humanistic and Structural Marxism

Humanistic and structural Marxism are two major strands of Marxist thinking. Humanistic Marxism is represented by such scholars as Georg Lukacs (1885-1971) and Antonio Gramsci (1891-1937). Structural Marxism is represented by Louis Althusser (1918-1990). To the casual observer, the differences between these two strands of Marxism might seem small. (Indeed, even to some Marxist theorists the differences between them also seem small). Both humanistic and structural Marxists embrace the overarching framework that Marx put forth. The differences lie more in emphasis. Humanistic Marxism tends to emphasize such things as agency and culture. It tends to focus more on the processes: by which people make sense of their worlds; by which people interpret and assign meanings to their worlds; and by which the symbolic world is created, maintained or changed. Humanistic Marxism tends to draw more heavily from the early writings of Marx for inspiration, when Marx wrote more about philosophy, culture and psychological processes of understanding (for example, when he wrote about alienation). In contrast, structural Marxists do not focus on such things. Instead, they focus on the structural organization of the world, with the economy at its heart. The structured social world has a reality in itself, and if Marxism is going to be a scientific theory of history, then the focus must remain on this rather than on psychological, or symbolic or cultural things.

The main difference between the structural and the humanistic Marxists is captured in the following lines written by Marx: "Men make their own history, but they do not make it just as they please; they do not make it under the circumstances chosen by themselves, but under circumstances directly found, given and transmitted from the past" (1978:595). Marx is saying that people make choices, and they are not simply mechanical robots programmed by society. But he also says the choices that people make are limited and defined by the larger society, specifically by history. The forces or structure of society and history bear down upon individuals and shape and determine how individuals understand and act in their worlds. Structural Marxists tend to focus on the second part of this quote; humanistic Marxists tend to focus on the first part. That is, structural Marxists see the large-scale structures of society – the organization of politics, ideology, the economy, institutions, etc. -- that are external to the individual as the main forces driving individual action and history forward. Humanistic Marxists on the other hand claim that the point is to understand how individuals make sense of their world and how they decide to act in one way or another.

Structural Marxism

Louis Althusser (1918-1990) is the main figure associated with structural Marxism. Althusser was French. He was born in the colony of Algeria and then moved to France. He fought for France in World War Two, was captured by the Germans, and spent several years of the war in a prisoner of war camp. After the war he earned his doctorate from the Ecole Normal Superieure in Paris and later taught there for many years. Althusser lived in Paris for much of his adult life. In the 1940s and 1950s he became a committed Marxist and an active participant in the French Communist Party. At this time, he fell in love and lived with Helene Rytman, who was herself a devout Communist. They eventually married in 1975. His most well-known writings on theory include a selection of essays in the book *For Marx* and *Reading Capital*, the latter co-written with Etienne Balibar, both were originally published in the early 1960s. Althusser suffered serious bouts of mental illness through much of his life. Specifically, he had major depression and was hospitalized on several occasions for his problems. The mental illness grew worse as he got older. By the late 1970s his illnesses became quite severe. He strangled and killed his wife in 1980, but before he was arrested, was sent to a mental hospital. He was not tried for the crime due to his mental incapacitation, and remained in the hospital, for the most part, until 1990, when he died of a heart attack.

Althusser is known for developing a complex type of Marxism called structural Marxism, though he consistently rejected this label. Structural Marxism combines some themes, though not specific ideas, of structuralism, with the theory of Marxism. We discuss structuralism more fully in Chapter Twelve. Here we can say just a few words about it. Structuralism is a form of social theory that begins with the belief that there are two types of explanations of social behavior and social order. One of these relies upon the concept of agency, the other on the concept of structure. The concept of agency was introduced in Chapter One. Agency theories claim that social theory should be built on the assumption that individual social actors make choices. They have "free" will. They decide to do this or that. As such, the task of the social scientist is to understand and explain this process of decision making. But critics, such as the structuralists, complain that such an approach cannot be scientific. It must inevitably rely upon the opinions of the social scientist to declare why an individual does what he does. Can anyone say with scientific certainty why an individual acts as he or she does? Critics complain that it is not possible. As a result, if one wishes to understand social behavior and social order scientifically, one needs to look outside of the individual and toward the structures of the social world.

This inspired social scientists to look around for such a theory. Some found it in a theory of signs developed in Europe called structural linguistics. European structuralism (and poststructuralism, see Chapter Twelve) in the social sciences over the last fifty years can trace its roots to structural linguistics. At the heart of this approach is the question: How do signs make meaning? How do we know the meaning of a stop sign, or a bed, or a rose, or a poem? For structuralists, the meaning of something is based upon the system of symbols in which the word or sign is embedded and used. Meaning is derived from this system and from the relationship of the sign to other signs and the system and not from the relationship of the sign to what it represents in the world. Structuralists also say sign systems are organized and meanings are made largely through binary opposition of meanings. We know up because it contrasts with down. We know black because it contrasts with white, etc. Again, language, sign systems, and consciousness, the theory claims, each has a structure to it. There are rules governing how individual parts of these systems operate. There are rules of grammar, for example. Moreover, structuralism claims the meanings of the individual parts of a system are derived from their relationship to the entire structure and to the other parts of the structure. The task then is to identify the structural elements and to figure out how they work together, i.e., to figure out the rules of the system of signs.

This led to the emergence of structural anthropology, first developed by Claude Levi-Strauss. Levi-Strauss sought to understand the structures of cultural practices. For example, he sought to identify the structures of myths, of cooking, of family systems, etc. Why is it that we eat some foods and not others? Why do we not eat dogs? Why is it that we cook some foods and not others? Why is it that we bake some foods, boil others, roast still others, and eat others raw? Similarly, one could map out the structured relationships of family members to one another. The relationship that one has to his or her uncle is structured. There are a structured, organized set of rules governing these cultural formations. More to the point: for Levi-Strauss the structures of a cooking system or of a family system are identical. That is, when one analyzes closely and deeply the various cultural patterns of a group of people, one finds only one foundational structure of consciousness that structures all of the cultural practices of a group. There is one shared deep structure.

Althusser is called a structural Marxist, but it should be recognized that while he appropriated a number of themes found in structural linguistics and structural anthropology, he most certainly did not use the theory of structuralism as developed in these fields in any sense. He did not subscribe to the basic claims of these forms of structuralism. Instead, he is called a structuralist because he drew upon similar conceptual themes of the structural linguists and anthropologists. The turning away from the individual self as the object of study and the focus on understanding conceptual systems or structures that organize and maintain social life are two such themes. Structural Marxists tend to focus on types of structures of the social world that are autonomous from the individual psychology, such as the economic, political and ideological structures. Althusser was a structural Marxist because he rejected the focus on agency, because he embraced a call for science, and most notably because he sought to understand the structures of the world from a Marxist perspective. Importantly, like the structuralists, Althusser believed it was necessary to understand the structure of the whole if one wished to understand the parts of that whole. The world has a structure to it; history has a structure to it. At the heart of both of these lies the economic structure of a society. We return to this below.

Althusser embraced Marxism as a science, and the form of that science was structuralism. He rigidly embraced the notion that Marxism was a science of history and of social behavior, and like all sciences it contained a method that must be rigidly adhered to if one wished to produce truths about the world. But Marxism was not like other conventional sciences. It was not a positivist science. Althusser said that one of the central points of Marxism is that it has offered a radically different type of epistemology, or theory of knowledge, one that rejects the dominant ways of knowing in capitalism. Althusser calls this alternative Marxist epistemology historical materialism.

He also claimed that one of the fundamentally important aspects of Marxism consisted of the breaks Marx had with the past, both in his own life and with earlier thinkers. Althusser said that Marx's later work was distinctly different from his earlier work. His later work was fully structural. That is, Marx was no longer interested in the psychological or philosophical or humanistic concerns of the individual, but instead was interested in understanding the laws of history. Althusser also argued that Marx's theorizing (both his earlier and later theorizing) was fundamentally different from that of people he was intellectually influenced by, most notably Hegel. Althusser complains that far too many people misunderstand Marx on this point. For example, Marx did not simply turn Hegel's idealism on its head and replace it with a materialism, but instead fundamentally reconceptualized the relationships between the material and ideal conditions. (He quotes from Marx's *Capital* to make his point: "With [Hegel] it is standing on its head. It must be turned right side up again, if you would discover the rational kernel within the mystical shell.")

Althusser believed that Marx fully embraced the concepts of dialectics and materialism, and he did so as well. To understand Althusser, one must appreciate the overarching significance of these two concepts. He was a materialist, but this materialism does not parcel out the world into two distinct realms, i.e., the realm of ideas and the realm of material conditions. The two are through and through part of the real material existence. The two are reflections of the dialectic that constitutes this and all realities (that is the kernel). In effect, Althusser sets about systematically to apply a complicated understanding of dialectical materialism.

He starts with the notion of totality. Society as well as our lived existence within it constitutes a totality. The structured whole is a "structure of dominance." The central part of the totality is the economic structure; in the modern world this is capitalism. But economics is only one structure. Society consists of multiple, overlapping structures. These include conventionally understood structures such as the economic and political domains, as well as the ideological domain (see below), and the various institutions (family, education, etc.). The world is comprised of multiple types of structures. There is a moral structure, a language structure, structures of being, etc. The totality consists of all of these as they are organized into a system of dominance, with the economic structure being central to all of them.

An essential element of the economic structure is the form of production. For Althusser, understanding the conceptual organization of production was needed. Production was important not simply to understand how the economy works, but it was important to understand how all the structures of the world work. Ideas are produced; families are produced; the political system is produced; science is produced; etc. And the form of production is determined by the economic structure.

The different structures of society combined in reality constitute the totality. But they are riddled with contradictions, and these contradictions which constitute reality are what Althusser calls overdetermined. The concept of overdetermination means that any one reality has many features to it and that one reality is not determined by any single one cause to the exclusion of the others, though the economic structure is ultimately the fundamental determining one. In other words, things are caused by many factors rather than by one factor and these factors can overlap, overdetermining a reality. The contradictions of capitalism are much like this. "Every contradiction is a contradiction in a complex whole structured in dominance" (2005:204-05). Contradictions are overdetermined. The most famous of the contradictions in capitalism according to Marx is that between labor and capital. But there are countless other contradictions rooted in a political and economic philosophy of capitalism. The very notion of agency and self, for example, are essentially contradictory. Social reality then is determined by the overdetermined contradictions (2005:101), which will eventually reach a crisis point which the system cannot contain.

One of the things that distinguishes Althusser from many other Marxists is his view of the state, i.e. the national government. Why do states exist and how and why do they function as they do? Marx famously claimed the modern state in democratic capitalist societies exists to serve the interest of the ruling class. But how does this happen? Two explanations have surfaced. One explanation, called the instrumentalist position, claims that the state serves the interest of the ruling class because the members of the ruling class are in fact consciously supporting the state. They are lobbying officials, or directly influencing or making policies. The instrumentalist perspective claims that the ruling class (the bourgeoisie) is personally and consciously doing things that maintain the state and the entire economic order. A very different explanation is that the state does things not because individuals from the ruling class tell it to do things but because it is structured and is part of larger structures that dictate that it must do things. This is a structuralist position. The state serves the interest of the ruling class not because the ruling class consciously does things to influence the state, but instead because the normal, structured workings of the system keep it going. Individual actions are inconsequential in this perspective. Althusser takes this position.

On a related note, Althusser also embraced anti-humanism (see Chapter Twelve). Humanism is the intellectual view that human beings possess some universal and timeless characteristics or attributes or traits that make them special, that gives them a special and central place in the universal. Humanism claims that humans intrinsically have a special value, a value that is distinctly different and superior to the value of any other thing, such as a plant or an animal. For example, the claims that men have "inalienable rights," as Jefferson says in the Declaration of Independence, is indicative of a humanism. Althusser rejects humanism in part because it is essentially a historical concept that claims to be one that is not historical. It was and is produced within a specific economic structure in a historical context. (This is a common form of argument found in Althusser.) The notion that humans have freedom, or any of the other notions associated with the Enlightenment, is historically bound. Humanism ultimately fuels an ideology (see below) that helps democratic capitalism survive. Humanism leads people away from looking at how and why the totality of capitalism has produced this form of thinking and leads people to believe in the timelessness of truths about humans.

Althusser claims that Marx may have embraced humanistic ideas in his earlier work but broke from the humanistic tradition in his later work. It is essential therefore for a genuine Marxism, for a genuine revolutionary theory rooted in dialectical materialism, to reject humanism. He writes: "It is impossible to know anything about men except on the absolute precondition that the philosophical (theoretical) myth of man is reduced to ashes" (2005:229). In sum, humans are produced through the particular totalities within which they live, and an understanding of social life must begin there.

Readers are sometimes taken aback by a rejection of humanism, and an embrace of anti-humanism. Some see anti-humanism as somehow evil, as it claims to reject the value of humans. But it is important to recognize that anti-humanism is not a rejection of the claims that humans have a special value. Rather, it is a claim that what makes humans valuable is the human claim of their value (see Heidegger, Chapter Twelve.) Humans create their worlds, and it is through this creation or production that value is realized.

Althusser is perhaps most well-known for his essay on ideology, "Ideology and Ideological State Apparatus" (2001). To understand his views of ideology it should be recalled his rejection of those that separate out or divide the dimensions of reality. Those that claim there are two distinct realms, such as the material world and the world of ideas, are wrongheaded, so too are those who claim a distinction between the base and superstructure, which are central parts of Marxists' theories of ideology. In reality, in the totality that is reality, these things are not in fact separate but in fact are parts of one reality. As such, Althusser embraces the claim that Marx once made that "ideologies have no history." By this it is meant that one cannot think of ideology removed from the lived, material existences within which it exists. Ideology does not have a history that is in any way distinct or different from the history of the material world, of capitalism. "Ideology," Althusser says, "has a material existence" (2001:112). Ideologies exist and operate through a number of places called "ideological state apparatuses" (ISAs). The term is a bit misleading in that it does not mean that all of the ISAs are directly controlled by the state. Instead, it means that they work toward maintaining the normal functioning of the state and thus serve to maintain the economic system of capitalism. Here is his list of ISAs: the religious ISA, the educational ISA, the family ISA, the legal ISA, the political ISA, the trade union ISA, the communications ISA (press, radio, television, etc.), the cultural ISA (literature, the arts, sports, etc.)(2001:96).

It is through these sites that forms of being are produced and reproduced that allow the system of capitalism to continue. A central way in which this occurs is through the production and reproduction of the self. The self is produced by and through ideologies, by and through ISAs. He notes that "The category of the subject (which may function under other names: e.g., as the soul in Plato, as God., etc.) is the constitutive category of all ideology, whether its determination (regional or class) and whatever its historical date – since ideology has no history" (2001:115-16). Without a subject, a self, there can be no ideology. Someone has to claim something. There has to be an author. Someone has to originate the ideas that make up an ideology for there to be an ideology. Ideologies, he says, "interpellates or calls out or hails the subject. "Ideology "acts" or "functions" in such a way that it "recruits" subjects among the individuals ... or "transforms" the individuals into subjects ... by the very precise operation which I have called interpellation or hailing, and which can be imagined along the lines of the most commonplace everyday police (or other) hailing: "Hey, you there!" " (2001:118). In sum, our selves and our notion of the self are produced and reproduced through ideologies. We are created, molded, made through these processes.

All of this may sound foreign to American students' ears. After all, we are raised to believe in the autonomous self. We are raised to believe that we are all unique and special and distinct. We are raised to believe that we are all like little gods, endowed with universal value. Yet Althusser is saying something different. He is saying that we should understand the self, the subject, historically and materially. We should understand that we are constituted through the workings of the totality and specifically through the workings of the ISAs.

Humanistic Marxism

Humanistic Marxism stands in contrast to structural Marxism. Two of the more well-known humanistic Marxists are Georg Lukacs and Antonio Gramsci. While their theories were quite distinct from one another, they did focus on similar themes within Marxism. Both focused upon culture and consciousness. Both focused upon how capitalism was influencing the ways that people thought about and engaged in their worlds. Both seemed drew more inspiration from the young Marx's writings rather than from his later writings. In short, while Althusser was focused on factors external to the individual, Lukacs and Gramsci were interested in understanding things such as being in the world and how people's consciousness was shaped and determined by the forces of the material world, specifically the economic structures.

Georg Lukacs

Lukacs (1885-1971) was a Hungarian Marxist philosopher, who spent considerable time in the German speaking world. He was an intellectual, a social theorist, and a literary theorist. He personally knew and communicated with many of the prominent European intellectuals from the early and mid-nineteen hundreds, including Max Weber and Georg Simmel, as well as influential figures in the art and theater worlds. Of note, he also was very engaged politically through his adult life, serving in various administrative and political capacities in the oppressive communist regimes in Hungary.

His most famous book is *History and Class Consciousness* (1968), which was written in 1923. The book came to have a major impact in Western Marxist thought with many Western European and American Marxists being influenced by it. The theoretical interpretations he offers in that book have often been referred to as Hegelian Marxism, and he has often been identified as such. He is called a Hegelian because he focused, at least in *History and Class Consciousness*, on dialectics and consciousness, two themes that are prominent in Hegel's thinking. Lukacs fully used dialectics throughout his studies. Moreover, he used a number of other central Hegelian terms, such as totality, which we discussed above in relation to Althusser's theorizing. Hegel focused on consciousness and being, and upon contradictions rooted in the relationships of these things to the lived realities. He was concerned not with material conditions, not with economics -- particularly as possible causal factors -- but instead was concerned with how and why people thought about, and understood, their worlds as they did. In short, he was arguably an idealist. Lukacs also focused on dialectics and upon consciousness, but he did so from a Marxist perspective.

Lukacs and Party Loyalty

Lukacs was politically active through his life and was a leading member of the Hungarian communist party and communist government. He also was committed to an allegiance with the Soviet Union-led Marxist regime in Hungary. His communist party commitments and loyalties had a negative effect upon his scholarly work. His book *History and Class Consciousness*, which is widely regarded as an important and highly creative work, was viewed quite negatively by the communist party members in power who were committed to what they saw as Marxist orthodoxy. The critics complained that Lukacs' work was not true Marxism but was instead a distortion of the true theory, largely because of its Hegelian emphasis. Lukacs subsequently sought to be more orthodox. As a result, Lukacs' later work became far less creative and innovative. Numerous scholars have noted that his later work was not as bold and imaginative as *History and Class Consciousness*. He is said to have surrendered his intellectual autonomy to party loyalty and discipline, much to the detriment of the quality of his scholarship.

His main influence upon Western social theory comes from the book *History and Class Consciousness*. Several significant theoretical ideas are put forth and elaborated in this book that influenced a number of more recent Western Marxists. (For example, the members of the Frankfurt School were influenced by his ideas.) Here we describe a few of the central ideas. We begin with the notion of reification. **Reification** is the noun, to reify is the verb. The concept of reification has two dimensions. First, reification is the process by which things that are made or produced by human beings are then thought of as they were produced by nature rather than being produced by humans. Second, one might think of reification as a form of frozen consciousness. Let us look more closely at these two ideas. According to Marx one of the ways that capitalism has been able to survive, given that it is said to be riddled with contradictions, is that people, and specifically the working class, are unable to see or to recognize the problems with it. They are unable to see or to recognize their own oppression and the various negative and harmful ways that capitalism works. It is through reification in part that this occurs. Marx wrote that one of the things that distinguishes capitalism from earlier modes of production was that it was able to hide from view the way it really works. When one buys a shirt at Walmart, one does not think about the ten-year old children in Viet Nam or Mexico who made the shirt. One does not think of the conditions under which they work and live. One does not consider the labor or the human element that went into the production of the shirt. In effect, the shirt is simply there on the shelf at the store. It becomes and is treated as if it existed in the same way a wild blueberry on a bush in the fields exists. You simply pick the blueberry. It is part of nature. It simply exists. Humans did not do anything to make it exist. The same is true for all commodities. We buy and sell things as if they are simply there, and this allows us to avoid seeing what Marx would say are the truly oppressive workings of capitalism.

But it is not simply commodities that are at issue here. It is also ideas and other things. Capitalism reifies our world in many ways. For example, Marx argues that private property is a social and a historical creation. It is not a part of nature like a mountain or the stars in the sky. Yet if one conducted a poll of Americans today, would they say private property is natural or would they say it is a human creation? My guess is that they would say it is a natural part of the world. Importantly, when one thinks of things as natural rather than as man-made, then the possibilities of changing these are questionable. It simply is. That is the way it is. As such, this would prevent people from developing a critical attitude toward capitalism, and it ultimately serves to maintain this economic system. Another example: Think about the concept of greed. Are human beings naturally greedy? Are they naturally selfish? In the capitalist society in which we live, we are instilled with the belief that greed is natural. Capitalism is built upon an assumption that people are greedy. It would not work if people were not greedy, or more accurately it would not work if people did not believe that people were greedy. Moreover, as it has been said -- by Gordon Gekko, played by Michael Douglas in the movie Wall Street as well as by many others -- that "greed is good." This is not the place to engage in a philosophical discussion about human nature, and about whether individuals are naturally greedy or not (though Marx himself does discuss his views of the concept of human nature). The point is that peoples' beliefs arise from the social contexts, specifically the economic organization of society, and when we think that greed is natural, we think that it is not only the way that it is, but that it is the way it should be and must be.

The second way of understanding reification is in terms of what I like to call frozen consciousness. This stems directly from what was just said. Our consciousness is molded by the economic context of capitalism. Of importance here is the fact that capitalism is a highly rational system. It assumes that individuals will operate rationally; that they will try to maximize their own self-interests through producing, buying and selling things. (Echoes of Weber's influences on Lukacs can be seen here.) This rational mode of being dominates our world. Whether we are working in a factory or buying a hamburger at Burger King, we are surrounded by rational systems and these systems demand that we think and act rationally. (I am speaking specifically of formal rationality here. See Chapter Four.) In short, reification is the idea that humans have become thing like. They have become like machines in capitalism for capitalism. They mechanically engage with their world. This form of consciousness is a reified one. People have become mechanical in their activities and are unable to recognize this. They go about producing and consuming things in a mechanistic, rational way. All of this also allows capitalism to continue without protest.

In addition to people becoming and thinking and acting in a more thing-like manner as a result of reification, people also surrender their autonomy to things. Things become like people in a modern, rational, technological capitalism, and people become like things. We empower our worlds to have control over us, whether it is computers, or facebook, or stop lights, or escalators at the mall.

Lastly, a key feature of reification concerns social relationships. Social relationships have become reified. "The relationship between people takes on the character of a thing" (Lukacs, 1968:83). Our social relationships have become rational, mechanistic engagements rather than human encounters. We not only treat ourselves as things, and not only treat others as things, but treat our relationships with others as things. For example, rational calculation which is the fundamental mode of being in the market economy saturates all areas of social relationships. Thus, a person who thinks of getting married measures the costs and benefits of doing so. The teacher calculates how he or she will engage with students (perhaps to get good student evaluations?). Human relationships have surrendered to the logic of the market and the logic of capitalism. We pay people to care for our children. This is reification. The origins of this can be traced to Marx's views of the factory and how individual factory workers become alienated from themselves and from each other. The factory worker has to treat the other factory workers as little more than things needed to get his or her work done.

In sum, capitalism produces forms of beings in which people, as producers and consumers, develop a false consciousness about their worlds as the result of the reification that comes along with capitalism. This works to maintain this particular economic system.

Antonio Gramsci

Gramsci (1891-1937) was an Italian Marxist. He became a devoted communist and an active member of the Communist Party in Italy in the early decades of the twentieth century. Like Lukacs, Gramsci was politically engaged throughout his life and believed the essence of Marxist theory lies in trying to make political change. The point was not simply to discuss or teach theory. Gramsci took to heart Marx's famous line, "Philosophers think about the world, the point is to change it." As an adult he became actively involved in journalism, serving as an editor and writer for radical papers. He also was actively involved in the Italian Communist Party and their activities. In Italy as in other European countries in the years between World War One (1914-1918) and World War Two (1939-1945) there were pitched and violent conflicts between the radical right wing fascists (such as Hitler) and the radical left communists. In Italy Mussolini, the right wing fascist, came to power in 1922. A few months earlier Gramsci had gone to Moscow to coordinate his revolutionary activities with the new communist leadership of the Soviet Union. He returned to Italy in 1924 and was arrested in 1926. He was sentenced ultimately to twenty years in prison. In prison he wrote what has come to be his most well-known book, *The Prison Notebooks* (1971). He was released from prison in 1934 because of his deteriorating health, and he died a few years later in 1937.

Gramsci's theory was not well known in the United States prior to the 1970s. This was in part because his writings were not widely available to the English speaking world of the United States. The first English translations of his writings appeared in 1957 (when *The Modern Prince and Other Writings* was published). But it was not until 1971 when *The Prison Notebooks* were published in the United States that his theoretical formulations started to become known to academics and others.

While Gramsci was unquestionably a Marxist, he did not believe that Marx's theory as it was formulated was necessarily and ultimately the final truth. He rejected those who seemed to believe Marx's theory should be understood in an orthodox way, that is, in a way not unlike a Christian would look at the Bible. Marx "is not a Messiah who left a string of parables laden with categorical imperatives, with absolute, unquestionable norms beyond the categories of time and space" (2000:36). Moreover, Gramsci interpreted Marx in distinct ways. Two of the ways he did so involve determinism and positivism. A deterministic Marxist would claim there is an inevitability to history and to where society is going. A deterministic Marxist would say that when Marx says capitalism will be overthrown and replaced by socialism and then communism, he meant it. Determinism is the position that claims things will automatically and inevitably happen. Individuals or groups cannot do anything about it. This is a highly mechanistic view of the social world. Gramsci strongly rejected this understanding of Marx. "History is not an oak tree," he says, "and men are not acorns." (2000:49). By this he means that history is not an automatic, natural process. Men (humans) make history, but of course not in situations of their own choosing. They make choices, and these choices influence the course of history. History is not scripted. In the same way, Gramsci rejected positivism, and he rejected any attempts by Marxists to graft positivism onto the theory. We have discussed positivism elsewhere. It is the philosophical basis of much of modern science. Positivism presents a philosophy that is outside of history. Marx is "neither a mystic nor a positivistic metaphysician" (2000:37). Positivism is one that presents a set of rules to follow to obtain truths about the world. For Gramsci, both positivism and determinism have the same problem: They both negate the real, living individual subject. They both negate the fact that men and women make their own histories. There is nothing mechanical about social life and history. As a result, much of Gramsci's theorizing is focused on trying to understand change.

He focused upon developing a "theory of praxis." **Praxis** is putting the theoretical ideas of Marxism into practice. (Non-Marxists sometimes use the concept of praxis, when they do, they simply mean putting theory into practice, whether the theory is Marxist or not.) It is living the theory through political engagement in one's daily life. It is a central concept in Marxism in general, and it is one that Gramsci used to build his entire theory. Relatedly, as a humanistic Marxist, Gramsci focused his theoretical attention on the themes of culture and consciousness, rather than on the structures of the economy and how it shapes or determines social realities. As a revolutionary he wished to understand how people do or do not develop ideas that are revolutionary.

All of this led him to reassessing the meaning of Marx's base-superstructure model of culture and consciousness. (Technically, the superstructure consists of the law, politics, and culture.) This is Marx's model that explains anything from cultural formations, such as movies and popular music, to the organization of cultural institutions, such as universities. One will recall that in Marx's model the base determines the superstructure and the superstructure reinforces the base. The ideas, beliefs, and culture of a society help to maintain the existing economic system with its inequality, and they help to support and maintain the position of the ruling class. Gramsci embraced this model but was highly critical of people that he believed distorted it. They distorted it by creating the idea that the base (e.g. the economic structures of a society) is fundamentally distinct from the superstructure. These two parts are not distinct in reality. They are only conceptually distinct. (He makes his argument in very much the same way that Marx himself did. (See Marx's Thesis One on Feuerbach.)) In one interesting passage, Gramsci writes that "material forces are the content and ideologies are the form" (2000:200) by which he means that the beliefs, consciousness, culture are part of an entire reality, and this entire reality also consists of material forces.) Moreover, he criticizes Marxists who claim that the superstructure is simply an automatic reflection of the base. "The claim ... that every fluctuation of politics and ideology can be presented and expounded as an immediate expression of the structure [base], must be contested in theory as primitive infantilism" (2000:190). There is not a mechanical relation between the two.

He builds upon this understanding in his development and use of the Marxist concept of **hegemony**. Superficially, many people use the concept to refer to ideology, or perhaps to a dominant ideology, or to dominance itself. However, Gramsci has a more careful understanding of the concept. Hegemony is fundamentally a form of dominance, but it also refers to leadership. It is the cultural and political dominance of a leadership group. In the case of capitalist society, bourgeois hegemony means the bourgeoisie, as the leading group, assert their understandings of the way the world is, and they proclaim the way the world should be seen by the entire population. Moreover, hegemony implies consent. It implies that the population in general accepts uncritically and unreflectively the existing order, which ultimately is based upon the ideas and practices of the dominant class, i.e. the bourgeoisie. Thus far, the concept sounds similar to the concept of ideology. But hegemony goes beyond ideology. While one could have a hegemonic ideology (e.g., "Jerry Springer is the opium of the people"), one can find hegemony in places other than in ideologies. "Hegemony organizes action through the way it is embodied in social relations, institutions and practices, and informs all individuals and collective activities" (Bottomore, 1983:202; see also Mouffe, 1979).

At the heart of Gramsci's Marxism lies the commitment toward revolutionary change. Much of his theorizing was oriented toward understanding the conditions that are needed for revolutionary change to occur. Toward that end, he wrote a good deal about leadership and specifically about the role of intellectuals in the revolutionary struggle. Intellectual leadership is vital. The working classes have to be guided into understanding the realities of their situation – realities defined by Marxists. "The active man-in-the-mass has a practical activity, but has no clear theoretical consciousness of his practical activity, which nonetheless is an understanding of the world in so far as it transforms it" (2000:333). To develop the needed critical consciousness, they will have to be led. "Critical self-consciousness means, historically and politically, the creation of an elite of intellectuals" (2000:334). Intellectuals will have to teach them. All of this may sound quite insulting to the working classes. After all, it suggests they need someone to tell them what reality is; they need someone to tell them what their problems are. But Gramsci had a more sophisticated understanding of this. As with everything, he saw social life as fluid rather than static. Social life is comprised of dynamic relations which can and do change. So too is the relationship between the leaders and the led. This should be an interactive, dynamic process. That said, the role of the intellectual and intellectual leadership is vital, he insists.

He defines intellectuals in a distinctive way: "All men are intellectuals … but not all men have in society the function of intellectuals" (1971:9). Whether one works in a factory or in a college classroom, one is an intellectual. There are two types of intellectuals: organic and traditional. These two types differ in terms of their function. Specifically, they differ in terms of their orientations to the hegemonic order. Traditional intellectuals uncritically accept the existing order. They function to maintain the existing social arrangements. Organic intellectuals, on the other hand, question the existing order. Moreover, organic intellectuals actively engage in praxis. They actively participate in activities that challenge the hegemonic order. It is the function of the group that defines whether it is traditional or organic. Both traditional and organic intellectuals can and do emerge from either the rich classes or the working classes. Gramsci believed it was important to nurture the growth of organic intellectuals, particularly to nurture the growth of these in the working classes. "Technical education," he says, "must form the basis of a new type of intellectual" (1971:9). This new intellectual must have a "new mode of being" must consists "in active participation in practical life, as constructor, organizer, "permanent persuader" and not just as a simple orator" (1970:10).

The Critical Theory of the Frankfurt School

If one went online today to youtube and then searched for videos related to "The Frankfurt School," one would of course find many. Some would be lectures by professors explaining what the Frankfurt School is all about. A few would be lectures or interviews given by the members of the School, such as Herbert Marcuse. Still other videos, and there are many, would be found that are almost hysterical in their hatred of the Frankfurt School. These latter videos tend to be produced by one or another politically conservative group. One of these videos described is captioned with the following: "A group of Marxists formed what has become known as the "Frankfurt School." Their goal is nothing less than to destroy Christian influence in the West." Another one is described by its producers as follows: "The origins of "political correctness" or "cultural Marxism" can be found in the early parts of the 20th century from the Frankfurt School, which was headquarters for the Communists scheming in Germany…" I mention these here not to dispute these critics. I will leave it to the readers to judge for themselves after reading this chapter whether these claims are in any way accurate. I mention them here as a way of introducing this theory. The theory obviously has produced quite a negative reaction in some circles, particularly some conservative political circles. It is clearly seen by some to have led to "political correctness" and the "culture wars" being engaged in the United States today. Why would such an obscure theory produce such reactions? I again will leave it to the readers to reach their own conclusions on this matter.

The Frankfurt School is the name of a group of Marxist influenced German scholars who came together in the early 1920s at the newly created Institute of Social Research in Frankfurt, Germany. Critical theory is the name of the theory developed by the members of this group. The Institute was initially funded by Felix Weil, the son of a rich grain merchant. Weil sought to create a Marxist research institute, but as we see below the members of the Institute strayed very far from conventional, orthodox understandings of Marx. Dozens of intellectuals came together at the Institute. These scholars met, held classes, lectured and produced research. The Institute became affiliated with the University of Frankfurt. The members came from many different academic disciplines, from philosophy to sociology, from literature to psychology (see Jay, 1973; Held, 1980). The prominent psychoanalyst Eric Fromm, for example, was a member of the Institute. In this chapter we focus on the ideas of three of the more well-known figures associated with the Frankfurt School: Herbert Marcuse, Theodor Adorno, and Max Horkheimer. Not all of the members thought alike on all issues. There was a great deal of variation in their ideas. Nevertheless, one can identify some central ideas and themes in the writings of the Frankfurt School, and specifically in the writings of these three men, and these common elements will be described below.

Of note, almost all the leading members of the Institute were Jewish. This is significant to an understanding of the history of the Frankfurt School because Hitler came to power soon after the Institute was founded. If one was to create a list of the groups hated most by Hitler, one would likely find communists (Marxists), intellectuals, and Jews at the top (along with gays and many other groups). The members knew they had to leave. The Institute was forced to move from Germany due to the impending Holocaust. They moved temporarily to other parts of Western Europe and then eventually relocated the Institute to the United States. It became affiliated with Columbia University in New York City. After World War Two the Institute formally relocated back to West Germany, but some of the main figures either remained in the United States or moved back and forth from Europe to America. (During the war many of the members served in the United States military.) In America, some of the members moved to California; some taking up academic positions at one or another campus of the University of California.

The Frankfurt School was relatively unknown in America until the 1960s. Their theory spread in the 1960s for a number of reasons. More and more of their work was being translated into English. Their theories were being taught at some of the major universities, and of course several of the main figures were themselves teaching and lecturing at American universities. The student protests of the 1960s were often inspired directly or indirectly by the ideas of Marcuse, Adorno, Horkheimer and the other members of the School. The ideas of the Frankfurt School spread in American universities in the 1960s and 1970s, particularly in sociology programs, but also in other areas, and their ideas arguably contributed to the growth of new disciplines such as African American Studies, Feminist Studies, and Cultural Studies. The explicit influence of the Frankfurt School seemed to have declined in the closing decades of the nineteen hundreds. However, it bears noting that many of the ideas of this School have become part of mainstream sociology today.

Overview

The overarching theme found in the writings of the Frankfurt School members is that modern, rational capitalism is inherently destructive and dehumanizing. It is destructive to social relations, to the natural environment, and to meaningful and fulfilling individual human life. Moreover, the workings of capitalism allow for peoples' superficial and immediate needs and pleasures to get met more and more, but these gratifications in fact prevent and distract people from recognizing the destructive and dehumanization that is occurring to themselves, to their social relationships, and to the natural environment.

As Marxists (really neo-Marxists), however loosely associated, the Frankfurt School had to confront two major, thorny questions. That is, Marxism in the twentieth century, if it had any hope of being seen as a viable form of sociological theory, had to address two problematic questions. The first concerns the fact that the communist revolution did not happen. Specifically, it did not happen when and where Marx arguably thought it was going to happen. Marx envisioned the communist revolution to occur in the most industrialized capitalist countries in the world. In the early and mid-nineteen hundreds that would be Western Europe and the United States. But the proletarian class did not rise up and start a revolution in the United States, nor did they do so in Europe (though in Europe the working class was throughout the modern era much more of a powerful political force than in the United States). So the first question is: Why didn't the revolution happen where and when it was supposed to happen? Why didn't the proletariat rise up in America and overthrow the system? Either Marx's theory was wrong, or the theory somehow needs to be adapted or modified to explain this. It was not simply that the revolution did not happen in the most industrialized capitalist countries. It was also that the communist revolutions in the twentieth century happened in countries that were pre-industrial, agricultural and barely capitalistic at all, that is, in countries where it was not supposed to happen, at least not yet. (Lenin, the leader of the Russian Revolution that resulted in the creation of the Soviet Union, actually wrote an essay in which he argued that Marx's theory can effectively explain such things. Nevertheless, it is a problematic point for Marxist theory.)

> ## Max Horkheimer
>
> Max Horkheimer (1895-1973) was born in Stuttgart, Germany. He grew up in a prosperous, Jewish family. His father owned several textile mills. Max studied psychology and philosophy at the University of Frankfurt where he was a student of the phenomenologist Edmund Husserl. He earned his Ph.D. in philosophy in 1925, and his doctoral dissertation was on the philosophy of Kant. He was a lecturer at Frankfurt until 1930, when he was appointed as Director of the Institute of Social Research which opened in 1925. He was influential in steering the Institute's Marxist theoretical directions. When Hitler rose to power, Horkheimer fled, first to Switzerland and then to the United States. He assumed a position at Columbia University in the 1930s, moved to California in 1941, and became a United States citizen. After the War, in 1949, he returned to Germany and resumed teaching at the University of Frankfurt, though he went back to America on several occasions in the post-War decades for several lengthy stays.

The second question was equally troubling: Why did the Marxist, communist revolutions in the twentieth century all turn out to be such disasters? Stalin's Soviet Union was a nightmare by almost everyone's account. Stalin, who took over after the death of Lenin created a monstrous bureaucratic and oppressive state. One need only look at North Korea today to see another glaring example of how disastrous communism has been when put into practice. Not many people in their right mind would wish to live in North Korea today or in the Soviet Union before it collapsed in 1991.

The Frankfurt School turned to the ideas of the young Marx to explain the first of these two questions. The term "the young Marx" is in contrast to the term "the old Marx." This refers to a distinction that is sometimes made in studies of Marxism between the way that Marx thought about the world when he was young and how he thought about the world when he was older. When he was young, he tended to focus upon issues related to philosophy, to culture and consciousness. When he was younger, he focused upon things such as alienation and ideology. He focused upon the effects that capitalism was having upon the individual human being. Later in his life, i.e. the old Marx, he became more focused on conducting economic analyzes. This is clearly seen in his major economic work *Capital* (1977), the three volume economic analysis which explains how and why capitalism will collapse due to internal contradictions. As we see below, the Frankfurt School focused their attention on culture and consciousness, on ideology and the like, and spent very little time examining the economics of capitalism. Nor did they spend much time focusing on class analysis, though they did spend considerable time trying to understand how and why the working class did not become the revolutionary force in the United States that Marx predicted it would become.

The Frankfurt School arguably grafted some of the central ideas of Weber onto Marx's theory to explain the second of the two problems noted above. The Soviet Union became a bureaucratic nightmare. The forces of bureaucracy and formal rationality, particularly when combined with technology, with centralized authority, and with the ideology of positivism, as described below, leads or can lead to a hellish society. Weber as much as Marx said this, though of course Weber was certainly no Marxist. Like many, Weber saw the real possibilities of a communist nightmare emerging as a result of these forces.

At the heart of the Frankfurt School's critical theory is as the name implies the need to be critical. The Frankfurt School say that criticism is crucial, but that one must recognize the nature of criticism has to change for

Theodor Adorno

Theodor Adorno (1903-1969) was born in Frankfurt, Germany to a wealthy wine merchant. His father was Jewish and his mother was Roman Catholic. She was from Corsica. By many accounts Adorno is said to be the most intellectually gifted of all of the Frankfurt School theorists. He was philosopher, musical composer, musical theorist, and cultural critic. He received his Ph.D. in philosophy in 1931. His dissertation was on aesthetics in the existential philosophy of Soren Kierkegaard. As a student, Adorno studied with a number of the more prominent and influential intellectuals of the day including Tillich, Cornelius, and the avant-guard music composer Alban Berg. Adorno left Germany in 1934 after the Nazi's came to power. He moved at first to Oxford, England and then to New York and southern California. He met Horkheimer in the 1920s and joined the Frankfurt School in 1938. Unofficially he was a member since 1931. After World War Two he returned to Germany and became a professor at the University of Frankfurt. He became the Director of the Institute of Social Research in 1958. He died of a heart attack in 1969.

it to be meaningful within a rational, capitalist world. One must develop criticisms not within the logic and structures of rationality that are dominant in this world. Instead, one must be critical of the very nature of criticisms that are allowed in this system, for these criticisms may well be serving to maintain rather than to challenge the system. When someone criticizes those in power, those in power might use these criticisms as evidence that we are indeed living in a free, democratic society. For example, when the members of the Democratic Party criticize members of the Republican Party today for one thing or another, this gives the appearance of real and meaningful democratic debate. The Frankfurt School argue that much of these disagreements are not meaningful. They give the appearance of being meaningful, and thus it is hard to criticize them. But the Frankfurt School say when one looks more closely and more deeply at these criticisms and at the workings of rational capitalism, one finds there more meaningful criticisms, i.e. criticisms of rational capitalism itself. Specifically, one needs to criticize a mode of reasoning and a mode of being produced by capitalism that creates the illusions of meaningful criticisms.

Three Influences on the Frankfurt School

The Frankfurt School was largely influenced by three major theorists -- Marx, Weber, and Freud, though they also were well versed and significantly influenced by other intellectual traditions in the German speaking world, such as German philosophy, and specifically existentialism and phenomenology. Here an overview is presented of the main ways that Marx, Weber and Freud influenced their theorizing. We begin with Marx. As was just noted, the Frankfurt School drew upon the writing of the young Marx. Many of these ideas were described in the chapter on Marx. Here we touch upon some of these and elaborate upon some others. The Frankfurt School firmly embraced Marx's dialectical materialist mode of understanding. Dialectics was a central element in their theorizing. An orienting idea for this form of theory was to look at the world through the contradictions that comprise it. But the contradictions they focused upon were less those related directly to the workings of the economics of capitalism and more on the philosophical level.

For example, democratic capitalism arguably can be both liberating and oppressing at the same time (see below). A second and perhaps more central example is their focus on the dialectics of experience. They were quite interested in human experience and in the ways the organization of the world bears down on this experience.

> ## Herbert Marcuse
>
> Herbert Marcuse (1898-1979), like Adorno and Horkheimer, was born into a wealthy Jewish family. He received his doctorate from the University of Freiburg in 1922 and then moved to Berlin where he worked in the antiquarian book business. In the late 1920s he read Martin Heidegger's *Being and Time*, one of the classics in existentialism, and then moved back to Freiburg to resume his studies under Heidegger. Marcuse studied with Heidegger for several years. However, Heidegger's support of the Nazis led to a break in their relationship. (Heidegger notoriously went on to be an official in the Nazi regime, and he never apologized or showed any remorse for doing so after the war.) Marcuse fled Germany in the early 1930s. After a brief stay in Paris, he moved to New York City in 1934. He remained in America for the rest of his life. He worked for the U.S. Military during the war (at which time he lived to Washington, D.C.). After the war, he taught at Brandeis University and then in the 1960s he moved to California to teach at the University of California, San Diego. In the 1960s he became an inspiration and celebrity to the student protest movement (and an object of scorn to the political leadership of California, including Governor Ronald Reagan). He died of a stroke in 1979.

In addition to dialectics, the Frankfurt School anchored their theorizing in an embrace of Marx's base superstructure model of consciousness and ideology. You will recall this is Marx's model to explain how people come to believe and think as they do, and the model shows how these forms of beliefs and thoughts are determined by the economic structures of society. The model explains how these beliefs and thoughts help to keep what Marxists see as an oppressive system of capitalism going. In traditional Marxism, the base is the economic system, and the superstructure consists of the law, politics and culture of society. In terms of the Frankfurt School, the core of the superstructure consists of culture, ideology, and modes of thinking. Marx argued that "the ruling ideas in each society are the ideas of the ruling class," and the Frankfurt School agreed. We saw examples of this in the chapter on Marx. It will be recalled that ideas in art, in science, in religion can all be explained using this base superstructure model. Rich people will fund ideas that are supportive of their views and that are supportive of the system which keeps them rich. Is it very likely that a rich person would give money to a church in which the preacher calls for a revolution against the rich people? Is it likely that a rich person would give money to a church in which the preacher says the rich people are bad or evil and unjust? No, and this is the point. Rich people will give money to a church in which the preacher says things that are either supportive of the rich, or at the least not threatening to them. Similarly, as we saw, what is deemed to be good taste in art, for example, is determined by rich people and not by working class or poor persons. Think about who decides what art is placed in the great museums in the country? The rich people's tastes are represented there. They ultimately determine what is and what is not good art. Yet who goes to these museums? In any major city in the country, school buses filled with children from the poorer and working classes are brought to the museums to be taught that the art they see is great art. The tastes of the rich are the proper tastes of all.

But there is much, much more that the Frankfurt School take from the base superstructure model. They are interested in far more than the content of beliefs. A central concern is the form of thinking and being produced by capitalism. The distinction between form and content is important to understand. When one pours water into a glass, the water takes the form of the glass. It fills the glass and is bound by it. A television show, a comedy perhaps, also has a structure or form to it, and all or most such shows have a standard format. This is the form or structure. But each individual show is unique. The content is different. In much the same way, our thinking has a form and a content. For the Frankfurt School, the key to understanding how capitalism is able to survive in the face of what they see as the endless contradictions in this system has to do more with the form of the thinking and beliefs of people and less with the content. For example, one might find revolutionary political lyrics in various forms of popular music, whether it is the hip hop group Public Enemy calling upon its followers to "fight the power" or the reggae star Bob Marley calling upon listeners to "get up, stand up" (or perhaps a more recent example might be music from Rage Against the Machine?). On the surface, this form of music does indeed look revolutionary. The contents of the songs are calling for revolution, but the Frankfurt School would say otherwise. The form of the music, in terms of music theory, is very basic and hypnotic. It is relaxing and not challenging; it encourages the listener to relax and to be mellow. The form or structure of reggae, for example, with its syncopated beat (which emphasizes the off-beat, e.g. the human heart is syncopated), is quite soothing. In effect, the content of the music appears to work toward getting the listener to become revolutionary, but the form does the opposite. For the Frankfurt School this is how much of popular culture operates. It convinces people that they are opposing the existing capitalist system, when in fact they are not. Instead, they are contributing to its maintenance by embracing music that appears critical.

As Marxists, the Frankfurt School wished to understand how capitalism was able to survive. The base superstructure model served as a starting point, as we just saw. But they build upon this by focusing upon the concepts of reification and mystification. Reification is a concept we encountered earlier. Marx used this concept, but the Frankfurt School used it more widely. As noted earlier, reification has two components to it. First, it is the idea or belief that man-made things are in fact not made by man, but are part of nature, and as things that are part of nature they cannot or should not be changed. The second part of reification, which is closely related to the first, is what I like to call frozen consciousness. That is, reified thought is that it is structured in a way that makes it uncritical. It is inflexible and unable to see things in a critical way. Reified thought is uncritical thought. It is thought that allows the existing system of inequality, capitalism, to continue because people support and defend it rather than challenge it. According to the Frankfurt School, as well as Marx, capitalism was also able to survive in part because it was mystifying. Mystification, which is closely related to reification, refers to the way that capitalism blinds people from seeing the true workings of this economic system. People are unable to see what is actually going on because of the workings of this system. This is mystification. In a very basic Marxist sense this refers to the fact that when someone buys some clothes at Target or Walmart (okay, maybe Aeropostale?) they do not think about or consider who made the clothes or how the clothes were made. They do not consider that it may have been made by a twelve-year old child in Viet Nam or Pakistan working under horrible conditions. They are blind to these facts. The Frankfurt School take this much further and not only focus on being blind to the processes of production, but also they argue that people become blind to their own oppressions under democratic capitalism. We are told we live in a free society, a democratic society, for example, where the majority rules, but the Frankfurt School would argue America is run by the ruling classes, and it is run by the demands of the logic of capitalism rather than by the demands of people. These forms of mystification and more prevent meaningful criticisms of capitalism from arising, and they allow for the continued uninterrupted operation of what the Frankfurt School would say is an oppressive capitalist system.

Together reification and mystification relate to the concepts of ideology and false consciousness. The Frankfurt School was focused almost exclusively on this dimension of reality rather than on the economic analysis or class analysis or upon the organization of production. Instead, they were interested in understanding, culture, consciousness, and consumption.

The Frankfurt School was also greatly influenced by Weber and specifically by his theory of rationalization. Remember that Weber believed that formal rationality was taking over from substantive rationality in the modern world. Formal rationality is the lining up of means and ends without considering values in a social context. This is the form of rationality one would see, perhaps, in a scientific laboratory or in a business operation, or perhaps in the military. The Frankfurt School in general accept Weber's claims about rationalization (though they do make some pointed criticisms of it (see Horkheimer, 1974:6) with some important modifications. They use a different set of concepts that echo in a general sense Weber's concepts of formal and substantive rationality. Horkheimer, for example, uses the term **subjective rationality** rather than formal rationality, and **objective rationality** rather than substantive (1974:3-5). Marcuse and others used the concepts of individualistic rationality and technological rationality to make a similar distinction. **Individualistic rationality**, he says, is based upon individual rational judgment, and is also based upon rational self-interest, e.g. the interest based upon market principles. **Technological rationality** is imposed by the technological structures within which we live (see Marcuse, 1964). The Frankfurt School theorists are not simply replacing a set of Weberian concepts with a different set of concepts. They view the nature of rationality, and specifically its relationship to practices – to lived realities – differently from Weber. The Frankfurt School theorists see Weber's conceptualizations of rationality – both formal and substantive - as imposed upon the individual, and this imposition negates the possibilities of true freedom. Marcuse makes such an argument. He is arguing in part that modern rational capitalism imposes both forms of rationality onto the subject, and as such denies the subject the possibility to be truly free. Individualistic rationality denies the lived context of human experience and technological rationality imposed the instrumentality of technology onto this human experience. Neither allows for the individual to make autonomous, moral judgments about his or her lived realities. We are required to conform to the logic of these structures, whether those of a smart phone or an escalator at a mall. A key difference between their understandings and Weber's concerning types of rationality is that they complain that Weber's way of understanding these two types of rationality is based upon a way of thinking that is formally rational in it structure, and as such is not and cannot be critical. The Frankfurt School also notes that one cannot separate out the forms of rationality from the real, lived historical and material context within which rationality is enacted. In other words, Weber divorces his understandings of rationality from lived and living history. It is lived experience that is central here, but this human experience operates within a broader, real context. Rationality must be understood in relation to the economic system in which it operates, in the case of the modern, western world, that system is capitalism.

The ideas of Sigmund Freud were the third major theoretical influence on the Frankfurt School. To understand this influence we need to first describe a bit about Sigmund Freud's theory. Freud (1856-1939) was an Austrian medical doctor. (He was a neurologist/psychiatrist.) He developed a theory of psychology and mental illness called psychoanalysis, which said that the cause and the treatment of mental illness was largely psychological rather than biological. He developed a theory of the mind and a theory of treatment that became very influential in the twentieth century. Almost all of the American psychiatrists, for example, in the 1940s and 1950s embraced psychoanalysis. Psychoanalytic theory had a great impact not only upon the mental health industry, but it also had a great impact upon many parts of American culture. Hollywood directors, for example, were sometimes influenced by Freud in the making of their films. Psychoanalysis also influenced various academic disciplines in the middle of the twentieth century, from literature to sociology. (In the last thirty years or so, partly as the result of the rise in the use of psychopharmacology, i.e. drug treatments, in psychiatry, and partly for other reasons, the acceptance, influence and use of psychoanalytic theory not only in psychiatry but in all of the other disciplines had declined greatly.)

So what is psychoanalysis? Freud develops his theory of the mind using two assumptions. The first assumption is that human beings are animals. Our overall functioning, when one digs down to the core, is basically the same as the functioning of a dog. Much like a dog or cat seeks pleasure, and seeks to avoid pain, so too do humans wish for pleasure, and seek to avoid pain. Moreover, just like animals are driven by instincts, so too are humans driven by the same. The second assumption is that human behavior is largely driven by the unconscious. That is, the human mind has two parts to it, the conscious and the unconscious parts. The conscious part is the part that we are aware of. When I ask you why you did something, you can tell me. When I ask you what you did this morning, you can tell me. These are all parts of the conscious side of the mind. This is the part of our past and present that we are aware of. But Freud argued that we also have an unconscious side of the mind. This is the part of the mind that we are not aware of, but this part nevertheless influences if not determines our behavior. We do not and cannot recall everything that has ever happened to us. If I asked you what you had for breakfast on April 20, 2005, could you tell me? No. The unconscious is that part of the mind that influences us and our actions without our awareness. That is, we may say we did something for this or that reason, but the real reason might be an unconscious reason, a reason that we are not aware of. We might be driven to do this or that by the unconscious. For example, you may say you smoke cigarettes because you enjoy the taste or whatever, but a Freudian might say you are doing it for an unconscious reason (perhaps oral gratification, see below).

He goes on to build a three-part theory of the psyche, or mind, using these two basic assumptions. The psyche he says has three parts, the ego, the id, and the superego. The ego is the part that is oriented toward reality. It is driven by the reality principle. It is largely conscious and is the part of the mind that is responsible for understanding reality and for negotiating that reality. The id is largely unconscious and is the site of our basic instinctual drives. Like an animal we have instincts. A dog is motivated by food, fear, sex, other desires, etc. So too is a human being. The id, Freud says, is driven by the pleasure principle. We are driven (unconsciously) to get are instinctual needs met. Specifically, we have unconscious wishes and desires that we seek to fulfill. Freud identifies two primary instincts in humans, Eros and Thanatos. Eros is, for our purposes, the sex or love instinct. We are driven unconsciously to fulfill our sexual wishes. Thanatos, an idea which he developed later in his live, is the death instinct, or more generally it is the aggressive instinct. In sum, we are driven by love (Eros) and death (Thanatos), but importantly most of these desires are hidden from our conscious. They are unconscious, but real nevertheless. Our unconscious wishes and desire based in the id push on us to be realized. They try to get us to do this or that. The superego is partly conscious and partly unconscious. It is the moral side of our mind. It is the side of the mind that morally evaluates whether some action is right and good or whether it is wrong and bad. The superego develops in the child as the result of parent's actions toward him or her. The individual learns what is good and bad, etc. In sum, the id and the superego are like the bad and good angels sitting on our shoulders. The bad angel tells you to go out and have fun, go out and steal, whatever. The good angel says you should not do that because it is wrong. The ego tries to manage these conflicts going on within the mind with the demands of the external realities. It may, for example, be acceptable to have sex at some times and places, but not others. If one had a weak superego and a weak ego, then one might try to have sex anywhere and anytime.

Freud also builds into his theory of psychoanalysis a theory of psycho-sexual development. (The theory is called psycho-sexual, but the term sexual is really referring to something broader than the narrow way we understand sex.) That is, he develops as part of his overall theory an explanation of how children psychologically develop and grow up to be adults. This is a stage theory. That is, he says in normal development children go through a sequence of five stages or steps in development as they get older. The stages differ in the ways, or the "places," that the child seeks and gets his pleasurable (instinctual) needs met. The first stage is the oral stage, lasting roughly from birth to one-year old or so. The infant gets his or her needs met through oral gratification, specifically from sucking at his or her mother's breast. The second stage is the anal stage, lasting from one to three years old. In this stage the basic psycho-sexual pleasure a child gets comes from control over bowel movements, i.e. going to the bathroom. This is the traditional stage of potty training. As the child grows, and as he or she gets these earlier needs met, he or she then moves on to the next stage. This stage is called the phallic stage and lasts roughly from three to six years old. The term phallic (phallus) refers to a symbol representation of a sexual organ or act. The Washington monument might be considered a phallic symbol in that it is long, narrow, hard and pointed. It is a symbol of a large penis. Better yet, a psychoanalyst might say a gun is a phallic symbolic. Not only is it long, narrow, and hard, but something shoots out of it! In this stage, the child gets pleasure through the use of symbols. It is the stage of significant language development. It is in this stage that a very significant development occurs. This is the Oedipus complex. Freud got the idea of the Oedipus complex from an ancient Greek myth. In that myth, Oedipus kills his father (not knowing it was his father) and then marries his mother (not knowing it was his mother). Upon realizing what he has done – that he killed his father -- Oedipus becomes so filled with guilt that he pokes his eyes out and goes blind. The Oedipus complex in human development follows the same theme. It is Freud's explanation for how little boys grow up to identify as men. Specifically, he says it is the process by which the little boy who is in love with his mother comes to realize that he has competition for his mother's love from his father. As an infant, the little boy has his mother all to himself. Indeed, the infant at the breast of his mother is one with her. As he gets a little bit older, he develops a distinct self, but he still seeks to have his mother all to himself. But his father is bigger than he is, and as such the little boy does not stand a chance in this competition for mother's love. What is the boy to do? Freud says the boy unconsciously wishes to destroy or kill the father such that he can have his mother's love all to himself. But the boy knows this is not possible, and the boy also feels guilty for wishing his father dead. As a result, the boy seeks to identify with his father rather than compete against him. If he cannot defeat his father, perhaps if he can act like him. By acting and being like his father, he unconsciously believes he will therefore still be able to get his mother's love. (In hindsight, Freud's entire theory is very sexist, and it has been harshly criticized by feminists. It is among other things based upon the assumption that male development is the normal mode of development. Psychoanalysts did develop a theory of girl's psychosexual development called the Electra complex, but Freud's theory was based not on that but on the boy's development.) Next, the period of latency is from six years old to puberty. This is a quiet or dormant stage. Not much is happening in terms of changes in the psycho-sexual system. The final stage is the genital stage, from puberty to adulthood. In this adult stage, assuming the person successfully goes through all of the earlier stages, the person gains pleasure through love and sex with a person from the opposite sex.

    Freud created his theory to account for mental illness, and while this is not our primary concern here a few words can be said about this. Mental illness could occur as the result of problems that develop within the psyche or within the process of psycho-sexual development. For example, if a person has a weak ego and a strong superego, the person might be overly moralistic or perhaps rigidly moralistic and might have problems interacting with others. A person could also become disturbed if they do not successfully move through the stages of psycho-sexual development. If someone does not get their needs met at one or another of the stages, then that person may not effectively move on to the next. He or she might get psychologically stuck in an earlier stage of development. For example, if a child is not properly potty trained during the anal period, i.e. if parents do not teach the child how to appropriately and effectively manage to learn to control his bowel movements, the child might grow up psychologically stuck in the anal stage, even as an adult. And as an adult this person might constantly seek to get these needs met, e.g. through an inappropriate or excessive need to control or manage personal situations.

Another key part of psychoanalytic theory is the defense mechanisms (also called ego defense mechanisms). According to Freud and psychoanalysts defense mechanisms are psychological techniques (often unconscious) that are used by the mind to defend itself against psychological threats. (Freud's daughter, Anna, who became an influential psychoanalyst in her own right, wrote one of the first books describing these.) Psychoanalysts have identified more than twenty defense mechanisms. We need not describe all of these here. The important point for us is to understand what these mechanisms are in general and how they work. I will use several examples to illustrate these things. Some defense mechanisms are identified as primitive, while others are seen as mature. Primitive mechanisms include things like denial and acting out and projection. Mature defense mechanisms include those such as sublimation. And there are some that lie between the mature and primitive, such as repression and displacement. Let me say a few words about a few of these. Projection is placing feelings or thoughts you may have about yourself onto another when these feelings or thoughts might be too painful to acknowledge. If you get into an argument with someone and call them stupid or irrational, you might be unconsciously thinking you yourself are being stupid and irrational, but you are psychologically unable to admit this. You project your feelings about yourself onto the other person. Displacement is a defense mechanism in which you direct your thoughts and feelings onto to some person or object that is not the true object of your thoughts or feelings. If you are angry at someone but are psychologically afraid to confront the person directly, you might redirect (displace) your feelings on to another person who you are not really angry at. This could be called the "kick the dog syndrome." That is, if you are angry with your boss at work and psychologically cannot tell him you are angry, then you might go home and yell at the dog for some silly reason. You might take your anger out on the dog. Perhaps the dog is sitting on the couch (again!). One last defense mechanism can be mentioned here: Sublimation. Sublimation is the channeling of threating thoughts or feelings into appropriate or socially acceptable ways. Thus, for example, the architect who wishes to believe and to have others believe he is sexually well endowed or sexually powerful and strong, might design the Washington Monument, or perhaps some tall skyscraper. Perhaps, a psychoanalyst might say, a plumber chooses to become a plumber because it allows him to sublimate his sexual desires. He puts pipes together, one thing into another, and allows fluids to rush through them! Modern society could not function, psychoanalysts would say, if we did not resort to the defense mechanisms of sublimation.

One of the themes one might have noticed in Freud's psychoanalysis concerns the various ways the impulses of the id and of the unconscious in general have to somehow to be managed or controlled for social order to be sustained. They have to be repressed, or put down, or contained. After all, what would happen if everyone simply acted upon their pleasurable wishes and desires, sexual or otherwise? We have to have psychological mechanisms built into to us to prevent us from acting like the animals we are. It is hard to image how society could survive if people acted on their animal desires without any sort of control. The defense mechanisms and the ego and superego operate in ways to check or contain the various desires and wishes pushing upon the self.

So far, we have been describing a theory of individual psychology, i.e. psychoanalysis. That is, the above might explain how or why an individual does what he or she does. But what about society and social order? How does psychoanalysis help to explain such things? For Freud and the psychoanalysts, society, social order, and civilization are based upon the effective repression or control of the instinctual drive. It is only through the use of psychological techniques that the desires and wishes associated with the pleasure principle and rooted in the id can be managed or contained. If people were allowed psychologically to seek to gratify their needs for pleasure in an unconstrained way, society would not exist. Humans would then be worse than a pack of dogs. Because of the aggressive instincts (Thanatos) humans would surely self-destruct and kill each other endlessly. Psychoanalysts argue that these instinctual drives are contained in civilization through the use of things like the defense mechanisms. For example, we may unconsciously channel our instinctual desires into appropriate social behaviors (e.g. sublimation). In short, society has to develop psychological techniques by which the wishes and desires of the id are repressed, controlled, managed.

By this point one might be asking, what does any of this have to do with sociological theory or with the critical theory of the Frankfurt School? The answer is: plenty. Recall that the Frankfurt School was in part interested in understanding how capitalism – a system they saw as filled with contradictions and irrationalities – was not only able to survive, contrary to Marx's beliefs, but was also able to flourish in the post-War War Two decades. America and Western European societies became largely consumer driven societies. It is toward consumption that the Frankfurt School focuses a good deal of their attention. It is toward an understanding of consumption that we can see the influences of psychoanalysis on their theory, and specifically on how psychoanalysis intersects with Marx and Weber. But to understand all of this we must first turn to a description of their interest in the themes of positivism, science, and technology. After that, we will relate these things to consumption.

Adorno's Negative Dialectics

The Frankfurt School members were heavily schooled in and influenced by the German philosophical traditions of the late eighteen hundreds and early nineteen hundreds. Much of this philosophy concerned such things as wishing to understand the experience of being and how this relates to the broader social and historical context. Many of the members were students of some of the great German philosophers of the time who focused on such things as phenomenology and existentialism, including but not limited to the great and controversial German existentialist Martin Heidegger. (Heidegger is widely considered one of the more important philosophers of the twentieth century. He also was an unrepentant Nazi and served in the Hitler regime.)

Of all of the members of the Frankfurt School, Theodor Adorno was seen as the one most philosophically inclined. Adorno grafted some of the important non-Marxist ideas related to experience and being, e.g. existentialism and phenomenology, onto the scaffolding of Marxism., and in the process modified both traditions. Adorno wrote a lot about philosophy, about popular culture, about music (he was trained in classical music), and other such things. Arguably, one of his most important contributions to the Frankfurt School's overall project was his development of the concept of **negative dialectics**, which he explains in a book by the same title (1973). The Frankfurt School largely embraced one or another form of Marx's dialectics, that is, of thinking of the world as composed of opposing or contradictory forces which necessarily produce new realities which then produce new contradictions. Marx, it will be recalled, took this concept from Hegel and turned it on its head. Marx turned it from being an idealist concept to a materialist concept. Adorno and the other members of the Frankfurt School largely agreed with Marx here. But Adorno dives into the concept of dialectics further and develops the concept of negative dialectics.

Negative dialectics is basically the idea that there is a reality independent of our being and there is an understanding of that reality, the latter is necessarily part of our experiencing our being. We understand reality through our actually lived engagement with it. A central and necessary part of the process of this engagement is that we construct concepts to understand the external world. But do these concepts mirror reality precisely? If there are three apples sitting on a table and I say, using word or concepts, that there are three apples sitting on the table, then it would seem that words can and do accurately represent reality. But this actually is a rather rare example. Yes, numbers may represent realities accurately, but most of human existence does not draw upon numerical concepts. When we apply the concept of goodness or beauty, of fairness or ethics, etc. is there a similar parallel between concepts and realities? No. There is generally a gap between the abstract concept and the reality. If I say something is blue, what shade of blue do I mean? What is pure blue-ness? The point is that there is always a difference between the concept and the reality. This difference arguably is a contradiction, a dialectic. This is the basis of what Adorno called the negative dialectic.

At the heart of his analysis lies the concepts of self and of ideology. Ideology he says is anchored in the very denial of this gap: "Ideology lies in the substruction of something primary, the content of which hardly matters; it lies in the implicit identity of concept and thing, an identity justified by the world even when a doctrine summarily teaches that consciousness depends on being" (1973:40). As we see below, Adorno and the Frankfurt School members see the dominance of positivism, anchored in capitalism, as a cause of this production of ideology, and ideology prevents people from being critical of the world. In keeping with a theme of the Frankfurt School, Adorno is saying that the modern ideology, nurtured by capitalism and fostered by positivism produces an uncritical self, a self which blindly submits to the dictates of capitalism. He writes: "In sharp contrast to the usual ideal of science, the objectivity of dialectical cognition needs not less subjectivity, but more. Philosophical experience withers otherwise. But our positivistic *zeitgeist* is allergic to this need. It holds that not all men are capable of such experience; that it is the prerogative of individuals destined for it by their disposition and life story; that calling for it as a premise of cognition is elitist and undemocratic" (ibid.).

Lastly, it needs to be emphasized here that for all of Adorno's abstract discussion of concepts, of existence, of ideologies, of being, etc., that at the heart of his approach is an embrace of materialism, in opposition to idealism. We see this, for example, in his critiques of Heidegger and existentialism, which he says tends to reify the concept of self and being. That is, such idealist philosophies abstract the living, material being, the living self from his or her actual living experience and moves them to a plane of concepts and ideas. But Adorno says we must start with the realities that we are living, material beings and not stray from this reality in our theorizing.

Positivism, Science, and Technology

It perhaps would not be an exaggeration to say the Frankfurt School members were alarmed at the unfettered -- at the seemingly unstoppable – influence and effect that positivism, science, and technology was having upon the world in the mid-twentieth century. Positivism and science were discussed in Chapter One; so we do not need to go over them in detail here. Suffice to say that positivism is a philosophical position that assumes there is one and only one way of correctly knowing things about the world. That way is through the objective observation of the world and through the use of a systematic logic. Positivism is the philosophy that explains why science should be trusted to produce truth. It is based upon the belief that one should identify and isolate causes and effects in the world and that one must rely upon objective, systematic observation of the facts in the world to see these relations and to make claims about how the world works. Positivism is the philosophical legitimation of modern science. When one thinks of positivism, one should think about how and why we believe science discovers truths through experiments.

A concept closely associated with positivism is scientism (see Chapter One). Scientism is a general way of understanding the world that people use on a day-to-day basis that is based upon the logical principles of positivism. That is, we all try to act in an objective, unbiased logical manner in our daily lives. Our daily decisions should be based upon objective, cool rationality, rather than by emotions or values or morality. Much like the scientist in the laboratory is not supposed to let his or her own emotions, values or morality influence (and thus distort and pollute) his research, so too on a daily basis people in today's world are supposed to act rationally. This is scientism. Think about the capitalist economic system. Capitalism demands that people act rationally when they are consumers or producers. If I am a business owner and I do not act rationally in my decision making about how to make something or other, how long am I going to remain in business? This mode of thinking and being found in the economic arena and in the scientific arena (and in the bureaucratic arena) is claimed by some to have come to dominate all areas of social life.

The Frankfurt School members were interested and concerned about all of these things. They were concerned that capitalism produces scientism and it demands, however subtly, that people embrace positivism as the only approach to discovering truths about the world. But they were particularly concerned about technology. Science is the basis of technologies, and technology in a capitalist world has become as much if not more a source of oppression as it has a source of liberation. When we think of technological advances, from smart phones to airplanes, from new medications to new automobiles, we tend to think progress. We tend to think that technology is wonderful and that it has liberated us from the shackles of nature. After all, without air conditioners, what would life be like in Florida? (Of course, the Frankfurt School was writing before the dawn of the information age, and before the era of the internet.) What is then so bad about technology? Technology might have given us the ability to fly to the moon, but it has also given us nuclear weapons. The German Nazis were very technologically sophisticated. They used technology in their death machines of the holocaust. Technology is a major reason for the current environmental disaster of global warming. But one does not have to look at such large-scale forces to recognize the effects of technology. One could look at more personal consequences. Technology is all about control, and controlling humans and human behavior is a big part of technology. Increasingly, we are being forced to surrender our own personal decision-making powers to those of technology. We must do what the technology tells us, and we should not, and cannot, complain. Humans are increasingly controlled and managed by technology. Are we being liberated by technology, or are we being enslaved to it? The Frankfurt School would likely say both. There is a dialectic here.

At the heart of this dialectic is the irrationality of rationality. The Frankfurt School claim that the embrace of positivism and scientism is the embrace of formal rationality or in what the members say is an embrace of technological rationality. It is an embrace of a way of thinking and being that surrenders human autonomy to pure logic, to a value-free logic. As we saw with Weber, the systematic application of formal logic, to the exclusion of any consideration of human values, leads to insanity, to the holocaust, to the dehumanization of the world. Marcuse captures some of this in the following:

> The idea of compliant efficiency perfectly illustrates the structure of technological rationality. Rationality is being transformed from a critical force into one of adjustment and compliance. Autonomy of reason loses its meaning in the same measure as the thoughts, feelings and actions of men are shaped by the technical requirements of the apparatus which they themselves have created. Reason has found its resting place in the system of standardized control, production and consumption. There it reigns through the laws and mechanisms which insure the efficiency, expediency and coherence of this system. (1941:146)

It bears repeating that the Frankfurt School are not opposed to technology and they are not opposed to rationality (though their critics sometimes say they are). They are opposed to the forms and uses of rationality and technology in a capitalist society that is oriented not toward the fulfillment of genuine human needs but to the fulfillments of the demands of the capitalist market and capitalist system.

Dialectic of Enlightenment

The *Dialectic of Enlightenment* is both the name of a book written by Horkheimer and Adorno (1993) and a phrase that captures another central theme in the Frankfurt School's theory. The Enlightenment, as we saw in Chapter One, is the period in Western European intellectual history from sixteen hundreds through the end of the seventeen hundreds. It is period in which new ways of thinking emerged, ways which gave birth to the great revolutions of the end of the seventeen hundreds – The French and American Revolutions, and which paved the path for the development of the modern world, and the world in which we currently live. One of the central themes of the Enlightenment was the primacy of reason. As we saw, the Enlightenment philosophers called for people to base their understandings and decisions on reason, rather than on things such as tradition or religion. There was great hope that an embrace of reason would lead to a better world – a better social, political, scientific, economic world. Our modern democracy, capitalism, and science are all rooted in reason and ultimately in Enlightenment thinking.

Yet the Frankfurt School say there is a dialectic or contradiction embedded in this Enlightenment. What is it? There are a number of contradictions. The most basic concerns the simultaneous forces of liberation and oppression rooted in reason or rationality (specifically formal types of rationality). Science, for example, has liberated us from nature (see above). Capitalism has given us prosperity (or at least it has given many if not most of us far more prosperity than people had hundreds of years ago). The Enlightenment liberates us on a philosophical level as well. It calls for liberty, freedom of thought and action. At the same time, it oppresses us in that it controls us. Rationality orders us to conform to bureaucracies. Technologies demand that we conform to their commands. At the heart of the dialectic is the dominating nature of rationality. Rationality dominates us. It commands us, for both good and ill. The Enlightenment elevates rationality to a position that cannot be questioned. It is simply the case that rationality dominates us. This is associated with another set of contradictions. This set revolves around the relationship of the individual to the belief system of rationality in a rational, capitalist world. This belief system becomes mythic in that it is not allowed to be questioned or challenged. As such, it turns the individual into nothing more than a puppet or a machine that is simply following the orders given to it by rationality. Yet at the same time, rationality, specifically in a rational, democratic capitalist world, demands that we as individuals make choices. It demands that we act as autonomous beings assessing situations and act upon these based upon our assessments. In short, it demands that we are free beings. And yet, how is it possible to do both? How is it possible to be both free and enslaved to rationality? These contradictions need to be managed somehow if capitalism is to survive. One way this occurs is through consumption.

Another facet of the dialectic of enlightenment involves the desired consequences of the applications of reason. On the one hand, the Enlightenment leads people to believe in a wonderful future, a utopia, if reason is embraced. On the other hand, the essence of this form of reason is that is has an essential character that is one of domination. The Enlightenment thus has a dual structure:

> [Part of which] as the transcendental, supraindividual self, ... comprises the idea of a free, human social life in which men organize themselves as the universal subject and overcome the conflict between pure and empirical reason in the conscious solidarity of the whole. This represents the idea of true universalism: utopia. At the same time, however, reason constitutes the court of judgment of calculation, which adjusts the world for the ends of self-preservation and recognizes no function other than the preparation of the object from mere sensory material in order to make it the material of subjugation. (Horkheimer and Adorno in Held, 1980:150)

Consumption and Commodity Fetishes

Consumption was another major theme found in the works of the Frankfurt School. They were particularly interested in the relationship among technology, the market and consumption. The Frankfurt School rightly noted that an understanding of capitalism in the mid-twentieth century, particularly in the decades after World War Two, required a refocus away from what were the traditional concerns of Marxists, i.e. the organization of production, and toward consumption. They were particularly focused upon consumption in the cultural domain, in anything from movies to classic music to popular music. All of their analyses were oriented toward an understanding of how these things helped to maintain the system of capitalism, and how cultural forms might possibly help to confront and challenge the capitalist system. They were particularly interested in understanding how popular culture, particularly pop culture in America – the movies, television, popular music, etc. – was organized and how this organization helped to maintain this system. Popular cultural forms, they complained, have become nothing different than any other product that is bought and sold. Culture has become commodified. Popular art forms have become no different from Coke-a-Cola.

Popular culture was now organized through a **culture industry** which fused elements of technology and rationality with the demands of the market and thus was organized not to inspire critical judgments in the consumers of these products, but instead to maintaining the system by providing cultural products that were superficially appealing to the consumers. These popular forms make the consumer happy and content and help blind them to the realities of capitalism. Much like Marx once said, "Religion is the opium of the people," now one might say, "Jerry Springer is the opium of the people." If the members of the Frankfurt School were alive today, they surely would say this. Listening to a song on itunes is like eating candy or doing a drug. It makes you happy and content. Is texting, tweeting, or looking at facebook much different? Technology has fused with culture, with rationality in the service of capitalism to produce mindless, fun, enjoyable entertainment.

They focused on popular culture because they believed this was a key toward understanding how capitalism – an oppressive system they saw as filled with contradictions – could manage to survive and flourish. The almost obsessive focus on consumption they said was like a fetish. They also complained that reason itself has become a fetish:

> Complicated logical operations are carried out [in industrial capitalism] without actual performance of all the intellectual acts upon which the mathematical and logical symbols are based. Such mechanization is indeed essential to the expansion of industry; but if it becomes the characteristic feature of minds, if reason itself is instrumentalized, it takes on a kind of materiality and blindness, becomes a fetish, a magical entity that is accepted rather than intellectually experienced. (1993:23)

A fetish is a concept originally related to Freud and psychoanalysis. It is an object that brings people (sexual) pleasure and in which people obsess over. For example, one might have a foot fetish in which he or she gets sexually aroused by feet. But the concept fetish here is less sexual per se and is broader. Here we are looking at the obsessions with consumption of commodities. A **commodity fetish** is when someone or an entire society is oriented toward getting pleasure through consumption, and they become obsessed with this. The focus on the pleasures of obsessive consumption prevents people from looking critically at the workings of capitalism and thus help to maintain the system. This notion is closely related to the ideas of reification and mystification which were discussed above. We have become lost in our consumption; our humanity has become lost in our consumption.

The Frankfurt School take their analysis of commodities and consumption much further. The lines between appearances and reality become blurred in consumer culture, and what matters is not the real thing, but the appearance of the thing. Superficiality rather than depth becomes the focus in consumer capitalism. "Real life is becoming indistinguishable from the movies," Horkheimer and Adorno tells us. "The sound film far surpassing the theater of illusion, leaves no room for imagination or reflection on the part of the audience, who is unable to respond within the structure of the film, yet deviate from its precise detail without losing the thread of the story; hence the film forces its victims to equate it directly with reality" (1993:126). Here they are noting the technology of movies is such that it seduces the viewer and brings him or her into it completely. Reality disappears in the instant. Most importantly, the line between appearance and reality disappears, and all that is left is appearances as reality. But it is not just the movies where this occurs. Society is saturated with these processes, in and out of the theater.

Consumer culture allows people to be uncritical and oblivious to the workings of capitalism in many other ways. For example, Marcuse wrote about **repressive desublimation** (1964). Here he modifies some basic concepts from psychoanalysis and grafts them onto his critical theory. It will be recalled that sublimation is a defense mechanism. It is the channeling of unconscious desires and wishes (often sexual) into appropriate social behaviors. It involves the masking of the real desires and symbolically turning these into acceptable and appropriate behaviors, e.g. smoking a cigarette, designing a skyscraper (see above). But Marcuse says that consumer capitalism is desublimated. By this he means that the riches of capitalism have provided people with the ability to get many of their basic pleasurable needs met through the marketplace. No longer does one need, for example, to channel their (conscious or unconscious) sexual desires into some symbolic behavior. Instead we can now get gratifications directly. We get pleasure through drinking a Coke-a-Cola or listening to itunes. Better yet, we watch pornography on the internet. (The Frankfurt School theorists were of course writing before the internet era, but their argument is as applicable if not more so to the new technology.) At first glance, this might seem like the internet is liberating from a psychoanalytic perspective. Freud complained about the repressions of the Western world, particularly the strict sexual controls of the Victorian era, and he complained about the psychological harm done by these to individuals. Wouldn't it seem liberating to have all of our pleasure met, as they are now? Marcuse says this is part of the problem. It appears liberating, when it is in fact oppressive or repressive. So how it is repressive? How is this bad? He says it is bad because the entire process through which people now get their pleasurable needs met is managed, controlled, manipulated by rationality and the marketplace. The pleasures look and feel good but are in fact nothing more than manipulations. Ultimately, this process is harmful to man's humanity, but the nasty thing about capitalism is that it appears to be the opposite.

This touches upon an overarching theme in the writings of the Frankfurt School. They often claim that capitalism produces a culture that appears to be good in one way or another. It appears to allow people pleasure and freedom, etc. But this appearance is the very opposite of what is occurring. Time and again, the Frankfurt School explain how consumer capitalism creates illusions that do not readily allow for criticism; it creates the illusions that criticisms of it, within the confines of its own logic, are meaningful. For example, think about the protest music of the 1960s, whether it is Bob Dylan, folk music, or any of the anti-establishment or anti-war songs of that era. On the surface, these songs appear to challenge the existing capitalist system. They appear to be critical. Yet the Frankfurt School members say, these songs do the opposite by appearing to be critical. Adorno, the music specialist, made a point of this. He noted that the structure of the music, e.g. its very simply musical form, three cord songs, etc. its hymn-able and memorable melodies, is seductive. The very structure of the music lulls the listener into a state of mindless contentment. Even if the lyrics proclaim revolutionary or critical ideas, or better yet *because* they proclaim revolutionary or critical ideas, the listener can relax and feel content. The listener is not encouraged or prompted through the structure of the music to think, and to be meaningfully critical.

Totalitarianism and the Individual

Moreover, the Frankfurt School complained about the totalitarian nature of consumer capitalism. They were particularly concerned that this totalitarian system was causing great damage to the individual (or to the dignity of the individual). It was bearing down upon the individual and negating his or her humanity. First, we must understand the concept of **totalitarianism**. The term totalitarianism usually refers to a country with a government that is all powerful. It is based upon the idea that the people exist to serve the state (i.e., national government) and not the other way around. The state has complete power over all facets of life. The fascist Nazi regime under Hitler was a totalitarian state, so too is the communist state of North Korea today. The Soviet Union was also a totalitarian society. Traditionally, democracies are thought to be the opposite of totalitarian societies. Whereas totalitarian societies reject freedom and reject the rights of the individual, democracy embraces freedom and the rights of the individual. So how could the Frankfurt School call democratic capitalist societies totalitarian? They claim (and this is particularly Horkheimer's view) that the fusion of formal rationality (or technological rationality) with capitalism, and the fusion of formal rationality with dominance, creates a totalizing oppressive force. Everyone must conform to the accepted truths of capitalism, of formal rationality. Otherwise, they are seen as mad, or otherwise deviant. In the same way that Weber's iron cage of rationality is not seen, but is real nonetheless, and is imposed upon individuals, so too is technological rationality. We have all become slaves, and we do not know it. Moreover, our status of being slaves is maintained by our belief in the claim that we are free. The Frankfurt School were very concerned about the effects that this has had upon the individual. Individual humanity, they argue, was denied, as people are turned into happy consumers acting rationally in their daily lives. There has been a "decline of the individual" in the modern era (Horkheimer, 1974).

Moreover, the decline of the free and autonomous individual is associated with yet another contradiction (dialectic): In consumer capitalism individuals are given a seemingly endless array of consumer choices. One could go to McDonald's or Burger King. One could buy an iphone or a Samsung Galaxy. One could buy Nikes or New Balance. The choices we have in capitalism are almost endless. Is not choice at the heart of freedom? Doesn't this mean that we are free in capitalism, in contrast to what the Frankfurt School claim? They would say that this is yet another way in which the system blinds people to the oppressive nature of capitalism. These choices allow us to think we are free, but in fact they do the opposite. The choices give the appearance of freedom, but in fact are instruments of conformity. After all, is there really any meaningful difference between Coke and Pepsi? A big Mac and a Whopper? Yes, there are differences, but are they meaningful? Does it matter if you chose paper or plastic bags at the supermarket? The idea of giving people choices, when the choices are empty, helps to maintain the illusion of real freedom.

The Authoritarian Personality

In the wake of the horrors of World War Two, some if not many of the members of the Frankfurt School sought to understand how democracy fell apart in the 1920s and 1930s in Europe and how fascism took over. Fascism first took hold in Italy in the 1920s under Mussolini and came to power in Germany in the early 1930s under Hitler and the Nazis. It was also embraced in many other European countries of the time. Democracy necessarily died under fascism and fascism led to the insanity of the holocaust where six million Jews and millions of Roma peoples were killed, along with millions of mentally ill, intellectually disabled, etc. Ultimately, World War Two led to the deaths of over fifty million people, including Russians, Poles, and American military members, to name just a few. In short, fascism led to the destruction of the western world and democracy. It was of course defeated by a coalition of the U.S., England and the Soviet Union.

As most of the members of the Frankfurt School were European Jews, it is probably not surprising that they wished to understand after the war how this nightmare could have happened, and most importantly they wished to understand whether something like it could happen again: Could democracy in a stable prosperous country such as the United States fall to fascism? Was the rise of fascism a unique historical event of the nineteen thirties or was there something about democracy, and specifically, democratic capitalism that nurtures its own demise and nurtures the rise of fascism within it? These are some of the questions many of the members of the Frankfurt School were asking in the shadow of World War Two.

The Frankfurt School's ideas on democratic capitalism and the possibilities of the rise of fascism can perhaps best be seen through two things. The first is a study titled *The Authoritarian Personality* (1950) done by Adorno et al. in America in the immediate post-World War Two era. The second consists of the various writings of Erich Fromm, a psychodynamic psychologist, who was associated with the School. We can begin by summarizing Adorno et al.'s study. Adorno and his colleagues conducted a study of personality and political ideologies in America. As noted, they wished to understand how fascism, and the associated virulent antisemitism, arose within democratic countries of Europe and specifically wished to understand whether it might arise again in the democratic capitalist country of America. They constructed lengthy survey questionnaires meant to measure whether respondents had one or another personality characteristic and personality types and whether there were similarities amongst certain personality types and commitment to fascist ideologies. They developed several scales to measure several distinct personalities: The antisemitism (AS) scale; the ethno-centrism (E) scale; the political economic conservativism (PES) scale, and the fascism (F) scale. Within their surveys, they included questions that would measure the degree to which a respondent ranked high or low on each of the scales. They then administered the surveys to approximately 2000 Americans (in California) from various groups, e.g. college students, labor union members, merchant marines, government workers, longshoreman, schoolteachers, prison inmates, psychiatry patients, nurses, etc.

The fascist scale was undoubtedly the most discussed and was the most controversial. The fascist scale was comprised of six dimensions: conventionalism; authoritarian submission; authoritarian aggression; anti-intraception (i.e. "opposition to the subjective, the imaginative, the tender-minded" (1950: 256); superstition and stereotypy; power and "toughness" (i.e., "preoccupation with the dominance-submission, strong-weak, leader-follower dimension; identification with power figures; overemphasis upon the conventional attributes of the ego; exaggerated assertion of strength and toughness" (ibid.: 256); destructiveness and cynicism; and projectivity (i.e. "the disposition to believe that wild and dangerous things go on in the world; the projection outward of unconscious emotional impulses" (ibid.:257)). Respondents who scored high on these dimensions were deemed to have fascist tendencies. The researchers found that a surprising number of respondents had such tendencies.

They also found that respondents who scored high on the fascist scale also tended to score high on other scales, such as the antisemitism scale, the conservative scale, and the ethno-centric scale. The authors note in their conclusion:

> The most crucial result of the present study .... Is the demonstration of a close correspondence in the type of approach and outlook a subject is likely to have in a great variety of areas, ranging from the most intimate features of family and sexual adjustment through relationships to other people in general to religion and to social and political philosophy. Thus, a basically hierarchical, authoritarian, exploitive parent-child relationship is apt to carry over into a power-oriented, exploitively dependent attitude toward one's sex partner and one's God and may well culminate in a political philosophy and social outlook which has no room for anything but a desperate clinging to what appears to be strong and a disdainful rejection of whatever is relegated to the bottom. The inherent dramatization likewise extends from the parent-child dichotomy to the dichotomous conception of sex roles and of moral values, as well as to a dichotomous handling of social relations as manifested especially in the formation of stereotypes and ingroup-outgroup cleavages. Conventionality, rigidity, repressed denial, and the ensuing break-through of one's weakness, fear and dependency are but other aspects of the same fundamental personality pattern ... "(1950: 971).

In short, the authors suggest that democratic capitalism, at least as found in the United States, produces fascist personality types which are in effect threats to democracy. The study was widely discussed in academic circles at the time, with some if not many scholars being critical of the methodology and claims made in it. Conservatives, in particular, complained that the study was biased. For example, it did not include any such liberal scale which might align with fascism. Conservatives suggest that perhaps there is as much if not more of a correlation between a liberal orientation with fascism as there is between conservatives and fascist personalities.

Erich Fromm was another member of the Frankfurt School who conducted his own research on the authoritarian personality. For example, in his book *Escape from Freedom* (1969 [1941]), Fromm presents a psychodynamic analysis of the modern democratic personality in an attempt to understand how democracies can and have slid into fascism. The democratic personality, in part due to its relation to particular social class positionings, is one that generally gravitates toward one of three types: 1) the automaton conformist; 2) the authoritarian; 3) the destructive personality.

The historic seedbed for these problems lies in the Protestant Reformation and with Luther. Protestantism elevated the self to a place of prominence. The self was not lifted out of its context. The thing of importance was the individual and his or her relation to God. (Echoes of Weber are loud here.) This fostered the growth of democratic capitalism, which in term amplified the tendencies that arose with the Protestant Reformation. Specifically, the freedom of the self in the modern world brought with it two contradictory things: The self was alone, detached, isolated, and the self was autonomous.

The anxiety of the detached self, combined with the workings of capitalism, produce anxieties and needs within the individual which Fromm says are channeled psychologically into personality structures such as the authoritarian personality. This situation produces anxieties, and it produces distorted social relations in which individuals are incapable of engaging in healthy love relations and instead, psychological, are led to engage in relations which are sadistic, masochistic or both. We connect with others and take pleasure through sadistic abuse of others, or through an embrace of the pain inflicted to us by others, or both. These pathological psychological needs brought about by the detached self and its frustrations are channeled through personality structures and produce such things the authoritarian personality and the conformist. Sadism, masochism, and sado-masochists are the hallmark features of personality types associated with fascism – including the authoritarian personality and the conformism.

While the Frankfurt School's research on the authoritarian personality was done over a half a century ago, it is worthwhile to ponder whether their concerns for the possible collapse of democracy and the resurgence of fascism is applicable today, particularly to America today. Unquestionably, Donald Trump is an authoritarian (many including myself argue he is a fascist). Equally as important, the Republican Party today has been taken over by radical elements which are authoritarian in character (and arguably fascist). Perhaps we might draw upon the writings of the Frankfurt School and their analysis of the authoritarian personality to make sense of what is happening in America today?

Culture and Nature

Another theme appearing in some of the writings of the Frankfurt School concerns the relationship of culture to nature, and specifically to how the rise of formal rationality or technological rationality relates to this relationship. Horkheimer and Adorno write about such things in the *Dialectic of Enlightenment* (1993). When we think of culture, we think of things produced by human beings as a result of intentional acts. Art, science, language, religion, technology and so much more are parts of culture. Nature, on the other hand, consists of things that exist and operate without being produced by humans. The trees in the forest, the tides in the sea, etc. are aspects of nature. And yet human beings are part of culture and part of nature. We are biological beings, we are animals, but we are more than this. What is and what should be the relationship humans have with nature and culture? These issues have been discussed and debated by philosophers since humans first walked on the earth. In the modern world, since the Enlightenment, reason, or formal rationality, have come to define how we understand the relationship between nature and culture. For the Frankfurt School, domination is an essential character of the form of reason or rationality (e.g. formal, instrumental, technological rationality) that has conquered the modern world. The essence of reason is that it is useful to manage and control the world. It dominates. Its very character is one of domination. Modern capitalism following from the Enlightenment embraces reason and thus domination, and specifically embraces a partitioning of nature from culture; modern capitalism embraces the domination of the nature by culture. Science and technology are and should be used to dominate nature. Nature is there to be used by people. This form of understanding is very destructive, according to the Frankfurt School. It is destructive to the natural environment. (They were writing well before the modern environmental movement arose, and well before such issues as global warming arose, but they undoubtedly would note their theories apply to such things.) But more. It is destructive to human beings. After all, we are part of nature. Our natures are negated by the conquest of reason and its dominating qualities. Our bodies are things separate from our beings and are there to be used. We need to liberate our bodies from this oppression – the oppression based on the divide between nature and culture and on a system which sees culture's role as one that must dominate nature. We need to reconceptualize and integrate nature and culture, but this can only be done by changing and replacing capitalism. For example, we need to reconceptualize sex. This does not mean however that the Frankfurt School embraced "free love" or pornography (see above). Paying for pornography on the internet or embracing free love is little different from the distractions discussed earlier: They make us happy and content and blind in the harmful world of capitalism. They argue that such activities are wrongheaded because they do not address the root of the problem, i.e. modern, rational capitalism.

What is to be Done?

We have thus far seen how the Frankfurt School like to criticize. They criticize everything from popular culture to capitalism. Yet it is easy to criticize. It is far more difficult to propose solutions to the problems one identifies. What do the Frankfurt School members propose as solutions to the many, many problems of rational capitalism? As Marxists they are calling for the end of capitalism. But what is to replace it? They certainly would not want a form of communism that looks anything like the oppressive totalitarian systems of the former Soviet Union or the current North Korea. What then do they propose? While they do present some clear and unequivocal ideas regarding what should happen, they never give us specifics. They call for the end of capitalism and for the liberation and emancipation of the individual, but again, how is this to happen and what will the future society look like? It appears they are calling for a new form of rationality, one that would replace the existing form of formal rationality, or individual or technological rationality, or subjective or objective rationality. But what would this look like? It would need to be critical. It would need to be dialectical. It would need to embrace the Marxist claim of praxis. Praxis, as we saw earlier, is the fusion of theory and practice. It is living one's theory. One will recall Marx's famous line, "philosophers think about the world, the point is to change it." Theory should be oriented to real life. Theory should be put into practice in daily life to change the world in fundamental ways, at least this is the implication of the Frankfurt School's theorizing. Issues and concerns about justice and values should infuse the reasoning process, and these should infuse social behaviors and social organization. Knowledge is not simply given to people from on high. It is not simply there to be imposed upon people. This form of knowledge, like the knowledge produced through formal rationality, negates the autonomous individual. What is needed then is for the development of a form of reasoning, a form of **critical reasoning**, which overcomes the limitations of existing forms of rationality, and this emerges within lived, social interactions.

Critical reason stands in opposition to objective and subjective rationality (as well as in opposition to individualistic and technological rationality). In some ways, one might hear the echo of Weber's distinction between formal and substantive rationality here. However, critical reason is not akin to substantive rationality. The essence of critical reasoning is the lived, social experiences which produce knowledge. It is a recognition that reason is produced by and for people, and when it is imposed upon people or when it is produced not by people but by a detached logic (operating within capitalism), then it negates our humanity. It appears that the implication of the Frankfurt School's theorizing is that one should engage in critical reasoning in which knowledge produced through social interactions is oriented toward meaningful social change. For example, think of a college class. A traditional class is one in which the professor hands out a syllabus on the first day and then lectures to students throughout the semester. The students are turned into consumers. They are turned into passive receivers of knowledge. Their humanity is thus negated. In such a setting, the class is structured to maintain the existing political system by teaching students to be passive and uncritical, to follow the commands of authority. The professor lectures, and the students quietly listen. But what if a professor thought the Frankfurt School's theory was correct? How would he or she then organize the class? Perhaps the professor might not hand out a syllabus, but instead tell the students that they will be responsible as a group for creating one, with advice or suggestions, if asked, by the professor. The same with grading and with the class format. Should the class be structured as lectures, or should there be discussions, or something else? Through the active engagement of the students, particularly if it is informed by the critical understandings of the Frankfurt School, the theory could be put into practice. Such a class would give responsibility to the students. It would likely not be organized as a traditional class. It would empower the students. It would call for the students to be autonomous agents, who critically evaluate things, such as the organization of the course, and who actively create their worlds. It is the process that is central to critical reasoning, unlike other forms of reason where the lived process is subordinated to a set of detached rational rules.

The Evolution of the Institute

The Institute for Social Research has gone through several generations since its founding around one hundred years ago. Through this time, the theoretical focus of the Institute has significantly changed. After the first members, including Adorno, Horkheimer, and Marcuse, died, the Institute was for a time led by Jurgen Habermas (1929-). Habermas is arguably one of the most significant social theorists and social philosophers in the world today. He was a student of the original Frankfurt School theorists but took Critical Theory in a different direction. His theorizing and philosophy eliminated, or at the very least reduced, the Marxist influences as well as the psychoanalytic influences found in the original theorists, while keeping the critical impulses of the founders, and Habermas elevated issues related to language philosophies and to American social philosophy, particularly incorporating the ideas of George Herbert Mead, pragmatism, and other such ideas (See Chapter Eleven for a detailed description of his theorizing.) More recently, scholars of the Institute such as Axel Honneth (1996) and Rahel Jaeggi (2018) also have pursued an intellectual course very different from the original members. They draw inspiration from Hegel rather than from Marx. Their theorizing is anchored more in contemporary moral philosophy and themes of interpersonal matters such as "recognition" or respect than it is in a Marxist informed critique of capitalism. (For some nice sympathetic criticisms of their work, the reader is referred to debates between the American feminist philosopher Nancy Fraser, who is more committed to the original critical impulses of the Institute, and Honneth and Jaeggi (2003, 2018).)

Summary

In this chapter we covered two distinct, yet related, sets of theories influenced by Marxism: structural and humanistic Marxism and the critical theory of the Frankfurt School. Two main currents of Marxism that emerged in the twentieth century are structural Marxism and humanistic Marxism. Althusser is a structural Marxism; Lukacs and Gramsci are humanistic Marxists. Althusser is influenced by structural anthropology and structural linguistics. He embraces Marx's concepts of dialectics and materialism but presents his own understanding of Marx's concepts. Althusser says that Marx did not simply use Hegel's concept of dialectics. Instead, Marx radically reconceptualized it. Materialism should be understood as including the realm of ideas in dialectical unity with material conditions. Althusser says that an analysis of anything in society must start with the concept of totality. The totality is defined by capitalism, and the task is to identify and analyze the site of production of the essential contradiction in capitalism, which is between capital and labor. Althusser says that society consists of multiple overlapping structures, with the economic structure being at its heart. The concept of production is central not only to economics but to the structuring of the totality. Things in reality are produced not as the result of one or another factor, but by a multiple over overlapping factors. Realities are overdetermined by these multiple factors. There are two theories of the state: instrumentalist and structuralist. Althusser favors the latter. He also embraces an anti-humanism and argues that Marx does as well. He develops a theory of ideology and ideological state apparatuses (e.g. family, schools, work, etc.) through which the self is seen as a product of ideologies.

Humanistic Marxism is far more popular today than structural Marxism. Two of the main figures associated with humanistic Marxism are Lukacs and Gramsci. Lukacs is identified as a Hegelian Marxist because of his rich use of dialectics. He is associated with theoretically elaborating the concept of reification. Gramsci embraced an anti-deterministic and anti-positivistic view of Marx. Social life and history are not programmed. People make their own histories. He embraces the concept of praxis and theorized about the social factors and conditions that would produce opposition to and ultimately a revolution against capitalism. He anchored his theorizing in an elaboration of Marx's base superstructure model. The base and superstructure are inextricably intertwined. Gramsci elaborated the concept of hegemony and saw it as central to understanding how capitalism operates in the modern world. He was committed to revolutionary change, and he analyzed the concepts of leadership and the role of intellectuals in the revolutionary struggle. He believed the revolution should and would be led by organic intellectuals.

A different theory, called critical theory, was produced by the members of the Frankfurt School, the informal name of the Institute of Social Research originally located in Frankfurt, Germany. Some of the major figures include Marcuse, Adorno, and Horkheimer. The Frankfurt School's theory is a revisionist Marxist theory, largely influenced by the young Marx rather than the old Marx, that incorporates ideas from Weber and Freud. The Frankfurt School sought to understand how capitalism, filled with its contradictions, was able to survive and flourish, and why communism in the Soviet Union became such a disaster. The School saw the central importance consumption, rather than the traditional Marxist focus on production, has had for the maintenance of capitalism in the United States and western Europe in the post-World War Two era. The School argued in part that unconscious psychological processes work in conjunction with the needs of capitalism, to create false ideas and beliefs in the minds of people, which allow capitalism to be maintained.

The Frankfurt School used Marx's base-superstructure model to understand ideology, consumption and culture. Capitalism survives in part because of mystification, reification, and commodity fetishism. The culture industry plays a major role in maintaining capitalism by feeding the masses with popular and high culture that serves to prevent the populace from developing critical perspectives. The culture industry is a fusion of rationalization, capitalism, and consumption. The Frankfurt School claim that the symbolic world of culture, including art, has been taken over by the culture industry and is driven by the pursuit of profit. The culture industry crafts its products, from movies to music, in rationalized and simplistic forms that simultaneously prevent the populace from developing meaningfully critical ideas while also creating the illusion of happiness and contentment of the populace. Consumer capitalism can be described as a totalitarian society, in which everyone is the same, but everyone thinks they are unique individuals. The logic of positivism, and the products of positivism – science and technology – operate under the conditions of technological rationality. The Frankfurt School were highly critical of positivism and technological rationality. These act in ways, much like Weber's formal rationality, to blind people from assuming a fully human, active position in the world.

The Frankfurt School have had a significant influence upon some forms of sociological theorizing in the last fifty years or so, though much of this influence is subtle or indirect. For example, many of the ideas developed by the Frankfurt School arguably have influenced recent critical race and gender identity theories (see Chapter Thirteen) as well as various forms of postmodern theories (see Chapter Twelve). It is somewhat curious that

Frankfurt School have had such an influence when one considers the many, many criticisms that have been leveled against them. Several of these criticisms can be noted here. One common criticism is that the Frankfurt School members are hypocritical because they embraced Marxism while at the same time they also were criticized as elitist. Almost all of the members come from wealthy backgrounds, and most thought highly, if not critically, of highbrow Western culture. They had "bourgeois" tastes in art and culture. Adorno spent much time developing a theory of aesthetics. He was particularly interested in music. He was a musician himself and wrote numerous critiques of classical music. While he criticized many composers, he also liked some others. (For example, he liked the odd serialism of Schoenberg. Adorno was a student of the avant guard composer Alban Berg, who was himself a student of Schoenberg.) At the same time, Adorno and the others were quite dismissive or disparaging of pop music. Adorno also harshly criticized jazz, claiming its structure did not foster critical engagement in the listener. Others criticized the Frankfurt School for having a theory that ultimately leads to irrationality. When rationality is questioned, what is the basis of claiming facts? Facts become nothing more than things to be debated in the political arena. You might say one thing is true, I might say that another is true. Who is to say? If facts are no longer treated as objective and independent of judgments of humans, then this leads inevitably to thinking in terms of political contests. Those who have the most power get to determine what the facts are. Conservatives complain that this has led to such confused and debatable concepts as "political correctness" and "racist micro-aggressions" that are heard today in public discussions. Critics complain that such concepts are irrational and falter when exposed to objective, rational argument, but the Frankfurt School's reasoning rejects such objective approaches. Relatedly, critics complain that the Frankfurt School theorizing is filled with confused concepts that are not readily subject to empirical, scientific investigation. (After all, if science is based upon formal rationality, if sociologists embraced this form of science, would they not be part of the problem?) (Though to be fair, the Frankfurt School members did engage in numerous research projects, some of great note, and these projects appeared generally to conform to the normative scientific standards of the time.) On the other hand, traditional Marxists have complained that the Frankfurt School are not true Marxists and that they have perverted Marxists ideas. Much as Marx complained that Hegel was an idealist, so too recent Marxists complain that the Frankfurt School were also idealists. They focused on culture to the exclusion of an analysis of the material conditions. Moreover, there was an absence of any analysis of class and class conflict in their writings. In addition, going back to the first criticism noted above, they showed at best a lack of interest in the working class and at most a disdain for this class. They looked down, in their elitist ways, upon the cultures of the working class.

Discussion Questions

1. How do you think the Marxist theorists covered in this chapter -- Lukacs, Althusser, or Gramsci -- would respond to the criticisms of Marx offered by Dahrendorf (see Chapter Seven)? Are Dahrendorf's criticisms sound, and do they mean that any and all attempts to salvage Marxist theory are doomed to fail?

2. Some scholars argue that the supposed differences between the humanistic and structural Marxists are in reality not differences but are instead simply two different ways of looking at the same thing? Are the humanistic and structural Marxists in conflict with one another, or can they be wedded? How?

3. The Frankfurt School argue that traditional forms of culture, for example, popular music, have the effect of supporting capitalism rather than challenging capitalism, even when the lyrics of popular music appear to be critical or revolutionary. The Frankfurt School argue that the simplistic and predictable structures of popular music are soothing and create pleasantness, rather than genuine criticism. They argue that critical lyrics only appear to be effective criticism, when in fact these criticisms found in popular music have the opposite effect. They allow the listener to feel he is being critical while at the same time the structure of the music encourages continued passivity and pleasantness. Is the Frankfurt School right about popular music? Is popular music really not critical in any meaningful sense? Can popular music actually serve as a vehicle to create critical consciousness, or does the very fact that it is part of the culture industry prevent it from being truly critical?

4. The Frankfurt School complain that Western Democracy, and specifically American Democracy, is a totalitarian system. It gives the appearance that everyone is free and independent. It gives the appearance that individualism is a cherished value. But in reality
The system enslaves everyone to mindless conformity through slavish compliance with the culture industry. Are they correct when they say America is a totalitarian society? Why or why not?

5. Marcuse once wrote an article on the repression of tolerance. He argued that the tolerance of cultural differences found in America and in developed capitalism in general gives the appearance that America is a free society. But

Marcuse argues that this appearance of tolerance actually works to blind people from the lack of true freedom in American society. Tolerance serves to blind people from understanding how consumer capitalism dehumanizes people. Is he right to say that tolerance, as it is realized in America, actually is a tool of psychological oppression?

Chapter Nine: Micro-Sociological Theories – Symbolic Interactionism, Goffman, and Phenomenology

This chapter describes three of the main micro-theories in sociology: 1) Symbolic interactionism; 2) the works of Erving Goffman; and 3) phenomenology and ethnomethodology. While these perspectives are quite different from one another, they share a common focus on the study of small-scale social interactions and on the social psychology of participants. The difference between macro and micro orientations should be remembered here. Macro-sociology explains social life, social behavior, social order by focusing on large-scale social forces, such as the organization of the economy or culture or society at large. A macro-sociologist, for example, might seek to understand divorce by examining the large-scale economic or structural context within which the divorce is happening. Perhaps divorce could be explained by the changing structures of the economy. For example, increasing unemployment surely puts increased pressure on marriage. Perhaps divorce could be explained by changing understanding of roles, e.g. the role of husband and wife, the ideas of masculine and feminine. Changes in these roles, brought about perhaps by changes in the structures of society, might produce more divorce. These are macro forms of explanations. Micro-sociology focuses not on large-scale social organization but instead on small, face-to-face interactions to explain social life. Micro-sociology explains social behaviors by focusing on how individuals act based upon their understandings of their immediate present environment, of the social realities of the here and now. A micro-sociologist examining divorce would be far more interested in understanding how the husband and wife understand themselves and their relationship in the lived present than they would be in understanding how the large-scale forces of social structure or the economy determine divorce rates.

The three perspectives described in this chapter share a micro-perspective, but they are nevertheless quite different from one another. Symbolic interactionism is currently much more popular in sociology than the other two. Symbolic interactionism is built upon the ideas of the American philosopher George Herbert Mead (1863-1931). Mead believed that individuals are common-sense making creatures. They are practical, problem solvers. He believed people act based upon the meanings they assign to their worlds, and they act based upon their understandings of who they believe themselves to be. People are symbol using creatures, and as such language and signs and their meanings are central to an understanding of social behavior. Individuals live in a social universe. Our individual selves are produced through the social interactions we have. Erving Goffman (1922-1982) is sometimes identified as a symbolic interactionist, but he is not. While he was greatly influenced by Mead, he was equally influenced, if not more so, by other scholars such as Emile Durkheim, Georg Simmel, and the rhetorician Kenneth Burke. Goffman developed a theory he called dramaturgy which uses the theater metaphor to explain social behavior. We are all acting throughout our daily lives in one or another play – at work, at home, at school, wherever. In a classroom, for example, the play is class. There are basically two roles: the role of students and the role of professor. We each have our parts, and we tend to do things so that the show goes on. The show must go on (but of course it does not always do so). Later in his life, Goffman abandoned dramaturgy and developed a different approach called frame analysis. Frame analysis is far less well known and far less often used today in sociology than his earlier theory of dramaturgy. Some scholars today claim that frame analysis is a continuation of his earlier theory, but it is not. In frame analysis, Goffman abandons the theater metaphor and instead focuses upon understanding modes or types of beings. For example, when one is practicing a violin, one is operating in a different mode of being than when one is on stage performing in an orchestra in front of an audience. Likewise, when one is talking to a friend one is operating in a different mode of being than when one is performing at work as a used-car salesman.

The third perspective covered in this chapter is phenomenology and ethnomethodology. Phenomenology is the name of a type of philosophy first developed by the German Edmund Husserl (1859-1938). It seeks to understand the structures of experiential consciousness. It identifies and analyzes the building blocks or the elements of our consciousness in the present that allow us to understand and to make sense and to act in our worlds. Phenomenology was first turned into a sociological theory by the German Alfred Schutz (1899-1959). As one can see, this tradition has deep German roots. Schutz later moved to America and taught a number of influential American sociologists, including Harold Garfinkel. Garfinkel (1917-2011) embraced phenomenological sociology and developed his own, unique version that he called ethnomethodology. The term ethnomethodology is a bit unfortunate in that it sometimes leads the reader to believe inaccurately that his theory was somehow related to "ethnicity." It was not, at least not directly. It is best to think of the prefix "ethno" here in relation to ethnography, a type of qualitative methodology in sociology and anthropology in which the researcher seeks to understand, to capture, the meanings people have of their present behaviors and present social circumstances.

Symbolic Interactionism

George Herbert Mead never used the term symbolic interactionism to describe his philosophy. It was Herbert Blumer, a sociologist who was a student of Mead's at the University of Chicago, who took the latter's philosophy and turned it into a sociological theory that he called symbolic interactionism. While their focus of attention was a bit different – Mead wished to create a philosophy (which he called a social psychology) and Blumer wished to use these ideas to create a science that sociologists could use to do research – their ideas about explaining social behaviors are more similar than they are different. As such, in this section the ideas of Mead and Blumer will both be discussed.

To begin to understand symbolic interactionism we might turn to the movies, and specifically to *Sunset Boulevard*. *Sunset Boulevard* is routinely found on the lists of the one hundred greatest movies of all time. It is a film noire classic. Made in 1950, it was directed by Billy Wilder. The main characters were Joe Gillis, played by William Holden, and Norma Desmond, played by Gloria Swanson. Gillis was a struggling script writer who has not had a job recently and was experiencing financial troubles. Desmond was an aging, washed-up, former silent film star, who lived in an old, broken down mansion in Beverly Hills. Desmond's servant/butler Max von Mayerling, played by the noted director Erich Stroheim, also played a prominent role in the film. Near the beginning of the film, Gillis, was being chased in his car by people seeking to repossess it. He tried to hide on Desmond's property. He meets Desmond and she convinces him to edit or rewrite a movie script that she had written. She had dreams of returning to stardom. She was once a famous star in the silent movie era, but now with talking movies she has not had a role in many years. Gillis reluctantly agrees to work for Desmond to write the script. Desmond instructs Gillis to move into the mansion or at least to be a guest in an apartment adjacent to the mansion. She buys him clothes and lavishes him with presents. As the movie progressed it is increasingly clear that Desmond harbors delusions that she is still a famous and influential actress, and that people can and will bow to her demands. Mayerling, her servant/butler, helps to convince her of these delusions by doing such things as writing fan letters to her under phony names. Gillis too allows her to maintain her delusions. As the movie progresses Desmond falls in love with Gillis, though Gillis does not have similar feelings. He only has continued to work for her, writing the script, because she pays him.

While Gillis is living in the mansion, he falls in love with a screen writer. Desmond finds out about this and she is emotionally crushed. Desmond eventually threatens to kill herself. Gillis then shatters Desmond's illusions by telling her that her ideas about having fans and about staging a comeback are delusional. She then shoots and kills Gillis. The movie ends when the police and media arrive at her mansion. She is shown walking down the stairs from her bedroom acting as if she is in a Hollywood movie playing a part. At the bottom of the stairs she then gives the famous line, "All right, Mr. De Mille, I'm ready for my close-up." It is clear she has become lost in the delusion that she had been living for so long.

Some of the main points in symbolic interactionism are reflected in this movie. Most notably, symbolic interactionism claims that we act based upon our understandings of who we are, how we define ourselves, and how we define our situation. How we define ourselves is determined by social interactions, and because these interactions change so too do our definitions of ourselves. Who was Norma Desmond? She was once a famous actress. Her fans in the silent movie era certainly filled her with the notion that she was an important Hollywood star. But now that the silent movie era has ended, what sustained her understanding of herself? Why did she not adjust in a more effective manner to her new position as retired or aging film star? Why did she continue to believe she was still a great and influential star, whom was greatly and widely admired? She was able to maintain this false impression of herself because of the ways that the people around her interacted with her. Gillis and Mayerling spent the most time around her and they both were invested for their own reasons at having her maintain her delusions. She finally goes insane, as is clear from her belief that she was actually in a movie at the very end of the film when she was not, only when Gillis interacts with her and tells her the public has forgotten about her and that she is not the star she things she is.

George Herbert Mead

George Herbert Mead (1863-1931) was born in South Hadley, Massachusetts. His father was a Congregationalist (Protestant) minister who went on to become a professor at Oberlin College. His mother, Elizabeth Storrs Billing, was a deeply religious Protestant, who served as the President of Mount Holyoke College for a time. Mead earned his bachelor's degree from Oberlin in 1883, and after working for a few years in various positions, including one as a school teacher, he began graduate studies at Harvard University. He never earned any graduate degree. At Harvard, he became friends with the older William James, who was a Harvard professor and prominent pragmatist philosopher, though Mead never took a course with the latter. After leaving Harvard, Mead became a professor at the University of Michigan, and there developed a friendship with John Dewey and other prominent pragmatist philosophers. Dewey then took a position at the University of Chicago, in 1894, and invited Mead to join him there. Mead accepted and assumed a faculty position at the University of Chicago where he remained for the rest of his life. Mead studied for several years in Germany, from 1888-1981, where he took classes with a number of important German psychologists and philosophers, including Wundt, Dilthey, and perhaps Simmel. Of note, Mead never wrote a book in his life, though he did write a number of articles. His class lectures were compiled by his former students into what has become his most well-known work, publishes as the book *Mind, Self and Society*. Mead was actively involved in the "progressive" political and social causes of the time, and indeed his philosophy captures much of the Progressive Era spirit of reform. He was a friend of the prominent reformer Jane Addams and participated in and supported the women's suffrage movement as well as the settlement house movement.

Main Ideas

Mead was an American philosopher who was associated with the pragmatist school of philosophy, an influential form of philosophy in the late eighteen and early nineteen hundreds. Other notable pragmatists include Charles Peirce (1839-1914), William James (1842-1910), and John Dewey (1859-1952). In many ways **pragmatism** reflects the stereotypical American character. It is built on the assumption that people are practical, problem solvers. They are common sense making and common sense using creatures. Pragmatism begins with an optimistic view that individuals identify problems to solve and then solve them. Quite American in belief! Pragmatism is oriented toward understanding how people understand their worlds – how they assign meanings to their worlds -- and how and why they act as they do. It begins with the assumptions that people live in real time. Life is seen as a process. It also begins with the commonsense assumption that the reality of ultimate concern for us is the reality in front of us in the immediate present. We may and do think about the past and the future, but we do so in the present. We also are conscious beings who use language to assign meanings to our present, and we act based upon the meanings we assign.

In the following pages, the particular ideas of Mead are described, because he was the pragmatist most influential on the development of the sociological theory called symbolic interactionism. Mead called his philosophical approach a form of social psychology, and indeed this is a good way of thinking about it. He wished to understand the psychological processes that are involved in social action. But he believes the social is fundamentally important here. Our psychologies are rooted in the social, and therefore one needs to develop a psychological theory that is rooted in the social.

Main themes

Several overarching themes must be kept in mind if one is to understand Mead. The first is the importance of the social. Any explanation of human behavior, any understandings of individuals or of group behaviors, must begin with the social, rather than with the individual. The social world has priority in the analysis of social behavior. As he notes: "Social psychology studies the activity or behavior of the individual as it lies within the social process; the behavior of an individual can be understood only in terms of the behavior of the whole social group of which he is a member, since his individual acts are involved in larger, social acts which go beyond himself and which implicate the other members of that group" (1962:7). Moreover, and as we see below, the individual emerges through the social; the social is not produced by the individual. The second set of concepts of importance are language, symbols and meaning. As we will see, Mead believes that people are meaning making creatures, and we act based upon the meanings we give to the world. These meanings are constructed through our use of language and symbols. The third concept is the assumption that people are naturally active, problem solvers. We do not passively react to our worlds. We actively engage through a social psychological process in this world. The fourth theme is time. To understand Mead's theory, there needs to be a recognition of the centrality of the concept of time – in contrast to space -- within it. We live in and through time. Life should be seen as a process, as something that is fluid and changing, and fluid and changeable. Echoing William James' phrase "the stream of consciousness," humans live in a never-ending emergent reality. The social world is a never-ending emerging process. Theory must begin with this assumption. These themes will reappear over and over in the coming pages. Lastly, it bares noting that Mead wished to create a social psychology that could be the basis of a science of behavior. He wished to understand and explain observable, social behavior. But to do so it was necessary to look to social psychology.

Influences

We can now turn to look at how he built his theory. The theory was built in part in reaction to the behaviorist psychology of the American John B.

Watson that was emerging around nineteen hundred. (Mead also was reacting against other noted forms of psychology at the time, including the important psychological theories of Wilhelm Wundt.) Behaviorism is basically a mechanical form of learning theory. Animals do or do not do things based upon such things as rewards and punishments. Behaviorism begins with two basic concepts: the stimuli and the response. The stimulus is the cause of an action. The response is how the agent reacts to the stimuli. If I accidentally put my hand on a hot stove, I will likely pull it back and yell out in pain. The hot stove is the stimulus; the yelling is the response. For Watson animals and people alike can be understood using this basic model. However, Mead complained that Watson's model might be good for explaining the actions of an animal, a dog or a chicken, but it does not work to explain the actions, at least most actions, of human beings. Watson's model assumes an automatic or mechanical reaction to a stimulus. This does not work Mead says because for most human behaviors there is something between the stimulus and the response. He called this the "black box." People generally do not automatically response to stimuli. They think about the stimuli and about the possible response and about other things, and then act. This box consists of consciousness, of our assigning meanings and understandings, of a stimulus before we respond. I may not think when I pull my hand back and yell after placing my hand on a hot stove, but I will think about whether I should drive ninety miles an hour in a forty-five mile an hour speed zone before I decide to drive in one way or another. Most human behavior is of this order. Consciousness, meaning and thought are involved. This is central to understanding human behaviors.

Concepts

Objects

For Mead consciousness does not exist without **objects** of consciousness. That is, there cannot be an empty consciousness. We cannot be conscious without having an object of thought in consciousness. The concept of object here is important. The object of thought could be anything. We understand our world and act in our worlds based upon the objects we identify. As Herbert Blumer notes:

> The position of symbolic interactionism is that the "worlds" that exist for human beings and for their groups are composed of "objects" and that these objects are the product of symbolic interaction. An object is anything that can be indicated, anything that is pointed to or referred to

– a cloud, a book, a legislature, a banker, a religious doctrine, a ghost, and so forth. ... The nature of an object – of any and every object – consists of the meanings that it has for the person for whom it is an object. This meaning sets the way in which he sees the object, the way he is prepared to act toward it, and the way in which he is ready to talk about it. (1998:10-11)

Symbols, Gestures and Significant Symbols

Symbols are ideas that represent things, such as a chair, a book, a person, a system of language, etc. For Mead, they have precise qualities. Symbols are fundamentally social in nature. They have shared meanings. If you speak a word, which is a symbol, you assume that the person hearing the word understands it in the same way that you mean. Language is the most important system of symbols for symbolic interactionist theory. It is important for many reasons, not the least of which concerns the concept of self, as we discuss below.

Mead distinguishes between symbols and significant symbols, and he distinguishes gestures from significant symbols. Let us start with the latter distinction and then move on to the former. We can use the concepts of objects, symbols, stimulus and response and return to Mead's argument about how human beings are animals but are distinctly different from other types of animals. Earlier it was noted that Mead says that the behaviorist psychology of Watson was inadequate to understand human behavior. This is related to the distinction between gestures and significant symbols. To understand the difference, we must begin by noting that both gestures and significant symbols involve social interactions, but in fundamentally different ways. Animals can use gestures, but only humans can use significant symbols. A **gesture** is an act by one animal that is a stimulus to another animal to respond. Mead uses the example of a dog fight to illustrate the concept:

> The act of each dog becomes the stimulus to the other dog for his response. There is then a relationship between these two; and as the act is responded to by the other dog, it, in turn, becomes a stimulus to the other dog to change his own position or his own attitude. He has no sooner done this than the change of attitude in the second dog in turn causes the first dog to change his attitude. We have here a conversation of gestures. They are not, however, gestures in the sense that they are significant. We do not assume that the dog says to himself, "If the animal comes from this direction he is going to spring at my throat and I will turn in such a way." (1962:43)

This **conversation of gestures** is an automatic process that involves the absence of thought and reflection.

In contrast, **significant symbols** produce the same effect in the person making or using the symbols as they do in the person receiving (hearing, seeing, experiencing, etc.) them. As Mead notes, a significant symbol, "has the same effect on the individual making it that it has on the individual to whom it is addressed or who explicitly responds to it, and this involves a reference to the self of the individual making it" (1962:46). Significant symbols are based upon shared understandings of the symbol, shared by both the person sending the symbol and the person receiving it. It necessarily involves the assumption on the part of the person sending the symbol that the person, the self, receiving it will understand it in the same way the first person intends. Significant symbols then involve one person putting themselves in the shoes of the person he or she is speaking with and imaging how the person is receiving and understanding the symbol. Moreover and importantly, significant symbols also prompt a reaction; the receiver is prompted to response, to act. The nature of the significant symbol fosters a reaction on the part of the party receiving it, but it is not a mechanical or automatic reaction. Humans can engage in such processes; animals cannot. Significant symbols lie at the heart of social interaction.

We have described the difference between gestures and significant symbols, but what about the difference between symbols and significant symbols? For Mead, the difference lies in the ways the symbol does or does not "call out" a response in a person. A symbol does not call out, or necessarily produce, a response, whereas a significant symbol does. Mead writes:

> [I]f one is speaking of a dog to another person he is arousing in himself this set of responses which he is arousing in the other individual. It is ... the relationship of this symbol [i.e. the dog], this vocal gesture, to such a set of responses in the individual himself as well as in the other that makes of that vocal gesture what I call a significant symbol. A symbol does tend to call out in the individual a group of reactions such as it calls out in the other, but there is something further that is involved in its being a significant symbol: this response within one's self to such a word as "chair," or "dog," is one which is a stimulus to the individual as well as a response. (1962:72-73)

The Importance of Meaning

The importance of the concept of meaning in symbolic interactionism has been suggested above. But it deserves to be highlighted. Meaning is central. We are meaning making creatures. We make meanings through the use of symbols in social interactions. "[T]here is a difference between the intelligent conduct on the part of animals and what we call a reflective individual. We say that the animal does not think. He does not put himself in a position for which he is responsible; he does not put himself in the place of the other person and say, in effect, "He will act in such a way and I will act in this way." If the individual can act in this way, and the attitude which he calls out in himself can become a stimulus to him for another act, we have meaningful conduct" (1962:73).

We are constantly assigning meanings to our lived realities. It is in the nature of our being that we do so. One may say we are compelled by our natures to do so. When we enter a situation, we say, whether self-consciously or not, "what is the meaning of this situation?" and then act based upon our answer to the question. When a college student walks into a classroom on the first day of class, she thinks – on one level or another of consciousness – "what is the meaning of this?" She looks around and sees all of the elements of a classroom – whiteboard, desks, other students, etc. – and she recognizes that it is a classroom and acts accordingly. In short, individuals "define the situation" and then act in the situation based upon how they define it.

For Mead, meaning, like so much of our human existence, is connected to the social process: "[T]he nature of meaning is intimately associated with the social process as it appears." "Meaning is implicit – if not always explicit – in the relationship of the various phases of the social act to which it refers, and out of which it develops" (1962, 76).

Mind and Self

Mead's most significant work was *Mind, Self and Society: from the Standpoint of a Social Behaviorist* (1962). This book was not written as a book. Instead, it is comprised of the edited transcripts of notes taken by his students in his courses on social psychology. In this work, he provides a systematic overview of his theory and of the concepts of mind, self, and society. I describe the concept of mind and his all important concept of self here and later describe his understanding of society. **Mind** for Mead is something akin to an organized set of attitudes about time and about choices that a person has. Mind is characterized by a "reflective intelligence" (1962:118). Perhaps a good way to understand what he means is to think about an expression that was once more commonly used in the past than it is today. In the past, people might say, "I have a mind to ..." act in this way or in that way. For example, a parent in disciplining his child may say, "I have a mind to ground you for a week." The mind anchors our response to the immediate situation by imagining the consequences of actions in that situation. The mind allows us to "isolate" objects, to select one rather than another object to focus upon, and to assess how or if the object is of some use. "We try to distinguish the meaning of a house from the stone, the cement, the brick that make it up as a physical object, and in doing so we are referring to the use of it" (1962:131). Our mind allows us to orient ourselves such that we can make decisions. Moreover, "It is that mechanism of control over meaning in this sense which has, I say, constituted what we term "mind" " (1962:133). Lastly, the mind emerges out of language and is fundamentally social. It arises within the social process.

The concept of **self** is arguably one of the most central in the entire symbolic interactionist theory. Mead and the symbolic interactionists understand the concept of self in a way that is different from the way that many others see it. The self has a number of unique characteristics. The self is fundamentally social. It is born out of the social, through social interactions. The self is a process and is not a thing. It is made and remade constantly through social interactions. It arises through social experience (1962:140). It is fluid and changing. The self is active. That is, the self actively creates and recreates itself through these endless interactions. The self is also a symbol. It is an object, and uniquely an object to itself. It is simultaneously an object and a subject. If someone were to ask you, "Who are you?" you would likely begin your response with "I am ...." The I is a symbol that represents the self. But we also refer to ourselves as "me." When I think, "What does that person think of me?" I am using the word me to refer to my self, as an object of my thought. Thus, the self has two parts, the I and the Me. More accurately, the self is both the I and the me (1962:277). The I is the active, impulsive side of the self. It is the side of the self that is the subject of the action. It is the side of the self that says, "I want this, I want that ...." The me is the part of the self that is viewed as an object to itself. I imagine how I think others may see me. I put myself in the shoes of others and imagine how they see me. Mead says we are engaged in a dialog between the I and the me on a constant basis, though more often than not it is not a conscious process. Think for a moment that you are at a party and wish to go up to someone to talk to them or to ask them out on a date. You very well might think to yourself, "I want to talk to that person, and ask them out, but what are others going to think of me if the person rejects me?" Similarly, ask yourself why is it that some students do not ask or answer questions in class. Undoubtedly, some persons in class that wish to ask or answer questions posed by the professor or teacher do not do so because they are likely thinking to themselves, "I want to speak in class, but I am afraid what others might think of me if I say the wrong thing." Again, it is this running dialog that propels us forward.

The self for Mead is not the biological organism of the person. It is not someone's body. We cannot have a self without a body, but the self is distinct from the body. To understand this better, we might ask whether a six-month old baby has a self? For Mead, this baby does not have a self. Why? The baby does not have a self because it does not yet use symbols, specifically significant symbols – most notably language, and the ability to use these symbols is necessary for the existence of self. When the individual develops language, and when he or she can use the words I and me, then the self develops. Is it then possible for someone to lose a self after they have had one? What about someone stranded on a dessert island? When Tom Hanks in the movie Cast Away gets stranded on a dessert island after his plane crashed, did he continue to have a self or did he lose it? After all, he no longer had anyone to talk to. The social disappeared – at least in terms of having other real people to talk to, but the self is produced through the social. He continued to have a self because he continued to use language. He talked to himself out loud, and undoubtedly without speaking. He had running conversations with himself. He treated himself as both subject and object. But it is hard to maintain the self without the actual social being present. Language, as a social thing, might substitute for real social interactions for a time, but eventually a person's self might become threatened without real social interactions. It is interesting to note that after a while in the movie, he imagined a volleyball to be a person-like thing. He found this volleyball and painted a picture of a human face on it, and he began to interact with it as if it was a person. He named his new friend Wilson (the brand name on the ball.) He became so attached to the ball that at one point when Hanks had built a raft to escape from the island, Wilson fell overboard and Hanks dove into the ocean, risking his life, to save Wilson. A symbolic interactionist might say he created Wilson as a person in an attempt to salvage his notion of self in the absence of contact and interaction with other human beings. He felt a need to create a social world, a world of another "person," Wilson, with which he could interact.

The Generalized Other

When we interact with others, we imagine how the others are understanding us. In one way or another, when we use language or other types of symbols we must assume or try to assume that the other person is understanding our words in the same way that we are intending them. This of course does not always happen. When it does not, there are adjustments. This is social life. But what does it actually mean to put ourselves in the shoes of another person when we are interacting with them? When I am having a fight with my wife, am I putting myself in her shoes as I interact? When I go to a café and buy a coffee, am I putting myself in the shoes of the person behind the counter? When I am walking down a city street, am I imagining how others see me, and then will I adjust my behavior based upon this imagining? Does a three year old on an airplane put herself in the shoes of the other passengers as she endlessly cries and misbehave and disturbs the other passengers? All of these instances and of course many more illustrate the complexities of this seemingly simply process of interacting and putting oneself in the shoes of the person he or she is talking to. The importance of some of these interactional circumstances are discussed below in relation to the concepts of roles and the play stage and game stage. Here I will call attention to the important concept of **the generalized other**.

We can begin by distinguishing the generalized other from what we might call the particular other. When I am having a fight with my wife, I am putting myself in her shoes in our interactions. I am imagining how she understands and hears me. I am imagining how she understands my words. I am not thinking of how "wives" in general or for that matter people in general might respond to me. I am thinking and responding to one particular person. But much of social life is not like this. Much of social life entails our interacting with people we do not know. Think about life in public places. When I am walking down the street, I do not know the other people on the street. But am I aware that other people – people I do not know – can see me, can judge me based upon how I walk, how I dress, how I act. Most people, or at least most adults, are influenced by other people, people in general through their daily life, particularly in public. People consider how they are being seen by others in general. Some people may wish to claim that they do not consider how others may see them when they decide to dress in one way or another or to do one thing or another. But the reality is, according to symbolic interactionists, most people in fact are highly influenced by how they imagine how others – in general -- see them. This is the generalized other. "The attitude of the generalized other is the attitude of the whole community" (1962:154). It is the imagining of how people in general see you.

It is a powerful social regulator. Can you imagine how someone who never thinks about how people in general see them would behave? If I did not care about how people in general saw me, might I not engage in all sorts of anti-social behavior? Can you imagine a society populated by people who never consider how other people in the society would see them? How would they behave?

But where does the generalized other come from? Is it there at birth? Does it arise with the emergence of the self? For Mead, a young child does not yet have a generalized other. A four year old has a self, but the self is not yet stable because of this lack of generalized other. It is only later in childhood that it is developed. It is only with the development of the generalized other that "the fullest development of ... the individual self" can arise (1962:155). Moreover, the stability of social order, of society, is dependent upon most individuals developing a generalized other. As such, it is to the process of psychological development we can now turn.

The Play Stage and the Game Stage

Mead gives us a developmental theory to explain how the adult self comes to be. He presents a stage theory of the development of the self in childhood. There are two stages – the play stage and the game stage. From the time a child first begins to use symbols, i.e. language, until some indefinite age, say eight or nine years old, he is in the **play stage**. The child in the play stage has a self; he or she can use symbols. But at this stage the child's self is not yet stable. In this stage, the child does not have a generalized other. The child interacts with, or is oriented toward, particular others. That is, a four year old might think about what mommy or daddy would do if the child did this or that, but he or she would likely not think about how other people in general would think about their action. As the name suggests, in the play stage the child here is engaged with others in a series of unstructured encounters. What is it like to play a game with a four year old child? The child does not care much about following the rules of the game. There is no concern for the stability of the game. The child is simply playing. In the play stage, the child is constantly trying on one role or another and imagining how others might respond to him or her in those roles. "A child plays at being a mother, at being a teacher, at being a policeman" (1962:150). The child imagines his role and imagines the reception of his role. In the play stage, the child "utilizes his own responses" (ibid.:150) to stimuli to create his or her self. The processes involved are largely rooted in the imagination of the individual child rather than through the actual social interactions an adult has with others. As a child, "He plays that he is, for instance, offering himself something, and he buys it; he gives a letter to himself and takes it away; he addresses himself as a parent, as a teacher; he arrests himself as a policeman" (ibid.:150-51). In short, this is a period of constantly trying out selves through imaginary encounters. At this stage the self is not yet anchored through social and symbolic interactions.

As the child gets a little older, he enters the **game stage**. In the game stage, a child has developed a generalized other. He or she now considers how people in general view and will view his or her actions. Mead uses the game metaphor to illustrate this stage. In a game of baseball (a favorite example of Mead's), for example, an individual must be able to take the "attitude of everyone else involved in the game" if he or she is to be able to effectively play the game. He has to take the role of not one other individual – a particular other -- but of all the other individuals in the game. If I am playing second base on a baseball team and there is a runner on first base, then a ball is hit to the third baseman, I will need to know what all the other players on the field are going to do if I am to make an effective play. I need to know, to anticipate, what the shortstop is going to do, what the runner or runners are going to do, what the first baseman is going to do. In short, in the game stage the individual takes the roles of everyone else and not just the role of one other. "[A]n organized structure arises in him" as a result, and this organized structure is the self, the stable self.

Roles

The concept of role is central to much of sociology. It could broadly be thought of as an organized set of expectations attached to a position. For example, the position of father has certain expectations attached to it. Together these constitute the role. The concept of role was central in the classic structural functionalist theory of Talcott Parsons (as we saw in Chapter Seven). But symbolic interactionists are critical of the ways that many sociologists – including Parsons -- conceptualize and use this concept. They complain that many sociologists tend to see a role as something an individual simply gets poured into and then conforms to mechanically, without thought or reflection. But an essential feature of symbolic interactionism is that social life is emergent, dynamic, fluid. So too is the self. Selves are not passive, and they are not passive in relation to roles. Individuals do not simply adopt the expected behaviors of the role in which they are placed, they actively engage with it, possibly trying to modify the role such that it is aligned with notions of the self. They engage in **role-making**. One only needs to recognize that roles change in history to recognize their fluid nature. Think of the role of college student. Were the expectations of being a college student – either in classroom behavior or etiquette or elsewhere – the same in nineteen hundred as they are today? The role has changed. How? Arguably, it has changed through a gradual process of role-making.

Roles are central to the social interactive processes that are the focus of symbolic interactionism. When we interact with another person, the situation might call upon us to interact fundamentally with the role that the other person is in rather than with the unique individual with which one is interacting. When a student talks to a professor after class, the student likely will be imagining the professor as embodying the role of a professor. He or she imagines how professors think and act. Only by imagining how "professors" would respond to the issue, can a student effectively proceed in the interaction. The student will interact based upon his or her understandings of how a professor is and should act, and the student interacts accordingly. Much of social life involves people interacting with strangers in various roles. When you go to a store to buy something, the person behind the counter is in the role of salesperson. You interact with that person based upon your understanding of the role of salesperson rather than upon your understanding of the individual person, as you do not know this person. You imagine what it is like to be a salesperson when you interact with him or her.

Earlier, we noted that in interactions one has to place oneself in the shoes of another and to imagine how the other person is understanding oneself as one communicates to him or her. This same process occurs when one is interacting with someone in one or another role. To communicate, the person must **take the role of the other** and imagine how this person in the role will understand and respond. When talking to a police officer, one has to place themselves in the shoes of the role of the officer to understand how he or she may act. Roles then are centrally important in the endless and ongoing production of social life.

Society and Social Order

Thus far we have described some of the basic ideas and concepts of Mead's philosophy and of symbolic interactionism. But how do these concepts explain social behavior and social order, which are both topics of central concern for sociological theory? Individuals are meaning making creatures. We act based upon the definition of the situation. We act based upon the understandings we have of the immediate present. We say, what is going on? and then act accordingly. Moreover, we develop a concept of self, a concept of who we are, through social interactions, and this self is dynamic and changing. We enter a situation and seek to understand it, and we seek to understand our concept of self in the situation. Further, we generally seek to engage in the situation in ways to maintain our concept of self. If I think I am a very bright student, I might speak up in class or I might try to do well on exams. Other students then might come to believe I am very bright and will interact with me as if I am very bright. Alternatively, imagine that you are convicted of a crime and are put into prison, even if you have not committed the crime. Your sense of self is that you are not a criminal. But what happens when you tell your fellow inmates that you are not a criminal? What happens when you tell the guards you are not a criminal and that you do not belong there? Will they believe you, or will they assume your claims are nothing more than the acts of a criminal? After all, don't all criminals say that? Aren't all criminals liars and con artists? And how will your fellow inmates and how will the guards interact with you? Will they treat you as if you are not a criminal and that you are wrongfully imprisoned, or will they treat you like a criminal? Surely, they will treat you like a criminal. And what will happen to your sense of self when everyone around you interacts with you as if you are a criminal? Will they trust you? If you asked the guard for special privileges because you are not like the other prisoners, what will he say? Surely, he will think you are trying to con him as prisoners do. All of the reactions by others will shape your understanding of self, and eventually because you cannot escape these reactions, you very well might develop a new understanding of your self. You might develop an understanding of your self that says you are a criminal, or at least a prisoner. (This example illustrates Erving Goffman's concept of total institutions and how these types of institutions affect the self. See below.) In short, the self is defined and constantly redefined through social interactions.

It is important to recall here that the self actively makes itself. Students often mistakenly believe that symbolic interactionism claims that people passively adopt the notion of self that others impose upon them. They are what people tell them to be. This is not what symbolic interactionism is saying. Remember, the self has an I and a me. The self actively engages with the social world. It is influenced by this world, but it is not determined by it.

But what about society and social order? How does Mead's social psychology explain the large-scale organization of society? How does it explain how social order is created, how it is sustained, how it falls apart? A key concept used by Mead to help account for such things is the generalized other, noted earlier. Mead writes in his description of society: "The very organization of the self-conscious community is dependent upon individuals taking the attitude of the other individuals. The development of this process ... is dependent upon getting the attitude of the group as distinct from that of a separate individual – getting what I have termed a "generalized other" (1962:256). This concept provides the glue, at least to some large extent, through which social order is made possible and is sustained.

What about the concept of society? How does Mead understand this thing called society? To understand this, it needs to be remembered that he believes the only reality that has meaning is the reality in which one acts and give meaning. In other words, the immediate present is all that really exists in any meaningful way. This is not to say that the past did not exist, and the future will not exist. It is to say that the meaning of the past and of the future is created in the present. It is the present and immediate context of social life that is the focus of attention for this theory. What then of society? Does society exist? **Society** for Mead is, like all of his concepts, an aspect of a living reality. It is emergent. Society exists when individuals share understandings and attitudes of others. Society exists when individuals develop shared understandings of the ways that others will react. Blumer in his essay "Society as Symbolic Interaction" describes society as "consisting of acting people, and the life of the society is to be seen as consisting of their actions." The "acting units" may be separate individuals, or collectivities "whose members are acting together on a common quest," or organizations "acting on behalf of a constituency." He continues: "Respective examples are individual purchasers in a market, a play group or missionary band, and a business corporation or a national professional association. There is no empirically observable activity in a human society that does not spring from some acting unit" (1998:85). For Mead, society consists of the organized set of responses to situations:

> I have tried to bring out the position that the society in which we belong represents an organized set of responses to certain situations in which the individual is involved, and that in so far as the individual can take those organized responses over into his own nature, and call them out by means of the symbol in the social response, he has a mind in which mental processes can go on, a mind whose inner structure he has taken from the community to which he belongs. (1962:270)

At the same time, society, institutions, and social structures that exist independent of the individual influence the individual. These things bear down upon the individual and shape the possibilities of the individual's response. But for symbolic interactionism it always comes down to the belief that individual selves actively make themselves through a process of interacting. Individual selves are fundamentally social and the social is both a product of individual selves acting and is a constraint upon this acting.

Biology, Evolution and Science

We end our description of Mead and symbolic interactionism with a brief note about the place of the ideas of biology, evolution and science in this perspective. It is worthwhile to note that biology, evolution, and science were central themes in Mead's philosophy, but they all but disappeared when Blumer and later (and more recent) sociologists turned Mead's ideas into the theory of symbolic interactionism. The intellectual perspective Mead took in developing his theory of social psychology was built upon basic claims of some of the major scientific theories of the time – of the early nineteen hundreds -- that could and have been used to explain social behavior. These include psychology, biology, and evolutionary theory. It was noted above that Mead was influenced by the behavioral psychologist Watson, and that Mead criticized Watson's ideas because the latter claimed that all animal behavior -- human and non-human – was fundamentally of the same nature. That all behaviors – animal and human -- could be explained by such things as stimulus and response, rewards and punishments, etc. Mead did not take issue with Watson's overall goal of seeking to develop a general theory of behavior. He simply argued that Watson's theory could not rightly be applied to humans. Thus, Mead would agree with Watson that such concepts as stimulus and response, rewards and punishments, and others do apply to both humans and animals. Both animals and humans are driven to seek pleasure and avoid pain, both seek out rewards and seek to avoid punishment. But it is how humans do so that is important for Mead. They do so differently from animals. Consciousness is central to an understanding of human behavior.

Likewise, Mead did not reject Darwin's theory of evolution, and specifically his claims that species evolve based upon their genetic adaptability to their environment. (However, he did reject other aspects of Darwin's theorizing, such as his explanations for animal emotions.) Adaptability is a central theme in Mead's theorizing. What in the nature of being human has allowed humans to survive (and flourish) from an evolutionary perspective? Humans have survived because they have developed an evolutionary ability to adapt to their circumstances through the use of such things as consciousness and language. We are driven to survive and to survive we adapt. As humans, consciousness and language are the tools that have emerged in evolution to allow us to do so. Mead writes: "Darwin regarded the animal as that out of which human conduct evolves, as well as the human form, and if this is true then it must be that in some sense consciousness evolves" (1962:19) This fundamental change leads humans, unlike other animals, to possibly alter their evolutionary trajectory. They can and do actively partake of their world and shape their world to their own ends.

Recap

To summarize the main themes in symbolic interactionism we can turn again to Blumer. Symbolic interactionism is based on three premises and six "root images." The three premises are:

1) "[H]uman beings act toward things on the basis of the meanings that the things have for them" (1969:2).
2) Meanings are derived from social interactions.
3) "Meanings by a person in his action involves an interpretive process" (1969:5) and as such meanings are modified in the course of actions.

The six root images are:

1) The nature of human society or human group life (1969:6): Symbolic interactionists see humans as being actively engaged in social life.

2) The nature of social interactions: "Society consists of individuals interacting with one another" (1969:7).

3) The nature of objects: "Objects are the products of symbolic interaction" (1969:10).

4) The human being as an active organism: "The human being is seen as an organism that not only responds to others on the non-symbolic level but as one that makes indications to others and interprets their indications" (1969:12).

5) The nature of human action: "The human individual confronts a world that he must interpret in order to act instead of an environment to which he responds because of his organization" (1969:15).

6) Interlinkage of action: "Human group life consists of, and exists in, the fitting of lines of action to each other by the members of the group" (1969:16-17).

Phenomenology and Ethnomethodology

Phenomenology and ethnomethodology are sometimes said to be approaches that examine the practices of daily life. They seek to understand how it is that people make sense out of their worlds in the immediate present and how people act in their worlds based on this understanding. We describe here some features of phenomenology and then turn our attention to ethnomethodology. More often than not people go through their day-to-day lives without reflecting in the present why they are doing this or that. Life goes on in a seemingly automatic way. When people enter a situation that they recognize as somehow typical or familiar, they do not have to stop and ask, "what is this situation?" They have experiences that allow them to make sense of the present situation without having to constantly question it. When a student walks into a college classroom on the first day of class, he or she may wonder what the particular class will be about, but he or she will likely not wonder that much about what will happen in the class. The student decides to sit in one of the desk chairs, and her fellow students do likewise. When the professor begins to talk, the student becomes silent (and they put away their smartphones, right!). How and why is it that the student knows how to behave this way? One might say it is because he or she has learned this behavior from sitting in classes for over twelve years. It has become habit. But what does that mean? The student still makes choices about what to do. The student knows that this class may be similar to other classes, but at the same time it is different and unique. It is different from a high school class. Perhaps the professor will conduct the class not as a lecture but as an on-going discussion. Perhaps that would be different. Moreover, the student on an ongoing basis is making sense of his or her immediate environment; he or she is making choices about how to respond to this environment. He or she is selecting one or another thing in his or her present to focus upon and selecting others not to focus upon. Phenomenology and ethnomethodology seek to understand the processes through which people make sense out of their immediate worlds and then act upon it based upon this sense making.

Phenomenology did not first emerge as a type of sociology. Rather it began as a form of philosophy. Phenomenological philosophy was created largely by Edmund Husserl, a German scholar writing in the early nineteen hundreds. Husserl was influenced by the rich philosophical traditions in nineteenth century German scholarship. This tradition often involved an examination of epistemology and of consciousness. Epistemology is the branch of philosophy that studies how we know things. How is it that we are able to know anything? How is it that we know the difference between a rock and an apple, and how is it that we know that we can eat one and not the other? How is it that we know the difference between past, present, and future? Philosophers from the Enlightenment through the present have grappled with theories that attempt to explain such things. Husserl's phenomenology is an example of this attempt. Husserl wished to understand the organization of consciousness in the immediate present. This organization or structure allows us to make sense out of our immediate worlds. The task is to understand the building blocks of this experienced consciousness. On a day-to-day and minute to minute basis we do not think of these building blocks as we engage in our worlds. We could not. Otherwise, we would be crazy. Much like a musician cannot think about the notes he or she is playing when playing them, a person in their daily lives does not typically think of his or her consciousness when engaging in the world. How is it that we understand our immediate world as we do? That is the question driving phenomenology.

Husserl wished to create a "science" of consciousness to attempt to answer these questions. But his view of science is not quite the same as the way we normally think of science. Normally today we think of science using experiments and statistics to make generalizations about the factual (empirical) world. But how can one use experiments and statistics to make generalizations about human beings who have consciousness, who make free choices all the time? Traditional, positivistic science, the forms of science found in chemistry or physics or biology, are not applicable to a scientific understanding of human beings because we have consciousness, we live in and through time, and we have freedom. Our being is emergent. It is not static. The task for phenomenology is to understand the ways that people understand their worlds and then make choices in their worlds based upon these understandings. A scientific understanding here must reject statistics and traditional experiments and instead should be based upon objective, factual observations of lived consciousness. Only in this way could one make claims about the workings of consciousness.

A central part of Husserl's approach is that any and all assumptions, particularly metaphysical assumptions, related to an understanding of human behavior should be avoided. He wished to create a presupposition-less approach. Metaphysics is the branch of philosophy that concerns things which cannot by their very nature be proven or disproven through scientific (empirical) means. Does god exist? Do humans have freedom? What is the largest number? These are all metaphysical questions. All too often sociological and psychological theories are built upon one or another metaphysical claim and are thus not truly or fully scientific in their approach. For example, Marx claims that the working class may not seek to have a revolution because they are suffering from "false consciousness." But what is false consciousness? Can one prove that it exists, or is it simply an assumption that cannot be proven or disproven? Likewise, the claims made by Parsons or Durkheim that social things exist because they serve a function is an equally questionable assumption. Sigmund Freud's psychoanalysis is yet another example. Freud argues that much behavior is motivated or caused by unconscious processes. We do things for reasons that we are unaware and that we cannot be aware of directly. But what is the unconscious? Is it real? Or is it a fictitious assumption? (Better still, where is the id?) Husserl wishes to develop an approach that avoids all such assumptions.

The founder of phenomenological sociology is Alfred Schutz. He was Austrian and was a student of Husserl in Germany before World War Two. Schutz moved to the United States in 1939. (He was Jewish and fled Hitler's horrific Nazi regime.) In 1932 he published (in German) the first influential book on phenomenological sociology titled *The Phenomenology of the Social World* (1967 [1932]). His theory is largely built upon the ideas of Husserl. However, he also was greatly influenced by Weber as well as by other European and American philosophers including Henri Bergson, William James, and Karl Jaspers, among many others. He believed Weber's approach which was based upon an understanding of the meanings of people's actions was generally correct. However, he believed Weber made far too many assumptions about these meanings. Weber imposed his own assumptions on actors he was studying and as a result misunderstood their behaviors. For example, Schutz complained that Weber did not critically examine the concept of motive enough. Weber believed that motives are the reason for willed behavior. However, Schutz says there are two fundamentally different types of motives. There are **in-order-to motives** and there are **"because" motives**. In-order-to motives is action that is oriented to a future event, but a because motive is related to a past event (1967:87). The only way to understand if one or another of these motives explains a behavior is to look more closely at the lived experience of individuals.

In many ways, phenomenology is almost the inevitable path to proceed if one wishes to develop a science that explains social behavior. After all, to explain social behavior scientifically one must start with objective understandings of facts related to individual behaviors and individual choice making. To do otherwise inevitably means that the researcher is imposing his or her assumptions, in one way or another, on the facts being observed and as such is distorting a true, scientific understanding of those facts.

Schutz took many of Husserl's ideas, as well as the ideas for others. He also developed many of his own. Several of these can briefly be described here. The first set of concepts relates to time. We live in and through time, and any sociological approach which does not begin with a genuine appreciation of this reality creates a distorted understanding. Moreover, time is continuous. We live in and through a stream of consciousness. The concept of stream of consciousness has been used by many throughout the ages, but it was the American pragmatist William James' embrace of it that greatly helped paved the way for its used in modern philosophy and sociology. Our consciousness is fluid and it exists only in time. It cannot be thought of as being composed of discrete parts. Time blends into other times. Time is fundamentally different from space. When one treats time as if it was the same as space, i.e. as having discrete parts that are separate and distinct from each other, each equally of the same size as the other, then one distorts an understanding of lived reality. This is related to a second concept, that of duree. (The English translation is duration). Henri Bergson uses the concept of duree to highlight this fundamental difference between time and space. (Bergson argues that modern philosophy from Kant on have erred because it has used the forms of thinking about space as universal forms, and has wrongfully claimed or assumed that the experience of time is the same as the experience of space and that the concept of time can be thought of as mimicking the concept of space, when in fact they are radically different forms of concepts that require radically different way of understanding.) All of this is meant to show that it is the flow of experience that needs to be understood if one wishes to understand social experience.

Phenomenologists also embrace the concept of **intentionality**. The question to ask is what is the intent? Consciousness requires content. We cannot have a consciousness without having a consciousness of something, and the consciousness of something implies that the person has an intent. He chooses one thing to think about and to do, and not another. His orientations are fundamentally intended. We are intentional beings. As such, the task is to understand the intentions of people's actions. It may seem as if we are not intentional when we pay attention to one thing and ignore another, and it may seem we are not intentional when we act based upon this selection, but phenomenologists claim we make choices and act upon them. This is the foundation of intentionality.

How is it then that we create our realities, and how is it that we act based upon these understandings? In other words, how do we make sense out of our lived present? We accumulate a **stock of knowledge** as we move through life that allows us to make sense of the worlds we experience. This stock of knowledge is not simply a knowledge of facts, but it is also a knowledge of circumstances, and even more a knowledge of practices as they relate to circumstances. A student knows what a classroom means and how he or she is expected to behave because of the stock of knowledge he or she has developed over the years related to earlier experiences involving classrooms. The student draws upon his or her stock of knowledge to make sense of the present. Another concept is **typification**. When we orient our consciousness (intentionally) in the present, we seek to understand what it is we are focused upon. We seek to relate this present focus to classifications of experiences we have earlier had so that we can understand the present. We typify the present circumstance by saying it is or is not like earlier examples. It is of the same or a different type. When a student walks into a classroom and the classroom has all the markings of a traditional class, e.g. the chairs are all lined up facing the front, there is a blackboard in the front of the room, etc., the student says to himself, this is a typical classroom, and as a typical classroom one knows what to expect.

Relevance is another concept used by Schutz. What is relevant to someone will influence how they understand and act in the present. One might find that the most relevant thing is to understand and engage with the immediate context of experience. On the other hand, one might find that it is more relevant to daydream or to think about what one will be doing tomorrow rather than to engage in the immediate. Schutz identifies four "regions" or zones of relevance (Schutz, 1970:112). The first region is the attention to the immediate present. This is the primary relevance. If you are a student in a class, your primary relevance is in understanding what the professor is saying and doing so that you can do as well as you hope to on the exams in the class and so that you can get the grade that you imagine. A second zone of relevances concerns the "tools" that one may use to achieve the goals associated with the primary relevances. To do well in the class, the student might say to himself or herself, "the way to do well in this class is to take good notes." The student then takes notes as best as he or she can with the intention of doing well. The third form of relevance "have no connection with the interests at hand" (1970:112). They are "relatively irrelevant." If, for example, the student in class thinks about how he or she looks, how he or she is being perceived by others in the class, then this is relatively irrelevant to the interest of getting a good grade. Lastly, the fourth zone of relevance is the "absolutely irrelevant." Here the student sitting in class is focused not at all on what is occurring in the class, but instead focusing upon what he or she will be doing over the coming weekend.

The **natural attitude** is another concept used by phenomenology. The natural attitude is the unreflective, taken for granted position one has in daily life. It is the orientation we take through much of our lives. We go about our daily lives seamlessly, in an unreflective way. While we can and do step out of our natural attitude and ask, "What am I doing?" or "What is going on?", most of the time we operate in our daily lives without such questioning. We make assumptions about the world and simply live in and through it. Specifically, we live in and through the lifeworld, another central concept in phenomenology. The lifeworld is the world of everyday life. It is "the total sphere of experiences of an individual which is circumscribed by the objects, persons, and events encountered in the pursuit of pragmatic objectives of living. It is a "World" in which a person is "wide-awake," and which asserts itself as the "paramount reality" of his life" (Wagner in Schutz, 1970:320).

Thus far we have been describing the individual's experience in living. But sociology is concerned not about understanding individual actions as an endpoint, but instead is interested in understanding the social. Individual action may be a way by which to understand the social, but it is simply a means to this end. Schutz recognizes this and devotes considerable time towards an explanation of the "intersubjective" nature of our being. He begins with the assumption that part of the world within which we live is intersubjective. We live with other people. The question then is how do we or how can we understand other people? We can never know completely the mind of another, but at the same time this does not mean the other's mind is utterly inaccessible to me (1967:99). Our consciousness allows for this understanding. One person may understand the meanings of another in the lived experience that both occupy by sharing such things as the life world, relevance structures, an understanding of motives (i.e., in-order-to vs because), typifications, stocks of knowledge, etc.

Various sociologists took the ideas of Schutz and of Husserl and developed their own versions of phenomenologically inspired sociology. Peter Berger and Thomas Luckmann's works (1966, 1967) are examples of this. Berger and Luckman build a sociology perspective on phenomenology, but they also add to it ideas from Durkheim, Weber, and Marx, among others. They claim that our understandings of the world, the meanings we assign to it, are emergent, and sociologists must begin here. We create our world through a three step process of externalization, objectification, and internalization. The first step is **externalization**. We put out into the world from inside of ourselves our intents, our inclinations, our desires, etc. We intentionally engage with the world. This is externalization. It is the orientation and engagement with the world from the inside out. We externalize ourselves, for example, when we say and do things.

Objectification occurs next. This is when we turn these externalizations into objects in the world that have realities independent of us. The artist objectifies his understanding of his world by painting a painting. This painting then takes on a life of its own and can be internalized by one or another person. **Internalization** is the reverse of externalization. It is the taking in from outside into the inside understandings of the world. It is through this process that Berger and Luckmann say we create our world and specifically our society.

Ethnomethodology

Harold Garfinkel (1967) and his colleagues and students developed a more influential tradition in sociology that is derived directly from phenomenology. Garfinkel called his approach ethnomethodology. "Ethno" refers to people; "methodology" refers to the procedures used. Together, these two ideas go to the heart of ethnomethodology. It is an approach that seeks to understand the methods by which individuals in the present use to understand and act in their worlds. Garfinkel criticizes other more traditional forms of sociology for making unwarranted assumptions about individual actions. These other forms he says wrongfully assume that individuals passively do things in response to the demands of the external social environment. These other sociologies treat individuals not as active agents but as pawns whose behaviors are determined and dictated by external social forces, often large-scale forces. Garfinkel complains that mainstream sociological approaches treat individuals as "cultural dopes" who do not make choices and agency. That is, these other approaches treat individuals as if they are little more than puppets reacting to the demands of society. He begins with the assumption that individuals are not cultural dopes but instead are active agents who on a minute to minute basis are making choices and decisions and acting upon these choices and decisions. I decide in the here and now what to focus upon, what is important, and how to act. The task of sociology is to understand the process through which an individual makes decisions and acts.

Ethnomethodology seeks to understand the ordinary, common daily activities of life. On a day-to-day basis more often than not people engage with others and their worlds in an unquestioning way. This practical activity of making meaning and acting upon meaning such that life can proceed is a focus of attention for ethnomethodology. How is it that people make sense out of their practical worlds? What assumptions and perspectives do they have that allow them to engage unquestioningly in their day-to-day lives?

A key concept in Garfinkel's approach is indexicality. **Indexicality** refers to the intentional focusing on one thing in the immediate present and the assignment of meaning to that one thing in its context. Think of indexicality as pointing. When you point to one thing and not another, or when you focus your attention on one thing and not another, this is indexicality. We intentionally focus on one thing or another and must select from the infinite number of possibilities one or another thing to focus upon. We then give this thing meaning in the context within which it is indexed. It would mean one thing to say, "look at that lion," if you were at a zoo and the lion was in a cage. It would mean quite another thing to say, "look at that lion," if you were walking down Broadway in New York City and you saw a lion walking down the street unleashed. Garfinkel uses the term indexical expressions to refer to indexicality that has been put into words.

Another key concept is **reflexivity**. We should begin here by noting the difference between the terms reflexive and reflective. Reflective refers to an orientation in which a person thinks back upon the past and assess it. In this sense the person is removed from the event that he or she is thinking about. He or she is removed in time or space from the immediate. The concept of reflexive involves no such separation. Reflexive refers to an orientation in the present in which a person thinks about the present and acts based upon this process. Reflexivity is being critically and self-consciously engaged in the present. Reflexivity is based upon the recognition that we live in time, and because we live in time we create our worlds as we engage in our worlds. As Anthony Giddens says (see Chapter Eleven), the reflexive nature of our being is such that a situation is both a "medium and an outcome." When we use an indexical expression, we are both describing our worlds and are creating or determining our worlds simultaneously. We make and remake our worlds simultaneously. It can be no other way.

Garfinkel was very interested in taking the abstract concepts related to phenomenology and using them in actual research. He conducted numerous research studies. At the heart of his research approach was the analysis of **accounts**. An account is a stated or unstated understanding of the organization of our immediate worlds. When we give an account, we are providing explanations for the ordering of our experienced worlds. More often than not, these accounts are left implicit. One of the tasks of the researcher, Garfinkel says, is to make these accounts explicit. By doing so we can come to understand the building blocks of social interaction and of social order. He produced numerous studies in which he sought to understand the decision making processes of professionals, specifically medical and mental health professionals. How do these professionals make decisions about diagnosing someone? How do they make decisions about determining whether someone has committed suicide or whether the death should be ruled otherwise? We traditionally do not question such things and assume the professionals are simply applying mechanical, rational procedures in their decision making. Garfinkel says the process of decision making is far more complicated than this and it involves an understanding of accounts given or implied in the works of these professionals.

Garfinkel provides numerous examples of studies and exercises he did to understand the process by which people use common sense, practical understandings of their immediate situations to act in their worlds as they do. All too often, he says, sociologists wrongfully impose upon people wrongful, implied assumptions about why people do what they do. To accurately understand social behavior, we must unpack the common place. In one exercise he asked his students to write down a short description of some behavior they observed at home or out of class. Students wrote down the short description. He then asked the students to write down what was actually happening rather than what was simply observed. He was pressing students to provide for more contextual information by which to understand the descriptions they had given. Students, he said, complained as he pressed for more information. The complaints together with the recognition that the descriptions hid within them complicated assumptions about the realities presented revealed the underlying structure of the common place. He was seeking accounts and was examining ways that accounts were presented in the immediate present.

Garfinkel is perhaps most well-known for his **breaching experiments**. In these exercises, he would have students conduct an exercise out of class, in some common everyday setting, in which the students intentionally acted in a manner that would undoubtedly disrupt the smooth flow of everyday life. For example, a student might go to their home and then pretend he or she is a stranger or a customer rather than a son, daughter, brother or sister. He or she would interact with others in this odd manner, and then would observe how others react. The point of such disruptions is that the common place assumptions that make up daily life and that make daily, practical interactions seamless tend to be hidden from view, and the task of ethnomethodology is to reveal these hidden assumptions or structures that underlie daily life. When the son treats his father in a formal way at home, the father will react. The father may get frustrated. The father might think the son is playing a game at first, but after a while he might become upset. The point is that he will resort to any number of techniques to restore normality in the flow of existence. The task of the ethnomethodologist is to identify the elements of this normality. The task is to identify and explain how these elements combine to allow for the smooth flow of everyday life.

Garfinkel (1967:42-43) provides a number of examples of these breaching experiments. Here is one:

(E) On Friday night my husband and I were watching television. My husband remarked that he was tired. I asked, "How are you tired? Physically, mentally, or just

bored?"
(S) I don't know, I guess physically, mainly.
(E) You mean that your muscles ache or your bones?
(S) I guess so. Don't be so technical.
   (After more watching)
(S) All these old movies have the same kind of old iron bedstead in them.
(E) What do you mean? Do you mean all old movies, or some of them, or just the ones
you have seen?
(S) What's the matter with you? You know what I mean.
(E) I wish you would be more specific.
(S) You know what I mean! Drop dead! (1967:43)

Ethnomethodology has spawned several different forms of research. **Conversational analysis** is perhaps the more popular of these. In conversational analysis the researcher transcribes conversational interactions between people and precisely codes the transcriptions. The researcher examines in the most micro way each and every element of the conservation, paying particular attention to what was unsaid. The length of pauses, for example, and when they occur, are important factors. The loudness of the voice, the inflections, the references, etc. all are chronicled and analyzed with the intent of understanding the underlying structures which allow for conversations and social order to continue seamlessly.

The Theories of Erving Goffman

Erving Goffman's theorizing is the third dominant micro approach to sociology (along with symbolic interactionism and phenomenology). It is difficult to categorize his theory. Many identify him as a symbolic interactionist or at least as someone who is writing in this tradition. But this is not quite accurate. He was not a symbolic interactionist. Unquestionably he was influenced by Mead and the other pragmatists and was influenced by his teachers at the University of Chicago, including C. Everett Hughes, who were inspired largely by Mead. Many of the concepts and themes used in his writings also might suggest he was an interactionist. He focused, for example, extensively on concepts of self and role and upon how the self attempts to define itself through interactions on an on-going basis. Nevertheless, it is clear he was influenced as much by a number of other scholars, who were not interactionists, and traditions, as he was by symbolic interactionism. He was greatly influenced by Hughes, Durkheim, Simmel, Kenneth Burke, Schutz and the phenomenologists, and many others from a wide range of academic fields.

A few words can be said regarding some of these influences. Simmel's influence upon Goffman consisted in part on his ideas of form and content. More generally, Simmel, like Goffman, tends to view social life from a perspective that sees ongoing gaps between forms of social life and the experiencing of individuals or groups within these forms. For example, there may be a gap between a person's understanding of who they are and who they wish to be -- that is, their understanding of self and the role they are placed in. This gap cries out for the individual to do things to somehow overcome it, to manage it, or to remove himself from the situation, or other things. As I describe below, Goffman's dramaturgical analysis is based in part upon this formulation.

One can also hear the echoes of Durkheim in Goffman's writings. This might seem strange particularly if one recalls from the chapter on Durkheim that he was focused on social facts, e.g. things external and coercive upon individuals. He was not concerned with such things as the self. Yet Goffman was very much interested in the self. So how could Durkheim be seen as an influence? Both Durkheim and Goffman were focused largely in one way or another upon the relationship of the self to society. Durkheim repeatedly wrote about social forces bearing down upon the individual, whether these related to anomic conditions or to conditions in which there was too much integration and/or regulation, in which the individual becomes lost in the collective. A major theme in Durkheim's work was the relationship of the society to the individual. Specifically, the form of society influenced the self -- whether it consumed the individual or whether it allowed the individual the opportunities to maintain distinct autonomy. Relatedly, Durkheim was very much focused upon the social structures and their impact upon the individual. Goffman too was most interested in understanding how the social environment influenced the individual self. Thirdly, Durkheim focuses upon (sacred) rituals, particularly in his work on the sociology of religion. Rituals are closely associated with such things as scripts and dramatic presentations, which are central to Goffman's earlier theorizing.

Goffman was also greatly influenced by the ideas of Kenneth Burke (1897-1993)(Gusfield, 1989). Burke was an American intellectual whose work cannot be neatly placed into one or another academic discipline. His focus was on language and how language works, but he was also deeply interested in traditional sociological concerns as well as philosophical concerns. He was an extremely creative scholar, though his writings are less than clear. (Interestingly, many of his ideas were later developed independently in one form or another by European scholars associated with post-modernism and post-structuralism (see Chapter Twelve).) Burke was a rhetorician, a theorist of language, a philosopher of language, a social theorist, a literary critic, among other things. His entire perspective cannot be presented here. Instead, just a few elements of it can be described. Burke developed two distinct forms of theories – of language and of social behavior – in his life. He called his earlier theory dramatism, and his later theory logology. His theory of **dramatism** is best seen in what is perhaps his most well-known book *A Grammar of Motives* (1945). Burke was seeking to understand in this book how and why we develop explanations for human behavior, with language being a form of behavior. He begins by making the distinction between motivations and motives. **Motivations** are the real and essential reasons that someone does something. **Motives** are the claims made by someone, either the person who engaged in the action, or someone else, for why the person does something. Can a scientific discipline based upon making claims by observing facts, i.e. empirical realities, say anything about motivations? After all, what is the real, true reason that anyone acts as they do? Motivations are beyond the realm of science. On the other hand, motives can be studied scientifically. If I say that a person does something for this reason, then this claim is an empirical fact. As one cannot study in any form of systematic, scientific way motivations, because it would be no different than scientifically studying the existence of god, then all that is left is the study of motives. This is one of Burke's projects: How are we to explain motives? Another is to recognize the nature and the complexities involved in trying to understand motivations.

He draws upon the theater metaphor, i.e. drama, to understand motives, and seeks to understand social life as if it was a drama. The question then is, how is the action in a play, or a movie carried forth? What moves the action forward? What is the motive of the actions in the play or the movie? Burke turns to his concept of the **pentad** to answer these questions. The pentad consists of five questions: "Any complete statement about motives," he tells us, "will offer some kind of answers to these five questions: what was done (act), when or where it was done (scene), who did it (agent), how he did it (agency), and why (purpose)" (1945:xv). What makes the action move forward then is not to be found in some deep part of the individual self. Instead, the action is carried forward by the act, by the scene, by the agent, etc. All of these elements of the pentad are factors that can account for the action. Burke focuses upon pairs of these five, which he calls "ratios." Thus, there is an act-scene ratio, or scene-purpose ratio, etc. He explains social actions using these or other ratios, recognizing that the same action could be explained using different ratios, or could be explained using all five elements of the pentad. In other words, what causes an action is not to be found in the essential elements of the self and its motivations, but instead must be found elsewhere.

A second major element of his dramatism is the focus on the **four "master" tropes**: metaphor, metonymy, synecdoche, and irony. Tropes are turns in the language. They are figures of speech. When one says "all hands on deck" one is using a trope. Specifically, this is called synecdoche. It is a different type of trope than when one says, "Boston beat New York last night" (referring to the Red Sox and Yankees baseball teams), which is an example of metonymy. Tropes are means by which language makes meaning by indirect reference rather than by direct reference to the actual world. Our language use is filled with tropes. The very statement "filled with tropes" is a trope. One fills a glass of water, literally. But how can one literally fill language? Burke uses the trope of "container and things contained" to capture the nature of tropes (which he seems to have taken from the philosopher Henri Bergson). Sociology, and sociological theory in particular, uses these literary devices regularly, and arguably could not do otherwise. Concepts such as social structure or society (or for that matter, the self) are tropes. The very notion of model building that some theorists rely upon (far less so today than in the past), such as the theory building of Parsons and structural functionalism is deeply tropic in nature. ("Deeply" tropic is itself tropic!), so too is Durkheim's frequent use of biological metaphors, and other such tropes, to understand sociology. As social theory inevitably relies upon tropes, the question is, which trope does Burke prefer? Burke, in keeping with his loose, very loose, Marxist leanings, embraces irony, which he often describes as dialectic-irony. Dialectics he says is a form of the trope of irony and is the one that social theorists should rely upon in their theory building.

Goffman combined these two elements of Burke's theorizing – the pentad and the master tropes – into his theorizing. Their influence can be seen in his early work on dramaturgical analysis and in his later work on frame analysis. A cornerstone of dramaturgy is using the metaphor of the theater to understand social life. Moreover, in all of his examples and studies in which he used his dramaturgical theory one is repeatedly brought back when reading them to questions about tropes. When, for example, he is describing how people behave in a mental hospital is he writing simply about a mental hospital, or is he writing about all mental hospitals, or perhaps about all total institutions? (Total institutions are described below. They include such things as army boot camps, monasteries, prisons, and lock mental hospitals, among other settings.) Perhaps he is not simply writing about total institutions, but instead making comments about modern society in general? Perhaps with the growth of rationalization and capitalism, our society has become more like one big total institution? He never says anything like this, but that is the point. It is what is implied and unstated, it is what lies behind and between the words, that is as significant as the words themselves. If one ignores the mechanisms of tropes, one very well will miss this significant feature of his work.

It was noted above that it is difficult to categorize Goffman's theorizing. His theory does not fit neatly into a symbolic interactionism, or any other conventional form of theorizing. It becomes even more difficult to categorize his theorizing when one recognizes that his theorizing changed over the course of his career. Here we focus on one major change that occurred. For much of his career Goffman worked on developing and defending his theory of dramaturgical analysis. Most of his better known books are written from this perspective, including *The Presentation of Self in Everyday Life* (1959 (1956)), *Asylums* (1961), and *Stigma* (1964). In these works, he builds upon the theater metaphor to explain social behavior. We are all playing roles and trying to carry off performances. In this respect, the sentiments of dramaturgy are captured in Shakespeare's famous lines from the play *As You Like It*: "All the world's a stage, and all the men and women merely players; They have their exists and entrances, And one man in his time plays many parts." Later in his life however Goffman significantly changes his theoretical perspective away from dramaturgy. This new or different perspective is seen in *Frame Analysis* (1974) as well as in *Forms of Talk* (1981). In these later works he abandons many of the basic elements of dramaturgy, and he leaves behind many of the basic themes. For example, the theater metaphor is gone in these later works. As he tells us on page one of *Frame Analysis*: "All the world is not a stage." (In point of fact, Goffman also says something that seems similar in his earlier works. In *The Presentation of Everyday Life* he writes, "All the world is not, of course, a stage, but the crucial ways in which it isn't are not easy to specify" (1959:72). The point is that he means something very different when he says it is not a stage in his earlier writings and in his later writings. In his earlier writings he is saying social life is not literally a stage. In his later writing he is saying the trope of the stage does not work to explain social life.)

Dramaturgy

We begin with an overview of **dramaturgy**, and then describe his theory of *Frame Analysis*. Several of the main themes of dramaturgy are briefly described here. These will be presented in greater detail below. These main themes appear over and over again in dramaturgy. One of these concerns the self and the role and the relationship between these. If in our daily lives we are forever playing parts in plays, whether as a person playing the part of a student at a university, or a person playing the part of cashier or customer at a Starbucks, the question surfaces: Who are we when we are playing these parts? In other words, is the self different than the role it is playing? If so, what is the self? And how and why does the self and role interact as they do? Are you nothing more than the role you are playing? For Goffman, people often or for the most part tend to try to carry off their performances and to convince the audience that they are who they claim to be. This is for him a driving force in social action. A second theme concerns techniques. Much of Goffman's theory focuses upon the various techniques individual have access to and use to carry off their performances and to manage the relationship between self and role. For example, if someone is placed in a role in which they are not comfortable, they might draw upon various techniques to create a distance from themselves and the role they are playing. They might try to create a role distance by convincing others they are not the role. When someone at the financial aid office refuses a request by a student and then says to the frustrated student "I am just doing my job," they are trying to let the student know that they are not the bureaucrat they appear to be, but are instead simply playing the role of bureaucrat. A third theme concerns deception. Goffman was very interested in things such as deceptions and deceit, specifically in relation to how a person may act in a way to manipulate others into believing something about the first person that is not true. One last central theme in his theory concerns the never-ending gaps between appearances and realities, between what is and what is thought or wished to be. I may wish to convince you that I am intelligent, but you may not believe it. But what behaviors of mine led you to believe this? And how do you respond in these beliefs? The chasms and contradictions of social life propel social life forward, as people adjust and make adjustments to these.

Goffman relies on a number of concepts in his theory of dramaturgy. As the theory is built on the theater metaphor, he says we can use some of the basic elements of the physical setting of the theater to help us understand the performances of social life. He identifies two main regions of social life: the front and the backstage. The **front** region consists of all the elements involved in the social interaction which can be viewed by the audience. It is akin to the front stage in a theater, which is the place on stage where the actors can be seen performing in front of the audience. The **back stage** is the place where the actors cannot be seen and where they are no longer performing, at least not for the original audience. When an actor leaves the stage and goes behind the curtain, he is no longer in character. The front region consists of two parts: the setting and the personal front. The setting and personal front can and are used by the actors to carry off their performances. Goffman calls these things that are used in this way expressive equipment. **Expressive equipment** are things that the social actor can draw upon to try to convince the audience that the actor is who he or she says he is. The setting is the "scenic part" of expressive equipment. The **setting** consists of the props on stage which allow the audience to understand what they are seeing. In a play about a classroom, for example, the setting might consist of desks and chairs, a blackboard (whiteboard, or today perhaps a computer?), and other things that tell the audience what the setting is. The personal front are the things attached or connected to the individual actor that are or can be used to convey the impression that he or she is who they say they are. The **personal front** has two parts: appearances and manners. Appearances are things attached to the person that convey, or not, to the audience that they are the character they are playing. The clothes a person wears, whether a person has a visible tattoo or piercing, the way one wears one's hair, are all examples of the part of appearances. These all convey in themselves to the audience something about the acting self. Manners consist of the way that one carries him or her self. The way that one talks, walks, interacts with others, are examples of manners. If one speaks with an accent, or speaks with improper English, these convey to the audience things about the person.

Actors in the front region are oriented toward managing the impressions the audience has of them. **Impression management** is a central part of dramaturgy. The actor tries to convince the audience that he or she is who he or she says. If I am performing on stage and playing the role of Hamlet, I will try to say and do things to convince the audience, to manage their impressions, that I am in fact not simply playing the role of Hamlet but in fact am Hamlet. If I am a professor giving a lecture in class, I will try to convince my students by managing their impressions of me that I am in fact a professor. But performers do not always succeed in having a good performance. Sometimes actors get booed by the audience. This relates to Goffman's distinction between expressions given and expressions given off. One tries to manage the impressions of others by expressing oneself in one way or another. Expressions given and expressions given off are two types of communication related to impression management. **Expressions given** are the intentional things a person does that lead the audience to believe he or she is who he or she says. **Expressions given off** are the unintentional things a person does that lead the audience to believe that person is or is not who he or she says. (Technically, Goffman says both of these forms of communication can be used intentionally, in that both can be used to present misinformation about the actor to the audience.) Often times, there is a gap between the expressions given and those given off and this results in the audience coming to believe the actor is not the character being portrayed. This in turn, leads the actor either to have a failed performance or to make adjustments.

We can return now to the concepts of role and self and the relationship between these two in dramaturgy. But this presents some conceptual problems. The first of which is: what is the **self**? Is there some sort of "true" self that somehow remains constant behind the various roles that one plays? Or is there no true self, and only roles that we play? Goffman describe the self as being both a performer and a character. The self as **character** is "a product of a scene that comes off, and is not the cause of it" (1959:252). The self as character is "a dramatic effect arising diffusely from a scene that is presented." He continues, "In analyzing the self then we are drawn from its possessor, from the person who will profit or lose most by it, for he and his body merely provide the peg on which something of collaborative manufacture will be hung for a time" (1959:253). The self as character, in short, is something akin to a puppet on a string, defined and created by the play within which it is enacted. It is a peg, much like the peg on a coat rack, where one hangs the coat. The self is a product of a scene.

Yet the self is also a **performer**. As performer, the self,

> has a capacity to learn, this being exercised in the task of training for a part. He is given to having fantasies and dreams, some that pleasurably unfold a triumphant performance, others full of anxiety and dread that nervously deal with vital discreditings in a public front region. He often manifests a gregarious desire for teammates and audiences, a tactful considerateness for their concerns; and he has the capacity for deeply felt shame, leading him to minimize the chances he takes of exposure. (1959:253)

So which is it, is the self a product or a producer? Is Goffman saying the self is a performer or a character? The self is a performer and it is a character. It is a product and a producer. It is created by the scene and it also creates itself. Goffman describes the self as a character and as a performer, as well as a "performing character." Again, the self is both performer and character. To say that it is both leads to confusions and contradictions. While he says it is both, most scholars say that while he might claim it is both, that he generally tends to view the self as a peg, a character. Indeed, this is one reason that many would not call him a symbolic interactionist.

To complicate matters further, Goffman elsewhere presents some alternative understandings of the concept of self. We see this in his book *Stigma* (1964), where he discusses the concepts of identity and self identity, though it is important to understand that the concepts of self and identity are distinct. In *Stigma*, he identifies three forms of self identity. The first is social identity. Social identities are those held by others who know me but who do not know me well. These are associated with the categories, particularly of roles, with which a person is associated. One might identify someone as a professor, or as a boxer, or as a mother, even if one does not know the person personally. The second type is personal identity. This is the identity known to others that are personally connected to the person. A friend knows another friend in a way that is different from the way a student knows a professor. The more personal form of identity associated with these more personal relations are the foundations of personal identity. In short, personal identities are those held by people close to the person. These first two forms of identity are essentially tied to interactions, whether distance or close. The third form of self identity is different. This form is ego identity which is the subjective sense of who a person believes himself or herself to be. This form of identity must be felt by the person holding this identity.

Role distance is another concept closely related to the issue of self. For Goffman, we have a self and we play roles. The only way for his theory of dramaturgy to work is to claim there is some self that is stable across the different lived situations. Thus, I may be a professor, a father, a baseball fan, but my behaviors in these roles are based, according to Goffman on the relation between the self, who I believe myself to be, and the role I am playing. At times, a person will be comfortable playing a role. The demands of the role will be compatible with the person's understanding of who he is. If a person thinks of himself as a tough, aggressive man, and the person is placed in the role of Army sergeant, then that person will likely be able to play the role without much difficulty. If, however, a person is placed in a role that is contrary to his or her own understandings of self, then the person will not be comfortable and will have to respond in some way. Thus, if the tough, aggressive man is put into the role of babysitter of a two-year old, a role which requires compassion, caring, etc., then the man might have a conflict within himself. Role distance is the gap between the person's understanding of self and the role that he or she is playing, and it is associated with the techniques used by the person to create a distance between him or herself and the role that he is playing. This is seen in the example provided above of the bureaucrat saying, "I'm just doing my job." The person is telling others that he or she is not the role that he is playing. He or she is someone different from that role.

Another set of concepts in dramaturgy are **crediting** and **discrediting**. As we engage in social life, as we play our roles, we seek to have our performances credited. That is, we seek to have our actions validated as successful. We seek to have recognition that we have succeeded in playing the role in the way we wished to play it. But often times we fail at this and the audience discredits our attempts. The audience judges them to be ineffective, and the actor must then somehow respond to these assessments. Goffman wrote about these things in his book *Stigma* (1964). He defines a **stigma** as the difference between a person's virtual social identity and a person's actual social identity. (Note again the difference between self and identity.) A virtual social identity is what a person ought to be; the actual social identity is what a person is seen as. When there is a gap between them there is a stigma. In a less formal sense, a stigma is an aspect of a person that is viewed negatively by others. A physical deformity, a speech impediment, even an ethnicity or race, could be viewed as a stigma. In years past, and still in some places in America today, being or acting as a homosexual is stigmatized. Goffman goes on to distinguish two types of stigmas: discredited and discreditable. A discredited stigma is one that by its nature is known to others. It cannot be hidden from view. It cannot be hidden from the audience. Having a physical deformity, for example, is a discredited stigma. A discreditable stigma is one that is not known, or is not necessarily known, by the audience. Having a speech impediment is a discredited stigma, but being homosexual is a discreditable stigma, at least in the past and in many though certainly not all places today. A homosexual can hide this reality from others, and in years past most did just that. Goffman was interested in how individuals managed the two different forms of stigma. Different techniques are needed for the different stigmas.

The issue of self and role is also prominent in his book *Asylums* (1961). This work is an ethnography of a locked mental hospital. Goffman observed the daily workings of a mental hospital in Washington, D.C. and used his theory to understand and explain the behaviors he had seen. We can begin our description of *Asylums* by looking again at the central place of the relationship of self and role in dramaturgy. The argument thus far is that the self and the role played by the self are distinct. Moreover, if one is placed in a role that makes him or her uncomfortable, what is one to do? In most situations, the person may struggle with the role, he or she might try to create role distance. Perhaps the person will leave the setting, and the role, to resolve any struggles? But this may or may not be possible. A bureaucrat can leave the office at the end of the day, and then be themselves at home. The college student who plays the role in class can then be themselves when they go home for the weekend. Most social life calls upon us to assume different roles through the day, week and year. We put one on and take it off. The point is that we can do so. The self is distinct from the role. But what if you were placed in a role that you could not leave? What if you were forced to be in one and only one role, one that you would have to play all the time each hour, day, week, year in and year out? What then?

This is one of the main points in *Asylums*. In a locked mental hospital, a person is placed in the role of the mental patient. If the person does not see him or herself as mentally ill when they first entered the mental hospital, what then happens? How do they see themselves after spending some time in this setting? When everyone around them, the nurses, the doctors, the fellow patients, treat the person as a mental patient and interpret all of his or her behaviors as indicators that the person is mentally ill, how is the person, the self, to respond? There is then little to no ways in which the individual can salvage his prior understanding of self. That is, there is little chance of maintaining a notion of self that is not mentally ill in the face of have an unending audience telling him he is in fact mentally ill.

It is not that the patient does not try to do things to maintain his prior concept of self within the institution. Goffman writes about secondary adjustments made by the patients toward that end. The concept of secondary adjustments is broader than this for Goffman. It refers to actions taken by patients or staff that are outside the normal understandings of how the institution does or should function. When a staff has the patient do a favor for them, this is a secondary adjustment. But here we are focused upon the secondary adjustments of the patients. Secondary adjustments by the patients are acts, often done in secret, that are meant to salvage the self. The patient's use of free spaces and the uses of stashes are two examples of this. Patients seek out free spaces, places where the patients are not under the direct view or surveillance of the staff. He describes an underground tunnel beneath some of the buildings in *Asylums* as one place where patients congregated outside of the gaze of the staff. There "one could be one's own man" (1961:231). Similarly, patients often collected personal positions and kept them in private stashes such that they could maintain some connections to their understanding of self as distinct from the role of mental patient.

Goffman's study of this one mental hospital was meant to be more than simply a study of one mental hospital. He was making a claim about how and why these forms of institutions operated as they did. A mental asylum is an example of a **total institution**. The asylum shares many characteristics with other total institutions such as prisons and monasteries. These are:

> 1) All aspects of life are conducted in the same place and under the same authority; 2) Each phase of the member's daily activity is carried on in the immediate company of a large batch of others, all of whom are treated alike and required to do the same thing together; 3) All phases of the day's activities are tightly scheduled, with one activity leading at a prearranged time into the next, the whole sequence of activities being imposed from above by a system of formal rulings and a body of officials; 4) the various enforced activities are brought together into a single rational plan purportedly designed to fulfill the official aims of the institution. (1961:6)

It is not simply that the overarching framework of the various forms of total institutions are similar. It is also that they particular workings of these institutions are also similar. They are similar in their effects upon the self, and they are similar in the techniques used. For example, Goffman notes that the new patient in the mental hospital, or the new member of other total institutions, is subjected to what he calls the mortification of the self upon first arrival. The **mortification of the self**, literally the killing of the self, refers to the mechanisms by which the institution strips the new patient of his or her former understanding of self such that a new notion of self can be imposed. One mechanism by which this is done is through **degradation ceremonies**. Upon admission to the mental hospital, or to the prison, etc., the patients are brought together in a bunch. They are told collectively to take their clothes off in the common room. All of their personal positions are taken from them. Their hair is shaven, and they are deloused or subjected to some general form of bath or cleansing. They are then given uniforms and numbers. This symbolic stripping away of the old self then allows for an easier imposition of a new self, a new self defined as the new role of patient, prisoner, etc.

Goffman's work on asylums, as well as his overall dramaturgical theory, is often associated with labeling theory that arose in the 1960s. Labeling theory is a theory of deviance developed by symbolic interactionists in the 1950s and 1960s which challenged conventional understandings of deviance. Labeling theory is captured in a line by Howard Becker, a symbolic interactionist and one of the scholars most closely associated with this theory of deviance. Becker said that "deviance is that which is so labeled." Deviance refers to any acts which are subject to negative sanction, from types of crime to mental illness. Traditionally, mental health professionals saw mental illness as either a biological or psychological reality and responded to it with this assumption. But if one recalls the basic elements of symbolic interactionism, then one must rethink this understanding. If our behavior is based upon our understandings of who we are, and if this is based upon our interactions, then mental illness should be understand as being a product of this interactive process. Moreover, the concept of mental illness itself is produced through social interactions. Therefore, mental illness is not the result of some biological or psychological process but is instead the result of interactions. It is the result of one person or persons identifying and labeling another person's actions as symptoms of mental illness and of the second person accepting this definition. Once accepted the person will, or may, act in ways that conform to this imposed definition. For example, if someone called their child stupid over and over again, might the child not come to believe he or she is stupid? How would this child then act? He might believe he is stupid and act in a stupid way. If you call someone mentally ill, and under the right or wrong circumstances, the person being called this comes to believe this is who he or she is, then how will the person act? This is the essence of labeling theory, although there are many more details of the theory that have been left out here.

This perspective leads and has led to, or at least is associated with, a number of highly critical approaches to the sociology of deviance and mental illness. One implication of the theory concerns the effectiveness of mental hospitals and of total institutions in general. (This perhaps is not such an immediate and direct concern today because most locked mental hospitals closed down fifty years ago. However, the huge expansions of prisons in America over this period makes the issue as relevant today if not more so than it was decades ago.) Do mental hospitals work? If a person who was not mentally ill was placed in a total institution such as a mental hospital, how would they be seen and treated by the staff and the doctors? According to labeling theory their behavior would be seen as symptomatic of their illness and they would be treated as sick. Moreover, the patient could not escape these labels and as a result would likely adopt a new understanding of self.

The patient would come to be mentally ill. As such, mental hospitals do not cure mental illness, they cause it.

Frame Analysis

Goffman largely abandons, or at least significantly modifies, many of the positions he developed in dramaturgy in his later work, most notably in *Frame Analysis* (1974). The later theoretical perspective found in *Frame Analysis* is far less used by scholars today than his earlier work in dramaturgy, and when it is used scholars tend to turn it into an extension of dramaturgical analysis rather than to see it as a competitor to it. (See for example the ways that David Snow (1986) uses the concept of frames in his work on social movements). In *Frame Analysis*, Goffman says he was influenced by Alfred Schutz, William James, and also by the Henri Bergson. His theorizing here strays far from any semblance to symbolic interactionism. (The concepts of self and role are barely mentioned in *Frame Analysis*, though he does specifically note in a response to a review essay of the book that he is not rejecting the concept of self here, but instead "decentering" the concept. He writes: "If the result of my approach can be construed as "decentering" the self, then I am happy to be in the vanguard, providing it is appreciated that this does not mean a lack of interest in the self, merely an effort to approach its figuring from additional directions" (1981:62).)

Frames are the basis of his understandings of social action. A frame is a mode of understanding. It is a perspective we take in understanding our world in one way rather than in another. Much like a picture frame, a frame here allows us to see and act in the world in one way rather than in another. Goffman cites the work of the anthropologist Gregory Bateson (1972) as a major influence for his concept of frame. Specifically, Bateson writes in his essay "A Theory of Play and Fantasy" about a visit to a zoo where he observed two young monkeys engaged in playing at fighting. They were not really fighting, but playing. But the playing had the earmarks of fighting. The monkeys knew that each of them was playing. And yet sometimes play turns serious. It can turn to real fighting. At some point the play fighting turned to real fighting, though it looked the same. The point here is that we have different frames through which we engage the world. The frame of fighting is different from the frame of playing, though the behaviors might look similar. These are different modes of experiential being.

Goffman sets as his task the identification of the various major types of frames used by people in daily life, and he seeks to understand how and why people move from one type of frame to another. There are two basic types of frames: Primary frames and transformed frames. **Primary frames** are the frames through which we operate within most of the time in daily lives.

Primary frames are the ones of ordinary, unreflective engagement with the world. They are not contrived to convince the audience or participants that persons are being somehow other than genuine in their actions. When you are speaking with a friend or buying something at the story, you are likely using primary frames through which you understand and engage in the world. **Transformed frames**, by contrast, are all those other frames within which we operate outside of the primary frames.

He identifies two types of transformed frames: keyed frames and fabrications. To understand **keyed frames**, we must understand the concept of **keys,** which are a central part of frame analysis. He is using a musical metaphor when writing about keys. That is, one can sing a song in the key of D or in the key of C, and if one is presented with music that is written in the key of C but one is unable to sing in that key, one can transpose the music and sing it the key of D. The same sequence of notes will be followed, but the music will be different. The music will sound the same in some respects, but in others it will be different. In the same way, a person rehearsing a part in a play might read the lines and act in the same way as if he or she were actually on stage performing the part. Rehearsing and practicing are keyed frames. Goffman identifies five major types of keyed frames. The first is the make-believe frame. Make-believe frames are when people engage in unstructured play, for example when children or adults pretend, they are someone else or somewhere else, particularly with others. When the little girl plays house with others, she is engaged in the make-believe frame. The second is contests. Contests include play, sports, and other types of competitions. When playing a game of basketball, one is in the contest keyed mode of being. One is consciously aware that one is playing a competitive game, and one knows that the way to behave is distinctly different from the way one behaves when not engaged in a keyed frame. Ceremonies are a third form of keyed frame. Ceremonies include things like rehearsals and rituals. When people participate in a wedding ceremony, as the best man, for example, they are acting in a mode that is distinct from the primary frame. The fourth keyed frame is technical redoings. These include things like practices, demonstrations, experiments, and psychotherapy. When a door to door vacuum salesman shows a housewife how his vacuum works, they are engaged in a demonstration. The salesman is fully aware that he is engaging with the customer in a way that is different than the way he would engage with a friend. Like all keyed frames, it is contrived, and parties are aware that it is contrived. Fifth, we have regroundings, which include things like charity, apprenticeships, and shills "Nevada Style." (He is using the term Nevada style shill to describe the ways in which a dealer at a card game acts to keep the game going.) Regroundings, Goffman tells us, are conceptually the most "troublesome" of all of the keyed frames. The main theme in regroundings is the alteration of motives: "The notion of regroundings, then, rests on the assumption that some motives for a deed are ones that leave the performer within the normal range of participation, and other motives, especially when stabilized and institutionalized, leave the performer outside the ordinary domain of the activity" (1974:74).

He identifies four types of **fabricated frames**, and these are structured in terms of whether they are oriented toward the self or to others. The first two of these are what he calls benign fabrications. Dreaming is a benign fabrication oriented toward the self. Playing a hoax on someone, e.g. "playful deceit," is an example of a benign fabrication oriented toward others. The second two are exploitive fabrications. The examples he gives for exploitive fabrications that are oriented toward the self are psychosis and hysteria, e.g. major forms of mental illnesses. Hypnotism is the example he gives for exploitive fabrications directed at others.

The point with all of this is that there are different modes of beings, and we move from one to the other throughout our daily lives. He identifies various elements of frames, such as the rims of the frames, e.g. the limits, as well as the concept of strips, the defined period of observation of the frame. And he seeks to understand how frames operate. Moreover, it is not as if these frames are mutually exclusive. One can be operating in more than one frame at a time, and one frame can be operating within another frame. He calls this **laminations**, which are layered frames.

Goffman's frame analysis, as noted earlier, is distinctly different from his earlier theory of dramaturgy. We no longer find the theater metaphor anchoring behavior, nor do we find the concepts of role and self as significant. Frame analysis has not been widely used since the publication of his book and has been harshly criticized by some scholars. Denzin and Keller (1981), for example, wrote a negative review of *Frame Analysis*. The main complaint made by Denzin and Keller (who are writing from a perspective sympathetic to symbolic interactionism) is that Goffman's frame analysis is a form of structuralism (see Chapter Twelve), and as such it fails to recognize that people have agency, and that people make decisions and act based upon these decisions. Denzin and Kellner say people are not puppets, and Goffman treats them as such in this form of theorizing. They write: "If a structuralist interpretation of *Frame Analysis* is warranted, and we believe it is, then Goffman's contributions to an interpretive social science becomes limited. His frames are frozen forms. His concept of reality is illusive and blurred. His posited transformations have no cause or process behind them" (1981:58). They also complain that his examples are from the "edge of most people's lives" and are not central to the daily live and experiences of people. In addition, "Goffman's actors are monads, with single frames looking out at the world. There is no interaction in *Frame Analysis*. Selves are relegated to the sidelines. They are not necessary for Goffman's project-at-hand. ... [W]e find the structural Goffman woefully lacking" (1981:59). Goffman wrote a reply to their review in which he rejected the claims that he was a structuralist. He notes that *Frame Analysis* draws upon the likes of Schutz and James and others in this work, scholars who are anything but structuralist. He rejects their criticisms that he fails to appreciate that people make choices, and says that people make choices within the constraints of the settings and modes of being within which they operate.

Summary

This chapter reviews three of the main micro-theories in sociology: symbolic interactionism, phenomenology, and Goffman's theories. Symbolic interactionism is based on the pragmatist philosophy of George Herbert Mead. Symbolic interactionism assumes that people are common sense making creatures and problem solvers. We assign meaning to our world and act upon this meaning. The social world is continuously being created and recreated. Symbolic interactionism says that people are fundamentally social and our abilities to use symbols makes us distinct from other animals. The self is a core concept in symbolic interactionism. The self has two parts to it -- the I and the me. It is a symbol and it is fundamentally social. It is created and recreated continuously through social interactions. People engage in their social worlds driven by their need to define the situation and to maintain a definition of the self. Phenomenology is a micro theory that originated in Europe. The first main phenomenological sociologist was Alfred Schutz. It is oriented toward understanding the structures of experiential consciousness. It seeks to understand the building blocks of lived consciousness that allow individuals to make sense and to act in the world. A third micro theory covered in this chapter was that of Erving Goffman. Goffman is most well-known for his theory of dramaturgy, which relies heavily upon the theater metaphor to explain social behavior. We are in our daily, social lives all playing parts or roles in one play or another. We try to manage the impressions others have of us so that others believe who we say we are. The dynamic relationship between self and role is central to dramaturgy. Sometimes the role we are playing is compatible with our notion of self; other times it is not. Goffman focuses on the situations and techniques which allow or prevent a performance from being effectively carried off. Later in his life, Goffman abandoned dramaturgy and developed frame analysis, though the latter has not become very popular. Frame analysis claims that people engage in this world either using primary frames or transformed frames.

Discussion Questions

1. Does history matter? That is, does a sociological explanation of social behavior need to assume that history matters, or can explanations of social behavior be effective if they ignore history? The micro-sociological theories covered in this chapter seem to say that explanations can be effective without considering history. Similarly, symbolic interactionism may say that history matters only if the social actors recognize it as important and only if they say it matters? For example, does one need to understand the history of slavery in the United States today if one wishes to accurately understand black Americans and the relationship between white and black Americans today?

2. Some scholars have argued that phenomenology leads down a rabbit hole. That is, this approach creates an impossible situation in which the researcher is trying to capture actually and completely an understanding of a lived movement. But is it really ever possible to do so? As soon as one tries to understand a lived movement, the movement is gone. This is one of the reasons the approach has not been more widely embraced. Do you agree or disagree with this criticism? Why?

3. Erving Goffman's theory of dramatism is quite popular in sociology today, but his theory of frame analysis is not (or at least it is not used in the ways he originally formulated it). Why do you think some scholars prefer dramatism to frame analysis? Do you agree or disagree with Goffman's assessment of the limits of dramaturgy?

4. What is the self? Does the self exist? How would the scholars covered in this chapter answer these questions?

Chapter Ten: Exchange Theories, Network Theories, and Rational Choice Theory

There are many stories about African communities before the Europeans colonized them. In some of these communities it would be customary for a member of the group or tribe who wished to ask the tribal leader for a favor, or who wished to ask him for permission to do this or that or for some other thing, to bring the leader a gift of some sort as a token of respect and deference. The leader accepts the gift as it was intended and then makes a decision on the request. The gift is exchanged for the decision. Presumably, sometimes the leader grants the request, whatever it may be, whether it is a request for permission to graze one's cattle on the leader's land, or to allow the tribesman's daughter to marry one or another person, or permission to use a water source, etc. But surely at other times the leader denies the request. Yet even with these denials, the custom of this exchange continued. A major change occurred to this ritual practice when the Europeans came and conquered. Now the leader of the community is a foreigner, a European colonizer. If a member of the community wished to make a request to this new leader, such as the request of a favor of the same type described above, he or she would have to go to this European and ask him. The custom of the tribe had been for the member to bring a gift to the leader. But now, when the member does so he is arrested by the European colonizers. Why? He is arrested because he broke the European law of bribery. His gift is deemed a bribe, an illegitimate and illegal act. The nature of exchange fundamentally shifts with colonization.

What is the nature of exchange and what is its place in creating, maintaining, or changing social order? After reading the rest of this chapter, you might wonder whether the above is such a good example to introduce you to the three theories covered here: exchange, network, and rational choice theories. The theories we cover in this chapter do focus on things such as exchange, but they do not do so by incorporating political themes, such as colonization. Nevertheless, the bribery example illustrates several major elements of the theories described below. One of these is that the process of exchange is a major element of social interactions: I give you something and in exchange you give me something else. Another is that we should think of exchange not simply in terms of behavior in the economic marketplace. It is true that in the marketplace, we always are exchanging one thing, e.g. money, for something else, e.g., a mocha grande from Starbucks or some such thing.

But more, we engage in all sorts of exchanges that are not economic. When you hold the door open for someone, and they say, "thank you," you are engaged in an exchange. You are giving the person something. You are making it easier for the person to pass through the door. And the person is giving something to you. What are they giving to you? A thank you. They are giving you a note of appreciation, of recognition, a validation.

In this chapter, we cover three related theories. We begin with a description of exchange theories. The major figures associated with this theory are George Homans and Peter Blau. We then describe exchange network theory, which is derived from exchange theory. The chapter ends with a review of rational choice theory. James Coleman is the major sociological figure associated with this theory. Rational choice theory shares some characteristics with the other two theories covered here, but it is different in many ways, as we see below.

Exchange Theory

The concept of exchange has been used by social scientists ever since the Enlightenment and the emergence of modern social science. Enlightenment philosophers recognized the central importance of exchange as part of their larger project of understanding how the social world is organized and how it should be organized. (For example, Adam Smith, the author of what is sometimes considered the bible of modern capitalism, *The Wealth of Nations*, says it is the nature of humans that we are driven to "truck, barter, and exchange.") In the twentieth century, many anthropologists and sociologists have noted its importance. The anthropologist Marcel Mauss, who was Durkheim's nephew, wrote a classic anthropology book, *The Gift: The Form and Reason for Exchange in Archaic Societies* (2000), which was first published in English in 1954. Mauss showed the central importance of the exchange of gifts for social stability in traditional societies. Similarly, the influential social philosopher and sociologist Georg Simmel, writing in the early nineteen hundreds, noted the central importance of exchange: "Most relationships among men can be considered under the category of exchange. … Now every interaction is properly viewed as a kind of exchange. This is true of every conversation, every love (even when requited unfavorably), every game, every act of looking one another over" (1971:43).

Homans' Exchange Theory

The first sociologist to develop a comprehensive sociological theory based upon exchange was George Homans. Homans was born in 1910 into a wealthy family in Boston. (He was from a social class sometimes called the Boston Brahmins, the group of dominant Protestant White Americans who came to America in the sixteen and seventeen hundreds and who maintained their wealth and dominance through the centuries.) He graduated from Harvard University and became a professor there in the Department of Social Relations, where he remained for the rest of his career. He died in 1989.

Homans was a colleague of Talcott Parsons, and in many ways his theory can be viewed as a response to, or rejection of, Parsons' structural functionalism. Homans believed structural functionalism was riddled with highly abstract concepts and questionable claims that made it less than scientific. Homans, for example, rejected Parsons' understandings of social structure and his voluntaristic theory of action claiming these concepts were less than clear and were less than capable of being scientifically measured and tested. The goal of a social theory, Homans believed, was to be scientific, and to be scientific the theory must be constructed in a way that allows for the concepts and propositions and hypotheses to be tested through empirical, fact-based research.

As a result, he developed his exchange theory. Exchange theory is based on the premise that social interactions can be understood as exchanges. The task for the theorist then is to identify the precise aspects of this exchange process. In many ways his theory can be thought of as combining the ideas of two major forms of thinking about social behavior, and in turning these forms into unified sociological concepts. His theory is built upon the ideas of behavioral psychology and basic market-based economic theory. To understand his exchange theory, we should first understand the major claims of these two theories – behavioral (operant) psychology and market-based economic theory.

Let's begin with a description of how Homans was influenced by market-based economic theory. By market-based economic theory, I am referring to some of the basic elements of the theory of the capitalist marketplace. In capitalism, the price of an object is dependent upon the demand for the object and the supply of the object. If something is quite plentiful and not many people wish to have it, then, all things considered, the price will be low. However, if something is very rare and many people wish to have it, the price will be very high. Gold is expensive because there is only a limited supply of it and there are many people who wish to have it. Similarly, the price will vary based upon the other possibilities. If you have a million rain jackets for sale and your store is in the desert, then presumably not many people would feel a need or a desire to buy a rain jacket and as a result the price would have to be quite low. Another way of thinking about this same thing is that the value of a thing that is bought and sold in the marketplace is reflected in the price, and the price of an object will rise or fall depending upon the supply and demand of the object. Hidden within these ideas are another set of ideas:

People make rational decisions about buying or selling things based upon their assessments of the costs and benefits (Homans calls benefits "rewards") associated with the thing being bought or sold. If something is costly but is deemed by someone to have little benefit to them, they will likely not have a great demand for it. For example, an expensive raincoat in the desert will not benefit the prospective consumer, and thus the consumer will not be willing to pay much for it. In sum, the above is nothing more than a short description of the basic assumptions underlying our capitalist economy. Homans builds his theory of social behavior upon this, but he fuses these ideas with those of behavioral psychology.

Behavioral psychology was developed by B.F. Skinner (1904-1990). The American psychologist Skinner developed a learning theory of behavior called operant conditioning which says that animals, from pigeons to people, can be taught to do just about anything if one provides the right reinforcements or punishments in a systematic or scheduled way. For example, a pigeon can be taught to peck at a lever in a cage by giving the pigeon food pellets (i.e., a reward) when the bird pecks the lever. Skinner did many studies with pigeons and other animals to demonstrate the principles of operant conditioning. We will not describe in any detail here all of the elements of Skinner's theory. Instead, a few basic concepts will be presented. The first set of concepts is stimulus and response. The stimulus is the thing that causes a reaction, and the reaction is the response. If I put my hand on a hot stove and then yell, the stimulus is the hot stove. The reaction is the yelling. The second set of concepts is reinforcements and punishments. A reinforcement is something given to an animal – a pigeon or person – after or while the animal has done an activity which the researcher desires the animal to do so that the animal will be more likely to do the activity again. A punishment is something given to an animal – a pigeon or person – after or while the animal has done an activity which the researcher desires the animal not to do so that the animal will be less likely to do the activity again. All of this may sound technical, but the idea behind it is very straightforward and commonsensical. To get a dog to do a trick, you reward it with a treat when the dog does the trick the way you want it to.

There are also two types of reinforcements and two types of punishments: Positive and negative reinforcements and punishments. Positive and negative refer to whether something is added or taken away to shape the behavior. If someone adds something, it is a positive. If someone takes something away, it is a negative. There are positive reinforcements and negative reinforcements, and positive punishments and negative punishments. Most of these are readily understandable. For example, when someone gets a raise at work, this is positive reinforcement. (Negative reinforcements are the rarest and sometimes the hardest to readily understand. An example might be when a college student lives with several other students, and the student cleans the bathroom to avoid having his or her apartment mates become upset with him or her. When the other students do not get upset, this reinforces the cleaning behavior of the first student.)

The last concept we can mention here is the schedule of reinforcements or punishments. A behavior could be reinforced or punished each and every time the pigeon or person does something. This is called continuous reinforcement. Alternatively, a pigeon or person's behavior could be reinforced or punished intermittently, say one every ten times the desired action occurs, or randomly, say sometimes it gets reinforced or punished every other time the act occurs, but at other times it gets reinforced or punished every tenth time. The classic example of the latter is gambling. If you go to Las Vegas and play the slot machines, you might win once and a while. It will be random. Your behavior is being positively reinforced and a random schedule of reinforcements. Lastly, Skinner notes that positive reinforcement on a random schedule is generally the most effective form of modifying a pigeon or a person's behavior. (It is not a coincidence that Las Vegas casinos use behavioral psychology!)

All of this, of course, sounds more like psychology than sociology, and it is. But Homans believes these same principles of behavioral psychology when combined with the principles taken from the theory of market economics, noted above, can explain social behavior. But how? He notes that behavioral psychology is a good place to start in building a sociological theory, but it is limited. It is limited because of its focus on one animal or person. When Skinner studies how a pigeon learns, the pigeon is not interacting with other pigeons or people (aside from the experimenter). But when people act and learn, they do so within the context of other people. As such, the situation is more complex. This is where the market theory comes in. People engage in relations with others based upon an assessment of costs and benefits of the actions with the others, and these are associated with reinforcements and punishments.

At the heart of this theory lies the notion of value. In the economic marketplace the price of a thing -- an apple, an automobile, land -- is said to be based upon its value, and this is determined by the relative supply and demand of the object. People buy and sell goods all the time. They also buy and sell services. If someone hires someone else to provide tutoring for their child to take the SATs or ACTs, they are hiring the person for the services he or she provides. Similarly, a medical doctor generally does not provide the patient with goods, rather he or she provides services. He or she provides and sells expert knowledge and judgment about medicine. In the economic marketplace, goods and services are what are exchanged. But in the social world outside of economics, are these the only things that are exchanged? Homans says no, and this is central to his theory. People exchange all sorts of things that are not goods and services, and these things are central to an understanding of social interaction and social order. What sort of things? Have you ever done something for someone because you liked them? Things such as approval and acceptance and friendship are some of the things people find of value and are things that are traded in social interactions. If I like someone and I want them to like me, I may seek to do something for them, perhaps help them with their homework or some such thing, to get them to like me. It is this type of exchange that Homans sees as central to social life. But it is not simply approval and acceptance that are exchanged. The number and types of things that can be and are exchanged in social interactions are enormous. For example, in the workplace a worker might exchange his or her effective work for money, for a paycheck. But he or she also might exchange it for things such as whether the setting is a pleasant place to work, or whether the job gives the worker prestige in the community, or perhaps he or she might value the work because it is interesting. All sorts of things can be and are exchanged in social interactions. Homans (1961) even says that justice (i.e. fairness) is a value that is exchanged.

Moreover, an individual could create a wish list of things he or she would like to buy in order of preference, i.e. in order of value. Individuals can and do rank their value preferences on all of the above and more. They have "hierarchies of value" (1961:393). Some things are more important or have more value to individuals than other things. Similarly, one could conceive of hierarchies of costs as well. In effect, there are preference hierarchies of costs and of values. A person behaves as he or she does based upon the calculations anchored in both of these.

In sum, people engage in exchanges with others on an ongoing basis in daily life. These exchanges are not unlike the exchanges in the economic marketplace. People assess the costs and benefits of an interaction and will act in ways that are favorable to them based upon this calculation. By costs Homans included the investments a person must make in the interaction. This investment could be time, money, etc. When a person engages in an exchange that is favorable to that person (i.e. when the benefits outweigh the costs), he or she is likely to continue that behavior. It has been positively reinforced.

In his book *Social Behavior: Its Elementary Forms* (1961), Homans sets out to describe the most basic, abstracted elements of the simplest forms of interaction. He begins by looking at how one individual interacts with one other, then he introduces a third person, and then he discusses groups. While the basic elements or logics of behavioral psychology and market economic principles are present in each of these forms of interaction, the processes of exchange become more complex as one moves from an interaction of two to interactions among three and then to that of a group. For example, in an interaction of two one person might be willing to offer his friendship to another in exchange for something from the other person. But if a third person is present, the cost and benefit calculations change. Now the person could offer friendship to all the members of the group or to one, and this offer of friendship can be offered to more than one without necessarily any additional costs. Or if the person offers friendship to one of the three and not to another, then this will also influence the exchanges among the three in ways that are different from the direct exchange between the two.

Homans presents the general propositions of his exchange theory. These are:

> 1. The Stimulus Proposition: If in the past the occurrence of a particular stimulus-situation has been the occasion on which a man's activity has been rewarded, then the more similar the present stimulus-situation is to the past one, the more likely he is to emit the activity, or some similar activity, now.
> 2. The Success Proposition: The more often within a given period of time a man's activity rewards the activity of another, the more often the other will emit the activity.
> 3. The Value Proposition: The more valuable to a man a unit of the activity another gives him, the more often he will emit activity rewarded by the activity of the other.
> 4. The Deprivation-Satiation Proposition: The more often a man has in the recent past received a rewarding activity from another, the less valuable any further unit of that activity becomes to him.
> 5. The Frustration-Aggression Proposition: The more to a man's disadvantage the rule of distributive justice [fairness] fails of realization, the more likely he is to display the emotional behavior we call anger. (1961:53-75)

All of the above have been discussed in one way or another above, except for numbers four and five. This fourth principle means that if a person always gets something for doing some act, then the value of that something for the person declines. It becomes less important and less powerful as a reward that motivates future actions. One might think of the analogy of food. If someone is rewarded with food for some behavior. Eventually the person will have eaten so much as to be "satiated" or satisfied, or full, and that person will not be driven to seek more food. The fifth principle focuses on fairness. People are driven by a desire to engage in what are seen as fair exchange interactions, but not all exchanges are seen as fair by one or both parties involved. When an exchange is seen as unfair a person will get frustrated and angry, just like the pigeon in the Skinner experiment gets frustrated, flapping its wings and exhibiting other such behaviors when it does not get the food pellet it expects after it pecks the food lever, a behavior which earlier had resulted in the food pellet appearing.

Homans' theory is almost exclusively focused on small-scale social interactions and group interactions. He is trying to develop a theory of the forms of "elementary social behavior." Toward that end, he focuses upon the aspects and dynamics of the exchange processes. But he also looks at group formation and to a far less extent discusses larger institutional organization. He discusses such things as leadership in groups and group cohesion, using his exchange model. A leader, for example, is said to have skills or attributes valued by a group, and these skills and attributes are not widely distributed. They are scarce. They are more valued, and this gives the leader power. Norms are also seen as centrally important in groups. "A norm is a statement made by a number of members of a group ... that the members ought to behave in certain ways in certain circumstances. The members who make this statement find it rewarding that their own actual behavior and that of others should conform to some degree to the ideal behavior described by the norm" (1961:46).

He does not write much about larger social structures, such as society in general or formal institutions. However, he does say a few things about these. The organization and workings of large and formal institutions, such as a university or an economy or a large corporation, can be understood using exchange theory. The same principles that apply in small interactions and in small groups, e.g. cost benefit analyses, etc., also apply to institutions. Institutions emerged out of the workings of these principles on the small-scale. But once institutions become formalized, new and complex forms of interaction do emerge. For example, conflicts can emerge in large institutions between the formal rules of the institution and the actual exchange processes that occur between individuals or groups within the institution. An individual might be expected to work hard or in a particular way in a factory according to the formal rules of the institution, but the exchange relations between the worker and other workers might be such that he calculates, as perhaps the others do, that it is more valuable to the worker not to work hard or in a particular way.

One last point needs to be made about Homans' theory. We should keep in mind that he is seeking to create a scientific theory. A scientific theory is one that is testable. It is one that a researcher could seek to assess whether it is true or false by doing empirical, fact based research. As such, all of the concepts of the theory need to be created in ways that allow them to be measured and tested. All of the elements of this theory could be, and need to be, operationalized. All of them could be put to the test by doing research on them. One could identify and measure, for example, one's value preferences; One could identify the value preferences of a group by observing group behavior, etc. In the same way that Skinner created a scientific psychology and the economists created theories of economics by identifying, observing and measuring behaviors (rather than things such as thoughts or feelings), so too Homans believes sociology should do the same.

Blau's Exchange Theory

Peter Blau picks up where Homans left off. Blau elaborates, modifies, and adds many elements to Homans' theory. Blau (1918-2002) was a German born, Jewish scholar. He fled Germany and came to America after Hitler came to power. He served in the United States Army during World War Two and earned the Bronze Star. After the war, he earned a Ph.D. from Columbia University, where he was student of Robert Merton. Blau went on to become an influential sociologist, producing a number of significant research works, including a widely cited work on bureaucracy. He taught at several universities, including the University of Chicago, the State University of New York at Albany, the University of North Carolina, and Columbia University.

Blau developed an exchange theory that is similar in some ways to Homans, but it is also different in many key aspects. It is similar in that Blau anchors his theory in behavioral psychology and the principles of the economic marketplace. However, it is different in its use of these theories. He draws far more on the metaphor of the economic marketplace to explain social behavior than he does on behavioral psychology. This is not to say that the basic claims of behavioral psychology are rejected. They are not. He readily notes that behavior should be thought of in terms of rewards and punishments, and costs and benefits. But the theory revolves around the metaphor of the market model. One can think of social interaction and social order in terms of some basic market principles, as noted earlier. People exchange things in the social marketplace. These things are assigned value. In the marketplace the three key determinants are price, supply and demand. Each of these affects the others; so too in the social marketplace, though rather than price one finds value in things associated with social relationships. For example, in social exchanges if I value being respected by someone, to get this respect I might seek to provide that person with something that I possess that they might wish to have.

This is not to suggest that Blau simply applies all of the principles of the economic marketplace to the social exchange process. He does not. Some important differences exist between economic exchanges and social exchanges. For example, social exchanges involve "unspecified obligations" whereas economic exchanges do not. When you buy something at a store, the exchange is clear and neither you nor the seller have any further obligation to one another. The relationship is ended. However, if someone does you a favor, they might say "you owe me," but they typically do not specify what it is that they are owed or when the debt needs to be paid. Moreover, most social exchanges do not even involve an explicit acknowledgement of debt. When you hold the door open for someone, and they say, "thank you," there is an exchange. But you do not say to the person "you owe me." In short, as we go through our daily lives, we engage in exchanges that involve unspecified obligations for future interactions with people in general. This relates very much to a second difference Blau sees between economic exchanges and social exchanges: "Only social exchange tends to engender feelings of personal obligation, gratitude, and trust; purely economic exchanges as such does not" (1967:94).

Another difference between Blau's exchange theory and Homans' is that Blau does not limit his theoretical analysis to small-scale social processes, as Homans does. Instead, he seeks to build a theory that explains not only small-scale social interactions but also the operations of larger forces in society. His theory seeks to account for the actions of institutions as well as the actions of small groups. Moreover, Blau builds his theory from the ground up. That is, he starts with an analysis of basic exchange relations between individuals and within small groups, and then from there he looks to apply the basic principles to the organization and dynamics of larger and larger social institutions. This is associated with perhaps the most important difference between the two. Homans grounds his theory in psychology, but Blau is interested in understanding the workings of social structures, rather than the workings of individuals. Moreover, the structures operate in distinct ways from the psychological processes which govern individual actions. "[N]ew social forces emerge in the increasingly complex social structures that develop in societies, and these dynamic forces are quite removed from the ultimate psychological base of all social life" (1967:20). Another difference between the two is that Blau's theory is more dynamic than Homans', and it addresses and incorporates issues of conflict and power. For Blau, much like in the economic marketplace where prices are fluid, rising and falling dependent upon supply and demand, social exchange processes are also fluid. There are multiple, ongoing dynamic tensions involved in these processes which lead to changes of one sort or another. Societies and social groups are filled with dialectics or contradictions. "There is a dialectic in social life, for it is governed by many contradictory forces" (1967:336). And these contradictions produce endless change.

Concepts in Blau's Exchange Theory

Blau builds his theory from an analysis of the social exchange process. We can now look a bit more closely at some of the main concepts of his theory. We begin by looking at several aspects or themes related to the basics of the exchange process. One of these is the recognition of two distinct types of rewards in social exchange: Intrinsic and extrinsic rewards. **Extrinsic rewards** are more like economic rewards. They are the rewards that one gets that are independent of the personalities of the persons involved in the exchange. Money, for example, is an extrinsic reward, but so too are things like prestige. Intrinsic rewards are not at all like economic rewards. **Intrinsic rewards** are those that cannot be removed from the persons in the relationship. Love, for example, and the pleasure of socializing with friends are intrinsic. He gives an example of a dinner party invitation to illustrate this:

> The person who accepts an invitation in order to enjoy the food and drink is an unambiguous case, and so is the one who does so for the sheer pleasure of seeing his old friends – extrinsic rewards motive the former, intrinsic rewards the latter. But consider the third person who comes to have an opportunity to meet high-status people, or the fourth who attends to enjoy the sparkling wit and intellectual sophistication at the dinner table. Compared to food and drink, the stimulating nature of the conversation of individuals is a reward that is intrinsic to the association, as is the enjoyment of their distinguished company. On the other hand, high prestige is evidently a characteristic that can be abstracted from the persons who possess it and used as an independent standard for evaluating the attractiveness of potential associates. The enjoyment of sophisticated conversation too implies that the level of sophistication serves as an extrinsic standard of attraction and of choosing between associates. From this perspective, the third and fourth guests are not drawn to the company at the dinner by its intrinsic attractiveness either but by the extrinsic benefits it supplies. (1967:37)

A second set of concepts concerns norms. Stable exchanges require two sets of norms: Norms of fairness and norms of reciprocity. **Norms of fairness** are the shared beliefs of members in an exchange relationship that the exchange is fair to both parties. Much like a buyer and a seller in the economic marketplace come to an agreement upon a fair price for an object, so too individuals do the same in social exchanges. But not all or even most exchanges are deemed fair by both parties. A buyer might feel that he has not received a fair value in the exchange with the seller. If I buy a used car from someone, I might come to believe I did not get a fair deal. For any number of reasons, parties might not believe an exchange was fair, though the norm of fairness exists. This gap between the norms and the reality is one of the forces that creates dynamic tensions which can lead to changes in social relationships. **Norms of reciprocity** concern the social pressures to give and not simply to take in social relationships, particularly in ways in which both parties feel the exchange is fair. Norms of reciprocity are essential to stable relationship structures.

People engage with others in exchange relations because they feel they will receive some reward as a result. However, the situation is a bit more complicated than this, and here Blau introduces the concept of **marginal utility**. The usefulness, or utility of a reward, is relative to how often one receives the reward. Specifically, the more one receives a reward, the less value the reward has for the individual. This is marginal utility. This principle has significant implications for exchange theory in many ways, some of which are described below. After all, if a reward loses its ability to serve as a reward, what would keep the behavior going? If I get rewarded with chocolate for being nice all the time, then sooner or later, I might say "I am sick of chocolate" and perhaps will cease being nice (or will continue to be nice because of other rewards.) In short, the principle of marginal utility suggests that things other than one set of rewards have to come into play to maintain an exchange relationship over time.

Trust is another central concept in Blau's exchange theory, and it is another way in which social relationships are seen as different from economic relationships. In economic relationships trust is not needed. In social relationships it is. For social relationships to be maintained each party has to trust that the other will somehow fulfill his or her part of the bargain. Each party has to assume that if one party gives another a benefit at one point in time, then at some later point the second party will return the favor in some way. Relatedly, in economic exchanges there is a determinancy. That is, when you buy a coffee at Starbucks, you are no longer obligated to the person behind the counter or to Starbucks. You are not obliged to return to buy another coffee from Starbucks. The economic transaction is self-contained. It is closed-ended. In contrast, social exchanges are not contained. They are open ended. There are diffuse, unspecified obligations in social relationships, and therefore trust is required to sustain the relationship. None of this is automatic. Indeed, it is dynamic. If and when trust breaks down or is not established, there will be conflicts in the social relationship or network of relationships.

Power and leadership are also important concepts in this theory. Power is central to an understanding of the dynamics of exchange relations. He builds his concept of power by noting the limitations of Weber's understanding of this concept. Weber's concept does not include any notion of rewards. Nor does Weber include an appreciation of the various options possibly available to participants involved in a power relationship. Blau defines power as "the ability of persons or groups to impose their will on others despite resistance through deterrence either in the forms of withholding regularly supplied rewards or in the form of punishment" (e.g. negative sanctions)(1967:117). Leadership is based in part upon power. To understand this, he describes the options available to an individual when he or she is commanded to do something:

> Individuals who need a service another has to offer have the following alternatives: First, they can supply him with a service that he wants badly enough to induce him to offer his service in return, though only if they have the resources required for doing so; this will lead to reciprocal exchanges. Second, they may obtain the needed services elsewhere, assuming that there are alternative suppliers; this also will lead to reciprocal exchanges but in different partnerships. Third, they can coerce him to furnish the service, provided they are capable of doing so, in which case they would establish domination over him. Fourth, they may learn to resign themselves to do without this service, possibility finding some substitute for it, which would require that they change the values that determine their needs. Finally, if they are not able or willing to choose any of these alternatives, they have no other choice but to comply with his wishes, since he can make continued supply of the needed service contingent on their compliance. In the situation specified, the supply of services inevitably generates power. The absence of the first four alternatives defines the conditions of power in general. (1967:118-119)

In short, at the heart of Blau's conceptualization of power lies dependence. When a person is in a relationship in which he or she needs something from someone else, and he or she does not have the above four options available to him or her, then a dependence-power relationship is created.

Reciprocity and Imbalance

A central element of Blau's theory is the idea that groups and societies exist as the result of the establishment and maintenance of exchange relations. But there is a dynamic nature to of these relations. Numerous "dialectics" or conflicts are part of exchange relations that can and do prompt changes. One of these is the degree of commitment each party in a transaction has to the relationship. The more committed participants are to the exchange relation, the more stable it will be. However, often, if not typically, one of the individuals is more committed to the relation than the other is, and this creates an imbalance. As a result, the person who is less committed has an advantage "since the other's commitment stabilizes the relationship, and since his lesser commitment permits him, more so than the other, to explore alternative opportunities. Hence, aside from their common interest in assuring that there is sufficient commitment, the two partners also have conflicting interests, because each is interested in having the other make a greater commitment" (1967:315-316). A second dilemma or contradiction involves an individual's attempt to gain favor with a group. He or she does so by trying to impress the group with qualities that will appear attractive to its members. But this creates a problem: "For an individual's endeavors to impress the rest of the group with his outstanding qualities in order to prove himself attractive to them and gain their social acceptance simultaneously poses a status threat for these others that tend to antagonize them. The very outstanding qualities that make an individual differentially attractive as an associate also raise fears of dependence that inhibit easy sociability and this make him unattractive as a social companion" (1967:316).

Other dilemmas exist. One of these concerns social approval. People wish for the approval of those they respect, but they also seek help from those same persons to improve their performance. But these things are incompatible, because "supportive approval fails to furnish an instrumental basis for improvements and critical appraisals imply disapproval" (1967:316). Likewise, the position of leadership in a group entails a dilemma or conflict because it requires the person commanding the power to gain the legitimate approval of those being commanded, but at the same time many of the things that are needed to gain dominance have the effect of antagonizing others and causing others to disapprove of the leader. Still another contradiction is as follows:

> If two individuals are attracted to one another, the first choice of either is to have the other make the greater commitment, but each prefers to make the commitment himself rather than let the relationship perish. The dilemma is how far to go in putting pressure on the other to make his commitment first, in as much as withholding commitment too long in order to gain a superior position in the relationship may endanger the relationship itself. (1967:317)

The principle of marginal utility, as noted earlier, presents another dilemma. Group commitment is based in part upon a member comparing the rewards he or she gets to those of others. If the individual feels a sense of relative depravation compared to others, he or she will seek greater rewards. Relative deprivation refers to the degree to which one compares the rewards he or she gets to others, and if others are seen to get greater rewards (for comparable costs), then a person will feel deprived. But as the individual gets more rewards, the principle of marginal utility says that these rewards will have less and less significance to him or her. This will weaken the ties and the exchange relations. There is also the dilemma of incompatible goal states. It is sometimes if not often the case that individuals have conflicting goals whereby the attainment of one goal prevents the attainment of another. For example, Blau notes that two prerequisites of leadership are positions of dominance and legitimate approval of followers, "but the practices through which a man achieves dominance over others frequently inspire more fear than love, that is, creates obstacles to obtaining the approval of followers" (1967:319).

Norms and Values

Blau, it will be recalled, was interested in developing a macro level theory, as opposed to the micro-oriented theory proposed by Homans. Thus, he was not simply interested in understanding the social exchange processes between two individuals, rather he wished to understand the processes of exchange between groups that constitute society. Moreover, as was noted earlier, he argues that "the complex social structures that characterize large collectivities differ fundamentally from the simpler structures of small groups" (1967:253). A key way that they differ is in the mechanisms of interaction that are required to sustain the relationships. In small-scale interactions, there is a direct relationship between individuals. In large-scale social structures, there is an indirect relationship. The issue then becomes: what are the mediating factors that hold these indirect relations together? Norms and values serve this end. Value consensus, for example, provides a mediating mechanism. We have already noted the norms of reciprocity and fairness above, but Blau sees norms in general, in addition to values, as being important in maintaining large-scale social structures. Normative standards "that restrict the range of permissible conduct are essential for social life" (1967:255). In short, norms and values mediate indirect relations. They serve to regulate and stabilize these relationships that are institutionalized into social structures.

Blau's Model of Social Structures

Blau builds a model of large-scale social structures upon all of the above concepts. The model is rooted in the idea that social exchange produces both integration and differentiation and these in turn produce organization. Organizations then engage in exchanges through the contradictory process of forming coalitions or asserting dominance. This dynamic tension produces political organization, which then may conflict with other organizations. In short, social exchange lies at the foundation of the structures and their interactions. These exchanges produce dilemmas and contradictions which call out for resolution and which produce change. At the same time, the norms and values serve to mediate relationships and to provide a basis of social stability and social order.

Developments in Exchange Theory

In the last thirty years or so a number of scholars have embraced one or another exchange theory rooted in the ideas of Blau or Homans. Two of the more influential theorists to do so are Richard Emerson (1925-1982) and his collaborator Karen Cook (1946-). Emerson relies more upon Homans' approach, but he also is focused upon developing a theory that can explain macro as well as micro social actions. He does so by using the term agent or actor in his theorizing to describe either an individual or a group. Like Homans, and like behavioral psychologists, Emerson is not interested in psychological motivations as such: " "[O]perant" [behavioral] psychology looked to be useful precisely because it contains so little "psychology" in the form of concepts specifically anchored to a complex psychological theory. For psychologists this might be a drawback. For sociologists it is a lucky by-product of the atheoretical philosophy of many operant psychologists" (1972b:87). Instead, his theory is built on the assumption that social actions occur in response to rewards or reinforcements agents receive. Emerson takes this further and focuses upon "power dependency relations" and upon exchange networks. Moreover, this theory differs from the earlier exchange theories in its specificity. He creates a highly precise, analytic model of social behavior, in which numerous mathematical equations are put forth to illustrate the exchange relations. This allows him to systematically state many "rules," "definitions," "propositions," "corollaries," etc. The intent is to develop a theory that allows for the creation of testable propositions. Theory he believes must be subject to empirical testing through research.

Power and dependency are at the center of exchange relations. One needs to understand power and dependency if one wishes to understand exchanges. Emerson's power dependency theory is based upon the definitions of power and dependence and the relationship between the two. Dependence is defined as follows: "The dependence of actor A upon actor B is (1) directly proportional to A's *motivational investment* in goals mediated by B, and (2) inversely proportional to the *availability* of those goals to A outside of the A-B relation" (1962:32). In other words, an actor is dependent upon another if the first wishes to get something (some reward, money, praise, etc.) from the second, and the actor is dependent upon the second to the extent that the first cannot get these rewards or other comparable rewards from some other source. If I want someone to be my friend, I might offer to help them with their homework. But that person may not wish to be my friend if they can find someone else that they like more to help them with their homework. Power is seen as follows: "The power of actor A over actor B is the amount of resistance on the part of B which can be potentially overcome by A" (1967:32). Power is a "property of social relations" and is not a property of an individual. Power here appears when one person makes a demand upon another, and the first person gets what he wants when the second person resists." And power and dependence are tied together: "The power of A over B is equal to, and based upon, the dependence of B upon A" (1967:33). But this relationship is not automatically balanced. At the heart of this approach is an analysis of the various ways in which the relationship can be imbalanced, and how actors can and do respond to the imbalances. Actions may or may not lead to a balanced exchange or to a change in the relationship. For example, if A has more power than B and B is not equally dependent upon A then several possible adjustments could occur:

1) B could reduce its "motivational investment" in goals mediated by A;
2) B could cultivate "alternative sources" for gratification of those goals;
3) A could increase "motivational investment in goals mediated by B;
4) A is denied "alternative sources" for achieving those goals. (1962:35)

Emerson also focuses on social exchange networks. "An exchange network can be defined as consisting of: (1) a set of actors (either natural persons or corporate groups), (2) a distribution of valued resources among those actors, (3) for each actor a set of exchange opportunities with other actors in the network, (4) a set of historically developed and utilized exchange opportunities called exchange relations, and (5) a set of network connections linking exchange relations into a single network structure" (Cook, 1983:277). He also maps out the various networks through which people engage in exchanges and shows how the structures and size of the networks influences how imbalances occur and are addressed by the actors in the network. The structure of exchange relations, for example, is different in a group of four people -- three of whom have relations with the fourth, while the fourth has individual relations with each other -- than it is a group of four people each of which has relations with only one other member of the group.

Emerson's colleague Karen Cook also elaborates and builds upon exchange theory. Her work has focused more on understanding the consequences of the structures of social networks upon social action and upon the role of trust in exchange relations. One issue for her concerns power. Which position in an exchange network is more powerful and which is less? For example, she demonstrates (1983) that the position in a complex structure of exchange networks, in which there are many actors, some interacting with many others, others interacting with very few, will determine the degree of power of the position in ways that are different than is commonly thought. She does this by first distinguishing between two types of connections: positive and negative relations. A positive connection between two actors, A and B, in a network is one in which the connection, i.e. the exchange, is dependent upon the relationship that B has with another member in a network, C. The exchange between A and B is contingent upon B's relationship to C even though A does not have any connection to C. This is much like the image of a middle man in an exchange between three people. The exchange between two of them, A and B, is dependent upon the exchange between B and C. A negative connection is one in which the exchange between A and B and not with C somehow costs C. When a person A buys something from one store, B, and not from another, C, this harms C because the person did not spend her money there. In this structure A has alternatives. A could choose either a relation with B or with C.

The conventional understanding of power in networks is that the position that is most central in a network is the most powerful. The position which appears to link all of the other positions in the network, the position through which all relations are directly or indirectly connected, is the most powerful. Other positions in the network may have as many if not more connections than this central position, but these other positions are peripheral. They are with positions that have fewer or no other connections. These relationships are not central to the entire network and do not link directly or indirectly all the positions together. Cook however notes otherwise. The power in a network is dependent not only upon structural position but also upon whether the network consists of positive or negative social relations. In a network of positive social relations, the more central position is the more powerful one, but in a network of negative social relations, the more central position is less powerful because it has fewer alternatives than the other positions.

In the last couple of decades, Cook (2003, 2005, 2009) has turned her attention to the study of trust in exchange relations. In *Cooperation Without Trust* (2005), Cook et al. argue that there is a relationship between power-dependency and trust. Trust is eroded in unequal power relationships. In complex networks, or in society at large, the decline of trust that comes with unequal power requires institutional mechanisms to be created to maintain trust. Thus, various governmental agencies supervise the banking industry. Professional associations supervise the professions, etc. But the institutional mechanisms put into place to ensure trust can actually undermine trusting relations. For example, in situations of declining trust, increased institutional mechanisms to ensure trust "through monitoring and sanctioning, ironically reduc[e] the possibility for ongoing trust relations" (2005:47). In addition, they argue that, contrary to many who claim that trust has declined in contemporary society and that this is harmful to social stability, trust is not essential to maintaining cooperative relations. For example, the concern that one has for one's own reputation is at least at some times more important to maintaining cooperative relations than is trust. The authors go further and argue that a lack of trust might even be better at maintaining relations, at least in some circumstances, than is trust. A lack of trust prompts people to question and challenge another's actions, and this arguably could serve to maintain stable relationships.

Rational Choice Theory

Coleman's Rational Choice Theory

Rational choice theory surfaced and then spread across several academic disciplines over the last several decades. One can find rational choice theorists in economics, political science, and sociology. The major sociologist associated with rational choice theory is the prominent American sociologist James S. Coleman (1926-1995). (His research on education, race, and inequality, was used in the 1960s, largely by liberals in Congress and the White House as the basis to enact a number of policies, most notably bussing, geared toward addressing segregation and inequalities between black people and white people in America, though in recent years his research has been used by arch-conservatives to support their own policies.) Coleman wrote the definitive book on sociological rational choice theory titled *Foundations of Social Theory* (1990).

In some ways, rational choice theory is quite similar to one or another version of exchange theory. Both rely upon the assumptions of the utility maximizing individual. That is, both begin with the assumption that individuals are purposive creatures seeking to maximize their self-interests through social actions. But there are many differences between the theories as well. For example, one of the differences concerns rationality itself. Blau argues that exchange theory explains both irrational as well as rational behavior. That is, exchange theory explains expressive as well as rational behavior. He writes:

> Human beings tend to be governed [within the rather broad limits that norms impose upon them] in their associations with one another by the desire to obtain social rewards of various sorts, and the resulting exchanges of benefits shape the structure of social relations. The question that arises is whether a rationalistic conception of human behavior underlies this principle that individuals pursue social rewards in their social associations. The only assumption made is that human beings choose between alternative potential associates or courses of action by evaluating the experience or expected experiences with each in terms of a preference ranking and then selecting the best alternative. Irrational as well as rational behavior is governed by these considerations. (1967:18)

On the other hand, Coleman claims that rational choice theory is actually more expansive than exchange theory. It can explain far more types of behavior than can exchange theory. In addition to arguing that one can find, at least in some forms of action, an "irrationality of rational behavior" (1990:198), one can also explain things such as bribery, threats, coercion, power, etc. using rational choice theory, according to Coleman. He claims that such things could not be explained by exchange theory.

Perhaps the most noticeably difference between the theories lies in the overarching models used by the respective theory for inspiration. Exchange theory, as we have seen, relies heavily upon behavioral economics and the market model. In contrast, Coleman relies far more on political and economic theories rooted in liberalism and in utilitarianism. His repeated reference to political philosophers stands in stark contrast with Blau and Homans.

Overview

At the heart of Coleman's theory lies his embrace of **methodological individualism**. Methodological individualism stands in contrast to methodological holism. Methodological individualism is the theoretical assumption that all social phenomena must ultimately be explained by examining the actions of individuals rather than groups. Moreover, it assumes that traditional sociological phenomena, such as societies, social structure, norms, etc. do not and cannot exist as entities independent from individuals, and that these phenomena cannot independently explain or account for social action. Individuals exist; societies do not. Rational choice theory whole heartedly embraces methodological individualism. **Methodological holism** is the opposite perspective. Methodological holism assumes that traditional sociological phenomena, such as societies, social structure, norms, etc. do exist, and that one or the other or a combination of both, form a unified whole, independent of individuals that comprise these wholes, which can explain social action in themselves. The structuralism of the European tradition of Levi-Strauss fall into this camp, as does some versions of Marxism (for example, that of Althusser), as well as the sociology of Durkheim.

Coleman's methodological individualism does not mean that he favors a micro approach to sociology. Theory should not focus upon social psychology or upon small-scale social interactions. He was indeed mostly interested in understanding large-scale, macro realities, but to understand large-scale social formations one must start with the assumptions of the rational actor. In other words, he seeks to fuse the micro and the macro using his methodological individualism. The assumptions of actors as being rational and purposive in their actions is the way to stitch together the micro and the macro. Specifically, assumptions of rational actors allow theory to move from the micro to the macro, but more. The macro in turn bears down upon the individual and influences his or her rational choice making. We see this below in the examples of norms and of trust. In short, social reality and specifically social formations are seen as emergent from individual actors acting rationally with each other.

One of the more distinct aspects of this rational choice theory is the degree to which it draws upon classical and contemporary political philosophy as well as economic theory. Coleman routinely creates conceptualizations through an engagement with arguments with political philosophers. He draws heavily upon the philosophy of utilitarianism. Utilitarianism is a largely British political philosophy from the eighteen and nineteenth century. The most famous philosophers associated with it are Jeremy Bentham and John Stuart Mill. It is a moral philosophy which claims that the most just society is the one that provides the most justice to the most people in that society. It also claims that the desire for pleasure (happiness) should be the basis of determining what is deemed good. In short, the best society is the one that provides the greatest goods for the greatest number of persons. The best society is the one that provides the most happiness for the most people. Mill creates a hierarchy of preferences that he says individuals naturally have, and he builds his political theory on all of this. One can see how this is closely aligned with rational choice, and exchange, theories.

Coleman also draws heavily upon the classical and contemporary liberal political philosophers. It is important here to understand the concept of liberal. When scholars use the term liberal, they are not using it in the way that the man or the woman on the street in America today might use it. They are not using it in a popular sense. When people in the general public today use the term liberal, they are typically referring in America to liberal Democrats, i.e. members of the Democratic Party. Here liberal suggest morally liberal, a support of gay rights and abortion, for example. It also suggests a support for a greater size and role of the federal government in one or another aspect of life. Political philosophers use the word liberal in a very different and often contrasting way. Here they are referring to a philosophical position that originates in the Enlightenment and which is rooted in the belief that liberty is a fundamental starting point for assessing the relative justness of a society. A liberal in this sense supports limited government and maximum amounts of choices for individuals. In this sense, a liberal is one who cherishes individuals and individual rights. A liberal in this sense is also one who embraces the values of free and critical thinking. In recent years we find that libertarianism as a political philosophy has (re)surfaced. Coleman also draws upon the writings of two of the more prominent recent moral and political philosophers writing on liberty and justice – John Rawles and Robert Nozick – in building his theory.

While drawing heavily upon these moral philosophers, Coleman also is confronted with the need to distance his theorizing from them. That is, the moral philosophers set about to provide the intellectual arguments for social conditions that would produce the most just society. They make moral arguments, grounded in the reasoning which can be traced back to the Enlightenment. Coleman, on the other hand, has a different task. His task is not to argue that one society or social setting is more just or more moral than another, and he is not seeking to create a theory that provides the foundations for how people *should* organize their society. He wishes to create a social scientific theory that explains how the world really works, rather than how the world should work. As such, he embraced a position of moral relativism: "It is important to emphasize that every ... observation is that of a particular social system [and not that of a moral perspective external to that system]. There is no absolute observation point, outside any social system, from which moral judgment may be made" (1990:387). Yet at the same time, his theory is built on the assumption that individuals act rationally, and that rational action is in part based upon the Kantian categorical imperative. Kant put forth a famous philosophical statement concerning the basis of morality that is called the categorical imperative. This is the position that you should act toward others in ways that you would like others to act toward you. It is a variation of the golden rule. It is rationally in someone's interest to embrace this moral position. This position inevitably complicates Coleman's desires to create an objective, moral free theory.

A final point could be made about morality and social theory. Coleman sees sociological theory as increasingly important in informing public debates and public policies. Rational choice theory is viewed as a tool that could be used to advance the cause of justice in society. While he is intentionally vague when it comes to proclaiming that sociologists should use theory to advance the cause of justice per se, he is clear that he wishes to create a "new social science" that combines theory and research to help improve society. Here he champions "reflexive consistency," which means systematically relating theory and research in a logically consistent way and applying these to real life social concerns (1990:614).

Basic Claims

Coleman begins with the assumptions that social actors are driven to maximize their utility. They are purposive in orientation and seek to achieve their interests through rational assessments of the situation. A significant element of the theory is resources. Whether an individual acts to achieve his rationally calculated interests or whether an individual achieves these is dependent in part upon the resources available to the actor. If I have an interest in buying a new iPhone but do not have the money (resources) to purchase it, then I will not be able to get one. In addition to resources and interests, an understanding of social action must recognize how the social context is affected by social action and how it affects social action. He identifies several concepts here. One of these is the amount of information an agent has. Rational assessments of one's situation is dependent upon how much information one has. One can still act rationally with limited information, but the action might be different than a rational action based upon much more information. Another concept is opportunity costs. In any action there is a cost associated with it. This cost is the inability to engage in a different action while doing the action. One can only do one thing at a time. As a result, the choice of doing one thing means that one is forgoing another. This is the opportunity cost. Externalities is another concept relevant here. Externalities are very much like unintended by-products of an action. When you drive to school, your car pollutes the air. It is a cost to the environment, and a cost to society in terms of public health and other things, but this cost is generally not factored into your rational assessment of whether to drive or not. Likewise, if I have a wonderful flower garden in my front yard, people who I do not know may enjoy the benefits of it without incurring the costs in terms of time and money and effort that I put into the garden. (If my intent in creating and maintaining the garden is such that others may think highly of me, then this would not be an externality. If my intent is the self-pleasure I take in producing this nice garden, then this would be an externality.)

Coleman presents a basic model of the "structure of social action" based upon rational choice theory assumptions and upon the concepts noted above. This model has three parts: 1) actors, 2) resources, and 3) "constitution" (i.e. "the initial distribution of control of resources among actors") (1990:132). In addition, the concepts of value and power are central to the model. "The power of an actor resides in his control of valuable events" and the "value of an event lies in the interests powerful actors have in the event." This are all tied together as follows: "Actors have initial control over resources and initial interests. This distribution leads to exchanges, which in a market structure allow specifying the value of each resource. Then each actor's power is the value of all those resources he controls, and the amount of each resource that an actor holds at equilibrium is determined by his interest in that resource, his power (that is, the value of the resources he controls), and the value of that resource itself" (1990:134).

Another way of describing his theory of (the structure of) social action is as follows: Individuals are propelled by interests and (an "initial distribution of") resources. This leads to exchanges by which value is allocated. Value is a reflection of power – over resources. The individual's power and interests and the value of the resource determine whether the social actor engages in a "market" exchange that maintains (or not) an "equilibrium [of the] distribution of control" over the resources (Coleman 1990:134).

Social Structure

As noted earlier, Coleman was far more interested in explaining large-scale, macro formations than he was in remaining on the micro. To understand the macro organization, or really any social structural formations, one needs to start with an analysis of the basic elements of rational action. But when one locates the actions of an individual or the interactions of two individuals within a broader social context, the theory inevitably must become more complicated. Coleman in fact devotes much if not most of his time examining the complexities of social structure, all the while using rational choice as the foundation of understanding. The theory relies implicitly upon the theme of emergence. Social structure emerges from the purposive, rational actions of social actors as they engage with one another. Structure emerges from individual actions.

He makes sense of numerous commonly used sociological concepts from this perspective. Norms, for example, emerge from the purposive actions of individuals, and not from the social structure itself. (This is not surprising from anyone who embraces the methodological individualist perspective.) As Coleman says, "I refuse to take norms as given ... I ask how norms can emerge and be maintained among a set of rational individuals" (1990:242). Norms are seen as "purposively generated in that those persons who initiate or help maintain a norm see themselves as benefiting from its being observed or harmed by its being violated" (1990:242). Norms are defined as follows: "A norm concerning a specific action exists when the socially defined right to control the action is held not by the actor but by others" (1990:243). Another concept is trust. Trust is developed and maintained through a similar process. Actors find it to be in their interest to trust some people at some times, and this along with norms and other things provides the groundwork for a stable social structure. A third concept is rights. Coleman, influenced as he is by political and moral philosophers, believes rights are an essential concept to consider when explaining social action and social order. All rights are socially determined and produced and there is not one set of rights that are universally valid or better than any other set of rights. Rights are defined as follows: "The actor has a right to carry out an action or to have an action carried out without dispute" (1990:50). Rights are socially agreed upon ways of doing things; the agreement is based upon the purposive, rational assessment of the individuals' self-interests. Another concept central to this theory is the corporate actor. He is very interested in understanding the workings of corporate actors, which consist largely of formal organizations or institutions, from businesses to states, i.e. national governments. The existence of corporate actors requires that individuals surrender some of their rights to others, and as a result it requires the existence of authority. This is all done by individuals seeking to maximize their interests. Corporate actors by themselves are then able to impose constraints upon individuals operating within their domains. Coleman here focuses on the importance of "constitutions." A constitution is an agreement amongst a group of people to surrender some personal rights such that the individuals can be better able to maximize their interests.

The Prisoner's Dilemma and the Free-Rider Problem

The **prisoner's dilemma** and the free-rider problem are two issues related to rational choice forms of theorizing that present some possible challenges to the logic and legitimacy of these approaches. These issues appear to suggest that when individual social actors act rationally and in their own self-interest within a social interaction, then the outcome of their actions might not be the most rational outcome for the individuals involved. It appears to suggest that the very assumptions of rational actors maximizing their interests is wrong. There is an irrationality to the rational choices people may make. Countless versions of the prisoner's dilemma have been given, but the core elements can be seen in the following example: Two partners in crime, person A and person B, are arrested and imprisoned for committing a crime together. Each prisoner is put in solitary confinement and cannot speak with the other. The prosecutor does not have enough evidence to convict the two of them on the main charge. As such, the prosecutor is hoping to get both convicted on a lesser charge. Toward that end, the prosecutor meets with each prisoner individually and offers each of them a deal. Each prison is given the opportunity to 1) confess, 2) to say he is innocent and that the other person did the crime; 3) or remain silent.

The prosecutor's offer is the following:

-If A and B each betray the other and each professes his own innocence, then each of them serves 4 years in prison
-If A betrays B but B remains silent, A will be set free and B will serve 6 years in prison (and vice versa)
-If A and B both remain silent, both of them will only serve 2 years in prison (on the lesser charge).

The Prisoner's Dilemma

	A Betrays B	A Remains Silent
B Betrays A	Outcome: A gets 4 years and B gets 4 years	Outcome: B is free and A gets 6 years
B Remains Silent	Outcome: A is free and B gets 6 years	Outcome: Both A and B get 2 years

The point of the game is to show that the rational thing to do is not always the best, most self-interested thing to do. Sometimes, acting in a less than rational way is in one's own best self-interest. Relatedly, the game is about cooperation and competition. Rational choice implies competition, but the game shows that cooperation rather than competition sometimes leads to the most rationally, self-interested results for the individuals. The rational thing for A and for B to do is to betray each other. But if they do this, it will not lead to the best outcome for each individual. If A betrays B, and B betrays A, then they both get 4 years. It will not lead to the most self-interested outcome. They each would get a better outcome if they both kept silent. In this case, they each would get 2 years.

    A rational choice theorist is forced to reconcile this game with their theory because the game appears to contradict the basic assumptions of the theory. Coleman specifically addresses the issue within the context of a discussion of collective behaviors. He discusses collective behaviors both to address the issues of concern related to the prisoner's dilemma and because he recognizes that many collective behaviors appear on the surface as anything but rational. They appear to be filled with irrational behavior. Collective behaviors include such things as social protest movements, crazes and panics -- "escape panics," bank and stock market panics, etc., fads and fashions, riots, etc. At the heart of his accounting for people's engagement in these apparent irrational actions lies the claim that people rationally transfer control over their behavior to others, and they do so to maximize their utility. That is, within stable situations, i.e. within settings without collective behaviors, people normal engage in trade-offs based upon rational calculations that these tradeoffs will ultimately be in the individual's best interest. Under these normal conditions a balanced or stable social order is created. But this does not always occur. Sometimes there is confusion, particularly regarding rationality and utility. At times, when people pursue their own rational self-interests, social imbalance occurs. This is how collective behaviors arises, he argues.

Within this context of collective behaviors, the issue of the free rider also appears. The **free rider problem** is the problem of explaining why someone who would benefit from the activities of a group even if he or she does not participate in the group's activities, which may be risky, would participate in these activities at all. For example, an African American in the 1950s and 1960s in the South had the choice of participating in one or another activities of the Civil Rights Movement. But if that African American recognized that he or she would benefit from the successes of the activities of other African Americans (and others) who participated in the protests, strikes, sit-ins, etc., without having to incur the costs, e.g. beatings, arrests, etc. that would result from participating him or herself, then why would he or she participate? The most rational, self-interested thing to do would be not to participate but to enjoy the gains or benefits of the successes (e.g. laws passed, etc.) of the protesters. In effect, why would anyone rationally participate in collective behaviors such as this? The rational thing to do would appear to be for individuals not to participate.

Coleman's solution to the prisoner's dilemma and to the free rider problems draws upon many of the basic concepts found in rational choice theory, such as some of those noted earlier. He claims that the prisoner's dilemma and the free rider problem can be solved when one recognizes the importance of trust, of norms, and of social capital. Coleman notes that the prisoner's dilemma is an artificial reality, and in reality social actors operate within a real context. These real contexts include more than two people. They include three or more, and they include the assumptions and beliefs of the peoples involved. These real life situations are such that, unlike the prisoner's dilemma, people will have some knowledge and information about other persons involved in the game. As such, the basic claims of the prisoner's dilemma that people act in a vacuum in a completely individualistic manner, ignorant of others, is simply wrong and inapplicable to real life circumstances.

Real life factors include such things as normative constraints, which are rationally produced beforehand. Participants in a real-life situation akin to the prisoner's dilemma will draw upon existing understandings of trust, rights and norms, and will rationally act accordingly. Also, the degree of information held by participants is a factor that needs to be considered. As noted earlier, what is and what is not rational must be understood within the context of the amount of information a person has in making decisions. A decision may be rational when made with limited information and knowledge, but the same decision may be seen as irrational or less than rational when it is made with more information and knowledge. In addition, people engage in activities, specifically in reference to the free rider problem, often to acquire "social capital," in the form of prestige, honor, or high status from others. These are all rational rewards which may propel an individual to act. In short, Coleman argues that the prisoner's dilemma and the free rider problems are not insurmountable conceptual problems for rational choice theory, but instead can be readily explained using the theory.

Summary

This chapter described several of the main versions of exchange theory, particularly those developed by Homans and Blau, as well as the related rational choice theory developed by James Coleman. Exchange theories assume that social life could be understood as an endless series of social exchanges. The theory is significantly influenced by behavioral psychology and by market-based economic theories. Exchange theory assumes people are motivated by reinforcement and punishments, or costs and benefits, and that the value and price of things exchanged are determined by a number of things, most notably supply and demand. Exchange theory claims that people exchange money and goods, but they also exchange a whole range of other non-economic things, such as love, power, prestige, friendship, etc. Homans' version of exchange theory, which was the first, was oriented toward developing a scientific theory of social behavior. It focuses on small-scale social interactions. Blau developed a more sophisticated exchange theory which focused less on psychology and small-scale interactions than it did on understanding social structures. He notes that there are some important differences between market-based exchanges and social exchanges. The differences are related to the differences between two main types of rewards: intrinsic and extrinsic. In his model, norms of reciprocity and norms of fairness are centrally important in maintaining social order. These norms are routinely violated, and as a result social life is dynamic. Social life is filled with contradictions and tensions. These contradictions explain the dynamics of social life. Trust and power, reciprocity and imbalance, and norms and values are all central concepts in his theory. Blau moves his theory from the micro to the macro. Richard Emerson and Karen Cook take the essential elements of Blau's theory and build upon them. They advance the theoretical ideas of power, dependency and trust in relation to exchange theory.

Rational choice theory was an influential theory in various social science disciplines in the closing decades of the twentieth century. The main sociological rational choice theory was developed by James Coleman.

Coleman embraced the concept of methodological individualism and rejected methodological holism. His theory is built upon several main traditions in political philosophy, most notably on the utilitarianism of Mill and Bentham, as well as the Enlightenment moral philosophers and the more contemporary liberal, moral philosophies of Rawls and Nozick. Rational choice theory assumes that people are fundamentally rational actors, and that social behavior and social structure can be explained with this assumption. Coleman explains social structure by focusing upon its emergent character. Norms, trust, rights and the corporate actor are major concepts in his theory. Rational choice theories are confronted with two conceptual problems: the prisoner's dilemma and the free rider problem. Coleman provides solutions to these problems.

Discussion Questions

1. Critics have sometimes complained that there is a type of faulty circularity in the logic of exchange theories and rational choice theories. That is, if anything from love, to power, to money can be exchanged and can also be used to explain exchanges, then is there anything that cannot be explained using this theory? If all behavior can be explained as the result of exchanges, then is the theory really saying anything at all?

2. Exchange theories and rational choice theories claim to be objective, unbiased, and scientific. But critics have sometimes complained these theories are not objective and unbiased, but instead have built into them conservative political biases. The theories tend to suggest that democratic, capitalist societies and the forms of relationships that are produced in these societies are good and normal, because they conform to the assumptions that people are at heart rational actors. Are these theories unbiased and objective, or are they biased and conservative? If they are biased, are they any ways to salvage the theories to make them less biased and conservative?

3. Should social theory be based upon methodological holism or methodological individualism? Why? What would Marx say about this?

4. Exchange theories and rational choice theories claim that the rational, self interested logic that one supposedly sees in the marketplace is a universal and natural feature of human beings. They assume this form of being is not determined by modern, rational capitalism, but is determined by the nature of human beings. Are they right to make such a claim, or are the wrongfully assuming the rational self interested actions of people in modern capitalism

are universal and natural? Are there many modes of being in this world, as claimed by phenomenologists, and if so, does this call rational choice theory into question?

Chapter Eleven: Integrative Theories – Bourdieu, Giddens and Habermas

In the last several decades, three broad forms of sociological theorizing have arisen. One of these forms is fundamentally uncritical and accepting of basic assumptions underlying social theory. This form of theorizing does not question or challenge the many conceptual, logical or meta-theoretical problems that confront the project of developing any sociological theory. It does not question the philosophical assumptions underlying conventional understandings of theory building. (For example, these theories may not question assumptions about the existence of the social that is independent of the self. They may not question the meaning or concept of self and agency. They may not question how or if one should understand history. Should one impose a logic upon history, as Marx does, or should one simply ignore history as irrelevant to the theoretical project? They might not question the nature of language. They might not question the meaning of social order. They might not question how theorists should resolve the tension between facts and values, etc.) Thorny issues are ignored or dismissed and are largely not engaged. Theories that continue to embrace the fundamental tenets of the classical theorists – Marx, Weber, Durkheim – are in this camp, as are a range of other current theories, from symbolic interactionism to exchange theories. A second form of theorizing revolves around the notion of the postmodern. Postmodern theories are discussed in Chapter Twelve. These radically reject conventional theorizing in part because of the fundamental conceptual, logical or meta-theoretical problems identified with them. Postmodern theories seek to tear down the basic scaffolding of conventional theorizing from the ground up and seek to reconstitute the entire project. This has led many critics to complain that postmodern theories lead to silliness, to incessant rejections, and that postmodern theories do not provide a solid, legitimate basis for theory building. A third form of theorizing does question the various fundamental problems associated with conventional theorizing, but at the same time it rejects what is seen as the cynicism of postmodern theorizing. This third form focuses upon addressing the thorny conceptual issues ignored or dismissed by the first group noted above. But it does not simply seek to reject the conventional approaches. Instead, it seeks to build more viable theories in their place.

In this chapter, three major examples of this third form of theorizing are presented. The theories of Pierre Bourdieu (1930-2002), Jurgen Habermas

(1929-) and Anthony Giddens (1938-) are described. Each of these in their own way seek to address many of the fundamental conceptual issues and problems underlying conventional theorizing. Here a couple of sets of such issues can be mentioned: agency-structure and micro-macro. The three theorists seek to overcome the problems associated with these sets of issues by developing approaches which claim to resolve them by integrating agency and structure, and the micro and the macro. These themes were discussed in Chapter One, but it is worthwhile to revisit them briefly here. The issue of agency and structure concerns the explanation of social behavior. How should a theorist explain social behavior and social order? Should he or she assume that social behavior is explained as the result of choices made by social actors (agency) or should he or she assume that social behavior is determined by external social forces, i.e. by the structures of the social world? Agency refers to the assumption that people are choice makers. People are not programmed to act in one way or another. They instead have will. They are meaning making and choice making creatures. Agency social theories are those that start with the assumption that people have agency. Structure refers to an organized system that is imposed upon the individual from outside of the individual. A classroom, for example, has a structure. It does not simply have a physical structure (chairs are arranged in rows, etc.), but it has a structure related to the social order. The structure is determined by such things as norms and power. Structural theorists focus upon any number of structures, from the structures of social institutions, such as the family or the economy, to the structure of language. These structures are said to determine individual behaviors. Structural theories claim that individual behaviors are products of the structures imposed upon them. In effect, people are more like puppets on strings than they are choice makers. The micro macro divide involves something different. Micro theories, such as symbolic interactionism, focus on individual or small-scale immediate interactions to explain social behaviors. Macro theories explain social behaviors by focusing on large-scale social organization. For example, Marx seeks to explain social behavior by analyzing the organization of the economy rather than focusing directly upon individual behaviors.

Social theories could be identified as micro or macro, and as agency or structural theories. We could place all theories on a chart (see Figure 11.1) where micro and macro are the vertical axis, and agency and structure are the horizontal axis. All theories could be located someplace on this chart.

	Macro Perspectives		
	Weber	Durkheim	
		Althusser (Marxist)	
Agency Perspectives	Gramsci (Marxist)	Marx	Structural Perspectives
		Blau	
		Homans	
	Goffman (Dramaturgy)	Goffman (Frame Analysis)	
	Symbolic Interactionism		
	Phenomenology		
	Micro Perspectives		

Where do the theories fit? Some examples:

Figure 11.1

Some theories are micro-agency theories. Symbolic interactionism is one such theory. Some theories are macro-structural theories. Durkheim's theory would be placed here. Still other theories are micro-structural. Goffman's theory is one such theory. Some theories might be placed in more than one location on the chart. Weber's theory, for example, might be considered an agency theory and a structural theory, but it arguably is also very much a macro theory. He after all was fundamentally concerned with explaining large-scale social issues, such as the rise of modernity. Marxist theory also might be located in various places on the chart, depending upon how one interprets Marxism. Some Marxists such as Althusser, for example, are structural Marxists. On the other hand, other Marxists such as Antonio Gramsci develop agentic Marxist approaches.

Some theorists today and in the past have sought to develop theories which could be located at the intersection of the two lines. That is, some, such as the theorists covered in this chapter, try to integrate the elements. Others have abandoned any attempts to develop theories that overcome the divides between agency and structure. Goffman, for example, explicitly does this in his book *Frame Analysis*:

> This book is about the organization of experience – something that an individual actor can take into his mind – and not the organization of society. I make no claims whatsoever to be talking about the core matters of sociology – social organization and social structure. Those matters have been and continue to be quite nicely studied without reference to frame at all. I am not addressing the structure of social life but the structure of experience individuals have at any moment of their social lives. I personally hold society to be first in every way and any individual's current involvements to be second; this report deals only with matters that are second. This book will have weaknesses enough in the areas it claims to deal with; there is no need to find limitations in regard to what it does not set about to cover. Of course, it can be argued that to focus on the nature of personal experiencing – with the implication this can have for giving equally serious consideration to all matters that might momentarily concern the individual – is itself a standpoint of marked political implications, and that these are conservative ones. The analysis developed does not catch at the differences between the advantaged and disadvantaged classes and can be said to direct attention away from such matters. I think that is true. I can only suggest that he who would combat false consciousness and awaken people to their true interests has much to do, because the sleep is very deep. And I do not intend here to provide a lullaby but merely to sneak in and watch the way people snore. (1974:14-15)

The theorists covered in this chapter – Bourdieu, Habermas, and Giddens – each in their own way seek to develop theories that are located, or perhaps seek to be located, at the intersections of the macro and micro and agency and structure. In addition, they also recognize what might be called the dialectic of social experience. This is more of a philosophical understanding of experience than that found in many other approaches. It is the recognition that individuals live in real time in real societies. In this way, individuals are and they are not. They exist and they are becoming at the same time. They exist in society and create society at the same time. The integrative theorists understand social reality through this lens, and they seek to develop theories that could be located at the crosshairs of the two lines in Figure 11.1.

Pierre Bourdieu

Bourdieu's earlier work consisted of anthropological studies of some ethnic groups in north Africa. Initially, he embraced a structuralist orientation, in the mold of scholars such as Levi-Strauss (see Chapter Twelve). Structural anthropology like Levi-Strauss took the extreme position that one cannot study agency or individual choice making from a scientific perspective, but one can, and should, study structures – for example of cultural formations -- scientifically. Structural anthropology set about trying to understand the structures of cultural formations, from the structuring of family and family relations to the structurings of myth. The task was to identify the basic elements of the structures of these cultural formations and to show how the elements are interconnected into unified structured wholes that dictate cultural practices.

Bourdieu soon rebelled against this. He came to believe that structuralists were wrongheaded in their approach (1990). They were trying to create an "objectivist" understanding, by avoiding any concern with individual psychology, or choice making or agency. They were trying to overcome the conceptual problems associated with attempting to scientifically studying individual consciousness, agency, choice making. They did this by rejecting a focus on such things. But Bourdieu says they then imposed this objectivist perspective onto the very people they were studying. In effect, the researchers were distorting understandings of the people they were studying while believing they were doing otherwise. "The logic inherent in the objectivist viewpoint inclines one to ignore the fact that scientific constructionism cannot grasp the principles of practical logic without forcibly changing their nature" (1990:90). In effect, structuralists were wrongfully seeing the people they were studying as nothing more than puppets on a string, marionettes, enslaved to the structures of their culture. Bourdieu recognized that the social scientist needed to appreciate the agency of the people that are studied. But he did not simply abandon a structuralist perspective and replace it with an agency perspective. Rather, he sees the very conceptualization of a divide between these two as misplaced and wrongheaded. Rather than seeing the theoretical situation as an either-or one, in which the scholar needed to embrace structuralism or agency, Bourdieu says we can and should transcend this divide. But how?

For him, the solution lies in the lived practices of people. These practices, or social behaviors, have a logic to them. There is a *logic of practice*. People simultaneously embody structure *and* agency through their social practices. In effect, we need to look at what people actually think and actually do, and by doing this the researcher can transcend the divide between agency and structure. But there is more to his analysis. He also believes the structuralist-agency problem is faulty in its conceptualization of the individual. It is based upon a faulty Cartesian image of the self as being composed of two distinct parts – the mind and the body. (Descartes actually believed the individual was composed of three parts – the mind, body, and soul!) For Bourdieu, this is an artificial distinction. If social scientists really wished to understand lived social behaviors then they must recognize that the individual in his or her living reality embodies the mind and body simultaneously and indivisibly. We cannot separate the two out. Again, it is through practices that we can get beyond this conventional misunderstanding of relying on the mind-body image. Lastly, and importantly, Bourdieu recognizes that humans, living humans, cannot be extracted from their living realities if we truly wish to understand them. Our reality, our being in reality, is such that we are intrinsically tied to the external world – our existence is our being. The internal and the external, our individual selves and the world outside of ourselves, comprise our reality. Abstracting one or another of these, distorts an understanding of social realities. This is the core philosophical basis of Bourdieu's theorizing.

A main theme in much of his theorizing is in developing a theory of "the logic of practice" that was largely focused on understanding social inequalities and how social inequalities are reproduced, or not – how they are maintained or challenged. This is most evident in his book *Distinctions: A Social Critique of the Judgement of Taste* (1984). This work summarizes a research project done by him on social class in France. He and his colleagues interviewed over one thousand French people to understand how people from the different classes, such as the middle class vs the working class, understood and appreciated various forms of art and other cultural productions. In their interviews the researchers sought to understand how people from the different classes looked at these forms of culture. In short, as the title suggests, Bourdieu wished to understand the cultural tastes of the different classes. It is through these tastes, through the aesthetic sensibilities, that members of various classes understood and perpetuated the class structure. The class structure is not simply there as an objective reality. It is lived and constantly being created. Classes are constituted through the structurings of the taste of the members.

Another big theme in his work is how these practices reproduce systems of inequality. He sought to understanding how social inequalities, whether race, class, gender, or some other form of inequality, are produced and reproduced. Bourdieu recognized that inequalities do not magically occur. Social classes, for example, are not simply objective categories that people fall into. Rather, people create through their practices the classes and the class system in which they live within an objective reality imposed upon them.

(This is not to suggest Bourdieu was developing some form of social constructionist understanding. He was not. There is an objective reality within which we live.) Social life is a fluid and dynamic process, constantly being created. Social processes have to occur for inequalities to exist. For example, how is it that African Americans were disproportionately poor compared to whites in the eighteen hundreds and are still disproportionately poor today? He saw that people had to do things on an ongoing basis to maintain one or another system of inequality. It was not simply that people at the upper end of a system of inequality, such as rich people in the economic system, had to do things to maintain an unequal economic system, but poor people as well had to do things to keep the system going. Bourdieu was interested in understanding the processes through which people produce and reproduce these systems of inequality. But this is not an automatic process, and it is not the case that systems of inequality automatically are reproduced. These systems can be and often are challenged. For Bourdieu, social class systems, or other systems of inequality, are not fixed and frozen, but are constantly being produced and, at least potentially, constantly being contested. In social life, there is an endless struggle between groups in systems of inequality.

Pierre Bourdieu

Pierre Bourdieu (1930-2002) was born in Southwest France and was raised in a lower middle class household. He was an excellent student. He attended the Ecole Normale Superieure in Paris for graduate school and while there studied with some of the more prominent French social scientists and philosophers, including the Marxist Althusser and the structural anthropologist Levi-Strauss. He was drafted into the French Army and served two years in Algeria, after the Algerian war for independence. He remained in Algeria after he left the army and conducted anthropological research on the Berber tribe. Aside from three years serving as a professor at the University of Lille, Bourdieu spent the rest of his life as an academic in Paris. In Paris he was appointed to several prestigious academic positions. Bourdieu published a number of important works in sociology. His book *Distinctions* has been listed as one of the most important works of sociology of the twentieth century by the International Sociological Association. He died in 2002.

One can see the influences of the French intellectual culture upon his theorizing. We have already noted the influence that structuralism has had upon his theorizing. But he was also influenced, as were most French social scientists in the mid to late twentieth century, by Marxism and by the phenomenological tradition (see Chapter Nine). Bourdieu was certainly no Marxist, but he did accept Marx's claims about the importance of conflict and power. He was influenced by Marx's views regarding the social processes involved in maintaining inequalities. Bourdieu also recognized the importance of economics in understanding all forms of inequality, but he rejected Marx's exclusive focus upon economics as the essential and only force that can explain inequalities. He was also influenced by phenomenology, broadly conceived. His focus on lived experience and how people make sense of, and engage in, lived experience, in real time, was central to his project. He wished to understand how people through lived experiences interpret their worlds and act in their worlds based upon these interpretations, and this orientation echoes that of phenomenology. Bourdieu understands social experience as fluid and dynamic, rather than as static and mechanical, as some theoretical traditions seem to do. But unlike the phenomenologists, the structuring of experiences are not merely unique to the individual. The structurings of the objective social conditions bear down upon the individual and the individual make sense and acts in his or her world through these structures.

Three central concepts in his theory are practice, fields and habitus. It is important to understand how Bourdieu uses the concept of practice. It is central to his theorizing. The word **practice** appears in the title of two of his books. The word practice has many meanings. One can practice at playing the violin, but one can also practice medicine. These are very different understandings of the word. One involves repetitive actions that are designed to prepare the person for a future performance. The other is the use of technical skills by someone of competence. And there are others. When Bourdieu uses the word practice, he is using it in a way that includes elements of all of these. We engage in practices in our daily lives. We do craft our behaviors; we practice our art of living. In some ways this is not unlike Goffman's understanding of social action. The actors perform; they skillfully engage in lived realities using techniques that enact their understandings of their worlds. For Bourdieu there is a "**logic of practice**" that needs to be appreciated if one wishes to understand social realities, and specifically if one wishes to understand how inequality is reproduced. He is not saying that people act logically in the sense of using rationality and the logic of science. Indeed, he is saying something very different. People are not machine like. "Practice has a logic which is not that of the logician" (1990:86). People instead employ practical or **fuzzy logic** in their day-to-day lives. By this he means that people create understandings of their world in their day-to-day lives that loosely might be called logical in a very general sense. People use common sense rather than formal logic in their dealings with the everyday world, and it is this common sense that comprises fuzzy logic. Fuzzy logic is not pure, rational thinking. Rather it is the logic one uses informally in one's daily actions. Fuzzy logic is also not often self-conscious. Often times, we are engaged in "logical" activity on a daily basis without self-consciously thinking about what it is we are doing. The task is to understand how people develop and use this fuzzy logic. (Bourdieu says we should understand this fuzzy or practical logic in practice, in lived practice. "Practical belief is not a "state of mind" ... but a state of the body" (1990:68), and bodies exist in lived realities.)

Another way of thinking of fuzzy logic is to contrast the idea of knowing how to play chess and knowing the formal rules of chess. If you read the rule book and understand it, do you know "how" to play chess? Formally, yes. But in reality, no. You have a formal understanding, not a practical one; not one anchored in fuzzy logic. Fuzzy logic is often implicit and unstated. One might also contrast the behaviors of someone playing a violin in an orchestra on stage, or a basketball player playing in a game, or a person driving a car, with a person practicing a violin in their home, or practicing basketball in the gym, or learning to drive. The basketball player, the violinist, and the car driver – in the game, on the stage, or on the road -- are all operating in what we might call "auto-pilot". This is akin to fuzzy logic. These people are consciously engaged in their worlds and are making decisions, but the process is not thoughtful. Similarly, one might contrast fuzzy logic with the form of logic employed by a student sitting in a classroom listening to a lecture. The student in the classroom experiences him or herself as a student in the classroom. He or she is self-conscious of his or her behaviors as she or he is doing them. This is not the use of fuzzy logic; it is the use of formal ways of being.

For Bourdieu, the sociologist should not merely be oriented toward understanding the logic of practices. He should be seeking to understand the rules or the "generative principles" governing and producing these practices. These principles, he says, can be understood as unified, and when put into practice tend to produce or reproduce inequalities, or they may challenge these inequalities. "Practical logic ... is able to organize all thoughts, perceptions and actions by means of a few generative principles, which are closely interrelated and constitute a practically integrated whole ... (1990:86).

Another concept central to Bourdieu's theory is **reflexivity**. As noted above, Bourdieu rejects common Cartesian assumptions; he rejects the divide between agency and structure; and he rejects the notion that individuals can be understood if they are removed from their lived realities. Reflexivity is a concept that is built upon the rejection of these claims. Reflexivity is an important concept in much of contemporary sociological theorizing. This concept should not be confused with reflective. Being reflective means to think about what one is doing. Reflexivity is fundamentally different. Perhaps Anthony Giddens, a theorist we will discuss later in this chapter, describes it best when he says that social life is both a medium and an outcome. This is reflexivity. Social life is fundamentally different from the natural world. In the latter, one thing causes another to happen. The natural world is composed of things that mechanically act upon other things. The nature of things in the natural world is that they are passive, waiting to be acted upon, or perhaps mechanically doing what its genetic profile dictated. It is a world of Newtonian physics. As it is acting, the rock does not think about its actions. But in social life, humans simultaneously create their worlds through the process of creating their worlds. We live in and through time. We are producing a reality that is constantly producing itself. This is reflexivity: the very nature of our very being is that we are constantly creating our being.

Practices, and specifically reflexive practices, are enacted on fields. **Fields** are structured sets of relations based upon particular topics or discourses. There is the field of art, the field of science, the field of popular culture, of music, of popular music, of classical music. There is a field of sports, of biology, of politics, etc. But there are also "fields of production" and "fields of consumption" (1984). While Bourdieu seems to suggest that fields are concrete and material things, such as the field of higher education, it might be better to think of these not as domains anchored in specific places and times, but as anchored in relationships. One might be in the field of art in a museum while talking to others about the art one is observing, but one too is arguably in a field of art while sitting at a café talking to others about art. The field is the structured relations of objective positions in a particular discursive domain. Bourdieu compares fields to games, but he notes a key difference. A game is self-consciously created, and members self-consciously participate. In contrast, in social fields, a participant engages in it without much thought. The participation is more automatic.

Fields are not static; they are changing and changeable. Also, social actors participate in many different fields., and many fields overlap. It is through practices on the fields that inequality is or is not reproduced. There are inequalities within fields and these inequalities may echo broader inequalities in society. For example, those at the top end of the art field may be more likely to be at the top end of the economy. It is in and through fields that contests over the organization of inequalities occur. Bourdieu identifies fields as sites of conflicts. "The field is … a field of struggles" (1992:101). For him, social life is an endless series of "symbolic struggles" – for example through cultural tastes -- for positioning in systems of inequality as they are realized through particular fields. When persons at the upper end of a field engage in relations with persons at the lower end of a field and when both parties accept that the first person is and should be at the upper end and the other should be at the lower end, then there is no conflict. However, when persons at the lower end question or challenge the rightfulness of the claims made by the persons at the upper end, then there is contestations and reactions. For example, one might ask about art. Who decides in our culture what is good art and what is bad art? Who decides what art should or should not be placed in one of the great museums? It is the rich people's tastes that are reflected in the museums and not the tastes of the poor people. If one demonstrates a knowledge of high art and if one can discuss in intelligent ways how a work of art is good art, such as Marcel Duchamp's "fountain" (i.e. a mass-produced bathroom urinal), or how and why Andy Warhol's stack of Brillo Boxes is considered an art sculpture, then this gives one an advantage in the system of inequality reflected in the art field. One's tastes are in accord with the tastes of the rich, the powerful, those at the higher end of the systems of inequality. Conversely, how might a poor person explain such art? Their explanations, or lack of explanations perhaps in the form of derision, help reinforce their locations at the lower end of the system of inequality.

Habitus is the third key concept (in addition to practices and fields). People engage in practices on fields that either reproduce systems of inequality or challenge these systems. They do so through their habitus. One may think of the habitus as the set of mental or cognitive structures that allow individuals to understand their lived worlds, though it should not be taken as a psychological construct per se. (Bourdieu writes: "Through the habitus, the structure of which it is the product governs practice, not along the paths of a mechanical determinism, but within the constraints and limits initially set on its inventions. This infinite yet strictly limited generative capacity is difficult to understand only so long as one remains locked in the usual antinomies – which the concept of habitus aims to transcend – of determinism and freedom, conditioning and creativity, consciousness and the unconscious, or the individual and society" (1990:55).) The habitus consists of "schemas of perception, thought and action." It is an "acquired system of generative schemes" (ibid.:55) through which we make sense out of, and act in, our worlds. We should remember that Bourdieu is focused on lived experience. As such, the habitus exists in the individual's engagement in his or her world. It is located where the individual meets the world in real time. It is the "internalization of the external and the externalization of the internal." The habitus is a "structured structure" and a "structuring structure," to use Bourdieu's curious phrasings (ibid.:53). It is a "system of durable, transposable dispositions ... which generate and organize practices" (ibid.:53). The habitus consists of generative principles that allow the individual to understand his or her world. It is comprised of the assumptions, predispositions, judgments, expectations, etc. that individuals carry around with them that allow them to make sense of their worlds and to act in their worlds.

It is through endless exchanges between people that systems of inequality are produced and reproduced on fields as people engage with each other through their practices and their habitus. Exchange lies at the heart of these social interactions. When people interact with one another, they often if not typically engage in a process of exchange. (The idea of exchange is central to a form of sociological theory called exchange theory (see Chapter Ten). But exchange theories have nothing to do with Bourdieu's theorizing. While Bourdieu draws heavily upon the idea of exchange, his theory is unrelated to exchange theories as understood in sociology.) We might exchange money at a Starbuck's for a coffee. I give the person behind the counter at a store some money and he or she gives me the object I just purchased. We engage in exchanges throughout our interactions with others. But we might also exchange, or trade on, our educational degrees. If one had an M.D. or a Ph.D., the person may directly or indirectly, implicitly or explicitly use this in a process of exchange with others. Other people may defer to the person with an M.D. or the Ph.D.; people might listen to, believe, or respect, what this person is saying, not because the person actually knows what he or she is talking about, but because of his or her educational credentials. In this case, the credentials are being exchanged for deference or attention. Exchanges occur throughout daily life. I say, "thank you" and you say, "you're welcome". If I do a favor for someone, I might then say, "you owe me." Social life is filled with exchanges. In anthropology, for example scholars have written about dowries that are used in marriages; money, goats, and women for marriage are exchanged in some societies. Gifts, as noted earlier, are also often exchanged in traditional societies.

But what is it that is being exchanged? For Bourdieu, this is a central part of the theory. For him, what is being exchanged in daily life is one or another form of **capital**. When we engage in exchange we use capital in the process. He is here using the metaphor of the market exchange loosely as a basis for understanding all sorts of exchanges and for understanding the reproduction of inequality. Drawing on the above examples, we can see that there are all sorts of different types of capital, for example: money, educational credentials, compliments, gifts, a polite thank you, and so many more. These are all examples of capital. Capital is the medium of the basic forms of exchange which maintain or contests systems of inequality.

Bourdieu identifies four types of capital. **Economic capital** is the first. This consists of money and financial assets (e.g. stocks, property, etc.) that a person has and can use to engage in the system of inequality. It is the most obvious and clear form of capital. When people have a lot of economic capital, they can use it to help them maintain their high position in the system of inequality, and ultimately they can use it to maintain the system of inequality itself. A rich person, for example, can spend money to lobby politicians or to help politicians get elected. **Social capital** is the second form. Social capital is comprised of a person's social network or systems of relationships. If one has many friends in powerful positions, he or she will have more social capital than if a person does not have friends in powerful positions. Marrying someone in a higher status group than one's own is drawing upon social capital. Being associated with one or another club, organization, university that is held in high regard by others is also reflecting social capital. Another example: Is it really a coincidence that a huge percentage of undergraduates at Harvard University come from private, highly expensive and elite prep schools? People can "trade" on their connections and relationships to advance their interests.

Cultural capital is the third and perhaps most well-known of the types of capital. Cultural capital consists of knowledge or possession of culture that are deemed valuable in a society. It largely revolves around the notion of taste. Indeed, his book *Distinctions* (1984) is based on an empirical study he conducted that examined how different economic classes have different cultural tastes, and how these differences help to perpetuate inequality. It involves knowledge and judgements about what is or should be regarded as good tastes, whether in terms of art in a museum, clothing styles, the way one talks and walks, or the types of food one eats. There are three forms of cultural capital. *Embodied cultural capital* is the first. It is attached to the body. Tattoos, jewelry, the way someone walks, the way someone dresses, the way someone talks, are all forms of embodied capital. One is not likely to find someone speaking the slang of the working or poor classes in the board rooms of the major corporations in America today. For that matter, one is not likely to find tattoos or nose rings on the leaders of corporate America today. A person says something about themselves, about their class location, about their location in systems of inequality of all types, through their embodied capital; it helps locate them in the system of inequality. *Objectified cultural capital* is the second form. This is the concrete form of cultural capital. If someone owned an original painting by Picasso, they would have a high degree of objectified capital. Third, there is *institutionalized cultural capital*. This refers to such things as academic qualifications, degrees, etc. Having a Ph.D., as was suggested above, carries weight, even if the person having it does not know much. Moreover, people will often listen and take seriously the words spoken by someone with a Ph.D. or an M.D. even if that someone is speaking on a topic well outside their area of expertise. Having a degree from Harvard University, for example, carries more weight, e.g. has more institutionalized cultural capital, than having a degree from a public, regional university, even if the person who graduated from Harvard knows no more than the other person.

The fourth form of capital (after economic, cultural and social) is **symbolic capital**. Symbolic capital is based on such things as status, duty, honor, prestige, but it is also found in such things as the exchange of gifts or of other such things. Someone that is viewed highly by others can trade on this in his or her interactions. Having prestige gives someone a greater ability to get their way and have their thoughts listened to than otherwise. But it is more than honor and prestige. Symbolic capital consists of those things which are exchanged that have value other than material or economic value. Bourdieu distinguishes economic exchange from symbolic exchanges, i.e. exchanges of symbolic capital -- in *The Logic of Practice* (1990). In a chapter titled "Symbolic Capital" he illustrates this principle by contrasting it with economic exchange and with Marx's views of the universal primacy of economics in understanding the social world. Bourdieu draws upon examples from anthropology to note that people throughout history into the present routinely exchanged things symbolically, not for financial gain but for other reasons, such as for the maintenance of social order and/or the maintenance of a system of inequality. Symbolic exchanges such as gifts (with little or no monetary value) between tribes for example, could be used to solidify stable, peaceful relations between the groups (1990:114). The exchange of gifts in traditional societies "[transmutes] the inevitable and inevitably interested relations imposed by kinship, neighborhood or work, into elective relations of reciprocity, through the sincere fiction of a disinterested exchange, and, more profoundly, at transforming arbitrary relations of exploitation (of woman by man, younger brother by elder brother, the younger by the elders) into durable relations, grounded in nature" (ibid.:112) In short, symbolic exchange is or can be oriented toward the maintenance of social relationships and of social order, but it is also distinctly different from economic exchange (though Bourdieu does say there is a fundamental relationship between symbolic exchange and economic exchange).

One can see how these forms of capital can be and typically are used to maintain systems of inequality. The cultural tastes, the social connections, etc. that a person has will directly contribute to locating that person in a system of inequality and will help to maintain, or not, a system of inequality. Bourdieu introduces a number of other concepts that a relevant here to understand this. One of these is **symbolic violence**. This refers to the imposition of a way of being upon people in the lower ranks or lower positions in a society that lead them to believe the existing system of inequality, and their place in it, are right or just. If a poor person is taught in schools or in the museums that the best tastes in art are the tastes of the rich and powerful – as it is their tastes that are reflected in the museum's art, then the poor person likely will not criticize, will not even question, the legitimacy of the system of inequality. The person may accept this as fact. This is symbolic violence. But people do not always accept the world as it is. Sometimes people at the lower end of a system of inequality come to believe there is something wrong with the system. Bourdieu calls this **hysteresis**. In other words, it is possible for a person to have a habitus that does not allow them to passively accept the existing system of inequality. Hysteresis is having a habitus that does not fit one's existing place in the system of inequality. **Doxa** is another concept in the theory. Doxa is a belief system related to the existing system of inequalities. It is a belief system that leads to people passively and uncritically accepting as legitimate the system of inequality as it is. Bourdieu describes it as follows: "Doxa is the relationship of immediate adherence that is established in practice between a habitus and the field to which it is attuned, the pre-verbal taking-for-granted of the world that flows from practical sense" (1990:68). But sometimes the doxa is threatened. Sometimes people, particularly those in the lower positions in society, experience hysteresis. Sometimes they see the symbolic violence perpetrated against them, and sometimes they protest. They develop alternative and oppositional beliefs about the world, about the system of inequality, about how the world is and how it should be. Bourdieu calls this **heterodoxy**. Heterodox beliefs challenge the existing beliefs that support the existing systems of inequality. Yet when heterodox beliefs arise or when they may appear threatening to the existing system of inequality and ultimately to the interests of those at the top of this system, members of society may invoke **orthodoxy**. Orthodox beliefs are reactions in defense of the existing system in the face of challenges to it by heterodox beliefs.

Anthony Giddens

Giddens developed an approach called **structuration theory**. It is difficult to neatly locate his theory within any of the conventional theoretical models described in this book. Similarly, it is difficult to identify without ambiguity or contradiction the main influences upon his work. Some claim he was powerfully influenced by Marx (see Ritzer, 2014:511), though he was most certainly no Marxist. Others suggest he was more influenced by functionalism (see Delaney, 2014:207), though he also was most definitely no functionalist. He severely criticizes Marxism, functionalism, and many other major sociological approaches, and also challenges many of the conceptual bases of such approaches (1984). For example, he rejects conventional model building used by some if not many theorists. There is a long history of such model building in sociology. Parsons' structural functionalism is one such example. Giddens develops a highly eclectic theory whose framework cannot be easily identified with any existing approach. Perhaps his theory is best thought of to be loosely in the mold of Weber, and loosely influenced by a range of phenomenological and existential philosophies and social theories. Like Weber, he refuses to present a simple, unified, whole picture of society. Like Weber, he embraces the importance of history for sociology, and like Weber, Giddens rejects any sort of deterministic logic or direction to history. (In contrast, Marx, according to many does impose a logical course to history.) He is influenced by phenomenological and existential schools of thought in the importance he gives toward understanding how and why individuals assign meaning in their lived realities. Similarly, his theory embraces the reality of a dualism of social existence. The dualism consists of the fact that we live in and through time, and as such we are always being and becoming simultaneously.

> ### Anthony Giddens
>
> Anthony Giddens (1938-) is widely considered one of the more influential sociological theorists alive today. He was born in London, England and was raised in a lower-middle class family. He received his doctorate from Cambridge University and eventually became a professor at this same university. From 1997 through 2003 he was the director the London School of Economics. He has published numerous books and has also served as an editor for several academic publishing companies. In 1985 he cofounded the Polity Press, which has become an influential academic press in the social sciences. In the last several decades, he has become more involved in British politics, having been given a nobility title of Baron. As a result, he was appointed to the House of Lords (as a member of the Labor Party) in the British government in 2004.

Giddens' theorizing can be broken down into three parts. One part involves the description and explanation of the main elements of his social theory, i.e. his theory of structuration. The second part concerns his understanding of agency and practices. The third part involves the application of these elements to an understanding of modernity.

Concepts in Structuration Theory

The concepts of social system and structure are central to the theory of structuration. Giddens does not use these terms as most social theorists do. He assigns different meanings to them. When writing about a **social system** he is generally referring to what most sociologists would consider social structure. For example, institutions such as families and schools are social systems. Systems are "reproduced relations between actors or collectivities, organized as regular social practices" (1984:25). Similarly, the concept of **structure** is used in an unconventional manner. For him, structure is not a rigid thing existing independent of individuals, removed from time and space. "Structure," he says, "is not external to individuals" (1984:25). But at the same time, it is something that exists in more than one time and place. Giddens notes that "structure refers ... to the structuring properties which make it possible for discernibly similar social practices to exist across varying spans of time and space, which lend them "systemic" form" (1984:17). Structures are comprised of **rules** and **resources**. Rules are defined in a particular way. Rules are not like the written rules of a board game, nor are they self-conscious rules. Rules are rather implicit and often unnoticed guidelines that we use to navigate our immediate worlds. They are the unstated and perhaps unknown, at least without reflection, principles that guide our understandings and our behaviors in the immediate present. When we enter a familiar situation, we implicitly call up the rules to be followed in the situation. We tend not to do so self-consciously, but we do rely upon these to engage in our worlds. There are two types of rules: Normative rules and codes of signification. **Normative rules** are, as the term implies, rules governed by norms. We are ruled by countless norms each and every day. Some of these we could state, others we likely could not. **Codes of signification** refer to the systems through which meaning is produced. Language, for example, is one such system. Resources are things that can be used by someone engaged in social practices that gives a person "command" over people or things. There are two types of resources: Allocative resources and authoritative resources. **Allocative resources** "refer to capability ... generating command over objects, goods, or material phenomena" (1984:33). Owning a factory or having money are examples of allocative resources. **Authoritative resources** refer "to types of transformative capacity generating command over persons or actors" (1984:33). The ability to tell someone else what to do is an authoritative resource.

Giddens says there is a **duality of structure**. That is, structure is both the medium and the outcome of the practices "they recursively organize" (1984:25). We create social structures through our engagement in and through them in real time. Structure is not something we are simply poured into. It is not something imposed from the outside. Giddens here is demonstrating again a desire to overcome the conventional agency structure divide in social theory. The divide does not exist. As he notes, "the constitution of agents and structures are not two independently given sets of phenomena, a dualism, but represent a duality" (1984:25). It is through the use of rules and resources in our lived realities that we engage with and simultaneously create and recreate the social structure. Structure is also both constraining and enabling. It prevents us from doing some things, but at the same time it allows us to do other things.

Another central concept in the theory of structuration is **time-space distantiation**. Time and space were briefly touched upon above, and we will revisit these again when we discuss his theory of modernity. Here it is worthwhile to describe the concept, as it is central to his overall theory. Social action occurs in time and in space, but what is the relationship of time to social action? What is the relationship of space to social action? What is the relationship of time and space, and their combined relationship to social action? These are all questions that go to the heart of Giddens' thinking. Perhaps the easiest way of understanding what he is getting at here is to imagine and to compare the ways that time and space are related to people in a post-industrial society, such as the United States today, to people living in pre-modern societies, say a Native American living in a hunting and gathering society a thousand years before Columbus set foot in the New World. The two worlds are fundamentally different. Neither time nor space was rationally ordered into neat, equal segments in the Native American world. In America today we have seconds, minutes, hours, days, etc. Each second is the same length as each other second. Each minute is the same as each other minute. Similarly, space is space. For the Native Americans they likely engaged in a world in which the notion of time and space were intimately and inextricably interconnected. Their realities, their lived experiences, where such that time and space were bound to the immediate lived worlds. Time and space each have meaning in relation to the lived realities and experiences of the people. In the modern world, by contrast, time and space have been lifted from lived experience. Time and space have been abstracted from the world. Twelve inches is twelve inches no matter where or when the twelve inches is found. It is only by doing these abstractions can we have institutions replicated across time and space. A McDonald's is the same in California as it is in New York. One shopping mall is the same as another. One school is the same as another. The only way that institutions could exist in more than one particular time and place at a time is if time and space were lifted out of their immediate present. This is what Giddens means by time-space distantiation. It is, as we will see, a fundamental characteristic of the modern world.

Giddens takes these concepts and builds them into a model of structuration. **Structuration** refers to the social processes involved in the production and reproduction of social life. Toward that end, he describes and analyzes numerous other concepts and relates these to one another. These include descriptions and analyses of structures, of modalities of structuration, of social practices, and of institutional order. We can look at each of these in turn.

There are three "structural dimensions of social systems": signification, domination and legitimation. Signification refers to the realm of the symbolic world (Figure 11.2). It is the structuring of meanings through words and symbols. Domination is the "very condition of existence of codes of signification" (1984:31). It is the foundation for the power of signification.

Giddens' Three Structural Dimensions of Social Systems

Structure(s):	*Theoretical Domain:*	*Institutional Order:*
Signification	Theory of Coding	Symbolic orders/modes of discourse
Domination	Theories of resource authorization; Theories of resource allocation	Political Institutions/Economic Institutions
Legitimation	Theories of normative regulation	Legal Institutions

Source: Giddens, 1984:31

Figure 11.2

Moreover, domination is an inherent part of social life, and it depends upon allocative and authoritative resources. The structures of legitimation are those forces which compel people to follow the conventions of society, whether willingly or not. The modalities of structuration are the tracks, the channels, or the medium through which the structures are realized in lived practices. There are three modalities. The first is the interpretive schemes that people use to make sense out of their symbolic worlds, e.g. the world of language. It is through the modality of interpretive schemes that the structure of signification is realized in practice. The control over resources – both allocative and authoritative is the second modality. The control over resources ("facilities") allows one person or group of persons to assert domination and control over others. It is through the modality of norms that the structure of legitimation is realized. It is through particular forms of social practices that the three types of structures and the three modalities are enacted. Signification is realized through the social practices of communications. Domination is realized through power, and legitimation is found in social practices through the use of sanctions. Finally, particular institutional orders are associated with the structures, modalities, and social practices. The institutional order of the symbolic realm, e.g. modes of discourse, are where the social practices associated with the structures of signification are found. The institutional orders of the political and economic institutions are the site for domination, and the legal institutions are the institutional order where legitimation is located.

The three types of institutional orders as well as the three forms of structures, practices, and modalities are not rigidly distinct in practice.

Similarly, none of the three necessarily is automatically more primary than the others. Giddens is providing here a model that is fluid. Some realities are such that the symbolic order is dominant and perhaps saturate the political and economic institutions and legal institutions. However, other realities accord the political and economic institutions more prominence, with the other orders are influenced by, dependent upon, or saturated by the former. The point is that in realities these orders and their associated attributes are conceptual models that can be used to understand the world and should not be used to force fit an understanding of any one reality into the boxes of the model.

The Individual and Agency

Agency is another concept central to this theory of structuration. As was suggested above, one should not consider agency as separate from structure and structuration. Giddens' entire social theory is built from the ground up, that is, from first trying to understand the individual and his or her actions and only then building upon this to develop an understanding of the larger social situation. He is heavily influenced by a number of diverse approaches to understanding the individual, including: the philosophy of existentialism; some versions of the psychology of psychoanalysis; the sociological and philosophical approach of phenomenology; and some philosophies of language, most notably by that of the late Wittgenstein.

One of the themes in Giddens' views of the individual and agency is that individuals often do things that have unintended consequences and these unintended consequences often lead to social order. "[A]cts have unintended consequences ... and unintended consequences may systematically feedback to be the unacknowledged conditions of further acts" (1984:8). In this regard, he notes the difference between agency and intention and complains that many wrongfully combine these two ideas. People have agency. They are conscious and they make choices. People also have intentions. They are self-consciously directed to doing one or another thing. But agency and intentions are not the same thing: "Agency refers not to the intentions people have of doing things but to their capability of doing those things in the first place" (1984:9). As people go about their daily worlds employing agency, they may or may not intentionally produce the world that they live in. This is a central feature of the theory.

He identifies three forms related to consciousness. The first is the unconscious. We all have an unconscious, and we all do things for reasons that can be found there. The unconscious was a central element in the theory of psychoanalysis (though Giddens claims he is using the concept in a different way). Giddens recognizes the existence of the unconscious but does not focus much attention on this. He is far more concerned about the other two forms. These are practical consciousness and discursive consciousness. **Practical consciousness** is the consciousness we have in our day-to-day experiences. When we go about our worlds and do not stop to think about what it is we are doing or why we are doing, we are operating in practical consciousness. Practical consciousness is rooted in common sense, in the practical understandings and management of day-to-day existence. **Discursive consciousness** is consciousness that we are aware of when we are engaged in it. It is thoughtful, reflective behavior. Giddens describes some of the differences amongst the three forms of consciousness by using an example given by the social philosopher Stephen Toulmin:

> To use Toulmin's example, a businessman who obtains money on false pretenses from a client can be said to have engaged in "conscious and deliberate fraud." On the other hand, if the same consequence follows quite inadvertently from the activities of the businessman, without his being aware of it, he "unconsciously" becomes the instrument of the other's financial discomfiture. Here the agent has to "think" about what he or she is doing for the activity to be carried out "consciously." "Consciousness" in this sense presumes being able to give a coherent account of one's activities and the reasons for them. (1984:44-45)

The distinctions are important because much of our lives are spent engaged in practical consciousness, and it is practical consciousness that provides the groundwork for the establishment and maintenance of social order. How does practical consciousness relate to social order? To answer this, we need to look at Giddens' assessment and criticism of Robert Merton's functionalist understanding of action and social order (1984)(Figure 11.3). Merton uses an example of the Native American Hopi rain dance to illustrate his functionalist claims. The Hopi claim to do the dance because they believe it will produce much needed rain. But why do Native Americans do rain dances even if the dances do not produce rain most of the time? Why would they continue with this behavior? Merton argues, as functionalists do, that a social behavior that continues must serve some social function. In this case, the dance binds the community together. It fosters solidarity. The point here is that it is a functional consequence of the activity produced by a social need. Giddens rejects the functionalist reasoning and instead says the Hopi rain ceremony produces community, but it not because it is functional to do so. Instead, the Hopi engage in the rain dance (purposive action) and this leads to unintended consequences (community).

This formulation is directly related to his views on the three types of consciousness as well as to his concept of rules, noted earlier. The point is that people engage in common sense, practical behaviors on a day-to-day basis which can and often does lead to the creation and maintenance of stable social formations and social order. Social order is created not by self-conscious design, but as a by-product of people engaging in common sense

---

Giddens' Explanation vs Functionalist Explanations

Giddens' explanation:

Social activity – purposive behavior ⟶ unintended consequences

-Purposive behavior can produce social order even if unintended

Functionalist explanation:

Social activity – functional need ⟵ functional consequences

-Social order is produced, even if unintended, because it is needed

See Giddens 1984:294

Figure 11.3

realities. In sum, he believes that habits and routines are central to the creation of social order. The routinization of actions produces social order.

Another central concept in Giddens' thinking about the individual and agency is **ontological security**. There are two parts to this concept: ontology and security. The word ontology comes from philosophy and most notably from the branch of philosophy called existentialism. Ontology refers to the study of essences. What is the essence of a table? Of a smart phone? Of a person? What are the essential qualities or properties of such things? What makes a table a table, a phone a phone, a person a person? Ontology is the study of such things. In relation to humans, ontology within existentialism focuses on the meaning of human existence. What is the essence of our being? What is the essential meaning of being a human being? Why do you exist? Is there any point to this existence? Giddens uses the term security to refer to the idea of trust. People who are secure trust the world about them. They trust they understand who they are and what the world is. People have a need to feel psychological secure in their worlds, on a very basic level, on the level of ontological security. The sense of ontological security is or at least can be developed through child development as parents provide a trusting, safe environment for their children. The same is true of the adult world. We like routines and predictability because they foster ontological security. As he notes, "Since anxiety, trust and everyday routines of social interaction are so closely bound up with one another, we can readily understand the rituals of day-to-day life as coping mechanisms" (1991:46).

Modernity and Political Economics

As much as Giddens builds upon theories of agency and of the individual, he has focused equally if not more attention upon the large-scale issues of modernity and political economy. As part of this project, he identifies numerous themes that are characteristic of the modern period, i.e. the period he says we live in now. Several of these themes have already been touched upon above. The issues of time-space distantiation, ontological security, and issues related to trust, noted above, are central to modernity. As he notes, "The dynamism of modernity derives from the separation of time and space and their recombination in forms which permit the precise time-space "zoning" of social life." He writes:

> All pre-modern cultures possessed modes of the calculation of time. The calendar, for example, was as distinctive a feature of agrarian states as the invention of writing. But the time reckoning which formed the basis of day-to-day life, certainly for the majority of the population, always linked time with place – and was usually imprecise and variable. No one could tell the time of day without reference to other socio-spatial markers: "when" was almost universally either connected with "where" or identified by regular natural occurrences. The invention of the mechanical clock and its diffusion to virtually all members of the population (a phenomenon which dates at its earliest from the late eighteenth century) were the key significance in the separation of time from space. The clock expressed a uniform dimension of "empty" time, quantified in such a way as to permit the precise designation of "zones" of the day (e.g., the "working day"). (1990:17)

He goes on to note that the "emptying of time" was associated with the "emptying of space." This time-space distantiation is closely associated with another concept: the **disembeddedness** of the modern world. The world has become disembedded. Disembedding mean "the "lifting out" of social relations from local contexts of interactions and their restructuring across indefinite spans of time-space" (1990:21). In other words, the groundings of social life in traditional societies were local and particular. Individuals and social relations were anchored in the immediate social encounters of daily life. But in modernity, this grounding has disappeared. Meanings then are no longer derived from reference to immediate time and place, but to forces removed from this immediacy. For example, "Disembedded mechanisms ... remove social relations form the immediacies of context" (1990:28). The use of money is an example. Money is a medium of exchange that negates the importance of the immediate situation. Its meaning is located beyond the immediate. A dollar is a dollar is a dollar – whether in Phoenix, Detroit or Seattle. (Though Giddens does not focus upon the disembeddedness of self, other scholars have noted that this is also a central feature of modernity (see the writings of the philosopher Charles Taylor (2004)). In short, the foundations or anchors have been cut off from social life in the modern world.

Time-space distantiation and disembeddedness are closely related to the issue of trust. **Trust**, and the associated concepts of security and risk, are key concepts in any understanding of the modern world. Giddens notes that the "environment" of trust, that is, the major ways through which trust is anchored, is fundamentally different in pre-modern and in modern times. In pre-modern times, the environment of trust was rooted in things such as kinship relationships, in local communities, in religious cosmologies or belief systems, and in tradition. In the modern world, the environment of trust is rooted in personal relationships, abstract systems (such as science), and future oriented thought, which he contrasts with the focus on the past and tradition found in pre-modern societies (1990:102).

Reflexivity is another concept that is characteristic of the modern world. The concept of reflexivity was introduced earlier in Chapter Nine on micro-sociologies. It specifically is a key concept used in phenomenological sociology. Giddens as well as many other contemporary theorists, particularly European, have recognized reflexivity as a central element of the contemporary world (see Touraine, 1981; Beck, 1992). "The reflexivity of modern social life consists in the fact that social practices are constantly examined and reformed in the light of incoming information about those very practices, thus constitutively altering their character" (1990:38). One can think of student evaluations of professors that are administered routinely by universities as an example of this process. Similarly, it is quite common for web sites today to urge those who engaged with the site or those who bought something from the site to complete a survey questionnaire reporting on their experiences. Were you satisfied with the transaction? If not, why not? Our world today is filled with such mechanisms, whether they are the explicit requests to complete surveys or otherwise. All of these are intended to help the respective organizations work more effectively, whether it is a university or a business.

Giddens has written extensively on the topic of modernity and its relationship to political economic systems. He embraces democracy and believes it to be the best of the political opportunities available now. Yet this does not mean the formal democracy in practice in England or in the Western world today is the mode of political organization that should be embraced. Giddens believes in the importance of civil society, the sphere of social life, outside of the formal political and economic domains, in which citizens can engage with each other as active citizens to debate and decide upon matters of mutual concern. He is critical of conventional political parties in England and argues for a "third way." The existing parties are the conservatives and the Labor Party. (These are very loosely comparable to the American political parties of Republicans and Democrats, though in England each of the comparable parties is arguably to the left of the respective American parties. Indeed, historically, the Labor party was a social democratic party, i.e. a very progressive party with deep labor and socialist roots. This is something not found in the American Democratic Party.) Giddens complains that the two parties are wrongfully stuck in a debate between Old Left politics and "market fundamentalism." The Old Left believes that government is the solution to all problems, and that bigger government is better. Market fundamentalism, which is the mode of political thought that has come to dominate so much of American society in the last thirty years, is the idea that the capitalist marketplace is the best solution for all social issues and problems. As such, government should be small and government should attempt to use the model of the market in governmental policy making to address problems, from issues related to education to the funding of heath care to medical research. He calls for a "third way" that reconceptualizes the debate between the two parties. This third way is not a middle way, but one that reimagines the possibilities. He calls for a new understanding of politics, economics, and of civil society. Ultimately, he embraces a large governmental sector, but also strongly champions the need for a vibrant civil society. (Giddens served as an advisor to British Prime Minister Tony Blair, who was the leader of the Labor Party, and who famously called for the Labor Party to abandon its traditional social democratic orientation in favor of a less radical perspective. Blair in many respects was doing what Bill Clinton claimed to be doing with the American Democratic Party.)

Jurgen Habermas

Jurgen Habermas developed his theory of communicative action in response to his training in critical theory at the Frankfurt School. Like the Frankfurt School, Habermas' theory is intended to be critical and emancipatory. His theory is highly critical of modern, rational capitalism, but as we see below his criticisms are very different from those offered by the Frankfurt School. It also seeks to be emancipatory. Habermas believes that theory can and should be used to change the world. He was oriented toward developing a theory that could and should be put into practice, and that practice should be oriented toward addressing and overcoming the fundamental problems identified with modern, rational capitalism. His project sought to fulfill the goals of the Enlightenment Project. He did not wish to abandon the fundamental claims of the Enlightenment (as some other recent theories, such as postmodernism. have sought to do (see Chapter Twelve)). The Enlightenment elevated reason to a place of central importance. It also elevated the value of the individual. Moreover, it led to the creation of modern democracy and the spread of the values of equality and liberty. These are all things that Habermas embraces. However, his critical analysis of capitalism shows that the Enlightenment Project has been perverted, largely as the result of rationalization and capitalism. The task then is to theorize how this situation has come about, and to theorize what should be done.

Habermas had some major differences with his teachers at the Frankfurt School. For example, the influence of Marx, which was so present in the

Jurgen Habermas

Jurgen Habermas (1929-) is one of the most prominent and influential theorists alive today. He was born in Dusseldorf, Germany. He was raised in a Protestant household. His father was the director of the Cologne Chamber of Commerce and was a Nazi sympathizer in the 1930s. Jurgen was enrolled as a child into the Hitler Youth after Hitler came to power. After the war, Habermas earned his doctorate in philosophy from the University of Bonn. In the 1950s he continued his studies under Horkheimer and Adorno and was associated with the Institute for Social Research (The Frankfurt School). He soon developed intellectual disagreements with the members of the Frankfurt School, believing in part that they were too cynical. He was a professor at the University of Heidelberg and then became chair of philosophy and sociology at Frankfurt in 1964. From there, he assumed the directorship of the Max Plank Institute in Starnberg (near Munich) in 1971. Then in the early 1980s he returned to the Institute for Social Research in Frankfurt to become its director. He retired in 1983, though he continues to publish and to give lectures and to speak out on matters of public concern.

writing of the Frankfurt School, declined tremendously in Habermas' writings. But the greatest difference between them lies in their focus. The Frankfurt School were largely focused upon understanding culture, specifically from a neo-Marxist perspective. That is, in one way or another, they subscribed to Marx's base superstructure model of culture, ideology, reification, etc. In contrast, Habermas focused on communication. He developed a theory of language, signs, and communications that could explain how the world works, and that could help people develop practices that could address and combat the negative forces of modernity (e.g. rationalization, capitalism, etc.).

Habermas has been influenced by many different intellectual perspectives. In addition to Marx (though he certainly is not a Marxist or neo-Marxist), he also is greatly influenced by Weber. Echoes of Weber's theory of rationalization can clearly be heard loud in both the Frankfurt School's theorizing as well in Habermas'. Habermas' approach also is not radically at odds with Weber's epistemological perspective, that is, with his theory about how a sociologist should go about understanding the world. Habermas was also greatly influenced by several American theorists and philosophers. One can see the influences of Parsons' theorizing in many parts of Habermas' theorizing, though of course the latter rejects many aspects of Parsons' theory as well, including the functionalist reasoning at its heart. Parsons' (and his students) conceptualization of systems and of social models can be seen in Habermas' theory. Symbolic interactionism also had a great impact upon Habermas. His overall theory of communication is greatly indebted to some of the main claims of symbolic interactionism, of Mead and the pragmatists. Relatedly and perhaps most significantly, Habermas was greatly influenced by language philosophy (as well as the philosophy of being and consciousness found in Germany), both those that emerged in Europe (and specifically Germany) and those that emerged in the United States. As communication became the central focus of his work, he sought to understand how language works in this process in the social world.

Communication and Understandings

More specifically, it is at the intersection of communication and rationality that Habermas focused his attention. He believes that at the heart of the concept of communication is the desire for understanding. When one party communicates with another, there is the implication that these parties are trying to understand each other. At least, this is the point of communication. As we see below, one of his concerns is that the ability to effectively communicate, i.e. to understand one another, in the world today has increasingly become problematic, due to large-scale forces of rationalization, the advances of capitalism, etc. Communication not only entails understanding, it also is deeply connected with rationality. "Communicative actions always require an interpretation that is rational in approach" (1984:106). The terms communication and rationality (and communicative rationality) are far more complex than might be suggested from the above.

And indeed, Habermas spends considerable time analyzing these terms. He does so with the intent of critically evaluating the modern world. That is, he seeks to understand how genuine rational, communication has become difficult to realize in the world today – in rational capitalism, and he seeks to know what people could do to realize this genuine communication today.

Habermas describes and analyzes three worlds as a key part of his theory to explain the ways in which rational capitalism affects the individual. Toward that end, he draws upon German philosophy and the notion of three worlds. We exist and live simultaneously in three worlds. The objective world is one of these. We must engage with objective realities that are independent of us in our daily lives. It is a reality that we have to manage to live in a world that has gravity, in a world in which water freezes at thirty-two degrees, in a world in which the sun rises and sets. This world operates under scientific laws independent of humans. The second world is the world of the social. Our world as humans is comprised of other humans. We are fundamentally social. It will be recalled that Habermas believes we naturally are inclined to seek understanding. The very use of language is based upon this assumption. The social world operatives under different sets of rules than does the objective world, and therefore our orientations to it are different. The third world is the subjective world. As humans, we necessarily engage with our selves as we live. We live in our individual worlds through which we assign meaning to it.

He devotes considerable time describing crucial differences between these three worlds (Figure 11.4). For example, he describes different forms of interest, knowledge and action associated with the three worlds. What is the interest one has when one engages in the objective world? It is a practical and instrumental interest. It is an objective interest to know that gravity exists, to know that water freezes at thirty-two degrees, and that the sun rises in the morning. I have an interest in understanding the objective realities of the world, if for no other reason than for survival. In the social world, I have an interest in coordinating my behavior with that of others. Toward that end, I have an interest in understanding how others act and I have an interest in cooperating with others. I also have an interest in the subjective world in emancipation, in being free and autonomous. Similarly, there are three forms of knowledge. Habermas calls the forms of knowledge of the objective world "empirical/analytic knowledge." This is basically the knowledge of the hard sciences, such as chemistry and physics and biology. It is the knowledge based upon conventional, positivist science. When a chemist does an experiment, he produces knowledge about the chemical world. In contrast, the knowledge produced by people in the humanities, such as historians and art professors, is what Habermas calls interpretive/hermeneutic knowledge. The art professor has knowledge about Picasso's art, and has knowledge about particular paintings by Picasso, but the form of knowledge he or she has here is different than that of the chemist. The knowledge is based upon interpretation. The art professor does not do a scientific experiment upon the Picasso painting to know what it means. Instead, he bases his understanding on knowledge of the background of Picasso, of the background of the art fields and traditions within it, and of art history. In the social world, the

Habermas – Summary of the Theory of Communicative Action

Worlds of Experience	Types of Interests	Types of Knowledge	Types of Action	Validity Claims
Objective World	Instrumental	Empirical/ Analytic	Teleological/ Instrumental	Truth
Subjective World	Practical/ Common Sense	Interpretive/ Hermeneutic	Expressive/ Dramaturgical	Truthfulness / Sincerity
Social World	Cooperation	Social Coordination	Strategic/ Normatively Regulated	Legitimacy/ Normative Agreement
Lifeworld	Meaning/ Emancipation	Critical	Communicative Action	Truth/ Sincerity/ Legitimacy

Figure 11.4

knowledge is of a different order. The knowledge is of the normative expectations. To navigate in the social world, one must have an understanding of the manner in which others will evaluate one's behavior. There is a moral component to this dimension. In addition to different types of interest and knowledge, there are also different forms of action associated with the different worlds. Action in the objective world is instrumental or teleological. Teleological action means that there is a pre-set mode of operating based upon logic that one employs. One simply and mechanically identifies the goals and the logical means of reaching the goals and then acts accordingly. The subjective world demands expressive or dramaturgical forms of action. This is action that is oriented the individual doing things to put forth an understanding of who he or she is in the specific setting in which he or she is acting. Here one is engaged in creative, expressive activities. In contrast, the social world revolves around normatively regulated action. The actor strategically assesses his or her social environment and assesses what is and what is not socially appropriate and acts accordingly.

(It should be noted that while Habermas describes these three worlds, he often describes them in different ways. One of the distinctive elements of this theorizing is that it constantly evolved throughout his life. When he read something new that he thought was of value, he would modify his theorizing and incorporate it. In terms of his model of three worlds, he sometimes locates elements of things such as morality and the concept of dramaturgy in different places. Above, for example, I note that the subjective world consists of dramaturgical action. Yet at times, Habermas suggests it is better to think of dramaturgical concepts as elements of the social world rather than the subjective world. At times, he identifies the concept of "presentation of self" as an element of the social world. The concepts of presentation of self and dramaturgy are of course directly taken from Goffman's theorizing. All of this makes for a precise understanding of the particulars of his theory a bit difficult. Nevertheless, whatever one's interpretation of the particulars the overall outline remains the same.)

Habermas also discusses a fourth, all-important "world." This is the lifeworld. The **lifeworld** is a concept taken from phenomenology (specifically from the founder of phenomenology, the German philosopher Husserl). The lifeworld is the composite of background assumptions we carry with us that allow us to understand the world (or any or all of the three worlds). It is comprised of bundles of patterns that allow us to comprehend the world: "We can think of the lifeworld as represented by culturally transmitted and linguistically organized stocks of interpretive patterns" (1987b:124). He writes: "Subjects acting communicatively always come to an understanding in the horizon of a lifeworld. Their lifeworld is formed from more or less diffuse, always unproblematic, background convictions. This lifeworld background serves as a source of situation definitions that are presupposed by participants as unproblematic" (1987a:70). The lifeworld then is the bedrock of understanding.

Another concept he uses is the **ideal speech situation**. This is a concept he takes from language philosophy. The ideal speech situation, for Habermas, is one in which the conditions have been met to allow for genuine communication between people. As the desired goal of humanity is to seek understanding and ultimately agreement, then the goal is also to realize the ideal speech situation, as this is where such understandings could arise. We can now relate the three worlds to the ideal speech situation that Habermas is looking for. It is important to note that for him an ideal speech situation is one that includes among other things the possibilities of critique. If a claim is not and cannot be criticized, then an ideal speech situation does not exist. What conditions are required in the respective worlds for an ideal speech situation to occur? There are three conditions or **validity claims** that need to be met, one for each world, in order for the conditions for an ideal speech situation to be met. Specifically, there are three "criticizable validity claims." That is, the basis for determining whether one is engaging properly in the respective worlds differs from one world to the next. The validity claim for the objective world is truth. When one is operating in the objective world, the key determinant should be the factual understanding of the objective world. One should base one's actions on an assessment of what is true versus what is not true. The validity claim for the subjective realm is sincerity or truthfulness. One is engaged in an autonomous, responsible, and free manner when one is being sincere in one's actions. The validity claim for the social world is legitimacy. By this he means that the "normative validity of a command" is deemed appropriate and legitimate. As Habermas notes, "The validity of the propositional content of an utterance depends ... on whether the proposition stated *represents* a fact (or whether the existential presuppositions of a mentioned propositional content hold); the validity of an intention *expressed* depends on whether it corresponds to what is actually intended by the speaker; and the validity of the utterance performed depends on whether this action *conforms* to a recognized normative background" (quoted in Held, 1980:334).

Again, when the three validity claims are simultaneously met for the three worlds, an ideal speech situation arises. Habermas looks to this situation as the one we should be striving to realize in practice. The lifeworld is associated with this ideal speech situation. It is through the lifeworld that we are able to enact this ideal situation. It is through the lifeworld that people can, at least possibly, engage with other people in genuinely human ways. It is through the lifeworld that people can engage with others as fully human. This brings us to one of the most central concepts in his theory: Communicative action. Communicative action is action that is oriented toward understanding. It stands in contrast to the actions found in the three worlds describe above – the objective, social, and subjective worlds – in that it is more foundational. Communicative action is oriented toward "reaching understanding." "The negotiation of definitions of the situation is an essential element of the interpretive accomplishment required for communicative action" (1987a:286). Communicative action is associated with the lifeworld and can be realized only in an ideal speech situation.

History and Society

Thus far, we have been describing his rather abstract theory about communication. This is the starting point, rather than the end point of the theory. Habermas connects all of the above to his theorizing about history. He connects the above with history and with an analysis of social structures.

We begin with history, then turn our attention to his theorizing about the lifeworld and the system. Habermas focuses on modern history. He identifies two major periods of modern, rational capitalism. The first is liberal capitalism; the second is organized capitalism. With the emergence of liberal capitalism in the early modern era, can the emergence of the modern nation state. During the preceding period of feudalism, nation states as we know them did not exist. The nation state and capitalism emerged on the backs of the Enlightenment, and with all of the values associated, including liberty and equality, and democracy. Capitalism also emerged within the context of Protestantism and the Industrial revolution. The Enlightenment values combined with Protestant values contributed to the growth of the values of individualism and the work ethic. Of note, it was in this period of liberal capitalism that the state became distinct and separate from the economy, in contrast to the feudal period. Moreover, the state was not involved in the economy during the liberal capitalist period.

All of this together led to several major changes, including the depoliticizing of the class conflict, and the rise of the public sphere. Marx of course saw the class conflict as essentially a political contest, or at least one that would lead to a political context. Habermas, on the other hand, argues that the class conflict was depoliticized because of the forces that produced a distinction between the state and the economy. As a result, capitalism was able to manage the essential conflicts regarding labor. Liberal capitalism also produced the public sphere, a central concept in Habermas' theory as we see below. The public sphere is technically not a place. It is a domain through which people can discuss matters of mutual concern outside of the major economic and political spheres. The public sphere is the domain in which people criticize one or another aspect of society, and debate issues of politics or social concern. Basically, it largely consists of those domains of public life that are social and that are not part of the economic or political realms. Voluntary associations, such as the parent teachers' association or the Knights of Columbus, bowling leagues, the Boy Scouts, religious organizations, civic organizations, etc., are all part of the public sphere (compare to Tocqueville; see Chapter Six). Importantly, so too is the media part of the public sphere. It is in and through the media that the public can engage in honest debate and discussions of matters of mutual concern. The public sphere emerged in the period of liberal capitalism.

Liberal capitalism gave way to organized capitalism in the twentieth century. Organized capitalism produced a new set of economic and political dynamics, which fundamentally altered the relationship of the state to the economy. Organized capitalism, particularly in the early nineteen hundreds increasingly produced monopolies within the economy. Corporations, from steel, to oil, to the railroads, increasingly became consolidated in the hands of one company or one group of companies cooperating with one another. A second economic issue involved the boom and bust economic cycles that were part of capitalism in the eighteen and early nineteen hundreds. Together, these things led to states becoming increasingly involved in the economic arena, which they continue to be to this day. The state became involved in the early nineteen hundreds in breaking up the monopolies through legislative and court actions. The state also became involved in managing the economic cycles of boom and bust, and of providing for the needs of the public in economic down turns. There is no better example of this than Roosevelt's New Deal programs to combat the Great Depression of the nineteen thirties. All of this produced a much larger state and a state which increasingly was tasked with providing for the needs (social, health, education, etc.) of its citizenry.

The Lifeworld and System

In keeping with his desire to explain the workings of modern, rational capitalism and of understanding how this system impacts individuals, social relations, and society in general, Habermas draws upon the evolutionary models developed by scholars like Parsons. While Habermas certainly rejected many of the questionable assumptions made by the structural functionalist Parsons, such as the claims related to functionalist reasoning, he nevertheless found much of value in Parsons' theorizing. Habermas embraces the claim that history can be characterized by growing complexity, by differentiations of component parts, and by the needs for mechanisms of integration. Much like the human being, in both its physical and psychological elements, is more complicated than an ameba or some other one cell creature, so too is modern society more complex than traditional societies. Similarly, there are more specialized and distinct parts in modern societies than there are in traditional societies. There is an increased division of labor. In all societies, as Parsons argued, there is a need for mechanisms that integrate the different parts of the society, if the society is going to be able to survive. The family unit has to be integrated somehow, for example, with the economic structures of a society.

Habermas starts here and identifies two major forms of integration: Social integration and system integration. Each society has to develop a means by which interpersonal relations manage to go on smoothly, and it has to develop a means of communications and coordination. This is social integration. Each society also has to develop a means by which institutional structures, such as the economy, is able to effectively work with the other institutional structures. This is system integration. He builds upon this conceptualization and upon his earlier formulations and identifies two key component parts of society: The lifeworld and the system. We have already discussed the lifeworld above. This is the domain of social life through which people can engage with others as people. It is the domain through which people can engage in communications and in which people can strive for understandings. The main vehicles through which people engage in the lifeworld are communication and ultimately language. The **system** is the term used to describe the large-scale, institutional forces in society. The two main components of the system are the economy and the state (or the political realm), and each has its own steering mechanism. **Steering mechanism** is a term Habermas uses to describe the main medium through which the parts of the system act, and it is the medium through which one part interacts with other parts. Much like a steering wheel on a car, the steering mechanisms of the system direct the economy and politics in one way or another. In the economic arena the steering mechanism is money; in the political arena the steering mechanism is power. Money and power are the media through which the economic and political systems assert themselves in society.

In traditional societies, e.g. pre-modern societies, the lifeworld and system were not separated, at least not separated anywhere as much as they are today. They were more or less integrated. Habermas says the modern world has brought about an **uncoupling of the lifeworld and system**. The two domains have become formally distinct in the practices of modern capitalism today. This produces a need for some mechanism by which the two domains are integrated with each other. For society to survive, the two must be integrated. Habermas would like the media of the lifeworld to be the vehicle of integration between the system and lifeworld. Language, communication, and the desire for understandings, could conceivably be the link between the two. That is, communicative action could conceivably be the mechanism by which the lifeworld relates to, impacts, shapes the system. However, he says something else has occurred. The media of the system, e.g. money and power, have become the link between the lifeworld and the system. These mechanisms allow the economy and political arenas to dominate the lifeworld. In other words, there has been a **colonization of the lifeworld**. The rational principles underlying the system and specifically the workings of the steering mechanisms of power and money are imposed upon the lifeworld. This is done largely through rationalization, and through the use of technology. There has been a **technicizing of the lifeworld** (1984). All of this is quite alarming for Habermas. The human element of society is being suffocated by the rationalizing, technologizing elements of money and power. One can hear clear echoes of Weber's theory of rationalization here, as well as Marx's concerns about the oppressive nature of capitalism.

In addition to his concerns about the colonization of the lifeworld, Habermas was particularly concerned about what we might call the colonization of the public sphere. The public sphere is of great importance for democracies, according to him. It is the public arena which is supposed to mediate between the state and society. In a democracy, citizens are supposed to engage with each other in "rational discussions," conversations, disagreements, etc. in public arenas. With the rationalization of society and the colonization of the lifeworld comes the conquest of the public sphere. In contemporary capitalism, Habermas argues the possibilities that people can honestly engage in the public sphere in truly democratic ways has been severely limited. Whether it is through the use of polling data or through manipulations of campaigns, meaningful public discussions of political issues have become almost impossible. Instead, these discussions are technologically managed. Politicians run for elections using the model of branding and commodities. They sell themselves like candy bars. Instrumental rationality driven by power and money have perverted the possibilities of the public sphere. All of this leads to **systematically distorted communications**. Our abilities to engage with others through communicative action has been cut off as the result of the technological and rationalized structures that shape the communications. Capitalism and rationality have combined to produce technologies that facilitate communications, for example, social media and the internet, but they have done so in a way that serves the needs and interests of the system, i.e. the economic and political realms, and not genuine human needs.

The Legitimation Crisis

In his book *Legitimation Crisis* (1975) and elsewhere, Habermas argues that modern rational capitalism produces numerous contradictions. Some of these can be managed to one degree by existing social arrangements, others he suggests cannot be. Most of these contradictions arise within or between three systems: the economic, the political, and the socio-cultural. He described a number of economic and rationality crises that arise in the economic and political arenas. For example, capitalism is an economic system that is anarchic in nature. It requires and produces chaos. It requires the lack of constraint for it to work. At the same time, this anarchy, this chaos, produces economic crises, such as boom and bust economic cycles and other such things that must be managed. The state increasingly is called upon to insert itself ever more as a managing agent of the economy. As such, one the one hand, capitalism requires unconstraint, but it produces a need for the state to constrain it. For example, the Great Depression which began in 1929 and continued through the 1930s arguably was a product of capitalism's excess. Roosevelt's New Deal greatly enlarged the role of the state in managing the economy. Roosevelt passed many measures to regulate the economy. It is not simply the New Deal that grew the government. Modern capitalism requires numerous and increasing things from the government. It requires the government to provide funds for education, particularly for higher education. It requires the government to provide basic needs for its citizens, from health care to welfare. It requires a large regulatory role. The growth of the state in America and in other industrial countries through the rest of the twentieth century suggests a recognition of this need for the state to manage the economy. Yet at the same time, capitalism demands freedom of the market, and demands the chaos that comes with it.

Habermas is more concerned about the "identity crises" which arise in the political and socio-cultural arenas. Specifically, a legitimation crisis arises in the political arena, and a motivational crisis arises in the socio-cultural arena. David Held, in his book on critical theory, describes the legitimation crisis:

> As the administrative system expands in late capitalism into areas traditionally assigned to the private sphere, there is a progressive demystification of the nature-like process of social fate. The state's very intervention into the economy, education, etc., draws attention to issues of choice, planning and control. The "hand of the state" is more visible and intelligible than "the invisible hand" of liberal capitalism. More and more areas of life are seen by the general population as politicized, as falling within its (via the government's) potential control. This development, in turn stimulates ever greater demands on the state. If the administrative system cannot fulfill these demands within the potentially legitimating alternatives available to it, while at the same time avoiding economic crisis, that is, "if government crisis management fails ... the penalty ... is the withdrawal of legitimation. (1980:291)

This is associated with a number of forces that produces a motivational crisis. For example, this crisis revolves around the contradictions between the autonomous, independent self that is produced and demanded by democratic capitalism and the needs for a state that becomes a larger technocratic manager of society and of individuals in the society. The individual is required in democratic capitalism to be a choice maker, but now the choices are managed, manipulated by the technological forces found in the economy and in the state.

Summary

This chapter describes three recent integrative theories. These theories try to conceptually bridge the gaps between the macro and the micro, and agency and structure. Bourdieu develops a theory of the logic of practice which is focused upon explaining the reproduction of inequality. Many say the theory is structural in orientation, but Bourdieu argues his theory has successfully overcome the divide between agency and structure. Three central concepts are habitus, fields and practices. Inequalities are reproduced (or not) through people employing their habitus in and on fields through practices. Inequality is reproduced or challenged as the result of the use of different forms of capital: economic, social, cultural, and symbolic. Giddens is associated with structuration theory. This theory builds upon innovative ways of conceptualizing social system, structure, rules and resources. Structuration theory says there is a duality of structure. Structure is simultaneously both a medium and an outcome. Three forms of consciousness are identified: practical, discursive, and the unconscious. Practical consciousness (which is similar to Bourdieu's concept of fuzzy logic) is key to understanding social behavior and social order. Giddens develops a theory of modernity which asserts that a number of concepts are central to the understanding of the world today. These include: ontological security; disembeddedness; time-space distantiation; trust; and reflexivity.

Habermas develops a form of critical theory which could be called the theory of communicative action. He was a student of the Frankfurt School, but disagreed with some of the claims of the School, and eventually developed his own independent theory. Habermas was influenced by many different theories, including language philosophies, Parsons' structural functionalism, symbolic interactionism, and Weber and Marx's theories. Habermas was concerned about the harmful and dehumanizing effects of rational capitalism and wished to develop a theory that could lead to changes which addressed these effects. He located communication and understanding, particularly as these things occur in language, at the heart of the theory. The theory builds on the realities of three worlds of experience: the objective, subjective and social worlds. Different types of knowledge, interests and actions are associated with the three worlds, and different types of validity claims which determine the correctness of these knowledge, interests and actions in the three worlds are described. The validity claims are truth, sincerity and legitimacy. The lifeworld is a fourth world. It is more foundational. It is through the lifeworld that individuals experience their worlds. For a genuine lifeworld to exist, i.e. for conditions that allow for full humanity to exist, the validity claims of the three other worlds must simultaneously be present. Habermas also provides a theory of history in which he identifies two periods of capitalism: liberal and organized. Class conflict was a central form of conflict during the period of liberal capitalism but was eventually tamed or managed due to a number of sociological factors, including the separation of the economic and political realms. The central point of conflict in the period of organized capitalism then shifts to other areas of social life, instead of economics. Concerns related to identity and culture and the environment now assume greater importance. New social movements arise, rather than class based movements, as a result. Habermas also creates a model of contemporary society that has two parts: the lifeworld and the system. He argues that the lifeworld has been colonized by the system. The lifeworld has two parts: the private and public sphere. The system has two parts: the economy and the political arena. The economy and political arenas are directed by the steering mechanisms of money and power, and these steering mechanisms have imposed themselves on the lifeworld, particularly on the public sphere. They have been colonized. This leads to systematically distorted communications, and it prevents people from being fully human. Habermas calls for the embrace and practice of communicative action to combat these forces. He also sees a legitimation crisis occurring in rational capitalism as a result of the above forces.

Discussion Questions

1. Scholars have criticized Habermas' ideas related to communicative action. They have sometimes said that his proposals to create a better society are vague and unclear. For example, what exactly would a society look like that embraces communicative action? Would it be democratic? Capitalist? What do you think Habermas would say here? What sort of world does Habermas hope to see? Is it realistic or not? Why or why not?

2. A question about Bourdieu's theory that some students have -- but are often unwilling to ask due to the fear of a negative reaction they might get if they asked it -- concerns the reasons for ongoing inequalities between groups, such as racial and gender groups. Specifically, some students might be inclined to reject Bourdieu's theory and instead embrace a biological theory of inequality. That is, some groups or richer than others due to innate, biological advantages. Some groups may be genetically assigned higher intelligence, than others, for example. This, of course, is a very emotionally charged type of statement, one that ultimately is based on traditional and classic forms of racism, sexism, etc. (Such forms are still around today, for example, one could look at Herrnstein and Murray's book *The Bell Curve*.) The question is: What would Bourdieu likely say in response to critics who say that the reason inequalities are reproduced is because of biology and not because of sociological factors?

3. What is the difference between Habermas' concept of the lifeworld and Bourdieu's concept of habitus? Describe the similarities and differences between the two concepts.

Chapter Twelve: Postmodern Theories

Is professional wrestling fake? Of course, everyone knows now that it is fake. But does it matter that it is? Does it really matter? The World Wrestling Entertainment (WWE), run by Vince McMahon and his family, has been around since the 1950s. Prior to the late 1980s, it carefully sought to create the image and the illusion that the wrestling matches were real, and not fake. But in 1989 the company, as a result of pressures from the government and elsewhere, had to admit the matches were not real. The company changed its name from the World Wrestling Federation to the WWE at that time. McMahon acknowledged for legal reasons that wrestling was not sport but entertainment. One could only imagine that he must have been concerned then about the future of the business. The business until then was supported in large part by the uncertainty in the mind of the audience over whether the matches were real or fake. That was part of its allure. Now that it was clear and official that the matches were staged, the uncertainty was gone. How was the business going to be able to continue, and how was it now to be successful when everyone now knows the matches are fixed? Yet something curious happened. No one cared. People continued to attend the matches and to watch on television (and online). Indeed, the fan base grew and grew. No one seemed to care whether it was real or fake. One could find articles in respected newspapers, to this day, wondering whether this or that retired professional wrestler was going to be admitted to the WWE Hall of Fame. In these articles, there were reports of how many world titles the wrestler had won, implying that the wins were real and admittance to the Hall of Fame was based upon real competitions. They of course were not. Professional wrestling seemingly can be both real and fake at the same time. The WWE now is a huge, publicly traded stock company. (His wife, Linda McMahon, who is a big supporter of Donald Trump, was appointed by Trump when he was president to lead a governmental agency.) It is more successful than it has ever been.

The blurring of the line between what is real and what is not real is no more apparent than in the words and actions of Donald Trump. He repeatedly says things that are not true. (Whether he knows these things to be untrue or whether he is delusional -- or whether he embodies some sort of hybrid form of delusional lying -- is a legitimate question for debate – a debate which has sadly not occurred.) The first four years of the Trump Administration was largely based upon endless distortions and lies and this has continued in his second term. His repeated claims of "fake news" captures this. (The attack on the press is not new. Many authoritarian leaders have done the same. Adolf Hitler, for example, often complained about the "lugenpresse," i.e. lying press.) Even though the vast majority of news stories in the mainstream press were not fake in any meaningful way, Trump said they were and he convinced millions of Americans that they were. (Sadly, in his second term the mainstream media has become far less critical and far more deferential to Trump's delusions and lies, a reality that does not bode well for the maintenance of a stable democracy.) Baudrillard and other postmodernists might say such things are an indication of the times within which we live.

What does this have to do with sociological theory? Plenty. It captures one of the many themes found in postmodern sociological theory – particularly the version developed by Jean Baudrillard, which is one of the approaches covered in this chapter. Postmodern theory, while incredibly diverse, generally shares the claim that the world today is fundamentally different from the world of one hundred years ago. The modern, industrial world has given way to the postmodern, post-industrial world, and with this has come many fundamental changes. One of these concerns the relationship of appearance to reality, of signs to what it is they represent. In earlier times signs drew their meanings from the things they represented. But now, some postmodern theorists, such as Baudrillard (see below), argue the meaning is no longer drawn from the reality of things. We are lost in a sea of signs, and these signs produce meanings by themselves, independent of the realities they supposedly reference. Much like it does not matter whether WWE is real or fake, our world is awash with signs that operate in the same way. I think of another old television show here: Jerry Springer. Real or fake? Does it matter? How about reality television shows? Real or Fake? But I also think of things perhaps that are more serious and are perhaps thought to be more real. I think of recent wars that the United States has been involved. American generals appear on television and provide briefing to the American people on the precision of the war's execution. They stand in front of computer monitors with videos showing precise missiles striking their targets. Never missing. It is antiseptic. It is emotionally numbing. War looks like a video game. Is it a video game? Real or fake? This is just another of the sets of provocative claims of postmodern theory.

The term postmodern theory is a catch-all term. It refers to many different and conflicting theories that many have placed under its name, though many of the theorists themselves reject such a label. The term is confusing as a result of this. It is also confusing because it is associated with some other theories, such as post-structuralism and deconstruction, which are arguably different from each other and which many of their proponents argue are different from what is called postmodern theory. Nevertheless, despite these difficulties, we are here lumping together a number of theories and theorists under the heading of postmodern social theories and, included in this are post-structural and deconstruction theories.

The term postmodern theory is also confusing because the term **postmodern** refers to different and contradictory things. Specifically, it is used to designate a particular style of cultural production, such as a style of art or architecture. One might look at a building and say it is in the architectural style of postmodernism, in contrast to gothic, or modern, etc. Alternatively, postmodern is also used to refer to a historical period, a period of postmodernity which is said to have followed the modern era. Postmodern has also been used to describe a type of social theorizing which is distinct from other types of theorizing described in this book, almost all of which may be called forms of modern social theory.

A few more words should be said on these three understandings of the word postmodern. In the world of aesthetic production (i.e. in the world of the creations of beauty), that is, in the art world, the world of architecture, music, literature, etc., there are terms used to describe different forms of art. For example, in painting there is a style called impressionism, which emerged in France in the late eighteen hundreds. Monet, for example, is an artist who painted in this style. In architecture too there are names for the various styles of buildings. The tall skyscrapers that appeared in America in the early and mid-nineteen hundreds often were identified as modern buildings – built in the modernist style. In contrast, one could go to Europe and look at the great historical cathedrals that were built hundreds of years ago. Some are identified as Gothic, with the high arches, gargoyles, and flying buttresses. This is the style. Other churches are in the Romanesque style, a style that preceded the Gothic. Romanesque is characterized by having rounded arched windows, among other things. There are many forms of artistic style. Postmodern is one of these forms. The art work of Andy Warhol, while generally considered to be "pop art" is also considered to be postmodern in form. Buildings created by architects such as Frank Gehry and Robert Venturi are often identified as postmodern. Indeed, a well-known architecture book by Venturi, Denise Scott Brown and Steven Izenour titled *Learning from Las Vegas* (1972) is a classic work in the theory of postmodern architecture. In this book, the authors praise the designs of the buildings on the Las Vegas Strip, as well as the planning of the buildings and of the city. They are championing postmodern forms of building and design. Similarly, one can find postmodern movies, literature and music. The movie director David Lynch's Blue Velvet and Ridley Scott's Blade Runner are sometimes identified as postmodern.

Postmodern aesthetics is characterized by its playfulness, by its lack of seriousness, by its appeal to popular tastes, by the practical and local. It is also characterized by its fundamental rejection of the principles that guided modern forms of aesthetics. Modernism sought to embrace reason and rationality and sought to create art and architectural styles on these principles. The rational ordering of space and the use of modern technologies would pave the way for a better world. Thus, we have skyscrapers. We have cities dominated by steel and glass towers, all embracing simple rational forms. Ornamentation was not needed or not wanted. It was not efficient. It was not rational. Modern architecture, embracing order and rationality, was rooted in universal, timeless principles. The local and the particular were not relevant. Thus, a modern skyscraper bears no immediate relationship to its immediate local and historical context. The skyscraper could be anywhere. It is abstracted from the context in its design. The French modernist architect Le Corbusier embodies these principles. He claimed he was trying to design buildings that would be "machines for living." He also drew up maps of his vision of Paris, a vision which called for the bulldozing of the city and the erection of countless, uniform high-rise buildings. (One can see this same idea in a number of large projects in the United States. Stuyvesant City in New York City is one example.) Postmodern aesthetics rejected the beliefs and aspirations of rationality. (Critics sometimes note that the postmodernists present an overly simplified and unified vision of modernism. Postmodernists are said to wrongfully reduces the complexities of modern art and architectural forms that appeared in the period of "high modernity" in the early nineteen hundreds into one simple formula. The critics note that modernism was far more complicated than some if not many postmodernists claim. For example, while rationality was a dominant theme in much modernist aesthetics, one could also find a radical rejection of rationality. The Dadaist style, for example, found in the work of the artist Marcel Duchamp embraced absurdity and the irrational. Duchamp is known for, among other things, creating a work of sculpture called The Fountain, which was nothing more than a mass produced, men's urinal. It is displayed as a work of art in many museums today. It is a decidedly modernist work of art, but at the same time it appears to have many of the features associated with postmodern art.)

There is no debate about the existence of an artistic style called **postmodernism**. It is recognized by almost all that this style of art exists. However, there is much debate about whether we have entered into a new historical period, one that is distinct from modernity, called **postmodernity**. One can identify several major periods of history. From the fall of the Roman Empire through the fourteen hundreds, there was the Dark Ages, otherwise known as the Middle Ages. In the fifteen and sixteen hundreds, there was the Renaissance. In the sixteen and seventeen hundreds, there as the Enlightenment (The Age of Reason), and from the eighteen hundreds through now, we have lived in Modernity (though Modernity is often said to begin in the sixteen hundreds). Some claim we have recently entered into a new historical period called postmodernity. Some mainstream, i.e. non-postmodernist scholars, in the post-World War Two era, such as C. Wright

Mills, argued that the character of American society at that time was becoming starkly different than the character that it had in earlier decades and earlier centuries. Postmodernist theorists in recent decades have made similar, albeit more dramatic, claims. The world of today is sufficiently different from the world of one hundred years ago as to warrant a new term to describe it: We have moved from a modern era to a postmodern era, they say.

Those who claim this often identify a number of things that are said to be unique to the contemporary world. We live in a world saturated by consumption. We live in a world of superficiality, where the only thing that matters is appearance. We live in a high technology world, a world of the internet. We live in a globalized world. We live in a post-industrial world in which the economy is no longer based on industrial production in factories, but instead on an economy that is based on services and information. We no longer build things but instead provide services and information. Whether a worker is as a software engineer or a shelf stocker at Walmart, service and information jobs rather than factory jobs are the more common forms of work today. We also live in a world of hyper-speed, and in a world where our understanding of time and space have been realigned. If you were blindfolded, put on a plane, then taken to a mall somewhere in America, and then your blindfold was taken of, could you say where you were? You would see the same stores. You would see the Apple store, the Aeropostale Store, and all the rest. The mall would look familiar. But it could be anywhere. Would you know where you are? What is the meaning of space in the world today if that is the case?

It was noted above that many people challenge this postmodern claim. Many critics of postmodern theorists who claim we have entered into a new historical era say that the changes identified by these theorists used to support their argument have in fact begun with modernity. There might be an amplification of the circumstances that emerged in the modern era, the critics say, but there are not any distinctive aspects of the era today that would warrant the label postmodern. Technology, for example, is a characteristic of the modern era and was central to industrialism. Relatedly, the world was already speeding up in the modern era, and the speeding up is not new to recent decades. Mass production, consumption and all of the other features said to be associated with a new era, with postmodernity, critics say can be found in the modern era. Many if not most conventional sociologists today would likely argue that we have not entered into a new historic era called postmodernity. It is true, they might say, that the globalized, high technology world, which is characterized by a consumer society and by a service and information based economy have a different quality about them today, but these new things have only amplified existing processes and not changed them. Most scholars would acknowledge that we now live in a post-industrial society, which is characterized by the above things, but not a postmodern society. In short, while there is general agreement that postmodernism exists as an aesthetic style, there is far less agreement about the reality of a postmodernity.

As a type of social theory postmodernism has taken ideas from these aesthetic fields, as well as from many other fields such as linguistics, philosophy, and conventional sociology, and it has also focused upon the dramatic changes in the real world in the last thirty years or so, i.e. the emergence of post-industrial, globalized, high-tech society. As noted, postmodern theorists do not all think alike. Postmodernism is associated with a wide range of theories and theorists. Some of the more well-known names associated with it are Michel Foucault, Jean Baudrillard, Jacques Derrida, and Gilles Deleuze and Felix Guattari, Francois Lyotard, among many others. Of note, many of the central figures of postmodern theory are French, and their theorizing was deeply influenced by French intellectual traditions and French culture and history. At the same time, a number of Americans have embraced postmodern social theory, but as we see below many of these have tended to modify or tame some of the more radical elements of this form of theorizing. For example, American theorists tend to humanize postmodern theorizing and they tend to steer it from its more radical implications towards a less dramatic liberalism (see below).

Thus far, we have described some central points related to postmodernism, but we have not yet mentioned any of the ideas associated with this form of theorizing. Here, we can mention a few general themes found in postmodern theorizing. After, we can describe in greater detail some of the common ideas in this form of theory. At its heart, postmodernism is an anti-theory. It is highly critical of most if not all of the major assumptions underlying conventional forms of theorizing and is highly critical of the organization of the contemporary world, i.e. of democratic capitalism. Postmodern theory is first and foremost rooted in an understanding of language and of symbolic forms rather than in an understanding of the traditional object of interest for sociology, such as institutions and social structures. This form of theorizing also recognizes that signs and language have assumed a more central place in the contemporary world, in the world of advertising, public relations, and media – social and conventional – than was the case in earlier decades and centuries. Postmodern theorizing also focuses upon a critical understanding of power and how power is used in relation to inequalities. But as we see, the concepts of power used in this theory is quite different from the way it is conventionally used. For example, it is intimately tied to language and symbolic forms. Postmodern theorizing also is oriented toward a critical assessment of self, identity and agency.

Main Influences

Postmodern theories are generally influenced by several intellectual traditions. One of these is structuralism. The word structure is commonly used in American sociology. Unfortunately, this creates a bit of confusion when one wishes to understand postmodern theory. The confusion is created because the meaning of the word structure in American sociology is fundamentally different from the meaning of structure as it is used in the theory of structuralism that serves as a significant inspiration for postmodern theory. When American sociologists use the word structure, they tend to refer to such things as institutional arrangements. Thus, the family has a structure; the economy has a structure; a football team has a structure. That is, there is an organized set of roles, norms, and values, which operate and that maintain the entity in question. The family has the roles of mother, father, son, daughter, etc., and each of these has attached to it sets of expectations. Combined this is the structure of the family. The structural functionalist theory of Parsons, described earlier, embodies this way of thinking of structure. But this is not the way that postmodernism understands structure.

Structuralism

Postmodern theory is greatly influenced by a **structuralism** that has its roots in European theories of language and signs, and specifically in the theory of structural linguistics. An early, major figure in structural linguistics was Ferdinand de Saussure (1959). Saussure (1857-1913) developed a theory of the sign. The sign could be anything from a word to a street sign. The sign has two elements to it, the signifier and the signified. The **signifier** is the part of the sign that is the object. It is the part of a sign that represents the meaning. It is the embodiment of the sign in some form, whether a word, an object, etc. The **signified** is the meaning side of a sign. It is the reference the sign is making. The question is: How does the sign make meaning? One might argue that the essence of the meaning of a sign comes from the relationship of the signifier to the signified. When someone says, "look at the brown dog walking down the street," my understanding of the meaning of these words might come from the relationship of the words of the sentence to the reality which they represent. The brown dog refers to an actual dog that is brown. But this is not how signs operate to produce meaning, the structuralists say. Meaning is produced by the relationship of one signifier to another signifier in the linguistic context of its use, and not between the relationship of a signifier to a signified. What is the meaning of a musical note? Doesn't a musical note only have meaning when it is located within a context of other musical notes in a song or a piece of music? The meaning is derived from the relationship between signifiers. Or the meaning of the word dog is found in its relationships – for example, a dog is not a cat, or a dog is in relation to the street it is walking on, etc. Structuralist theorists also claim our forms of thought and language are based upon binary oppositions. We necessarily compartmentalize our worlds into oppositions, black/white, up/down, presence/absence, etc. Black has meaning because it stands in opposition to white. (One can hear perhaps the echoes of Durkheim's thinking about the sacred and the profane here.) Perhaps most importantly, Saussure's theory of signs claims that sign systems, e.g. language systems, could be "scientifically" studied in and of themselves. That is, sign systems have a unity to them, a structure, and to study them one should not look at how the signs relate to social life or social practices. That is, the meaning of a sign system is derived from an understanding of the sign system and not from social life or social practices that may be associated with these signs. Sign systems have a structure that is independent of such things and the task is to discover the structure of these systems.

As an example, one could envision trying to determine the structure of the sign system related to furniture in a room. How is one to understand the furniture in a room? How is one to understand the meaning of a bed in a bedroom? A nightstand? A dresser? One assigns meaning to these things because one relates these to the other things in the context. The bed is related to the dresser, etc. One knows from this the meaning of the bed, and the meaning that this is a bedroom. But what if one found a bed in an unusual setting? There was once a public arts exhibit in a Boston subway a few years ago. On the middle of the subway platform there was a queen size bed. The bed was covered with sheets and blankets and pillows, just as one would find a bed in a bedroom. And there was a person in pajamas sitting in the bed under the covers, reading, as if she was in her own bedroom. Persons waiting for the subway could look and wonder what this work of art meant. It was a statement about structuralism. The meaning of the bed is different when it is placed in a context of signs in the subway than when it is placed in a context of signs in a bedroom. Another example: Stop signs. A stop sign has one meaning when one finds it on a post on a corner of a street. But doesn't it have a very different meaning when it is found on the wall of a college dormitory room? If you entered a dormitory room and saw such a sign, would you stop? The meaning is derived from relations to other signs, and it is derived from the context of its use. This is structuralism.

The first major social scientist to use and apply structuralist theory to the study of social life and social organization was the anthropologist Claude Levi-Strauss (1908-2009). Levi-Strauss took the ideas of structuralism and developed a structural anthropology. He did his anthropological research in Brazil (1961) and sought to understand the cultural practices of "primitive" groups, e.g. their family structures, their myths, their cooking patterns, by using structuralism. He argued that despite the superficial differences between the structural patterns of these various cultural forms, e.g. cooking, family, myths, etc., within any one tribe, there was a deep, shared structure underlying all of these patterns. That is, there is a deep structure in our minds that allow us to make sense out of cooking, myths, etc., and that these cultural formations all have the same deep structure to them. He believed the "primitive groups" in Brazil would give him the clearest view of these deep structures. As he noted upon return from Brazil: "I had been looking for a society reduced to its simplest expression. That of the Nambikwara was so far reduced that all I found there was men" (quoted in Homans, 1961:385).

I have created an example seen in Figure 12.1 below to illustrate the basic idea of structuralism. In the left side of Figure 12.1, you can see a basic culinary structure presented by Levi-Strauss. That is, think about how and why we eat certain foods in the ways that we do (and why we eat some things and not others such as dogs). We eat some foods raw but cook others. (Levi-Strauss actually goes further and presents a structure of the different ways that we prepare food, e.g. boil, roast, raw, etc., but we will not cover this here.) In Figure 12.1 below, I have presented Levi-Strauss' basic structure of

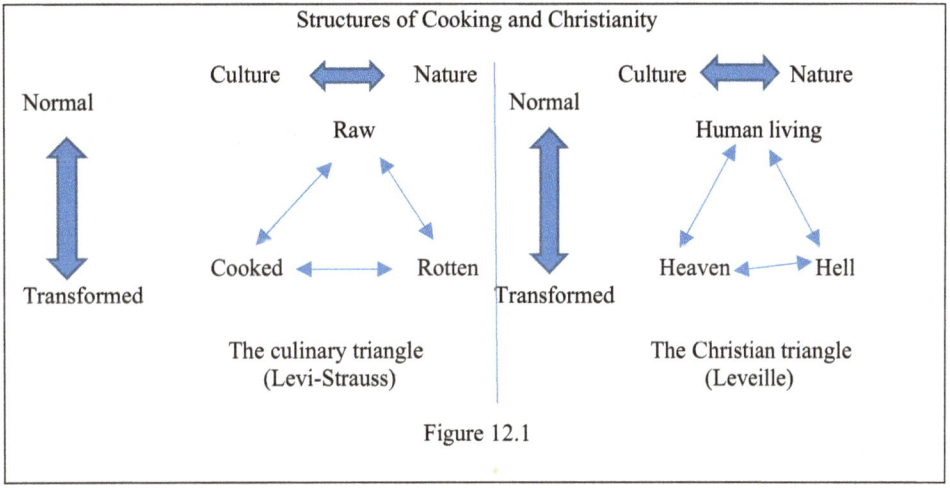

Figure 12.1

the cooking or culinary system on the left. On the right of the first structure, I have created my own structure. This is the basic structure of Christianity. You can see how the two structures are identical.

Levi-Strauss believed the deep, shared structure of one group or tribe was no different from the deep, shared structure of any other group or society. He wished to understand the universal structure of the mind of human beings. Thus, even though the cultural practices of native peoples in Brazil are dramatically different from the cultural practices of Americans in the early twenty first century, when one digs deep enough, according to Levi-Strauss, one will discover the same fundamental structures of the mind shared by both, and by all, groups.

Postmodern theory is influenced by structuralism, but it goes beyond it in some significant ways. And these ways are seen in its relation to another theory called post-structuralism. Postmodern theory is related to post-structuralism. Post-structuralism is derived from structuralism but makes a few crucial changes to the theory. Post-structuralism claims like structuralism that there is a structure to our cultural practices and to our consciousness. However, post-structuralists reject the structuralist claims that the structure is an enclosed system incapable of change, and most importantly they claim that there is no one deep, shared structure to the consciousness of all people and all groups, from the "primitives" in the rain forest of Brazil to the residents of New York City today. Instead, they argue that structures of consciousness can be and are different from one group to another. When Columbus sailed to America in the late fourteen hundreds and encountered the native people living there, did the native peoples think about the world, did they see their worlds, in the same way that Columbus saw his world? No. There were two distinct forms of consciousness. The post-structuralists say there is no deep shared structure to consciousness, but instead there are different structures. Moreover, the differences exist not only from one culture to another, as in the example of Columbus, but in history amongst the same people. As such, one might ask whether the structure of consciousness of Europeans today is the same as it was one thousand years ago. The post-structuralists would say it is different.

Existentialism

Another significant element of structuralism, and specifically of the structural anthropology of Levi-Strauss, is that it avoids the messy problem of motivations and intentions and agency. The task of the structuralist is to study scientifically (objectively) the sign patterns of a cultural phenomenon. One of the reasons that structuralism is appealing to some social scientists is that it appears to give the social scientist an approach that avoids or overcomes essentially thorny issues of interpretation of motivations, and thus appears to be more objective and scientific. This is directly related to the influences that phenomenology and existentialism have had upon postmodernism. Postmodern theory is greatly influenced by these approaches. But this influence is in reaction against, not supportive of, these two theories. These approaches were described in an earlier chapter (see Chapter Nine). Here we can briefly look at how they influenced postmodernism. It will be recalled that postmodern theory has its roots in France in the mid to late nineteen hundreds. In France, several major theoretical traditions were dominant at the time, including Marxism, structuralism, and phenomenology and existentialism. Structuralism appears to be a theory that is the polar opposite of phenomenology and existentialism. While phenomenology and existentialism seek to understand experiential consciousness and meaning making in the present, structuralism rejects all such quest as non-scientific or as metaphysical quests, i.e. pursuits that have no answers that could be scientifically proven. Again, the question of motivation and intent arises. Individuals in the present make sense of their worlds and act in it. But why do they do what they do?

Phenomenologists and existentialists tend to believe that the self as agent is crucial to understanding this. The intentional self, the meaning making self, is central to both approaches. But if one wishes to develop a science of sociology, one has to develop an approach that is not trapped by questions that cannot be answered through scientific means. Ultimately, phenomenologists and existentialists are led, or are conceptually forced, into defining the essence of the self, or they are led to capture the eternal present. That is, they are forced into claiming certain universal or transcendent features of this thing called self that all individuals possess, and that all individuals enact in the immediate present. This leads to a universalistic psychology in which it is claimed that all people share. However particular and unique the structures of consciousness appear in the immediate lived present, as phenomenologists seek to uncover, behind this approach lies certain claims that the structuralists (and post-structuralists) reject. Or on the other hand, they are led to endlessly try to capture the lived experiences of a social actor in the moment, in the present. But the present is fleeting and impossible to catch. (Postmodernists call this the "metaphysics of presence.")

Postmodern theory also often draws inspirations from certain forms of existential philosophy, for example, from the ideas of the twentieth century German philosopher Martin Heidegger (though it tends to reject other forms of existentialism, such as that proposed by Sartre), and from the eclectic thinking of the nineteenth century German philosopher Friedrich Nietzsche. Nietzsche is sometimes referred to as the godfather of postmodern theory. His philosophy is a rebellion against the Enlightenment, and against the modern world as it was unfolding in his time. Nietzsche opposed the Western embrace of reason and rationality, and he opposed given primacy to these things at the expense of morality and aesthetics. He rejects the Enlightenment claims that the foundation for understandings and for action should be reason and rationality, and the claims that morality and aesthetics should be based upon reason and rationality. He saw people in the modern world becoming spiritually enslaved to reason. This enslavement was negating our true humanity. Our true humanity, as biological and as moral beings, is that we are, or we should be, free. Our true essence is our will. Specifically, we are or should be driven by the "will to power." We should be driven to asserting our true selves in our worlds and can only do this if we cast of the constraints that reason and rationality (and conventional morality) have imposed. Nietzsche also is highly critical of religion, and specifically Christianity. God is dead, as he and many other philosophers from that time proclaimed. And when god is dead all things are possible. That is, what should be our morality if god is dead? If god is dead, why shouldn't someone kill someone else to take their money? What is the foundation of values and morality in a world in which god is dead? Moreover, if god is dead, what value do individual people have? What intrinsic value do they have? Individuals can have value, they can assign value to themselves, through their actions, their will.

Nietzsche was harshly critical of Christian morality and Christian ethics because he thought that it too enslaved people. It was the morality of the herd, he says. He viewed this morality, as well as democratic sensibilities which view individuals as having intrinsically equal value, as harmful to people's humanity. He sees this morality as a means of bringing down the creative, the powerful, those asserting their wills, to the level of the passive and submissive masses, who quietly conform to the enslavement of reason and to the Christian morality. He calls for a **transvaluation of values** in which individuals tear down the traditional ethics of the Western world, built upon reason and Christianity and replace these with new, undefined ethics, rooted in the assertion of will. Morality and aesthetics at the service of power become for Nietzsche the driving force for people, or at least these should be the driving force if people wish to truly realize their humanity. A new form of morality is needed, one that is not enslaved to reason. Toward this end, Nietzsche champions the ubermensch, the superman, as the model of being in his new world. This new person would assert their will, would live life as a work of art, and would not be enslaved to traditions of reason or religion.

Some if not many postmodern theorists share Nietzsche's concerns about the modern world. They see reason and the dominant forms of morality in place today as oppressive forces rather than as the liberating forces they are typically portrayed to be. These theorists also see conventional social scientific theories as contributing to these very problems, and as such a new form of theorizing is needed.

Marx and Weber

Postmodern theory has also been influenced, often indirectly, by the ideas of Weber and Marx. Weber's concerns about rationalization ripple through much of postmodern thinking. Marx's themes of power and inequality and his critique of the dehumanizing effects of capitalism also can be found in postmodern theory. Many of the major French post-modern theorists were schooled in Marxism in the French universities and many were, for however brief period of time, Marxists and/or members of the French Communist Party. However, postmodern theorists saw many fundamental problems with Marxism, and as a result ultimately rejected it. Several of these can briefly be mentioned here. Postmodernists rejected the totalizing view of Marxism. Marxism was simply another, wrongheaded grand theory (see below) that claimed to explain everything. Such forms of theorizing, the postmodernists claim, are no different from religions or other totalizing beliefs that wrap the diversity of lived experiences into one neat theoretical mold. It is time to move beyond this form of thinking. Relatedly, Marx's claim that he had discovered the "science" of history is equally rejected by postmodernists. So too do postmodernists reject Marx's materialism and his claims that economics and the productive system are the keys to understanding the workings of society. In the postmodern world, the realm of symbols and consumption are the key things to understand, rather than materialism and production. Lastly, Marxism is rejected by postmodernists because the former is anchored in the Enlightenment which is seen as a major source of the problems of the contemporary era. (However, some would claim that Marxism has a dialectical relationship with the Enlightenment.) Postmodernists reject the Enlightenment Project, the historical project which seeks to enact the principles found in the Enlightenment.

Despite such criticisms, postmodern theory embraced several themes found in Marx's theory. The importance of capitalism, of power, of inequality are all recognized by postmodernists. Both Marxists and postmodernists see rational capitalism as an oppressive, dynamic force. Similarly, Marx's theory of ideology, while generally rejected by postmodern theorists, has had a significant impact upon this thinking. The claim that the symbolic realm, the realm of ideas and ideology, has a major role to play in maintaining the current systems of inequality, is an idea shared by both Marxists and postmodernists. (It bears noting that there are some scholars who attempt to fuse Marxist ideas with postmodern ideas. The Marxist literary critic Frederick Jameson (1991), for example, shows how postmodern cultural forms can be understood within the context of Marxism. These forms of culture work to blind people from seeing the workings of capitalism, and as such allow capitalism to continue.)

Themes in Postmodern Theory

Despite the significantly different perspectives amongst postmodern theorists, a number of themes tend to reappear in the various approaches. One of these themes is superficiality. Postmodernists often claim that the current era is one in which the superficial rather than depth is a prominent feature of the era. Image rather than reality dominates. In this age of hyper-advertising, of public relations, of mass entertainment, of the internet, the superficial appearances are all that matters. Theorists argue that modernity was characterized by depth. There was a quest to understand the deep meanings behind the appearances. Modern social and psychological theories reflect this. This is seen, for example, in Freud's psychoanalytic theory. In its quest to uncover the true, i.e. the deep, explanations of people's behavior one had to dive deep into the unconscious. Behaviors and thoughts are only appearances cloaking a truth that lies hidden beneath, within the unconscious. Likewise, Marx claimed to have discovered the deep essential truths of history which propels all forward. These truths are often hidden by false consciousness, ideology, or mystification, or reification, etc. The postmodern era, in contrast, is characterized by the surface, by the **superficial**, by its emptiness. What meaning does the Campbell Soup can lithographs produced by the pop artist Andy Warhol have? There is no meaning, no depth. We live in a world of appearance. The images are not hiding some deeper realities. There are no deeper realities to be found. The appearances are the reality. What you see is what you get.

Fragmentation is another theme of the postmodern. The world has become fragmented – largely due to capitalism, rationalization, technology, and globalization. Time and space and experience have all become broken into small, disjointed bits, and each bit has no apparent connection to other bits. For example, only a small number of characters are allowed in a text. Communications online are short, and often anonymous. People post comments to pages and respond to others who they do not know. The image of a webpage is scattered with advertising and with other things. One can move from one webpage to another in seconds, and again, and again. Postmodern art and architecture sometimes highlight this theme. Sometimes these forms combine elements from various other styles into one form. For example, a postmodern building might combine architectural elements from modernism, but also elements from the beaux arts style, from the Greco-Roman classical style, etc.

A third theme of postmodern theory revolves around **power**, inequality and difference. Postmodern theorists are highly critical of modern capitalism and are particularly critical of the inequalities that exist today. But the inequalities of concern are as much if not more about inequalities related to race, gender, gender identity or gender orientation, and other such things, than they are about economic class inequalities per se. Power is seen as central to inequality. It is the power of the symbolic realm that is of significance for postmodern theorists. Power is said to be part of interactions in ways that allow members of powerful groups to maintain their positions of power. The powerful, using the control over symbolic processes, attempt to define their own group and their own group's actions in ways that help maintain their powerful position, in the same way that these powerful groups use the control over symbolic processes to define less powerful groups in ways that help maintain these groups in less powerful positions. At the heart of these understandings of power is the fusion of power, action, symbolic forms, and biological beings. Power is enacted through actions by living beings in the present through the use of language, and it is through this that systems of inequality are maintained or challenged.

A fourth, central theme found in postmodern theories revolves around the ideas of post-self theories and around the debates regarding humanism and anti-humanism. We need to recognize here two distinct forms of postmodern theorizing related to the issues of post-self theories and to the humanism-anti-humanism debate. One form of theorizing is centered in Europe, the other in the United States. As was noted earlier, many of the central figures in postmodern theory came from France. However, there are a number of American postmodern theorists, and while they tend to share many ideas and themes with the Europeans, they also (often implicitly) differ from them on the matters of post-self theories and of humanism vs anti-humanism. European postmodern theories tend to embrace post-self theories and they tend to embrace forms of anti-humanism. In contrast, American postmodern theories tend to reject, or at most express ambivalence towards, post-self theories, and they tend to implicitly embrace humanism rather than anti-humanism. But what are post-self theories, and what is the issue of humanism vs anti-humanism?

In other chapters of this book, the theoretical issues and concerns related to agency have been noted. For example, is it possible or worthwhile to try to develop a scientific theory of agency? These issues were often discussed in relation to the agency-structure debate in sociology. Post-self theories of the postmodern reject all attempts to develop theories of agency. They also reject all scientific psychologies that claim that there is a scientifically knowable form of human consciousness or human psychology. These critics reject all such claims and go further. They often seek to understand the history of the self. How and why in history did people begin to develop scientific claims that say that human beings, human experience, could and should be understood scientifically in the same way that rocks or trees in a forest could be understood. Self theories necessarily have to build and rely upon models of the mind to explain motivation and intent, and post-self theories claim that such theorizing is at best wishful thinking, at worst it is part of the problem of the current age. Proclaimed scientific understanding of individual psychology and human experience is little more than another mechanism of rational control over individuals that stifle human beings' humanity.

The issue of humanism vs anti-humanism is a central theme in postmodern theory. As noted, European postmodern theory tends to embrace anti-humanism, while American postmodern theory often (though often implicitly) embraces humanism. So what is humanism? **Humanism** is the belief that there is something special and distinct about human beings. Human beings have some essential value that makes them automatically more important than anything other on this planet. Humanism says that people have value because they are people, and that people have more value than animals and rocks and trees. Humanism also is often associated with the claims that the essence of our humanity lies in our morality, our reason, and our sense of beauty. We are conscious and we make judgments about such things. We are more than mere rational, calculating machines. Humanism claims that all humans share certain fundamental attributes by nature. Humanism lies at the heart of the Enlightenment Project. The elevation of the individual self to the position of ultimate value in the universe was a part of this Project. The Enlightenment Project, as noted earlier, gave birth to the great revolutions of the late eighteenth century -- the American and the French Revolutions. Enshrined in the key documents of these revolutions one can find deep humanistic sentiments. For example, Jefferson wrote in the Declaration of Independence, that "We hold these truths to be self-evident, that all men are created equal, that they are endowed by their Creator with certain unalienable Rights, that among these are Life, Liberty and the pursuit of Happiness." The claim that humans have rights simply because they are humans is a classic humanistic position. It is really of secondary importance here whether the rights are endowed by a god or by nature. What is important is that these rights are said to simply exist prior to and separate from individuals. No one has to do anything to produce these rights.

Anti-humanism rejects the claims of humanism. It is sometimes thought or assumed that anti-humanist positions are by their very nature evil (or at the very least, that these positions lead to evil political consequences in real life (see the discussion about anti-humanism and Nazi-ism below)). After all, how can one be opposed to claims that humans are special, and that humans have inalienable rights? How can one oppose the claims that humans have a value that is essentially different and greater than the value of a tree or a chicken? Yet anti-humanistic, postmodern theorists claim that it is humanism and the associated principles of the Enlightenment that are in fact the evil ones, but because humanism is cloaked in warm sensibilities of the greatness of human beings it has allowed believers to ignore the harmful consequences that have arisen in modernity as the result of it. The massive security state apparatus in America today, or the endless wars America has and is fighting in, or the massive destruction to the environment, or the great inequalities and poverty in the age of plenty, are merely a few examples of what are said to be the consequences of humanism. Humanism, the critics say, is harmful too because it gives the appearance of goodness and nobility, but in reality it is harmful to individuals and to society.

The existential philosopher Martin Heidegger engages in this debate in his essay "Letter on Humanism" where he complains that the humanists are not only wrongheaded because they rely upon metaphysics in their theorizing ("Every humanism is either grounded in a metaphysics or is itself made to be the ground of one" (2003:178)), but more importantly because they do not value humans enough, even though they proclaim that they do. The proper value of humans, Heidegger says, lies in the recognition that humans create values. Humans assign value to humanity. Human values are not simply there to be found. He embraces an anti-humanism. He writes (in defending his deplorable Nazi actions during World War Two):

> Through this determination of the essence of man the humanistic interpretations of man as *animal rationale*, as "person," as spiritual-ensouled-bodily being, are not declared false and thrust aside. Rather, the sole implication is that the highest determinations of the essence of man in humanism still do not realize the proper dignity of man. To that extent the thinking in [Heidegger's book] *Being and Time* is against humanism. But this opposition does not mean that such thinking aligns itself against the humane and advocates the inhuman, that it promotes the inhumane and deprecates the dignity of man. Humanism is opposed because it does not set the *humanitas* of man high enough. (2003:181)

Postmodern theorists also tend to embrace an **anti-essentialism**, refusing to accept any and all essentialist claims, whether they are claims about the essential value of human beings or claims about the essential truths found through rational inquiry, or the essential truths found in one or another theory.

Another common position taken by postmodern theory is the rejection of meta- or **grand theories** (Lyotard 1984). Meta-theories are large-scale, all-encompassing explanations. These theories claim to explain everything. They are powerful and seductive. Freud's theory of psychoanalysis is a meta-theory, as is Marxism, and Darwin's theory of evolution, and most religions. The Enlightenment Project is seen as a meta-theory. Such theories allow individuals to surrender themselves to their truths. This abdication prevents humans from being truly free. Postmodern theorists claim that modernity was characterized by the embrace of meta-theories, but in the time of postmodernity, we should abandon our faith in any and all such approaches to knowledge. Instead, we should look at the local and the particular and the unique for knowledge.

We conclude this section with a brief note on something that was touched upon earlier. This is the issue of postmodern theories of the self. It was noted that European postmodern theory, largely rooted in structuralist sensibilities, rejects any sort of attempts to create a postmodern psychology. Postmodern psychologies have arisen in the United States. Postmodern psychology is seen by these theorists as an oxymoron, a term that is essentially contradictory. The point of postmodernism is to abandon the rational project of capturing the essential, timeless qualities of the self in one or another scientific psychological theory. At the same time, postmodern theories of the self tend to implicitly if not explicitly fall back into a humanist perspective, which also is fundamentally at odds with some of the major impetuses in postmodern theorizing. Critics complain that these American attempts at humanizing postmodernism negate its radical impulses and turn it into a fuzzy liberal project.

We can now turn our attention to a description of some of the ideas of two of the more well-known scholars associated with postmodern theory: Michel Foucault and Jean Baudrillard.

Foucault

If one walked into a bookstore – if one can even find one today, as there are fewer and fewer now in this internet age – and looked for books written by Michel Foucault (1926-1984), one might find his works in the philosophy section. But in a different bookstore one might find his books in the history aisle. A third bookstore might place his works in the sociology section. And yet others might place him with cultural studies, or postmodernism, or sex and gender. That he might be found in any of these sections is a testament to how difficult it is to categorize his works. Most of his writings were histories, but he did not write traditional histories. They were all laced with a sophisticated theoretical and philosophical perspective, though this perspective is not sometimes readily seen as one reads the histories. He wrote histories of mental illness, prisons and criminal justice, of medicine, of the human sciences (i.e. social and behavioral sciences), and of sexuality. While the theoretical frameworks used in each of these works differed from one to the next, there are some shared themes that one can readily identify in all of his work. These themes include power, knowledge, reason, morality, the body, and most notably the themes of the increasing and increasingly harmful use of power/knowledge put into the service of disciplining subjects into conformity in the modern era.

Foucault was influenced by many of the themes noted earlier – by structuralism, by Nietzsche and Heidegger, by phenomenology, existentialism, and Marxism. He adamantly insisted he was not a structuralist and was not influenced by structuralism, because he never employed the formal framework of structuralism in any of his works. For example, he did not rely upon mapping out conceptual binary oppositions into a defined grid within which cultural formations were enacted. Though it is correct to say that he did not systematically employ structuralists' concepts or methods, it is equally true that one can readily see a number of important, general structuralist tendencies in his work. Indeed, most of his research can be seen as structural histories of consciousness. In most of this work he sought to identify the structures of the consciousness of Europeans in the modern age, and specifically sought to show how these structures fundamentally changed from one historical era to the next. Thus, medical doctors in the fifteen hundreds saw their world and acted in the world in a fundamentally different way than the medical doctors of the eighteen hundreds. Because Foucault sought to understand the changing structures of consciousness, he is often called a post-structuralist rather than a structuralist. It will be recalled that structuralists such as Levi-Strauss sought to discover the universal structure of consciousness that all people in all places at all times share. Foucault is making a different argument. The structures change in time and place. There is no universal, timeless structure to our consciousness.

Michel Foucault

Michel Foucault, born Paul-Michel, was born in Poitiers, France in 1926. He was raised in an upper middle class household. He was a bright student growing up but was somewhat rebellious. He attended the prestigious Ecole Normal Superieure and eventually earned his doctorate. There he was a student of Althusser and other prominent French intellectuals. His focus of study was on the philosophy and history of psychology and psychiatry. He taught at a number of universities in various countries throughout his life but spent much of his career in Paris. In the 1970s he traveled to California, and specifically to San Francisco, and was greatly impressed. He would return to California on a number of occasions. (Near the end of his life he was given an appointment at the University of California, Berkeley but died before teaching there.) Foucault was a homosexual. He actively supported a number of political causes, most notably prisoners' rights. He died of AIDS in 1984, before most knew what the disease even was. When he was alive, he was recognized the world over as one of the most interesting, influential, and controversial scholars of the second half of the twentieth century.

Foucault was also influenced by Marxism and by Nietzsche and Heidegger. In his youth he was for a very short time a member of the French Communist Party. He left the party, he says, after becoming quite disenchanted with its authoritarian and disciplined orientation, and because of its homophobic tendencies. He was certainly no Marxist for most of his career. (Among other things, he rejects the central Marxist ideas of dialectics and materialism.) Yet even though he left the Party, he nevertheless was greatly influenced by Marxism. Specifically, he was very influenced by his teacher, the structural Marxist Louis Althusser. Many of the themes found in Althusser's theorizing – such as the anti-humanism, the opposition to theories based upon the self and agency, as well as Althusser's structural orientation -- also appear in Foucault's, though the latter leaves out all of the Marxist claims in the process. He was also strongly affected by the works of Nietzsche and Heidegger, and this becomes more apparent in his later works, particularly his work on the history of sexuality. The focus on being, the body, and morality and their intersections all were themes in his work that were largely derived from Nietzsche and Heidegger.

Foucault was interested in developing a method to study history and social life. He wished to develop a method of understanding history which did not require an understanding of individual historical selves doing things. He sought to create a history which did not rely upon assumptions about the motivations of individual subjects. He was interested in writing "histories without subjects." The post-structuralist sensibilities are clear here. It is striking that in most of his histories the action is carried forth not as the result of individual motivations or choice making, but instead by the structures of consciousness within which the actors operate. We largely do not see individuals doing this or that to move history forward. Instead, the structures of consciousness and their intersection with power/knowledge and social realities propel the action. He was also focused on the growth and spread of knowledge and reason in Western history and on how these things have increasingly become tied to power and disciplinary structures.

Several themes stand out in Foucault's writings: power/knowledge; discursive practices; and sex, the body, and morality. **Power** is a central theme in his histories. But Foucault sees power in a particular way. Power is ever-present in social realities. Moreover, power is found between people, concepts, or things. It is essentially a relational concept. Power also for Foucault is neither a positive nor a negative thing. It simply is part of reality. Power also has within it necessarily resistance. Without resistance there is no power. He was particularly interested in understanding the concept **power/knowledge** which is of course the fusion of power and knowledge. Knowledge cannot be understood without appreciating how power is implicated in its existence. While power/knowledge has historically always been in operation, Foucault is particularly concerned in understanding the historical changes in the formation of power/knowledge and is interested in understanding how in the modern world power/knowledge has increasingly become linked with disciplinary controls over the self, the subject, and sexuality. Discourse, practices, and discursive practices are a second set of concepts that ripple through his works. Discourse refers to specialized language for a group of people. Thus, one might have the discourse of baseball, where people talk about hits and runs in certain, particular ways. Or there is the discourse of science, or of sociology. In each discourse there is a particular vocabulary, and a particular way of framing the conversations to allow them to be understood by others who participate in the discourse. Discourses allow certain things to be said and they allow certain things to be thought; and they prevent things from being said and thought. For Foucault, discourse is closely tied to the concept of practice. In some ways Foucault used the term practice in ways not unlike the way Bourdieu uses the term (or vice versa). Practice involves informed and scripted behaviors related to particular domains of life. He was particularly interested in understanding discursive practices. Indeed, most of his histories involved such things in one way or another. **Discursive practices** are the actions of people using words that shape people's understandings and actions. The scientist producing truths about the world are engaged in discursive practices, for example. Foucault wished to understand the intersection of power/knowledge and discursive practices, particularly as these become powerful forces of social control, and increasingly so in the modern world. Another set of themes that are central to his theorizing, and which became even more so in his later work, are those of sex, the body, the self, and morality. Above, I noted that Foucault was influenced by structuralism. This seems to be opposed to the themes of sex, the body, the self, and morality, at least when one reflects within the traditional division of agency and structure and micro and macro. However, in his later work, he focused on how power/knowledge and discursive practices have throughout history in different ways imposed themselves on the individual and have defined sex, the body, the self, and morality in one way or another. In his later work, he seemed more influenced in understanding how the self as biological (sexual) subject is formed within the context of power/knowledge and discursive practices.

Foucault's Histories

Most of Foucault's histories contain similar themes and they contain the same periodization. They all break down European history into the same several periods, and they all examine how people thought and acted differently in these different periods. The first period covers the era prior to the sixteen hundreds. The second, which he calls the Classical Period, which is basically the Enlightenment, lasts from sixteen hundred through the end of the seventeen hundreds. The next period is the modern era which began in the late seventeen hundreds and which either has recently ended or which is nearing its end. Foucault suggests in several places that at the time of his writing that we have perhaps begun to enter a new era, which some have called postmodernity. But he was never completely clear about this claim.

Each historical period had within it a particular way of knowing, or a historically specific structure of consciousness which allows people to see the world in one way rather than another. He calls this the **episteme**. Thus, the episteme of the middle ages, e.g. before the Classical Age, was fundamentally different from the episteme of the Classical Age. His task in all of his works was to identify the elements of the structures of consciousness and to show how these have changed. He shows how these structures are related to social activity and practices, and specifically to practices regarding social control and order. We can look briefly at a few of his histories to get a sense of what he was doing.

Madness and Civilization

In his book *Madness and Civilization* (1965), Foucault presents a history of psychiatry and of how the seriously mentally ill were treated in Europe over the last few hundred years. He shows how the understanding and the response to mental illness significantly changed from one historical period to the next. He presents an argument in this book that is in stark contrast to traditional histories of psychiatry. Traditional histories paint a picture of historical progress in the understanding and treatment of the mentally ill. That is, traditional histories see the advances of the science of psychiatry (and other mental health professions) as leading to treatments that are both more effective and more humane, more compassionate, than those of earlier historical eras. In contrast, Foucault argues that the history of psychiatry gives the appearance of more effectiveness and of being more humane, when in fact it is the opposite. The growth of the science of psychiatry has led to more oppressive forms of control over the mad in the modern era.

Prior to the sixteen hundreds, he says, the mad were treated rather benignly, rather gently. That is, they were not subjected to harsh scientific treatments of psychiatry and were not subjected to the harsh disciplinary forces of the state. He uses the metaphor of the "ship of fools" to describe how madness was understood and how the mad were treated in the period before the sixteen hundreds. The ship of fools were largely mythic boats upon which the mad were placed. These ships, and the mad on them, were then left to wander up and down the rivers and canals of Europe stopping at various ports along the way. At the ports, the local residents would greet them warmly, give them provisions, and send them on their way. In this period, "Madmen then led an easy wandering existence" (1965:8). The point is that the mad were treated gently at the time. They were not subjected to confinement, not shackled and imprisoned, not subjected to discipline or treatment, scientific or otherwise. But this began to change in the sixteen hundreds. At that time, deviants of all sorts – that is, people who could not work, were rounded up and herded together in undifferentiated "Hospitals." Foucault calls this the Great Confinement. The homeless, the poor, the sick, the disabled, the mentally ill were all locked up together in these institutions for the first time. They were removed and isolated from the rest of society. What did all of the groups have in common, and why were they all rounded up? It was their inability to work, to labor, that they held in common. Moreover, Foucault argues that this view of labor was a moral one: "Labor in the houses of confinement ... assumed its ethical meaning" ... "It was in a certain experience of labor that the indissociably economic and moral demand for confinement was formulated" (1965:57). This fusion of economic and moral sentiments produced the great confinement. By the seventeen hundreds, the mad were rounded up and warehoused in these hospitals. Treatment was harsh or non-existent. The mad was put into chains in the corners of these institutions, and largely forgotten.

However, all this changed as the Enlightenment progressed. The Enlightenment humanistic values coupled with the embrace of science and reason led to the emergence of the first modern mental hospitals in the late seventeen hundreds. The psychiatrist, as both humanitarian and scientist, saw and treated the mad with compassion and with reason. The patients where metaphorically freed from their shackles and were not treated with medical science. The first modern form of psychiatric treatment was called moral treatment. It emerged in the late seventeen hundreds. Moral treatment was created by the medical doctor Philippe Pinel in France (and by Samuel and William Tuke in England) in the late seventeen hundreds. At the heart of this treatment was the belief that the mad could be cured through humane, scientific treatment. The modern asylum, or mental hospital, was born. Foucault notes that madness was reconceptualized at this time. With the Enlightenment came an increasing belief in the value of reason. The world was increasingly being defined or judged by reason (science, economics, etc.). Madness too was seen through the lens of reason. Madness now was defined as an absence of reason. It stood in contrast or in opposition to reason. The task then for the humane medical doctor was to restore reason in the patient. Modern treatments sought to do just that. For Foucault, however, this is problematic because it forces the mad to submit to the power of the medical doctors, and the doctors invoke their science and compassion to justify their power. Foucault suggests that this historical change appears on the surface to be a good thing, but the fusion of reason and power leads to a form of control over people, over the mad, which is hard to challenge. It was not a great advance. It was the opposite: a tool of oppression. The mad increasingly lost their autonomy to the growing power of reason and to the professionals who use this in the guise of compassion and science.

The Order of Things

Arguably, Foucault's most important book was *The Order of Things* (1970). (Foucault himself has said this is the case.) *The Order of Things* is a history of the modern human sciences which uses the same historical periods as his other work. The human sciences include all of the social and all of the behavioral sciences, e.g. psychology, sociology, economics, etc. He makes the provocative argument in this book that the subject of study for the human sciences, i.e. the subject of "Man" as both the subject of his own actions and as the object of study, is a product of the modern era, and specifically the product of the Enlightenment. Man in this sense did not exist prior to that time. The Enlightenment led to the birth of Man in the late seventeen hundreds. Man as conceived as a thing, as an object, with universal, shared properties that transcend time and space is a historical creation. It is a creation that serves as the foundation of all human sciences of the modern world. Foucault traces the conceptual structures in history that allowed for Man to be created. He specifically looks at the structures, and convergences of structures, of three academic fields: life (biology), language (semiotics), and labor (economics), and argues that the ways that the organization of the conceptual structures of these disciplines changed from the period before the sixteen hundreds to the Enlightenment (i.e. the Classical Age) provided a context or provided a seedbed for the emergence of the Man as the object (and subject) of study. The structures of the three discursive fields fused together to produce Man.

In short, Man, as is conventionally understood in the modern era, is characterized as having certain universal and timeless attributes, not unlike any object of nature as characterized as having attributes shared by other objects of the same. A table or an orange is defined by the things they share with other tables and oranges. Man too came to be defined this way in the modern world. He is making a very provocative claim here. He is saying the foundation for the modern human sciences, from psychology to sociology to economics, which are anchored in theoretical claims about the self, and about motivations and intentions, is a historical creation. As such, psychology, for example, should not be thought of as a permanent academic discipline which will inevitably exist in centuries to come. If the object of study is historically created, it is possible for this object to be historically destroyed.

Foucault goes on to describe numerous contradictions and conceptual problems that arises when in history scholars treat the subject of Man as an object, as a scientific object. (He describes this modern scientific project as "the analytic of finitude" and the contradictory problems associated with it as "the problem of the doubles.") The fundamental problem resides in the existentialist concerns about understanding lived, meaningful experience. It is not possible to capture the lived, meaningful experience scientifically. Yet this is the demand of science.

His argument ends with some speculations about the future of the human sciences. Perhaps, he says, we are now coming to the end of the modern era. Perhaps a new structure of consciousness, a new episteme, is or will be emerging. Perhaps this will spell the end of the era of Man, the end of the human sciences as we know them:

> As the archaeology of our thought easily shows, man is an invention of recent date. And one perhaps nearing its end. If those arrangements were to disappear as they appeared, if some events of which we can at the moment do no more than sense the possibility – without knowing either what its form will be or what its promises – were to cause them to crumble, as the ground of the Classical thought did, at the end of the eighteenth century, then one can certainly wager that man would be erased, like a face drawn in sand at the edge of the sea. (1970:387)

Discipline and Punish

In *Discipline and Punish* (1977), Foucault gives us a history of the prison and of the changing forms of discipline and punishment that have been administered to criminals. As in his other histories, he shows how society responded to criminals in very different ways in the different periods of modern history. Prior to the Enlightenment, the actual body of the criminal was punished. Torture was the common means of punishment. The book begins with a detailed and gruesome description of an episode from the 1750s in which a person convicted of murdering a king was drawn and quartered, that is, tortured in the public square. The punishment was a public spectacle with a large audience. All this changes however by the end of the seventeen and early eighteen hundreds. Here we encounter the emergence of the first modern prisons. These early prisons were places designed to discipline the criminal, to rehabilitate through the employment of disciplined, rational structures. Of note, the body was no longer the site or target of punishment, but now the mind was the target of discipline. Moreover, it now occurred beyond the view of the public. It became a private affair.

The issues of power and its fusion with knowledge are central to this book. The issue of power, of course, permeates all of Foucault's writings, but here it takes center stage. The forms of power used to manage and control the criminal population changed. It is no longer the brute, public force of public tortures or executions, but now the hidden, controlled forces of disciplinary structures on the minds of people. Power is still a central force here, but it is less obvious, less visible. Yet for Foucault, power is central to understanding any and all social realities. One cannot understand realities without recognizing the ever-present existence of power:

> The individual is no doubt the fictitious atom of an "ideological" representation of society; but he is also a reality fabricated by this specific technology of power that I have called "discipline". We must cease once and for all to describe the effects of power in negative terms: it "excludes", it "represses", it "censors", it "abstracts", it "masks", it "conceals". In fact, power produces; it produces reality; it produces domains of objects and rituals of truth. The individual and the knowledge that may be gained of him belong to this production. (1977:194)

Discipline and Punish is not simply a history of prisons; it also can be seen as a metaphor. Foucault is clear here when he says the arguments being made in the book are not simply about prisons, but about social order and disciplining at large, throughout society. In this vein he discusses the concept of the **panopticon**. In the late seventeen hundreds, the British philosopher Jeromy Bentham drew up architectural plans for the ideal prison, which he called the panopticon. It was designed to be the most efficient, most rational, mode of managing the prison population with the fewest number of guards. It was designed as a circle, much like a wagon wheel, with the guard tower in the middle and the cells on the other rim looking inward such that the guard in the middle tower could see all the cells. Foucault makes much use of the metaphor of the panopticon to describe the world of today. "Our society," he tells us, "is one not of spectacle, but of surveillance" (1977:217). The disciplinary forms embodied in the modern prison have spread out throughout society, and they subject all to disciplinary power today. **Carceral** (modeled in disciplinary prisons) networks "reaches all the disciplinary mechanisms that function throughout society" (1977:298).

Sex, the Body, the Subject, and History

Toward the end of his life, Foucault turned his attention explicitly to the themes of sex, the body, and the subject and how these things have been produced throughout history. In this later work we see a focus not on the disciplinary structures of the world. Instead, he focuses upon how power/knowledge and discourse/practices in history and in the present have insinuated themselves into the individual, biological subject. He specifically was interested in understanding how the self as a biological and human being can respond to these forces today. Sexuality was central to this project. He embarked upon a series of studies of the history of sexuality. In these histories he looked at sex not from a moral framework, but from a framework of technique. How has sex been understood and used in history, and how has this changed? How has pleasure been understood and used in history, and how has this changed? How has the subject been understood and used in history, and has this changed? These are a few of the thematic questions he addresses in his later work.

Foucault here looks at the history of sex and argues, in line with his earlier histories, that sex was understood very differently in earlier periods of history, and people practices sex in very different ways. As Dreyfus and Rabinow note in their critical description and analysis of his work: "Sexuality is a historical construct, not an underlying biological referent" (1982:168). He describes two periods of Western history – the ancient Greek world and the modern world --and compares how sex was understood and practiced in these two periods. In the ancient Greek world, sex was not given a particularly special place. It was instead seen as just another source of biological pleasure. It was not distinguished as such from general pleasure. It was not then seen as something that was a moral concern. Foucault says that sex in the ancient Greek world must be understood within the overarching Greek philosophical orientation. That orientation included an embrace of the notion of balance. Excess was not embraced. The good life was one in which the ancient Greeks maintained a controlled balance in their lives. It was not that sex was bad or good. Sex was, and sex was pleasurable. The point is that it was managed within the context of this overarching philosophy, a philosophy which focused upon techniques to manage the self.

In the modern Western world, beginning with the Protestant Reformation of the fifteen and sixteen hundreds, Foucault says sex was looked at quite differently. It became a religious and moral issue. But the issue of morality was again a technique used to control the population. Foucault makes much of the role of the religious confessional in the early modern era in managing sex. Confessions were oriented toward getting the penitent to confess in detail his sins, specifically his sexual sins. This was a form of interrogation bent upon controlling sex. Foucault argues that this need to control and to discipline sex evolved into the scientific control over all things biological in the modern era. In the modern era, sex has become an instrument of science, particularly medical and psychological sciences, to control, to discipline the individual body. Here Foucault discusses two concepts: bio-power and technologies of the self. It will be recalled that Foucault sees power as ever present, and as such it exists in the actual biological realities of human existence. **Bio-power** is the use of biology in the service of "administering" of controlling the individual and groups. Bio-power is a technology of the self. Foucault wished to understand how technologies, i.e. how disciplinary structures rooted in the power/knowledge intersection, are used on the body, specifically in relation to sexuality, as a form of control and as a form of creating order. He is as concerned about the oppressive nature of this as he is concerned about the various modern forms of expert controls used in modern societies. In his later work, he argued that the need to control biology was reflected not only in medicine and psychiatry, but also in population studies, and other fields. The point is that the disciplinary control over the biological subject expanded to a wide range of areas, particularly to a wide range of scientific areas that are used to control and manage the population.

Baudrillard

Jean Baudrillard (1929-2007) was a French intellectual who is usually seen as a major figure associated with postmodernism and post-structuralism. Like Foucault, Baudrillard was greatly influenced by structuralism and Marxism. Also, like Foucault, he eventually came to reject both approaches, though again like Foucault the influences of these two traditions are clearly seen in all of his work. Earlier in his career he attempted in part to merge structuralism and Marxism (1981) but soon abandoned the task. He found Marx's theory was flawed in many ways. Marx's criticisms of capitalism were problematic because they relied upon the same assumptions used by the capitalist economists being criticized. The focus on production, for example, or the assumptions that the essence of human beings is that they are productive agents, e.g. homo economicus, Baudrillard thought were wrong (Baudrillard; 1973, Poster, 1988). A truly critical approach, he believed, must get outside of the traditional assumptions and categories that are used by conventional economists. Likewise, he thought that the structuralist theory which sought to describe universal, timeless structures of culture or consciousness was wrongheaded because the theory itself was located in history and the ways that signs and symbols work in society changes from one historical period to another.

 As a result, Baudrillard set about to create a new theory, one that was attentive to the realities of the world today. Rather than focusing on production, as Marx did, Baudrillard believed it was essential if one wished to understand the world in the late nineteen hundreds to focus on consumption. Consumption rather than production was the key to understanding society today. In addition, the symbolic realm was also seen as key to understanding the world. In this age of mass communications, of advertising, of signs bombarding us everywhere, in which we are endlessly called upon to consume this or that, Baudrillard saw signs and the symbolic as centrally important.

View of History and his Theory of the Code

Baudrillard built a theory of history. Specifically, he developed a theory of the history of the sign and argued that the place of the sign in society fundamentally changed from one historical period to another. In ancient time, in pre-modern times, in the times before the Renaissance, signs were deeply embedded in the daily lives of people. People engaged in symbolic exchange. Think about life in a small village ten thousand years ago, anywhere in the world. How did people act and interact? The symbolic realm was the basis of social interaction and social order. It was not the material realm that was central. People exchanged things symbolically, whether exchanging wives or sacrificing to the gods, exchange was fundamental to the social order. The importance of religious rituals reflects this. Symbolic exchange – the exchange of values, norms, status, etc. – served as the foundation of society. To understand the centrality of symbolic exchange in traditional cultures and to illustrate how signs are used in such a different way in traditional cultures compared to modern cultures, we can refer again to the example of the comparison of the exchange process that may occur in a traditional village and the exchange process that occurs in the post-industrial world of today (see the beginning of Chapter Ten). The tradition in the village might be that the member brings a gift to the chief when the member makes the request. The chief then decides. What would happen today if a citizen of the United States offered a gift to a congressman in the hopes that the congressman would make a decision on his or her behalf? Wouldn't it be called a bribe? But in traditional societies, at least in some, it is not viewed as a bribe. Indeed, the giving of a gift to the chief in exchange for a favorable action by the chief is a custom, a standard practice. The point here is that the nature of signs and symbolic exchange is radically different in these traditional societies than it is in our society.

Here symbols were deeply entrenched in the daily lives of the members of the community. Symbols were not in any way separated out from these lived realities. It is important here to remember the structuralist theory of language, which Baudrillard is drawing loosely upon here. Structuralism says there is a distinction between the signifier and the signified. For Baudrillard, this distinction was not present in these pre-modern societies.

However, this all changes in the Renaissance (the fourteen and fifteen hundreds), and these changes continued into the industrial era. Here the sign becomes separated from the lived realities of people. Money develops, for example. A gap then arises between appearances and realities, between signifiers and signifieds. The nature of signs as a mediating vehicle then changes. It is not embedded in daily life but removed from it. The organization of the sign system itself, which is removed from the daily, embedded practices, becomes central. As a result, theories of representation become important -- for example, theories of representation of art, of science, etc. In art, the notion of perspective becomes a part of Western art. Perspective is the use of geometrical understandings to create the illusion of three dimensions on the two-dimensional space of a painting. Thus, a way to depict someone in the distance in a painting is to paint them smaller, and the way to depict someone closer to the viewer of the painting is to paint them larger. Perspective is a technique developed; it is a technique of signs. The new mediating role of symbols entails a very different form of social and political organization.

Baudrillard also brings in here suggestions of Marx's notions of use value and exchange value. It will be recalled that use values refer to the usefulness of a commodity. A heavy winter jacket does not have much use value in the desert. Exchange value, Marx and other economists such as Adam Smith say, is what the commodity is worth to others, i.e. how much they are willing to exchange for it. Baudrillard suggests that in pre-modern societies use values dominate, but with the growing surpluses in the Renaissance and beyond, exchange value becomes more central.

The industrial era and the emergence of modern capitalism is the third major period of the history of the sign. Baudrillard seems very much to be thinking about the late eighteen hundreds through the first half of the nineteen hundreds here. In this period, the separation of the signifier from the signified becomes complete, and the sign becomes dominated by the signifier. Appearance takes over from what it represents. We can think of the emergence of mass production and advertising here. This is an era of surplus. It is an era where consumption takes over from production, where exchange value takes over from use value, and where the signifier takes over from the signified, as the central forces of the era. All of these things lead to a new form of value: sign value. **Sign value** concerns the worth of the sign in itself. Sign value is related to things like status, prestige, tastes, and other such concepts. It is also related to the sociological concept of conspicuous consumption, developed early in the nineteen hundreds by the sociologist Thorsten Veblen. Conspicuous consumption is the idea that people can and do buy things for symbolic reasons to enhance their perceived status in a community. When a poor person buys a BMW or dresses in expensive clothing, these are examples of conspicuous consumption. The sign values of the car or clothes are what matters, and not whether the person driving the car or wearing the clothes are in fact rich or not.

Sign value is also related to the Marxist idea of fetish. The idea of a fetish was originally associated with objects from which people derived intense pleasure, classically sexual pleasure. One hears, for example, today people having foot fetishes or underwear fetishes, etc. These are objects which people derive sexual satisfaction from. In sociology, and specifically in

Marxist studies, fetishes are often described in terms of consumption. Marx and Marxists argued that capitalism produces consumption fetishes where people become so engrossed in consumption that they lose sight of everything else. They lose sight of concepts of justice, of morality, of meaning, and become obsessed at gaining gratification through consumption. For Baudrillard, the sign value acts in this way.

Baudrillard identifies a fourth historical period. This began in post-World War two decades and has continued since then. It is what some might call the post-modern period. It is organized along the principles not of production, as in the third period, but along the principles of simulation. Here the forces of the third period become intensified and the separation of the sign from all concrete reference becomes complete. Here signs have no reference to realities other than to their own realities. It is the era of the simulacrum and of hyperreality. The **simulacrum** (the plural is simulacra) is a copy without an original. Post-industrial capitalism is characterized by free floating signifiers detached from real reference. Appearance is all that remains, reality not only disappears but appearance becomes reality. We live in a mass produced, manipulated world of signs that have meaning only in reference to signs. The present is a world filled with simulacrum. The thing that is represented now is meaningless.

The only reality is the sign itself. Relatedly, the original now loses any and all meaning. All that is left are copies, and copies of copies. Think for a second about a can of Coke-a-Cola. What does it mean to say the "original" can of Coke-a-Cola? What is the meaning of the first can of Coke ever in existence? Today, originals have no meaning. The only meaning is to be found in copies of copies. I think of the wars the United States now engages in. It is common place during these wars for a general to appear on television in front of a video monitor in which he plays a tape of a recent successful bombing of a target. It looks and feels no different from a video game, or a game on your smart phone. Image is *all* that matters. One might ask: which is more real Disneyland or the world outside of Disneyland? In the world of today, Baudrillard seems to say, the fabricated world of Disneyland, the world in which all are happy and blind consumers of signs, is the reality. Moreover, it is not simply the reality, but it is the only reality. The world outside of Disneyland no longer exists. He writes:

> Disneyland is there to conceal the fact that it is the "real" country, all of "real" America, which is Disneyland (just as prisons are there to conceal the fact that it is the social in its entirety, in its banal omnipresence, which is carceral). Disneyland is presented as imaginary in order to make us believe that the rest is real, when in fact all of Los Angeles and the America surrounding it are no longer real, but of the order of the hyperreal and of simulation. It is no longer a question of a false

representation of reality (ideology), but of concealing the fact that the real is no longer real, and thus saving the reality principle. (1983:25)

Baudrillard says we live today in a world of hyperreality. **Hyperreality** refers to much the same thing as simulacrum. The elimination of deep meanings, the elimination of the significance of reality or the meanings behind the signs, has led to a reality that is nothing but the **free floating signifiers** and simulacrum. It is an intensive reality of the consumption of empty signs. This is the hyperreality. The emptiness of the present lost in the consumption of these signs is hyperreality. We are trapped in this reality.

Baudrillard claims that the world today is organized by a "code." He is referring to some sort of code that organizes the symbolic meanings in this world of hyperreality. Unfortunately, he never tells us much about this code. It is the organizing principle of the symbolic realm, the only realm left, but how and why is it organized? Capitalism surely is not the driving force any longer of organizing the symbolic realm, if it ever was.

The World Today and What is to be Done?

The contemporary world according to Baudrillard has a number of features. One set of features is excess and ecstasy. This is a world of world of hyper-consumption, of free-floating signifiers, of simulacra. It is a world of excess. More is deemed better. We are all called out to be consumers, and to consume. He says this is a world of ecstasy. By ecstasy he is referring to a world of intense pleasure. The objects of our desires, the commodified signs of consumption, call to us, and instill in us ecstasy. As we live in a world in which the referent no longer is meaningful, ecstasy refers to ecstasy and nothing more. We seek ecstasy, we strive for striving sake ever more for ecstasy. It is a world that has spun out of control, and we have become lost in the signs of consumption and in the pleasures of this consumption. This is related to another theme characterizing the world of today: implosion. Whereas the modern world may be characterized by explosion, by an almost never-ending push outward to destroy, the postmodern world is characterized by implosion, by endless consumptions of emptiness. This is little more than the corroding through excess. He gives examples of cancer and obesity to illustrate these trends. Another set of themes, closely related to the above, in his work on desire, pleasure and seduction. In the world of simulacra and hyper-consumption, we are called out by the organized sign code to gain pleasures through consumption of signs. We are seduced by the objects of our consumption and are defined by them.

The contemporary world is also characterized by the "death of the subject." (The influences of his structuralist and post-structuralist teachers are clear here.) Baudrillard sees the self as being produced by the seduction of the objects. It is made out of these and thus it is fragmented. The fragmented self has no anchor, no center. Consuming one thing, one set of signs, we become someone; consuming something else, we become something else. The subject as an anchored entity defining and making itself and its world has been eclipsed by the code and by the simulacra. Mark Poster describes Baudrillard's position:

> The pessimistic implications of [Baudrillard's book] *Simulacra and Simulations* are brought home in Fatal Strategies. Here Baudrillard attempts to think the social world from the point of view of the object, a seeming oxymoron. Like the post-structuralists, Baudrillard assumes that the era of the representational subject is past. One can no longer comprehend the world as if the Kantian categories of time, space, causality, etc. are necessary universal paths to truth. Baudrillard takes this to imply that the subject no longer provides a vantage point on reality. The privileged position has shifted to the object, specifically to the hyperreal object, the simulated object. In place of a logic of the subject, Baudrillard proposes a logic of the object, and this is his "fatal" strategy. (1988:6)

So what then is to be done? It will be recalled that Baudrillard has his intellectual roots in Marxism, though he long since abandoned the theory. He nevertheless retained the critical impulses associated with Marxism. Baudrillard is critical of what has occurred in consumer capitalism. He is concerned about traditional issues of justice and is concerned about what he takes to be the oppressive qualities of this new world order. What then does he say we should do about it? We can no longer hope for or champion a working class revolution, or any such thing, as he has said we no longer live in a world organized on the principles of production and economics. We can no longer hope for a better world built upon the embrace of one or another grand theory. What then is left?

Baudrillard and Resistance

Baudrillard does not give us much of a clear indication of what is to be done in the face of the postmodern, at least he does not give us a clear understanding of what he thinks should be done. He embraces play. All that is left is the play of free floating signifiers. Perhaps we could play with this to affect change? But how, and what sort of change is or should be sought? At one point, he embraces passivity or silence or at best refusal to participate. This is seen at the end of his essay, "The Masses: The Implosion of the Social in the Media." He writes:

"Our relationship to this system is an insoluble "double bind" – exactly that of children in their relationship to the demands of the adult world. They are at the same time told to constitute themselves as autonomous subjects, responsible, free, and conscious, and to constitute themselves as submissive objects, inert, obedient, and conformist. The child resists on all levels, and to these contradictory demands he or she replies by a double strategy. When we ask the child to be the object, he or she opposes all the practices of disobedience, or revolt, or emancipation; in short, the strategy of a subject. When we ask the child to be a subject, he or she opposes just as obstinately and successfully a resistance as object; that is to say, exactly the opposite: infantilism, hyperconformity, total dependence, passivity, idiocy. Neither of the two strategies has more objective value than the other. Subjective resistance is today given a unilateral value and considered to be positive – in the same way as in the political sphere only the practices of liberation, of emancipation, of expression, of self-constitution as a political subject are considered worthwhile and subversive. This is to take no account of the equal and probably superior impact of all the practices of the object, the renunciation of the position of subject and of meaning – exactly the practices of the mass – which we bury with the disdainful term *alienation* and *passivity*. The liberating practices correspond to *one* of the aspects of the system, to the constant ultimatum we are given to constitute ourselves as pure objects; but they do not correspond at all to the other demand to constitute ourselves as subjects, to liberate, to expressive ourselves at any price, to vote, to produce, to decide, to speak, to participate, to play the game: blackmail and ultimatum just as serious as the other, probably more serious today. To a system whose argument is oppression and repression, the strategic resistance is to demand the liberating rights of the subject. But this seems rather to reflect an earlier phase of the system; and if we are still confronted with it, it is no longer a strategic territory: the present argument of the system is to maximize speech, to maximize the production of meaning, of participation. And so the strategic resistance is that of the refusal of meaning and the refusal of speech; or of the hyperconformist simulation of the very mechanisms of the system, which is another form of refusal by overacceptance. It is the actual strategy of the masses. This strategy does not exclude the other, but it is the winning one today, because it is the most adapted to the present phase of the system." (1988:218-219)

While it is rather unclear what he hopes to see happen, it is clear that he does not believe resistance to the existing order will or should take conventional forms of political opposition. After all, conventional understandings of politics are historically contingent, and as we no longer live in a modern world which operates under the principles of production or for that matter under the principles of conventionally understood political economics, we cannot employ the same strategies now as was employed then.

In short, Baudrillard provides many rich insights into the workings of the contemporary world. However, some of his ideas are confused – ideas such as "the code" – or imprecise. His theory provides a nice array of creative and critical concepts useful to criticizing the world today, but he does not provide any suggestions for addressing the problems of the world today that are in any way helpful. After all, what is to be done?

Summary

In this chapter we covered some of the main ideas associated with postmodern theory, and we explored the ideas of Foucault and Baudrillard. Some of the main themes in postmodern theory are: fragmentation; superficiality; the rejection of grand theories; power, inequality, and difference; and anti-humanism. Postmodern theories were influenced by structuralism, and specifically the European structural linguistics and structural anthropology. Foucault was a French intellectual who is variously described as a philosopher, a historian, a social theorist. He wrote many critical histories, including histories of mental illness, of prisons, of medicine, of the social sciences, of sexuality, and more. Many of the same themes are found in each of these histories. He claims the structure of thought in each historic era, i.e. the episteme, differs from each other historical era. People see their worlds differently in these different eras. Foucault argues that the modern western world, with origins in the Enlightenment, looks like it is better than earlier periods in terms of things such as morality and freedom, but in fact it is worse. The growth of reason as the dominating force in the modern world is not the liberating force that many think it is. Instead, this growth has led to the oppression of humanity. Foucault describes the fusion of power/knowledge in this regard. Humanity in the modern world is being oppressed by Reason. Humans are subjected increasingly to disciplinary forces directed by Reason. Baudrillard was a French intellectual. He is generally considered one of the most extreme postmodern theorists, and many criticize his theorizing for among other things his exaggerations and hyperbole. He is influenced by structuralism and by Marx, though he rejects and goes beyond both of these. Baudrillard claims the power of signs in the world today has become so great that the meaning of signs has become detached from the real world, and we are all therefore living in a world detached from reality. A new reality has emerged. We are now living in a world of free floating signifiers. He also says the simulacrum has taken over. Simulacrum are copies without originals.

It should be noted here that there are many other scholars with many different and conflicting ideas who are identified with postmodernism. While they all have differing theoretical perspectives, they tend to share certain assumptions and tend to be influenced by similar intellectual traditions, as noted earlier. They also all are confronted with three common criticisms that have routinely be leveled against them by traditional social theorists and traditional sociologists today. These criticisms are often leveled again Foucault and Baudrillard. One common criticism of postmodern theory concerns the political implications of the theorizing. Postmodern theorists tend to profess to be radical and highly critical of contemporary society, of democratic capitalism. They also tend to claim to reject the foundations of all other forms of social theorizing. For example, they tend to reject any claims to grand theory. Yet critics have said that the political implications of this form of theorizing ultimately leads to either of two political positions, neither of which is accepted or acceptable by the postmodern theorists themselves. Critics complain that one position that postmodern theory could lead to if embraced is highly conservative if not fascist. Fascism is the oppressive political systems seen in Hitler's Nazi Germany, in Mussolini's Italy, and any number of other dictatorships since that time. Fascism is a form of political ideology where power determines morality, and all else. What is considered right or just is based upon who has the most power. Hitler said that the Germans were the master-race and the Jews needed to be killed, so by this way of thinking it was morally right. Fascism also rejects the basic claims of the Enlightenment and what it sees as the decadence, the failings, of modernity, much in the way that postmodernists also complain about such things. Similarly, fascist rail against rationality and champion irrationality, much as postmodernists do. Critics sometimes claim that it is not a coincidence that some of the main inspirations of postmodern theorists – including the philosophers Nietzsche and Heidegger – were either fascists or where scholars who influenced fascists. Hitler and the Nazis were influenced by both, and it should be noted that Heidegger himself was an unapologetic Nazi official in Hitler's regime. Postmodern scholars today universally reject such claims. Postmodern theorists claim to detest fascism and all things associated with it. Yet if they are not fascist, what then are they? This brings us to the second possible political position: Critics say that postmodern theory, if it is not fascist, is nothing more than warmed over liberalism disguised as something else. For example, while some postmodern theorists proclaim to be anti-humanists their political perspectives appear very much to embrace humanist sensibilities. Foucault, for example, seemed very much to embrace the Enlightenment values of liberty and equality and the value of the individual. Though he cloaks such understandings in theoretical garb that is seemingly at odds with conventional Enlightenment thinking, when push comes to shove, his position appears to be that of a liberal, that of a person who champions tolerance and acceptance of differences.

A second common criticism leveled against postmodern theory, often by conventional sociological theorists, is that postmodern does little more than wrap ideas that others have offered over the years into complicated and confusion concepts that look like they are new and innovative but in fact are saying nothing that is new. For example, the claim that the structure of consciousness can and does change from one historical time period to another has been claimed by many either directly or indirectly, from Marx to Durkheim. Similarly, the claim that there is a relationship between forces of power and knowledge in a society as is claimed often by postmodern theorists is also not new. Moreover, postmodern theorists who claim we have entered a new historical era that is fundamentally different than the modern era have been criticized for not convincingly demonstrating those features of the new era that are in fact unique in different. As noted in the introduction to this chapter, most if not all of the features said to be unique to a postmodern world can be identified as having existed in the modern, industrial world.

A third set of criticisms of postmodern theory is that it is nihilistic or fatalistic. Critics say this form of theorizing is nothing more than endless criticisms, and that it provides no meaningful way forward, either for the development of theory or for social or political action. It rejects the Enlightenment. It rejects a faith or hope in reason. It rejects theory. It rejects the possibilities of developing knowledge free from power, etc.

Lastly, critics complain that postmodern theory is riddled with contradictions, and that the advocates of this form of theorizing embrace rather than try to overcome these contradictions. Critics say this is hardly satisfactory. For example, postmodern theories tend to claim to reject grand theories, but postmodern theorizing itself tends to be a grand theory of sorts. Similarly, Foucault claims to reject traditional histories that implicitly view the history of the western world as one of progress. For example, traditional histories would claim that modern psychiatric theories and practices are better, more effective, and more humane than the theories and practices used in the eighteen hundreds, and those were better than those used in the sixteen hundreds, etc. Yet Foucault's history does little more than turn this picture up-side-down. There is still a historical trajectory imposed on history by Foucault, but instead of steady progress it is one of steadily increasing oppression in the guise of progress.

Discussion Questions

1. Scholars point to numerous contradictions found in postmodern theories and claim that these theories should be dismissed or rejected because of them. Can you identify two distinct contradictions in postmodern theory, and can you imagine how the postmodern theorists might defend their claims against these criticisms?

2. Do we now live in a period of history that is distinctly different from the modern era, and one that should now be called the postmodern era? Does the growth of the internet create social conditions that are fundamentally different from the social conditions of fifty years ago? What are they? Do we live in a new world, or are the changes we see around us simply the same changes that began in the modern world, only more intense?

3. Does postmodern theory lead either to fascism or to liberal democracy? Does it have a meaningful and defendable radical political position? If so, what is it?

4. What is the Enlightenment Project? Is it the source of the major problems in the world today, as some postmodern theorists claim? Or is the Enlightenment Project our only hope to produce a justice and prosperous world, or is there some other alternative?

Chapter Thirteen: Critical Identity Theories – Race, Gender and Queer Theories

We can frame our discussion here of critical theories of race and gender by looking at two distinct, but related, things. The first of these is a brief review of the ways in which the founders of American sociology thought of race, and specifically the sociology of race. The second is to briefly describe rather recent events related to the Black Lives Matter movement.

When one looks at the founding figures in American sociology in the early nineteen hundreds, it is striking from the perspective of today to see how these figures understood and thought about race and gender and about the sociology of such things. To begin, we can look at their understandings of race. When we do so, we find that some if not many of the founding figures were, in hindsight, very much racist in their beliefs (Morris, 2015), at least by contemporary standards. That is, one finds over and over that they embraced the "classic" form of racism that says that black people are genetically inferior to white people. This classic form says that blacks are genetically determined to have inferior character, temperament and intelligence than white people. To understand this more fully we can begin by looking at how the earlier sociologists thought of sociology itself. What was the purpose of developing this new field? What was the point? This is revealed in the first volumes of the American Journal of Sociology.

The first volume of the American Journal of Sociology, the first sociology journal in America, was published in July 1895 by the University of Chicago Press. Since its founding it has been a dominant force in American sociology. Sociology was a new field in America in the late eighteen hundreds. The very first article in this first volume was written by Albion Small, one of the founders of American sociology. Small played a significant part in the creation of the Department of Sociology at the University of Chicago and served as chair of the department for many years. He is sometimes credited with writing the first sociology textbook, though some say that honor goes to his colleague Robert Park. In Small's essay "The Era of Sociology" (1895:1-15), he describes the task of this new field of sociology. The task should be the advancement of sociology as a social science with the aim of ameliorating or helping to address problems of, or potential threats to, social order that were accompanying the quickly changing industrial, urban America of the turn of the century.

The essay is striking when compared to sociology today. There are thematic similarities and stark differences between then and now, both in terms of what the world is like and in terms of what the place of sociology is and should be within it. For example, Small championed social science as a discipline that should be oriented toward understanding and addressing the ills of contemporary society. Today, one finds some if not many sociologists embracing similar sentiments. But the differences, at least between Small's views and those of some sociological theorists today, are glaring. One difference concerns the relation of fact to value (see Chapter One). Small sees no problem with sociology embracing an empirical, scientific orientation. Indeed, the objective, unbiased scientific basis of the science of sociology is foundational for him. A second, though related difference lies in his views about the place of sociology in society and specifically its place in maintaining social order and in fostering appropriate (and ordered) change. It is through the systematic use of the sociological knowledge gained from empirical research that the discipline can help American society maintain order, or help to regulate change, in the midst of the great sea changes which were afoot at the birth of the twentieth century -- with industrialization, immigration, urbanization, etc. Embedded in this perspective is a view that sociology should serve to combat the real or potential irrational impulses or passions of the masses, who may in fits of irrationality embrace such harmful and destructive things as communism or some such radical alternative view of social organization. Small's vision of sociology is that it should be one that gives intellectual ammunition to people – particularly "men of affairs" -- to fend off the threatening impulses of "popular judgment" or even of Marxist sentiments. Here he distinguishes between "popular" sociology and scientific sociology. Popular sociology is a dangerous thing. It is the naïve and often inaccurate popular understandings of how the social world works; it is fueled by impulsive passions and unchecked sentiment. It is these public beliefs that are less than rational and systematic that should be countered by the science of sociology.

The goal is not simply to offer correctives to the half-truths or errors of popular sociology. The goal is to contribute to the betterment of society. Sociology should serve this end: "Precisely because permanent enlargement of human welfare is not a matter of shreds and patches, but a gain which depends upon the development of a superior type of manhood, capable of superior cooperation, do we maintain that the programme most directly adapted to the furtherance of that end is suppression of the riot of imagination and substitution of the order of investigation" (1895:7). Small, in effect, in keeping with the tenor of Progressive Era ethics, is embracing an ameliorist role for sociology. Its role is to identify and investigate the problems and threats to social order such that those in power can utilize the sociological research findings and respond and correct these problems: "If sociology is to be of any influence among practical men, it must be able to puts its wisdom about things that interest ordinary men in a form which men of affairs will see to be true to life" (1895:14). The content of the new journal, he tells us, will vary "from discussions of methodology to treatment of plans for social amelioration ..." (1895:14).

The essay is striking when compared to contemporary sociology for many reasons. One of these is that the utter whiteness and maleness of Small's perspective stands out, perhaps subtly. This is mentioned here not to criticize Small for advancing a perspective that is rooted in his maleness and his whiteness. Rather it is useful for us to understand how Small and the early sociologists think so that we may make better sense of sociological theory today. It is useful to recognize how such things as maleness and whiteness influenced (and influence) understandings of the social world. His white and male perspective is seen, often subtly, throughout the essay. We see it in a passage where he describes how the large-scale, systemic forces of the modern world can bear down upon individuals, knowingly or not, and how these present problems to them. The modern world is more "intrusive" than in earlier times. He describes how the "ranchman in Montana," "the manufacturer in Illinois," "the miner in Nevada," and "the rolling-mill operative in Pennsylvania" are impacted by large-scale, economic and political forces: "[A]ll these and the rest represented by them learn to disregard the fixed factors in human relations, and instead to watch other players in the game of life as exclusively as opponents at the chessboard or rival teams on gridiron or diamond" (1895:2). Stated or implied, this social world consists of men, and of men only. The proper concern and interest of sociology therefore is of men, and of men only. The game of social life is a game of men working, perhaps mostly white men working and interacting with other men, presumably white men.

Race is all but absent in the essay, though as we see below it was a major concern or major point of interest for some if not many of the early figures in American sociology. The existence and experience of race, of people of color, is all but absent in the essay. It does not appear to be a matter of importance in making sense of the social world. One might wish to claim that Small implicitly includes images of black Americans or others in his views of the American men, of the ranchers, machinists and carpenters, but, by and large, people of color are almost non-existent in the essay. They do appear, however, in a few noted places in the article. They appear a few times in some of the very lengthy quotes by a Benjamin Kidd, cited by Small. Small copies these long quotes to illustrate support for his own ideas about the need and value of a scientific sociology. Kidd criticizes what he sees as dangerous, popular distortions of history and society found in the popular press. The members of the press, e.g. the journalists (or at least the specific one he notes), are "ignorant," and they present faulty ideas about history and society.

They are not only ignorant, but they are naïve in that they make faulty judgments that would lead them to be believed by the ignorant masses. The press would mislead the reader, would impress the people, including non-Western, non-white people, who do not accurately understand the world: "He will find the same critic equally impressed by "the spectacle of the half-naked ascetic sitting under his banyan, and giving out to brown men, ignorant as fishes, thoughts which today form the only antiseptic in the minds of a third of the human race ..." (1895:9-10). He appears to be referencing people from places such as India or Africa. Perhaps the ascetic is the Hindu or Buddhist priest who is championing spiritualistic orientations? These religions and traditions are deemed "ignorant," waiting to be corrected by the white, male, western (social) scientist, objectively proclaiming the truths of the world.

It would be an error however to think that Small's article accurately captures the totality of the image of race and inequality held by the founding fathers of American sociology. Small's view is but one, albeit important, slice of the views of the founders. Indeed, the pioneers of American sociology in the late eighteen and early nineteen hundreds did in fact think and write quite a bit about race. One might even argue that they focused on race more than they did on many other topical areas in sociology. But they did so in ways that through the eyes of the present are clearly racist or at least could reasonably said today to be so. This is seen, for example, in one of the first, if not the very first, main textbooks in sociology, *Introduction to the Science of Sociology* by Robert Park and Ernest Burgess (1921), written in 1909. Park and Burgess were colleagues of Small and were also founding members of the discipline. In this text, they wrote about race in many places. They often times wrote about it in their lengthy accounts regarding the debates over the relative influence of nature or nurture on human behavior and in their accounts of inequality. At points, they suggest that much human behavior must be understood as being caused by forces of nurture (or culture or history). Thus, we are told when thinking that there may be a genetic difference in temperament between whites and "savage" races to remember that the differences between "these savages and the poorer white European classes is non-existent .... [I]t is sufficient for my purpose to have secured the admission that the peasants of Europe do not as a whole use their mental powers in a much more logical or abstract manner than do primitive people. I maintain that such superiority as they have is due to differences (1) of environment and (2) of variability" (1921:47). (Note that the authors here are comparing poor whites and not whites in general to "primitive people," i.e. people of color. Presumably, the rich whites are by nature, by biology, superior in their eyes.) Yet the authors also repeatedly invoked suggestions or outright claims that explanations for inequality between black people and white people are to be found in biological or cultural deficits within black people themselves. At some points, the clear racist claims – at least from the perspective of today – are explicit: "The Negro is, by natural disposition, neither an intellectual nor an idealist, like the Jew; nor a brooding introspective, like the East Indian; nor a pioneer and frontiersman, like the Anglo-Saxon. He is primarily an artist, loving life for its own sake. His métier is expression rather than action. He is, so to speak, the lady among the races" (1921:68-69). A few paragraphs earlier, Park writes: "The temperament [i.e. genetic disposition] of the Negro, as I conceive it, consists in a few elementary but distinctive characteristics, determined by physical organization and transmitted biologically. These characteristics manifest themselves in a genial, sunny, and social disposition, in an interest and attachment to external, physical things rather than to subjective states and objects of introspection, in a disposition for expression rather than enterprise and action" (1921:68). (Echoes of the classic, vile racist stereotypes of little Black Sambo or of Amos and Andy or of countless others are clear here.) One could chronicle many similar sentiments throughout the text. In short, either people of color are ignored or they are painted as racist caricatures.

This has produced two strands in American sociological theorizing in the early and mid-nineteen hundreds, both of which ultimately led to ignoring any meaningful engagement with race (from today's perspective). One of these strands was simply to ignore race as an important topic to consider. The other was to focus upon it through the lens of racist sciences (often rooted in Darwinian ideas) that emerged in the eighteen hundreds and continued through the first half of the nineteen hundreds. We should not discount the role of scientific racist understandings in sociology in the first half of the nineteen hundreds (and we should also not ignore its role today). Scientific racism focused on the natural rightness of systems of inequality, and the natural rightness of inequalities between racial groups. Scientific racism as an acceptable form of scholarship was significantly wounded as a legitimate enterprise in America and in Europe as a result of the rise of fascism. Hitler, his Nazi followers, and the fascist movement of the mid-nineteen hundreds warmly embraced scientific racism, and created gross and evil policies and practices based upon them, ultimately leading to World War Two, the deaths of fifty-five million people, the holocaust, and the eugenics programs.

We can get a better understanding of the ways that early American sociologists understood race by briefly reviewing a few more of the ideas of Robert Park, one of the more important early figures in the discipline. Park (1864-1944) is often considered the founding figure of the sociology of race in American sociology. He began his career as a journalist and then earned a doctorate in philosophy and sociology. He went on to work as a ghostwriter and political advisor to Booker T. Washington in Alabama, where he stayed for a number of years. After that, he became a professor of sociology at the University of Chicago. According to Aldon Morris (2015) in his insightful intellectual biography of W.E. B. Du Bois, *The Scholar Denied*, Park's work with Washington was not incidental to his beliefs about race. Indeed, the two men had similar views.

To better understand this, we can briefly summarize Morris's description of the differences between Washington and Du Bois. Washington and Du Bois were leading black Americans with contrasting views on how best to improve the lot of black Americans in the late eighteen hundreds and early nineteen hundreds. Morris contrasts the approaches to advance the cause of equality for black Americans made by Washington and by Du Bois. Du Bois championed the idea of educating the "talented tenth" of the black population in the best classic, liberal arts education available such that black leaders could be developed to lead the struggle for equality. He wished to create a class or group of black intellectuals as leaders of the movement for equality. This leadership would demand equality and would demand that white people make the changes necessary in law, policies and practices to create this equality. He also believed that black Americans should have the same opportunities to the highest levels of education in America as white Americans had. Washington rejected this idea. Washington instead argued that the best way to improve the lot of black Americans in the late eighteen hundreds and early nineteen hundreds was for black people to learn the industrial arts, to learn practical employable, manual skills such that blacks could get (working class) jobs and build wealth gradually. That is, they should be taught the trades, like plumbing and carpentry and farming. It was only by black people learning the manual trades that they will be able to lift themselves up over time, according to Washington. Black Americans, he said, should be encouraged to internalize the work ethic that white Americans supposedly had. He was opposed to focusing on having black people engaged in classic liberal arts education, education that focused on abstract ideas rather than concrete employable skills.

One perhaps can see how and why Washington became quite popular amongst the white elites at the time, and one could also see (as we describe below) why the approach advocated by Du Bois was so rejected by the white population. If nothing else, Washington's approach toward addressing the dire state of black Americans in the late eighteen and early nineteen hundreds implicitly or explicitly absolved white Americans from any responsibility related to this, and as such it absolved white America from any responsibility for correcting this situation. It allowed white Americans to believe they were not responsible for creating or maintaining these racial inequalities and they were thus not responsible for correcting these. White people thus were not called upon to acknowledge their responsibilities in this matter and were not called upon to do anything to change the situation. Washington's whole perspective also implicitly or explicitly fits nicely with racist sensibilities that blacks should be relegated to lower positions in society and that they should not aspire for the same things as whites. Afterall, the manual labor jobs championed by Washington echo the manual work done by blacks during slavery for hundreds of years.

According to Morris, Park, while working for Washington, comfortably embraced these ideas. Park as we saw earlier harbored racist sensibilities, and he also subscribed to Washington's views on the betterment of black America, as opposed to Du Bois's. (Morris argues that this is one of the reasons that Du Bois was blocked from entering white academic sociology during his lifetime.) Morris sheds further light on Park's views: "For Park, racial temperaments are key determinants differentiating racial groups. Contrary to scholars who argue that biology is almost absent from Park's analysis of race, his concept of "racial temperaments" reveals that he conceptualized races mainly in biological terms. Defining racial temperament, Park states, "This temperament, as I conceive it, consists in a few elementary but distinctive characteristics, determined by physical organization and transmitted biologically." Thus, his concept of race is consistent with the social Darwinist thesis that basic racial characteristics are biologically inherited" (2015:117).

Park was not alone in his beliefs. Many of the other prominent early sociologists had similar ideas. (It should be noted that not all early sociologists in America subscribed implicitly or explicitly to some of the harsher forms of biological determinism and its relation to inequalities. Edward Ross, another central figure in the development of sociology in the late eighteen hundreds and early nineteen hundreds, embraced fully the ameliorist role of sociology in society; Ross also forcefully rejected the ideas of social Darwinism and of Spencer – see Chapter One.) We can see this with the acceptance by many of eugenics and all that is implied by this. Eugenics is the theory of selective breeding to improve the human species. Much like in the agricultural domain where certain traits of cows, wheat, corn, chickens and pigs are encouraged to be passed on genetically through selective breading, so too the human race could be improved in this same way. Eugenics argued that people with genes deemed inferior, e.g. racial minorities, mentally ill, physically ill, etc., should be prevented from having children because this would lead to the worsening of the genetic stock of a people. Eugenics is closely aligned with Darwinism and with social Darwinism, which claim that inequalities are natural and good. The influential British polymath Francis Galton (1822-1911), a cousin of Charles Darwin, was an early proponent of eugenics. Eugenics was a popular theory in the early nineteen hundreds. However, its popularity in America and in Western Europe declined dramatically as the result of Hitler and the Nazis, as they embraced this theory and implemented horrendous practices based upon it.

But in the early nineteen hundreds, eugenics as part of the broader orientation of scientific racism was viewed quite favorably by many if not most American social scientists. Galton himself published articles in American sociology journals promoting his ideas, giving pointers to sociologists on how to use these in their field, and these were generally received quite well. He published one such article in the tenth volume of the American Journal of Sociology. And Galton was not alone. Many influential early figures in American sociology embraced these ideas. One of these was Franklin Giddings (1855-1931), the influential sociology professor at Columbia University. The point here is that eugenics is deeply racist, particularly in the hands of all those mentioned herein (and so many other supporters could be cited).

We can also frame our understandings of sociological theory and race by briefly describing the Black Lives Matter protests. The Black Lives Matter movement began after George Zimmerman, a white man, was acquitted in court of shooting to death Trayvon Martin, an unarmed black American teenager in Florida in 2013. The killing occurred on the grounds of an apartment complex where Zimmerman lived. Zimmerman followed Martin as he walked through the apartment complex grounds. He confronted Martin. An argument ensured, and Zimmerman killed Martin. Zimmerman was acquitted based upon the Florida "stand your ground" law, which made it legal for someone to kill another in self-defense. Since then (and before this), there have been numerous murders of young black American men by mostly white police officers. The Black Lives Matter movement arose to protests these. They have engaged in various forms of protests, from politely calling for national discussions on racism and police actions to disruptions of public meetings of politicians. The "official" Black Lives Matter.com webpage describes the movement: "We affirm that all Black Lives Matter: Black Lives Matter is an ideological and political intervention in a world where black lives are systematically and intentionally targeted for demise. It is an affirmation of Black folks' contributions to this society, our humanity, and our resilience in the face of deadly oppression." Alicia Garza, one of the founders of the webpage, describes the history of the movement: "I created #BlackLivesMatter with Patrisse Cullors and Opal Tometi, two of my sisters, as a call to action for Black people after 17-year old Trayvon Martin was post-humously placed on trial for his own murder and the killer, George Zimmerman, was not held accountable for the crime he committed. It was a response to the anti-Black racism that permeates our society and also, unfortunately, our movements." The Black Lives Matter movement is ideologically informed by critical race theory, including the ideas of some of the theorists noted below.

While Black Lives Matter protests continued from its founding, these protests grew dramatically in the summer of 2020. At that time, an unarmed black man George Floyd was pinned to the ground by a white police officer, with several other police standing guard. The white police officer put his leg on Floyd's neck and the latter laid on the pavement. With the help of two other police officers, the first officer held him down for over eight minutes, throughout which time Floyd was repeatedly saying "I can't breathe." The officer looked nonchalant as he had one of his hands in his pockets. Floyd stopped moving. The officers did nothing. He kept his knee on Floyd's neck. Floyd died.

This incident ignited a huge wave of protest across the country. Millions of people marched in Black Lives Matter protests for several weeks. In the midst of this period, serious rioting broke out in many major American downtowns. This shocked the nation. The protest then tended to orient toward tearing down statues deemed to represent the white oppression of people of color, most notably, statues of confederate leaders were attacked and taken down, either by force or by legal actions of the respective governments. Statues of others, such as Columbus, were also targeted.

Throughout this period, videos were posted online on social media over and over again showing white police killing young black men across the country. The breadth of the problem was hard to ignore. The problem was not simply police brutality against young black men, but it was implicitly and explicitly more than this. It was about the continued inequalities, between black Americans and white Americans, and the "oppression" of the former by the latter, and the seemingly unwillingness of white Americans to recognize this reality as a problem that needs to be addressed. Moreover, a theme of the Black Lives Matter movement was that white people, whether they were consciously racist or not, were culpable for the existing state of race relations in America today, and white people had an obligation to do things to change the situation.

These themes arguably are inspired not only by the lived experiences of black Americans, but also by the growth of critical approaches to race taught in the universities, as well as by a number of influential texts that have appeared in recent years. One book that has had a direct impact upon Black Lives Matter is *The New Jim Crow* by Michelle Alexander (2020). Alexander is a lawyer by training. Her book examines the massive rise of black incarceration that occurred in the late nineteen hundreds. She examines the courts, the police, and the prisons and shows how the systematic workings of these systems have produced a situation that in many ways is parallel to the racial oppressions found in the Jim Crow south prior to the Civil Rights movement of the 1960s. While it is technically not a work of sociology, Alexander's book is infused with contemporary sociological understandings of race. Critical race theory, which is discussed below, is another academic and critical approach to race that arguably informed Black Lives Matter, both in its call to recognize the systematic bases of racism today and its call to engage in political practices to combat it.

Overview

This chapter is on critical race and gender theories and on queer theories. Race, and gender, and issues related to LGBT+, and others are now treated very differently in sociological theorizing today than they were in the earlier history of American sociology. It is not simply that race and gender, for example, now are seen as vital issues in theory, but it is also the nature and form of theorizing itself that is different. Critical race and gender theories are not seeking merely to describe existing realities or to maintain the existing social order, and particularly the existing system of inequalities. Nor are most bent upon proposing theories to incrementally change one or another feature of society all the while maintaining the overall system of inequality. (Park and Burgess and the early generation of American sociologists seemed to embrace one or the other of these views.) Instead, critical race and gender theories are seeking to explain and to counter inequalities in race and gender. Relatedly, the conceptualization of epistemology and of the relationship of theory to method is often starkly different in these theories than it is in much conventional sociological theorizing. For example, these theories often implicitly or explicitly do not swear allegiance to science and to scientific objectivity as such; instead, they often develop and champion alternative epistemologies that challenge such things.

A chapter such as this poses a few conceptual or definitional issues that need to be addressed. One of these concerns the idea of critical race and gender theories versus race and gender theories. There are theories of race and/or gender which could be viewed as not being critical. Such theories adhere to conventional approaches to sociology and simply see race or gender as just some other categories of sociological analysis, not unlike the family, or institutions, or culture, etc. These traditional approaches adhere to the traditional notions that sociology is and should be an objective science, and it should not seek in itself to challenge and change the social world. On the other hand, there are theories that are decidedly critical, and most of the theories covered below are from this perspective. These approaches do not see race or gender as simply topics to be objectively studied by social science. Instead, they see the task to critically investigate how and why inequalities of race and gender exist, and they seek to do so in order to challenge and combat these inequalities.

A second conceptual issue involves the awkwardness of the term. The term critical race and gender theory is a bit awkward in that associated terms have been used in academics to refer to things other than the theories covered here in this chapter. It is awkward partly because the name is often associated with a specific, non-sociological theory, one that is found in legal studies. While critical race theories in legal studies share many of the themes, as we see below, with sociological theories, they differ in some respects. Legal scholars have developed the concept of critical race theory to mean a form of understanding of the law and how it works which locates the topics of race, inequality, and power at its heart. Critical race theory in this sense – in the popular sense today – that is, coming out of legal studies, is described below in more detail. As we will see, many of the ideas of this form of theorizing are and have been noted by sociologists developing their own versions of critical race theories. Yet the sociological approaches are generally a bit different. Sociological theories tend to focus in more elaborated ways upon the workings of social structures and cultures and how these operate to produce racial realities. A last conceptual issue to note concerns the term critical theory: when sociologists use the term critical theory, they tend to be referring to the ideas of the Frankfurt School (see Chapter Eight). The critical race and gender theories discussed in this chapter have little to do – at least not directly -- with the Frankfurt School's theorizing, though they are influenced by it (particularly in the early developments of the theory).

Another complexity involving this chapter concerns the relationship of race to gender theories. Should they be treated separately or within one chapter? Many would argue that these theories are fundamentally distinct and as such should be assigned separate chapters. However, some would argue there are sufficient parallels or overlaps between them to justify both being covered within one chapter. In addition, the intersections of race, gender, and class inequalities suggest a need to recognize how these theories inevitably are related. As we see below, Patricia Hill Collins and others use the term intersectionality to describe the ways in which more than one of the categories of race, gender, sexuality (and class) intersect in real life, and therefore the intersection must be understood in its own terms. One has a gender, a race, a class, etc. at the same time, and one experiences their intersections in daily practices. None of this is to deny the real differences in the experiences of the group members, for example, they are different in the particular historical and structural locations of women and people of color in the social world. Whether one wishes to cite biology, or marriage, or life circumstances, women and people of color are located in distinct social positions.

This chapter focuses upon some of the themes shared by race and gender theories and by critical race and gender studies. Several themes can be identified. This first theme revolves around: the recognition of the inequalities; the assertion that they are unjust; and the claim that sociological investigations could lead to understandings of these inequalities and to solutions to them. A second theme revolves around the systematic ways that the social context – the political, social, cultural, economic context – operates to produce or to maintain systems of inequality between women and men and/or between races. A third theme consists of a focus on the structured experiences and experiencing of racism, sexism, etc. Here the focus is on philosophy, psychology, social psychology. This theme is oriented toward knowing how such things as racism and sexism are experienced and how they are enacted by people in positions in power, often if not typically in an unknowing way. A fourth theme involves a recognition and theoretical understanding of the inter-connections of issues of race and gender, as well as belief in the importance now to see these things in a global context.

Critical Race Theories and Not So Critical Race Theories

An important distinction needs to be made here: between 1) theories about race and 2) critical race theories. While most theories of race that have arisen in the last thirty years or so can be located under the broad umbrella of critical race theories, some cannot. By race theories, in contrast to critical race theories, I am referring to theories that deny or dismiss the significance of such things as racism and discrimination as fundamental causes of inequalities between races today. Inequalities from this perspective must be located in other social conditions, such as economic arrangements. William Julius Wilson (1935-) makes such an argument in his provocative book *The Declining Significance of Race* (1980). The argument is described below. Critical race theorists roundly reject such arguments and instead claim that one cannot understand race and inequality today without locating racism and associated concepts at the heart of the theorizing. Many recent theorists, from Howard Winant (1994) to Cornel West (2001) argue that "race matters," and that it should be theorized. These and others are presented below.

Wilson's argument is described here as an example of a sociological approach that accounts for inequalities between blacks and whites in America that decidedly does not employ a critical race theory perspective, thought it arguably takes a "critical" perspective on the existence of racial inequalities. Wilson is a sociology professor at Harvard University and has spent his career conducting research and developing theories to account for inequalities between races, particularly between black people and white people.

If we use the summary points discussed below of traits of critical race theory as our guide, then Wilson would most certainly not be identified as a proponent. He would likely reject many of the items on the list. He would likely say many of these are wrong or misplaced. He is less interested in such things as consciousness, race identity, and the psycho-social and/or political processes involved in the ongoing production of racism, discrimination, and inequality than he is in understanding the economic and political structures which have and are producing and maintaining inequalities between the races. Similarly, he is not interested in challenging conventional social science epistemologies as critical race theorists are (as we see below). At the same time, his work has been consistently critical of the continuing inequalities between races in America. Much of his work focuses on understanding the enduring urban poverty in the black American community. Importantly, he argues in several books that racism and discrimination are no longer the main forces causing and reproducing these inequalities. One of his better known books is titled *The Declining Significance of Race* (1980). In that book, he argues that racism and discrimination once – during Jim Crow and slavery -- were major factors that accounted for these inequalities in the past, but changes to the economic, political, social and cultural landscape have led to the decline of these factors. Instead, the relatively recent (in 1980) changes in the economic and political fields now are the main reason for the continued inequalities.

He opens the book with the following passage:

> Race relations in American have undergone fundamental changes in recent years, so much so that now the life chances of individual blacks have more to do with their economic class position than with their day-to-day encounters with whites. In earlier years the systematic efforts of whites to suppress blacks were obvious to even the most insensitive observer. Blacks were denied access to valued and scarce resources through various ingenious schemes of racial exploitation, discrimination, and segregation, schemes that were reinforced through elaborate ideologies of racism. But the situation has changed. However determinative such practices were for the previous efforts of the black population to achieve racial equality, and however significant they were in the creation of poverty-stricken ghettoes and a vast underclass of black proletarians – that massive population at the very bottom of the social ladder plagued by poor education and lower-paying, unstable jobs – they do not provide a meaning explanation of the life chances of black Americans today. The traditional patterns of interaction between blacks and whites, particularly in the labor market, have been fundamentally altered. (1980:1)

In that book and elsewhere, he traces the historical outline of black poverty and argues that the social, political and economic structures have changed over the last two hundred years in ways that have resulted in the diminishing importance of racism as a primary cause of continued inequalities. Discrimination is not an explanation that works now. "My own view," he says, "is that historic discrimination is far more important than contemporary discrimination in explaining the plight of the ghetto underclass" (1987:32). He complains that others continue to wrongly cite discrimination as the major factor for black poverty today. However, proponents of the "discrimination thesis" are unable to account for many facts in recent history, facts that run counter to the discrimination claim. Proponents "find it difficult to explain why the economic position of poor urban Black people actually deteriorated during the very period in which the most sweeping antidiscrimination legislation and programs [the 1960s] were enacted and implemented. Their emphasis on discrimination becomes even more problematic in view of the economic progress of the black middle class during the same period" (1987:30). He presents evidence that the unemployment of black people both in absolute terms and in terms relative to white unemployment was lower in the 1940s and 1950s than it was in the 1970s and 1980s.

In the *Declining Significance of Race*, he lays out the argument. He identifies three distinct periods in American history and argues that the economic and political context in the three periods has shifted, and this shift accounts for the decline in the significance of racism and discrimination as an explanation for inequalities. The first period was the "planation economy and racial-caste oppression." This period lasted through slavery and into the early post-Civil War period. This was a period in which black Americans largely lived in the rural south. Economic and political power was fused and in the hands of white people, and white people created and maintained a form of caste system based upon racism and discrimination. This was followed by a second period: the industrial stage which was characterized by "industrial expansion, class conflict, and racial oppression." It lasted from the last quarter of the nineteenth century through the Great Depression of the 1930s. This was the period of massive industrialization, particularly in Northern cities. It was also the period of massive migration of black Americans from the rural South to the urban North. They were fleeing the oppressions and poverty of the South and looking for good jobs in the growing factories in the North. This was also the period of a massive immigration from Southern and Eastern Europe. Italian, Polish, Jewish, Irish people and many others flooded into the cities of the North. In this context, Wilson argues, discrimination was used as a tool by both the white workers and the white factory owners to further their own interests. The white workers prevented black people from joining unions. They were seen a threat to the white workers. On the other hand, the factory owners supported this situation because it served their interests by creating a force – unemployed black people – that could threaten the interests of the white working class. Unemployed black people thus could be used by the owners as a threat to the white workers: If the latter demanded higher wages, the owners could turn to hire black people and pay them less. Black people could possibly take their jobs, in part because the owners knew they would not have to pay black people as much as they paid white workers.

The political system at this time was safely in the hands of white people, but it becomes more complicated, as white workers, white owners, and white Southerners all had different interests. The power then becomes fragmented. The third period is "associated with the modern, industrial, post-World War II era, which really began to crystallize during the 1960s and 1970s, and may be characterized as the period of progressive transition from racial inequalities to class inequalities" (1980:3). This period is called the modern industrial stage. Importantly, basic changes to the economic structure occur in this third stage. The factories of the North increasingly closed and moved out; they moved overseas looking for cheaper labor, for less regulation, and for greater control. This is a period of transition from an industrial to a post-industrial economy. The post-industrial economy is built upon service and information types of jobs rather than industrial, factory jobs. However, these service and information jobs – jobs at WalMart, Home Depot, software companies, research companies – are of two distinct types. There are high-end, high paying, good benefit jobs, such as the position of a software engineer at Apple Computer. These jobs require significant education and training. But there are also low-end, low paying, poor benefit jobs, such as those at WalMart and McDonald's. These jobs do not require much education or training; they do not provide decent pay or benefits. Importantly, Wilson argues that the factory jobs left the cities, and the large black population that now resides there do not have the necessary education or training to get the high-end service jobs. They do not have access or opportunity to get good jobs, and as a result are stuck in poverty.

What is needed then, according to Wilson, is greater educational opportunity and job training for the urban black population. The overall argument was controversial when it was raised. It was embraced by a number of conservative white people, in part because it allowed white people to believe they had no direct responsibility in causing or in maintaining inequalities between black people and white people. (Echoes of Booker T. Washington can be heard here.) It also allowed conservative white people to propose policies that ignored or denied the existence or impact of racism and discrimination. Wilson's argument, for example, was used to oppose Affirmative Action. (It should be noted that he was very uncomfortable with such conservative support. He says he is a "social democrat," that is, a liberal democrat.) It also was harshly rebuffed by the critical race theorists, to which we now turn.

Critical Race Theories

We describe here three distinct, but overlapping, forms of critical race theories. These are: 1) the critical race theories (CRT) in legal studies; 2) critical race theories in sociology; and 3) critical race theories associated with post-colonial globalization studies. We begin with the legal studies perspective.

Critical race theory (CRT) emerged in the 1970s and 1980s when some minority law professors developed an alternative and more critical understanding of inequality and racism, specifically in relation to the law. Derrick Bell is often seen as one of the first important champions of this new perspective, along with others like Alan Freeman, Charles Lawrence and Kimberly Crenshaw, to name but a few (Crenshaw et al. 1995). At its heart CRT emerged in response to two currents. The first of which was the civil rights movement of the 1950s and 1960s. CRT scholars took issue with the liberal civil rights movement and specifically with the goal of working toward a "color blind" society in which as Martin Luther King famously said a person should be judged not by the color of their skin but by the content of their character. As Gary Peller, one proponent of CRT, noted in a recent essay in the online journal Politico, "We reject color-blindness as an ideal." The problem with the liberal perspective according to CRT scholars is both practical and theoretical. On the practical side, CRT scholars noted in the late nineteen hundreds and have continue to note into the present that while the civil rights movement did much good for black people, the gains achieved as a result of this movement have been largely halted. One need only look at the continued inequalities between blacks and whites to see this, whether in terms of economics, criminal justice, or other fields. CRT argues that a new theoretical and practical paradigm and program needs to be championed to pick up where the civil rights movement left off. But more importantly, CRT also complains about the theoretical perspective of the civil rights movement. Proponents of CRT argue that it is an illusion to think that the passage of laws and the pronouncement of judicial decisions, such as the famous U.S. Supreme Court of 1954, Brown v. Board of Education, will solve the problems of racism and racial inequalities. One of the problems – and there are many – that CRT proponents have with this liberal orientation is that it focuses on specific and identifiable instances of intentional discrimination, and it focuses on individual instances within law to the exclusion of an analysis of how law is tied to the rest of society. When laws are created and implemented that prevent such intentional discrimination, so the liberal logic goes, then racial equality will be achieved and all will be well. CRT says that we need to reconceptualize the notion of racism, and we should not pretend or wish that the entire concept of race will or should disappear – as is the position of the traditional civil rights movement as well as their liberal white supporters -- once we create laws and policies that abolish things such as segregation. By focusing only on the immediate and demonstrably intentional acts of discrimination, liberals allow the system of inequalities to be perpetuated, albeit often in more subtle forms. What is needed, according to

CRT is to focus on such things as "systemic racism" and on things such as "unconscious racism" (see Lawrence in Crenshaw et al., 1995).

The second major influence upon the development of CRT was the tradition of critical legal studies (CLS) within law schools which emerged in the wake of the leftist movements of the 1960s. CLS was largely a white led approach toward a critical examination of the law – how it is developed, how it works, and how it should work. CLS was largely anchored in Marxism or at least was heavily influenced by the Marxist tradition, a tradition that was brand new to the American academy in the 1960s. (Prior to the 1960s and in stark contrast, for example, to Europe, Marx was not taught very much at all in American universities and in American law schools. Indeed, Marxism was excluded from the academy.) CLS was also influenced by the earlier American theory of law called legal realism that was popular in the early and mid-nineteen hundreds. Legal realism, while most certainly not radical or Marxism, argued that to understand law and judicial decision making one needs to look at the social, historical, cultural and political context within which the decision making occurs. This context influences the decision making and an effective analysis of law cannot or should not be understood removed from the social context within which it exists. This argument stands in contrast to the traditionally dominant perspective in American legal scholarship which says that one should not look at such things, but instead should focus on the immediate legal case at hand and assess its logic, its coherence, and its practicality. The champions of CLS grafted this form of thinking – found in legal realism -- onto the more radical theoretical traditions associated with Marxism.

CRT draws upon these two main influences – CLS and a critique of the liberal civil rights movement – and mixes with it some influences from postmodern theory and poststructuralism, such as the ideas of Derrida and Foucault (Delgado and Stefanic, 2017). CRT has become established, even if as a minority presence, in many law schools today. The theory, while specifically emerging in the legal field, has in recent years been used in other fields such as education and sociology (though as we see below, sociologists have developed somewhat parallel ideas around the same time as CRT).

We can now discuss some of the central themes and concepts in CRT. One of the foundational claims of CRT is that race is a social construction. It is not rooted in biology, but is rooted in history, culture, economics, and politics. What is and is not a race is determined not by biology but by social factors. For example, three hundred years ago the English thought of the Irish as a different race. Today, the English and Irish are thought to be in the same race, the white race. This change did not happen because of advances in the biological sciences, but as the result of changing social circumstances. As we have seen elsewhere in this text, the idea that race is a social construction is not a radical one in the social sciences today. (However, some scholars argue that the concept of social construction is too conceptually or philosophically muddled and should be abandoned or radically re-examined.) But it becomes perhaps more central to the CRT project than it has in sociological theories. The associated assumption to the idea of race as a social construction is the idea that there are no meaningful biological or genetic differences between one race and another. If one embraces this idea of the essential equality of human beings of different "races", then this has significant implications for understanding and explaining inequalities between races and for proposing ways of addressing these inequalities. How is one then to explain inequalities, for example, between black and white Americans today, if one assumes that race is a social construction? There are several possibilities. One possibility is to say that there is something defective in the cultures of minority groups that is keeping them disproportionately poor. This is an old argument in sociology and is one that has been challenged because it "blames the victim". That is, such an explanation absolves white people from any responsibility for this inequality. CRT fundamentally reject these accounts. Another possibility is to say that inequalities are maintained because of the beliefs and practices of white people. This is the tact largely taken by CRT in accounting for inequalities.

A second theme is the claim that racism is not an unusual thing in America. Instead, it is ever-present. It permeates all or most of social life, even if we do not realize it. It is a ubiquitous reality in America that must be recognized and studied if we wish to understand American society and if we wish to create a better world. It saturates society.

Another theme piggybacks on the above: To understand inequalities we must understand racism, and to understand racism we must understand that its essence does not lie in individual, intentional, conscious beliefs and actions but instead lies in the cultural milieu of society *and* most importantly within the individual unconscious (cf Lawrence in Crenshaw, 1995). We have to understand "unconscious racism," according to CRT. As such, CRT theorist and their allies often proclaim, "To the extent that [the] cultural belief system [of America] has influenced all of us, we are all racists" (ibid.:237). Therefore, to understand and to address racism, we must focus not on individual, intentional actions but instead upon the systematic (and often) unintentional workings of society. (This, of course, is a highly controversial idea -- one which we discuss further below.)

Another focus of concern for CRT is the importance of giving due attention to the attitudes, beliefs, desires of black people or other people of color themselves and specifically to those segments of people of color which are poorer or more oppressed than others. The idea is to give the voiceless a voice by locating their agency as central to the analysis. As such, the focus in CRT is to reject the idea that rich white or rich black lawyers know what is best for poor black communities or what these communities need. Instead, the focus should be on championing the actual needs of the people as specified by themselves rather than the imagined needs of the lawyers when arguing law (cf. Bell, 1995b).

CRT also, as noted earlier, is anchored in the rejection of traditional liberalism and on the rejection of the theories and tactics taken by the mainstream civil rights movement to advance the cause of black people. CRT embraces a far more radical tact. While CRT acknowledges some of the gains of the civil rights movement, it argues that the latter is fundamentally flawed in that it is anchored in a goal of color-blindness. The civil rights movement strove to demand that black people are treated in the legal arena the same as white people. Most notable, the goal was to have individuals treated the same whether they are black or white. It was a goal of eliminating race and all considerations of race from policies and laws. The belief was that by doing so racial inequalities and racism would disappear and equality would arise in its place. A color blind world was the goal. CRT says this is a wrongheaded approach. Instead of negating race and instead of aspiring to create a system of laws and practices that demand that race is not to be taken into account, CRT says that because race and racism saturates society, that it must be recognized and taken into account regularly. We should not strive to eliminate or ignore race, but instead should recognize its centrality in the contemporary social world. CRT says that if one looks at the myriad of laws and court decisions made over the last fifty years which ostensibly are race neutral, i.e. that have no explicit racial element to them, one finds regularly that there are racial, i.e. racist, elements implicitly embedded within them. Laws proclaiming to be race neutral regularly produce affects which are decidedly not race neutral and are harmful to people of color. (While CRT often focuses on the non-intentional processes involved here, today we are confronted routinely with laws being created by people who proclaim the laws are race neutral and which superficially appear race neutral but in reality are in fact decidedly not race neutral when one looks at the broader context. There perhaps is no better example of this than the recent and current laws being passed by Republican state legislatures around the country designed to repress the votes of people of color (echoing the laws of the Jim Crow era, but in far more subtle and far more sophisticated ways). The authors of these laws proclaim they are passing these laws to ensure the integrity of the electoral process, but the facts are obvious: they are designed to reduce the numbers of votes cast by black people and people of color, who vote overwhelmingly for Democratic candidates today. One will find no explicit reference to race in these laws and the creators and supporters of the laws regularly insist the laws are not about race at all.)

Intersectionality is another theme common to CRT. This is a theme in sociology commonly associated with the works of Patricia Hill Collins (see below), but it also is quite common in CRT. Intersectionality basically means that one cannot understand any realities of inequalities, be it race, class or gender, without taking into account all three of these dimensions at the same time, specifically in the lived experiences of an individual. The experiences of a rich black man is different from that of a poor black woman; likewise, the experience of a rich black women is different from the experience of a rich white women. To effectively understand racism and racial inequalities one must be regularly attentive to the overlapping of race, class and gender and how these intersections impact one's life experiences.

CRT also takes an innovative and controversial (the reasons for which are discussed below) approach to epistemology. Epistemology is the philosophy of knowledge -- how we know things. (We discuss epistemology in greater detail in Chapters Seven and Twelve.) The traditional epistemological position of Western science and Western social science is anchored in the belief that there is an objective world outside of ourselves, outside of our experiences, which is independent of any judgments about it. It just exists independent of any claims made about it by people. For example, people may say the sun revolves around the world. But this is not true. The objective reality is that the earth revolves around the sun. And the earth revolves around the sun whether we say it does or not and whether we believe it does or not. At the same time, we have understandings of this objective world, and these understandings are distinct from the actual objective world. The traditional epistemology is that there is a distinction between the *appearance* (i.e. our understandings) of the objective world and the *reality* of the objective world itself. It is through the systematic, rational and objective observation and study of the appearance of the objective world that we can hope to develop a truer understanding of the objective world. The objective world is constant; our understandings of the appearance of this world can and does change. Words and symbols may represent the objective world, but words and symbols are not the objective world. This is the core of the traditional epistemology position of science: The difference between appearances and realities.

CRT champions a theory of epistemology that is at odds with this dominant theory – a theory which is the basis of mainstream science and mainstream social science today. This traditional epistemological position is also found in mainstream legal reasoning. However, like some versions of Marxism (see Chapters Two and Eight) and versions of postmodernism (see Chapter Twelve), CRT rejects it. CRT says that we cannot and should note separate out: facts from values; objectivity from assessments (appearances) of the objective worlds; objectivity from political considerations. CRT says these things are inextricably intertwined. Facts cannot be separated from value assessments. The traditional appeals of white legal scholars to separate these things out looks on its surface to be value free and politically neutral, but CRT says in fact, in reality, their proclamations of neutrality are themselves tools to maintain racial dominance. A new epistemological stance is needed, according to CRT. As the editors of *Critical Race Theory* (1995) note in their introduction: "Scholarship – the formal production, identification, and organization of what will be called "knowledge" – is inevitably political" (1995:xiii). For CRT, facts cannot and should not be separated from values. The authors note that they "reject the prevailing orthodoxy that scholarship should be or could be "neutral" and "objective" " (ibid.). For CRT, power and knowledge are intertwined and the point that the production of knowledge is essentially a political program to advance the interests of racial equality.

In recent years, CRT has been subjected to relentless, though often ill-formed and ill-informed, criticisms in popular political culture in America. Specifically, members of the Republican Party have identified it as a target that must be opposed at all cost, presumably because the Party has deemed this strategy to be politically useful. Republicans around the country in various states have passed laws banning the teaching of CRT in public schools. (Most of these laws ban CRT from being taught in K-12 schools, but some states, such as Idaho, have banned it from public higher education as well.) We will not here engage with the ill-founded criticisms leveled by politicians and their supporters. Yet at the same time, there are a number of legitimate scholarly criticisms that can be raised regarding CRT. A few of these are mentioned here. One over-arching criticism of CRT pertains to judicial decision making. CRT says that the traditional approach to the analysis of judicial decision making that focuses only on the immediate case at hand, and the logic of the particular case, and whether legal rules are being adhered to, is fundamentally flawed and that the wider social, political, cultural, and economic context (as these apply to race) must be considered in the analysis of judicial decisions and in the deciding of cases itself. CRT says that one must consider as well as the impact of any particular judicial action as well as its intent. (Some CRT proponents such as Lawrence (in Crenshaw, 1995) say that CRL does not embrace the impact argument over the intent argument, but instead reconceptualizes the entire framework. Despite this claim, it is clear that CRL favors strongly the impact side of the debate.) Critics could argue however that when we stray from the facts at hand in making judgments, we open the door to rampant speculation and opinion. Reasoned judgment and rationality go out the window and these are replaced by opinions rather than facts. Critics note that this is a very dangerous position that ultimately leads to the fusion of power and reason. The winner of an argument is based upon power rather than on the persuasiveness of their reasoning. This directly relates to a second criticism. Critics argue that when one says that truth and power cannot be separated, one is led down a very dangerous road – one in which "might is right" and this is fundamentally anti-democratic. At its heart critics might note that this is the essence of fascist sensibilities.

Another problem raised by critics is the epistemological problem of claiming that "we are all racists" and that there is an unconscious racism. There is an assortment of philosophical problems with these positions. One of these directly relates to the criticism noted above. The problem is the illogic of going from the general to the specific. For example, to present aggregate data as scientific evidence that black people are treated unfairly in the criminal justice system does not mean that when one looks at an individual action of someone and claim that the individual is acting in a racist way even if he or she does not intend to do so is logically faulty. If you took a poll of fourth graders and asked them what their favorite ice cream flavor is and eighty percent said it was chocolate, and then you pointed to one of the students and said that individual student's favorite ice cream flavor was chocolate, then you would be making a logical mistake. One can make general claims, i.e. claims about systematic workings of groups, but one cannot legitimately use such claims to explain an individual action.

It seemingly is almost inevitable that scholars who champion the claims of the legitimacy of the concept of "systemic racism" or some such concept are led back to individual explanations for this phenomenon. But when one is led back to an individual explanation, one is confronted with another conceptual difficulty. This is the scientific problem of the unconscious. CRT often claim that individuals are unconsciously racists. But this is problematic. From a scientific perspective the reliance upon the concept of the "unconscious" is problematic as it cannot be seen or objectively studied. The very nature of the unconscious renders it impervious to scientific study. As such, claims of unconscious racism are not that different from claims that (human) nature or God causes something to happen. To say that some individual white person is racist because they engaged with an individual black person in a way that somehow is harmful to the black person even if the white person had no racist intent is no different than saying that the cause of the white person's action was due to God's will. If a college professor asks a black student to leave a lecture because the student is being disruptive, is the professor racist? If the professor did not believe she was racist and did not believe she was acting in a discriminatory way in this instance, was the professor racist? If one wishes to adhere to the logic of science, then the answer is: we cannot prove the professor was unconsciously racist any more or less so than we can prove the professor acted because of her genetic (natural) programming or because God made her do it. Another example: How are we to account for violent criminal acts? Is it scientifically legitimate to say that someone commits a violent criminal act because he (or she) is genetically programmed by nature to do so? Where is the proof of this? At best, this is a scientifically dubious proposition (though admittedly one that is often made by scientists, criminologists and sociologists). These are all metaphysical speculations and not scientific claims. (Of course, CRT itself is not proclaiming itself to be a scientific endeavor, but instead is claiming to be a judicial position and as such CRT may claim scientific standards do not apply to their field, at least not in the same way as they may in scientific fields, such as sociology.)

One might also note that such CRT claims that "we are all racists" generally are based upon the belief that a culture itself is or is not racist. Critics note that this too is problematic. One problem concerns the reality of a "culture" that is somehow independent of the individuals that constitute this culture. (This is not unlike Durkheim's arguments in favor of his view of sociology (see Chapter Three).) Durkheim claims that society has a sui generis reality and that the study of this reality is central to what sociology should be. But for Durkheim, this sui generis reality is distinct from individuals, and he does not invoke concepts such as the unconscious in his theorizing.) Is culture independent of individuals or are they intertwined somehow? However one answers such questions, one is posed with endless conceptual problems.

Critical Race Theories and Sociology

The first American sociologist to recognize the importance of race for the sociological enterprise and to locate race at the heart of a study of social life was W.E.B. Du Bois (1868-1963). Though his academic work was not recognized as central to the discipline during his lifetime, in recent decades sociologists increasingly have come to see the importance of his contributions to sociology and to sociological theory. Du Bois was raised in Great Barrington, Massachusetts, and was one of the first, if not the very first, black American to receive a Ph.D. from Harvard University. He also studied in Germany (alongside Weber) at the University of Berlin. He was a very prolific scholar, having written many, many articles, books, and reports throughout his life. He spent much of his life as a professor at Atlanta University (now Clark Atlanta University), a historically black college, in Georgia. Du Bois was also very active politically in his life (and this cannot be separated from his beliefs about what theory is and should be, as we see below). He was a leader of the Niagara Movement in 1905, which brought together a number of prominent black Americans as well as some white reformers largely in reaction against the policies and programs championed by Booker T. Washington, which was discussed above. Du Bois was also one of the founding members of the National Association for the Advancement of Colored People (NAACP), which became during the Civil Rights movement of the 1950s one of the more important organizations championing racial equality.

Du Bois's scholarship and ideas were largely marginalized during his life (Morris, 2015; Rabaka, 2010) despite the fact that he arguably developed and employed theoretical and methodological ideas and research practices that were ahead of his time. Morris (2015) makes a persuasive argument that the racism of the white founders of American sociology (see above) led to Du Bois being largely ignored during his lifetime even though Du Bois developed important ideas and developed and employed theoretical and methodological perspectives well before these same things were adopted by white, mainstream sociology. For example, he developed and used a number of research methods that only later were used by the dominant white sociologists of the early and mid-nineteen hundreds. He used statistics (even if it was basic descriptive statistics – as was the case of the field at the time) in his research well before it was used by white sociologists. Similarly, he creatively used multi-modal methods, combining quantitative and qualitative research approaches in his work, again well before white sociologists did so (Rabaka, 2010).

He was also well ahead of his time in his development of some theoretical ideas related to race. He located the concept of race at the heart of his scholarship. He examined the many dimensions of race and most importantly believed one needed to place this at the heart of any sociological understanding of America. The opening lines of Chapter Two of what is his most well-known book, *The Soul of Black Folks*, makes this point clear: "The problem of the twentieth century is the problem of the color-line, - the relation of the darker to the lighter races of men in Asia and Africa, in America and the islands of the sea" (1969:54). Locating race at the heart of a sociological analysis was crucial to his theorizing.

His theoretical orientation was framed around several themes. First, he was animated by the political and moral project of advancing the cause of equality and justice for black Americans through his social scientific research. Second, he was focused on developing social psychological understandings of being black in America and of racism and how it is experienced. Third, he believed that in order to tackle these first two themes one needed to focus on the broader economic context of American society and how this relates to this social psychology. We can briefly look at each of these.

Du Bois was significant for his theoretical views and arguably more so for his extensive, rich and insightful empirical research on the state of black Americans. He published numerous studies on black Americans, from his book *The Philadelphia Negro* to his essays including, "The negro as he really is," a multi-method study of Dougherty County and the city of Albany, Georgia. In these studies, he fused detailed statistical descriptions within insightful ethnographic interpretations. Of note, he was interested in explaining the social forces that caused the deep poverty and social ills afflicting black Americans. He regularly turned to the structures of the economic and social order for such explanations, as well as to the blocked opportunities available to this population. He makes such points in his essay "The negro as he really is." He writes that the "ignorance of the ex-slave is far deeper than crude estimates indicate." The ex-slave does not know about the world, about economics, about government, etc. He or she does not know "of all those things as to which it was for the interest of the slave system to keep the laboring class in profound darkness. Those very things then which a white boy absorbs from his earliest social atmosphere – starts with, so to speak, are puzzling problems of the black boy's mature years. And this, too, not by reason of dullness but for lack of opportunity" (2011:45).

Later in the same essay, he explains more fully the harmful social psychological processes imposed by slavery, Jim Crow, and racism. The essay seeks to account for the "rise of the black freeholder" in a county in Georgia, "and his struggle for survival":

> … To the car-window sociologist, to the man who seeks to understand and know the South by devoting the few leisure hours of a holiday trip to unraveling the snarl of centuries – to such men very often the whole trouble with the black field-hand may be summed up by Aunt Ophelia's word: "Shiftless!" And yet they are not lazy, these men; they work hard when they do work, and they work willingly. They have no sordid selfish money-getting ways but rather a fine disdain for mere cash. They'll loaf before your face and work behind your back with good-natured honesty. The great defect as laborers lies in their lack of incentive to work beyond the mere pleasure of physical exertion. They are careless because they have not found that it pays to be careful; they are improvident because the improvident ones of their acquaintance get on about as well as the provident. Above all they cannot see why they should take unusual pains to make the white man's land better or to take more care of his mule and corn. (2011:49)

For Du Bois the economic and social structures were at the root of the problem of race inequality. But it was his insights into the social psychological dynamics produced by these things that were particular profound. Two of the central concepts he uses to describe these dynamics are the veil (or "the veil of race") and double consciousness. Both of these are explained in *The Soul of Black Folks* (1963 [1903]). The **veil** is something metaphorically worn by black people in America while interacting with white Americans. The veil shrouds the black individual's individuality. As such, white people do not "see" the living, unique individual when interacting with a black person. Instead, white people see "a black person", i.e. a member of a racial group, that is, a person devoid of individuality, of humanity. The veil is part of the color line that separates the races, but it is more. The veil appears to suggest that it prevents white people from seeing and from meaningfully understanding black people. But more importantly and more explicitly, Du Bois is interested in knowing how this veil affects black people. He begins the book: "To the real question, How does it feel to be a problem [being a black American]? I answer seldom a word" (1963:44). The veil creates social psychological dynamics by which black people are entangled with a **double consciousness**. He writes:

> After the Egyptian and Indian, the Greek and Roman, the Teuton and Mongolian, the Negro is a sort of seventh son, born with a veil, and gifted with second sight in this American world, -- a world which yields him no true self-consciousness, but only lets him see himself through the revelation of the other world. It is a peculiar sensation, this double-consciousness, this sense of always looking at one's self through the eyes of others, of measuring one's soul by the tape of a world that looks on in amused contempt and pity. One ever feels his twoness, -- an American, a Negro; two souls, two thoughts, two unreconciled strivings; two warring ideals in one dark body, whose dogged strength alone keeps it from being torn asunder. (1963:45)

One curiosity related to Du Bois's sociological theorizing lies in his embrace of Marxism. While recent scholars debate the commitment Du Bois had to communism and to Marxist theory, Du Bois himself has at times been quite clear about this. The problem of the twentieth century was not only the problem of the color line, but it was also the problem of the color line within capitalism. (He traveled to the Soviet Union in the 1920s, soon after the Russian Revolution, and strongly supported the new communist state.) In his Autobiography, he inserts a rather curious two page "interlude" titled "Communism," between Chapters Five and Six. There he writes:

> I have studied socialism and communism long and carefully in the lands where they are practiced and in conversation with their adherent, and with wide reading. I now state my conclusion frankly and clearly: I believe in communism. I mean by communism, a planned way of life in the production of wealth and work designed for building a state whose object is the highest welfare of its people and not merely the profit of a part. [paraphrasing Marx, he adds] I believe that all men should be employed according to their ability that wealth and services should be distributed according to need. (1968:57)

In light of this, it is rather curious why we do not see Marxist theory developed, employed and integrated into most of his writings and specifically in his empirical research projects. (He does provide an economically informed sociological understanding in his study *Black Reconstruction in America, 1860-1880* (1998) but even here his explicit use of Marxist theory is at best limited.)

Lastly, while scholars studying Du Bois regularly and rightly note that Du Bois was largely marginalized or dismissed by the leading mainstream white sociologists in the early and mid-nineteen hundreds due to racism, it bears noting that in addition to racism, it is possible if not likely that he was also marginalized or dismissed become of his embrace of communism. In the mid-nineteen hundreds, we must remember, the leaders of the United States were fanatically opposed to all things Marxist and all things communists and anyone associated with such things was marginalized or dismissed. It is likely that both the racism of the times and Du Bois's commitment to Marxism combined to fuel opposition to his work and ideas or to fuel the denial of its significance.

Recent and Contemporary Critical Race Theorists in Sociology

In the last several decades numerous sociologists studying race have picked-up where Du Bois left off. These scholars tend to reject some of the claims of less critical scholars such as William Julius Wilson and embrace some of the same themes found in the critical race theory that is anchored in legal studies. Critical race theorists outside of legal studies, from Cornel West (2001) to Howard Winant (1994) and beyond, roundly reject Wilson's arguments that race no longer matters. The opening lines of one of Winant's books could not be clearer on this point: "Race shows no sign of declining significance. Quite the contrary: in a range of manifestations wider and wider than the most fertile imaginations could have dreamed up, race continues to operate as a fundamental factor in political and cultural life all around the world" (1994:1).

We can turn now to elaborate some of the central claims of sociological critical race theories. Many of these echo the themes found in the legal studies tradition of critical race theory noted earlier; some are in addition to these. One theme in recent critical race theory is the insistence that race lies at the heart of contemporary society. Therefore, any sociological understanding of society must include the topic of race. It cannot be excluded. "Race is understood as a phenomenon whose meaning pervades social life. Race operates both micro- and macro-socially; not only the individual psyche and relationships among individuals, but also collective identities and social structures are racially constituted" (Winant, 1994:115). Importantly, the social psychological dynamics of race, for people of color in particular, first described and analyzed by Du Bois with his notion of "double consciousness," is greatly elaborated. Scholars now not only describe the contradictions and oppressions that come with this reality. For example, such processes place people of color in untenable boxes, as objects for white people or as victims; these processes cast people of color as not fully human, as objects (West, 2001). These scholars take it further and theorize political responses to the situation. The theoretical response, as a result, must be a political one in which people of color are turned into active agents, and this is largely the position taken by critical race theorists. This perspective calls for a focus on the experience of people of color, and specifically their experience in a world in which the dominant group is white people. It calls for the invigoration of the subjectivity of people of color in part by locating people of color as the subject and authors of their own experiences and not merely the objects of the dominant white group. Part of this perspective is the recognition that race, as a fundamental concept in social life, not only involves the experiences of people of color but also involves the role of the dominant white group in doing things that maintain inequalities and/or in doing things that critical race theorists view as racist or that are built upon racist formulations whether knowingly or not.

In 2003, a number of prominent social scientific scholars of race published a book titled *Whitewashing Race: The Myth of a color-Blind Society*. The book, written by Michael Brown et al., was largely a reaction to claims made by many conservative commentators, politicians, and scholars that race itself (and racism) was by now no longer a significant factor in accounting for inequalities between races. Conservatives saw the problems of inequality, specifically the disproportionate poverty amongst black Americans and Latinos, as caused by deficits in these populations and they believed it was not caused by the dominant white group's beliefs or actions. Either there was deemed to be something wrong or defective in the psychology or the culture of black Americans or other peoples of color, or less often but more perniciously conservatives would sometimes claim there was a genetic and biological cause and explanation for inequalities between racial groups: Black Americans, in effect, had an inferior generic makeup which gave them a faulty character or less intelligence than white people and that explains inequalities. (See Murray and Herrnstein's "best seller" *The Bell Curve* for a blatant racist account that proclaims the black Americans are less intelligent than white Americans and that this is largely caused by genetics. As such, nature is the cause and explanation of inequalities.) Typically, the fault, according to these commentators, lies with individual people of color or with biology and not with social organization or social structure, and certainly white people were absolved of any involvement (or responsibility) in maintaining the continued inequalities. White people may have engaged in racist and discriminatory practices in the past, but not now, the argument goes.

Brown et al. systematically critiques such arguments and instead claim that any understanding of the inequalities among races and any attempts to address these inequalities must begin with the recognition that one cannot effectively understand inequality and poverty in the black American community or in other communities of people of color without recognizing the place of white people in believing and doing things that maintain this inequality.

Race is a relationship, not a set of characteristics that one can ascribe to one group or another. Racial inequality stems from a system of power and exclusion in which whites accumulate economic opportunities and advantage while disaccumulation of economic opportunity disempowers black and Latino communities. Therefore, the first task in challenging America's color line is to change the terms of discourse. (Brown et al., 2003:228)

One must recognize the role of white people in creating and in maintaining the ongoing inequalities. However, white people are not inclined to recognize racism, and importantly are not inclined to recognize their role in such things. White people reside in a world of white privilege in which they are granted ongoing, and often subtle, benefits simply from being white. As Brown et al. note, "the last thing a fish notices is the water" (2003:34). White people in the normal course of life do not recognize the privileged position in which they live, in relation to peoples of color. And this allows white people to avoid thinking they have any role to play in creating or maintaining these inequalities. It also allows them to focus not on the social arrangements and structures of which they are part, but instead to focus on the individual members of the black American community for explanations of this continued inequality: The problem lies, so this form of reasoning goes, in and with these other people, and not with the white population. It is a white privilege not seen or recognized by white people that is part of the calculus of ongoing inequalities.

Brown et al. also make the important claim that inequalities between races today must be understood in terms of more than simply intentional discrimination. Unintended, systematic discrimination is more important to consider. That is, racism and discrimination can and does occur on a regular basis even though it is not intended. "The idea that racism is simply a collection of intentionally bigoted individuals is fundamentally flawed, both theoretically and empirically" (2003:64). As they note, "the specific intentions and choices of individuals regarding racial discrimination or exclusion are frequently irrelevant to the emergence and maintenance of social and economic inequalities in the United States" (2003:17). They use the example of "neglect" as it is used in the legal system to illustrate their point. One can be found guilty of a crime due to one's negligence. A company that makes a defective product that kills someone may be held responsible for its negligence. The company may not have intended to inflict the harm, but it did so. In the same way, discriminatory harm is being done by white people without their intent (2003:180). Moreover, the problem should not be seen as a problem of individuals acting in discriminatory ways. The more important source of continued inequalities is the racism and discrimination embedded in the workings of institutions, rather than within individuals. "[R]ace permeates America's institutions – and its distribution of opportunities and wealth" (2003:34). Brown et al. argue that unintentional, institutional discrimination is a major force in maintaining inequality. And this discrimination is steeped in history. American history has created a situation in which white people have "accumulated" wealth, power, etc. while black peoples and other people of color have suffered "disaccumulation" as a result.

Importantly, the processes of discrimination, in history and in the present, often involve compounding. One act, or one instance, of discrimination builds upon an earlier one, and this process exacerbates the situation. "Most of the current gap in life-chances and various measures of performance between blacks and whites reflect the legacy of past decisions – decisions that cumulatively resulted in a profound imbalance in the most fundamental structures of opportunities and support in America" (2003:227). Similarly, as they note while discussing the workings of discrimination within the criminal justice system: "Small disadvantages at each successive stage in the justice process result in big disparities over the long run" (2003:141).

The authors critically assess the unintentional, institutional discriminatory practices within the realms of education, the criminal justice system, employment, and politics to make their case. They systematically refute conservative arguments made over these issues, and instead demonstrate the systematic and enduring problems of inequality. A number of social and political proposals to address these issues are then offered. They note that their proposals are not radical. Instead, they are firmly liberal in their political orientation. For example, they call for much greater government spending on such things as education and job creation.

Michael Omi and Howard Winant together and separately (1986, 1994, 2001) have put forth an influential sociological theory of race that at its heart builds a conceptual bridge that links individual actions with those of large-scale, structural forces. Their theory is built upon the concept of racial formation (1986). **Racial formation** theory is based upon the claim that race is fundamentally a socially constructed concept. "From a racial formation perspective, race is understood as a fluid, unstable, and "decentered" complex of social meanings constantly being transformed by political conflict" (1994:59). Importantly, this construction must be understood critically within a historical and political framework. "We define racial formation as the sociohistorical process by which racial categories are created, inhabited, transformed, and destroyed" (1986:55). Winant explains further:

> Racial formation theory was developed as a response to postwar understandings of race, both mainstream and racial, that practiced "reductionism": [this means] the explanation of racial phenomena as a manifestation of some other, supposedly more significant, social relationship. Examples of racial reductionism include treatment of racial dynamics as epiphenomena of class relationships, or as the result of "national oppression," or as variations on the ethnicity paradigm established in the United States in the early twentieth century after successive waves of European immigration. ... In contrast to these approaches, racial formation theory suggests that race has become a fundamental organizing principle of contemporary social life. At its most basic level, race can be defined as a concept that signifies and symbolizes sociopolitical conflict and interests in reference to different types of human bodies ... There is no biological basis for distinguishing human groups along the line of "race" ... (1994:115)

A starting point for this theory is, as suggested above, the claim that the concept of race must be understood independently from the concept of class, and the former cannot be explained in terms of the latter. "The subordination of race to class has never been viable" (1994:33). One must therefore "inquire into the sources and contours of racial dynamics" (1986:35).

Winant argues that the sociology of race must begin with the concepts of racial hegemony and racial projects, and these must be understood within the historical, political and global contexts within which they occur. "A racial project is simultaneously an interpretation, representation, or explanation of racial dynamics and an effort to organize and distribute resources along particular racial lines" (1994:24). Racial projects can be used to maintain a system of racial dominance, or they can be used to challenge a system of dominance. Conservative white people today may draw upon racial projects to defend the status quo, while black Americans may draw upon racial projects to challenge the status quo. He uses Gramsci's concept of hegemony here (see Chapter Eight), though he does so without relying on its Marxist foundations. Winant defines hegemony as "a form of rule that operates by constructing its subjects and incorporating contestation" (1994:113). The theory is less about agency and more about the "interrelated structural and signifying dimensions of hegemony" (1994:112). In short, racial dominance occurs within particular historical, political and global contexts through the use of racial projects oriented toward either maintaining or challenging racial hegemony.

Winant summarizes some of the essential elements of the theory of racial formation: "1) race is understood as a phenomenon whose meaning pervades social life. ... 2) racial formation theory addresses the surprising expansion and intensification of racial phenomena occurring in the contemporary world, the new global context ... 3) racial formation theory suggests a new conception of racial history and racial time" (1994:115-16). There are two distinct forms of racial time. One of these is genealogical. This is the concept of time,

> in which the social construction of race is a millennial phenomenon whose origins lie in an immense historical rupture encompassing the rise of Europe, the onset of African enslavement, the conquista and colonization of the Western Hemisphere, and the subjugation of much of Asia. Across the centuries, there has been never-ending dispute over the meaning of race, controversy that was integral to the struggles of the oppressed and enslaved with their rulers. By now we have substantial scholarship on these matters that quite effectively explain the framing of supposedly unified collective identities (e.g. Europe) in terms of externalized "others." (1994:115-16)

The second form of historical time is contingency. This refers to historical racial time that is context driven: "Particular racial meanings and social structures are always context-driven" (1994:117).

Critical Race Theories and Postcolonial Studies

Another form of critical race theory can be found in the field of postcolonial studies. Postcolonial studies did not emerge within sociology or the social sciences, though it was as is deeply influenced by these fields. Rather it emerged within the humanities, in literature, in history, in culture studies, and in "area studies" – in academic disciplines devoted to the study of one or another, typically non-Western, cultural area of the world. Major figures associated with postcolonial studies include Edward Said (1935-2003), Frantz Fanon (1925-1961), Gayatri Spivak (1942-). Postcolonial studies look at race and race relations through the lens of history, colonization, imperialism, politics, and culture. It specifically is rooted in or draws upon the fields that study literature and the meaning of the symbolic world. It also is greatly influenced by critical approaches to the social sciences, including

Marx, globalization theories (Chapter Fourteen), and post-structural and postmodern theories. The relationship of power and knowledge, which as we saw in Chapter Twelve in the works of Foucault, is often central to postcolonial studies. Specifically, this field of study looks to know how dominant groups, in this case European and Americans, describe through texts those groups they dominate, through colonialism and imperialism. (Colonialism is the form of relationship between European powers, most notably France and England, and their subjugated colonies from the seventeen hundreds through the early to mid-nineteen hundreds. England, for example, ruled India, China, and broad swaths of the Arab and Islamic world, while France also ruled over vast swaths of the Arab and Islamic worlds (as well as over many countries in sub-Sahara Africa. Imperialism is a less direct, but more powerful form of domination of one country or region by another. Imperialism is said to be a more common mode of domination today.). The understandings put forth by European and Americans of the colonized people are gross distortions of these people. Postcolonial studies often seek to examine these views from a critical perspective. It seeks to explain how these understandings emerged in a political context and how they served the political ends of the Europeans and Americans.

One such example of this is found in the works of Edward Said. Said was a Palestinian Christian who spent much of his career as a professor in the humanities at Columbia University in New York City. His most well-known book is *Orientalism* (1979). The term **Orientalism** refers broadly to the field of study or inquiry, often found within universities, which focuses upon the culture and peoples of "the Orient." By the Orient, Said is mostly focusing upon the Middle East. That is, Orientalism is focused on understanding the Arab and Islamic worlds (though Said included Jews as well as Arabs as "Semitic" under the rubric as well). But more broadly it is the field of study that seeks to understand all parts of the world that are non-Western. Said focuses upon the period from the late seventeen hundreds through the middle nineteen hundreds, and this period is broken down into two parts. From the late seventeen hundreds through the early nineteen hundreds, Europeans, and specifically the French and English were the colonial rulers over much of the Middle East, over much of the Arab and Islamic worlds. The French and British empires were largely broken up by the early and mid-nineteen hundreds. From the mid-nineteen hundreds to the present, the United States assumed power and influence over these areas, though it did so not by direct colonization, but by indirect dominations. This is largely the period of imperialism.

Said demonstrates how French and European scholars, politicians, and others crafted an image of the "Oriental" that was fundamentally a gross distortion of reality. It was racist. Said shows how and why these images were produced and what ends they served. The image of the Oriental was that of "the other." **The other** that is portrayed in texts, in political documents, in novels, in scientific works, as that which is opposed and different from the European (and later American). The other lacks subjectivity. The people defined as other by the Orientalists (that is, the European scholars writing about the Middle East, the Arab and Islamic worlds), are passive objects. They lack humanity, autonomy, will. They are "not quite as human as we are" (1979:108).

More specifically, Said systematically shows how the European Orientalists created an image of the Orientals that was reductionist. The Europeans painted a picture of the Arab and Islamic people and culture as if it was one simple and unified entity in which the particular individuals and groups within this larger world had no distinctive elements, no distinctive histories, no distinctive realities. The complexities of the real world were reduced to simplistic views that conformed to the needs and desires of people who were the colonial masters of the Orient. These Europeans filtered their understandings through this lens of colonial masters, and this led to multiple gross and racist distortions of the subjugated peoples. One such mischaracterization concerns the European beliefs concerning the place of Mohammed in Islam. Mohammed is considered the Prophet in Islam. He lived from 570-632 A.D. in what is now Saudi Arabia, and he initiated the religion of Islam. He claimed to have received the work of God (Allah) and these words became the Koran, the most Holy Book in Islam. Said writes about how the Europeans in the eighteen hundreds understood his importance through their own realities and their own lens and as a result distorted a genuine understanding of Mohammed's place in the lives of Islamic people. He writes that "domestications of the exotic" is a common practice between cultures, and that the Orientalist of the European West did so as well. He continues: "but what is more important still is the limited vocabulary and imagery that impose themselves as a consequence. The reception of Islam in the West [in the eighteen hundreds] is a perfect case in point ... One constraint acting upon Christian thinkers who tried to understand Islam was an analogical one; since Christ is the basis of Christian faith, it was assumed – quite incorrectly – that Mohammed was to Islam as Christ was to Christianity... " (1979:60).

Such distortions and inaccuracies have consequences. In responding to the recent historian R.W. Southern, Said writes:

> The best part of Southern's analysis, here and elsewhere in his brief history of Western views of Islam, is his demonstration that it is finally Western ignorance which becomes more refined and complex, not some body of positive Western knowledge which increases in size and accuracy. For fictions have their own logic and their own dialectic of growth or decline. Onto the character of Mohammed in the Middle Ages

was heaped a bundle of attributes that corresponded to the "character of the [twelfth-century] prophets of the "Free Spirit" who did actually arise in Europe, and claim credence and collect followers." Similarly, since Mohammed was viewed as the disseminator of a false Revelation, he became as well the epitome of lechery, debauchery, sodomy, and a whole latter of assorted treacheries, all of which derived "logically" from his doctrinal impostures. (1979:62)

In short, the European scholars grossly misunderstood and distorted their understandings of the Orientals. They created simplistic caricatures of a people. It was an image of a people who were denied subjectivity, denied individuality. It was an image of a passive people. It was also an image of a culture and a people that was timeless, a culture that did not change and was static. It was an image of a closed system. In writing about the Orientalism found in American and European thought in the mid-nineteen hundreds, Said says that Islam and the culture said to be based upon it is viewed as a "closed system of exclusions. … [E]ach of the many diverse aspects of Islamic culture could be seen …. As a direct reflection of an unvarying matrix, a particular theory of God, that compels them all into meaning and order: development, history, tradition, reality in Islam are therefore interchangeable" (1979:298). Said rejects such claims; they are wrong and are little more than gross mischaracterizations. Another part of Orientalism consists of a description of several "dogmas" embraced in the twentieth century. One of these is the assumption of an "absolute and systematic difference between the West, which is rational, developed, humane, superior, and the Orient, which is aberrant, undeveloped, inferior." A second dogma is that Western scholars rely upon "abstractions about the Orient based on texts representing classical Oriental civilization" rather than on actual evidence from empirical research of the Orient today. "A third dogma is that the Orient is eternal, and incapable of defining itself; therefore it is assumed that a highly generalized and systematic vocabulary for describing the Orient from a Western standpoint is inevitable and even scientifically "objective." A fourth dogma is that the "Orient is at bottom something either to be feared (the Yellow Peril, the Mongol hordes, the brown dominions) or to be controlled (by pacification, research and development, outright occupation whenever possible)" (1979:300-301).

All of these faulty images were born out of the historical and political realities of colonization, and Said argues they cannot be understood separate from this context. His contention is that "Orientalism is fundamentally a political doctrine willed over the Orient because the Orient was weaker than the West" (1979:204). These images were born out of a need of Europeans to make sense and to legitimize their colonization of the Orient.

Said's is not a sociological theory in itself. But the themes found in his work and the systematic documentation used to support his arguments resonate greatly with some of the recent and current trends in sociological theorizing. There has, it has been said, a linguistic or cultural turn in sociological theorizing in recent decades, and Said's work sits comfortably within this turn. (He rightly calls himself a "humanist" scholar rather than a social scientist.) In addition, the critical focus on race, history, politics, and globalization all lend support for sociological theorists to draw upon his ideas related to race and inequality.

Another major figure associated with post-colonial studies is Frantz Fanon (1925-1961). He was born in Martinique, a French speaking Caribbean island. He studied in France and became a medical doctor, specializing in psychiatry (and psychoanalysis). His life was cut short by leukemia. Fanon viewed racism, inequality, and colonialism from a different perspective than that of Said, though neither approach these topics from a traditional social scientific or sociological perspective. Whereas Said focused mostly upon symbols and texts, upon literature, and upon culture studies, Fanon focused mostly on psychology, politics and praxis. He was influenced by many of the major intellectual figures in France, including Jean-Paul Sartre and the structural psychoanalyst Jacques Lacan, as well as scholars such as Jaspers and Nietzsche. More generally, he was influenced by phenomenology, existentialism, and Marxism. His first major book was *Black Skin/White Masks* (1967). In this book he provides a nuanced view of the fundamental problems and contradictions of being a black man in a world defined by white people, and he critically assess ways to personally address, cope and respond to these. The book is essentially an affirmation of blackness and black experience in the face of white racism and dominance, and it is a call for black people to assert and to define themselves on their own terms, and not on the terms imposed upon them by white people. At the center of the analysis is the conviction that white people are the cause of the problems of black people, and specifically of problems of psychology and notions of self amongst black people. In *Black Skin/White Masks* he presents numerous descriptions from personal experience and from printed sources of white racism. As with Said, black people are views as the Other. Their subjectivity is denied. They are relegated to an inferior position. They are seen as essentially inferior. But Fanon goes much further. For him, white people view black people as a danger, as a threat. This threat is due to black people being seen by white people as the embodiment of nature, while white people are the embodiment of culture (though Fanon does not use such terms): "To suffer from a phobia of Negroes is to be afraid of the biological. For the Negro is only biological. The Negroes are animals… [in the white man's eyes]" (1967:165). "The white man is convinced that the Negro is a beast; if it is not the length of the penis, then it is the sexual potency that impresses him. Face to face with this man who is "different from himself," he [the white man] needs to defend himself. In other words, to personify The Other" (1967:170).

Fanon analyzes the ways in which black people may respond to the overwhelming experiences of white racism, but most of the responses are futile and do not resolve the inner psychological tensions imposed upon black people due to racism. Instead, most possible responses exacerbate rather than resolve the psychological problems. For example, the black person might seek to copy or act like the white person in hopes of avoiding the white person's scorn. But this cannot and will not work, because the white person will not and cannot be convinced the black person is not black. After all, the white person is in the position of power to define this. On the other hand, the black person may retreat and seek to conform to his or her subjugated role, in which case he or she is again in a losing situation. Fanon writes, for example, about the prospects of embracing reason to possibly curry favorable impressions of white people. But this is futile: "Every hand was a losing hand for me. I analyzed my heredity. I made a complete audit of my ailment. I wanted to be typically Negro – it was no longer possible. I wanted to be white – that was a joke. And, when I tried, on the level of ideas and intellectual activity, to reclaim my negritude, it was snatched away from me" (1967:132).

For Fanon, the solution to this seemingly impossible situation of racist subjugation is self-assertion. It is through action, and only through action, that a black person will be able to assert and affirm his or her humanity. "Man is human only to the extent to which he tries to impose his existence on another man in order to be recognized by him ... [T]he former slave wants to make himself recognized" (1967:216). Later, he writes, "As soon as I desire I am asking to be considered. I am not merely here-and-now, sealed into thingness. I am for somewhere else and for something else. I demand that notice be taken of my negating activity insofar as I pursue something other than life; insofar as I do battle for the creation of a human world – that is, of a world of reciprocal recognitions" (1967:218). Fanon believes the only way to meaningfully and humanly respond to being placed in a position of Otherness, of being placed in a position of object, is for the black person to demand from white people a recognition of the black person's essential humanity.

But what sort of action might Fanon have in mind? It must first be recognized that the process of racist domination and the responses to it are not fundamentally psychological processes, at least they are not psychological processes that can be understood removed from the lived social, cultural, political, economic and historical contexts. These processes are fundamentally social and not individual in nature. For example, he criticizes psychoanalytic theory, and specifically the psychoanalytic concept of the inferiority complex, for two interrelated reasons. First, it wrongfully interprets all psychological phenomena through the lens of an abstract theory, removed from any considerations of reality – specifically political, cultural, and social realities -- and real racist oppressions. Second, this abstract theory is subtly, or not, infused with assumptions that the Western ways are the normal ways, e.g. the Western form of the family is deemed normal, and anything different is therefore deemed by definition abnormal. The point for Fanon is to tie some psychoanalytic concepts to a recognition of social reality. As he notes, "The rifle of the Senegalese soldier is not a penis but a genuine rifle, model Lebel 1916" (1967:106).

The type of action he champions to address racism is political. People of color should assert themselves politically. This is the most human thing to do. This is the way to possibly create alternative postcolonial forms of political and social orders which would overcome the racist legacy of colonialism. These things are described in his book *The Wretched of the Earth* (1963), which was largely written in response to his involvement in the Algerian fight for independence from France in the 1950s. (The Algeria struggle for independence was a major episode in French history and it greatly divided the French people. In some general ways it was not unlike the American war in Viet Nam.) *The Wretched of the Earth* in many ways was more like a political analysis of how to create an effective revolution than it was an academic treatise on race relations. Nevertheless, a central part of his argument concerns action, and specifically violence: "The colonized man finds his freedom in and through violence" (1963:86). But it is not random violence. It is violence oriented toward a revolution that seeks to create a new form of society. He hoped that in Algeria and anywhere else that American and Europeans continued their colonial or imperial rule, that colonized people would fight for decolonization, and in the new decolonized society there will emerge "new men": "Decolonization never takes place unnoticed, for it influences individuals and modifies them fundamentally. It transforms spectators crushed with the inessentiality into privileged actors, with the grandiose glare of history's floodlights upon them. It brings a natural rhythm into existence, introduced by new men, and with it a new language and a new humanity" (1963:36).

Critical Gender Studies: Feminist Sociological Theory

Arguably the first modern woman sociological theorist was Harriet Martineau (1802-1876). Martineau was also clearly a feminist (Rossi, 1973). However, whether one should consider her to be an early feminist sociologist is arguable. That is, she presents a framework for the study of sociology. She presents many feminist arguments regarding the ways that women were treated, and she presented arguments regarding the positions in society in which women should be accorded, but she does not synthesize these two strands – political and scientific -- into what we today might call a feminist sociological theory. The framework of her overall sociological approach was presented in Chapter One. Here I focus upon her feminist ideas.

While it is true that she did not systematically fuse feminist ideas into the architecture of her theorizing, one can fine numerous sociological insights regarding the position of women in society, and specifically regarding the fact that men had so much power in relation to women. For example, she provides insightful analyses of the similarities and differences in the ways that white people maintain their dominance over slaves and the ways that men maintain their dominance of women. At the same time, it is clear in retrospect that she embraced two potentially conflicting ideas regarding women. On the one hand, she was a fervent advocate for equality between the sexes, in all ways, and forcefully condemned social conditions that failed to treat women fairly and equally to men. In her chapter on "Women" in *Society in America* (1962), she makes these views quite clear:

> If a test of civilization be sought, none can be so sure as the condition of that half of society over which the other half has power, -- from the exercise of the right of the strongest. Tried by this test, the American civilization appears to be of a lower order than might have been expected from some other symptoms of its social state. The Americans, have, in the treatment of women, fallen below, not only their own democratic principles, but the practice of some parts of the Old World. (1962:291)

She goes on to show how women are treated unfairly in school, work, politics, and in the home. She made repeated complaints about the women's lack of vote. "[I]s it to be understood that the principles of the Declaration of Independence bear no relation to half of the human race?" (1962:308). On the other hand, she often wrote about the nature of women and how it is different (and in some ways superior) to the nature of men. For example, in her first published work in the Unitarian journal 1822, she notes that some of the best writings "on the subject of Practical Divinity" are by women. She continues, "I suppose it is owing to the peculiar susceptibility of the female mind, and its consequent warmth of feeling, that its productions, when they are really valuable, find a more ready way to the heart than those of the other sex; and it gives me great pleasure to see women gifted with superior talents, applying those talents to promote the cause of religion and virtue" (Quoted in Yates, 1985:20).

Feminist sociological theory has come a long way since then. One recent theorist is Dorothy Smith. Dorothy Smith (1926-), a British born sociologist, received her doctorate from the University of California, and has spent her career as an academic in Canada. She created a feminist sociological theory that draws upon key concepts from phenomenology and Marxism, though she most certainly could not be considered either a phenomenologist or a Marxist (1987: 9). Smith develops a **standpoint theory** of sociology. Standpoint theory rejects the sociological position that claims that theory can or should seek to objectively describe and explain the world. It rejects the positivistic, scientific assumptions, and instead claims that the standpoint of persons -- the perspective people take and their social location -- must be understood as central to the theoretical claims they make. And sociological claims traditionally and historically have been made by men:

> Established sociology has objectified a consciousness of society and social relations that "knows" them from the standpoint of their ruling and from the standpoint of men who do that ruling. To learn how to know society from sociology … is to look at it from those standpoints. It is to take on the views of ruling and to view society and social relations in terms of the perspectives, interests, and relevances of men active in relations of ruling. (1987:2-3)

For Smith conventional sociological theory, produced by men, reflect men's sensibilities, though it claims to reflect not the sensibility of men but to reflect objective reality. Smith rejects this perspective. The standpoint of men does not reflect an objective reality but instead reflects the men's understanding of this objective reality, and it reflects the ideas of the dominant group, the men. What is needed is a sociological approach which locates the standpoint, the perspective, of women at its heart. The standpoint of women, in contrast to the standpoint of men, appreciates and focuses upon the lived realities of women and their understandings of their world. None of this, she says, can be understood without an analysis of the relations of ruling which structure the ongoing inequalities between men and women and which support the men's standpoint in sociology. By **relations of ruling** she means "a complex of organizing practices, including government, law, business, and financial management, professional organizations, and educational institutions as well as the discourses in texts that interpenetrate the multiple sites of power" (1987:3). The relations of ruling today, characterized by the dominance of men, "involves a continual transcription of the local and particular actualities of our lives into abstracted and generalized forms" (1987:3). What is needed is a theory from the standpoint of women, by women, that builds from the local, lived, particular, everyday experiences and realities of women. This will necessarily require an understanding of the workings of the relations of ruling.

Smith argues that the relations of ruling which produce and maintain the dominance of men and which accords their standpoint the only legitimate one within sociology is in part supported through discourse and text. As such, it is important to know how these texts work (1990); how they are created; how facts are created by people from particular standpoints, and specifically by men and by women in the context of power relations.

A feminist sociology, she says, must begin with the recognition that women have a bifurcation of consciousness. This bifurcation, or split, refers to the fact that women exist in a conflicted reality. On the one hand, they exist in the objectified world created by men through the standpoint of men. It is the world that is claimed to be objective, fact based. On the other hand, they exist in a personal, immediate world of lived social relations: The everyday world of women. This bifurcation is made concrete when the experiences of women in the world is appreciated. That is women, in contrast to men, often move between two worlds in their practical daily lives, the public and the private (or domestic) worlds. Women are mothers, work in the home, but they also work outside the home. They live and work in these two domains, and these two domains call up two distinct forms of consciousness. The task of a feminist sociological theory is to understand this bifurcation and to appreciate the lived realities of women in their practical lives, and most importantly to situate all of this with the relations of ruling.

This form of understanding leads Smith to embrace what she calls **institutional ethnography** as the proper form of research stemming from her theory. However, she has a nuanced sense of both the term "institutional" and "ethnography." By institutional she means a complex of relations forming part of the ruling apparatus, organized around a distinctive function – education, health care, law, and the like. In contrast to such concepts as bureaucracy, "institution" does not identify a determinate form of social organization, but rather the intersection and coordination of more than one relational mode of ruling apparatus" (1987:160). Similarly, she presents a particular understanding of ethnography: "Ethnography does not here mean, as it sometimes does in sociology, restriction to methods of observation and interviewing. It is rather a commitment to an investigation and explication of how "it" actually is, of how "it" actually works, of actual practices and relations." Institutional ethnography is an approach that seeks to understand the everyday lives of women through a recognition of how their worlds are directly, though perhaps subtly, impacted and structured by the relations of ruling.

In recent decades, numerous feminist sociological theories have appeared. Smith's is merely one of these. A number of recent trends can be identified in these theories. One of these is an increased philosophical sophistication. Indeed, many of the more profound writings in feminist sociological theory are the products of philosophers rather than sociologists. Another trend is an increased appreciation of the importance of understanding the intersections of race, class and gender. Recent black feminist sociological thought in particular has often incorporated these themes. Still another theme is a focus on understanding and of according significance to the women's voice. Recent sociological feminist theory often argues for the need to understand the perspective, or standpoint, of women, as we saw in the writings of Smith. Recent theorizing also tends to challenge conventional social scientific epistemology. The traditional, "objective" scientific perspective championed by some sociologists is often rejected and replaced by a perspective that calls for an understanding of the lived realities of women, as well as calling for theory to be seen as not a descriptive tool but a political one. Theory is seen by many recent feminist sociologists as a tool in which to understand the oppressions experienced by women and as a tool to be used to combat these. In the following pages, I describe the works of the contemporary American philosophy Judith Butler as well as the writings of the sociologist Patricia Hill Collins, each of whom embodies some of the themes noted above.

Patricia Hill Collins (1948-) is a professor at the University of Maryland. She puts forth a black feminist sociological theory (2000). Like Smith, she too argues for the importance of a form of standpoint theory. A sociological theory that claims to understand the realities of an oppressed group -- and for Collins women and black people are two of these groups -- must place the standpoint of the persons of that group at the front and center of the theory. It is the particular, lived experiences and the particular perspectives that are attached to it that are central to standpoint theory. At the heart of standpoint theory is the rejection of conventional social scientific approaches that treat minorities or persons of oppressed groups as merely objects or pawns of forces outside of their control. Instead, standpoint theory asserts the central importance of recognizing the oppressed subject as a living, choice making subject, as someone who is fully human. Collins is largely interested in theorizing about black women. For Collins, when one embraces standpoint theory and seeks to understand the perspectives of these others, one must also recognize that lived reality is comprised of intersections of dominance in the realms of race, class, gender, and sex (2000:145; 2004). **Intersectionality** is a central concept in her theorizing. "Intersectionality refers to particular forms of intersecting oppressions, for example, intersections of race and gender, or of sexuality and nation. Intersectional paradigms remind us that oppression cannot be reduced to one fundamental type, and that oppressions work together in producing injustice" (2000:21). Intersectionality is closely related to another key concept, the **matrix of domination**. This "refers to how these intersecting oppressions are actually organized" (2000:21). Later she writes, "The term matrix of domination describes [the] overall social organization within which intersecting oppressions originate, develop, and are contained. In the United States, such domination has occurred through schools, housing, employment, government, and other social institutions that regulate the actual patterns of intersecting oppressions that Black women encounter" (2000:246).

To understand the position of black women Collins argues that one needs to appreciate the social context of their lives. This includes an appreciation of the forces of history. For example, traditional scholarship has often failed to understand black women and the impact of history upon them, and instead has treated black women as passive objects who are little more than pawns to powerful forces around them. Instead, a more accurate understanding would be to look at how women actively create their worlds and their social arrangements in history in the face of overwhelmingly oppressive forces. As one example, she notes that the ideas of gender roles, of family, of motherhood in the black community all were fundamentally shaped by the African cultures of black Americans who were brought to America as slaves, and these were altered due to the oppressive system of slavery. These things provided black women with a different social context than white women. For black women the central divide was not between the private realm and the public realm, as claimed by white feminist, but instead was between the oppressive white world and the world of the black community. Developments of the black family emerge in a fundamentally distinct context. The formation of this institution as well as others must be understood as effective actions taken by an oppressive group to survive, and ultimately as forms of resistance to this oppression.

An underlying theme in Collins' theorizing is the importance, really the necessity, of understanding the unique and particular perspectives of black women. Conventional approaches to the study of black women that tend to put all black women into one conceptual basket are rejected. She rejects this form of creating black women as The Other, and instead asserts the need to appreciate the human subjectivity of individual black woman's lived experiences. This simplistic device of creating binary categories of the researcher as subject and of the persons being studied as objects leads to misunderstandings of social reality. It fundamentally distorts a sociological understanding of black women.

Collins argues that women and black people and the working and poorer classes are oppressed, and these oppressions are at one and the same time distinctive and overlapping. It is only by understanding these distinctions and these overlapping elements that one can truly know the oppressions of any one group, such as black women. She does not devote much attention to the specific defense of the claim of the existence of oppression other than to point to history and to the glaring facts of massive inequalities in found in so many dimensions of social life that exist today, such as those between black people and white people, men and women, rich and poor, and heterosexual and non-heterosexual. Her focus is on black women, and here she does provide more detailed explanations of how the oppression is maintained. She specifically focuses upon the cultural arena, and the production of what she calls controlling images, which are basically racist, sexist, highly negative stereotypes about black women:

> Portraying African-American women as stereotypically mammies, matriarchs, welfare recipients, and hot mommas help justify U.S. Black women's oppression …. As part of a generalized ideology of domination, stereotypical images of Black womanhood take on a special meaning … These controlling images are designed to make racism, sexism, poverty, and other forms of social injustice appear to be natural, normal, and inevitable parts of everyday life. (2000:76-77)

These images are produced largely by men, and specifically rich, white men. They are spread through the culture and serve to maintain the oppression of black women.

She also develops a black feminist epistemology, that is, a black feminist form or theory of knowledge. This epistemology has several central features to it. One of these is the assumption that ideologies are rooted in interests. "Ideology refers to the body of ideas reflecting the interests of a group of people" (2000:7). Another is the rejection of positivism. This is closely related to the rejection of an objectivist perspective of truth. Truth, for Collins, is conditional. What is true is what is deemed to be true, and what is deemed to be true is dependent upon social organization and upon the relative power of those proclaiming truths. Truth and knowledge are social productions. As such, definitions themselves have a "politicized nature" (2000:138) to them. She writes:

> In the United States, the social institutions that legitimate knowledge as well as the Western or Eurocentric epistemologies [e.g. positivism] that they uphold constitute two interrelated parts of the dominant knowledge validation processes. In general scholars, publishers, and other experts represent specific interests and credentialing processes, and their knowledge claims must satisfy the political and epistemological criteria of the contexts in which they reside. Because this enterprise is controlled by elite White men, knowledge validation processes reflect this group's interest. (2000:271)

The task of theory then is twofold. On the one hand, one must embrace and champion subjugated knowledge. That is, the knowledge of subjugated, oppressed people, such as black women, most be recognized and accorded validity as arbiters of truths. On the other hand, one must also seek to understand the social forces that produce subjugated knowledge, and these can and are found outside of academia. As black women were historically shut out from the conventional academic institutions, which serve as the traditional, legitimating foundations of knowledge, they were led to produce knowledge in other, non-academic contexts, through music and literature, for example. There are several distinctive dimensions of black women's experiences that serve as the bedrock of black feminist epistemology:

> Black feminist intellectuals must be personal advocates for their material, be accountable for the consequences of their work, have lived or experienced their material in some fashion, and be willing to engage in dialogues about their findings with ordinary, everyday people. ... Historically, living life as an African-American woman facilitated this endeavor because knowledge validation processes controlled in part or in full by Black women occurred in particular organizational settings. When Black women were in charge of our own self-definitions, these four dimensions of Black feminist epistemology – lived experience as a criteria of meaning, the use of dialogue, the ethic of personal accountability, and the ethic of caring – came to the forefront. (2000:286)

In short, knowledge and truth are socially determined within a context of power (and interests). The task of a black feminist epistemology is in part the rejection of the epistemology of the dominant white men (e.g. positivism) and in part the resistance to succumbing to the abstract logic of this dominant approach. This requires the development of an alternative black feminist epistemology which is built upon a different reality and a different set of principles, including dialog, lived realities, interdisciplinarity, the focus upon knowledge in the service of subjugated people and social change, etc.

An essential part of Collins' black feminist sociology is that it should be fundamentally political in nature. "The overarching purpose of U.S. Black feminist thought is ... to resist oppression, both its practices and the ideas that justify it" (2000:25). The task of sociology is not to objectively describe or explain the world. The task instead is for it to change the world. But this belief in the function of change cannot be divorced from championing subjugated knowledge. That is, the point is not simply to change the world. The point is for black women to try to understand the nature of their knowledge and the means through which they produce it. But more. It is for the black feminist to assert the legitimacy of their epistemological perspectives and their knowledge claims and to demand that black women be given a legitimate political voice, and this can be done through black women assuming positions of power and influence in knowledge producing settings, such as universities. In short, the political agenda is at the heart of black feminist sociology, just as it should be according to Collins, for any oppressed group.

Queer Theory

A very different type of theory seeking to understand identity and inequality has emerged in the last thirty years. This theory is called **queer theory**. The name itself, of course, is provocative. In part, the name is used as a way for scholars and activists to re-appropriate a term that traditionally is used negatively or as an insult. (This is not unlike black Americans in the 1960s who championed the slogan "black is beautiful.") Queer theory turns the term queer into a positive and affirmative one. Queer theory is different from traditional race and gender theories. It is also different from sociological theories of gays and lesbians. It is also not a theory that began within sociology. Instead, it emerged within the fields of philosophy and literary studies. Queer theory is rooted in conceptually understanding the sources of gender categories and the associated forms of oppression that come with these. Some of the main figures associated with this theory are Judith Butler (1990), Eve Kosofsky Sedgwick (1990), and Teresa de Lauretis (1987)(see also Seidman, 1996, 1997).

Queer theory seeks to present a radical alternative to conventional approaches to gender and sex. The theory is built upon many of the ideas found in post-structural and postmodern theories and is influenced by scholars such as Michel Foucault. It sees the very formation and existence of dichotomous gender categories (e.g. male and female) as essentially oppressive – oppressive to any and all persons who are not straight males and who are instead women, gay, lesbians, transgendered, etc. Queer theory has built into it a call to political action to challenge and to overthrow the existing dominant forms of gender categories.

Queer theory begins with a recognition of the opposing ways of understanding gender and the inequalities of gender. One way, the traditional way, is based upon an essentialist claim that gender and sex are tied together by nature. Gender roles which are the social behaviors associated with genders are said to be produced by nature, by the biological sex of the person. In other words, the essentialist view is that men and women are biological different, and the gender differences between them are the result of these natural, biological differences. A very different way of understanding the differences between men and women is by embracing an anti-essentialist claim. That is, the differences in gender between men and women are not the product of biology but instead are the products of the social world. Scholars sometimes if not often associate the concept of social constructionism with this. Gender, it is sometimes claimed, is socially constructed. The idea of social construction is widely used in American sociology today (for good and ill). It traces its roots to symbolic interactionism as well as to phenomenology (see Chapter Nine; Berger and Luckmann, 1966; Goffman, 1961; Mead,

1962). The essence of social constructionism is that our beliefs about our worlds are determined not by a direct understanding of the world but through the mediation by symbols and specifically language. The important part of our worlds is not the world itself but the ways in which people see, understand, interpret this world. The world is a constructed place. The idea of social constructionism can readily be seen in the labeling theory of deviance, within the field of the sociology of deviance. The sociologist Howard Becker once proclaimed, "Deviance is that which is so labeled," by which he meant in part that no behavior in itself is deviant. A behavior only becomes deviant when others assign a label of deviance to it. Countless examples of the social construction of behavior can be found in the field of deviance. For example, homosexuality was once officially considered a mental illness by the mental health professions, and was listed as such in the first edition of the psychiatric diagnostic book, the Diagnostic and Statistical Manual of Mental Disorders (DSM), which appeared in the 1950s and 1960s. However, in the more recent editions of the DSM, homosexuality is not listed in itself as a mental illness. Homosexuality is not deviant in itself. It is only deviant when it is labeled as such.

It would be a mistake however to too quickly identify queer theory with social constructionism. While in a general way, queer theory is a form of social constructionism, it is built upon a decidedly more complicated theoretical and philosophical framework than social constructionism. Butler, for example, argues in her book *Gender Trouble* that gender is constructed, but it is not constructed in the way this term is sometimes used. She writes:

> To claim that gender is constructed is not to assert its illusoriness or artificiality, where those terms are understood to reside with a binary that counterposes the "real" and the "authentic" as oppositional. As a genealogy of gender ontology, this inquiry seeks to understand the discursive production of the plausibility of that binary relation and to suggest that certain cultural configurations of gender take the place of "the real" and consolidate and augment their hegemony through that felicitous self-naturalization. (1990:45)

This framework stands in opposition to the theories – symbolic interactionism and phenomenology – that are traditionally seen as the foundations of social constructionist ideas. Instead, it is built upon many of the ideas associated with Foucault and with postmodern theory, as is described in Chapter Twelve.

The works of Judith Butler will be used here to illustrate several of the central ideas in queer theory. The first of these ideas is **anti-essentialism**. Essentialist claims, whether in regard to gender or to any other facet of social existence, assert that there are timeless truths to be found beneath the appearance of reality. Moreover, these truths are seen as certain, unchanging and unchangeable. Essentialist claims reject the assumptions of pre-given foundations to our understandings. For example, if one says that the self is this or the self is that by its very nature, one is making an essentialist claim. If one says a man is this or a woman is that by its nature, one is making an essentialist claim. Essentialism claims that there are certain assumptions that should be accepted as true regarding the reality of one or another thing. What is the essence of gender? Of identity? Of desire? Essentialism claims the true meaning and true realities of any particular experienced reality lies in the hidden, essential nature of the things making up that reality. What does it mean to be a man? Or a Woman? What is the essence of this? In keeping with the post-structuralist influences, queer theory rejects all essentialist claims. For example, Butler challenges Freud's psychoanalytic theory and its assumptions of the essential naturalness of heterosexual desires. These sexual dispositions Freud claims are essential and natural. Butler responds: "But what is the proof Freud gives us for the existence of such dispositions? If there is no way to distinguish between the femininity acquired through internalization [e.g. socialization] and that which is strictly dispositional, then what is to preclude the conclusion that all gender-specific affinities are the consequence of internalizations? On what basis are dispositional sexualities and identities ascribed to individuals, and what meaning can we give to "femininity" and "masculinity" at the outset?" (1990:82-83).

Butler's anti-essentialism leads her to argue that the quest for origins is a harmful and misguided project. The quest for origins is the idea of the essential start or beginning of something or other. She writes: "Gay is to straight *not* as a copy is to original, but, rather, as a copy is to a copy. The parodic repetition of "the original" ... reveals the original to be nothing other than a parody of the *idea* of the natural and the original" (1990:43). Anti-essentialism appears again in her discussion of psychoanalytic theory. In psychoanalytic theory the origin of the individual self is traced back to the point where the infant separates from the mother after weaning. The assumptions of essences and origins produce necessarily fabricated or false stories used to sustain the overarching theories. Butler discusses this at one point in regards to the "laws" of psychoanalysis and heterosexual desires:

> The self-justification of a repressive or subordinating law almost always grounds itself in a story about what it was like *before* the advent of the law, and how it came about that the law emerged in its present and necessary form. The fabrication of those origins tends to describe a state of affairs before the law that follows a necessary and unilinear narrative that culminates in, and thereby justifies, the constitution of the law. The story of origins is thus a strategic tactic within a narrative that, by telling

a single, authoritative account about an irrecoverable past, makes the constitution of the law appear as a historical inevitability. (1990:48)

A central feature of many versions of queer theory builds upon this anti-essentialism. Notably, many embrace an anti-humanism (see Chapter Twelve). Butler does so. In one of her criticisms of traditional feminism, she complains about the humanistic assumptions of that perspective:

What is the metaphysics of substance, and how does it inform thinking about the categories of sex? In the first instance, humanistic conceptions of the subject tend to assume a substantive person who is the bearer of various essential and nonessential attributes. A humanist feminist position might understand gender as an *attribute* of a person who is characterized essentially as a pregendered substance or "core," called a person, denoting a universal capacity for reason, moral deliberation, or language. The universal conception of the person, however, is displaced as a point of departure for a social theory of gender by those historical and anthropological positions that understand gender as a relation among socially constituted subjects in specifiable contexts. This relational or contextual point of view suggests that what the person "is," and, indeed, what gender "is," is always relative to the constructed relations in which it is determined. (1990:14)

Queer theory is also influenced greatly by **post-structuralism**, and specifically by the ideas of Michel Foucault. Post-structuralism, you will recall, is derived from structuralism (see Chapter Twelve). Structuralism, for example, in the works of Levi-Strauss, is based upon the claim that the mind has an organized structure to it, and is based upon the assumptions that the meaning of a sign is derived from its relation to other signs, specifically, from binary oppositions: Hot is the opposite of cold; Up is the opposite of down, etc. Post-structuralism accepts the claims of a structure to our consciousness, but rejects the claims of binaries, and rejects the claims of the universality of the structure of consciousness. Structures can and do change in history or from one society to another. Queer theory rejects the claims of the universal and timeless presence of binaries (e.g. male and female). Moreover, queer theory sees binaries as fundamentally problematic in that they are the basis of gender oppression. The binary between men and women is created and used by men to maintain their dominance. For queer theory, discourse and thought in general is fused with power, and the embrace of binaries, particularly in relation to gender, cannot be understood outside of power.

The theory also rejects structuralism for its totalizing conceptualizations. Structuralism presents a model of consciousness that is all inclusive. It is a closed system in which all elements are contained and in which all elements relate to other elements. As with binaries, this assumption of totality is troubling for queer theory. Butler writes about these things in the context of the works of the structural linguist Saussure as well as the structural anthropologist Levi-Strauss:

> The *totality* and closure of language is both presumed and contested within structuralism. ... All linguistic terms presuppose a linguistic totality of structures, the entirety of which is presupposed and implicitly recalled from any one term to bear meaning. This quasi-Leibnizian view, in which language figures as a systematic totality, effectively suppresses the moment of difference between signifier and signified, relating and unifying that moment of arbitrariness within a totalizing field. The poststructuralist break with Saussure and with the identitarian structures of exchange found in Levi-Strauss refutes the claims of totality and universality and the presumption of binary structural oppositions that implicitly operate to quell the insistent ambiguity and openness of linguistic and cultural signification. (1990:54)

Abandoning structuralism for poststructuralist sensibilities, queer theory seeks to understand the "domains" or "matrix of intelligibility" that shapes the way people understand gender and perform gender.

The concepts of the subject, self and identity are also central. Building upon the anti-essentialist and post-structuralist claims, queer theorists tend to see the self not as a unified and timeless thing. Butler rejects the pre-discursive existence of the self and argues that the self is produced through lived social engagement. She complains that theories that assume the subject has "some stable existence prior to the cultural field that it negotiates" is wrongheaded. Instead, "the culturally enmired subject negotiates its constructions, even when those constructions are the very predicates of its own identity." Identity "is asserted through a process of signification, [it] is always already signified" (1990:196).

Butler also sees the importance of critically interrogating the concept of desire and its relation to the self. She turns to a critique of psychoanalysis to illuminate these ideas. Psychoanalytic theory has many years ago put forth a theory of desire and its relation to gender. In psychoanalysis, gender is rooted in the binaries of heterosexual desires. One is either a male or a female, and there are natural desires associated with each. These desires are pre-discursive. As such, they lay the foundation for a theory that supports the naturalness of two genders and the normalness of heterosexuality. Desire, like the subject, is constituted through discourse. Because it is constituted through discourse, she rejects the assumptions of the naturalness of two genders as well as the normalness of heterosexuality. Instead, there is a "heterogeneity of the subject, and individuals have a natural "biological polysexuality"

(1990:101). Desires are channeled into the binaries of heterosexuality only through cultural, discursive practices.

Queer theory in general and Butler's approach in particular places importance on the relationship of discourse to power, and the relationship of both to behavior, or performativity. For Butler, as for other poststructuralists such as Foucault, power is central to an understanding of social formations. Power is inextricably tied to discourse and to the production of sexuality, and specifically to the production of heterosexuality. She notes that "sexuality is culturally constructed within existing power relations" (1990:42). Also, in discussing Foucault's work *The History of Sexuality*, she writes, "the body is not "sexed" in any significant sense prior to its determination within a discourse through which it becomes invested with an "idea" of natural or essential sex. The body gains meaning within discourse only in the context of power relations. Sexuality is a historically specific organization of power, discourse, bodies, and affectivity" (1990:124-25).

Power, for Butler, is a constant. It should not and cannot be ignored or denied in any study of gender and sexuality. It is not something that one should or could seek to eliminate. Power is something that should be appropriated by those challenging what she sees as the oppressions rooted in the heterosexual order of things. Moreover, the meanings of sexuality and gender lie in performances. It is through social actions that gender and sexuality are realized, and this realization either can be in support of the binary of heterosexuality, and thus in support of oppression, or it can challenge this dominant discourse. Butler champions the latter.

To understand her calls to challenge and destabilize the binary of heterosexuality through action, one should appreciate her post-structuralist sensibilities. Her rejection of essentialism leads to a rejection of any attempts that seek to challenge or change any presumed essential condition, regarding sexuality, desire or gender. Her concept of performativity arises in this context. She makes the distinction between expressivity and performativity. Expressivity implies something deeper, something more essential that lies beneath the appearance. Expressivity is the mode of action founded upon conventional beliefs concerning of gender, sex and desire. Butler challenges this entire orientation and believes an alternative to expressivity is therefore required. **Performativity** is that alternative. It is the realization of the intersection of discourse and power through practices. And it is at this site of performativity that the hierarchical binaries of heterosexuality should be challenged. She writes: "When the disorganization and disaggregation of the field of bodies disrupt the regulatory fiction of heterosexual coherence, it seems that the expressive model loses its descriptive force. That regulatory ideal is then exposed as a norm and a fiction that disguises itself as a developmental law regulating the sexual field that it purports to describe" (1990:185). In short, queer theory calls for adherents to engage in behaviors that challenge the comfortable binaries of heterosexuality. For example, she calls for the use of parody as well as the use of drag to further this aim:

> If the anatomy of the performer is already distinct from the gender of the performer, and both of those are distinct from the gender of the performance, then the performance suggests a dissonance not only between sex and performance, but sex and gender, and gender and performance. As much as drag created a unified picture of "woman," … it also reveals the distinctiveness of those aspects of gendered experience which are falsely naturalized as a unity through the regulatory fiction of heterosexual coherence. In imitating gender, drag implicitly reveals the imitative structure of gender itself – as well as its contingency. (1990:187)

Queer theory calls for political engagement. This engagement, through performativity, is the direct consequence of the theoretical formulation of queer theory. Realities lie in and through action and being. Realities do not lie behind such things. Butler writes: "The foundationalist reasoning of identity politics tends to assume that an identity must first be in place in order for political interests to be elaborated and, subsequently, political action to be taken. My argument is that there need not be a "doer behind the deed," but that the "doer" is variably constructed in and through the deed" (1990:194-95).

Summary

This chapter described several of the critical race, gender and sexual identities theories that have arisen in the last several decades. An important distinction was made between traditional theories and critical theories related to these topics. Several early and traditional approaches were described. A distinction was made between theories of race and critical race theories. Wilson's theory was presented as a theory on race that is not categorized as a critical race theory. Wilson adheres to conventional sociological assumptions about epistemology and methodology, which are rejected by the more radical critical race theories. Wilson argues that economic and political structures rather than cultural forces and racism account for continued inequalities between races. Du Bois's theorizing on the other hand was described as an early critical race theory. Du Bois saw the importance of race in American society and saw the necessity of understanding it from a social psychological and an economic and political perspective. The term critical race theory was then explained, and it was shown that the term itself is traditionally assigned to a specific theory found in legal studies. This classic form of critical race theory (CRT) was explained and discussed. This was followed by a description of several sociological theories that might also be called critical race theories. Here, the critical race theories of West, Omi and Winant, and Brown were described. These theories assert the continued significant of racism and discrimination in explaining inequalities today. Many of these argue that race operates independently from social class, and because of this, theorizing about race itself is necessary to understand inequalities. Moreover, these theories tend to focus on the relationship between the dominant white group and minorities as central in any understanding. They largely are relational in focus. Racism and discrimination are also seen as systematic, rather than, or in addition to, being a conscious and individual force. The postcolonial theories of Said and Fanon were then briefly described. Postcolonial theories largely originate in the humanities rather than the social sciences and they focus on the symbolic realm, such as literature, to examine how dominant groups in the West have created caricatures of people of color so that the dominant groups could maintain their dominance. Postcolonial studies scholars like Fanon argue that the theoretical response should be through political action which challenges the domination.

This chapter also described several critical gender theories, as well as queer theory. We began with an overview of the early work of Martineau, then covered the more contemporary theories of Smith and Collins. Smith develops a standpoint theory of gender which integrates phenomenology and elements of Marxism. She argues that one must look at the relations of rulings that appear in everyday life if one wishes to understand and to combat gender inequalities. Collins builds upon standpoint theory but develops a theory of intersectionality that argues that one must understand the interrelated dynamics of inequalities found in the domains of race, class, and gender. The chapter also describes Butler's version of queer theory. Queer theory is greatly influenced by the post-structuralist theory of Foucault. It argues against the conceptual binary of male and female, and champions multiple sexual identities. Queer theory also embraces the call to action in the form of performativity.

Discussion Questions

1. Which should be understood as more foundational, or more basic, or more universal when sociological theorists seek to understand inequality – race, class, or gender? Are these categories necessarily interlinked or not? How or why? Which category should be the cornerstone of understanding inequalities? Why?

2. What are the similarities and differences between the sociological organization of race inequalities, gender inequalities, and sexual inequalities?

3. Many critical race and gender theories claim that discrimination occurs without intention. That is, the claim is that there are unconscious forces operating within people in dominant groups that cause them to discriminate, unknowingly, against others. This is associated with the concept of institutional discrimination. Yet some social scientist question whether this is a legitimate social scientific concept. Social scientific concepts must be capable of being objectively studied. Empirical evidence or facts must be the basis of these studies. But concepts such as institutional discrimination are highly interpretive and not readily subject to empirical study. Is institutional discrimination a valid social scientific concept?

4. Queer theory claims that natural differences between male and female desires is in fact the product not of nature but of society. But one might ask, should social theory ignore nature? Can any social theory be complete if it does not recognize the biological reality of human beings? How should social theory address nature and the biological reality of human beings? Are we not animals, with instinct? Is it possible to incorporate nature into a theory? Why or why not?

Chapter Fourteen: Theories of the Changing Present World – Globalization and the Environment; From Wallerstein to Castells and Beyond

Sociological theorizing being done in the last few decades is quite different from the theorizing done in earlier decades and earlier centuries. We have seen a glimpse of some of these changes in the last several chapters -- on integrative theories, critical identity, race and gender theories, and postmodernism. In this chapter we pick up where we left off in these chapters. Here we review a few of the most recent trends in sociological theories. To frame this chapter, we begin by distinguishing two distinct current approaches to theorizing today. One of these is the more conventional. This conventional approach tends to embrace either one or another form of scientistic form of theorizing or it embraces the micro traditions in theorizing, most notably in the form of symbolic interactionism. The scientistic (or if you will, positivistic) form of theory embraced by numerous contemporary sociologists ultimately proclaims the method to be the theory. That is, the sociologist today should be a researcher who does his or her work based upon the ideas of science. Theory will or does emerge, from the perspective of this approach, from the production of research findings. In some ways, one might consider this approach an anti-theory theory in that it relies upon the philosophy or theory of methods. The true workings of the social world, it is argued, will be revealed through the systematic application of scientific methods in an understanding of that world. The true workings will not be revealed through abstract theories which may or may not be untestable. (How, for example, can one test Marx's theory of false consciousness?) The second form of conventional theorizing today is the embrace of the micro-traditions of symbolic interactionism and associated theories. In classic American forms of intellectual orientations, this approach is rooted in an embrace of the common sense, of the practical (see Chapter Nine).

Both of these conventional approaches are limited or limiting in their orientation. The focus on the particular, in each case, either in particular facts or in particular, lived interactions, encourages theory to ignore or to deny the social whole. This then automatically means that theory in this tradition is unable to be effectively critical of this whole or of the structural workings of society. Moreover, history vanishes in these conventional approaches. The past is not of concern, nor is conceptualizing the past. What matters is the explanation of the observed present. This denial of history, which is sadly widespread in American sociology in general today, and within American sociological theory in particular, takes sociology far from its roots in the eighteen hundreds when many, such as Weber and Marx, believed, the task was to understand and explain the modern world – how it came about, what the consequences of it will be, etc.

In this chapter, we do not focus on either of these conventional approaches. Instead, we turn to several other recent and current theories that often are less inclined to accept the limitations just noted of the conventional approaches. Here, we look at a number of other perhaps more theoretically dynamic forms of understanding that have emerged in the last thirty years or so. We focus here on two distinct, yet sometimes overlapping, currents in recent theorizing. One current can be called concretizing theories. Concretizing theories generally seek to apply the critical and/or historical understandings of the social whole to the real particular lived realities. By concretizing theories, I am referring to those which claim that theory now cannot or should not be developed in the abstract. Such abstract theories are like model building in which some timeless model of society is developed. Instead, the concretizing theories claim that theory must be grounded in the workings of the real world. The development of theoretical concepts must be tied to the real understandings of the real world as it exists today. But this understanding must be informed by a critical or historical understanding of the social whole. Globalization theories, environmental theories, and critical race and gender theories fall into this camp. We look at the first two of these below. A second recent current focuses upon what may be called historically contingent theories. These theories begin with the recognition that different historical eras require different theoretical conceptualizations. The theories of the industrial era, from Marx to Durkheim, may not be applicable to the post-industrial world of today. These recent theories focus on identifying the major and distinctive social themes found in the present social world, recognizing that these themes are historically specific and were not, and may not be in the future, significant factors in explaining social realities. We touched briefly on this form of theorizing in Chapter Eleven, where we went over the theorizing of Giddens. Giddens, you may recall, claims that the essential forces of the contemporary world, including things such as reflexivity and disembeddedness, are distinctive to this world and are not applicable to earlier time periods. In this chapter we explore some other theories seeking to identify the distinctive dynamics of this contemporary world.

Concretizing Theories: Globalization

An increasing number of globalization theories have emerged in the social sciences in the last forty years or so. These theories, often interdisciplinary in focus, seek to understand the world-wide processes by which the world has and is increasingly becoming interconnected. They seek to understand the forces propelling globalization forward as well as the consequences of this process. In this section, we describe two very different globalization theories. The first is Immanuel Wallerstein's world systems analysis. Wallerstein is influenced by Marx in his theorizing and is critical of the current process of globalization. He sees the structure of the globalization process as favoring rich and powerful countries and disfavoring poor and week countries. The second is Samuel Huntington's the clash of civilizations. Huntington is a political scientist who like Wallerstein is concerned about the globalization process. Huntington makes a cultural argument, claiming that the process of globalization is going to lead to conflicts between major civilizations in the world.

World-Systems Theory

Immanuel Wallerstein (1930-) is an American sociologist who has spent much of his career elaborating a theory of globalization that he calls world-systems theory or world-systems analysis. He presents a detailed description of the theory in his four volume work, *The Modern World System, Vol. 1-4* (1974, 1980, 1989, and 2011), which was written over a span of fifteen years. The unit of analysis for his research and for his theory, i.e. what it is he is studying, is not the traditional unit studied by most sociologists. Most study units such as individuals, or groups, or even one or another society. Wallerstein instead is seeking to understand modern world history and as such is interested not in individual countries but in the world system that ties all of the countries in the world together. The theory largely focuses on the political and economic structures tying all of the countries together, and it focuses upon the relationship between the political and economic realms of the international system. It is a work of political economy.

Wallerstein is often identified as a Marxist or as a neo-Marxist, and his theory has within it many of the classic positions taken by Marx. One of these positions shared by Marx and Wallerstein is the claim that the economic structure of a society (or world) is the fundamental driving force in history. So too is the claim that capitalism is fundamentally based upon exploitation. For Wallerstein and for Marx the endless drive for profit is a fundamental characteristic of capitalism. Both theorists also argue that capitalism is riddled with contradictions which ultimately will not be able to be contained, and these contradictions or conflicts will lead to crises and ultimately the collapse of capitalism, though their understandings of how these conflicts will lead to the downfall of capitalism are markedly different. One could point out many other common themes found in the two perspectives.

Yet Wallerstein's theory is quite distinct from traditional Marxism in many respects. One difference revolves around social classes. For Marx, the essential contradictions of capitalism would appear in the conflict between two economic classes – the proletariat and the bourgeoisie. This conflict would ultimately lead to a political revolution led by the proletariat and to the end of capitalism. For Wallerstein, social classes, and specifically the industrial working class, are not the central force in global capitalism. Instead, he writes about "peoplehood" which may be comprised of several dimensions which are distinct from class. Peoplehood is associated with race, with nationalism, and with ethnicity. There are different peoples in different countries and these countries, as we see below, are positioned in one or another place in the international capitalist system. It is this that is central to Wallerstein's theory, and not the economic class conflict between the working class and the rich persons within one society. On a closely related note, he identifies the household rather than the individual worker as the central and most basic economic unit of the capitalist system (2004:32-36). "There are classes in a capitalist system ... [b]ut ... wage workers are ensconced in households" (2004:35). Households consist of many persons, and they operate under principals that are different from those governing the operation of one individual worker. He also differs from Marx in his understanding the role of industrialization in the history of global capitalism. For Marx, capitalism and industrialization went hand in hand. They emerged together. Wallerstein, however, traces the origins of the modern, capitalist world system to the fourteen hundreds, well before industrialization began. Another difference between Wallerstein and Marx concerns their understanding of the role of the state (or national government). While both saw the state ultimately as a tool used by the bourgeoisie to maintain the economic order and to further their interests, Wallerstein's analysis of the state is far more detailed. For example, he argued that the state has and can maintain the economic order by serving the needs of the bourgeoisie, but it does so in different ways in different countries depending upon the position of the respective state in the world economic system. States in less developed countries, for example, are rather weak and subject to the demands of the more powerful states and the more powerful groups in those states. In another way, the powerful and rich states are in a better position to aid the powerful economic actors (corporations and rich people) within them by helping these actors move their costs to the poor states.

Wallerstein builds his theory on a number of central concepts -- the most fundamental of which is the division of labor. The division of labor allocates some jobs to some people, and other, different types of jobs to other people. There are bankers and there are farmhands. There are software engineers in Silicon Valley, California, and people working in clothing factories in Pakistan. But Wallerstein focuses less upon the division of labor within any one country, than he does on the division of labor between countries in the international system. The types of jobs found in the United States are quite different by and large from the types of jobs one finds in a Nigeria or some other country in Africa. Moreover, it is not simply that the types of jobs are different, but these differences are associated with the different types of things produced in the different countries. One country may produce agricultural products, another may produce manufactured goods, and another might produce services and information. The division of labor also entails a hierarchy of power, with some positions, and some countries, having control over other weaker countries. In addition to the division of labor, Wallerstein notes that capitalism, which is the world economic system today, is based upon accumulation. Specifically, the accumulation of capitalism is the central force propelling society forward. In other words, rich people and rich corporations wish to make more and more money. The capitalism system demands it, and the system fosters it. But for Wallerstein, capitalism is not simply characterized by accumulation. It is characterized by endless accumulation: "We are in a capitalist system only when the system gives priority to *endless* accumulation of capital" (2004:24). The cost of production is another central concept found in his theory. Capitalism is driven to maximize profit, and one way to do this is to try to reduce the costs of production. A central cost of production is labor. Corporations are driven to seek out cheap labor. This fuels the endless process of global capitalism, as corporations move their factories and companies from developed countries, such as the United States, to undeveloped or less developed countries, in search of cheaper labor. This process is perhaps most obviously seen in the United States as it shifted from an industrial to a post-industrial economy. Clothing, shoes, computers, and automobiles are increasingly being made in less developed countries and are being made increasingly less in more in developed countries.

At the heart of all of this lies the notions of exploitation and surplus value. We may define exploitation as the difference between the value of a worker's labor and the value of the product made by the worker in the marketplace. This is also known as surplus value. Capitalism is built upon this concept. Corporations seek to increase the surplus value of the productive process, and in global capitalism they are propelled to do so by seeking out cheaper labor in other countries. The endless pursuit of capital accumulation leads corporations to an endless pursuit of exploitation.

State and Economy: Quasi-Monopolies, Economic Management

The role of the state is central to Wallerstein's theory. Specifically, the relationship of the state to the capitalist economy and to corporations or firms is key. It is traditionally believed that the state plays or should play a minimal or non-existent role in a capitalist economy. This is the idea of a laissez-faire economy. The belief is that the economy and society will be better off if the state does not intervene in the economy, or at the very least if it intervenes as little as possible. Wallerstein says these claims are simply not accurate descriptions about how capitalism works. Instead, he says the state plays and it must play an integral role in the economy and in relation to corporations and firms for capitalism to work. The state has to intervene in the capitalist market because if it did not, capitalism would collapse. A laissez-faire system would simply not work. "The totally free market place functions as an ideology, a myth, and a constraining influence, but never as a day-to-day reality. One of the reasons it is not a day-to-day reality is that a totally free market, were it ever to exist, would make impossible the endless accumulation of capital" (2004:25). The rush to bargain down prices in a completely open, competitive marketplace, would produce an unworkably low and an increasingly lower rate of profit, which is unsustainable. As a result, corporations rely upon the state to regulate the market in ways that make it sustainable. Wallerstein says that sellers always prefer a monopoly (2004:26), as this would of course give them the maximum accumulation of capital but notes that this is not generally realistic in practice. Instead, corporations (sellers, firms) become quasi-monopolies. States can and do manage the economy to favor some corporate actors, thus allowing them to assume a position that resembles a monopoly, though in reality is not technically one. States do various things to produce and maintain these quasi-monopolies. One of these is to rely upon the system of patents, which allow corporations exclusive control and ownership over patents and inventions. "State restrictions on imports and exports (so called protectionist measures)" (2004:26) are another way in which the state produces or supports quasi-monopolies. In addition, state regulations of various sorts also aid quasi-monopolies, as smaller competitors are unable to absorb the costs associated with complying with these regulations.

The state is also vital to the maintenance of capitalism because it subsidizes many of the costs that would otherwise have to be paid by corporations, and these costs would be prohibitively expensive. We are speaking here of externalities. Externalities are aspects of the economic production process that are not recorded as costs to the corporations even though they are in fact costs. These costs do not appear, in effect, on the accounting balance sheets of the corporations, but they are nevertheless costs associated with production. Who then pays for such things? Society or the general population does. There are three main externalized costs: costs of toxicity; costs of exhaustion of materials; and costs of transport (2004:47). Costs of toxicity are things like pollution of the environment. While there are now some regulations governing these things, by and large corporations are not required to pay for their pollution of the environment. The cost of exhaustion of materials is the destruction or eradication of one or another element of the natural environment. "A good example of materials that have not been adequately replaced is the world wood supply. The forests of Ireland were cut down in the seventeenth century. And through the history of the modern world-system, we have been cutting down forests of all kinds without replacing them. Today we discuss the consequences of not protecting what is considered the *last* major rain forest in the entire world, the Amazon area in Brazil" (2004:48). The third cost is that of transportation. Wallerstein notes that while corporations pay some for the use of public roadways, trains, etc., they do not pay the full costs associated with transportation. Transportation costs are subsidized by the public.

In addition to all of these, the state also does a number of other things that are essential to the maintenance of capitalism and that are necessary for corporations to survive. One of these is the state's regulation and control over its boundaries. It establishes import and export policies, and it establishes tariff (import taxes) upon corporations, thus regulating the markets in favor of corporations in the society. A second thing the state does is to ensure property rights of the corporations through laws and policies. A third way is that it intervenes in the economic area in ways that serves the interest of corporations, for example through the regulation of the labor market, including such things as labor laws, health and safety regulations, etc. At first glance, it might appear that these things work against the interests of corporations, but Wallerstein argues otherwise. "[M]any entrepreneurs have ... seen that in the long run, state interference may be of use to them ... Ensuring long-term labor supply, creating effective demand, and minimizing social disorder may all be in part consequences of such state interference in the workplace" (2004:47).

History: From World-Empires to World-Economies and Beyond

History lies at the heart of Wallerstein's theory. In any period of history, one or another type of world-system dominates. Specifically, there are two different types of world-systems: world-empires and world-economies. To understand this, we must first understand what Wallerstein means by the word world. He is not using the word world to mean necessarily the entire globe. He is,

> not talking about systems, economies, empires of the (whole) world, but about systems, economies, empires that are a world (but quite possibly, and indeed usually not encompassing the entire globe). This is a key concept to grasp. It says that in "world-systems" we are dealing with a spatially/temporal zone which cuts across many political and cultural units, one that represents an integrated zone of activity and institutions which obey certain systemic rules. (2004:16-17)

In other words, a world may not be global, it may cover only part of the globe. But this world must be held together by rules grounded in a shared economic situation. As such, the ancient Roman empire spanned many different cultures and societies, but it was a world in that all the diverse parts of it were tied together through political economic structures.

He divides history into two great periods. First, there was the period of **world-empires**. This lasted until 1450 or so. This was followed by the period of the world-economy, which we are currently in. World-empires include ancient Indian and Chinese civilizations, ancient Rome and Greece, European empires, etc. World-empires are characterized by a central political authority that rules through its military, i.e., through its use or threat of use of force. The political order of the empire is maintained by the military. Peoples under the rule of empires are forced to pay taxes to the centralized power. Empires can and do encompass many different cultural groups, but these groups are required to pay tribute and taxes to the centralized political leaders. Wallerstein argues that this system creates economic problems that ultimately lead to its demise. The problems are in part associated with an unsustainable circle in which the leaders impose taxes and tributes to support the military. The increased taxes and tributes prevent the economies from expanding. Dissent and dissatisfaction in the populace grow. The leadership is forced to rely more and more on the military to maintain order and control, particularly of the far flung regions under its command. Increased military expenditures require increased taxation and tributes, and the cycle continues.

The period of world-empires was replaced by **world-economies** beginning in the fourteen hundreds. The emergence and spread of the capitalist world economy is key here. The modern **world-system** is defined and united by the division of labor and by the dictates of capitalism. It is also characterized by "bureaucratic state machinery in certain areas" (1974:63). Capitalism demands the unending pursuit of accumulation of capital. In contrast to world-empires, there is no single political system ruling over the entire world. In this modern system, the defining political entities are nation states rather than empires. But the force holding the system together is economics, capitalist economics.

Wallerstein identifies three different regions or types of economic states within the world-economies: the core, semi-periphery, and periphery. The **core states** are those that are rich, stable and dominant in the international arena. They include countries such as the United States, Germany, France, England, Canada, etc. They have well paid labor forces and large consumer markets. The governments are stable and offer much protection to corporations and to the workings of capitalism, in the form of such things as externalization of costs (see above). Core states offer much protection for the quasi-monopolies. **Periphery states** are poor, unstable and weak in the international arena. Workers in the periphery states have little choice in employment. They are basically forced to work in very low paying jobs that are part of the international economy. Importantly, the governments of the periphery states are weak and unstable, particularly when compared to the core states. The semi-periphery states are those between the core and periphery. **Semi-periphery states** are states that have moved from the periphery. As the result of the world-economy, these semi-periphery states have become more stable and stronger, and their economies have developed, though they continue to be distinctly less powerful and weaker than the core states. The semi-periphery is "needed to make a capitalist world-economy run smoothly" (2000b:89).

Things that are produced in one type of state are not the same as those produced in another. In the peripheral countries, for example, the economies tend to be based on agriculture and the harvesting or mining of basic natural resources, such as in the areas of timber, mining, etc. In effect, these states are export oriented economies. The raw products are shipped to core countries. They are then processed or manufactured into consumer goods, and consumed by members of these societies, or they are exported back to the periphery. The iron or copper mined in Chile is, for example, shipped to the core countries and made into machinery. The bananas grown in Costa Rica are shipped to New York and consumed there. On the other side, the economies of the core countries were built upon manufacturing and industry and are now built on service and information types of jobs. Either way, the products of the core countries are either consumed by the core countries or are exported to the periphery.

The structure of these relations between the core and the periphery is one of dependence. Wallerstein's theory is a form of dependency theory in which the structure of the international economic system places the peripheral countries in a position of dependence upon the core countries. The poorer countries have been absorbed into an international economic order which is controlled and managed by the core countries in the core countries' interest, and specifically in the interest of capitalism and the corporations holding quasi-monopolies.

Phases of the Modern World-Systems and Modern History

In addition to dividing history into periods of world-empires and world-economies, Wallerstein identifies several distinct periods of world-economies, and these periods have distinct forms. The first period spanned from the mid-fourteen hundreds through the mid-sixteen hundreds. This was the period of agricultural capitalism. It was during this period that the modern nation state begins to emerge. Spain was the dominant power. This was followed by mercantile capitalism, which lasted from the mid-sixteen hundreds through the mid-seventeen hundreds. Mercantilism is characterized by a form of capitalism that has a lack of industrial forms of production and a lack of commercial banking. That is, in mercantile capitalism manufactured goods were not made in factories, but in the home. In addition, much of the focus was on the organization and control of trade – this was an important period of European colonization – rather than on the organization and control of production. The lack of commercial banks meant that the rich persons would make their investments directly in companies rather than indirectly through organized investment banks. The Netherlands and France became the dominant countries in this period. The next, third, period began in the mid-seventeen hundreds and lasted through 1917, at the end of the First World War (and at the time around the Russian Revolution). This era is characterized by industrial capitalism. (It was the period of the industrial revolution), and Great Britain was the dominant country. The United States became the dominant power in the next period, the fourth period, which began after World War Two and continues through the present, though as we see below Wallerstein argued that 1968 was a major turning point. This fourth period was one of multinational capitalism, in which multinational corporations consolidated their powers.

Wallerstein believes, in the spirit of Marx, that global capitalism has within it contradictions which will force it either to fundamentally change or to collapse. The force producing the essential contradictions is the incessant demand for the accumulation of capital coupled with the structural pressures for profits to decline. There is a cyclical process in economics based upon these principles. Here he embraces the theoretical concept of Kondratieff waves. Kondratieff was an early twentieth century Russian economist who argued that the global capitalist system goes through fifty to sixty-year cycles of expansion and contraction. There are two phases to each cycle. In the A-Phase, the global economy expands. New products and new markets are created and expanded. New countries, during these periods, are brought into the periphery (from being external to the global system). The rates of profit grow as the corporations in core countries find ways to reduce costs. More and more things are produced. This is the period of economic expansion. Around thirty years after the start of the A-Phase, a new phase begins. This is the B-Phase, a period of decline or contraction. The B-Phase lasts another thirty years or so. In Phase B, global capitalism experiences stagnation (or recession or contraction). It reaches the point of overproduction. Commodity prices fall, labor prices rise, some corporations go out of business, leaving fewer still active.

These Kondratieff waves repeat themselves in modern history. It is the nature of global capitalism that they do. However, "a Kondratieff cycle [or wave], when it ends, never returns the situation to where it was at the beginning of the cycle" (2004:31). These cycles spiral in history to points of increasingly significant contradictions, which will eventually lead to the demise of the existing system of global capitalism. Wallerstein identifies the "world revolution of 1968" as a major turning point here. Specifically, this was the time in which the most recent Kondratieff wave moved from the A-Phase to the B-Phase. The world since 1968 has been in a state of "chaos" and will continue to be in crisis for the next "twenty-five to fifty years" from 2004 (when he wrote this).

The B-phase of this cycle has multiple dimensions. It begins with the world revolution of 1968. He argues that in or around 1968 there were revolutions, protests, and turmoil in countries around the world, from the Paris student uprisings in May, 1968 to students in Chicago protesting the Democratic National Convention; from wars of liberation waged in Viet Nam to rebellions and revolutions throughout Latin America, African, and Asia. The causes of this new phase are based on global economic conditions but are also related to cultural factors as well. Three economic factors associated with costs of production are remuneration, inputs, and taxation. First, remuneration. Remuneration refers to paying for the labor. Global capitalism pushes corporations to seek to lower their costs, but in this B-phase of the cycle they are unable to do so. The costs of remuneration, inputs, and taxations cannot be reduced. Indeed, they are increased, thus threatening the profits of the corporations. In earlier phases of global capitalism corporations could and did reduce their costs of labor by exporting production to peripheral countries with very low labor costs, or by turning countries that were external to the entire global capitalist system into peripheral countries. However, in this B-phase of this cycle of global capitalism, there are few if any countries left that corporations could turn to in search of very, very cheap labor. The corporations have exhausted this possible way of addressing the issue of costs.

The costs of inputs have also increased. Inputs refer to the costs of machinery and materials of production. But there are three hidden costs associated with inputs and these three are increasing. First, there are costs associated with disposal of waste. It is clear there is a world-wide environmental crisis, and the days are long gone when corporations could simply externalize their waste costs for free. Second, there are costs associated with renewing raw materials. There is only so much oil and coal in the ground that can be used. There is a limit to natural resources that can be used, and because global capitalism is reaching this limit the costs of production associated with this can only go up. Third, there are infrastructure costs. Infrastructure refers to "all those physical institutions outside the production unit which form a necessary part of the production and distribution process – roads, transport services, communications networks, security systems, water supply" (2004:82). These are costly, and either are paid for by the public through taxation and public works or by private corporations. Either way, they are an unavoidable burden.

Taxation is the third economic cost of production, along with remuneration and inputs, that has and will rise. The rise of taxes is associated with things that the state needs to do to ensure a stable environment within which the economy can operate. These include such things as security forces (police and military), the building of infrastructure (roads and bridges, etc.), employing a bureaucracy, etc. The rise of taxes is also associated with "political democratization." That is, the populace in democracies is demanding more educational, health, and social security from the state.

Wallerstein argues that these three costs have all been rising over the last fifty years and they cannot be contained. "On the other hand, the sales prices have not been able to keep pace, despite increase in effective demand, because of the stead expansion in the number of producers and hence of their recurring inability to maintain oligopolistic conditions. This is what one means by a squeeze on profits" (2004:83).

He says nineteen sixty-eight was a turning point. By that time, a "liberal centrism" was dominate in political systems around the world. This liberal centrism was the fruit of the movements for change in the decade. This liberal centrism was oriented toward salvaging the capitalist world economic system, through modifications (rather than through revolution). However, he says by 1968 it was apparent that the liberal centrism could not contain the contradictions in the system. It could not contain the increasing problems in the economic realm as noted above – related to remunerations, inputs, and taxation – but equally as important, it could not contain the political crises that were emerging. The liberal centrist approach gave way to a more polarized political context which increasingly pitted extreme, opposing political views against each other. This polarity is characterized as one between "The spirit of Davos and the spirit of Porto Alegro" (2004:88).

Davos refers to the annual global summit or meeting of the rich and powerful from throughout the world. They come together at Davos, Switzerland to discuss the state of affairs of the world, particularly to discuss the international economic and political order. The participants overwhelmingly if not universally embrace the existing system of global capitalism. They ultimately reflect a commitment to unfettered global capitalism, which is a capitalism that operates with as little government intervention as possible. In short, they embrace a conservative perspective. Porto Alegro refers to a city in Brazil where the World Social Forum (WSF) first met. It meets now annually, moving from city to city around the world. The WSF is a grass roots organization that is highly opposed and antagonistic to the ideologies espoused by Davos. The WSF is the largest global meeting for the alter-globalization movement (sometimes referred to as the anti-globalization movement), the movement opposed to the current globalization processes which are rooted in liberal capitalism. WSF see global capitalism as having caused great harm to people throughout the globe. WSF advocates a different social, political, economic world system from capitalism. It embraced grass roots activism and participatory democracy. It also champions the rights of indigenous peoples around the world faced with the imposition of global capitalism upon their life, culture, etc. The WSF sees the concentration of wealth and power in the hands of a small minority of people and countries as fundamentally anti-democratic, and it advocates for a system that puts the needs of people before the needs of profits.

It is this ideological divide that Wallerstein says has increased and likely will continue to increase in the near future. The concepts of liberty and equality are central to this struggle. He equates liberty with democracy and argues there are two distinct elements of liberty. There is the liberty of the majority and the liberty of the minority. The liberty of the majority "is located in the degree to which collective political decisions reflect in fact the preferences of the majority, as opposed to those of smaller groups who may in practice control the decision-making process" (2004:89). Liberty of the minority is quite different. "It represents the rights of all individuals and groups to pursue their preferences in all those realms in which there is no justification for the majority to impose its preference on others" (2004:89). A simple example of this might be the right of marijuana users to get high. The majority might support keeping the drug illegal, but the minority who use the drug would favor legalization. An embrace of the concept of the liberty of the minority would favor the minority's views here. But Wallerstein likely is referring to larger issues than this, likely to such things as the rights of indigenous groups, for example, Native peoples in the Brazilian rain forest, whose rights might be ignored by mining and forest companies seeking to use their lands. This ideological divide presents an "enormous and never-endingly difficult of deciding what is the line between the liberty of the majority and the liberty of the minority." Wallerstein notes that "in the struggle over the system (or systems) that will succeed our existing world-system, the fundamental cleavage will be between those who wish to expand both liberties – that of the majority and that of the minorities – and those who will seek to create a non-libertarian system under the guise of preferring either the liberty of the majority or the liberty of the minority" (1994:89).

Equality is the second issue. He notes that many scholars claim that there are inherent tensions between liberty and equality, but they are in fact "the reverse side of the same coin" (1994:89): "To the degree that meaningful inequalities exist, it is inconceivable that equal weight be given to all persons in assessing the preferences of the majority. And it is inconceivable that the liberty of the minorities will be fully respected if these minorities are not equal in the eyes of everyone – equal socially and economically in order to be equal politically. What the emphasis on equality as a concept does is point to the necessary positions of the majority to realize its own liberty and to encourage the liberty of the minorities" (1994:89). The choice becomes one of embracing a "hierarchical system bestowing or permitting privilege according to rank in the system" (as is championed by Davos) or "for a relatively democratic, relatively egalitarian system" (as is championed at the WSF). Wallerstein does not say what will happen, but he expresses an optimism that the conflicts rooted in global capitalism are now producing self-conscious debates about the existing and future global political and economic order, and that these debates are a good thing.

Huntington's Clash of Civilizations

Globalization theories are often interdisciplinary in nature. They often draw upon ideas from various academic disciplines, from economics to sociology. Sometimes the theorists themselves are sociologists, sometimes they are from other disciplines such as political science. In this section, we review the globalization theory of the political scientist Samuel Huntington (1927-2008). Huntington was a professor at Harvard University for much of his life. He first presented his theory of the clash of civilizations in an article in the Foreign Affairs journal (1993) and then a couple of years later in a book of the same name (1996). Rather quickly, the article and book created much debate and criticism. It has again gained attention in more recent years due in part to the seemingly endless Islamist terrorist attacks occurring against the West, as well as the Islamic terrorist attacks against other non-Islamic parts of the world (such as sub-Sahara Africa).

Huntington's theory is fundamentally different than Wallerstein's in several ways. It focuses more on culture and identity whereas Wallerstein's theory sees economics as the key. Huntington's theory is built on what he calls civilizations. Civilizations are the key force driving global relations forward. Wallerstein in contrast focuses upon nation states and their relationship to capitalism and corporations. Perhaps the greatest difference lies in their theoretical assumptions or in their ideological positions. Wallerstein embraces a neo-Marxist perspective, however loosely defined, while Huntington instead embraces a perspective that one might call conservative (though Huntington himself was an advisor to the Democratic Party).

The thrust of Huntington's argument lies in the claim that there will be a **clash of civilizations** in coming years, specifically between Western civilization (which included the United States, Western Europe, and other countries) and other civilizations. This clash will be rooted in culture. He writes: "It is my hypothesis that the fundamental source of conflict in [the] world will not be primarily ideological or primarily economic. The greatest divisions among humankind and the dominating source of conflict will be cultural" (1993:22). It is significant to note that he presented his theory soon after the Soviet Union fell apart in 1988-1991. For much of the twentieth century the major international conflict was between ideologies. In the mid-nineteen hundreds, there were major conflicts and wars between the three dominant ideologies: Democratic capitalism, Nazi-ism/fascism, and communism. From the end of World War Two through the 1980s, the conflict was between two of these ideologies – communism and democratic capitalism, as Nazi-ism was defeated in the War. With the end of communism, a new line of conflict has emerged (or re-emerged). This new conflict is no longer between ideologies. It is now largely a conflict rooted in religion and culture. It is the conflict of civilizations. A civilization is defined "both by common objective elements, such as language, history, religion, customs, institutions, and by the subjective self-identification of people" (1993:24).

Huntington identifies "seven or eight major civilizations": Western (including the United States, Western Europe, and others), Confucian (including China, and Southeast Asian countries), Japanese, Islamic (including Arab Islamic countries and non-Arab Islamic countries), Hindu (largely the country of India), Slavic-Orthodox (including Russia, and Eastern European countries such as Poland), Latin American, and "possibly African civilization." He says "possibly" Africa because he questions whether there is a sufficient unity to the culture of sub-Sahara African to make a claim of a single civilization. These seven or eight civilizations will increasingly be coming into conflict with one another because of a number of historical and structural features of the globalization process which have been strengthening civilization identity rather than weakening it. People are increasingly being identified, and are increasingly identifying, with one or another of the civilizations due to these features.

Six main factors have enhanced civilization identities and have simultaneously fostered growing differences and conflicts between the civilizations. The first of these is that "differences among civilizations are not only real; they are basic" (1993:25). Things like religion, and history, culture and tradition, are not things that one can put on and take off like a coat. Nor are they like political parties in which a person could be a Democrat today and a Republican tomorrow. Civilization identities are basic and are products of centuries The second factor is that "the world is becoming a smaller place" (1993:25). The increasing interactions and contacts between peoples of various civilizations intensify civilization consciousness, and they intensify "awareness of differences between civilizations and commonalities within civilizations." Huntington quotes from Donald Horowitz to highlight this point: "An Ibo may be … an Owerri Ibo or an Onitsha Ibo in what was the Eastern region of Nigeria. In London, he is a Nigerian. In New York, he is an African" (1993:26). The third main factor supporting and enhancing civilization consciousness and identity, and fueling differences amongst civilizations, is that "The processes of economic modernization and social change throughout the world are separating people from longstanding local identities. They also weaken the nation state as a source of identity" (1993:26). Individuals in the modern world who are increasingly exposed to or immersed in other civilizations or in the overall world of globalization potentially lose their cultural anchor of identity. A person from India attending graduate school or living in England might increasingly wonder who he or she is. An embrace of his Indian culture may result.

A fourth factor is that "the growth of civilization-consciousness is enhanced by the dual role of the West" (1993:26). As the Western world has asserted its dominance around the world through culture (Hollywood, movies, etc.), politics, economics, etc. this heightens a perception of threats to the civilization identities experienced by persons from other places. People might feel their own culture and identities are threatened as, for example, the English language and McDonald's become accepted in their countries. This threat encourages people to embrace and to assert their civilization identities. The fifth factor is that "cultural characteristics and differences are less mutable and hence less easily compromised and resolved than political and economic ones" (1993:27). This is related to the second factor noted above, but it is distinct. Huntington argues that the nature of civilization identity does not readily allow for a compromise between groups. You are either a member of one civilization or another, not both. You either have one religion, culture, tradition, history, or you have another. You cannot have both. You cannot be Christian and Muslim at the same time. This inevitably results in people being forced to take sides. The last factor is that "economic regionalism is increasing" (1993:27). Here he presents evidence that challenges the commonly held view that says that the globalization process involves more and more countries trading and engaging in economic interactions with one another, with more and more different peoples throughout the world. The world, according to this belief, is becoming smaller and more united. Huntington says that this is not the case. Instead, what has been happening is that more and more countries and peoples within one or another civilization are increasingly trading and engaging in economic relations with other peoples or nations within their own civilization, and they are not engaging in countries and peoples from other civilizations as much. Brazil is trading more with Argentina; Canada is trading more with the United States. Globalization in effect is happening on a regional basis rather than on a global one. This of course reinforces civilization consciousness.

The heightened civilization consciousness will produce the possibilities of future conflicts between civilizations. Huntington presents a rather traditional (and some might say dated) view of history that suggests that civilizations have lives. They are born, they grow, and they die. Civilizations gain and lose power through history. They expand and contract. They become more powerful and less powerful. He assesses the current situation of the United States (and Western civilization) in the world today and expresses a number or concerns. He also gives several policy recommendations for the United States to effectively address the changing international landscape of civilizations, and specifically the changing role of the United States within it.

His concerns and policy suggestions are based upon what he sees as threats to the stability and interests of the United States (and Western civilization). Echoing the ideas of the American historian Carroll Quigley, Huntington also says there are a number of indicators of "mature civilizations on the brink of decay" (1996:304), including economic and demographic indicators. External threats include anything from military conflicts to international economic power. But Huntington says that "[f]ar more significant than economic and demography are problems of moral decline, cultural suicide, and political disunity in the West." He goes on to list the "oft-pointed-to manifestations" of this moral decline:

> 1. increases in antisocial behavior, such as crime, drug use, and violence generally;
> 2. family decay, including increased rates of divorce, illegitimacy, teenage pregnancy, and single-parent families;
> 3. at least in the United States, a decline in "social capital," that is, membership in voluntary associations and the interpersonal trust associated with such membership;
> 4. general weakening of the "work ethic" and rise of a cult of personal indulgence;

5. decreasing commitment to learning and intellectual activity, manifested in the United States in lower levels of scholastic achievement. (1996:304)

These problems are associated with a more fundamental problem in Western society, according to Huntington. This is the problem of "multiculturalism." (This is an argument that has been raised by numerous conservative scholars in recent decades, perhaps most notably by Harold Bloom in his 1987 book *The Closing of the American Mind*, in which he criticizes multiculturalism found in higher education). Huntington writes:

Historically American national identity has been defined culturally by the heritage of Western civilization and politically by the principles of the American Creed on which Americans overwhelmingly agree: liberty, democracy, individualism, equality before the law, constitutionalism, private property. In the late twentieth-century both components of American identity have come under concentrated and sustained onslaught from a small but influential number of intellectuals and publicists. In the name of multiculturalism they have attacked the identification of the United States with Western civilization, denied the existence of a common American culture, and promoted racial, ethnic, and other subnational cultural identities and groupings. (1996:304)

Huntington is concerned that multiculturalism is an "internal rot" that is doing great harm to traditional American culture, and ultimately is weakening the cohesiveness of Western civilization.

Concretized Theories: Sociological Theories of the Environment

Sociological theories of the environment as well as the sub-discipline of the sociology of the environment have only been around for the last fifty years or so. These theories are in the broad scope of history quite young and the field is constantly changing and developing. Three historical currents came together to give birth to sociological theories of the environment. The first of these is the historical evolution of the ways in which the relationship of culture to nature has been understood in the modern Western world. Nature is the part of our world that exists and operates outside of human intent. Culture is that part of our world which is produced through human activity. But what is the relationship of culture to nature? Are they distinct from each other? Are they at odds, in conflict, with each other? Are there other ways of understanding this relationship? Is the divide between the two a wrongheaded way of understanding the environment? The culture and ideologies of the Western world, specifically the ideas of the Enlightenment, go to the heart of this matter. The Enlightenment championed reason and culture as separate from nature, and it championed the idea that culture should dominate and control nature. (This idea actually can be found in the Book of Genesis in the Bible.) Industrial capitalism embraced this idea, and many if not most of the technological inventions that have occurred have allowed people to have greater and greater control over nature, and they have allowed people to be increasingly "freed" from nature, from the constraints of nature. We now have air-conditioners that regulate temperature and airplanes that allow us to move about quickly, not to mention the internet and modern medical technologies. But in the last fifty years or so, this traditional understanding of the relationship of culture and nature has increasingly been challenged.

The second current giving birth to sociological theories of the environment was the birth of the modern environmental movement. Beginning in the 1960s and continuing into the present, activists and scholars sought to change public policies regarding the environment. Rachel Carson's book *Silent Spring* (1962) is often identified as a major early work in environmental activism. Environmental movement organizations from Greenpeace to the Sierra Club arose and engaged in protests to affect change. More and more, environmental concerns came to the concern of the public and of the politicians.

The third current is the history of sociological theory itself. As we have seen, the foundations of sociological theory going back to the nineteenth and early twentieth century have increasingly come under attack, or at least they have been significantly challenged from many different directions. Many of these challenges have been described in earlier chapters. The lack of agreement in sociology in recent years about the basic premises of sociological theory, let alone about the basic theories themselves, has provided an intellectual space in which alternative forms of theorizing can and have emerged. Sociological theories of the environment have emerged within this context, as these three currents have come together.

Theories in Environmental Sociology

There is no one universally shared theory of environmental sociology. There are several competing approaches. This lack of cohesion mirrors the lack of agreement amongst sociologists in general over sociological theories. As noted throughout this text, some sociologists subscribe to Durkheim's ideas, others to Marx's, others to symbolic interactionism, etc. Most take some ideas from some theorists, and some ideas from other theorists, and combine these into individualized, cohesive understandings. The lack of cohesion in environmental sociology is likely caused in part by some of the same factors that cause the confusions in sociological theory in general. The lack of cohesion in environmental sociology perhaps is also due in part to the newness of the sub-discipline. It has only been around for fifty years or so, and it has seen significant and frequent changes since that time.

There are two broad types of theories of environmental sociology. These two are distinguished from one another in terms of their conceptualization of the relationship of society to the environment. The first set of theories embraces a traditional sociological conceptualization of the distinction between society and the environment. In this formulation, scholars seek to understand how society and social forces impact the natural world, or they seek to understand how the natural world impacts society and social forces. Or they seek to understand both. The important point is that the two – society and nature -- are seen as distinct and in relation to one another. Environmental theories that take a critical view of capitalism, often inspired by conflict theory and specifically by Marxist ideas, fall into this camp of traditional sociological conceptualizations. So too do politically conservative theories, most notably the theory of ecological modernization theories. On the other hand, a second set of theories of environmental sociology begin by rejecting the assumption of a divide between society and the environment, or at least they begin with the assumption that society and the environment are inextricably intertwined part of one reality and cannot and should not be divided conceptually. Theories of this sort tend to focus on the importance of such things as meaning, values, justice, and inequality. Below we look at a few theories from each of these two camps.

Society vs the Environment

Murray Bookchin developed a neo-Marxist perspective on the environment in the 1960s which he called "**social ecology**" (1991, 1995, 2005). His perspective is sometimes described as libertarian socialism or anarchistic. He described himself as a social anarchist. Bookchin attributes the destruction of the environment in capitalism to the needs of this system for inequalities and hierarchy. He opens his book *The Ecology of Freedom* by noting that, "The very notion of the domination of nature by man stems from the very real domination of human by human" (2005:1). Inequalities produced by capitalism wreak havoc on the environment. For example, poorer people in poorer countries are forced to clear cut forests to survive, and to engage in one or another practice that is fundamentally destructive to the environment. The exploitive nature of capitalism leads the bourgeoisie to view the environment as well as the poorer people as objects to be used, and together this view leads the bourgeoisie to contribute to the destruction of the environment. For Murray the solution is to end capitalism. Much of his theorizing (and political activism) was oriented not simply to describe and explain the world but was oriented towards changing it.

Allan Schnaiberg (2005) presents a different form of Marxist inspired theory. He developed the influential concept of the **treadmill of production** to describe the processes within capitalism that by their nature destroy the environment. The treadmill of production is based in part upon two basic elements of the economy – withdrawals and additions. Withdrawals are all those parts of nature that are taken and used in the economy. We extract iron from mines and trees from forests. We withdraw fish from the sea and clean air from the atmosphere. Basically, withdrawals are the raw materials used in production. In the economic process we also add things to the natural environment. We pollute. We create garbage, etc. The basis of our economy is this cycle of withdrawals and additions. But Schnaiberg notes that this is not now a stable process. Capitalism must expand by its nature. It must seek more profits. As such, it must endlessly withdraw more and more from the environment, and must also as a consequence add more and more to the environment. He identifies three main sectors of society – capital, labor and the state -- and notes that they all are caught in this treadmill of production and are all inclined to support this treadmill.

Bookchin and Schnaiberg are both critical of reformist strategies for addressing the destruction of the environment. Reformist strategies, in contrast to radical ones, call for modest or minor changes to one or more laws or practices rather than for major society-wide changes.

The problem for Bookchin and Schnaiberg lies in the economic system of capitalism and any genuine solution must call for an end to this system itself or at the very least must lead to a major revision of the current form of capitalism. Bookchin, for example, criticizes some reformist tactics as recycling noting that these sorts of things individualize the problem. They allow individuals to think that individual actions on a daily basis can be an effective response to the destruction of the environment when in fact these actions not only do little to address the problem but in fact do the opposite. They perpetuate the ongoing destruction of the environment by distracting individuals from focusing their attention on what needs to be done to meaningfully address the issue. Bookchin was particularly critical of various alternative lifestyles and various theories of the environment calling for a naïve and simplistic embrace of nature. He writes:

> It is inaccurate and unfair to coerce people into believing that they are personally responsible for present-day ecological disasters because they consume too much or proliferate too readily. This privatization of the environmental crisis, like the New Age cultures that focus on personal

problems rather than on social dislocations, has reduced many environmental movements to utter ineffectiveness and threatens to diminish their credibility with the public. If "simple living" and militant recycling are the main solutions to the environmental crisis, the crisis will certainty continue and intensify. (in Maniates, 2014:352)

In contrast to the neo-Marxist theories just described, a second form of environmental sociology that begins with the traditional separation of society and the environment is built upon one or another neo-liberal economic orientation. Neo-liberalism, contrary to what the term may suggest, is a conservative approach. Neo-liberalism embraces a laissez faire capitalism and believes social issues and problems can and should best be solved by using market mechanisms. The applications of the mechanisms of supply and demand are said to be the most effective way to address environmental issues. The major neo-liberal theory of environmental sociology is **ecological modernization**, and two of the more well-known ecological modernization theorists are the Dutch sociologists Arthur Mol and Gert Spaargaren (Mol, 1995; 2001; Mol and Spaargaren, 2005). Ecological modernization theorists do not see capitalism as the cause of environmental problems, as, for example, the treadmill of production theorists do. Instead, ecological modernization theorists believe that capitalism can be the solution to environmental problems of things such as pollution. Similarly, the use of technology is not in itself the cause of the problem. Instead, technology can, will, and should be the solution. Ecological modernization is an optimistic approach. The openness and "reflexive" nature of capitalism allows the system to effectively respond to environmental problems. (We discussed reflexivity in Chapter Eleven. Briefly, reflexivity is the idea that a person, group, institution or system acts in a self-conscious manner, using knowledge and theories in an active, creative, and ongoing manner. It is the opposite of engaging in knee-jerk reactions. It is reacting in a way that considers the reality in which the act occurs and how it relates to the agent doing the action and the world around it.) A corporation, for example, must constantly consider how and why it acts as it does. If it does not, it will go out of business. If a corporation pollutes, the public might view the corporation negatively. But the corporation wishes to be seen in a favorable light. The corporation therefore will monitor its own behaviors in ways that will allow it to know how it is being viewed. Knowing it would be harmful to its own image to pollute and to be seen negatively by the public, the corporation might then not pollute. This open and critical nature of capitalism, the ecological modernization theorists argue, leads corporations and individuals to effectively address environmental problems.

Ecological modernization theorists also note that the adaptability of capitalism is also found in the forms of reasoning used to make decision in this system. That is, in capitalism the traditional forms of reasoning and decision making by corporations and others are based upon economic, political, technological and social factors. But capitalism has produced a new form of reasoning: ecological rationality. This form of rationality is attentive to the possible harm done to the environment as the result of possible actions taken by corporations and is now said to be part of corporate decision making. Ecological rationality, it is argued, has joined these others as a basis for decision making within corporations. Now, corporations do not simply assess the economic, political, technological and social factors in their decisions, but also environmental factors as well.

Society and the Environment United

The above theories begin with the assumption that society and the environment are distinct and separate (though Bookchin's anarchistic approach perhaps could be seen otherwise). A different form of sociological theory of the environment has emerged from scholars who tend to look at the complexities involved in the real unity of society and the environment. Approaches in this tradition tend to focus on the themes of value, meaning creation, justice, or inequality. Here just a few of the perspectives in this tradition are described.

Some theorists have argued that one needs to understand values if one wishes to understand the relationship of society to the environment, and the environment to society. The work of Ronald Inglehart (1977, 1990) is relevant here. Inglehart argues that a value shift has occurred in western countries beginning around the early 1970s. Prior to that time, people embraced what he calls materialist values. Since that time, people have embraced **postmaterialist values**. Materialist values concern such things as physical security and safety, health, and economic security. Post-material values in contrast revolve around things such as aesthetics, freedom, and quality of life (Bell, 2012). There has been a generational shift in value orientations, and this shift is attributed to the growing prosperity of the Western countries.

Arguably the first major attempt to develop a theory of the sociology of the environment that was rooted in a rejection of the conventional divide between society and nature was the new environmental paradigm developed by William Catton and Riley Dunlap (Dunlop, 1979 and 1980; Catton and Dunlop, 1980; Dunlop, 1980). Dunlap and Catton are widely recognized as being important figures in the development of the sociology of the environment sub-field of sociology. Their theorizing begins with a criticism of conventional sociological understandings of the environment. The conventional understanding, embodied in the writings, for example, of Robert

Park, a sociologist at the University of Chicago in the early twentieth century, who was one of the early, founding fathers of modern American sociology, saw one set of factors operating on human society and a different set operating on the environment. Park said that human societies, because of such things as the division of labor, allow humans an independence from the environment. Technology also frees people from the environment. Moreover, the structure of human societies is determined not by nature but by culture. Dunlap and Catton call this traditional sociological thinking of the relationship of society and nature the **human exceptionalism paradigm** (HEP). They later changed the term to human exemptionalism paradigm (though they continued to use HEP to designate it). Catton and Dunlap disagree with this perspective and advocate for an alternative one which they call the **New Ecological Paradigm** (NEP) for the sociology of the environment. NEP rejects the assumptions of HEP. HEP fails to recognize the commonality of the human world with other animal species. HEP also emphasizes cultural and social factors and ignores biological environmental factors as causal forces in the social world. Lastly, HEP ignores or downplays the constraints of the environment on human activities and social organization, and instead views the environment as this passive entity outside and removed from the social world. The environment in HEP is seen as simply something that can be used or manipulated. In contrast, NEP recognizes that the environment can be understood as something that can be used or manipulated, but that the environment and its relationship to human societies is more complicated than this. For example, the environment can influence and determine social arrangements and social actions.

Riley and Dunlap went on to elaborate their NEP in the late 1980s and early 1990s Dunlap (1993). They created a model of environmental sociology that has three parts, which could be conceptualized as a Venn diagram in which the parts overlap (Hannigan, 1995:16). The three parts of the model reflect the different ways that humans interact, engage or use the environment. The first part they call the "supply depot." The environment is used by humans for natural resources, from coal to timber. The second part is the "living space." In this part, human societies live. They build houses, roads, etc. This is the part in which humans engage with the environment on a daily basis in ways that allow them to live. The third part is called the "waste repository." Here, the environment is used as a place to put human waste, from industrial pollution to garbage. The three parts are in tension with one another, and they all operated within the limited space of the overall environment. Thus, as one part grows, this puts pressure on the other parts. Moreover, as all three grow, this puts increasing pressure on each of the parts because the environment itself is limited.

Theories of the Present Age

In addition to theories of the concrete, such as globalization theories, environmental theories, and critical theories of inequalities and identity (Chapter Thirteen), a number of theorists in the last several decades have focused upon trying to understand the distinctive or unique character of the present age, or the present historical era. These theorists seek to understand the historical changes that have led to the present and that have led to the present being distinctly different from eras of the recent past. It is clear to many that we live in a world that is very different and becoming ever more so each passing day from the industrial, modern world of the early nineteen hundreds – the period, for example, to which the classical sociological theorists were responding. Many of the theories described above, i.e. globalization, theories of the environment, etc., focus upon understanding the present age, but their focus is not the present age in itself, and it is not on understanding the historical dynamics which have produced the present. They are less concerned with theorizing about the essential dynamics of the present age than they are in understanding one or another aspect of this. We have covered a few theorists in earlier chapters (specifically the integrative theories of Chapters Eleven and the postmodern theories of Thirteen) who were devoted to the task of understanding how the present is different from the past. Much of Giddens' theory, for example, is devoted to this task. In this chapter we describe several other theorists – specifically Beck, Touraine, and Castells -- who are specifically focused upon understanding how the present age is distinctly different from the earlier, industrial, modern capitalist age.

    The work of the German sociologist Ulrich Beck (1944-2015) is a classic example of an approach that seeks to understand the uniqueness of the present age. Beck's theory has several basic claims. One of these concerns the risk society (1992). His theory of the risk society could very well have been described within the above section on environmental theories because his concept of the risk society and the theory surrounding it revolve around risks related to the environment. He argues that the essential dynamics driving society forward in the late twentieth century are fundamentally different from those of society in the nineteenth century. In the nineteenth century the central forces concerned class and inequality. This was the period of industrialization. It was a period in which the concern was for material wealth. People were driven to work to get the material things needed to survive. The central dynamic force of the industrial era was a conflict over material wealth. Industrial class conflict reflects this. The forces today are different. Poverty and want, he says, are no longer the driving forces, at least not in wealthy societies. The affluent societies of today, produced by capitalism, create new dynamics and new forces. Today, these new dynamics revolve around risks, rather than class conflict, and specifically environmental risks to the health and safety of people. Whether it is chemicals in the food, the destruction of the environment, nuclear power or weapons, radiation, or other such environmental threats, we live in an age of risks.

The present age is different from the earlier one. It is different largely because of the changing relationship between nature and society (see above) in the two periods. In the nineteenth century, nature was seen as being outside of society, and society was outside of nature. But now nature and society are inside of each other. An awareness has developed that they are inextricably intertwined. Nineteenth century social theory is no longer applicable to an understanding of the world today because it is based upon the early, outdated understanding of the relationship between nature and society. Beck writes:

> At the end of the twentieth century, nature is *neither* given *nor* ascribed, but has instead become a historical product, the interior furnishings of the civilizational world, destroyed or endangered in the natural conditions of its reproduction. But that means that the destruction of nature, integrated into the universal circulation of industrial production, ceases to be "mere" destruction of nature and becomes an integral component of the social, political and economic dynamic. The unseen side effect of the societalization of nature is the *societalization of the destruction and threat to nature*, their transformation into economic, social and political contradictions and conflicts. ... Whereas the concept of the classical industrial society is based on the antithesis between nature and society (in the nineteenth century sense), the concept of the (industrial) risk society proceeds from "nature" as integrated by culture, and the metamorphosis of injuries to it is traced through the social subsystems. (1992:81)

Of note, Beck is not saying that we have moved into an era beyond modernity. Rather we now are entering a new form of modernity which he calls the **risk society**. The risk society is characterized by two features, risk and reflexivity. In some ways these themes echo those presented by the British sociologist Anthony Giddens, though Beck developed his ideas independent of Giddens and he elaborates his theory in a very different manner than does Giddens. When Beck writes about risks, he is talking about environmental risks to health and safety. We have moved from a type of society that was oriented to the production of wealth, in earlier class based societies to a type of society that is now oriented toward the production of risks. His theory revolves around how risks are produced, managed, and controlled. It also revolves around understanding the processes by which people are aware of or understand the risks.

He contrasts the characteristics of the risk society with those of class societies nineteenth century). They operate under very different principles. For example, class based conflicts are explicit and readily visible. The working class can identify the problem, e.g. the problem of the owners not paying them enough. The problem can readily be seen and identified. In the risk society on the other hand, the risks to health and safety produced by chemicals in the air, in our bodies through food, by radiation, etc., are not readily seen. Moreover, class based conflicts allow for particular groups to form to address the problem. Unions, for example, can and have arisen to do so. In contrast, in risk societies the risks are not specific to one or another group and as such do not readily lend themselves to the political forms of organization found in class based societies. These risks do not readily allow for one group to pit itself against another to address the concerns. The risk of pollution harms the rich as well as the poor. It is true, as Beck rightly notes, that there is some overlap in terms of risks and class positions. That is, poorer groups often are subjected to environmental risks at a higher rate that richer groups. But Beck says in the broad scheme of things the two factors – risk and class – operate under different logics.

Part of Beck's argument concerns the increasing dominance of technological and economic rationality. This echoes Weber's concerns about the growth of formal rationality in the modern world. Beck notes that the standard way in which environmental risks are identified and managed today is through the use of science. Scientists conduct studies to determine the relative risk to health or safety of one or another product or activity by corporations (or governments). They produce their statistical findings. And these are deemed true and formally legitimate. Beck however argues that this ignores a "social" rationality, which is distinct from the scientific (or formal) rationality presented by scientists. The social rationality is that of the laymen and women who respond to environmental risks in personal, common sense ways. Rather than relying and trusting the truths of the claims of the scientists when they proclaim the probability or risk of one thing or another happening, laypersons rely upon personal experiences to form their arguments. Beck champions this social rationality.

This is very much related to the second element of his theorizing: reflexivity. In addition to risk, the present age is characterized by reflexivity. As was noted above, Beck does not believe we have entered into a new historic era, one that is distinct from modernity. Instead, we have entered a new form of modernity, one that he calls **reflexive modernity**. Beck uses the concept of reflexivity in much the same way that Giddens does. An understanding of social life requires a recognition that people's behaviors are simultaneously the "medium and outcome" practices. Giddens defines reflexivity not merely as "self-consciousness but as the monitoring character of the ongoing flow of social life" (1984:3). This monitoring characteristic can be seen in many areas of social life, from individual decision making to institutional actions. For example, in universities as well as in corporations today there are seemingly endless self-reviews, often in the form of surveys or evaluations. In universities, various offices repeatedly ask members of the university to complete surveys to tell the offices how they are performing. Student evaluations of professors serve much the same function. Beck notes that the world today has become saturated with reflexivity, and this reflexivity is associated with the risk society. There is, for example, a "reflexive politicization" (1992:77) in which risks are produced and maybe managed through ongoing monitoring of the practices involved.

The concept of reflexivity is closely associated with another that is central to Beck's theorizing. This is the changing nature of the individual. According to Beck (and Giddens), the individual in reflexive modernity has become disembedded. The mooring of self identity and of the individual have been cut. In the industrial era individual identities were formed, at least within the economic and political arenas, in terms of class affiliation. In earlier times, identities were formed through traditions. These are no longer options for anchoring the self. The self now has to create and recreate itself. In post-industrial, reflexive modernity individuals define themselves, and they do so on an ongoing basis. Even biographies are created, rather than given, today. "Biographies ... are becoming reflexive" (1992:131). But like other aspects of reflexive modernization, this process of individual reflexivity contains contradictions. There are "*inherent contradictions in the individualization process.*" On the one hand, the individual in the reflexive modern world "is indeed removed from traditional constraints of existence in the labor market and as a consumer, with the standardization and controls they contain." As such, he or she is free to create him or herself. However, at the same time "new dependencies arise." The individual is subjected to the forces of fashion, social policy, etc.: "The place of *traditional* ties and social forms (social class, nuclear family) is taken by *secondary* agencies and institutions, which stamp the biography of the individual and make that person dependent upon fashions, social policy, economic cycles and markets, contrary to the image of individual control which establishes itself in consciousness" (1992:131).

A second theory of the present age is that of the French theorist Alain Touraine (1925-2023). Touraine is often credited with being one of the first scholars to identify a new era, a post-industrial society. His arguments are oftentimes seen as being similar to those put forth by the American sociologist Daniel Bell (1919-2011). In his book *The Coming of Post-Industrial Society* (1976), Bell argues that America was moving from a society rooted in industrial production to one that was oriented toward information and services. Bell identifies several basic components of this new post-industrial society that were thought to be emerging at the time: 1) There was a shift in the economy from manufacturing to services; 2) Science and information becomes important, new industries emerge; and 3) A new powerful social class was emerging – the class of the technological elites.

Some of Touraine's ideas are similar to Bell's, but his overarching theorizing is very, very different. The mode of thinking is very different. Touraine is also often associated with social movement studies, and specifically with contributing to the development of "new social movement theory." Like Beck (and Giddens), Touraine sought to understand the unique characteristics of the late twentieth and early twenty-first centuries. He believed the essential dynamic of the social world today is different than what it was in earlier times. In pre-industrial societies, the essential dynamic rested in the political. But then economics and the social, rather than the political, became the central elements of the industrial era. "The industrial revolution and capitalism freed themselves from political power and emerged as the "basis" of social organization" (2007:1). Issues revolving around "social classes and wealth, bourgeoisie and proletariat, trade unions and strikes, stratification and social mobility, inequality and redistribution" became central, driving forces. But today, in the post-industrial era the economic and the social have been replaced by the cultural as the central dynamic of the age.

Touraine notes that not only have the essential dynamics of society changed, but so too have the forms of theorizing sociologists use to understand society changed. Sociologists now should not be looking at institutions but instead at relationships. Social relations become central. He writes in one of his books on social movements:

> Let us recall what was our starting-point: sociology studies social relations. Its main method should, therefore, make possible the direct observation and analysis of these relations. If one is to take as the object of study a situation, a trend or an opinion, one is already distancing oneself from the main field of sociology. This is why the old division of society into "institutions" – the family, political power, the company, the town, etc. – has long been abandoned and replaced by new subdivisions which can all, directly or indirectly, be defined in terms of social relations: organizations and their relations of authority; political decisions and the influences leading to them; class relations and systems of order considered in their function of exclusion and elimination. But these social relations are not readily visible, indeed, they are more or less masked by order and domination. Sociology's chief problem is to bring these relations to the surface, so as no longer to be the dupe of the categories of social practice. (1981:139)

Touraine examines the rise of post-industrial society (1974) and shows how this new form of society affects the self and identity. "[I]n a post-industrial society, in which cultural services have replaced material goods at the core of production, it is the defense of the subject, in its personality and in its culture, against the logic of apparatuses and markets, that replaces the idea of class struggle" (quoted in Castells, 2010:22). The self in the post-industrial era has lost its traditional moorings and is forced to create itself. Touraine shows how the fundamental shifts in the essential workings of post-industrial society contribute to this. He does so by first distinguishing the concept of society from that of modernity (2007). Society is a part of modernity. It is influenced by the forces of modernity, including those derived from the Enlightenment. These forces include the embrace of Reason and the embrace of the concept of the individual, the primacy of self, individual rights, etc. Modernity is characterized by what he calls historicity. **Historicity** refers to the capacity of societies in the modern era to "self-reproduce": "[S]ociety [in modernity] has a growing awareness of producing itself, rather than being defined solely by quasi-natural evolutionary processes. ... [O]ur societies regarded themselves as being self-created, offspring of their own efforts, not only by employing material resources in the service of major projects, but in setting as their main objective the construction, consolidation and defence of societies whose interest ... include equality opportunities, is the most important principle for assessing forms of behavior and defining good and evil" (2007:46). In short, historicity in some respects is akin to the concepts of reflexivity described by Giddens and Beck.

A central aspect of modern societies, according to Touraine, is that the principles of organization are fundamentally different than those which governed earlier societies. In pre-modern societies, religion or tradition or political forces were imposed from outside of the lived social realities. In modern societies, the essential governing and regulating forces are internal to it. This creates a number of dynamics. One of the things it does is that it changes the forms of contestations. In earlier societies, class conflicts or conflicts between those with power – over economics, politics, tradition – and those without led to classic oppositional contests. The working class, for example, mobilizes against the bourgeoisie. With the fundamental shift that has occurred in post-industrial societies these conflicts are no longer salient. Instead, a main focus becomes the individual and individual self creation. This is related to the claims made by Giddens and Beck regarding the disembedded character of the contemporary world. The self is no longer anchored in tradition or in other social formations. As a result, the individual is compelled to create itself in the contemporary world.

All of this is closely related to Touraine's claim of the death of the idea of society and of sociology (2007). The idea of society was central to the modern industrial world. But with the conquest of capitalism, with globalization, and with the internet age, the idea of society no longer has meaning, at least it no longer has meaning as the central force driving decisions and social policy. "What we are living through is not the collapse of a sandcastle, but the exhaustion of social policy focused on society, its functions and its integration. We are already caught up in the transition from a society based on itself to self-reproduction by individuals with the help of transformed institutions. Such is the meaning of the *end of the social*" (2007:67). He says that sociology was born in a different age, in an industrial age in which the idea of the social and the idea of society was central. But Touraine says one of our main concerns now is "to challenge the categories that formed the basis for classical society that has come to the end of its road. The sociology of systems must give way to a sociology of actors and subjects" (2007:52).

Manuel Castells (1942-) is another theorist who focuses his attention on trying to understand the uniqueness of the current age, and in trying to clarify how the essence of this age is fundamentally distinct from that of the earlier industrial age. Castells is a Spanish sociologist who is currently a professor at the University of Southern California. He was a student of Touraine, and some of themes found in Touraine's writing are also found in Castells', though in the latter these are often much more systematically described and more clearly elaborated. Castells presents his argument in his three volume work *The Information Age: Economy, Society, and Culture* (1996, 1997, 2010 [1996)]). His theory integrates a number of central themes, including: networks, information and technology, globalization, identity, social movements, capitalism, and the state. These themes are tied together through the various domains of social life: political, economic, social, cultural.

His theory is based upon an understanding of the structure of the capitalist economy, and upon how this structure of organization is distinctly different in the information age, which he says began around 1970, compared to the earlier industrial capitalist era. The change was largely brought about by informational technology, including the internet. A new economy has arisen, and this new economy has several distinct features. It is informational; It is global; and it is networked (2010:77). In this new economy, a new "paradigm" has arisen. A new set of principles now govern the workings of the world. This new technological paradigm has five distinct features to it:

> 1. Information is central to it. It is the raw material. Technologies of information act differently from earlier forms of technology. They act on information, "not just information to act on technology." Technologies do not simply respond to information. Information responds to technology.
> 2. New technologies have had a "pervasiveness of effects."

3. Informational technologies have their own networking logic, which is "well adapted to increasingly complexity of interaction and to unpredictable patterns of development."
4. Informational technology is based upon flexibility. Processes, organizations, and institutions can be modified or altered by "Rearranging their components."
5. There is a "growing convergence of specific technologies into a highly integrated system" (2010:71-72).

In short, his most foundational claim is that the society of today, and the world itself, is distinctly different that the world of one hundred years ago. We have moved from a period of industrial capitalism to an informational age. This new age began to emerge in the 1970s and has increasingly taken root ever since. It is not simply that we have moved from a society that used to primarily manufacture and consume industrial goods for mass consumption to one that now produces and consumes information and services. Rather, this new informational age and this new **network society** operate under a distinctly different logic than the logic that governed industrial capitalism. The logic that now rules is the logic of the networks. For example, in industrial capitalism, political power, conventionally understood, was a major force in the organization of society. But in the informational age power is displaced, relocated. He writes:

> The network morphology is ... a source of dramatic reorganization of power relations. Switches connecting the networks (for example, financial flows taking control over media empires that influence political processes) are the privileged instruments of power. Thus, the switchers are the power-holders. Since networks are multiple, the inter-operating codes and switches between networks become the fundamental sources in shaping, guiding, and misguiding societies. (2010:502)

Networks are at the heart of his theory. So what are networks? We might think of a network as a system of connected relational chains. Person A (or group or institution or thing) might have a relationship with person B; person B might have a relationship with person C; person C might have a relationship with person D, etc. But the forms of the network are very diverse. Person C, for example, may also have a relationship with person A. Alternatively, Person C might have a relationship with person A, but may not have a relationship with person B. One can easily see this in online communications, or in real friendship groups. Nodes are central parts of networks. A node is a location in a network whereby three or more other parties have a relation with the party in the node, but do not directly have relations with one or another. The node is in effect a medium through which others engage the network.

There are many types of networks. There are financial networks, friendship networks, religious networks, virtual community networks, work networks, professional networks, economic networks, etc. With the growth of technology, and specifically of informational technology related to the internet, networks have become more prominent features of the social landscape. But for Castells, a more crucial issue concerns networks in general and what flows through the networks. The idea of flows is central to his theorizing. We can think of flows as the thing circulating through the veins of the network, not unlike how blood flows through the veins of a human body. Money, for example, is the thing that flows through financial networks. People flow through airport networks, etc.

Networks of course are not new to the world. They did not just appear on the scene with the emergence of the informational age. Networks have always been around. For example, in industrial capitalism, networks were central. The flow of money and goods defined industrial capitalism. But Castells is making the point that the nature of the flows in the informational age as well as what flows through the networks are very different now. Information is now the life blood of many, many networks in the information age. This is easy to understand when one considers the internet. But information is also what circulates on Wall Street, along with capital, in the financial markets, which now are also highly integrated into the internet networks. We now have an informational capitalism rather than an industrial capitalism. In the professions too, whether medical, legal, education, information flows through the networks. In work, in the economy, in culture, in organizations, in mass media, in the internet, in social movements, the flow of information characterizes the contemporary world, and this world is globalized. But is not simply information that flows. Society now is comprised of all sorts of networks and flows, though informational flows are central. Castells notes that society now is "constructed around flows: flows of capital, flows of information, flows of technology, flows of organizational interaction, flows of images, sounds, and symbols" (2010:442).

This relates to another dimension of his theory. This concerns his understandings of the changes in time and space in the information, networked age. The social meanings of time and space have changed in history. Let us begin with space. Many social thinkers have written about such things, often these are Marxists. The French philosopher Henri Lefebvre wrote several volumes about this. David Harvey, the Marxist geographer, wrote about the "spatialization of time" in his book *The Postmodern Condition*. Castells shares with these scholars the belief that the social understandings of time and space change in history, and that as the result of technology, information, and capitalism we now view and experience time and space, and their relationship to one another, in a different way than we once did.

Let us start with space. Castells says that "space is crystallized time." He goes on to provide a more detailed definition: "space is the material support of time-sharing social practices" (2010:441). Space should be thought of in terms of social practices and these practices occur necessarily in time. He notes that "any material support bears always a symbolic meaning. By time-sharing social practices, I refer to the fact that space brings together those practices that are simultaneous in time" (2010:441). There are two distinct types of spaces: the space of flows and the space of place. He says the "spatial logic" of the two are very different. They differ in terms of the meanings of each and in terms of how each is experienced. In the informational age spaces of flow have become dominant. **Spaces of flow** are settings through which flows occur in networks. Spaces of flows are defined and organized by what flows through them. Technically, "The space of flows is the material organization of time-sharing social practices that work through flows" (2010:442). Cities, for example, now are nodes in various networks in which many things flow -- information, capital, services, etc. The global interconnection of networks is constituted by many, many spaces of flow. These spaces essentially have meaning in reference to their networks and not to specific and particular locale in which they exist.

There are three layers of spaces of flow:

1. The first layer, which is "the first material support of the space of flows, is "constituted by a circuit of electronic exchanges."
2. "The space of flows is constituted by its nodes and hubs."
3. "The spaces of flow refer to the spatial organization of the dominant, managerial elite (rather than classes) that exercise the directional functions around which such space is articulated." (2010:443-445)

In short, spaces of flow have come to have a major organizing role in society today.

The concept of **spaces of places**, in contrast to spaces of flows, is more conventional. Spaces of places refer to locales that have meanings directly connected to the immediate and personal experiences of persons experiencing them. One's childhood home, for example, could be considered a space of place, as perhaps a sacred mountain in one or another traditional religion. The meanings and understandings of place within the logic of the space of places is locally derived and particular to the experiences of the living actors experiencing the place. Here place has meaning in reference to individuals or groups and their biographies or histories. In contrast, spaces of flows have meaning in relation to the networks. A McDonald's restaurant, for example, likely does not have personal significance. One McDonald's is like another. So too is one shopping mall like another.

Castells claims that spaces of flows are taking over. But they have not, and perhaps cannot, eradicate spaces of places. Indeed, one of the central conflicts in the contemporary world is the conflict between spaces of flows and spaces of places, or more precisely between the logics associated with each type of space. A central conflict concerns the dominance of the elites, as noted in the third layer, number three, above. The elites manage and control the spaces of flow, while the people (including those formerly associated with the working class) operate within the spaces of places and have no power over the spaces of flow. He writes:

> The fundamental form of domination in our society is based on the organizational capacity of the dominant elites that goes hand in hand with its capacity to disorganize those groups in society which, while constituting a numerical majority, see their interest partially (if ever) represented only within the framework of the fulfillment of the dominant interests. Articulation of the elites, segmentation and disorganization of the masses seem to be the twin mechanisms of social domination in our society. Space plays a fundamental role in this mechanism. In short, elites are cosmopolitan, people are local. The space of power and wealth is projected throughout the world, while people's life and experience is rooted in places, in their culture, in their history. Thus, the more a social organization is based upon ahistorical flows, superseding the logic of any specific place, the more the logic of global power escapes the socio-political control of historically specific local/national societies. (2010:446-447)

In a similar vein, Castells described changes to time in the information age. A **timeless time** has emerged. Much like our understandings and experience of space are shaped by society, so too is our understanding and experience of time. The change in time can be illustrated by the changes in the physical presentation of time. In the mechanical era, we had mechanical watches. In the digital era, we have digital clocks. In the industrial era there was the mechanical clock; one could see the hour and minute hand moving around the circle on the dial of the face of the clock. One could locate the present in relation to the past and to the future. If the minute hand was on the three, then one could see it was after the two and before the four. One could see how close it was to either. Time bore a relationship. In the informational age, there is a digital clock with the time appearing suspended. One does not see, literally, the past or the future on the face of a digital clock. One sees a timeless now. A similar point is made about time itself. Much as he does with his discussion of space, he draws upon some of the many theorists who have written about changes to time (from Giddens to Harvey, see above). Time is not simply being relativized. Rather, the change is more profound. "It is the mixing of tenses to create a forever universe, not self-expanding but self-maintaining, not cyclical but random, not recursive but incursive: timeless time, using technology to escape the contexts of its existence, and to appropriate selectively any value each context could offer to the ever-present" (2010:464).

Castells describes how the notion of time has changed in various domains in society. Time has changed: in work, with flex-time, etc.; in terms of biological rhythms, for example, of the human body; in terms of death, as we seek to eliminate this timely fact of life through the use of technology; in the use of the internet; and in other ways. "The timelessness of multimedia's hypertext is a decisive feature of our culture, shaping the minds and memories of children educated in the new cultural context" (2010:492). He continues:

> If encyclopedias have organized human knowledge by alphabetical order, electronic media provide access to information, expression, and perception according to the impulses of the consumer or to the decisions of the producer. By doing so, the whole ordering of meaningful events loses its internal, chronological rhythm, and becomes arranged in time sequences depending upon the social context of their utilization. Thus, *it is a culture at the same time of the external and of the ephemeral.* (2010:492)

For Castells, time has become both flat and empty. It has become all that there is and nothing that is there. It is a new form of time called timeless time. But as with space, this new time, this timeless time, has not conquered all. As with space, timeless time impacts some part of society, while real time, old fashioned time, continued to impact other parts. And perhaps not surprisingly, "timeless time belongs to the space of flows, while time discipline, biological time, and socially determined sequencing [i.e. real, old fashioned time] characterize places around the world, materially structuring and destructuring our segmented societies" (2010:495). The space of flows "dissolves time by disordering the sequences of events and making them simultaneous, thus installing society in eternal ephemerality. The multiple spaces of places, scattered, fragmented, and disconnected display diverse temporalities, from the most primitive domination of natural rhythms to the strictest tyranny of clock time" (2010:497).

A central part of his analysis concerns identity and social movements in the network society. He describes these things in Volume Two of his trilogy (1997). Social movements abound in the modern world, from the environmental movement to the women's movement, from the radical Islamists movement to the labor movement. Castells is associated with the theory of social movements called new social movements theory. New social movement theory arose in Europe in the last thirty years. Its major proponents are people such as Touraine, Alberto Melucci, and Manuel Castells. (Habermas is also sometimes associated with this new theory.) New social movement theory arose in reaction to the perceived limitations of what was in the 1970s and 1980s the major form of theorizing about social movement. At the time, Americans such as Charles Tilly and Doug McAdam developed approaches to social movement that were rooted in resource mobilization, rational choice, and political process models. These forms of theorizing did not see factures such as identity and culture as being centrally important in understanding social movements. New social movement theory, on the other hand, believed that the social movements that were appearing in Europe and American in the last forty years or so were centered around the issues of culture and identity. In addition, they argued that the organization and style of these movements were distinctly different from the movements of earlier generations. New social movements attributed these differences to the major changes occurring with the emergence of the post-industrial era – noted by Castells, Beck, etc. described above.

Castells says that the network society is based upon "the disjunction between the local and the global for most individuals and social groups" and by the "separation in different time-space frames between power and experience." This creates a situation in which "reflexive life-planning becomes impossible, except for the elite inhabiting the timeless space of flows of global networks and their ancillary locales. And the building of intimacy on the basis of trust requires a redefinition of identity fully autonomous vis-a-vis the networking logic of dominant institutions and organizations" (1997:11). Subjects in the network society are "in the process of disintegration" and social movements arise in response to this.

He identifies three forms of identity: legitimizing identity, resistance identity, and project identity. Legitimizing identities are those created by existing institutions and imposed upon individuals to support the continued dominance of the institutions. Resistance identities are "generated by those actors that are in positions/conditions devalued and/or stigmatized by the logic f domination" (1997:8). Project identities are new identities that people build that "redefines their position in society and, by so doing, seek the transformation of overall social structure" (1997:8). Social movements form when social situations move people from legitimating, to resistance, to project identities.

Identity construction operates very differently for individuals in groups that are located in different places in the network society. The "elites" have one basis of identity, while the masses have another: "[O]n the one hand, the dominant, global elites inhabiting the space of flow tend to consist of identity-less individuals ("citizens of the world"); while, on the other hand, people resisting economic, cultural, and political disenfranchisement tend to be attracted to communal identity" (1997:356). Communal identities are aligned with project identities. People then come together to form social movements.

Summary

This chapter describes three interrelated, contemporary forms of sociological theorizing: globalization theories, environmental theories, and theories of the changing present. Two forms of globalization theories were described. One of these was the world-systems theory of Wallerstein. World systems theory is based on Marxism and seeks to explain how the global capitalist economic system is structured to maintain global inequality and to maintain the power and wealth of the rich countries. The theory also identifies contradictions in this global capitalist economy. In contrast, Huntington's theory of the class of civilization is based more upon a cultural argument which claims there will be increasing tensions between world civilizations due to several historical factors. There are two broad types of theories of environmental sociology. These two are distinguished from one another in terms of their conceptualization of the relationship of society to the environment. The first set of theories embraces a traditional sociological conceptualization of the distinction between society and the environment. Within this first set of theories are conflicting positions. On the one hand, environmental theories developed by the likes of Bookchin and Schnaiberg are critical of capitalism and see this economic system as largely responsible for the destruction of the environment. On the other hand, the ecological modernization theorists Mol and Spaargaren see capitalism and market forces not as the problem but as the solution to environmental problems. A second set of theories of environmental sociology begin by rejecting the assumption of a divide between society and the environment, or at least they begin with the assumption that society and the environment are inextricably, intertwined part of one reality and cannot and should not be divided conceptually. The second set of theories challenges and ultimately rejects the traditional view that separates society from the environment. One example of this second type of theory is found in Inglehart and his concept of postmaterial values. But this second form of theorizing is most elaborated in the works of Catton and Dunlap. They initially developed a model which they called the human exceptional paradigm, and then changed it to the new ecological paradigm. In this later model, they try to conceptualize the interactive dynamics of society and the environment.

Several theories of the changing present were also covered in this chapter. These included those of Beck, Touraine, and Castells. These theories all begin with the assumption that the essential dynamics of the post-industrial era are fundamentally different than the dynamics of the industrial era. In the industrial era, the main dynamics were rooted in material concerns, and the central point of conflict was rooted in class conflict. In the post-industrial era, new dynamics emerge. Beck argued that we now live in a risk society, in which the control and management of risk has become the central theme of the era, rather than concerns over class and class conflict. Reflexivity, he says, is also a central feature of the world today. Touraine argues that the post-industrial world is one in which the control over historicity is the central issue, and this is closely related to the disembedding of the self. The self has lost its anchoring in the post-industrial world. Touraine argues that those who control historicity, i.e. the technocrats, have great power in shaping and controlling individual selves. Castells, a student of Touraine, argues that networks are central features of the world today. He describes the changes that have occurred in the way that time and space are understood and experienced in the world today and describes the differences between spaces of flows and spaces of places. The organization of power has fundamentally changed in the world of networks. Power now is in the hands of elites who control the spaces of flows. This leads to a conflict between individuals, whose identities have been destabilized in the new networked world, in the world of spaces of flows, and the elites who control the spaces of flows. Individuals embrace the spaces of places and seek to assert their identities through these, but at the same time they are necessarily operating within spaces of flows controlled by elites. Castells and Touraine say that new social movements emerge as the result of the changing social dynamics of the post-industrial world.

Discussion Questions

1. What should sociological theory do about nature and specifically about the relationship of nature to culture? Is it possible to have a legitimate theory of society that does not incorporate a place for nature within it? If nature is needed, how should it be built into a theory?

2. Huntington and Wallerstein present conflicting theories about globalization. Which do you think is a more accurate theory? Why?

3. Beck, Touraine, and Castells argue that classical sociological theories, such as Marx's, are no longer relevant today because the social organization of the world today is fundamentally different than the world of the time of Marx. We no longer live in an industrial world defined by class and class conflict. Instead, we live in a post-industrial world that operates under a different set of dynamics. Are these theorists right, or is Marx still relevant? Explain.

References

Abrams, Philip. 1968. *The Origins of British Sociology: 1834-1914*. Chicago: University of Chicago Press. Quoted in *Sociological Theory* by George Ritzer (seventh edition). Boston: McGraw-Hill, p. 38.

Adorno, Theodor. 1973. *Negative Dialectics*. Translated by E. B. Ashton. New York, New York: Continuum Press.

Adorno, Theordor, Else Frenkel-Brunswik, Daniel Levinson, and R. Nevitt Sanford. 1950. *The Authoritarian Personality*. New York, New York: W.W. Norton.

Alexander, Michelle. 2020. *The New Jim Crow*. New York, New York: New Press.

Althusser, Louis. 2001. "Ideology and Ideological State Apparatus," in *Lenin and Philosophy and Other Essays*, pp. 85-126. New York, New York: Monthly Review Press.

Althusser, Louis. 2005. *For Marx*. New York, New York: Verso Press.

Aron, Raymond. 1996. *Main Currents in Sociological Thought, Vol. 1*. New Brunswick, New Jersey: Transaction Publishers.

Aron, Raymond. 2001. *The Opium of the Intellectuals*. New York, New York: Routledge.

Bateson, Gregory. 1972. "A Theory of Play and Fantasy," in *Steps to an Ecology of Mind*, pp. 177-193. New York, New York: Ballantine Books.

Baudrillard, Jean. 1973. *The Mirror of Production*. Translated by Mark Poster. St. Louis, Mo.: Telos Press.

Baudrillard, Jean. 1981. *For a Critique of the Political Economy of the Sign*. Translated by Charles Levin. St. Louis, Mo.: Telos Press.

Baudrillard, Jean. 1983. *Simulations*. New York, New York: Semiotext(e).

Baudrillard, Jean. 1988. *Jean Baudrillard: Selected Writings*. Edited by Mark Poster. Stanford, Ca.: Stanford University Press.

Beck, Ulrich. 1992. *Risk Society*. London, England: Sage Publications.

Becker, Gary. 1992. *The Economic Approach to Human Behavior*. Chicago, Illinois: University of Chicago Press.

Bell, Daniel. 1976. *The Coming of Post-Industrial Society*. New York, New York: Basic Books.

Bell, Derick. 1995a. "Serving Two Masters: Integration Ideals and Client Interests in School Desegregation Litigation," ," in *Critical Race Theory*, edited by Kimberle Crenshaw et al., pp. 5-19. New York, New York: The New Press.

Bell, Derick. 1995b. "Brown v. Board of Education and the Interest Convergence Dilemma," in *Critical Race Theory*, edited by Kimberle Crenshaw et al., pp. 20-29. New York, New York: The New Press.

Bell, Michael Mayfeld. 2012. *An Invitation to Environmental Sociology*. Fourth edition. Los Angeles, Ca.: Sage.

Bellah, Robert, Richard Madsen, William M. Sullivan, Ann Swidler, and Steven Tipton. 1996. *Habits of the Heart: Individualism and Commitment in American Life*. Updated (Second) edition. Berkeley, Ca.: University of California Press.

Berger, Peter and Thomas Luckmann. 1966. *The Social Construction of Reality*. New York, New York: Anchor Books.

Berger, Peter. 1967. *The Sacred Canopy*. New York, New York: Anchor Books.

Blau, Peter. 1967. *Exchange and Power in Social Life*. New York, New York: John Wiley and Sons.

Blumer, Herbert. 1998. (1969). *Symbolic Interactionism: Perspective and Method*. Berkeley, Ca.: University of California Press.

Bookchin, Murray. 1991. *The Ecology of Freedom: The Emergence and Dissolution of Hierarchy*, rev. ed. Montreal, Quebec, Canada: Black Rose Books.

Bookchin, Murray. 1995. *The Philosophy of Ecology: Essays on Dialectical Naturalism.* Montreal, Quebec, Canada: Black Rose Books.

Bookchin, Murray. 2005. *The Ecology of Freedom: The Emergence and Dissolution of Hierarchy.* Oakland, Ca.: AK Press.

Bottomore, Tom (editor). 1983. *A Dictionary of Marxist Thought.* Cambridge, Massachusetts: Harvard University Press.

Bourdieu, Pierre. 1990 (1980). *The Logic of Practice.* Stanford, California: Stanford University Press.

Bourdieu, Pierre. 1984. *Distinctions: A Social Critique of the Judgment of Taste.* Translated by Richard Nice. Cambridge, Massachusetts: Harvard University Press.

Bourdieu, Pierre, and Wacquaint, Loic. 1992. *An Invitation to Reflexive Sociology.* Chicago, Illinois: University of Chicago Press.

Bowles, Samuel and Herbert Gintis. 2011. *Schooling in Capitalist America.* Chicago, Illinois: Haymarket Books.

Brown, Michael, Martin Carnoy, Elliot Currie, Troy Duster, David Oppenheimer, Marjorie Shultz, and David Wellmam. 2003. *Whitewashing Racism: The Myth of a Color-Blind Society.* Berkeley, Ca.: University of California Press.

Burke, Kenneth. 1945. *A Grammar of Motives.* Berkeley, Ca.: University of California Press.

Butler, Judith. 1990. *Gender Trouble.* New York, New York: Routledge.

Carson, Rachel. 1962. *Silent Spring.* New York, New York: Houghton and Mifflin.

Castells, Manuel. 1997. *The Power of Identity. The Information Age: Economy, Society and Culture, Volume II.* Malden, Massachusetts: Blackwell.

Castells, Manuel. 1998. *End of Millennium. The Information Age: Economy, Society and Culture, Volume III.* Malden, Massachusetts: Blackwell.

Castells, Manuel. 2010 (1996). *The Rise of the Network Society. The Information Age: Economy, Society and Culture, Volume I.* Second edition. Malden, Massachusetts: Blackwell.

Catton, William and Riley Dunlap. 1980. "A New Ecological Paradigm for Post-Exuberant Sociology." American Behavioral Scientist 24:15-47.

Cohen, G. A. 1978. *Karl Marx's Theory of History: A Defence.* Princeton, New Jersey: Princeton University Press.

Coleman, James S. 1990. *Foundations of Social Theory.* Cambridge, Massachusetts: Belknap Press of Harvard University Press.

Collins, Patricia Hill. 2000. *Black Feminist Thought.* New York, New York: Routledge.

Collins, Patricia Hill. 2004. *Black Sexual Politics.* New York, New York: Routledge.

Collins, Randall. 1975. *Conflict Sociology: Toward an Explanatory Science.* New York, New York: Academic Press.

Collins, Randall, 1993. "What Does Conflict Theory Predict about America's Future? 1993 Presidential Address." Sociological Perspectives 36 (4)(Winter), pp. 289-313.

Comte, Auguste. 1988 [1842]. *Introduction to Positive Philosophy.* Edited by Frederick Ferre. Indianapolis, Indiana: Hackett Publishing.

Cook, Karen, Richard Emerson, Mary Gilmore, and Toshio Yamagishi. 1983. "The Distribution of Power in Exchange Networks: Theory and Experimental Results," American Journal of Sociology, 89 (2): 275-305.

Cook, Karen. 2003. *Trust in Society.* New York, New York: Russell Sage Foundation.

Cook, Karen, Russell Hardin and Margaret Levi. 2005. *Cooperation Without Trust?* New York, New York: Russell Sage Foundation.

Cook, Karen, Margaret Levi, and Russell Hardin. 2009. *Whom Can We Trust? How Groups, Networks, and Institutions Make Trust Possible.* New York, New York: Russell Sage Foundation.

Coser, Lewis. 1956. *The Functions of Conflict*. New York, New York: The Free Press.

Crenshaw, Kimberle, Neil Gotanda, Gary Peller, and Kendall Thomas, eds. 1995. *Critical Race Theory: The Key Writings*. New York, New York: The New Press.

Dahrendorf, Ralf. 1959. *Class and Class Conflict in Industrial Society*. Stanford, California: Stanford University Press.

Davis, Kingley and Wilbert Moore. 1945. "Some Principles of Stratification." American Sociological Review 10:242-249.

de Condorcet, Marquis. 2003 [1793]. "Sketches for an historical Picture of the Progress of the Human Mind," in *From Modernism to Postmodernism: An Anthology*, edited by Lawrence Cahoone, pp. 63-69. Malden, Ma.: Blackwell Publishing.

Delaney, Tim. 2014. *Classical and Contemporary Social Theory*. Boston, Ma.: Pearson.

De Laurentis, Teresa. 1987. *Technologies of Gender*. Bloomington, Indiana: Indiana University Press.

Delgado, Richard and Jean Stefancic. 2001. *Critical Race Theory: An Introduction.* New York, New York: New York University Press.

Denzin, Norman and Charles Keller. 1981. "Frame Analysis Reconsidered," Contemporary Sociology 10 (1): 52-60.

De Saussure. 1959. *Course in General Linguistics*. Translated by Wade Baskin. New York, New York: McGraw-Hill.

Dreyfus, Herbert and Paul Rabinow. 1982. *Michel Foucault: Beyond Structuralism and Hermeneutics* (second edition). Chicago, Illinois: University of Chicago Press.

Du Bois. 1968. *The Autobiography of W.E.B. Du Bois*. New York: New York: International Publishers.

Du Bois, W.E.B. 1969 [1903]. *The Soul of Black Folks*. New York, New York: Signet.

Du Bois, W.E.B. 1998. *Black Reconstruction in America, 1860-1880*. New York, New York: The Free Press.

Du Bois, W.E.B. 2011. *The Sociological Souls of Black Folk: Essays by W.E.B. Du Bois*, edited by Robert Wortham. Lanham, Maryland: Lexington Books.

Dunlap, Riley and William Catton. 1979. "Environmental Sociology," Annual Review of Sociology 5:243-73.

Dunlap. Riley. 1980. "Paradigmatic Change in Social Science: From Human Exemptionalism to an Ecological Paradigm." American Behavioral Scientist 24:5-14.

Dunlap, Riley. 1993. "From Environmental Problems to Ecological Problems," in C. Calhoun and George Ritzer, eds. *Social Problems*. New York, New York: McGraw Hill.

Durkheim, Emile. 1965 (1915). *Elementary Forms of the Religious Life*. New York, New York: The Free Press.

Durkheim, Emile. 1979. *Suicide*. Translated by John Spaulding and George Simpson. New York, New York: The Free Press.

Durkheim, Emile. 1982. *The Rules of Sociological Method*. New York, New York: The Free Press.

Durkheim, Emile. 1984. *The Division of Labor in Society*. Translated by W.D. Halls. New York, New York: The Free Press.

Elster, Jon. 1985. *Making Sense of Marx*. Cambridge, England: Cambridge University Press.

Emerson, Richard. 1962. "Power-Dependency Relations," American Sociological Review 27 (1): 31-41.

Emerson, Richard. 1972a. "Exchange Theory, Part I: A Psychological Basis for Social Exchange." In J. Berger, M. Zelditch and B. Anderson (eds.), *Sociological Theories in Progress, Vol. 2*. Boston, Ma.: Houghton Mifflin: 28-57.

Emerson, Richard. 1972b. "Exchange Theory, Part II: Exchange Relations and Networks." In J. Berger, M. Zelditch and B. Anderson (eds.),

Sociological Theories in Progress, Vol. 2. Boston, Ma.: Houghton Mifflin: 58-72.

Fanon, Frantz. 1967 [1952]. *Black Skin, White Masks*. Translated by Charles Lam Markmann. New York, New York: Grove Press.

Fanon, Frantz. 1963. *The Wretched of the Earth*. New York, New York: Grover Weidenfeld.

Foucault, Michel. 1965. *Madness and Civilization*. New York, New York: Vintage Books.

Foucault, Michel. 1970. *The Order of Things*. New York, New York: Vintage Books.

Foucault, Michel. 1977. *Discipline and Punish: The Birth of the Prison*. New York, New York: Vintage Books.

Fraser, Nancy and Axel Honneth. 2003. *Redistribution or Recognition: A Political-Philosophical Exchange*. London, England: Verso Books.

Fraser, Nancy and Rahel Jaeggi. 2018. *Capitalism: A Conversation in Critical Theory*. Oxford, England: Polity Press.

Fromm, Erich. 1969 (1941). *Escape from Freedom*. New York, New York: Henry Holt.

Garfinkel, Harold. 1967. *Studies in Ethnomethodology*. Oxford, England: Polity Press.

Gerth, H.H. and C. Wright Mills. 1958. "A Biographical View." *From Max Weber: Essays in Sociology*, edited by H.H. Gerth and C. Wright Mills., pp. 3-31. New York, New York: Oxford University Press.

Giddens, Anthony. 1984. *The Constitution of Sociology*. Berkeley, Ca.: The University of California Press.

Giddens, Anthony. 1990. *The Consequences of Modernity*. Stanford, Ca.: Stanford University Press.

Giddens, Anthony. 1991. *Modernity and Self-Identity*. Stanford, Ca.: Stanford University Press.

Giddens, Anthony. 2010. *The Third Wave: The Renewal of Social Democracy*. Malden, Massachusetts: Polity Press.

Goffman, Erving. 1959. (1956). *The Presentation of Self in Everyday Life*. Garden City, New York: Anchor.

Goffman, Erving. 1961. *Asylums*. Garden City, New York: Anchor.

Goffman, Erving. 1964. *Stigma*. Englewood Cliffs, New Jersey: Prentice-Hall.

Goffman, Erving. 1974. *Frame Analysis: An Essay on the Organization of Experience*. Boston, Ma.: Northeastern University Press.

Goffman, Erving. 1981. "A Reply to Denzin and Keller," Contemporary Sociology 10 (1): 60-68.

Goffman, Erving. 1981. *Forms of Talk*. Philadelphia, Pennsylvania: University of Pennsylvania Press.

Gramsci, Antonio. 1971. *Prison Notebooks*. New York, New York: International Publishers.

Gramsci, Antonio. 2000. *The Antonio Gramsci Reader*. Edited by David Forgas. New York, New York: New York University Press.

Gusfield, Joseph. 1989. *Kenneth Burke: On Symbols and Society*. Chicago, Illinois: University of Chicago Press.

Habermas, Jurgen. 1971. *Knowledge and Human Interests*. Boston, Ma.: Beacon Press.

Habermas, Jurgen. 1975. *Legitimation Crisis*. Boston, Ma.: Beacon Press.

Habermas, Jurgen. 1987a. *The Theory of Communicative Action. Volume One*. Translated by Thomas McCarthy. Boston, Ma.: Beacon Press.

Habermas, Jurgen. 1987b. *The Theory of Communicative Action. Volume Two*. Translated by Thomas McCarthy. Boston, Ma.: Beacon Press.

Habermas, Jurgen. 1989. "The Public Sphere" pp. 231-236 in *Jurgen Habermas on Society and Politics: A Reader*. Edited by Steven Seidman. Boston, Ma.: Beacon Press.

Hamilton, Alexander, James Madison, and John Jay. 2003 [1787]. *The Federalist Papers*. New York, New York: Signet Classics.

Hannigan, John. 1995. *Environmental Sociology: A Social Constructionist Perspective*. London, England: Routledge.

Held, David. 1980. *Introduction to Critical Theory*. Berkeley, Ca.: University of California Press.

Heidegger, Martin. 2003. "Letter on Humanism," pp. 174-194 in *From Modernism to Postmodernism: An Anthology*, edited by Lawrence Cahoone. Malden, Massachusetts: Blackwell Publishing.

Hill, Michael. 1989. Introduction to *How To Observe Morals and Manners* by Harriet Martineau. New Brunswick, New Jersey: Transaction Publishers.

hooks, bell and Cornel West. 1991. *Breaking Bread: Insurgent Black Intellectual Life*. Boston, Ma.: South End Press.

Homans, George Caspar. 1961. *Social Behavior: Its Elementary Forms*. New York, New York: Harcourt, Brace, and World.

Honneth, Axel. 1996. *The Struggle for Recognition*. Cambridge, Ma.: MIT Press.

Horkheimer, Max. 1974 [1947]. *Eclipse of Reason*. New York, New York: Continuum Press.

Horkheimer, Max and Theodor Adorno. 1993 [1944]. *Dialectic of Enlightenment*. New York, New York: Continuum Press.

Huaco, George. 1966. "The Functionalist Theory of Stratification: Two Decades of Controversy," *Inquiry* 9:215-240).

Huntington, Samuel. 1993. "The Clash of Civilizations?" Foreign Affairs 72 (3): 22-49.

Huntington, Samuel. 1996. *The Clash of Civilizations and the Remaking of World Order*. New York, New York: Simon and Schuster.

Inglehart, Ronald. 1977. *The Silent Revolution: Changing Values and Political Styles Among Wester Publics.* Princeton, New Jersey: Princeton University Press.

Inglehart, Ronald. 1990. *Culture Shift in Advanced Industrial Society.* Princeton, New Jersey: Princeton University Press.

Jaeggi, Rahel. 2018. *Critiques of Forms of Life.* Cambridge, Ma.: Harvard University Press.

Jameson, Fredric. 1991. *Postmodernism or, The Cultural Logic of Late Capitalism.* Durham, North Carolina: Duke University Press.

Jay, Martin. 1973. *The Dialectical Imagination: A History of the Frankfurt School and the Institute of Social Research, 1923-1950.* Berkeley, Ca.: University of California Press.

Kant, Immanuel. 2003 [1781]. "An Answer to the Question: 'What is Enlightenment?'" in *From Modernism to Postmodernism: An Anthology*, edited by Lawrence Cahoone, pp. 46-49. Malden, Ma.: Blackwell Publishing.

Lawrence, Charles. 1995. "The Id, the Ego, and Equal Protection – Reckoning with Unconscious Racism," in *Critical Race Theory*, edited by Kimberle Crenshaw et al., pp. 235-257. New York, New York: The New Press.

Levine, Donald. 1971. "Introduction," to *Georg Simmel: On Individuality and Social Forms*, edited by Donald Levine, pp. ix-lxv). Chicago, Illinois: University of Chicago Press.

Levi-Strauss. 1961. *Tristes Tropiques.* Translated by John Russell. New York, New York: Atheneum Press.

Locke, John. 1975 [1689]. *An Essay Concerning Human Understanding.* Oxford, England: Oxford University Press.

Lukacs, Georg. 1968. *History and Class Consciousness.* Translated by Rodney Livingstone. Cambridge, Ma.: MIT Press.

Lyotard, Jean Francois. 1984. *The Postmodern Condition.* Minneapolis, Minn.: University of Minnesota Press.

Maniates, Michael. 2014. "Individualization: Plant a Tree, Buy a Bike, Save the World?" in *Environmental Sociology: From Analysis to Action*, third edition. Edited by Leslie King and Deborah McCarthy Auriffeille, pp. 343-364. Lanham, Maryland: Rowman and Littlefield.

Marcuse, Herbert. 1990 [1941]. "Some Social Implications of Modern Technology," in *The Essential Frankfurt School Reader*, pp. 138-162, edited by Andrew Arato and Eike Gebhardt. New York, New York: Continuum Press.

Marcuse, Herbert. 1964. *One Dimensional Man*. Boston, Ma.: Beacon Press.

Martineau, Harriet. 1962. *Society in America*, edited by Seymour Martin Lipset. Garden City, New York: Anchor Books.

Martineau, Harriet. 1985. *Harriet Martineau on Women*. Edited by Gayle Graham Yates. New Brunswick, New Jersey: Rutgers University Press.

Martineau, Harriet. 1989 [1838]. *How to Observe Morals and Manners*. New Brunswick, New Jersey: Transaction Publishers.

Marx, Karl. 1977. *Capital, Vol 1-3*. New York, New York: Vintage Books.

Marx, Karl. 1978. *The Marx-Engels Reader* (second edition). Edited by Robert Tucker. New York, New York: W.W. Norton.

Matsuda, Marie, et al. 2003. *Words that Wound: Critical Race Theory, Assaultive Speech, and the First Amendment*. Boulder, Colorado: Westview.

Mauss, Marcel. 2000. *The Gift: The Form and Reason for Exchange in Archaic Societies*. New York, New York: W.W. Norton.

Mead, George Herbert. 1962 [1934]. *Mind, Self, and Society*. Chicago, Illinois: University of Chicago Press.

Merton, Robert. 1967. *On Theoretical Sociology*. New York, New York: Free Press.

Merton, Robert. 1969. *Social Theory and Social Structure*. New York, New York: Free Press.

Mol, Arthur. 1995. *The Refinement of Production: Ecological Modernization Theory and the Chemical Industry*. Utrecht, the Netherlands: Van Arkel.

Mol, Arthur. 2001. *Globalization and Environmental Reform: The Ecological Modernization of the Global Economy.* Cambridge, Massachusetts: MIT Press.

Mol, Arthur and Spaargaren, Gert. 2005. "From Additions and Withdrawals to Environmental Flows: Reframing Debates in the Environmental Social Sciences." Organization and Environment 18:91-107.

Morris, Aldon. 2015. *The Scholar Denied: W.E.B. DuBois and the Birth of Modern Sociology.* Berkeley, Ca.: University of California Press.

Mouffe, C. (editor). 1979. *Gramsci and Marxist Theory.* London, England: Routledge and Kegan Paul.

Omi, Michael and Howard Winant. 1986. *Racial Formation in the United States: From the 1960s to the 1980s.* New York, New York: Routledge.

Park, Robert and Ernest Burgess. 1921 [2016]. *Introduction to the Science of Sociology.* Reprint. Publisher Unknown and Unlisted. See CPSIA and www.ICGtesting.com.

Parsons, Talcott. 1949. *The Structure of Social Action. Vol. 1 and 2.* New York, New York: The Free Press.

Parsons, Talcott. 1951. *The Social System.* New York, New York: The Free Press.

Parsons, Talcott. 1966. *Societies: Evolutionary and Comparative Perspectives.* Englewood Cliffs, New Jersey: Prentice Hall.

Polanyi, Karl. 1957. *The Great Transformation.* Boston, Ma.: Beacon Press.

Poster, Mark. 1988. Introduction to *Jean Baudrillard: Selected Writings.* Stanford, Ca.: Stanford University Press.

Putnam, Robert. 2000. *Bowling Alone.* New York, New York: Simon and Schuster.

Rabaka, Reiland. 2010. *Against Epistemic Apartheid: W.E.B. Dubois and the Disciplinary Decadence of Sociology.* Lanham, Maryland: Lexington Books.

Ritzer, George. 1997. *Postmodern Social Theory*. New York, New York: McGraw Hill.

Ritzer, George and Jeffrey Stepnisky. 2014. *Sociological Theory* (9th edition). New York, New York: McGraw Hill.

Rossi, Alice. 1973. *The Feminist Papers*. New York, New York: Columbia University Press.

Rousseau, Jean Jacques. 2003 [1750]. "From Discourse on the Sciences and the Arts," in *From Modernism to Postmodernism: An Anthology*, edited by Lawrence Cahoone, pp.32-37. Malden, Ma.: Blackwell Publishing.

Rousseau, Jean Jacques. 1954 [1762]. *The Social Contract*. Translated by Willmoore Kendall. Chicago, Illinois: Henry Regnery Co.

Said, Edward. 1979. *Orientalism*. New York, New York: Vintage Press.

Schnaiberg, Allan. 1980. *The Environment: From Surplus to Scarcity*. New York, New York: Oxford University Press.

Schutz, Alfred. 1967 (1932). *The Phenomenology of the Social World*. Translated by George Walsh and Frederick Lehnert. Evanston, Illinois: Northwestern University Press.

Schutz, Alfred. 1970. *Alfred Schutz: On Phenomenology and Social Relations*. Edited with an introduction by Helmut Wagner. Chicago, Illinois: University of Chicago Press.

Sedgwick, Eve. 1990. *Epistemology of the Closet*. Berkeley, Ca.: University of California Press.

Seidman, Steven. 1996. *Queer Theory/Sociology*, ed. Oxford, England: Blackwell.

Seidman, Steven. 1997. *Difference Troubles: Queering Social Theory and Sexual Politics*. New York, New York: Cambridge University Press.

Simmel, Georg. 1950. *The Sociology of Georg Simmel*. Translated by Kurt Wolff. New York, New York: The Free Press.

Simmel, Georg. 1971a. *On Individuality and Social Forms*. Edited by Donald Levine. Chicago, Illinois: University of Chicago.

Simmel, Georg. 1971b [1918]. "The Conflict in Modern Culture," in *On Individuality and Social Forms*, pp. 375-393. Edited by Donald Levine. Chicago, Illinois: University of Chicago.

Simmel, Georg. 1971c [1918]. "Subjective Culture," in *On Individuality and Social Forms*, pp. 227-234. Edited by Donald Levine. Chicago, Illinois: University of Chicago.

Simmel, Georg. 1971d [1918]. "Fashion," in *On Individuality and Social Forms*, pp. 294-323. Edited by Donald Levine. Chicago, Illinois: University of Chicago.

Simmel, Georg. 1971e [1918]. "The Metropolis and Mental Life," in *On Individuality and Social Forms*, pp. 324-339. Edited by Donald Levine. Chicago, Illinois: University of Chicago.

Simmel, Georg. 1971f [1918]. "The Poor," in *On Individuality and Social Forms*, pp. 150-178. Edited by Donald Levine. Chicago, Illinois: University of Chicago.

Simmel, Georg. 1971g [1918]. "The Stranger," in *On Individuality and Social Forms*, pp. 143-149. Edited by Donald Levine. Chicago, Illinois: University of Chicago.

Simmel, Georg. 1990. *The Philosophy of Money*. Edited by David Frisby. Translated by Tom Bottomore and David Frisby. London, England: Routledge. Second Edition.

Small, Albion. 1895. "The Era of Sociology," The American Journal of Sociology, 1:1: 1-15 (July).

Smith, Adam. 1976 [1776]. *The Wealth of Nations*. Edited by Edwin Cannan. Chicago, Illinois: University of Chicago Press.

Smith, Dorothy E. 1987. *The Everyday World as Problematic: A Feminist Sociology*. Boston, Ma.: Northeastern University Press.

Smith, Dorothy E. 1990. *Texts, Facts, and Femininity: Exploring the Relations of Ruling*. New York, New York: Routledge.

Snow, David, E. Burke Rochford, Steven K. Worden, Robert D. Benford. 1986. "Frame Alignment Processes, Micromobilization, and Movement Participation," American Sociological Review 51: 464-481.

Spencer, Herbert. 1886. *Social Statics*. New York, New York: D. Appleton and Company.

Spencer, Herbert. 1967 [1876]. *The Evolution of Society: Selections from Principles of Sociology*, edited by Robert Carneiro. Chicago, Illinois: University of Chicago Press.

Taylor, Charles. 2004. *Modern Social Imaginaries*. Durham, North Carolina: Duke University Press.

de Tocqueville, Alexis. 1955 [1856]. *The Old Regime and the French Revolution*. Translated by Stuart Gilbert. New York, New York: Anchor Books.

De Tocqueville, Alexis. 2000 [1835]. *Democracy in America*. Translated by Harvey Mansfield and Delba Winthrop. Chicago, Ill.: University of Chicago Press.

de Tocqueville, Alexis. 2003 [1835]. *Democracy in America*. Translated by Gerald Bevan. London, England: Penguin Books.

Touraine, Alain. 1974. *Post-Industrial Society*. Unknown: Wildwood House Press.

Touraine, Alain. 1981. *The Voice and the Eye*. Cambridge, England: Cambridge University Press.

Touraine, Alain. 2007. *A New Paradigm for Understanding Today's World*. Malden, Ma.: Polity Press.

Tumin, Melvin. 1953. "Some Principles of Stratification: A Critical Analysis." American Sociological Review 18:387-394.

Venturi, Robert, Denise Scott Brown, and Steven Izenour. 1972. *Learning from Las Vegas*. Cambridge, Ma.: MIT Press.

Wallerstein, Immanuel. 1974. *The Modern World-System I: Capitalist Agriculture and the Origins of the European World-Economy in the Sixteenth Century*. New York, New York: Academic Press.

Wallerstein, Immanuel. 1980. The Modern World-System II: *Mercantilism and the Consolidation of the European World-Economy, 1600-1750*. New York, New York: Academic Press.

Wallerstein, Immanuel. 1989. *The Modern World-System III: The Second era of Great Expansion of the Capitalist World-Economy, 1730-1840*. New York, New York: Academic Press.

Wallerstein, Immanuel. 2000. "The Construction of Peoplehood: Racism, Nationalism, and Ethnicity," pp. 293-309 in *The Essential Wallerstein*. New York, New York: The New Press.

Wallerstein, Immanuel. 2000b. "The Rise and Demise of the Capitalist System," pp. 71-105 in *The Essential Wallerstein*. New York, New York: The New Press.

Wallerstein, Immanuel. 2004. *World-Systems Analysis: An Introduction*. Durham, N.C.: Duke University Press.

Wallerstein, Immanuel. 2011. *The Modern World-System IV: Centrist Liberalism Triumphant, 1789-1914*. Berkeley, Ca.: University of California Press.

Weber, Marianne. 2017. *Max Weber: A Biography*. New York, New York: Routledge.

Weber, Max. 1958. "Class, Status, Party" in *From Max Weber: Essays in Sociology*, edited by H.H. Gerth and C. Wright Mills., pp. 180-195. New York, New York: Oxford University Press.

Weber, Max. 1958a. "Science as a Vocation" in *From Max Weber: Essays in Sociology*, edited by H.H. Gerth and C. Wright Mills., pp. 129-156. New York, New York: Oxford University Press.

Weber, Max. 1968 (1921). *Economy and Society. Volume 1 and 2*. Edited by Guenther Roth and Claus Wittich. Berkeley, Ca.: University of California Press.

Weber, Max. 1976. *The Protestant Ethic and the Spirit of Capitalism*. New York, New York: Charles Scribner's Sons.

Wilson, William Julius. 1980. *The Declining Significance of Race*. Chicago, Illinois: University of Chicago Press.

Wilson, William Julius. 1987. *The Truly Disadvantaged*. Chicago, Illinois: University of Chicago Press.

Winant, Howard. 1994. *Racial Conditions: Politics, Theory, Comparisons*. Minneapolis, Minn.: University of Minnesota Press.

Winant, Howard. 2001. *The World Is a Ghetto: Race and Democracy since World War II*. New York, New York: Basic Books.

Wolff, Kurt. 1950. Introduction to Georg Simmel's *The Sociology of Georg Simmel*. Translated by Kurt Wolff. New York, New York: The Free Press.

Yates, Gayle Graham. 1985. Introduction, pp. 1-28, in *Harriet Martineau on Women*. Edited by Gayle Graham Yates. New Brunswick, New Jersey: Rutgers University Press.

www.ingramcontent.com/pod-product-compliance
Lightning Source LLC
Chambersburg PA
CBHW080352030426
42334CB00024B/2848